AA

MAXI SCALE ATLAS
BRITAIN

Scale 2.4 miles to 1 inch, 1:151,000

3rd Edition September 1992
2nd Edition October 1991
1st Edition May 1990

© The Automobile Association 1992

The Automobile Association retains the copyright in the original edition © 1990 and in all subsequent editions, reprints and amendments to editions listed above.

Produced by the Publishing Division of The Automobile Association.

Mapping produced by the Cartographic Department of The Automobile Association. This atlas has been compiled and produced from the Automaps database utilising electronic and computer technology.

Published by The Automobile Association, Fanum House, Basingstoke, Hampshire RG21 2EA.

Printed by Grafica Editoriale, Bologna, Italy.

The contents of this atlas are believed correct at the time of printing, although the publishers cannot accept any responsibility for errors or omissions, or for changes in the details given. They would welcome information to help keep this atlas up to date; please write to the Cartographic Editor, Publishing Division, The Automobile Association, Fanum House, Basingstoke, Hampshire RG21 2EA.

A CIP catalogue record for this book is available from the British Library.

ISBN 0 7495 0604 0, ISBN 0 7495 0607 5

Information on National Parks provided by the Countryside Commission for England & Wales.

Information on National Scenic Areas – Scotland provided by the Countryside Commission for Scotland.

Information on Forest Parks, provided by the Forestry Commission.

The RSPB sites shown are a selection chosen by the Royal Society for the Protection of Birds.

Picnic sites are those inspected by the AA and are located on or near A and B roads.

National Trust properties shown are those open to the public as indicated in the handbooks of the National Trusts of England, Wales and Northern Ireland, and Scotland.

Route planning

- Don't drive if you are tired
- Stop regularly for fresh air and exercise
- Plan long drives in advance
- Use the map on this page to plan your route
- Check and note your route details using the atlas section
- Avoid urban areas – they are always slower
- Use motorways where possible – they are generally faster
- Tune to local radio to avoid hold-ups and road works
- Never drink and drive . . . .

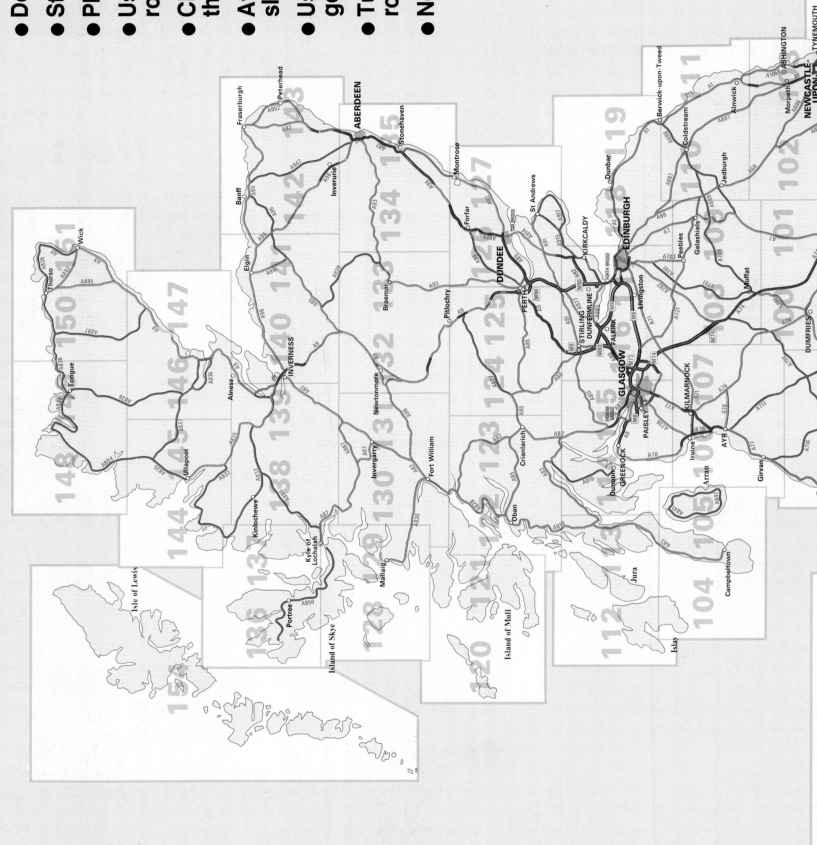

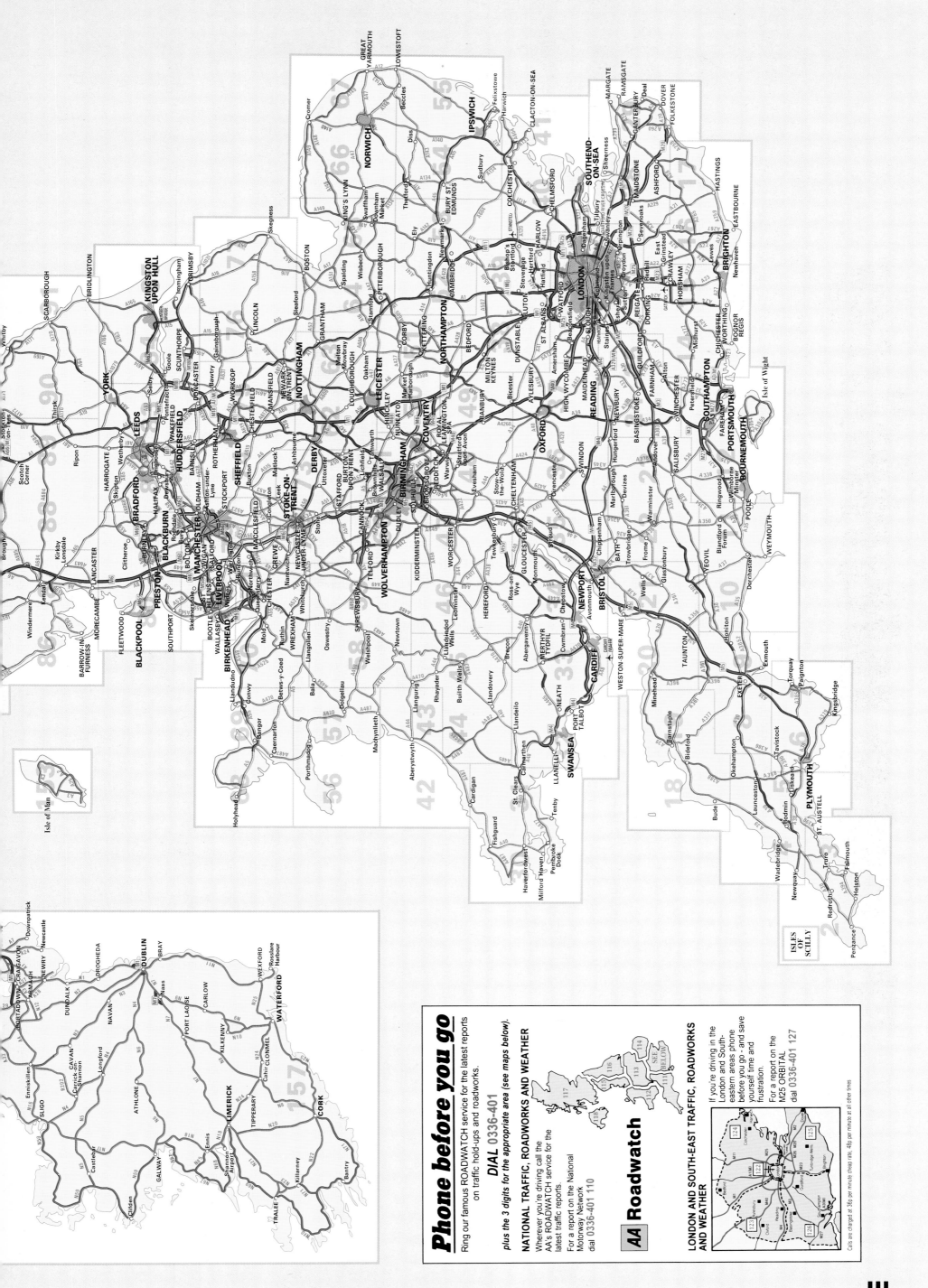

Phone before you go

Ring our famous ROADWATCH service for the latest reports on traffic hold-ups and roadworks.

DIAL 0336-401

plus the 3 digits for the appropriate area (see maps below).

NATIONAL TRAFFIC, ROADWORKS AND WEATHER

Wherever you're driving, call the AA's ROADWATCH service for the latest traffic reports.

For a report on the National Motorway Network dial 0336-401 110

AA Roadwatch

LONDON AND SOUTH-EAST TRAFFIC, ROADWORKS AND WEATHER

If you're driving in the London and South-eastern areas phone before you go - and save yourself time and frustration.

For a report on the M25 ORBITAL dial 0336-401 127

Calls are charged at 36p per minute cheap rate, 48p per minute at all other times

III

Using this atlas

Atlas and Routeplanner

Whether you are planning a holiday for the family or a day out from home, or making a trip for business or pleasure, the Maxi Scale Atlas, with its clear, easy-to-read mapping, is an essential guide.

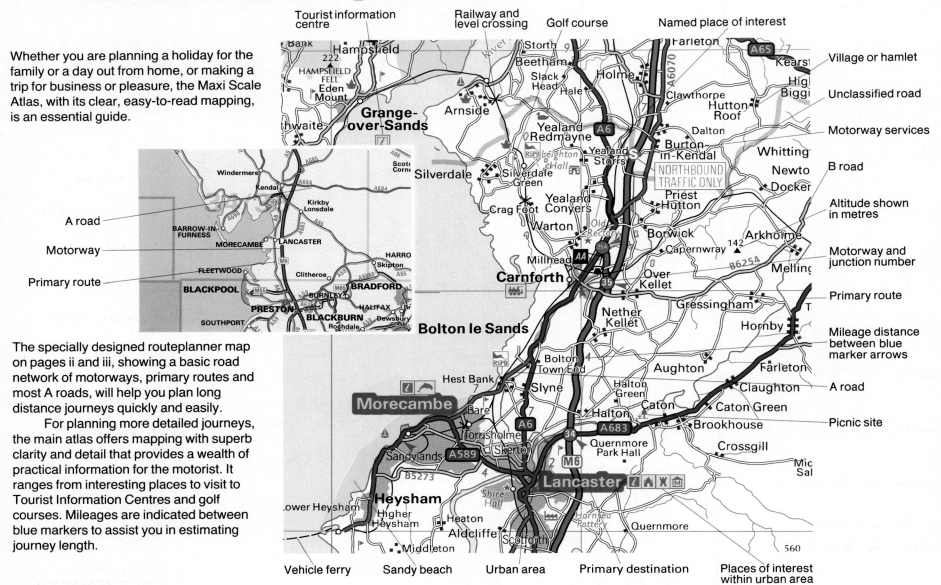

- Tourist information centre
- Railway and level crossing
- Golf course
- Named place of interest
- Village or hamlet
- Unclassified road
- Motorway services
- B road
- Altitude shown in metres
- Motorway and junction number
- Primary route
- Mileage distance between blue marker arrows
- A road
- Picnic site

- A road
- Motorway
- Primary route

The specially designed routeplanner map on pages ii and iii, showing a basic road network of motorways, primary routes and most A roads, will help you plan long distance journeys quickly and easily.

For planning more detailed journeys, the main atlas offers mapping with superb clarity and detail that provides a wealth of practical information for the motorist. It ranges from interesting places to visit to Tourist Information Centres and golf courses. Mileages are indicated between blue markers to assist you in estimating journey length.

- Vehicle ferry
- Sandy beach
- Urban area
- Primary destination
- Places of interest within urban area

London

A routeplanning map of London, on pages 158-159, shows all major roads, underground and British Rail stations, and provides a simple guide to finding your way around the city.

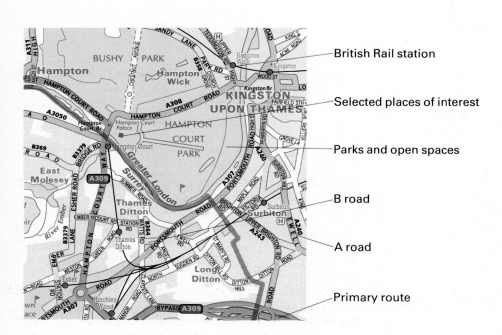

- British Rail station
- Selected places of interest
- Parks and open spaces
- B road
- A road
- Primary route

Index

Over 30,000 places are indexed alphabetically between pages 160 and 188. Each entry is followed by its county in *italics*, the relevant atlas page number in **bold** type and the National Grid reference (see opposite for explanation) to help you find its exact location on the map.

- Place name
- County
- Page number
- National grid square
- Map grid reference

Motoring symbols

M4	Motorway with number
11	Motorway junction with and without number
3	Motorway junction with limited access
S	Motorway service area
	Motorway and junction under construction
A4	Primary route single/dual carriageway
S	Primary route service area
BATH	Primary destination
A1123	Other A road single/dual carriageway
B2070	B road single/dual carriageway
	Unclassified road single/dual carriageway
	Road under construction
	Narrow primary, other A or B road with passing places (Scotland)
	Road tunnel
	Steep gradient (arrows point downhill)
Toll	Road toll
5	Distance in miles between symbols

V	Vehicle ferry – Great Britain
CHERBOURG V	Vehicle ferry – Continental
H	Hovercraft ferry
	Airport
H	Heliport
	Railway line/in tunnel
	Railway station and level crossing
	Tourist railway
AA	AA Shop – full services
AA	AA Roadside Shop – limited services
AA	AA Port Shop open as season demands
	AA telephone
	BT telephone in isolated places
	Urban area/village
628	Spot height in metres
	River, canal, lake
	Sandy beach
	County/Regional boundary
	National boundary
88	Page overlap and number

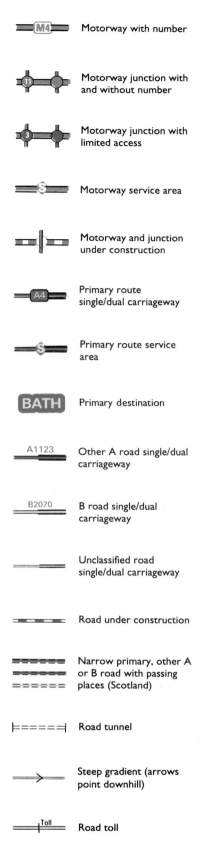
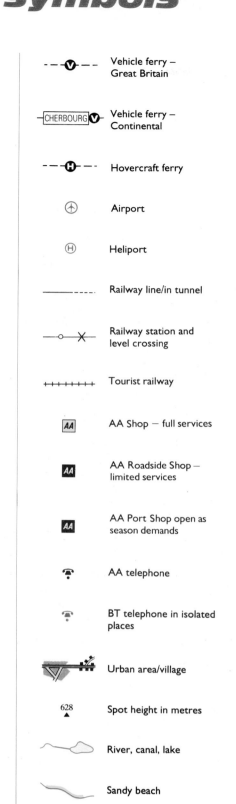

Tourist symbols

	Tourist Information Centre
	Tourist Information Centre (seasonal)
	Abbey, cathedral or priory
	Ruined abbey, cathedral or priory
	Castle
	Historic house
	Museum or art gallery
	Industrial interest
	Garden
	Arboretum
	Country park
	Agricultural showground
	Theme park
	Zoo
	Wildlife collection – mammals
	Wildlife collection – birds
	Aquarium
	Nature reserve
RSPB	RSPB site
	Nature trail
	Forest drive
	National trail
	Viewpoint
	Picnic site

	Hill fort
	Roman antiquity
	Prehistoric monument
1066	Battle site with year
	Steam centre (railway)
	Cave
	Windmill
	Golf course
	County cricket ground
	Rugby Union national ground
	International athletics stadium
	Horse racing
	Show jumping/equestrian circuit
	Motor racing circuit
	Coastal launching site
	Ski slope – natural
	Ski slope – artificial
NT	National Trust property
	Other places of interest
	Boxed symbols indicate attractions within urban areas
	National Park (England & Wales)
	National Scenic Area (Scotland)
	Forest Park
	Heritage Coast

National grid

The National Grid system covers Britain with an imaginary network of squares using blue horizontal lines called northings and vertical lines called eastings. These lines are numbered along the bottom and up the left hand side of the atlas pages.

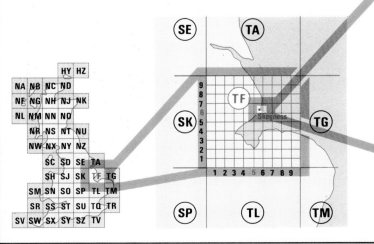

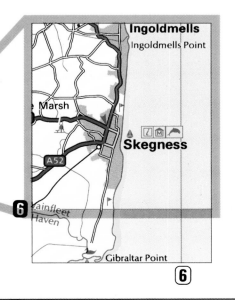

Our example, Skegness, left, is shown in the index as

Skegness *Lincs*.................77 TF**5**6**6**3

The two letters are not needed for simple navigation, but can be helpful if you want to use the map in relation to the rest of the country and other map series.

The 4-figure grid reference at the end of each entry will help you locate a place on the map.

For quick reference, the four figures are arranged so that the 1st and 3rd are highlighted in **bold** type. Using Skegness to illustrate this, the 1st figure, **5**, shows which number to locate along the bottom of page 77 and the 3rd number, **6**, which number up the left hand side. Where these two lines join indicates the square in which you will find Skegness (56).

To pinpoint the position more accurately, use the 2nd and 4th numbers. The 2nd, 6, tells you how many imaginary tenths along the bottom line to go from the 1st number, whereas the 4th number, 3, tells you how many tenths up the line to go from the 3rd number. Where the two lines intersect, you will locate the town of Skegness.

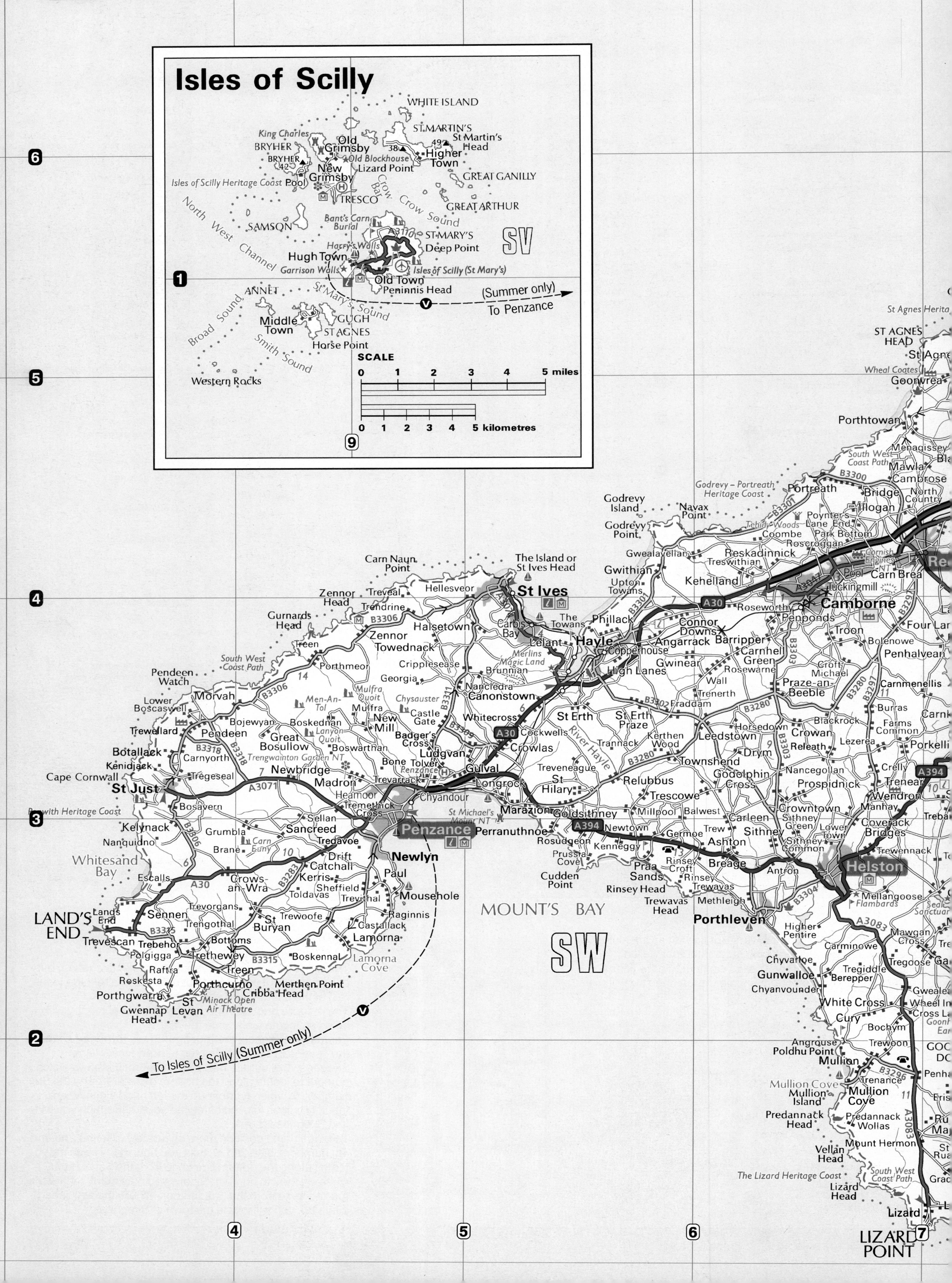

Isles of Scilly

WHITE ISLAND

King Charles
BRYHER
Old Grimsby
ST MARTIN'S
St Martin's Head
BRYHER 42
New Grimsby
Old Blockhouse
Lizard Point
Higher Town
GREAT GANILLY
Isles of Scilly Heritage Coast
Pool
TRESCO
Crow Bay
Crow Sound
GREAT ARTHUR
Bant's Carn Burial
SAMSON
A3110
ST MARY'S
Deep Point
Harry's Walls
Hugh Town
Garrison Walls
St Mary's Sound
Isles of Scilly (St Mary's)
Old Town
SV
North West Channel
ANNET
Peninnis Head
(Summer only) To Penzance
Broad Sound
Middle Town
GUGH
ST AGNES
Horse Point
Smith Sound
Western Rocks

SCALE

0 1 2 3 4 5 miles

0 1 2 3 4 5 kilometres

9

St Agnes Heritage
ST AGNES HEAD
St Agnes
Wheal Coates
Goonvrea
Porthtowan
Menagissey
Mawla
Cambrose
B3300
Bridge
North Country
Illogan
Godrevy – Portreath Heritage Coast
Portreath
Poynter's Lane End
Park Bottom
Reskadinnick
Treswithian
Cornish Engines
Red
Carn Brea
Godrevy Island
Navax Point
Gwealavellan
Upton Towans
Tehidy Woods NT
A30
Tuckingmill
Roseworthy
Camborne
Four La
Carn Naun Point
The Island or St Ives Head
Godrevy Point
Kehelland
Penponds
Troon
Bolenowe
Penhalvean
Zennor Head
Treveal
Trendrine
Hellesveor
St Ives
Gwithian
Phillack
Connor Downs
Angarrack
Barripper
Carnhell Green
B3303
Burras
Carnk
Gurnards Head
B3306
Halsetown
The Towans
Carbis Bay
Lelant
Hayle
Copperhouse
High Lanes
Gwinear
Rosewarne
Wall
Trenerth
Praze-an-Beeble
Croft Michael
Carnmenellis
11
Treen
Zennor
Towednack
Crippleslease
Merlins Magic Land
Brunnian
Canonstown
Whitecross
St Erth
St Erth Praze
Fraddam
Leedstown
Horsedown
Crowan
Releath
Lezerea
Porkelli
South West Coast Path
Porthmeor
14
Men-An-Tol
Mulfra Quoit
New Mill
Castle Gate
Badger's Cross
Nancledra
B3302
Kerthen Wood
Drym
Godolphin Cross
Nancegollan
Sithney
Trenear
A394
Pendeen Watch
Morvah
B3306
Georgia
Mulfra
Lanyon Quoit
Boswarthan
Ludgvan
Gulval
Crowlas
Trannack
Townshend
Prospidnick
Manhay
Treba
Lower Boscaswell
Bojewyan
Boskednan
Great Bosullow
A30
Cockwells
Treveneague
Trescowe
Crowntown
Coverack Bridges
Trewellard
Pendeen
Trengwainton Garden NT
Bone Tolver
Trevarrack
St Hilary
Relubbus
Millpool
Balwest
Carleen
Crelly
Botallack
B3318
Carnyorth
7
Newbridge
Madron
Penzance H
Longrock
Trewennack
Kenidjack
Tregeseal
Heamoor
Tremethick Cross
Chyandour
St Michael's Mount NT
Marazion
A394
Goldsithney
Newtown
Germoe
Sithney Green
Lower Sithney Common
Helston M
Cape Cornwall
A3071
Bosavern
St Just
Kelynack
Grumbla
Brane
Carn Euny
Sellan
Sancreed
Tredavoe
Penzance
Perranuthnoe
Rosudgeon
Kenneggy
Trew
Ashton
Breage
Anton
B3304
Mellangoose
Flambards
Nanquidno
Whitesand Bay
Escalls
A30
Drift
Catchall
Kerris
Paul
Mousehole
Newlyn
Prussia Cove
Cudden Point
Praa Sands
Rinsey
Rinsey Head
Trewavas Head
Methleigh
Porthleven
B3083
Seal Sanctuary
Trewennack
Higher Pentire
Carminowe
Tregiddle
Berepper
Tregoose
Ga
LAND'S END
Land's End
Sennen
Trevorgans
Crows-an-Wra
Trethewey
B3315
Sheffield
Trevithal
St Buryan
Trewoofe
Boskenna
Raginnis
Castallack
Lamorna
Lamorna Cove
MOUNT'S BAY
SW
Chyvarloe
Gunwalloe
Chyanvounder
White Cross
Cury
Mawgan Cross
Gwealea
Trevescan
Trebehor
Polgigga
Raftra
Roskesta
Bottoms
Treen
Merthen Point
Cribba Head
To Isles of Scilly (Summer only)
Angrouse
Poldhu Point
Mullion
Trewoon
GOO DO
Porthgwarra
Gwennap Head
St Levan
Porthcurno
Minack Open Air Theatre
Mullion Cove
Mullion Island
Predannack Head
Mullion Cove
Predannack Wollas
Penha
B3296
Eris
Ru
Ma
Vellan Head
Mount Hermon
St Rua
The Lizard Heritage Coast
South West Coast Path
Lizard Head
Grad
Lizard
LIZARD POINT
7

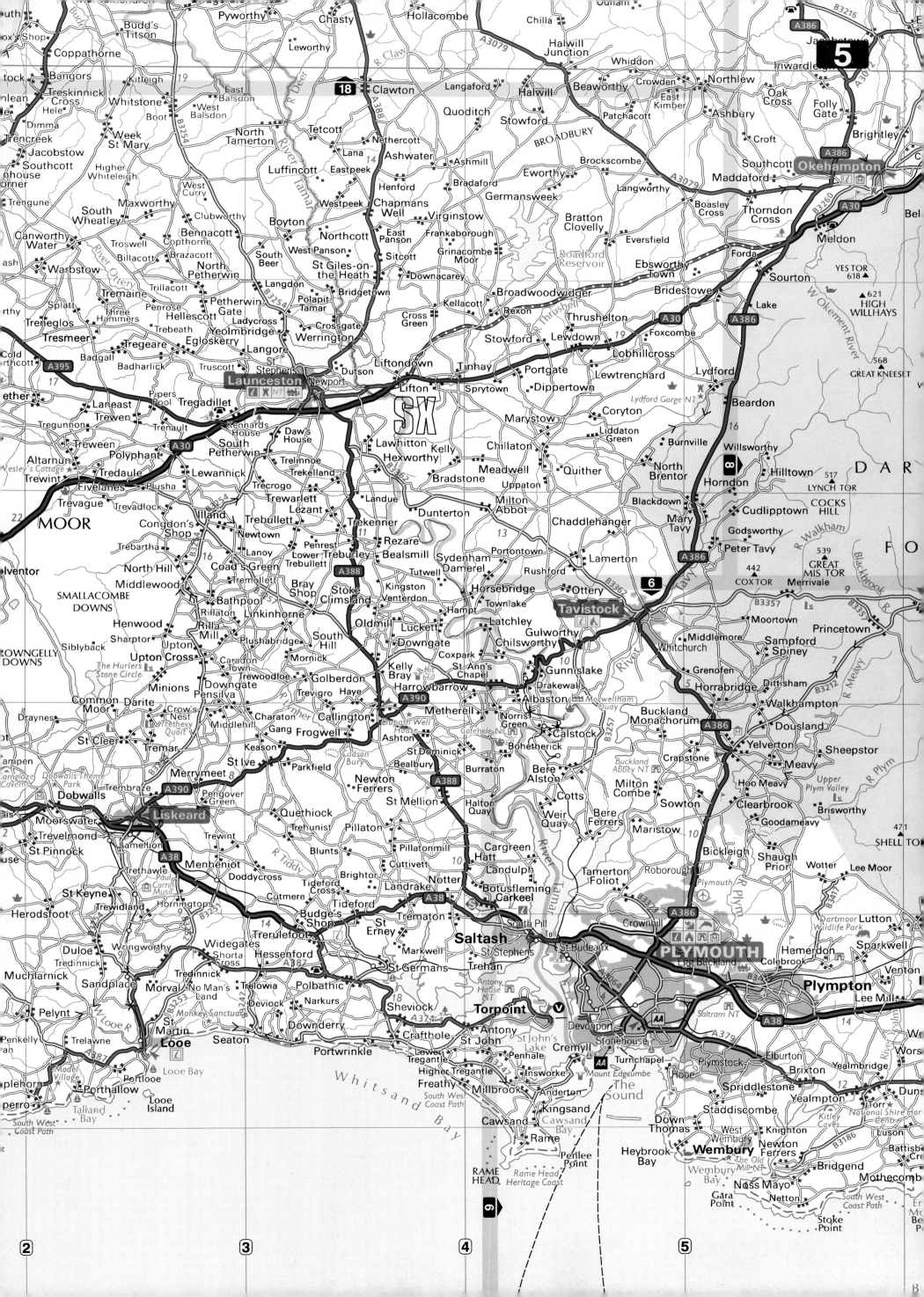

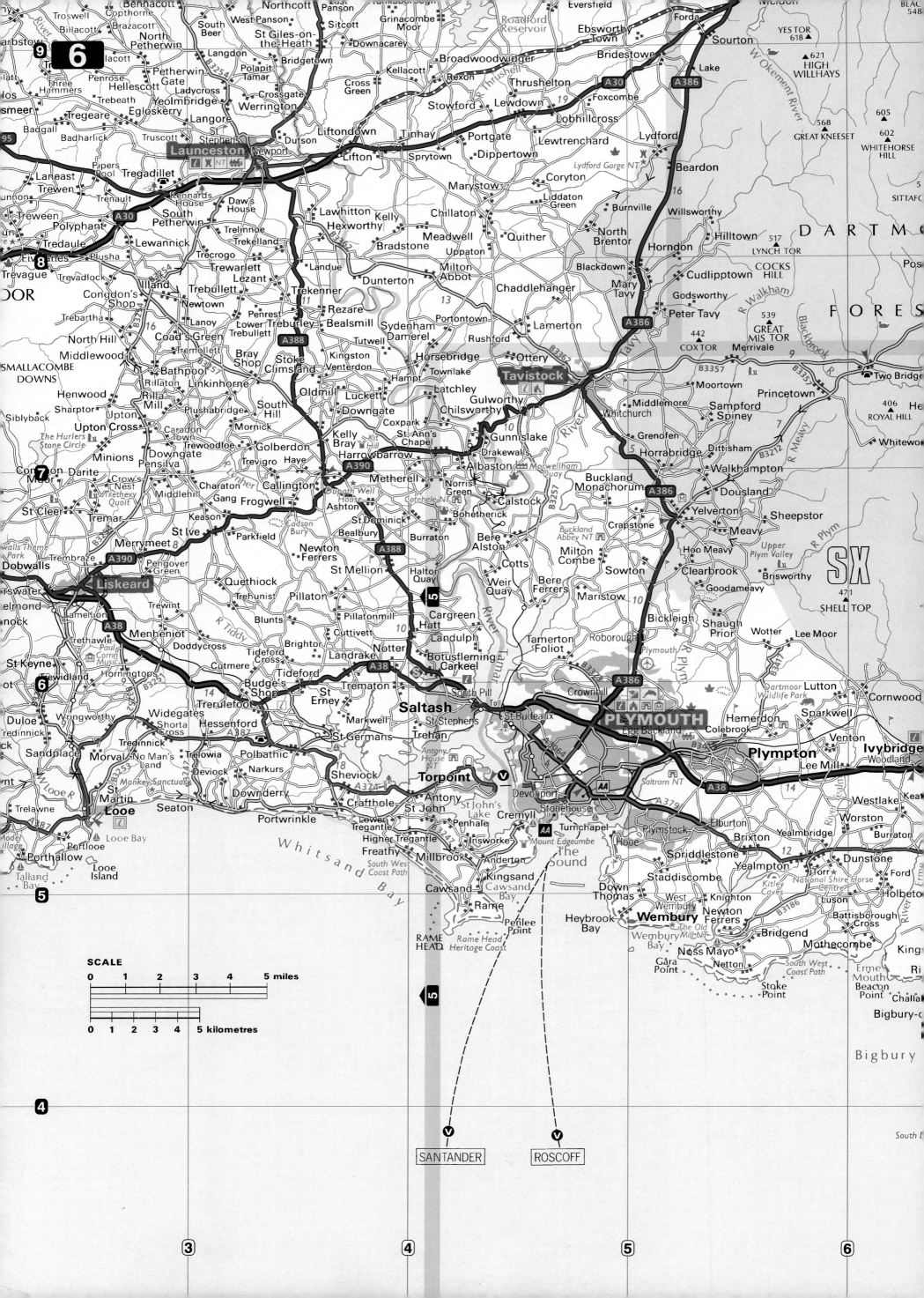

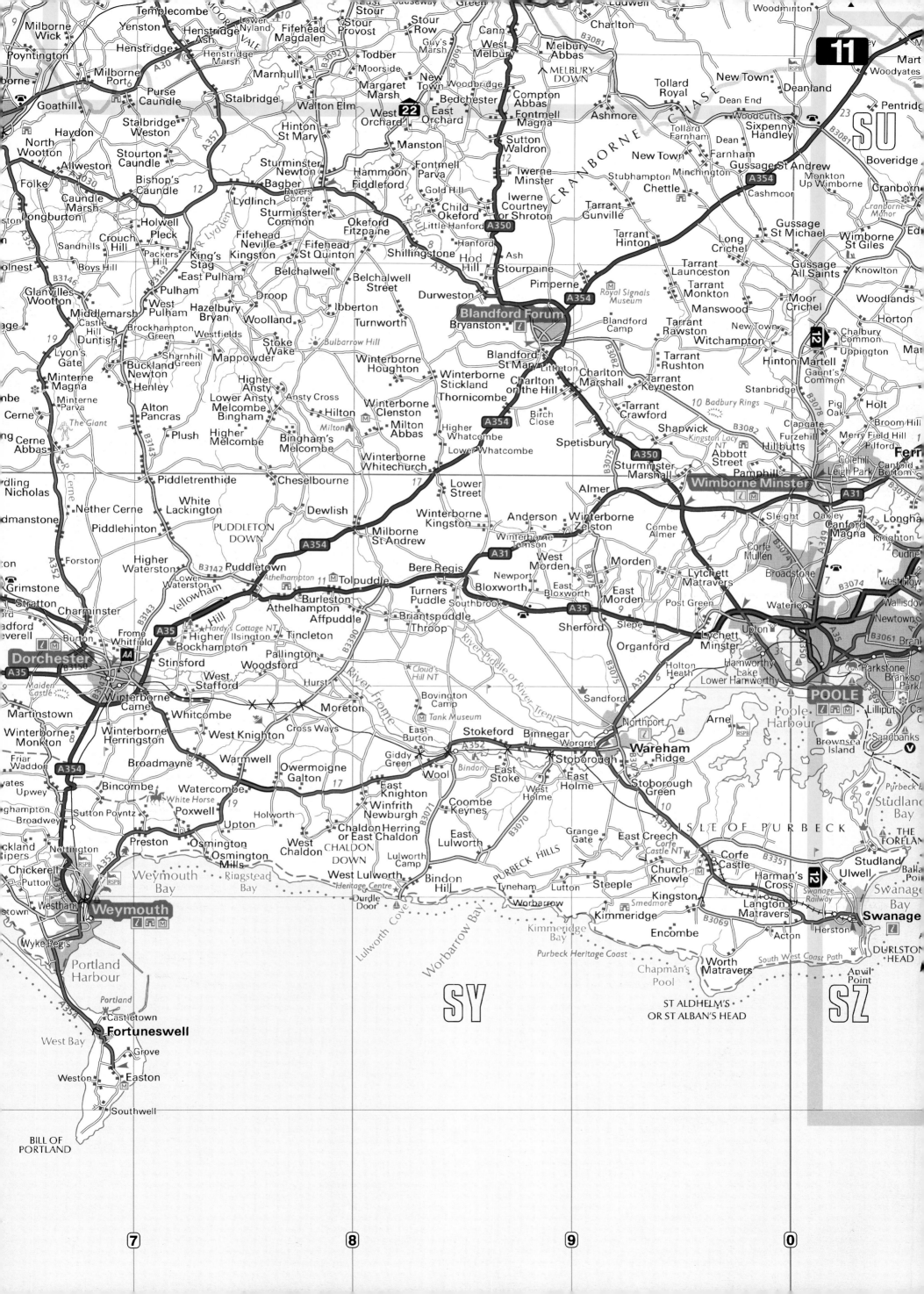

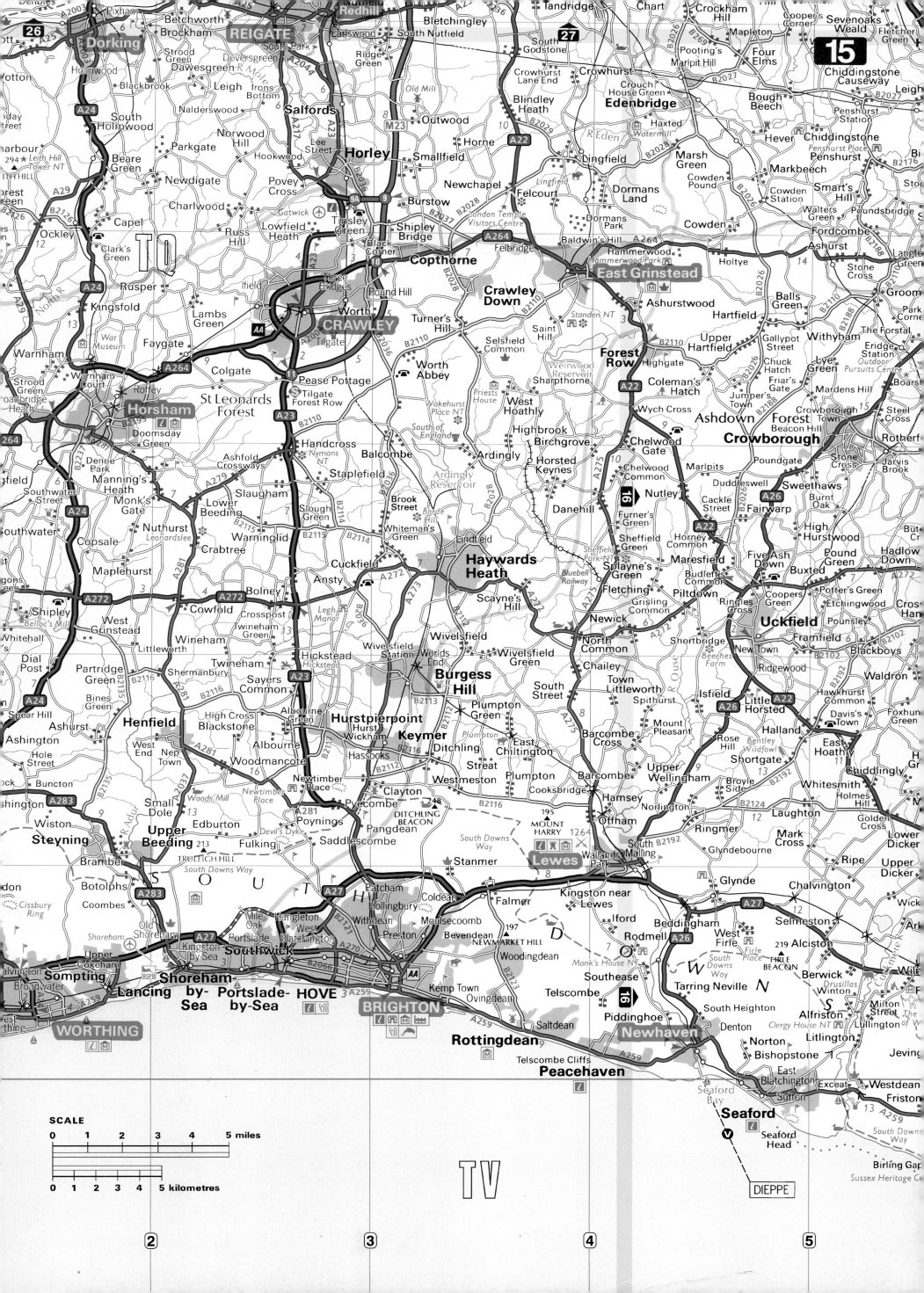

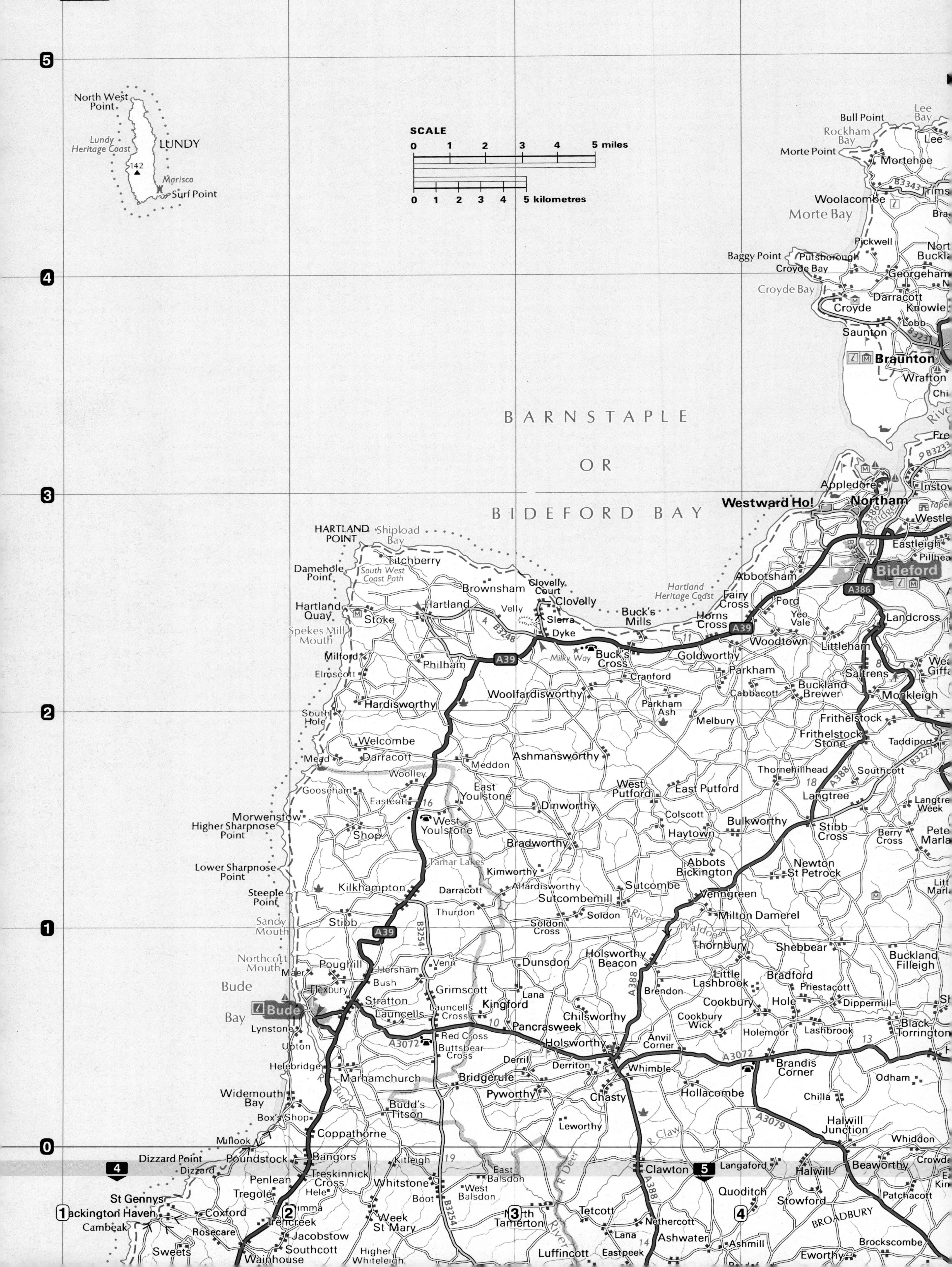

5

North West
Point

*Lundy
Heritage Coast*

LUNDY

▲142

Marisco
✠ Surf Point

SCALE

0 1 2 3 4 5 miles

0 1 2 3 4 5 kilometres

Bull Point Lee
Bay
Rockham Lee
Bay
Morte Point
Mortehoe Mortehoe

Woolacombe
Morte Bay

Pickwell
Baggy Point Nort
Buckl
Putsborough
Croyde Bay Georgeham
Croyde Bay
Darracott
Croyde Knowle
Lobb
Saunton
Braunton
Wrafton
Chi

4

B A R N S T A P L E

O R

B I D E F O R D   B A Y

River

Appledore Northam
Westward Ho! Westle

Eastleigh
Bideford

3

HARTLAND
POINT *Shipload
Bay*
Titchberry
Damehole
Point *South West
Coast Path*
Brownsham Clovelly
Court
Hartland Clovelly Buck's
Velly Mills Horns
Sierra Cross Abbotsham
Hartland
Quay Stoke Dyke Buck's Woodtown
*Spekes Mill
Mouth* Cross Goldworthy Littleham
Milford Philham Milky Way Parkham
Elmscott Woolfardisworthy Cranford Cabbacott Buckland
Hardisworthy Parkham Brewer Monkleigh
South Ash Melbury Frithelstock
Hole Darracott Meddon Frithelstock
Welcombe East Ashmansworthy Stone Taddiport
Mead Youlstone West Thornehillhead Southcott
Woolley Putford East Putford 18
Gooseham Dinworthy Langtree
Eastcott West Colscott Langtre
Morwenstow Youlstone Bradworthy Haytown Bulkworthy Week
Higher Sharpnose Shop Stibb Berry Pete
Point Kimworthy Abbots Cross Marl
Lower Sharpnose Darracott Alfardisworthy Bickington Newton
Point Thurdon Sutcombemill St Petrock Litt
Steeple Kilkhampton Soldon Sutcombe Venngreen Marl
Point Soldon Milton Damerel
*Sandy Stibb Cross River Waldon Shebbear Buckland
Mouth* Holsworthy Thornbury Filleigh
*Northcott Poughill Venn Beacon Little Bradford Priestacott
Mouth* Hersham Dunsdon Lashbrook Hole Dippermill
Bude Maer Bush Grimscott Lana Brendon Cookbury Black
Flexbury Stratton Kingford Chilsworthy Cookbury Holemoor Lashbrook Torrington
Bude Launcells Launcells Pancrasweek Wick Anvil
Bay Cross Holsworthy Corner Brandis
Lynstone Red Cross Derril Derriton Whimble Corner Odham
Upton Buttsbear Bridgerule Hollacombe Chilla
Helebridge Cross Pyworthy Chasty Halwill
Marhamchurch Junction Whiddon
Widemouth Budd's Leworthy Broadbury
Bay Titson R Claw Beaworthy
Box's Shop R Deer Crowde
Coppathorne

0

4 Dizzard Point Poundstock Kilkeigh 19 Clawton 5 Langaford Halwill
Dizzard Bangors East Quoditch
Penlean Treskinnick Whitstone Balsdon Stowford Patchacott
St Gennys Tregole Cross West Tetcott Quoditch
1 ackington Haven Hele Boot Balsdon Nethercott Brockscombe
Cambeak Coxford imma Week th Lana Ashwater Eworthy
Rosecare Trenhcreek Jacobstow St Mary Tamerton Eastpeek Ashmill
Sweets Southcott Higher B3254 Luffincott
Wainhouse Whiteleigh

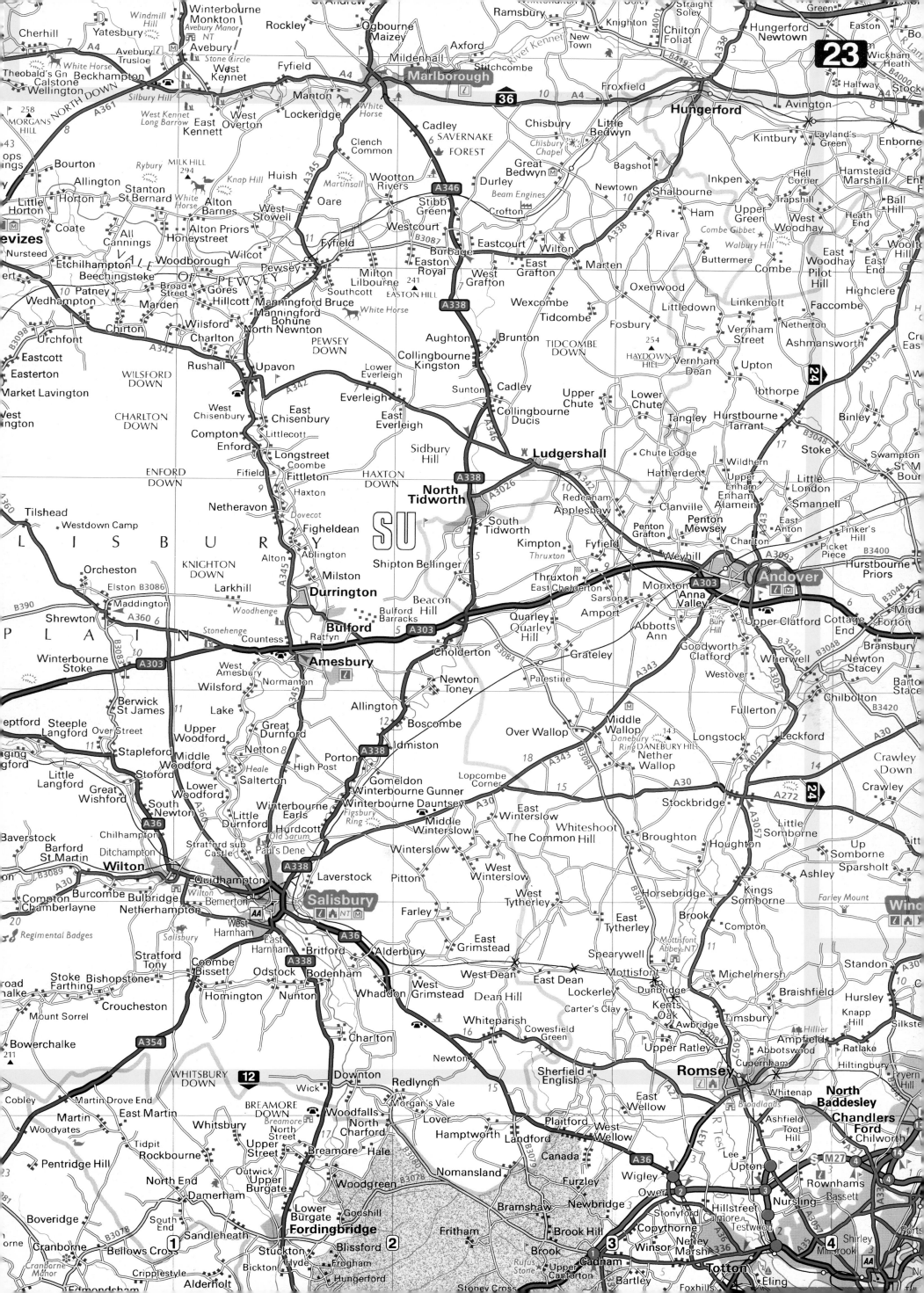

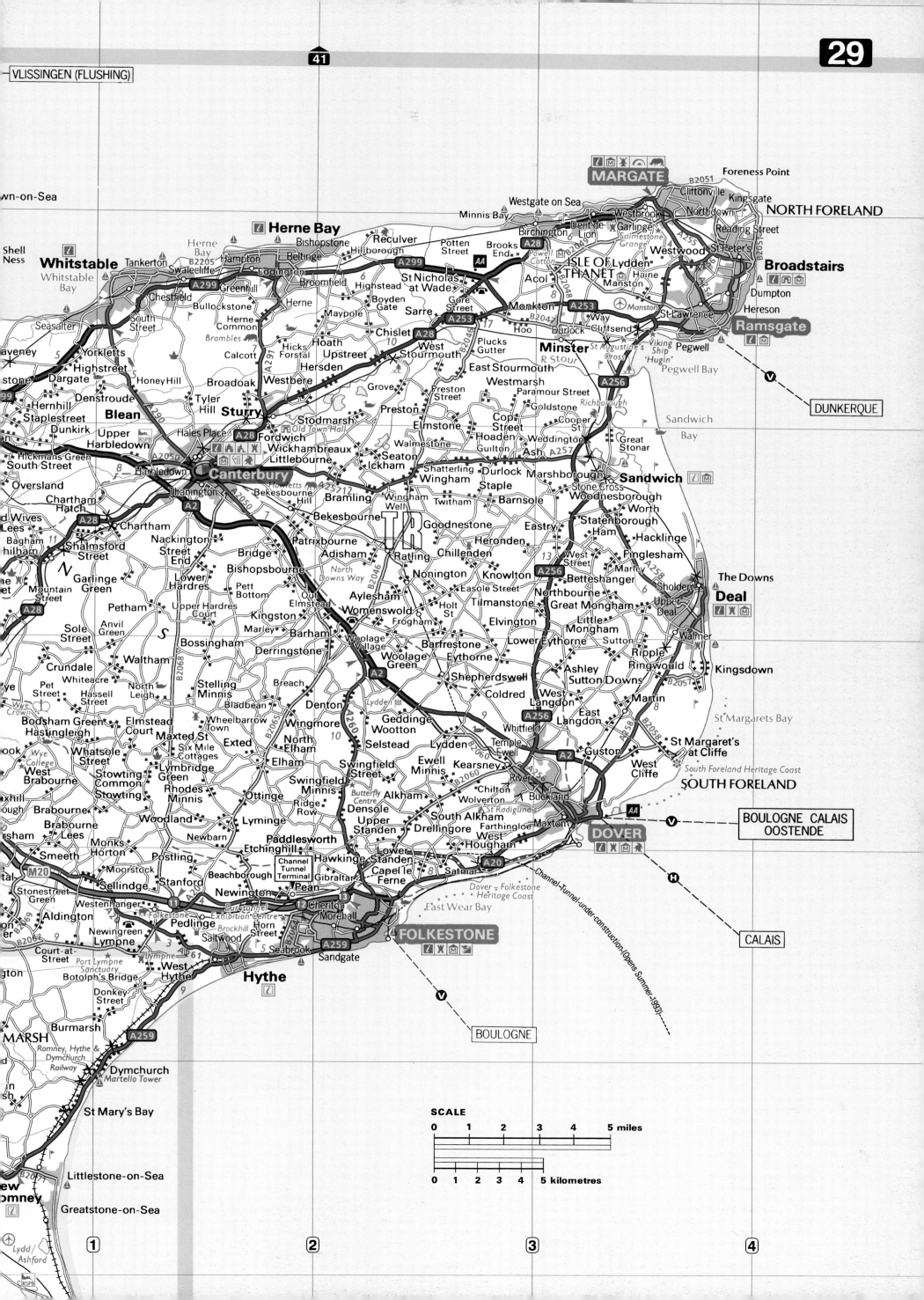

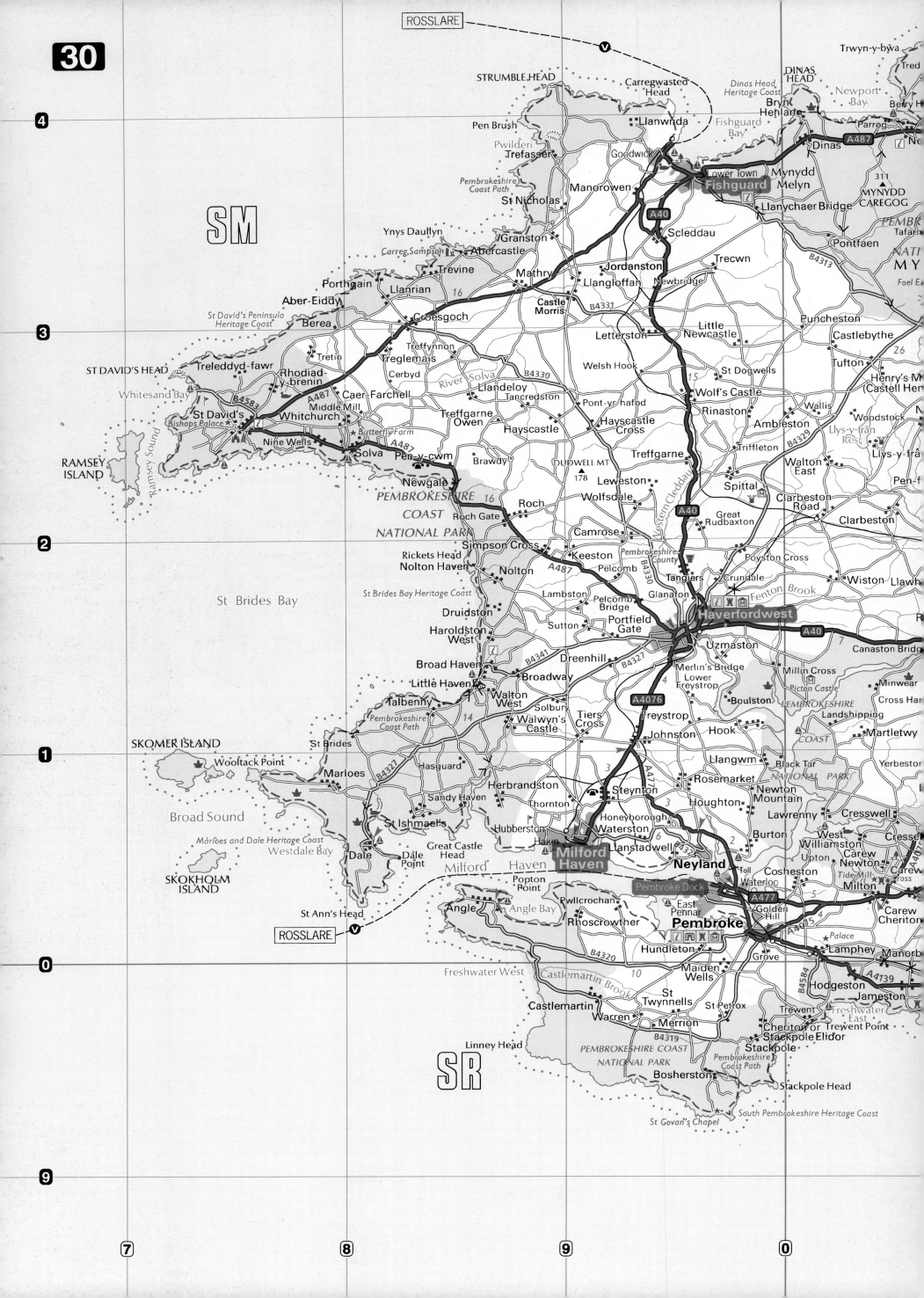

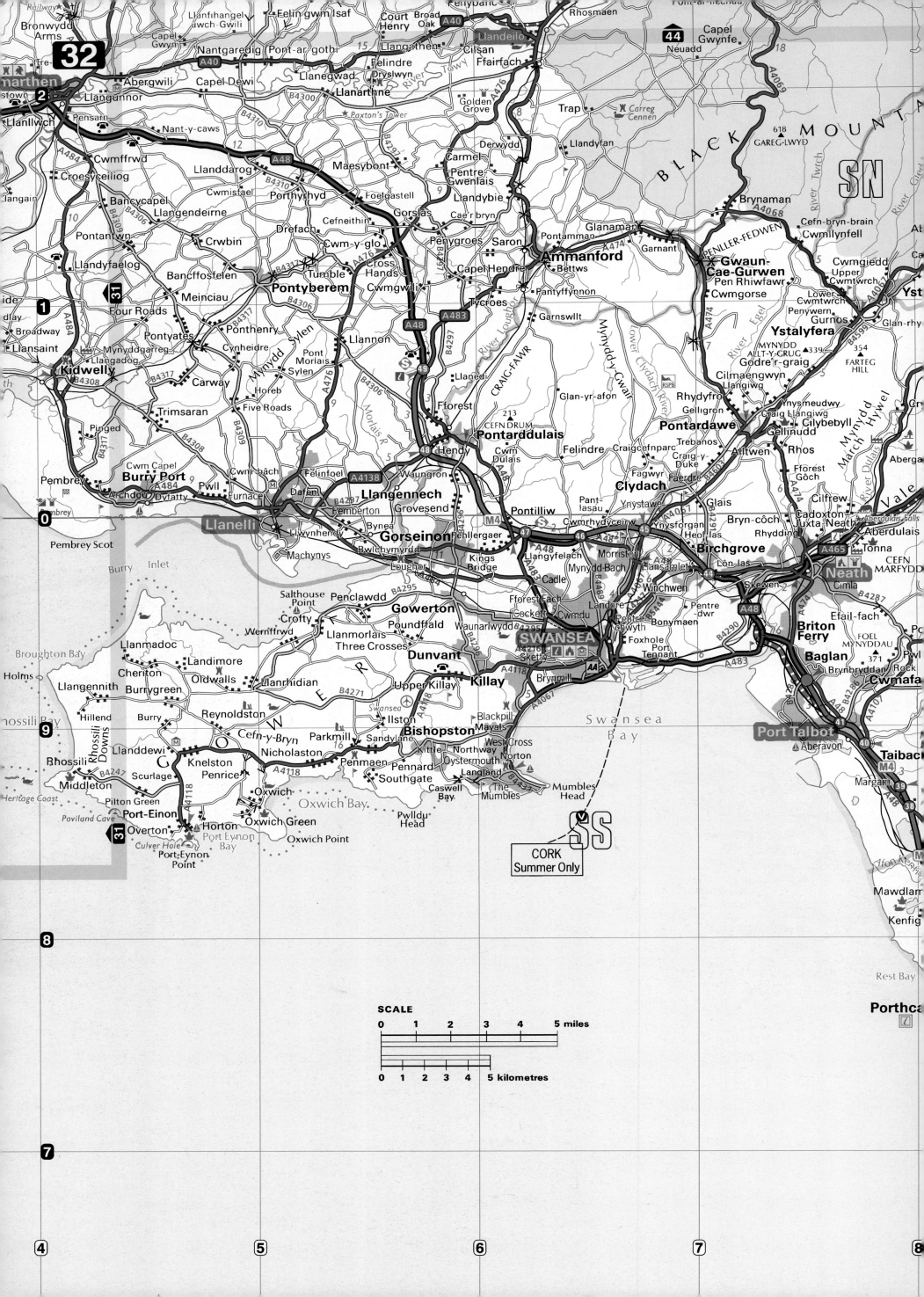

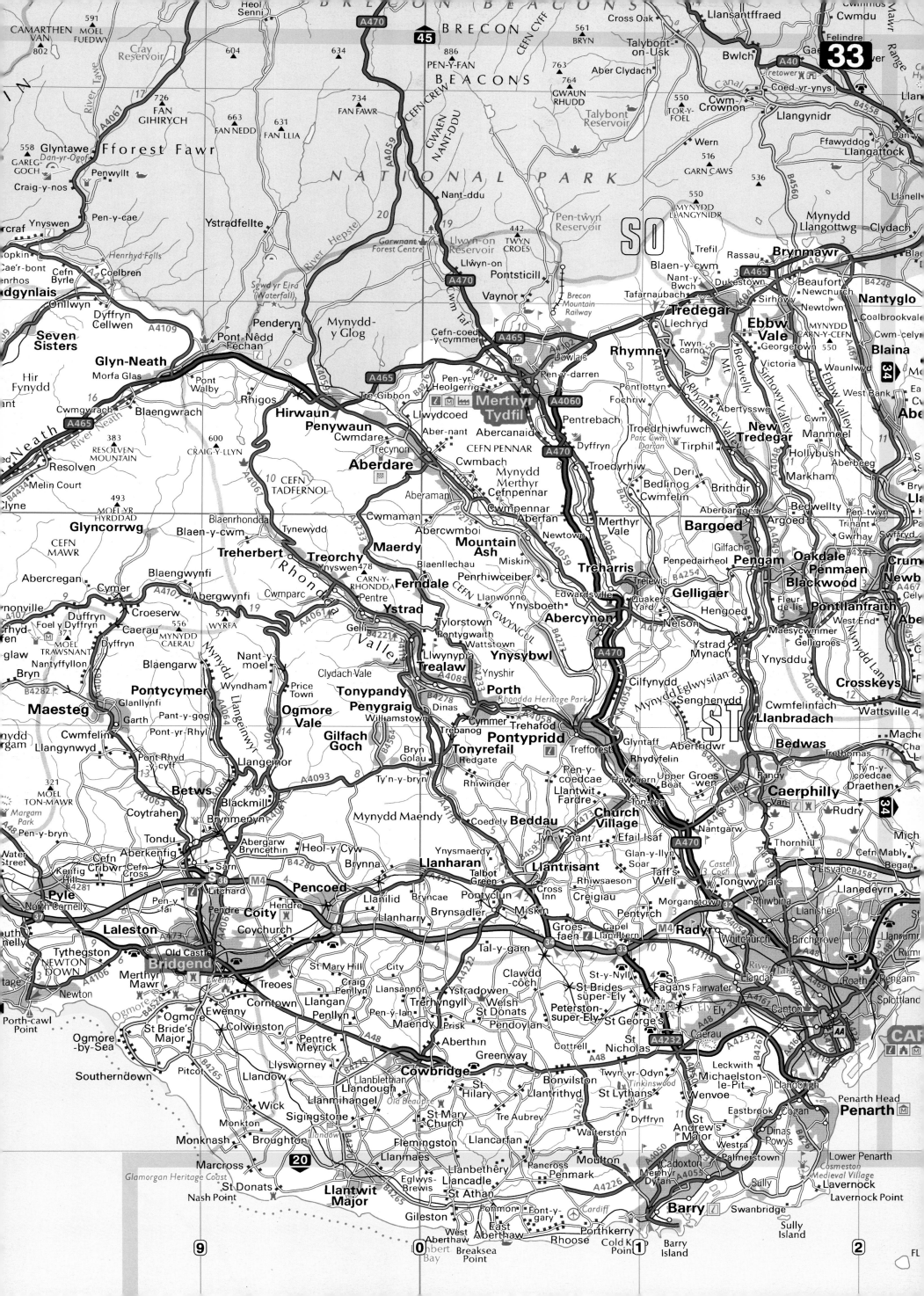

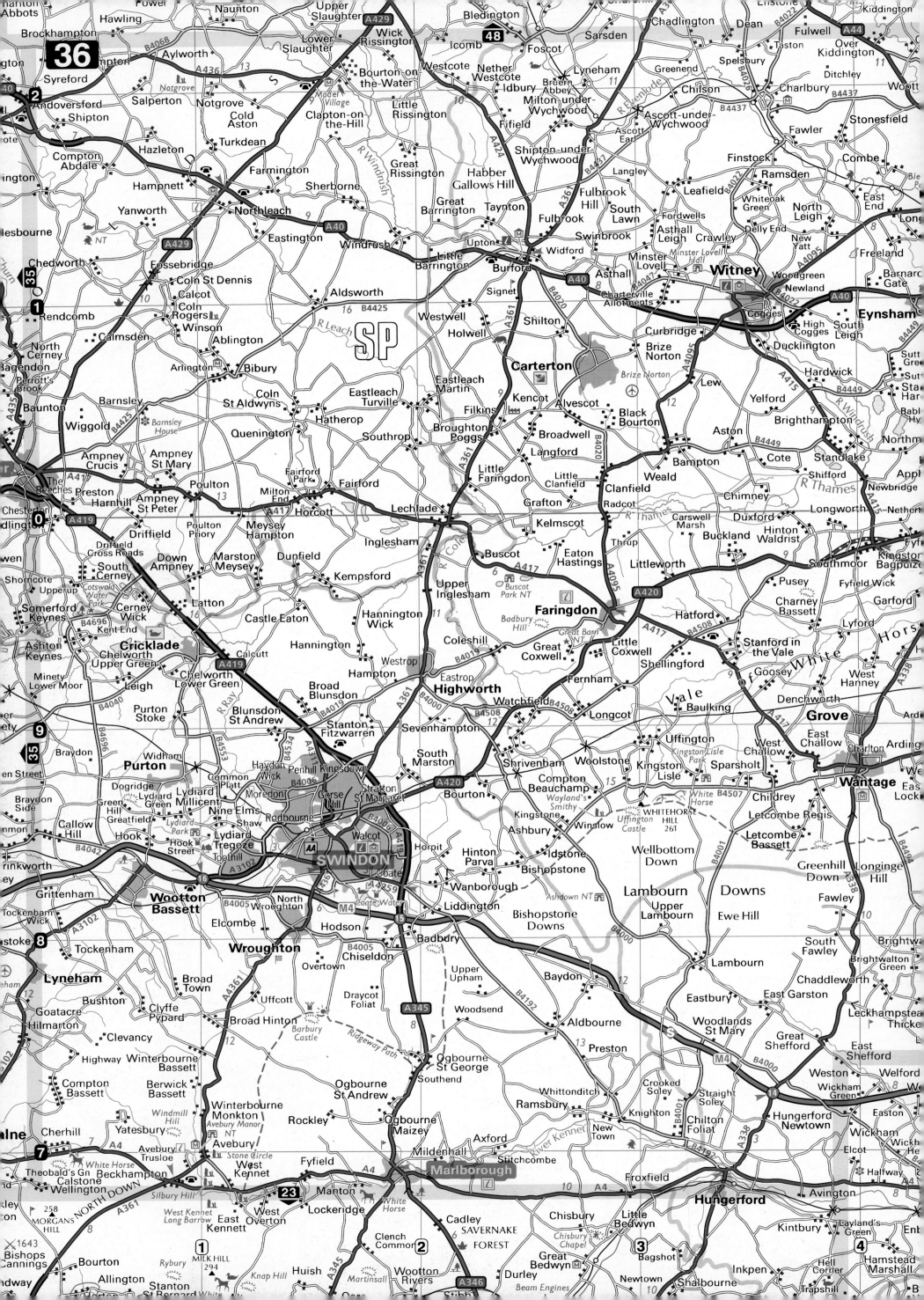

R Stour
Stratford St Mary
Bergholt
Street
Lower Street
Lower Street
Felixstowe ℹ️

Boxted
Langham
Dedham
Brantham
Stutton
Holbrook
Erwarton
Shotley Gate

Horkesley Green
Boxted Cross
Castle House
Dedham Heath
Cattawade
Holbrook Bay
Parkeston Quay
A45

Boxted Heath
Langham Heath
MANNINGTREE
Lawford
River Stour
Wrabness
55
AA
Parkeston
Bath Side
Harwich Harbour
The Redoubt

Great Horkesley
Langham Wick
New Mistley
Mistley
A120
Upper Dovercourt
Harwich
Landguard Fort
Landguard Point
V

West Bergholt
Langham Moor
Ardleigh Heath
Mistley Heath
Bradfield
Ramsey
B1352
B7351
Dovercourt
ℹ️
V
ZEEBRUGGE

Mile End
Ardleigh
Little Bromley
Bradfield Heath
Wix
Little Oakley
Great Oakley

Horkesley Heath
Fox Street
Burnt Heath
Horsleycross Street
Goose Green
Wix Green
B1414

Parson's Heath
Crockleford Heath
8
B1029
Horsley Cross
19
Pennyhole Bay
ESBJERG GOTEBORG HAMBURG HOEK VAN HOLLAND

West Bergholt
A12
A604
A134
COLCHESTER
A120
Great Bromley
A120
Tendring Heath
Tendring Green
Stones Green
17
Horsey Island

Greenstead
A133
Elmstead Market
Hare Green
Little Bentley
Goose Green
Beaumont
The Naze

Trexden
AA
New Quay
Wivenhoe Cross
Beth Chatto
Elmstead Heath
Frating Green
Tendring
B1035
Thorpe Green
Thorpe-le-Soken
B1034
Kirby-le-Soken
Walton on the Naze

Shrub End
B1026
B1025
Old Heath
WIVENHOE
Elmstead Row
Frating
16
Weeley
B1033
B1033
Kirby Cross
Frinton-on-sea

chester dge
Blackheath
Rowhedge
High Park Corner
Alresford
Great Bentley
Weeley Heath
B1033

Malting Green
Fingringhoe
Tenpenny Heath
B1027
Aingers Green
B1414
Cook's Green
Great Holland
TM

Abberton
Thorrington
Little Clacton
Great Holland

Langenhoe
South Green
Samson's Corner
B1029
Hurst Green
Holland-on-Sea

Abberton Reservoir
Peldon
Great Clacton
A133
Holland-on-Sea

Great Wigborough
MERSEA ISLAND
B1027
St Osyth
Rush Green
CLACTON-ON-SEA ℹ️

West Mersea
East Mersea
Point Clear
Jaywick

Shinglehead Point
Colne Point

Bradwell Waterside
Sales Point

Bradwell-on-Sea
B1021

Tillingham

Dengie

Asheldham

outhminster
neyhills

urnham-on-Crouch
Holliwell Point

Foulness Point

Courtsend

allsea sland
Churchend

FOULNESS ISLAND

TR

SCALE

0   1   2   3   4   5 miles

0 1 2 3 4 5 kilometres

29

inster

0
V
VLISSINGEN (FLUSHING)
1
2
3

C A R D I G A N

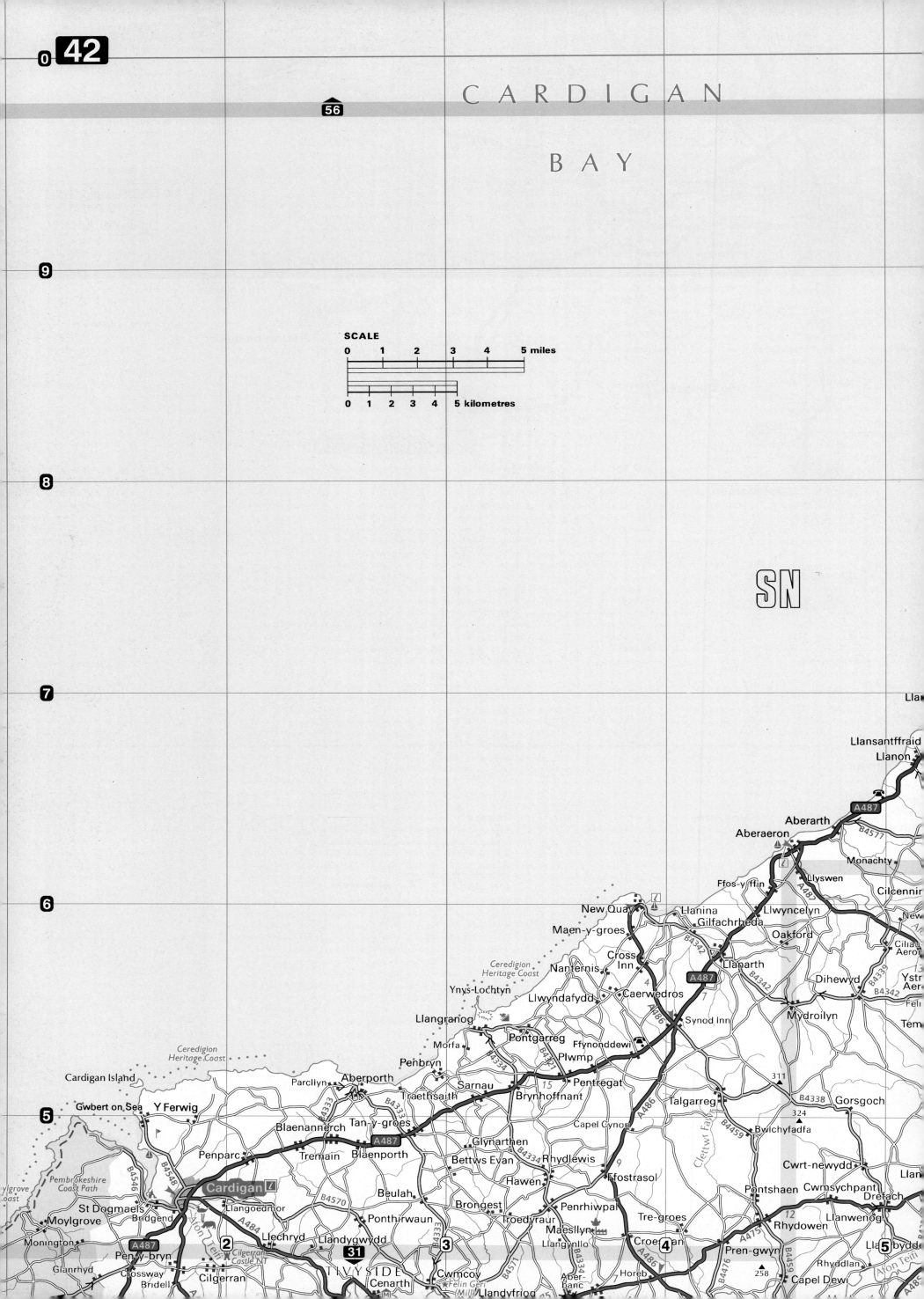

⬆ 56

B A Y

9

SCALE

| 0 | 1 | 2 | 3 | 4 | 5 miles |

| 0 | 1 | 2 | 3 | 4 | 5 kilometres |

8

SN

7

Llan

Llansantffraid
Llanon

A487

Aberarth
Aberaeron
B4577

Monachty

Ffos-y-ffin
Llyswen
Cilcennin

6

New Quay
Llanina
Gilfachrheda
Llwyncelyn

New

Maen-y-groes
Cross Inn
B4342
A487
Oakford
Cilia
Aeror

Ceredigion Heritage Coast
Nanternis
Llanarth
Ystr
Aero

Ynys-Lochtyn
Llwyndafydd
Caerwedros
4
A486
7
Dihewyd
B4339
13

Llangranog
Synod Inn
Mydroilyn
B4342
Tem

Pontgarreg
Ffynonddewi
Morfa
Plwmp
B4334
B4321
311

Penbryn
B4334
A486
Talgarreg
B4338
Gorsgoch

Cardigan Island
Parcllyn
Aberporth
Sarnau
Brynhoffnant
15
Pentregat
A486
B4459
324
Bwlchyfadfa

Ceredigion Heritage Coast
Traethsaith
B4333
B4333

Gwbert on Sea
Y Ferwig
B4571
Capel Cynon
9
Clettwr Fawr
Cwrt-newydd
Llan

Blaenannerch
Tan-y-groes
Glynarthen
A487
A486
Bwlchyfadfa
Cwmsychpant
Drefach

Penparc
Tremain
Blaenporth
Bettws Evan
Rhydlewis
B4334
Pontshaen
Rhydowen
Llanwenog

Pembrokeshire Coast Path
Cardigan
B4570
Hawen
Efostrasol
Tre-groes
Llan

ylgrove
Coast
B4546
B4568
Beulah
Brongest
Penrhiwpal
Croe an
A475
5

St Dogmaels
Bridgend
Llangoedmor
A484
Ponthirwaun
Troedyraur
Maesllyn
Llangynllo
A486
Pren-gwyn
B4459
Rhyddlan
Afon

Moylgrove
2
Llechryd
Llandygwydd
3
Aber-banc
4
258
Capel Dewi

Monington
Pen-y-bryn
Crossway
Bridell
Cilgerran Castle NT
Cilgerran
Cenarth
31
Cwmcoy
Felin Geri Mill
Llandyfriog
B4571
B4334
Horeb
A486
Glanrhyd
TIVYSIDE

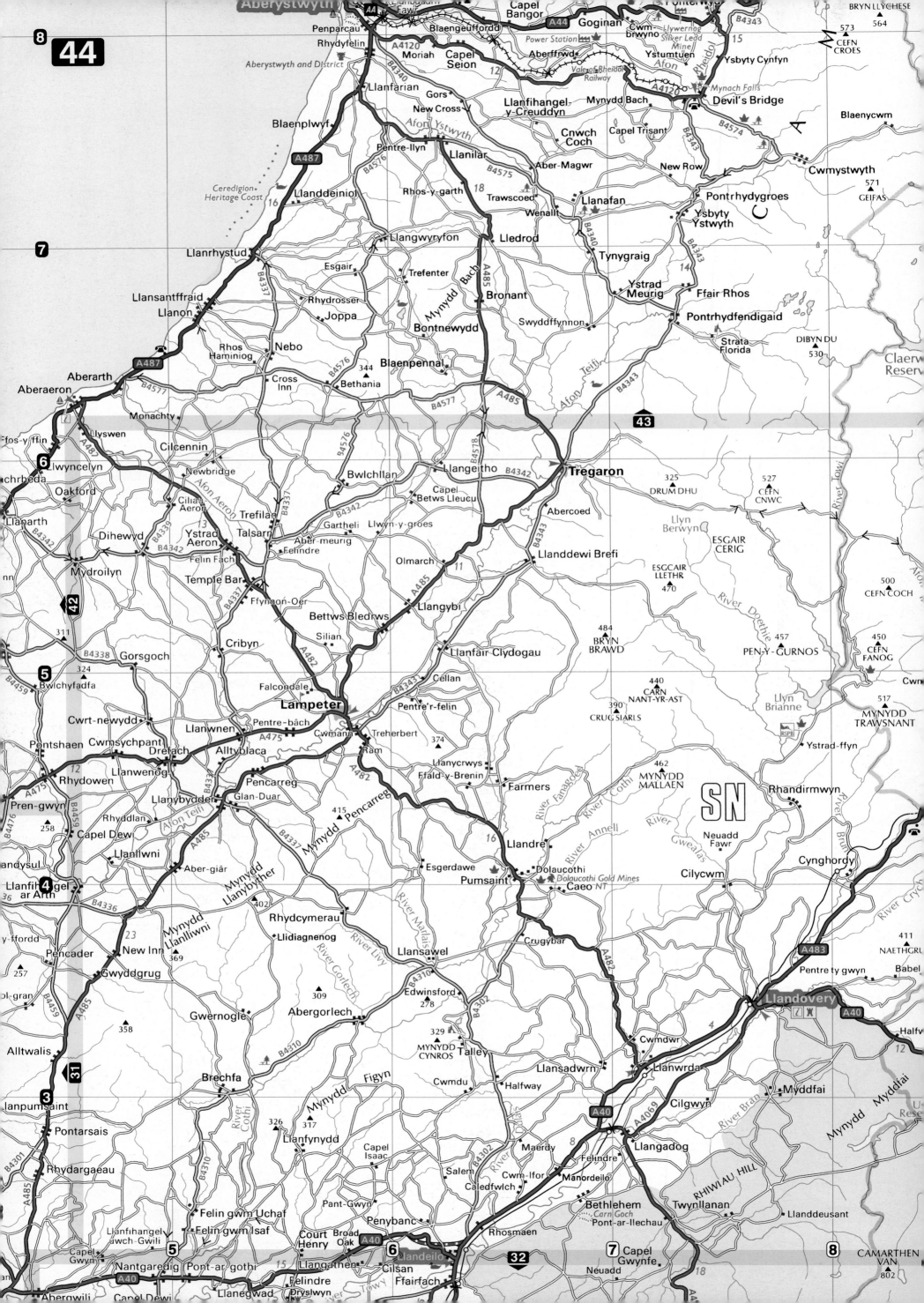

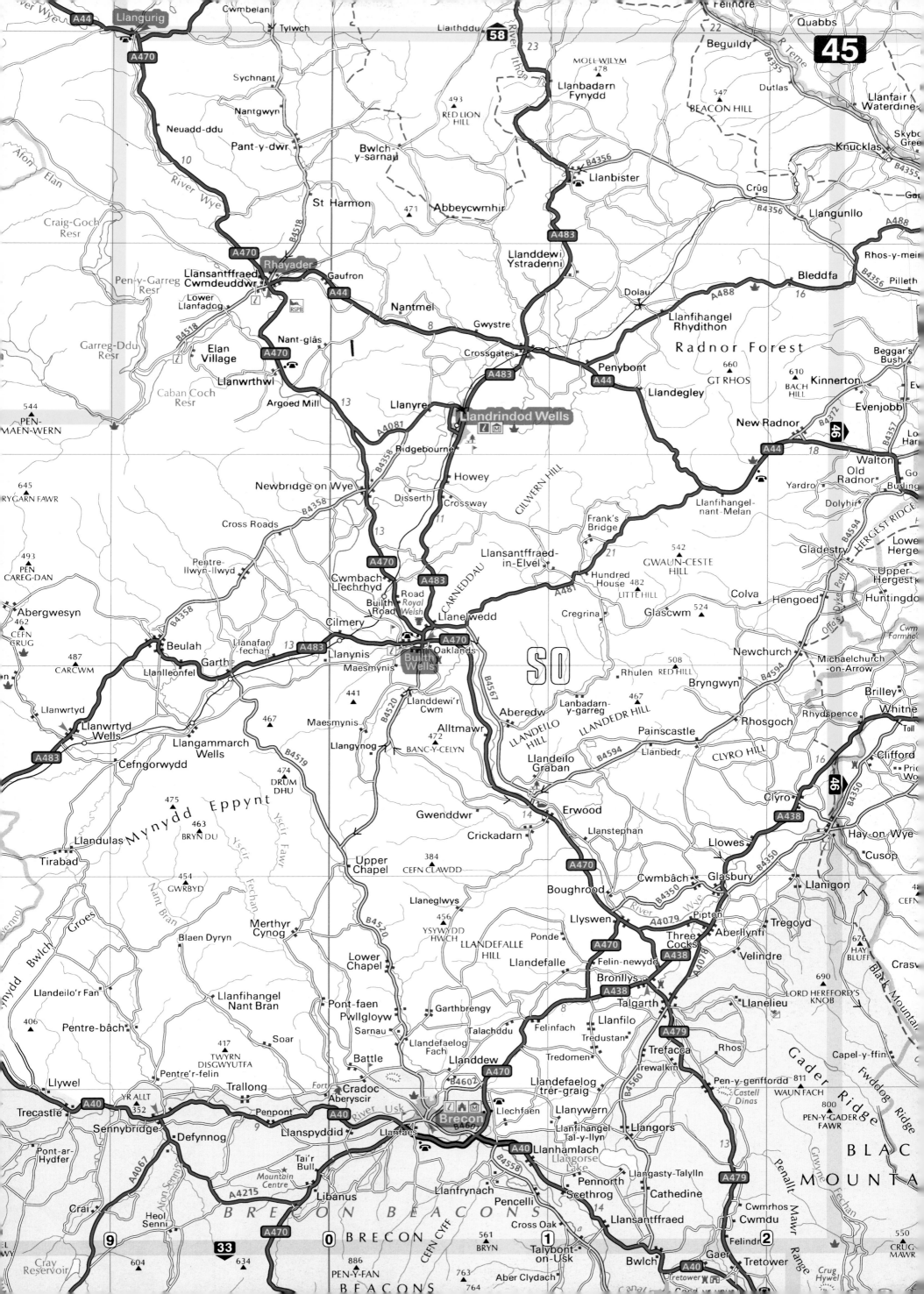

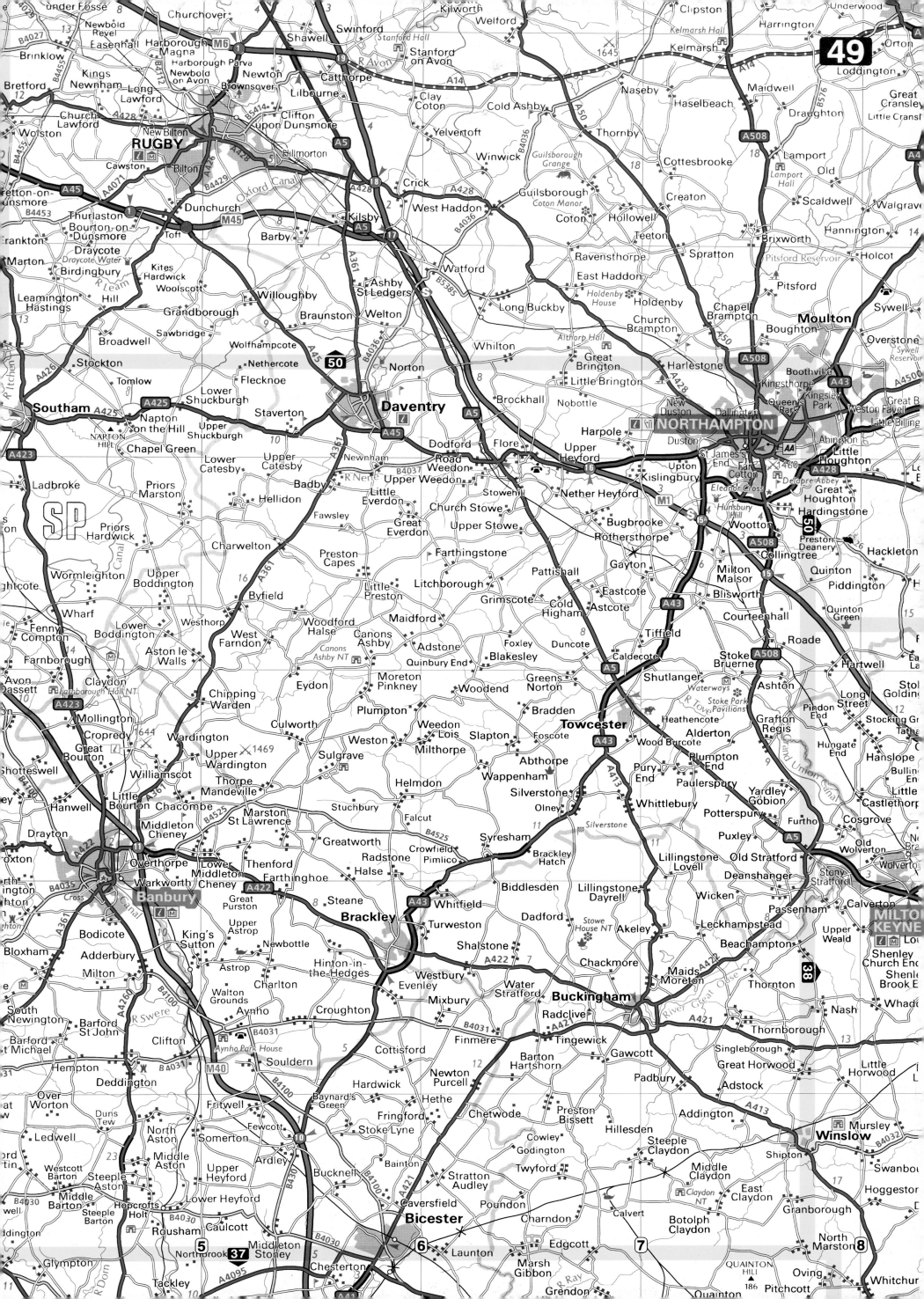

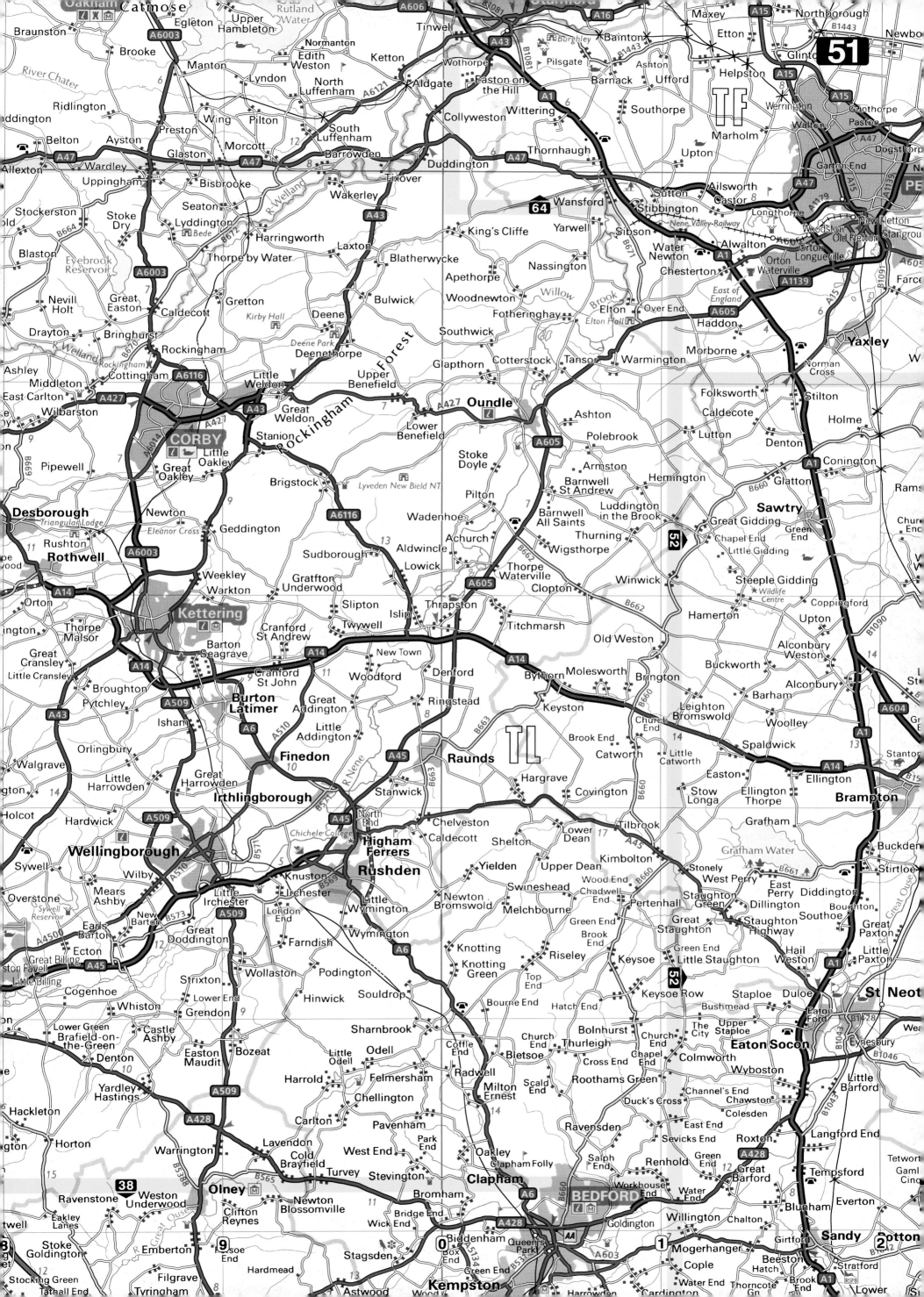

5

68

4

3

2

1

0

SCALE

0   1   2   3   4   5 miles

0   1   2   3   4   5 kilometres

42

C A R D I G A N

B A Y

SH

PENINSULA

LLEYN

Pontllyfni
Llanllyfni
Nebo
Aberdesach
Nasareth
Clynnog-fawr
Capeluchaf
Gyrn-goch
Pant-glas
Trevor
Y GYRN-DDU
522
Upper Clynnog
Bryncir
Llanaelhaearn
Tre'r Ceiri
A487
Trwyn y Grolech
Glan-Dwyfach
Carreg Ddu
Pistyll
Llithfaen
B4417
St Cybi's Well
Rhoslan
Porth Nefyn
Llwyndyrys
Pencaenewydd
Llangybi
Morfa Nefyn
Nefyn
Llanarmon
Porth Dinllaen
Fron
B4354
Chwilog
Llanystumdwy
Groesffordd
Rhos fawr
Edern
Bodfuan
Penarth Fawr
Cri
Rhos-y-llan
A497
Llannor
Abererch
Porth Ysgaden
Llandudwen
Efailnewydd
Tudweiliog
Dinas
Rhyd-y-clafdy
Denio
Pen-ychain
Carn Fadrun
Garn
Porth Colman
Bryn mawr
Penrhos
Pwllheli
Llangwnnadl
Meyllteyrn
Llaniestyn
Pen-y-graig
B4417
B4415
Botwnnog
Llanbedrog
14
Sarn
B4413
Mynytho
Lleyn Heritage Coast
17
Nanhoron
Trwyn Llanbedrog
Bryncroes
Porthoer
Llandegwning
St Tudwal's Road
Rhydlios
Rhoshirwaun
A499
Anelog
Llangian
Penycaerau
Plas-Yn-Rhiw NT
Abersoch
Y Rhiw
Llanengan
Uwchmynydd
Llanfaelrhys
Sarn-bach
St Tudwal's Island East
Aberdaron
Porth Neigwl
Marchros
St Tudwal's Island West
Aberdaron Bay
Porth Ysgo
Bwlchtocyn
Porth Ceiriad
Bardsey Sound
St Mary's
BARDSEY ISLAND

Old Welsh Country Life
19
20
21
7
13
37
R Erch

1   2   3   4

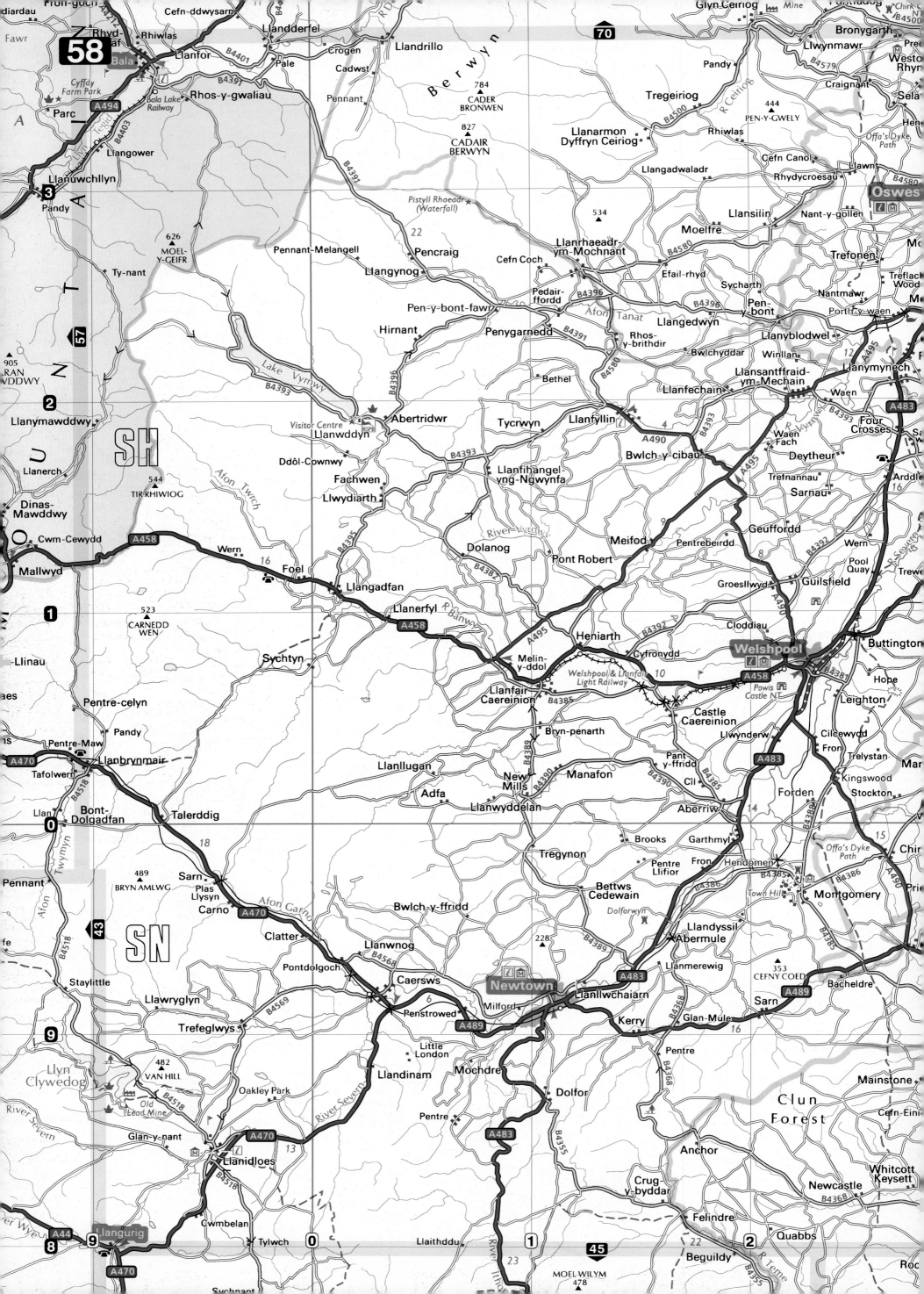

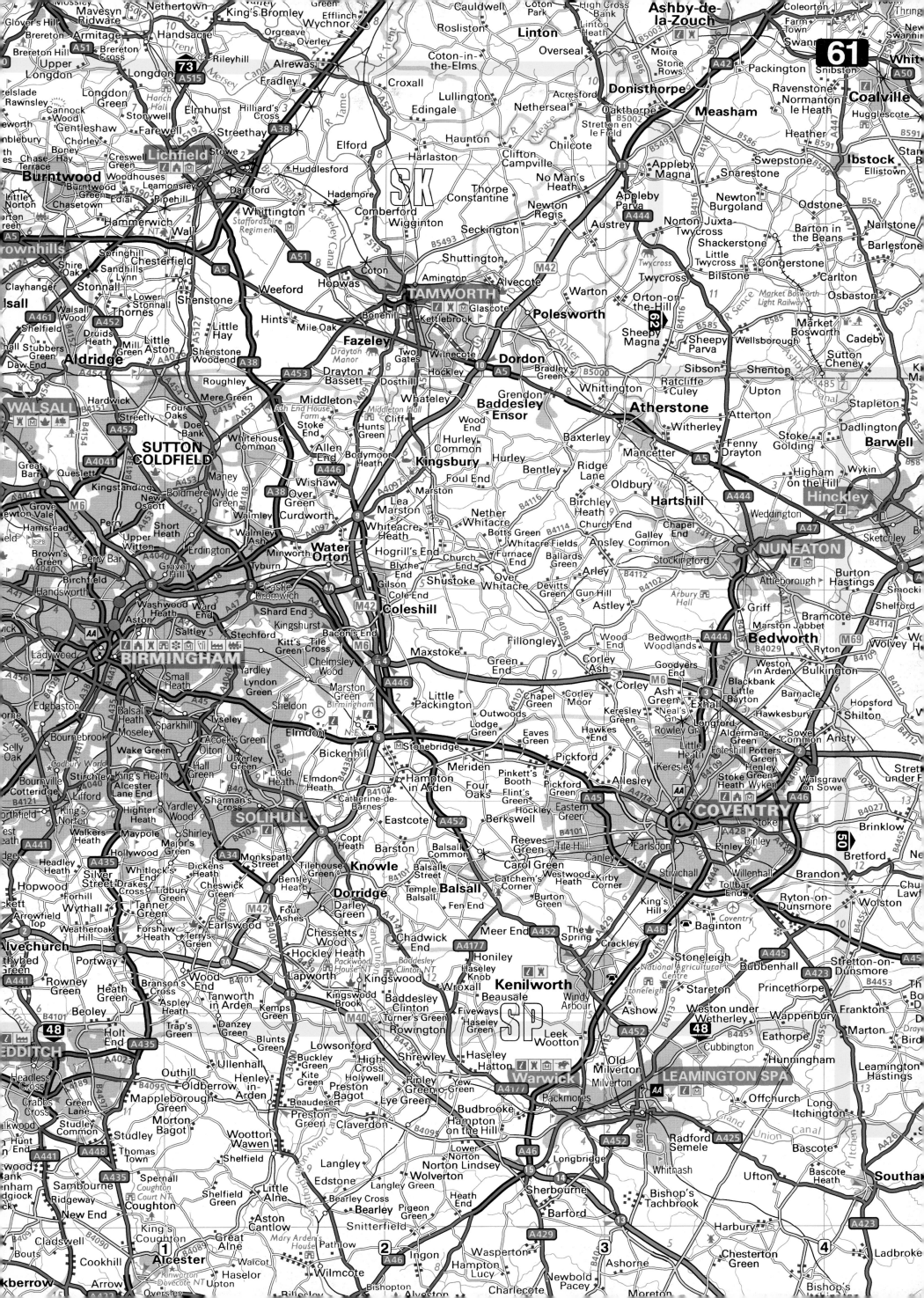

SCALE
0 1 2 3 4 5 miles
0 1 2 3 4 5 kilometres

East Runton
Cromer
Overstrand
Sidestrand
Felbrigg Hall NT
Crossdale Street
Metton
Northrepps
Trimingham
Southrepps
Gimingham
Roughton
Thorpe Market
Mundesley
Lower Street
Paston
Trunch
Knapton
Bacton
Edingthorpe
Walcott
Bradfield
Old Hall Street
Antingham
Swafield
Edingthorpe Green
Witton
Ridlington
Happisburgh
North Walsham
Spa Common
Ridlington Street
Whimpwell Green
Meeting House Hill
Honing
Crostwight
Happisburgh Common
Tungate
Felmingham
Briggate
East Ruston
Hempstead
Tuttington
Skeyton Corner
Bengates
Lessingham
Ingham Corner
Swanton Abbot
Westwick
Dilham
Stalham
Ingham
Sea Palling
Worstead
Smallburgh
Stalham Green
Frankfort
Low Street
Calthorpe Street
Scottow
Sloley
Pennygate
Hickling
Horsey Corner
Sco Ruston
Tunstead
Wood Street
Sutton
Hickling Green
Horsey
Market Street
Crowgate Street
Barton Turf
Hickling Heath
Hill Common
Neatishead
Barton Broad
Catfield Common
West Somerton
St James
Irstead
Catfield
Hickling Broad
Horsey Windpump NT
Threehammer Common
Sharp Green
Potter Heigham
Winterton-on-Sea
Hoveton
Ludham
Martham
Belaugh
Johnson's Street
Bastwick
East Somerton
Wroxham
Upper Street
Repps
Hemsby
Upper Street
Thurne
Hemsby Hole
Woodbastwick
Broadland Conservation Centre
Ormesby Broad
Newport
Horning
Clippesby
Rollesby
Ormesby St Michael
Scratby
Ranworth
Pilson Green
Burgh St Margaret
California
Salhouse
Cargate Green
Ormesby St Margaret
Panxworth
South Walsham
Upton
Billockby
Filby
Caister-on-Sea
Town Green
Thrigby
Mautby
Little Plumstead
Burlingham Green
Acle
Stokesby
West End
West Caister
Great Plumstead
Hemblington
North Burlingham
Damgate
Runham
Witton
Lingwood
Beighton
Tunstall
A47
Thorpe End
Blofield
Moulton St Mary
THE BROADS
Runham
NORWICH
Brundall
Halvergate
GREAT YARMOUTH
Postwick
South Burlingham
River Yare
Southtown
Strumpshaw
Southwood
Freethorpe
Burgh Castle
Surlingham
Buckenham
Wickhampton
Berney Arms
Gorleston on Sea
Hassingham
Freethorpe Common
Bradwell
Rockland St Mary
Cantley
Witton Green
Belton
Elm Grove
Claxton
Limpenhoe
Reedham
Hobland Hall
Langley Street
Hardley Street
Nogdam End
Fritton
Browston Grn
Thurton
Lower Thurlton
St Olaves
Hopton on Sea
Chedgrave
Norton Subcourse
Thorpe
Herringfleet
Loddon
Hales
Thurlton
Somerleyton
Blundeston
Corton
Seething
Raveningham
Haddiscoe
Pleasurewood Hills
Gunton
Maypole Green
Toft Monks
Wheatacre
Oulton
Kirby Cane
Bull's Green
Aldeby
Burgh St Peter
Oulton Broad
LOWESTOFT
Stockton
Gillingham
River Waveney
Kirkley
Bungay
Beccles
A146
Carlton Colville

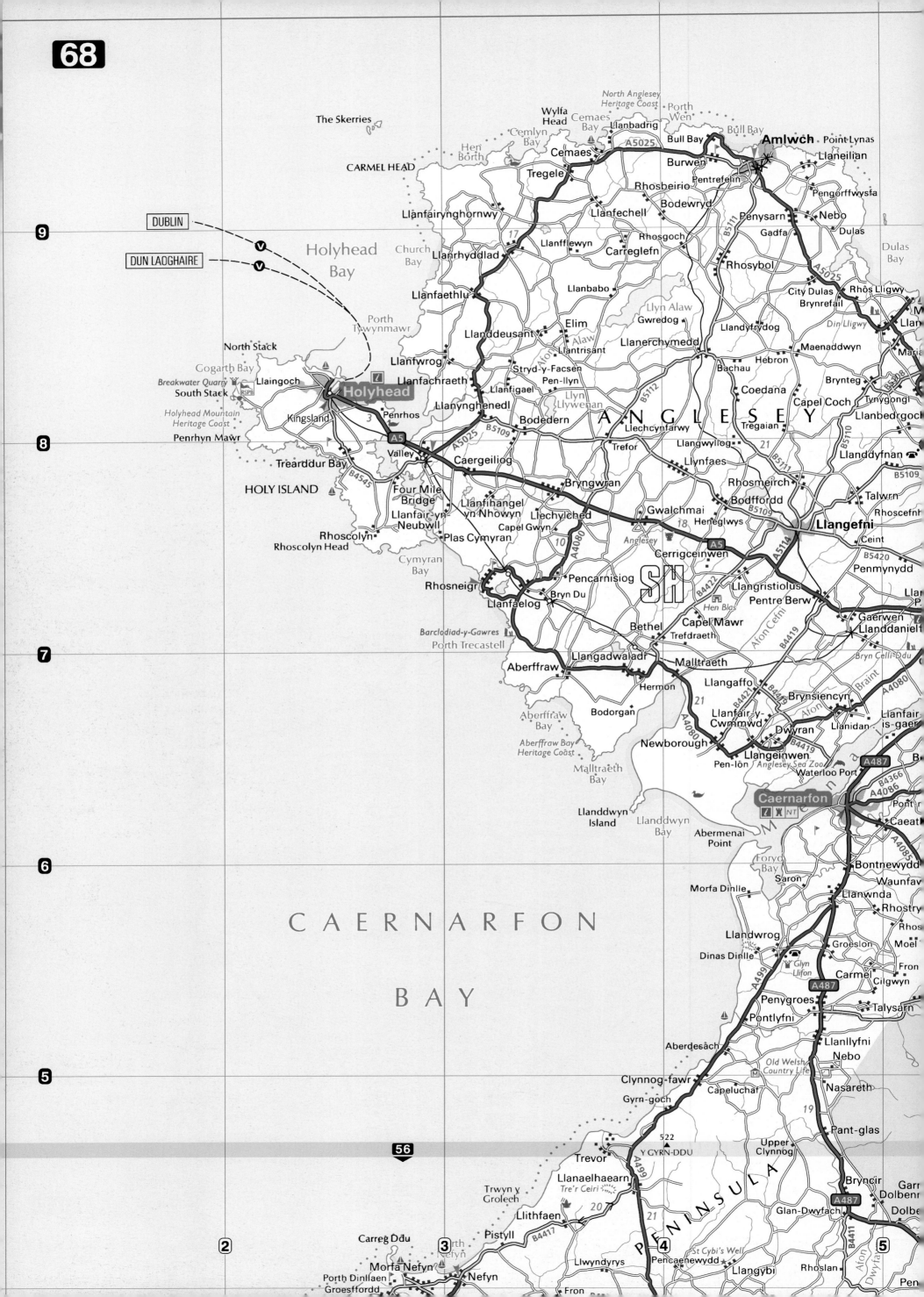

The Skerries

North Anglesey
Heritage Coast
Wylfa
Head   Cemaes   Porth
Bay   Wen
Cemlyn   Llanbadrig
Bay
CARMEL HEAD   Hen
Borth   A5025   Bull Bay   Bull Bay
Cemaes   Burwen   Amlwch   Point Lynas
Tregele   Llaneilian
Rhosbeirio   Pentrefelin
Llanfairynghornwy   Llanfechell   Bodewyd   Pengorffwysfa
Penysarn   Nebo
9   DUBLIN   Rhosgoch   Gadfa   Dulas
Llanfflewyn   Carreglefn
DUN LAOGHAIRE   Rhosybol   Dulas
Holyhead   Church   Llanrhyddlad   Bay
Bay   City Dulas   Rhôs Llïgwy
Brynrefail
Holyhead   Llanfaethlu   Llanbabo   Llyn Alaw
Bay   Din Llïgwy
Llandyfrydog   Maenaddwyn
Porth   Elim   Gwredog   Brynteg
Tywynmawr   Llanddeusant   Llanerchymedd   Hebron
North Stack   Llantrisant   Bachau   Capel Coch
Gogarth Bay   Llanfwrog   Coedana   Tynygongl
Breakwater Quarry   Stryd-y-Facsen   ANGLESEY
South Stack   Laingoch   Pen-llyn   B5112   Llanbedrgoch
RSPB   Holyhead   Llanfigael   Llechcynfarwy
Holyhead Mountain   Llanynghenedl   Trefor   Llangwyllog   Tregaian   Llanddyfnan
Heritage Coast   Penrhos   Bodedern   Llynfaes
Penrhyn Mawr   Kingsland   3   A5   A5025   B5109   Rhosmeirch   Talwrn
Valley   Caergeiliog   Bryngwran   Bodffordd   Rhoscefni
Trearddur Bay   B4545   Gwalchmai
B5109   Heneglwys   Llangefni
HOLY ISLAND   Four Mile   Llanfihangel   Llechyliched   18   A5   Ceint
Bridge   yn Nhowyn   A5
Llanfair-yn-   Capel Gwyn   Anglesey   Penmynydd
Neubwll   10   A4080   Cerrigceinwen   B5420
Rhoscolyn   Plas Cymyran   SH   Llangristiolus   Pentre Berw
Rhoscolyn Head   Pencarnisiog   B4422   Hen Blas
Cymyran   Bryn Du   Capel Mawr   Gaerwen
Bay   Rhosneigr   Bethel   Llanddaniel
Llanfaelog   Trefdraeth   B4419
Barclodiad-y-Gawres   Llangadwaladr   Bryn Celli Ddu
Porth Trecastell   Aberffraw   21   Malltraeth   A4080
Aberffraw   Hermon   Llangaffo   Brynsiencyn
Bay   21   Braint
Bodorgan   Llanfair-y-   Llanfair
Aberffraw Bay   Cwmmwd   Dwyran   Llanidan   is-gaer
Heritage Coast   A4080   Newborough   Llangeinwen
Malltraeth   Pen-lôn   Anglesey Sea Zoo   A487
Bay   Waterloo Port   B4366
Llanddwyn   A4085
Island   Llanddwyn   Caernarfon   A4086
Bay   Abermenai
Point   Caeat
Foryd   Bontnewydd
Bay   Saron
Morfa Dinlle   Llanwnda   Rhostry
C A E R N A R F O N   Waunfav
Llandwrog   Groeslon   Moel
Dinas Dinlle   Glyn   Carmel   Fron   Rhos
Llïfon   Cilgwyn
B A Y   Penygroes
Pontllyfni   Talysarn
Aberdesach   Llanllyfni
Nebo
Old Welsh
Country Life
Clynnog-fawr   Nasareth
Gyrn-goch   Capeluchaf
Pant-glas
19
56   522
Y GYRN-DDU   Upper
Trevor   Clynnog
A499   Bryncir
Llanaelhaearn   A487
Trwyn y   Tre'r Ceiri   Glan-Dwyfach   Dolbenn
Grolech   20   Garr
A487   Dolbe
Llithfaen   21   PENINSULA
Carreg Ddu   Pistyll   B4417   St Cybi's Well   A411
2   3   4   Pencaenewydd   5
rth   Llwyndyrys   Llangybi   Afon   Dwyfa
Nefyn   Fron   Rhoslan
Morfa Nefyn   Nefyn
Groesffordd

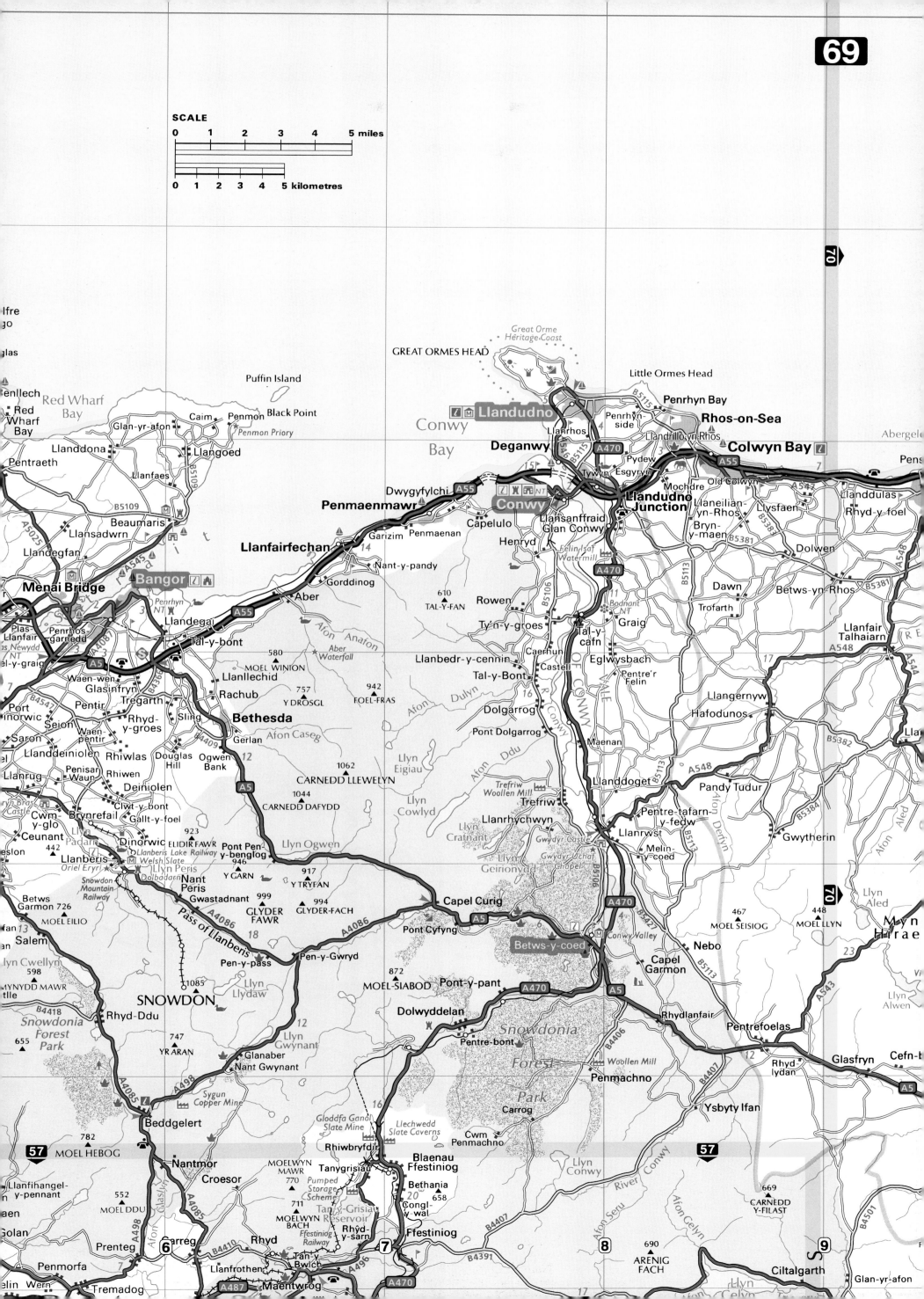

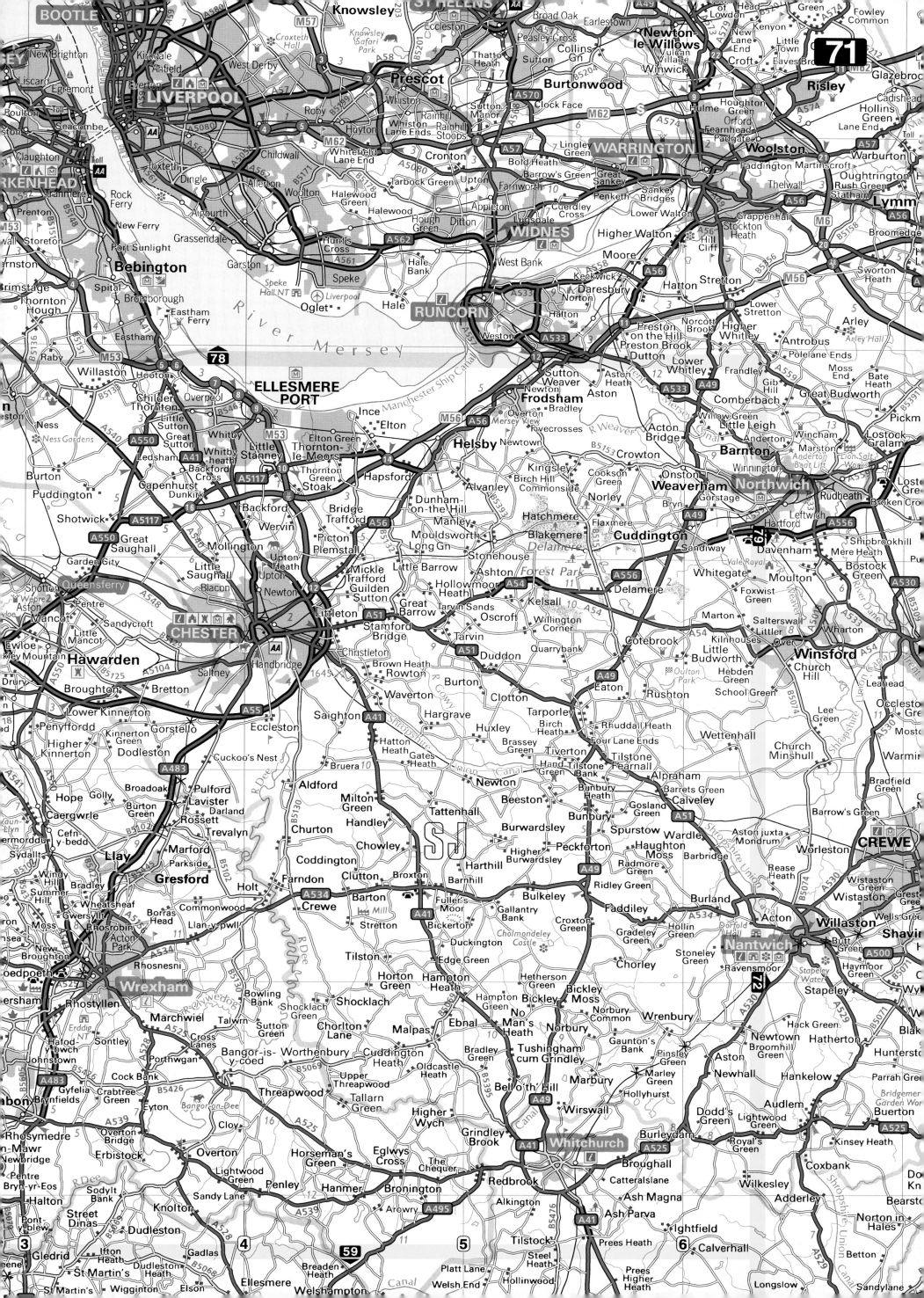

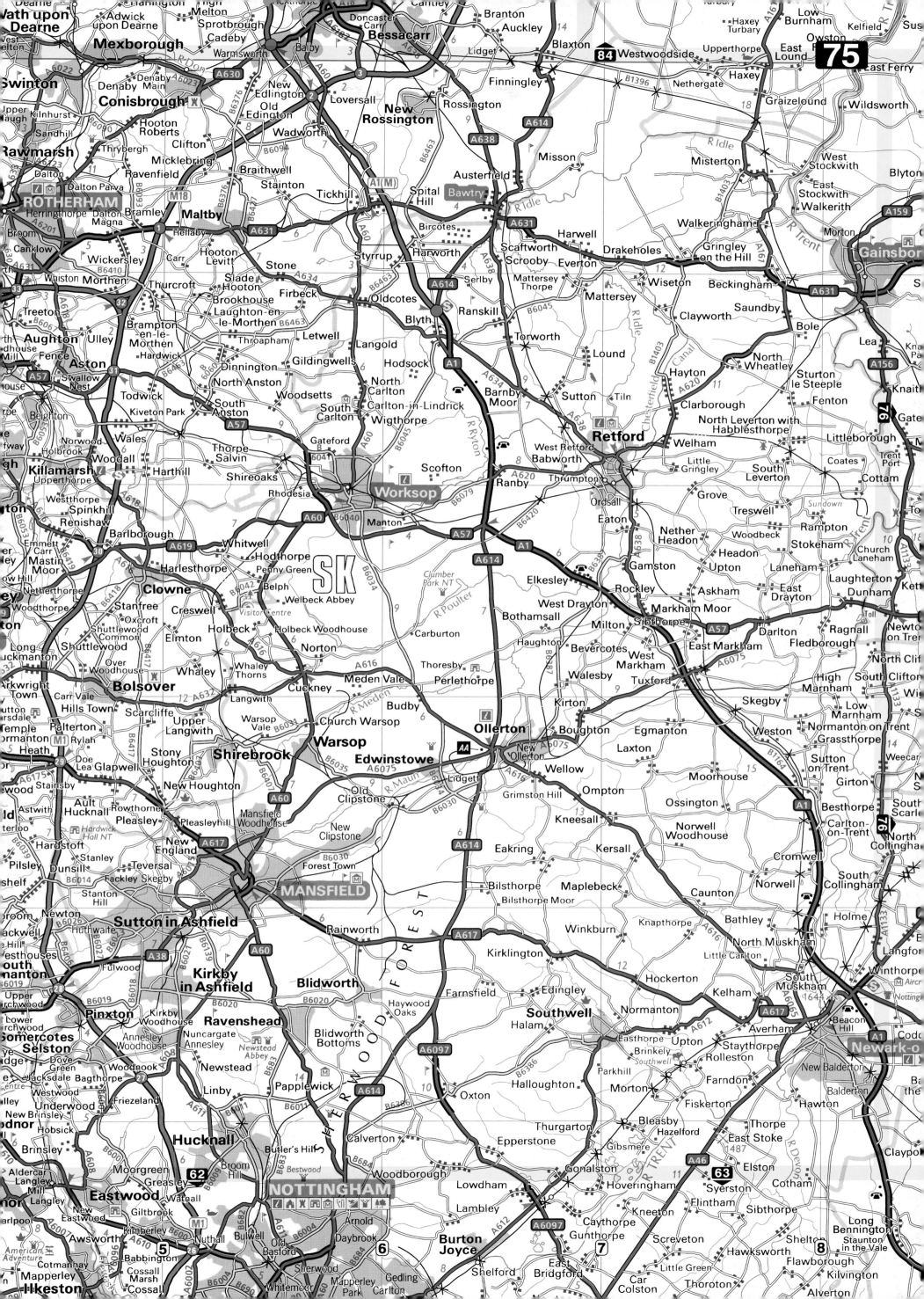

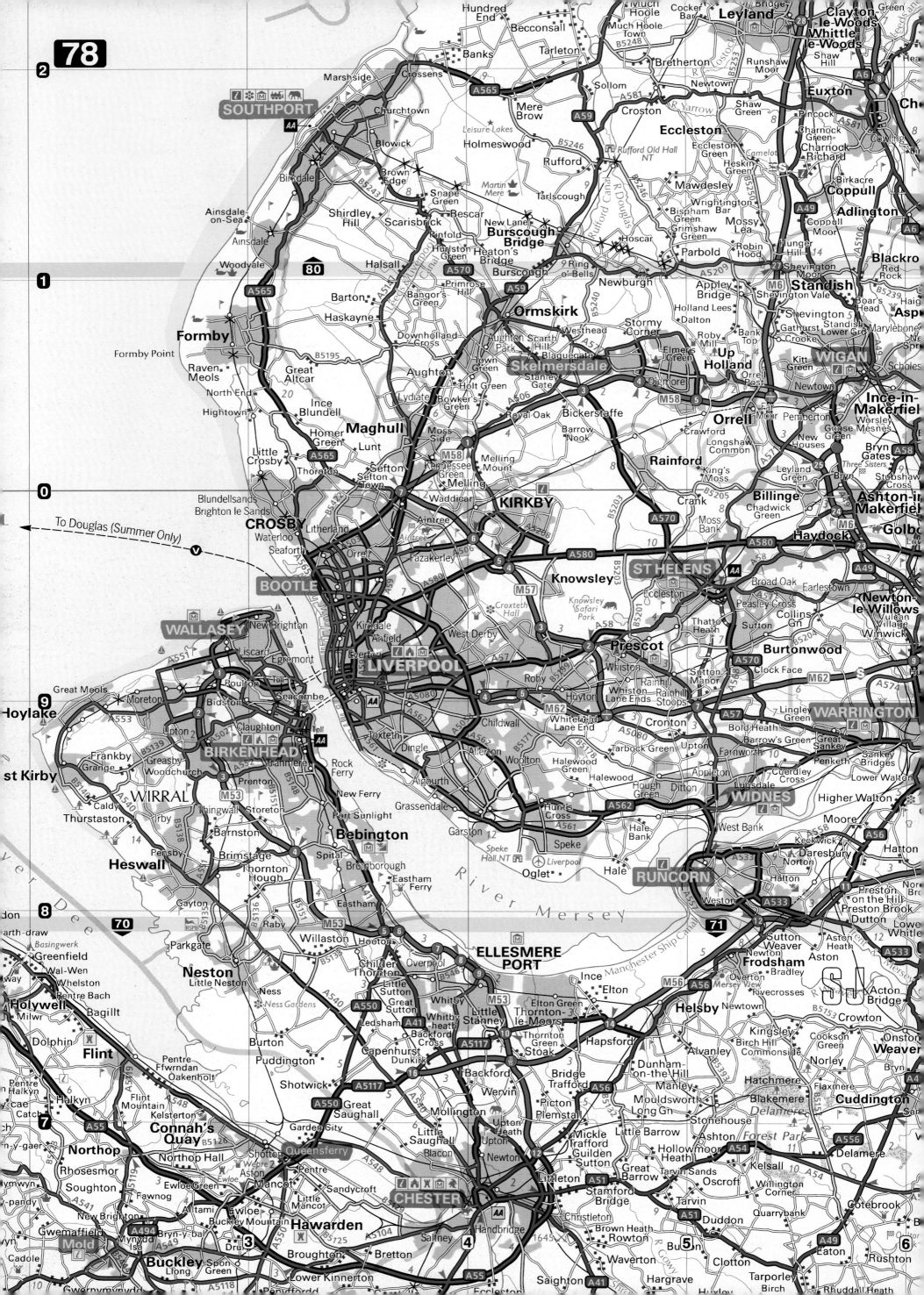

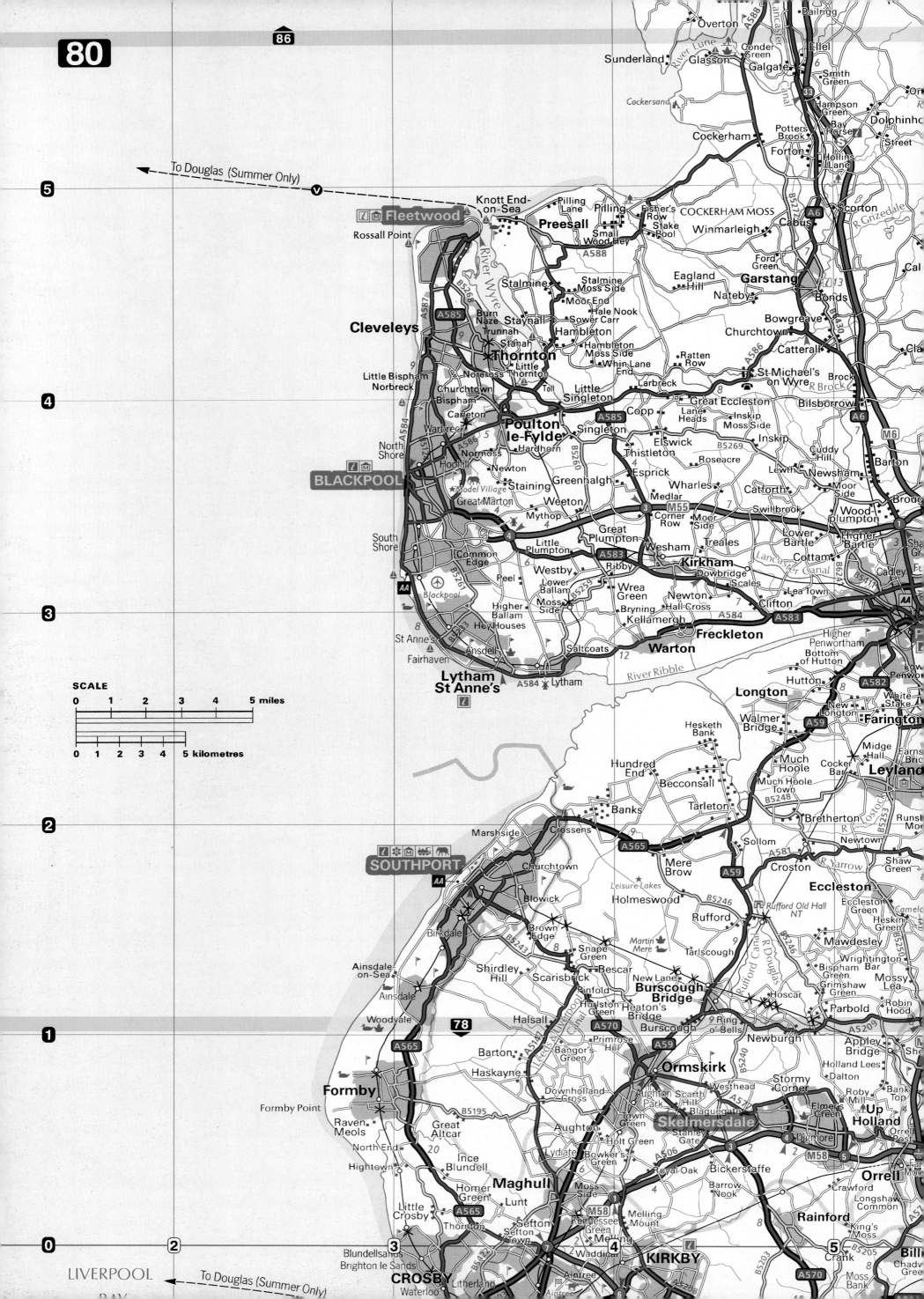

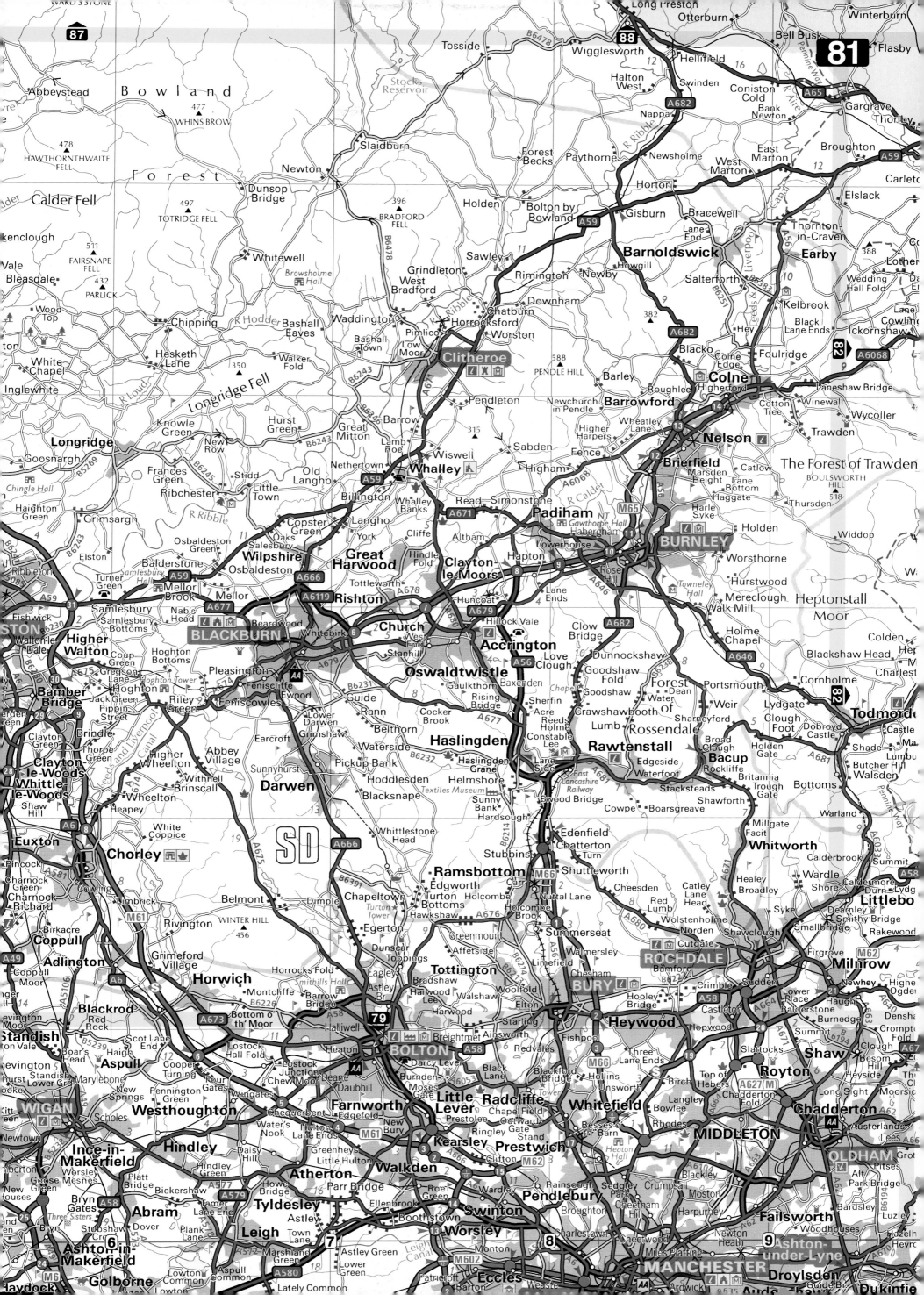

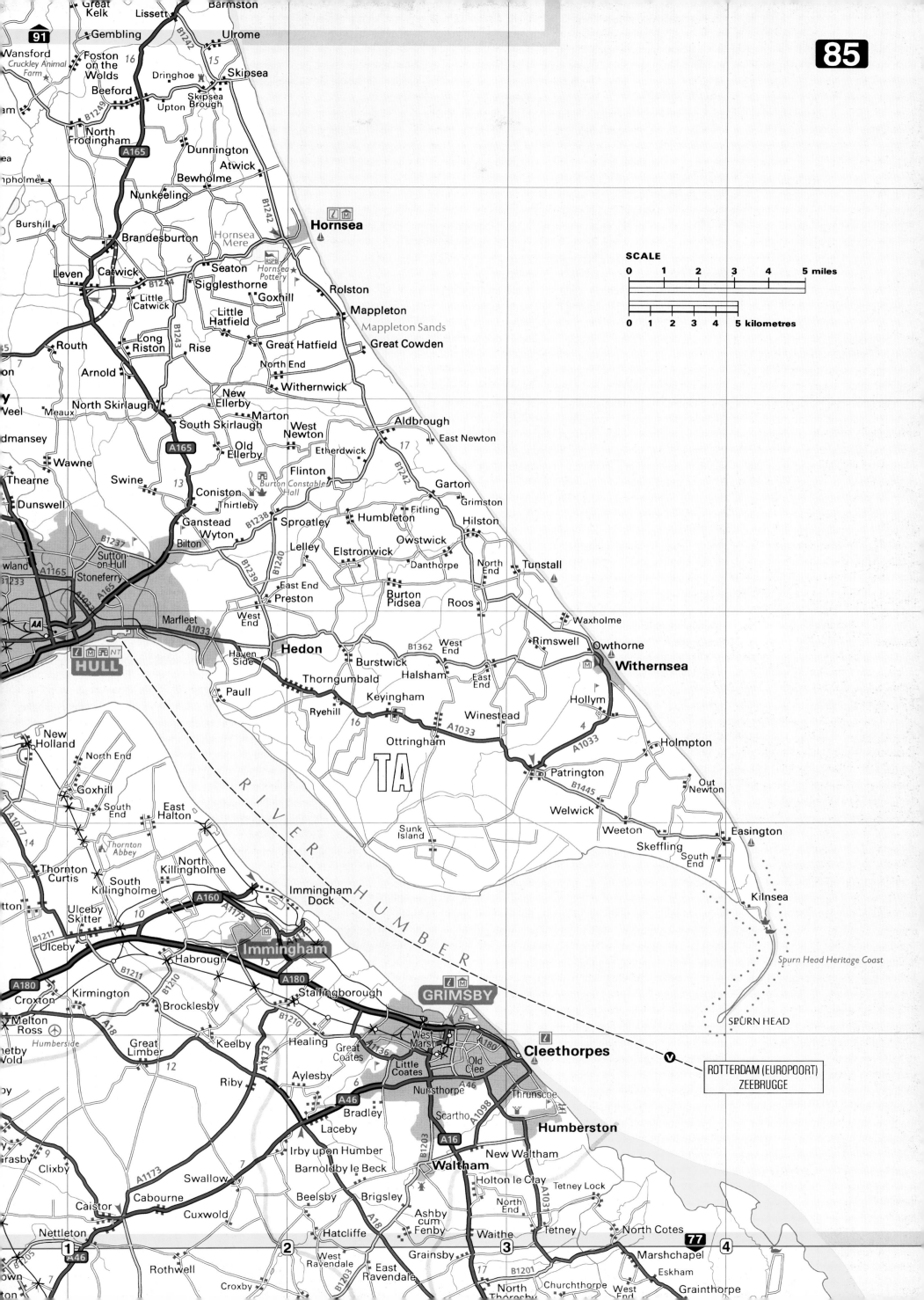

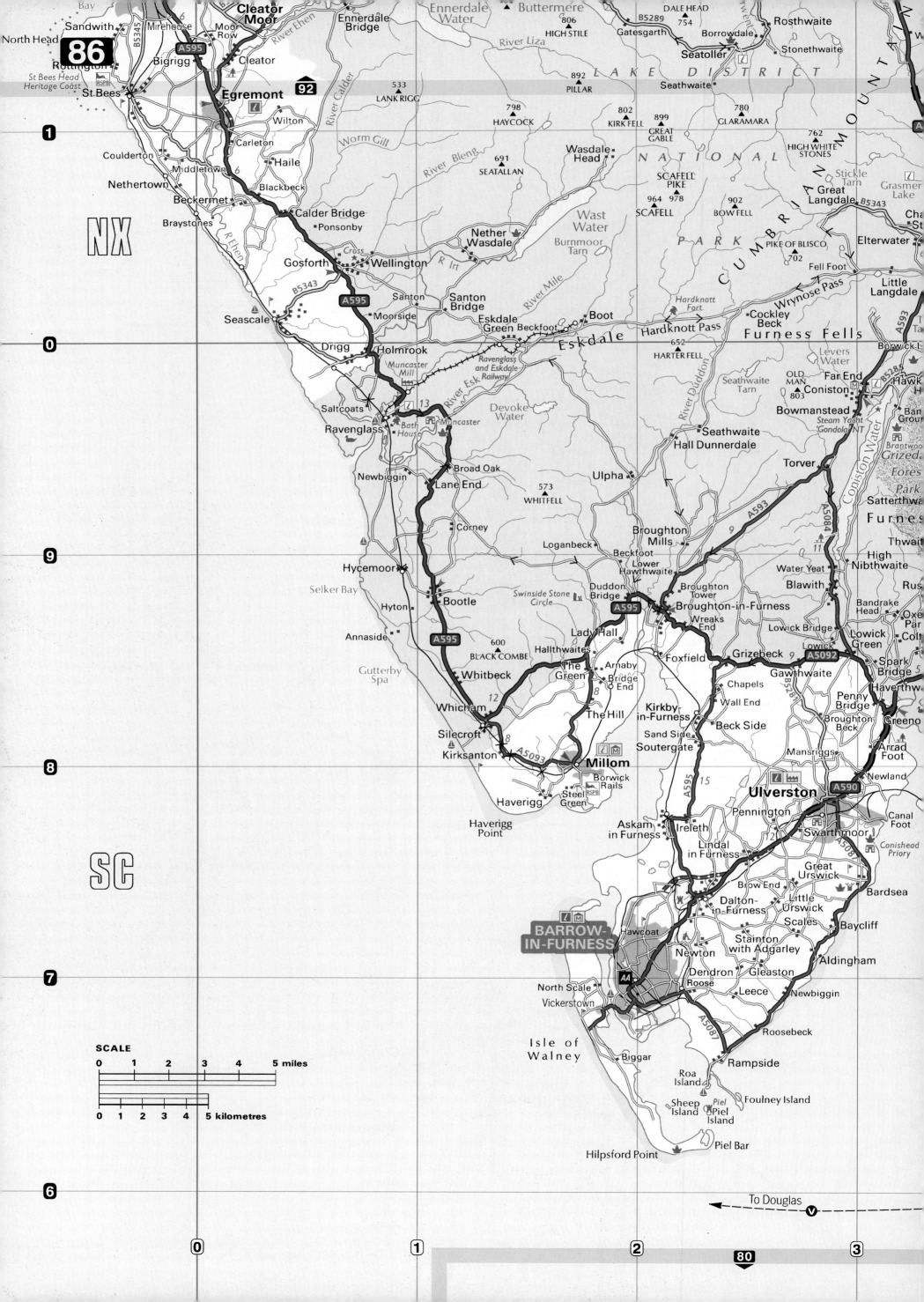

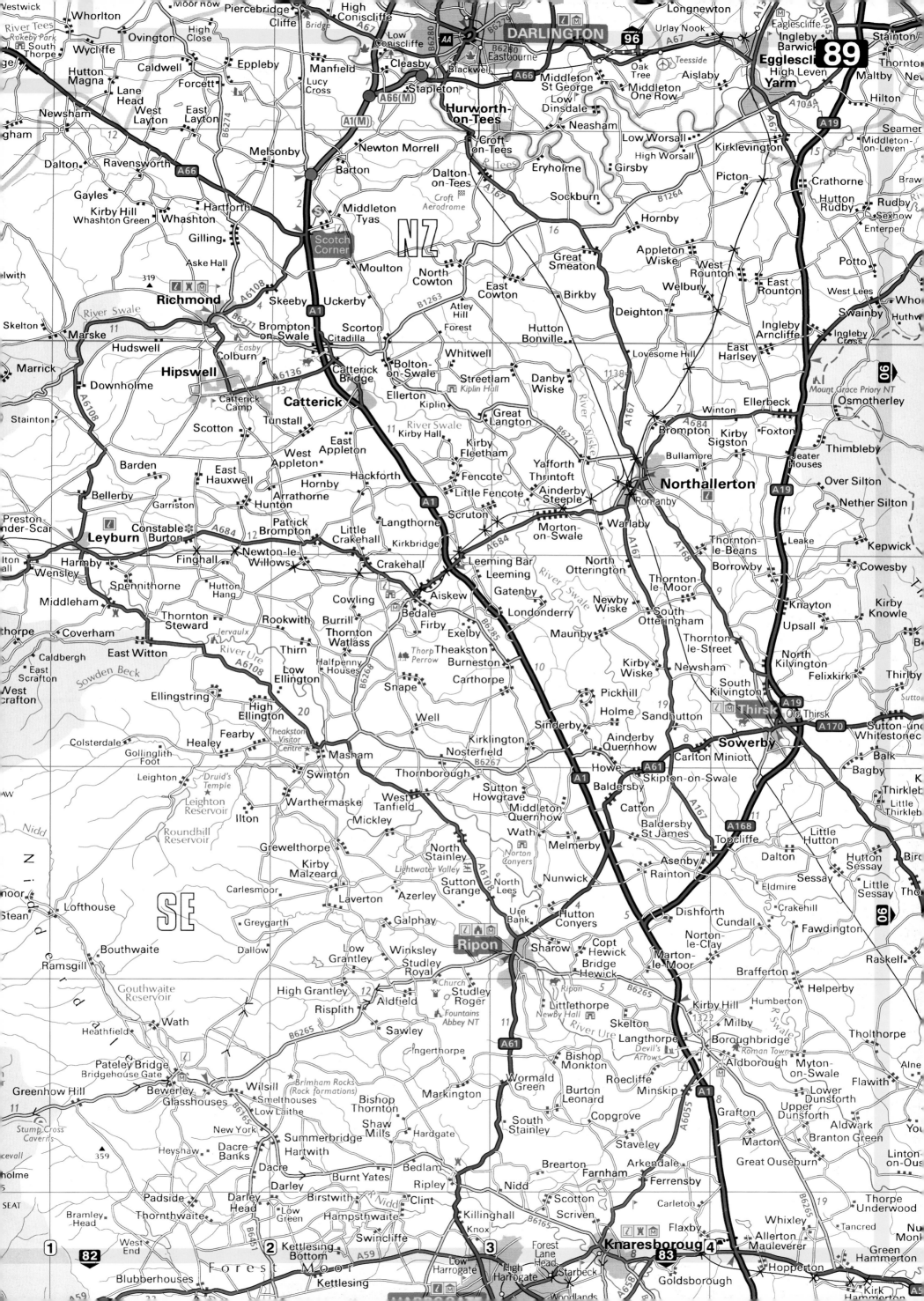

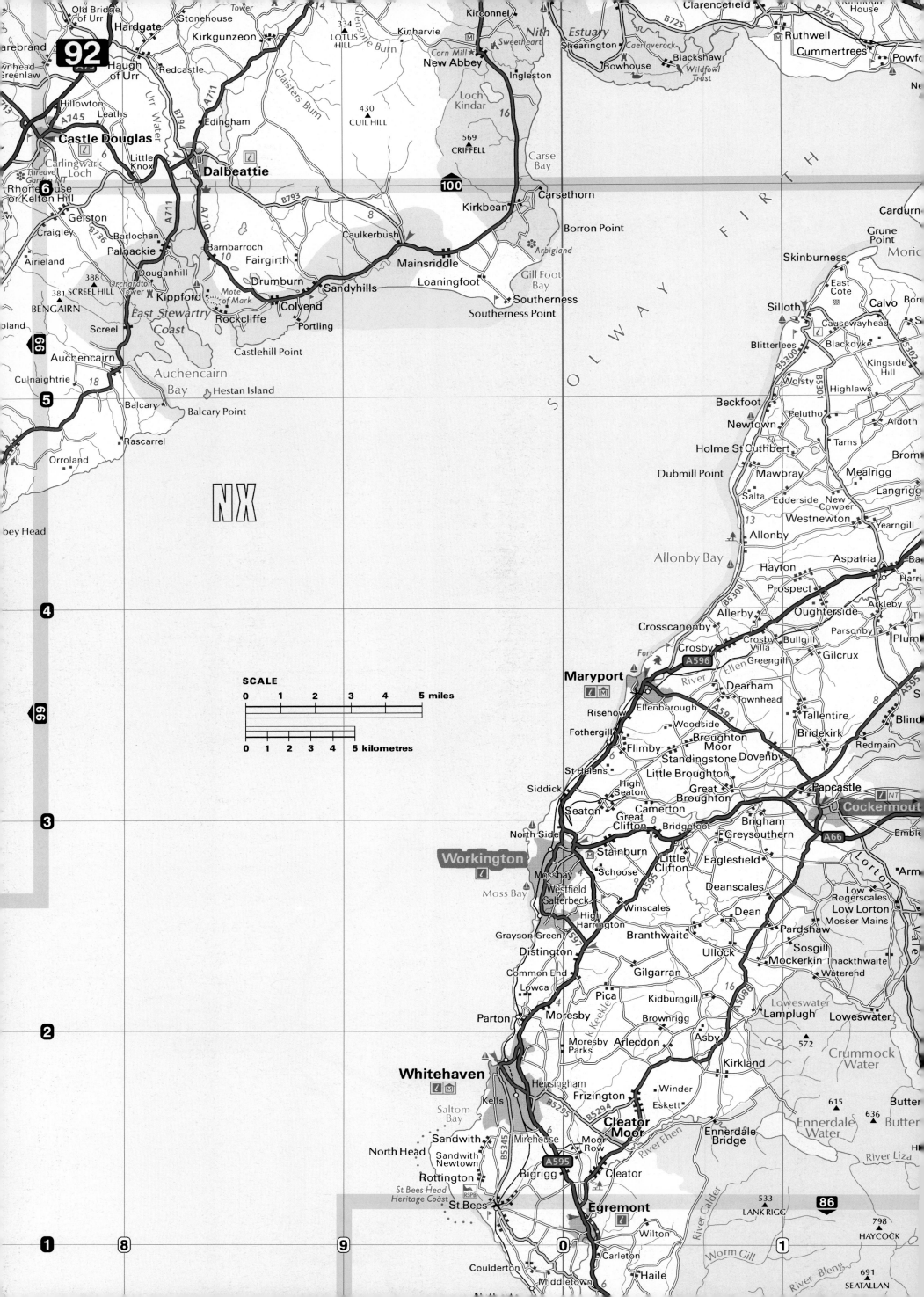

BERGEN
STAVANGER

GOTEBORG

ESBJERG
Summer Only

SCALE

| 0 | 1 | 2 | 3 | 4 | 5 miles |

| 0 | 1 | 2 | 3 | 4 | 5 kilometres |

...AND

...ham

NZ

...asington
Colliery

...horpe

...eterlee

Horden

Blackhall Colliery
Blackhall Rocks

A1086

...den

Monk
Hesleden

Hart
Station

A179

...raton   Hart

A19

High
Throston

Elwick

Middleton

HARTLEPOOL

Dalton
Piercy

Hartlepool Bay

Brierton

B1277

Seaton Carew

Greatham

A689

A178

Graythorpe

Tees Bay

Newton
Bewley

Energy Information
Centre/Power Station

Billingham

A1185

Warrenby   Coatham

Cowpen
Bewley

Redcar

Haverton Hill

Marske-by-the-Sea

A1085

Port
Clarence

River Tees

Teesport

Saltburn-by-the-Sea

Toll

A66

Kirkleatham

Grangetown

New
Brotton

Hummersea Scar

A19

South
Bank

Lazenby

Yearby

A174

Brotton

Skinningrove

Boulby

Staithes

North
Ormesby

Lackenby

New Marske

Upleatham

Skelton

Kilton

Street
Houses

AA   Eston

Wilton

Dunsdale

New
Skelton

Carlin
How

Loftus

Port Mulgrave

MIDDLESBROUGH

A1085

Normanby

North
Skelton

Kilton
Thorpe

Easington

Dalehouse

Hinderwell

...naby
Tees

Acklam

Ormesby

Tocketts

Boosbeck

Lingdale

Liverton
Mines

Roxby

Runswick
Bay

Marton

Ormesby Hall NT

Margrove
Park

Stanghow

Handale

Borrowby

Newton
Mulgrave

Ellerby

Goldsboro

North Yorkshire
Heritage

5   Nunthorpe

A171

Stainton

Hemlington

6   Hutton

Pinchinthorpe

Guisborough

90   7   Moorsholm

Liverton

Scaling

B1266

8

Lythe

Thornton

Nunthorpe
Village

Hutton
Lowcross

Hutton
Hall

Cleveland Way

Gerrick

A171

A174

Maltby

Newby

Newton under
Roseberry

8

Bennane Head
Pinwherry
Colmonell
B734
River Stinchar
Muck Water
106
Loch
Moan
Heronsford
Water of Tig
Barrhill
346
CARWALL

Ballantrae
B7044
Laggan
Feoch Burn
A714
Corwar

A77
Lochton
B7027
22
Glentr
Villa

437
BENERAIRD
Drumlamford
Loch
Dornal
Loch
Ochiltree
Creebank

321
CARLOCK
HILL
387
ALTIMEG HILL
BENBROKE HILL
Loch
Maberry
Clachaneasy

Glen App
Cross Water of Luce
Laggangairn
Standing Stones
Southern Upland Way
Knowe
River
Bladnoch

To Larne
Milleur Point
17
184
URRALL FELL
G

Corsewall Point
Penwhirn
Reservoir
Glenwhilly
Black Burn

Lady
Bay
Portencalzie
Cairnryan
Main Water of Luce
Tarf Water
271
ARTFIELD FELL
Carseriggan

Barnhills
B738
Braid Fell
Barfad

South Cairn
Kirkcolm
A77
New Luce
214
CULVENNAN
FELL
Shennanton

Ervie
Loch
Connell
Low Barbeth
Beoch Burn
Loch
Ronald
Tarf Water

Knocknain
Low Salchrie
Black
Loch
Chlenry
Dernaglar
Loch
Clugstor

Leswalt
B7043
Lochnaw
Innermessan
White
Loch
Castle Kennedy
A75
Craighlaw
Kirkcow

Balgracie
A718
Stranraer
Aird
164
CRAIG FELL
Carscreugh
Fell
Loch

Auchnotteroch
Castle Kennedy
A75
10
Dunragit
Glenluce
Glenluce
Castle
of Park

Broadsea
Mark
Kildrocher House
Piltanton Burn
Whitecrook
Castle
Loch

Portslogan
Bay
Lochans
181
CAIRN PAT
8
14
B7077
B7084
Milton
A747
Fell
Loch

Black Head
A716
A77
19
Stair Haven
Auchenmalg

Portpatrick
Stoneykirk
18
North Milmain
Mull of
Sinniness
Mochrum
Loch
Culshabbin
Barra

B7042
Sandhead
Auchemalg
Bay
Chapel Finian
13

Cairngarroch
Kirkmadrine
Church
A747
Elrig

Money Head
Mochrum

NW
A716
High Ardwell
Ardwell
Port William

Ardwell Bay
Ardwell
House
Chapel Rossan

Drumbreddon
Balgowan
L U C E   B A Y
Barsalloch Fort
Barsalloch Point

Logan
B7065
Port Logan Bay
Port Logan
Point

Garrochtrie
Kilstay

Clanyard Bay
Clanyard
Drummore

Laggantalluch Head
Kirkmaiden
High
Drummore
Killiness Point

Barncorkrie
B7041
Maryport

Cardryne

Cardrain
West Cairngaan

RSPB
MULL OF GALLOWAY

3

0   1   2   3

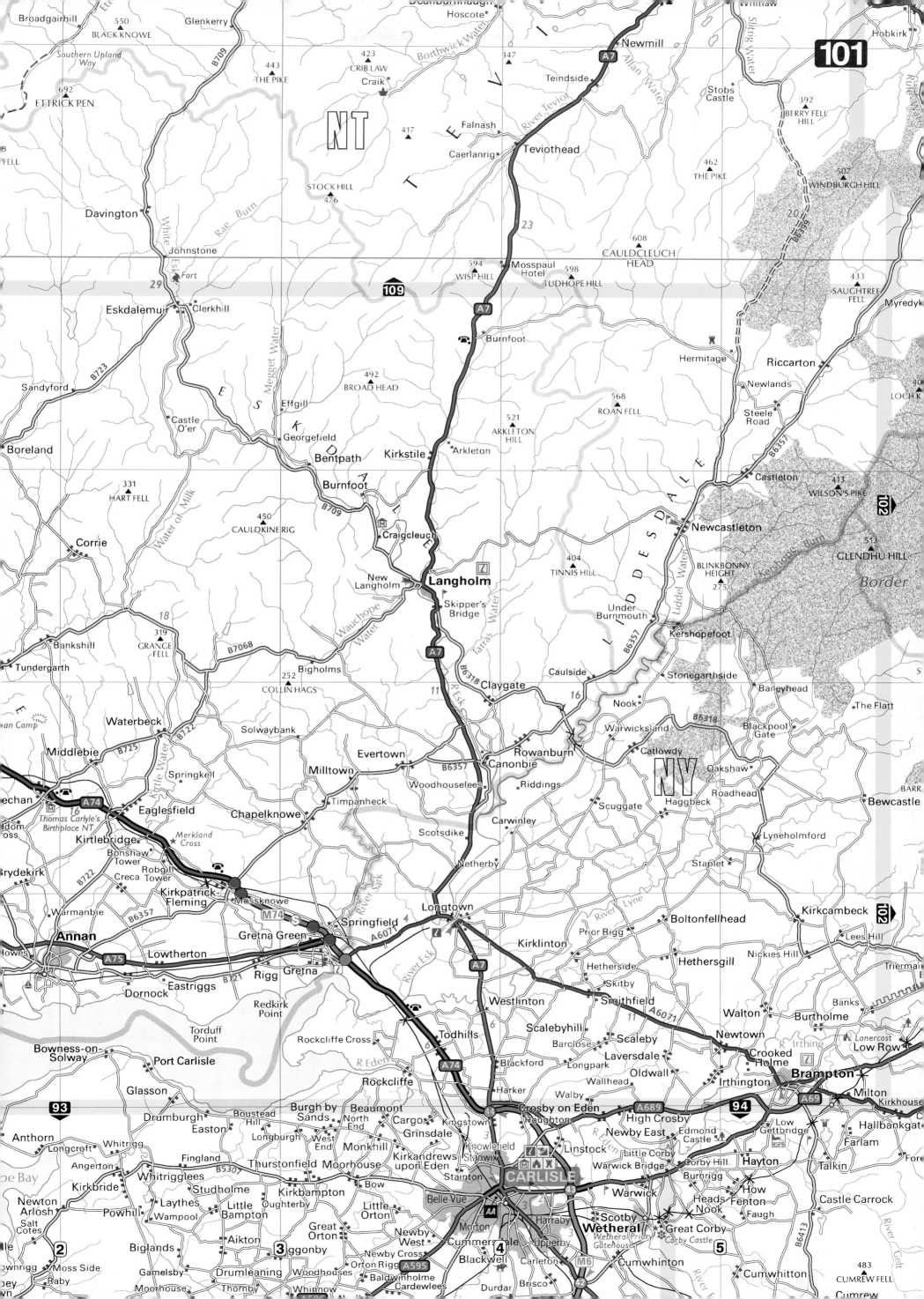

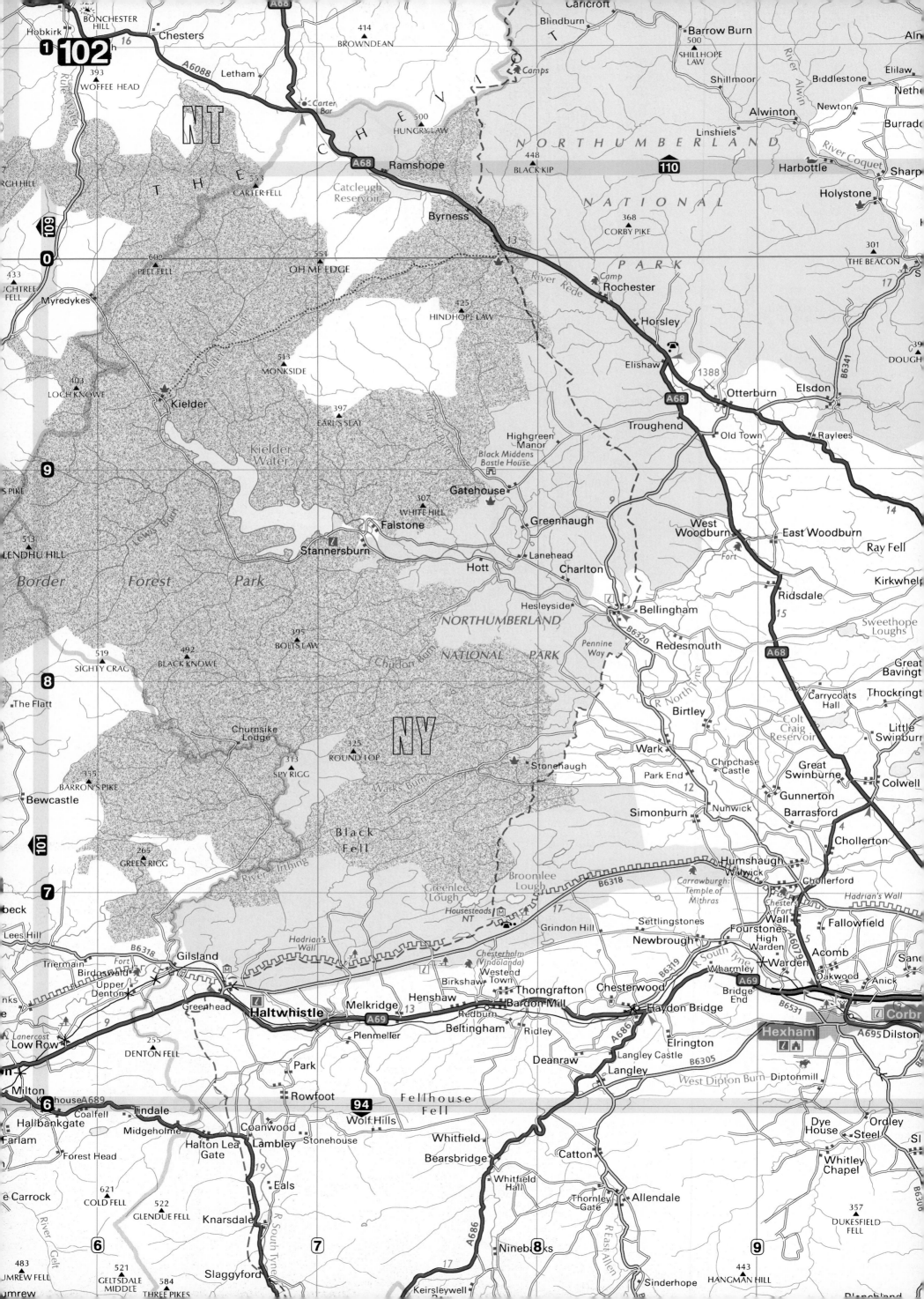

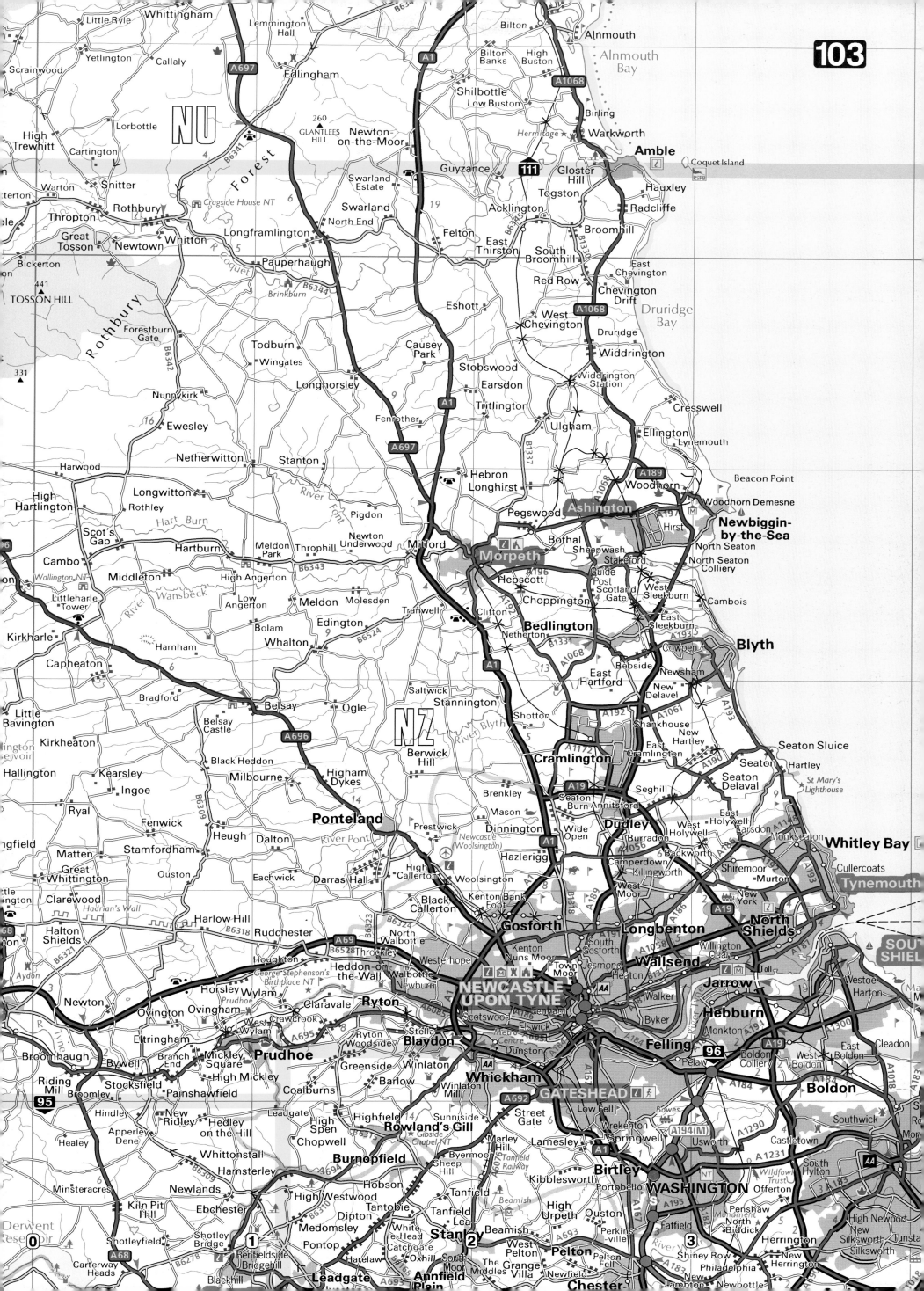

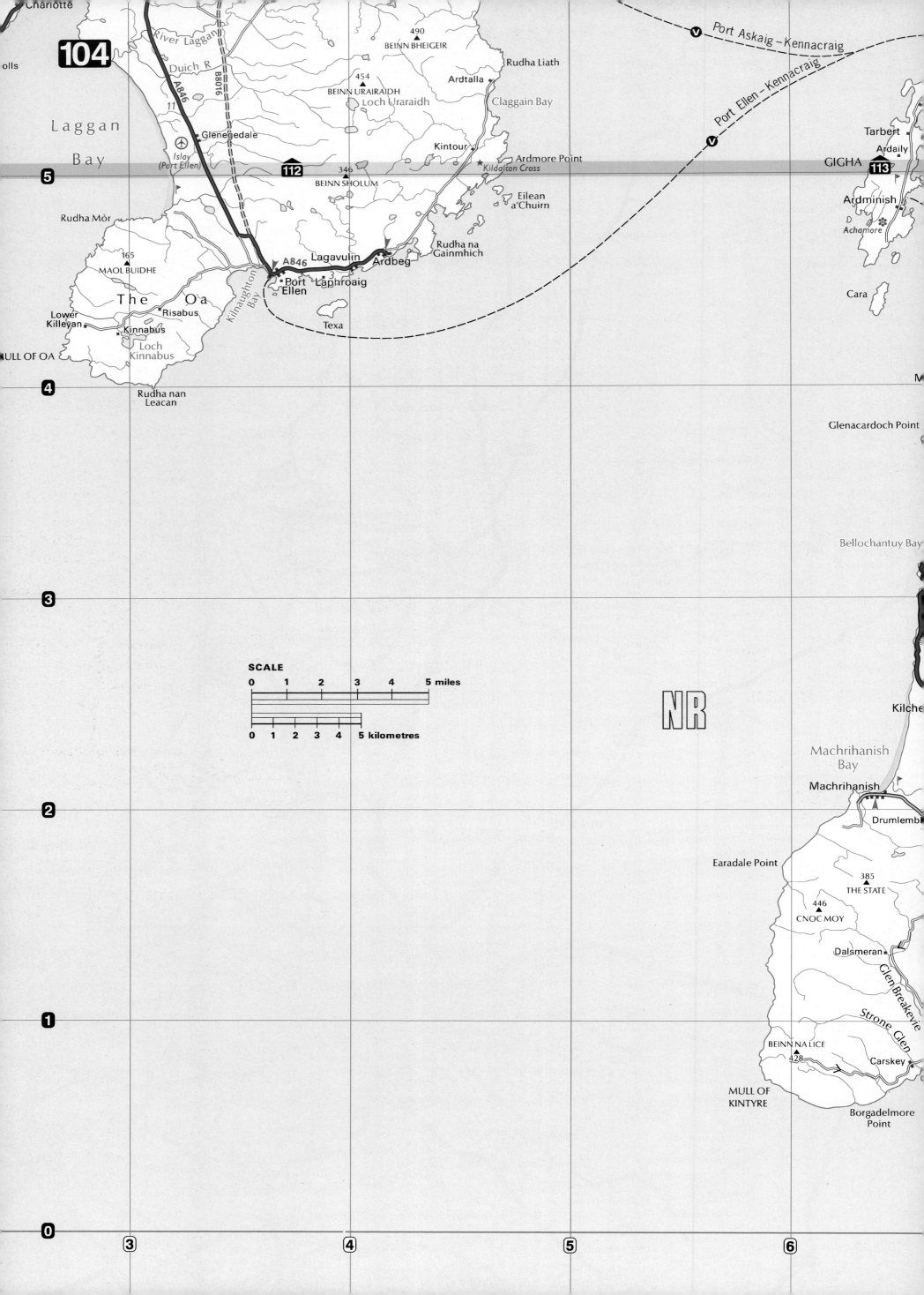

Chariotte

River Laggan

Duich R

A846
B8016
11

490
BEINN BHEIGEIR

Rudha Liath

Ardtalla

454
BEINN URAIRAIDH

Loch Uraraidh

Claggain Bay

Laggan

Bay

Glenegedale

Islay
(Port Ellen)

Kintour

Ardmore Point

112

346
BEINN SHOLUM

Kildalton Cross

Eilean
a'Chuirn

Rudha Mòr

165
MAOL BUIDHE

A846

Lagavulin

Ardbeg

Rudha na
Gainmhich

The Oa

Risabus

Kilnaughton Bay

Port
Ellen

Laphroaig

Lower
Killeyan

Kinnabus

Texa

MULL OF OA

Loch
Kinnabus

Rudha nan
Leacan

Port Askaig – Kennacraig

Port Ellen – Kennacraig

Tarbert
Ardaily

GIGHA **113**

Ardminish

Achamore

Cara

Glenacardoch Point

Bellochantuy Bay

NR

Kilche

Machrihanish
Bay

Machrihanish

Drumlemb

Earadale Point

385
THE STATE

446
CNOC MOY

Dalsmeran

Glen Breakerie

Strone Glen

BEINN NA LICE
428

Carskey

MULL OF
KINTYRE

Borgadelmore
Point

SCALE

0   1   2   3   4   5 miles

0   1   2   3   4   5 kilometres

West

Portachoillan

Ronachan Point

Clachan

A83

Ronachan

Loch Ciàran

Ballochroy

Gigha

Loch Garasdale

247
CRUACH MHIC GOUGAIN

264
CNOC-AN T-SAMHLAIDH

Cour Bay

Cour

Crossaig

Claonaig

Skipness
★Chapel
Skipness Point

Sound of Bute

Ardscalpsie Bay

Kingar

nan Bay

(Summer Only)

Cock of Arran

SOUND

Lochranza

Catacol

114

Glen Chalmadale

8

Rhunahaorine Point

Rhunahaorine

38

Tayinloan

Glen Catacol

North Arran

834
CAISTEAL ABHAIL

Mid Sannox

B842

Grogport

Barmollack

Penrioch

Pirnmill

Corrie

Carradale Water

CRUACH NAN GABHAR

354

Whitefarland

17

715
BEINN BHARRAIN

Loch Tanna

Glen Forsa

874
GOATFELL

A841

Imachar

Belloch

A33

Arnicle

Bart Water

B879

Carradale

Dippen

Carradale House

Carradale Point

Ballekine

Dougarie

Forsa Water

792
BEINN NUIS

Glen Rosa

Brodick NT

Merkland Point

6

106

Glenbarr

Torrisdale Square

Carradale Bay

A R R A N

Brodick Bay

319

BEINN AN TUIRC

454

Stone Circle

Auchagallon
Machrie Bay

Machrie Farm

Glenloig

B880

512
A'CHRUACH

Brodick

Strathwhillan

Cleongart

408
BÒRD MÒR

Saddell

Tormore

Machrie Moor

11

Corrygills

Clauchlands Po

lochantuy

Z

Saddell Bay

Moss Farm Road Stone Circle

503
BEINN BHREAC

Lamlash

Margnaheglish

Lamlash Bay

Holy Island

Tangy Loch

396
SGREADAN HILL

Ugadale

Ballymichael

Torbeg

Shiskine
Birchburn
North Feorline

Cordon

A841

4

Ballachgair

Drumadoon Bay

Blackwaterfoot
South Feorline

Glen Scorrodale

Cairn Ban

Auchencairn

Kingscross

Knockenkelly

Glen Lussa
Peninver

Ardnacross Bay

Kilpatrick
Kilpatrick Dun

Whiting Bay

Whiting Bay

Kilmichael

Brown Head

Kilmory Water

Glen Ashdale

Largymore

A83

Drumore

B842

Corriecravie

A841

Largybeg

Campbeltown

i

Torr a' Chaisteal Fort
★

Sliddery

Lagg
Kilmory

Levencorroch

Dippin

Dippin Head

B842

Campbeltown Loch

Island Davaar

16

Torrylin

Cairn

Bennan

Kildonan

6

843

Bennan Head

Pladda

K

NS

Kildalloig

352
BEINN GHUILEAN

Achinhoan

10

Conie Glen

Kerran

Glen

B842

Ru Stafnish

106

Macharioch

Polliwilline Bay

Southend

Sanda Sound

Dunaverty

Sheep Island

Sanda Island

Ailsa Craig

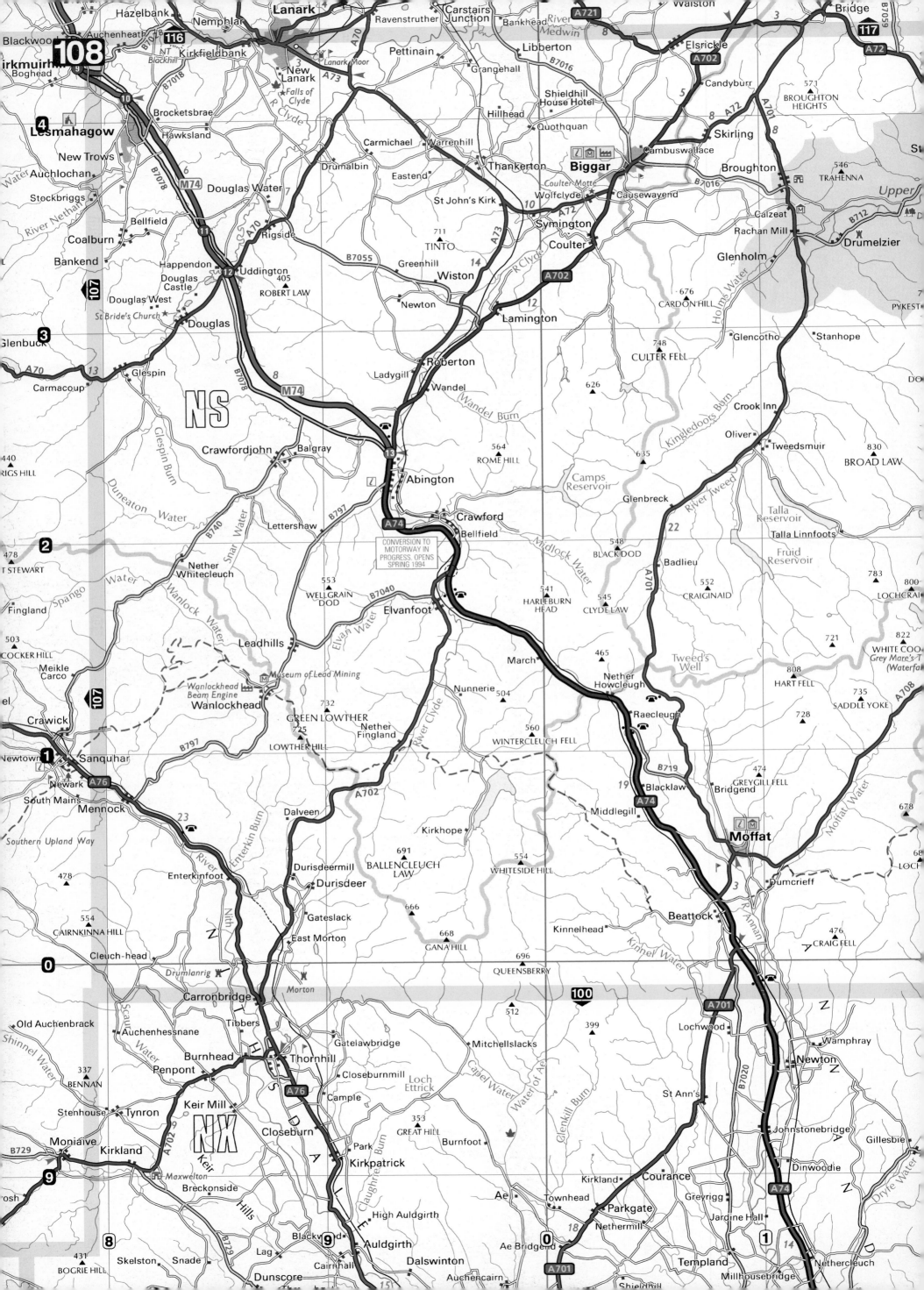

SCALE

0 1 2 3 4 5 miles

0 1 2 3 4 5 kilometres

ithe Barn
1333
A1
A6105
B6461
Tweedmouth
East
Ord
A698
119
Murton
Thornton
Unthank
West Allerdean
Ancroft
B6354
Berrington
Bowsden
B6353
The Lady
Waterford Hall
ford
on
Fenton
Town
Nesbit
Doddington
wtown
land
ng
Humbleton
Wooler
Earle
Middleton Hall
North
Middleton
South
Middleton
AND
PARK
Ilderton
Roseden
Roddham
Liburn
Tower
DUNMOOR HILL
567
Hartside
Prendwick
Alnham
Elilaw
Netherton
Burradon
Sharperton
Hepple
Great
Tosson
BEACON
17
Bickerton
Swindon
TOSSON HILL
11
0

North Northumberland
Heritage Coast

Barracks
Town Ramparts
Berwick-upon-Tweed
Spittal
Huds Head

Scremerston
Cheswick
Goswick
Haggerston
Beal
Kyloe
East
Kyloe
Fenwick
Buckton
Smeafield
Holburn
Detchant
Middleton
St Cuthbert's
Cave NT
Hetton
Steads
North Hazelrigg
South Hazelrigg
B6349
Belford
Outchester
Spindlestone
Bellshill
Warenton
B6348 Adderstone
Warenford
NU
A1
Newstead
Ellingham
North
Charlton
Doxford
South
Charlton
Ditchburn
Harehope
Eglingham
Beanley
Powburn
East
Bolton
Bolton
Abberwick
Broome Park
Lemmington
Hall
Edlingham
GLANTLEES
HILL
260
Newton-
on-the-Moor
103
Swarland
Estate
Swarland
North End
Longframlington
Pauperhaugh
Brinkburn
B6344
Forest
B6341
1

CAUSEWAY
FLOODED
AT HIGH TIDE
HOLY ISLAND
Holy
Island
Lindisfarne
Priory
Castle Point
Lindisfarne Castle NT
Guile Point

North Northumberland
Heritage Coast

Staple
Sound
FARNE
ISLANDS
Inner
Sound
Budle
Bay
Bamburgh
Budle
Waren
Mill
Easington
B1342
B1341
B1340
Glororum
New
Shoreston
Burton
Bradford
Elford
Seahouses
North
Sunderland
Lucker
Newham
Chathill
Tughall
Swinhoe
Beadnell
Beadnell Bay
Preston
Brunton
High Newton
by-the-Sea
14
Christon
Bank
Falloden
B6347
Embleton
Embleton
Bay
Dunstan
Steads
Dunstanburgh
Castle NT
Rock
Dunstan
Craster
Rennington
Stamford
Howick
Hall
Howick
Cullernose Point
17
B6346
Littlehoughton
Broxfield
B1340
B1339
Longhoughton
River Aln
Denwick
Boulmer
Alnwick
Hawkhill
Lesbury
Seaton Point
B6341
Bilton
Alnmouth
7
Bilton
Banks
High
Buston
Alnmouth
Bay
A1
Shilbottle
Low Buston
A1068
Birling
Hermitage
Warkworth
Amble
Coquet Island
RSPB
Guyzance
Gloster
Hill
Hauxley
Togston
19
Acklington
Radcliffe
Broomhill
Felton
East
Thirston
South
Broomhill
Red Row
East
Chevington
Chevington
Drift
A1068
3
West
Chevington
Drudge
Druridge
Bay
Eshott
2

River Till
River Breamish
River Coquet
River Aln

A697
New
Bewick
Wooperton
Old Bewick
CATERAN HILL
267
16
Brandon
Branton
Fawdon
Ingram
Glanton
Glanton Pike
COCHRANE
PIKE
334
Great
Ryle
Shawdon
Hill
Whittingham
Little Ryle
Yetlington
Callaly
Scrainwood
Lorbotle
Cartington
High
Trewhitt
Warton
Flotterton
Snitter
Rothbury
Thropton
Newtown
Whitton
Cragside House NT
6
4
Longframlington
5
Forestburn
Gate

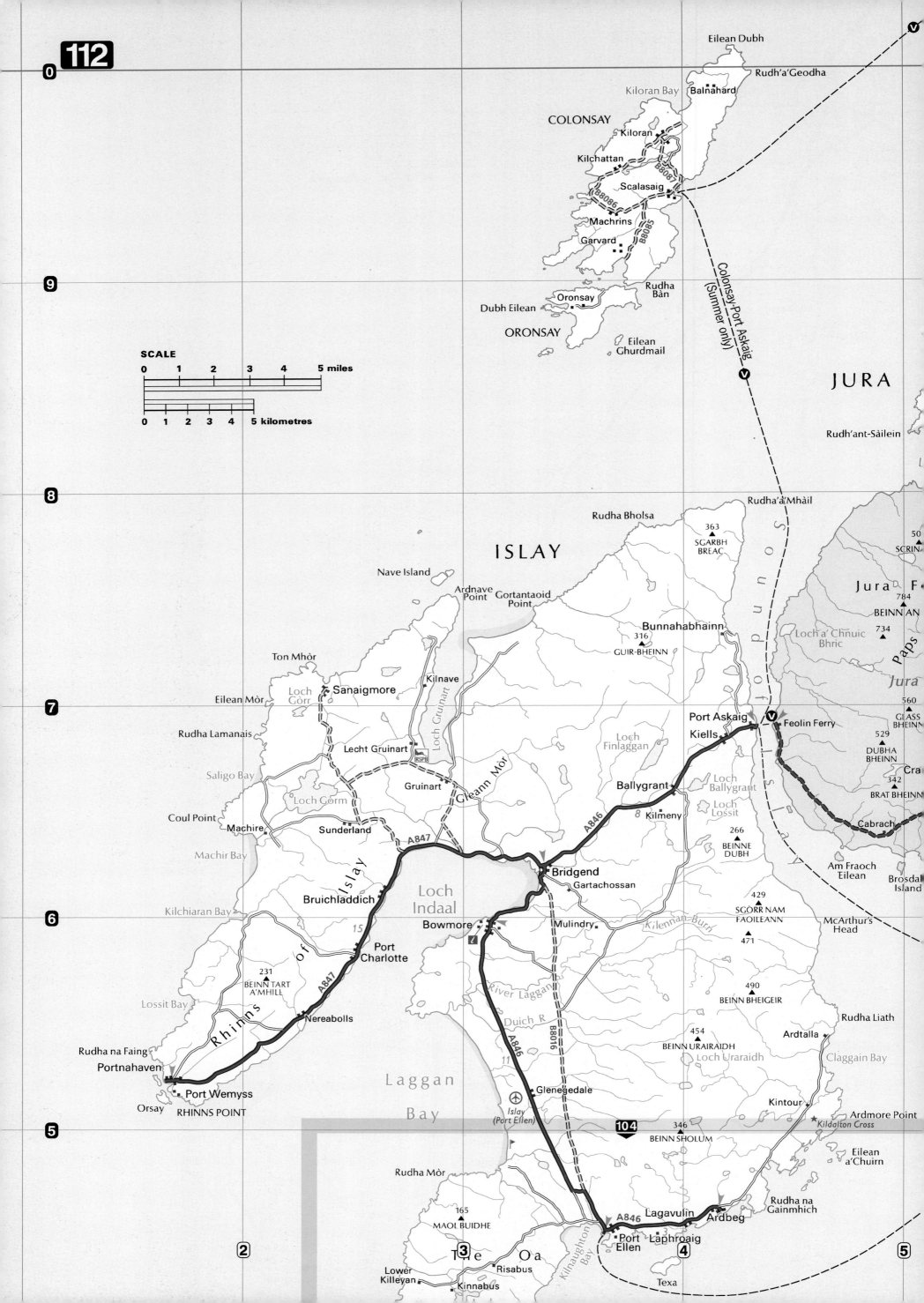

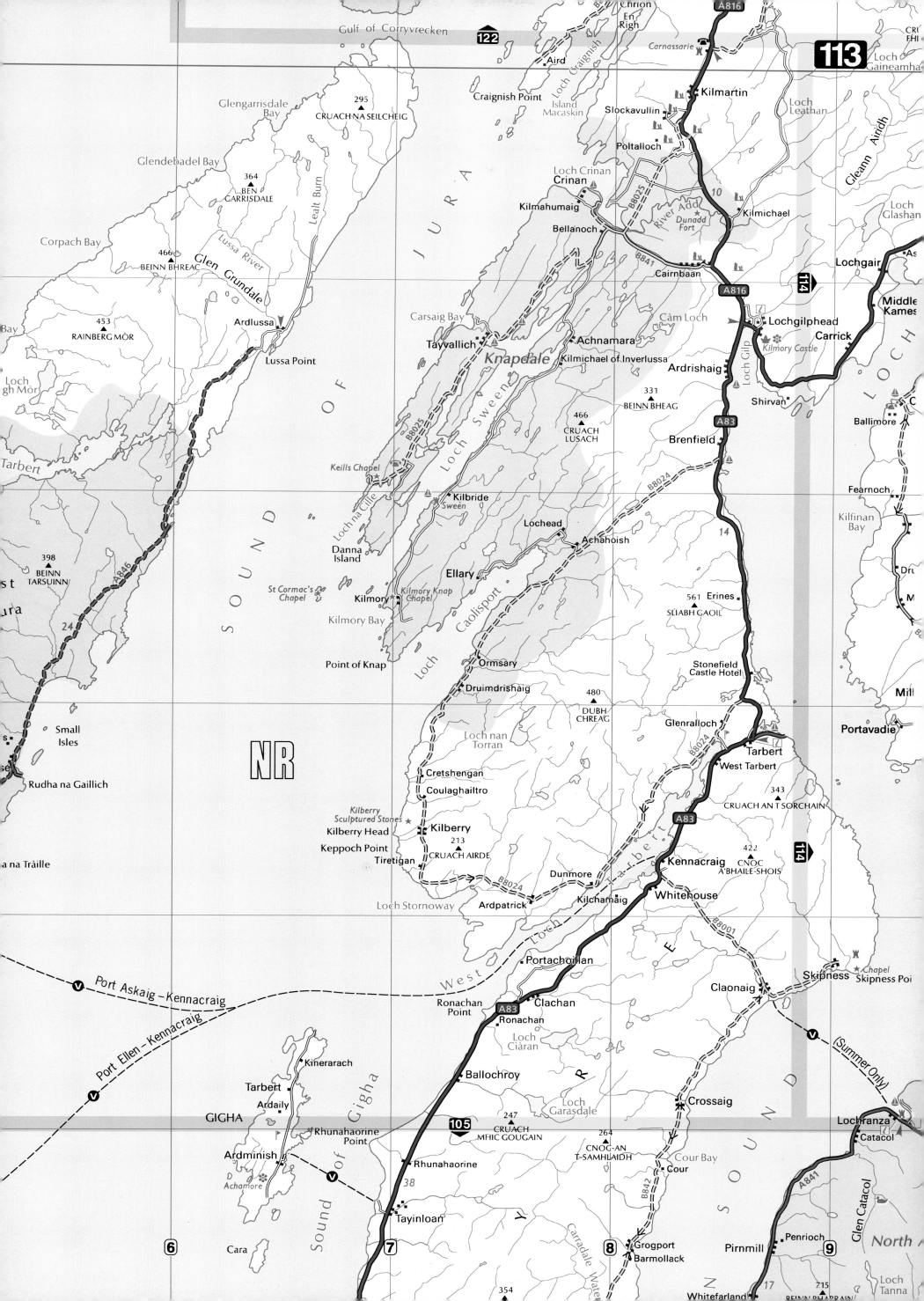

SCALE

0 1 2 3 4 5 miles

0 1 2 3 4 5 kilometres

NU

Dunbar

Broxburn
1650
Barns Ness
East Barns
Chapel Point
Skateraw
nhill
stead
Dry Brook
12
Thorntonloch
Innerwick
Crowhill
319
Reed Point
Pease
Bay
Siccar Point
Fast Castle Head
Dunglass
Collegiate
Church
COCKLAW HILL
Cockburnspath
Oldhamstocks
Water
A1
196
BROWN RIG
ST ABB'S HEAD
Ecclaw
Southern
Upland Way
A1107
391
HEART LAW
St Abbs
Grantshouse
Coldingham
Coldingham Bay
Eye Water
Butterdean
21
Houndwood
22
Eyemouth
Quixwood
262
Heugh Head
Cairncross
Abbey St Bathans
A6112
HORSELEY HILL
Reston
Ayton
Edin's
Hall Broch
14
B6438
Burnmouth
Ellemford
325
Auchencrow
Whitchester
COCKBURN
LAW
Marygold
B6437
MERMUIR
B6355
Lintlaw
Lamberton
Marshall Meadows Bay
us
Primrosehill
Preston
Chirnside
B6355
North Northumberland
Heritage Coast
B6365
Cumledge
Edrom
15
Foulden
Tithe Barn
A1
399
Church
Chirnsidebridge
1333
DIRRINGTON
GREAT LAW
A6105
Broadhaugh
Edington
Whiteadder
A6105
Manderston
Water
Crumstane
Allanton
Hutton
Barracks
Duns
Blackadder
Water
Paxton
B6461
Town Ramparts
Berwick-upon-Tweed
Gavinton
Blackadder
B6460
Sunwick
Tweedmouth
Spittal
B6456
Sinclair's
Hill
Fishwick
Loanend
East
Ord
Huds Head
Nisbet
Hill
Whitsome
Hilton
13
Polwarth
Fogo
110
6
Horndean
Murton
Unthank
111
A6105
Forgorig
A6112
Thornton
A698
Scremerston
Charterhall
Ladykirk
West Allerdean
B6525
Cheswick
Greenlaw
Swinton
Norham
Shoreswood
A1
Simprim
Upsettlington
Grindon
7
11
8
Ladykirk
Ho.
9
Shellacres
Felkington
0
Ancroft
A1
Goswick
Lambden
Leitholm
10
6
B6354
Grindonrigg
Berrington
Haggerston
Hume
River Tweed
Duddo
Beal

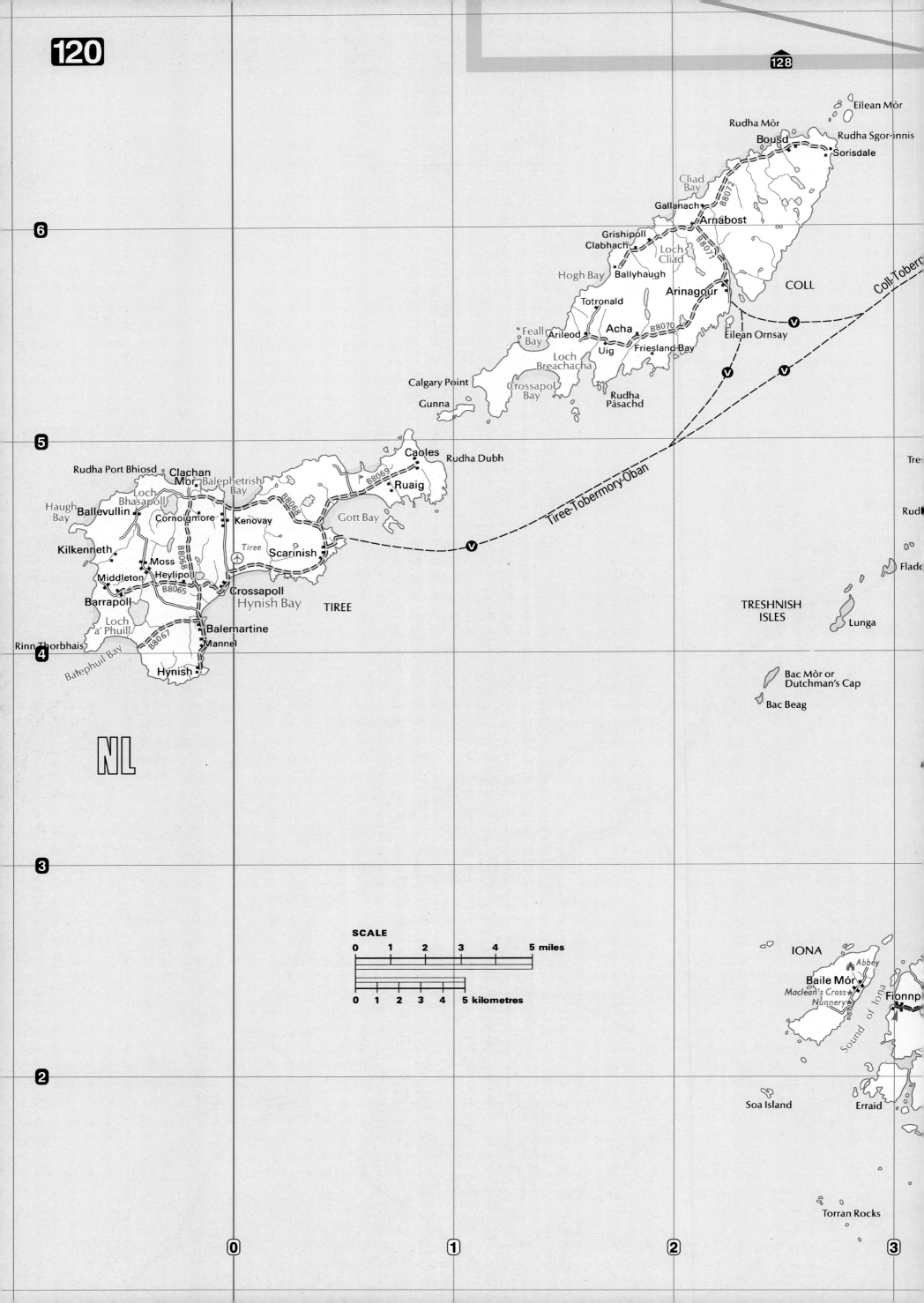

128

Eilean Mòr
Rudha Mòr
Bousd
Rudha Sgor-innis
Sorisdale
Cliad Bay
Gallanach
B8077
Arnabost
Grishipoll
Clabhach
Loch Cliad
B8071
COLL
Coll-Tobern
Hogh Bay
Ballyhaugh
Arinagour
Totronald
Feall Bay
Arileod
Acha
B8070
Uig
Friesland Bay
Eilean Ornsay
Calgary Point
Loch Breachacha
Gunna
Crossapol Bay
Rudha Pàsachd
Tiree-Tobermory-Oban

Rudha Port Bhiosd
Clachan
Caoles
Rudha Dubh
Tre
Mòr
Balephetrish Bay
B8069
Ruaig
Loch Bhasapoll
Haugh Bay
Ballevullin
B8068
Gott Bay
Rud
Cornoigmore
Kenovay
Tiree
Kilkenneth
B8068
Scarinish
Moss
Flado
Middleton
Heylipol
Crossapoll
TRESHNISH ISLES
Barrapoll
B8065
Hynish Bay
TIREE
Lunga
Loch a' Phuill
Balemartine
Rinn Thorbhais
Mannel
B8067
Hynish
Batephuil Bay
Bac Mòr or Dutchman's Cap
Bac Beag

NL

IONA
Abbey
Baile Mòr
Maclean's Cross
Nunnery
Fionnp
Sound of Iona

Soa Island
Erraid

Torran Rocks

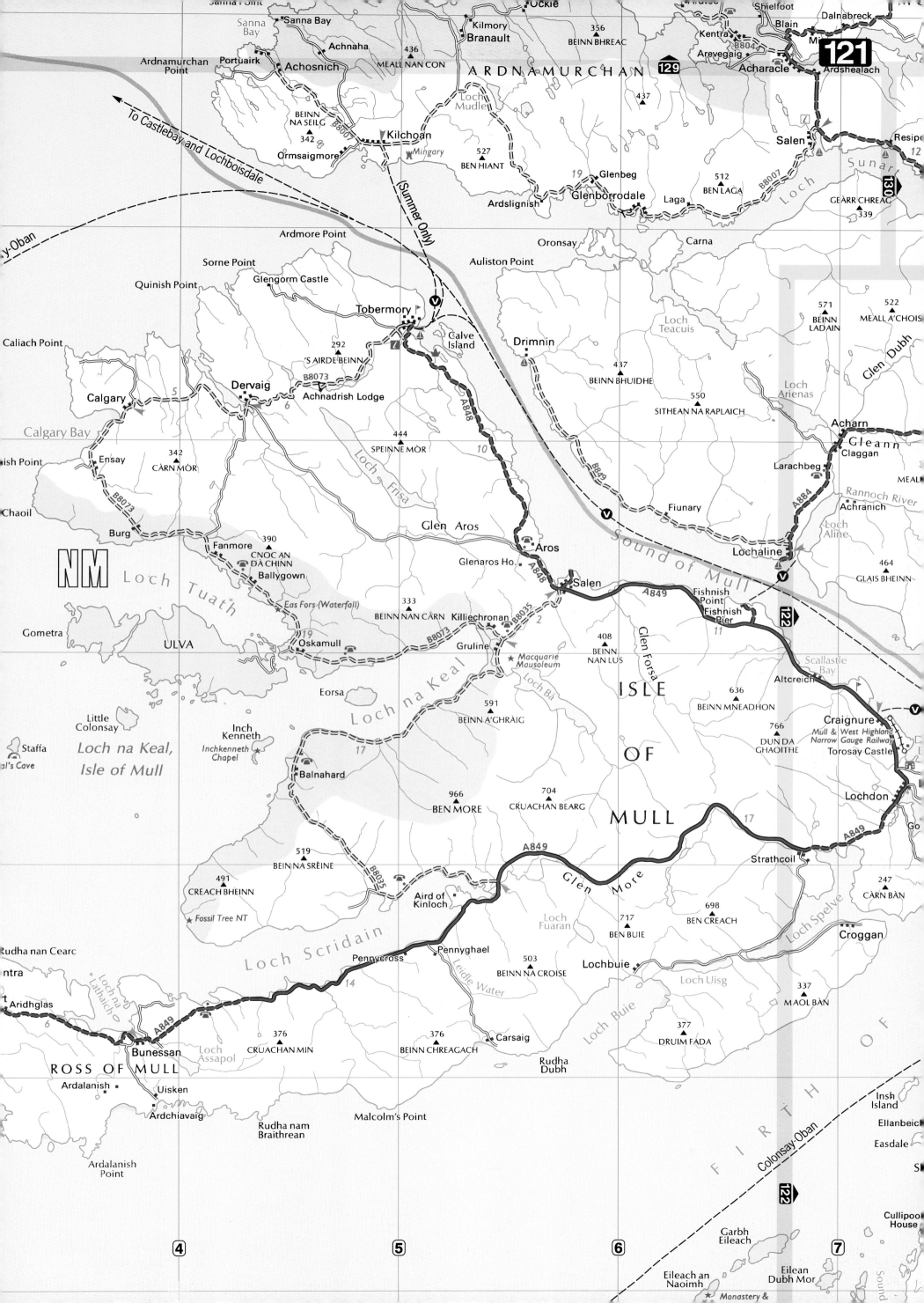

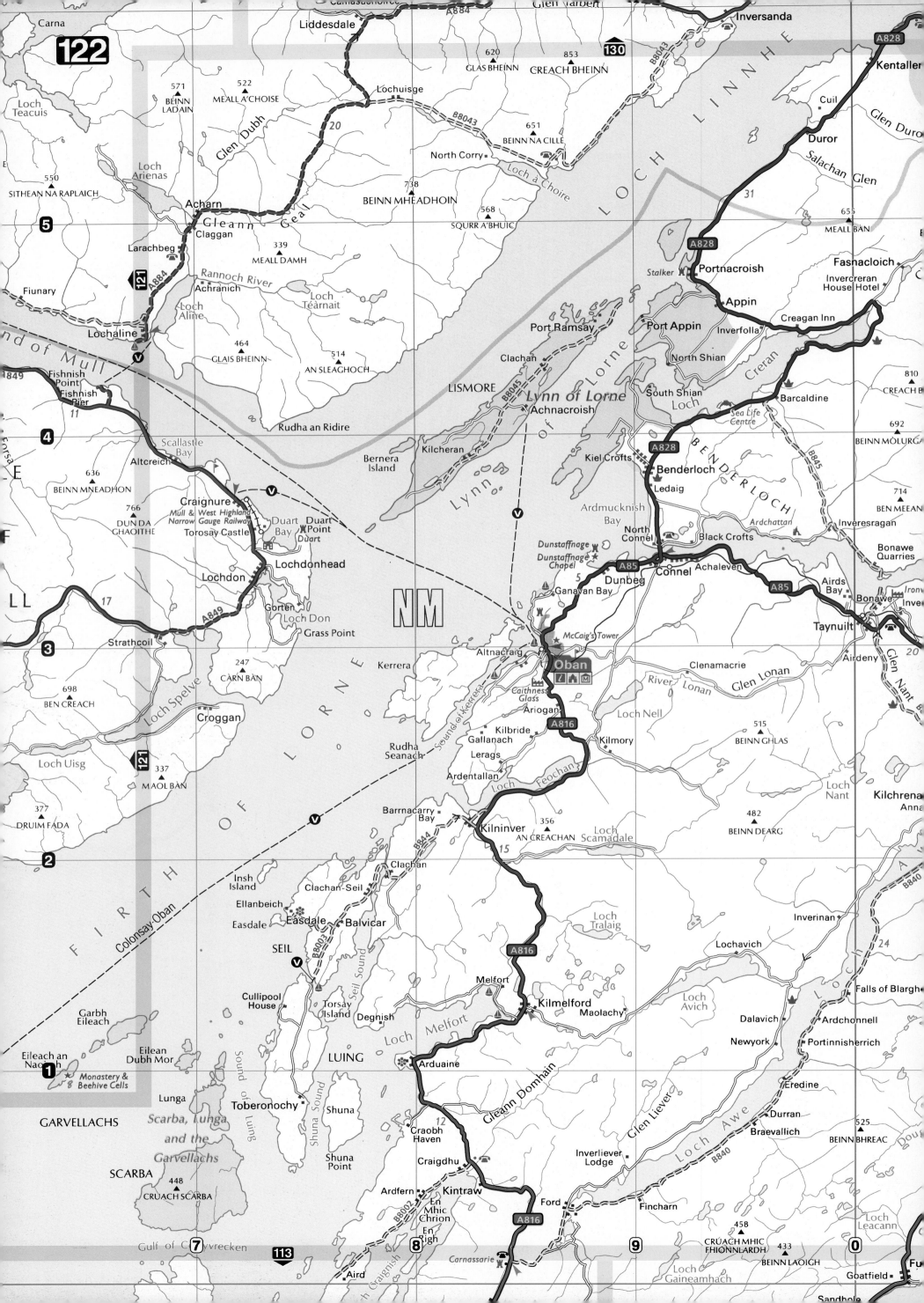

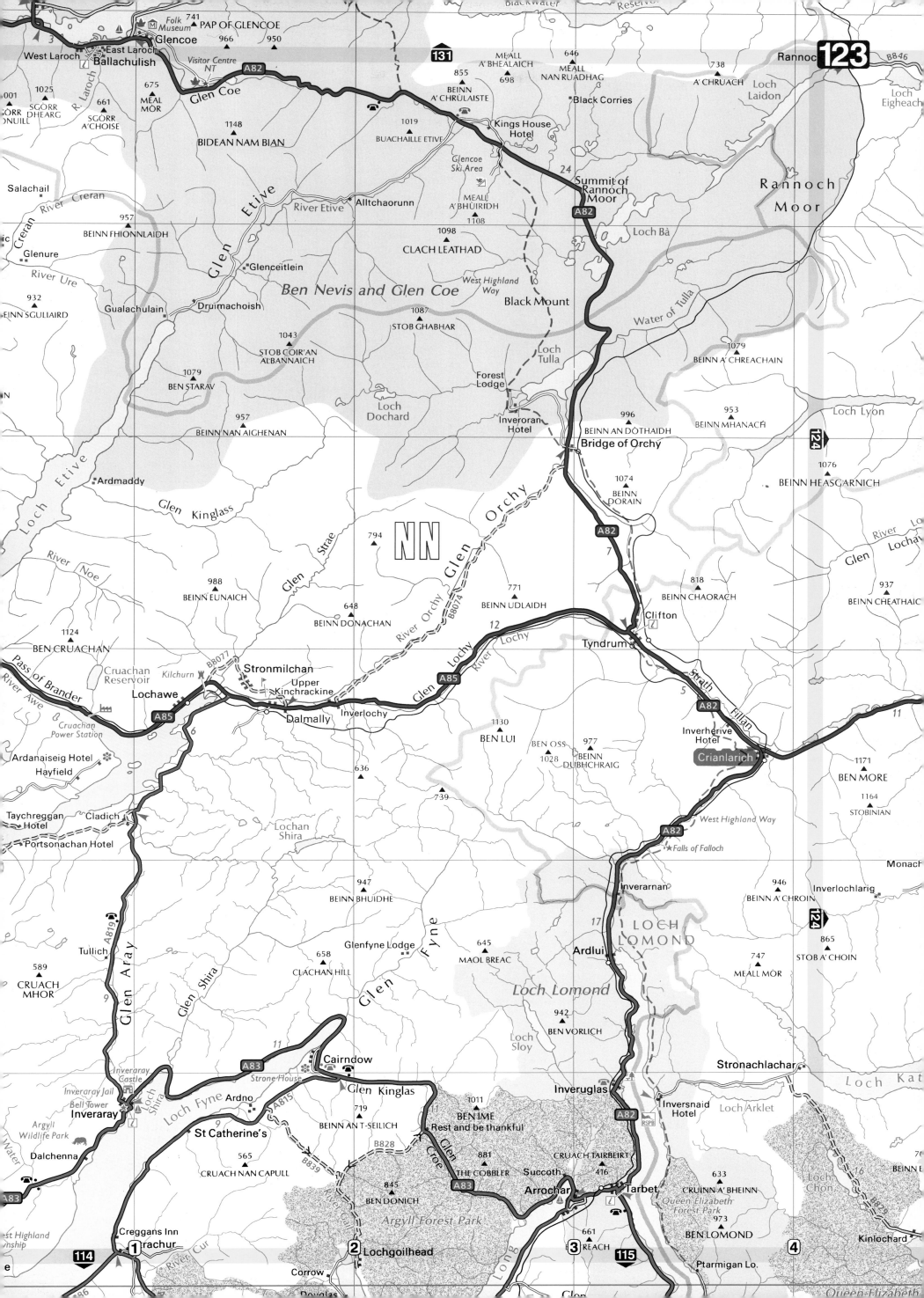

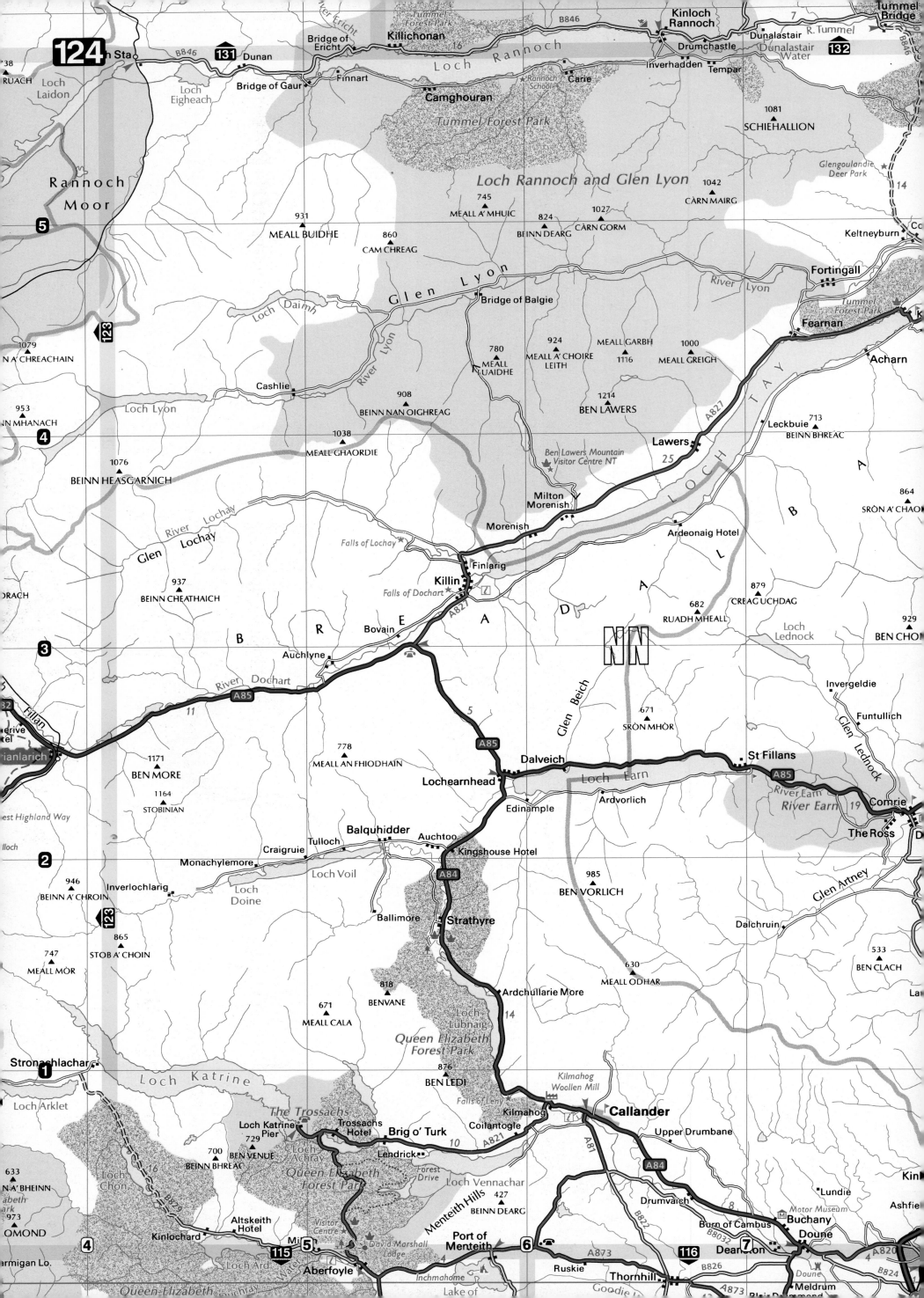

Murthill
Shielhill
Doocot
Netherton
Kinnaird Castle
Barnhead
Basin
Scurdie Ness
R
134
Finavon
Crosston
Farnell
135
Maryton
Ferryden
Oathlaw
13
Battledykes
Aberlemno
Craig
Pitkennedy
Melgund Castle
8
Westerton
Usan
A94
Carse Gray
Kemp's Castle
Clochtow
B9134
11
Braehead
Boddin Point
inshoe
Lunanhead
B9113
Restenneth Priory
Reswallie
Bolshan
132
Lunan
haram
Forfar Loch
A932
Balgavies
WUDDY LAW
LUNAN BAY
Guthrie
Glasterlaw
Forfar
Burnside
Kinnell
Boysack
Inverkeilor
Dunnichen
Letham
Pitmuies
13
Kingsmuir
Friockheim
Red Head
Balmuir
Leysmill
A92
Bowriefauld
Idvies
Chapelton
Cauldcots
B965
Craichie
Letham Grange
Inverarity
Redford
Colliston
6
Marywell
Whigstreet
B9127
Greystone
Auchmithie
Kirkbuddo
B961
B9127
St Vigeans
Hatton
Hayhillock
Carmyllie
Elliot Water
Carlingheugh Bay
auld
B978
14
Arbirlot
The Deil's Head
14
259
Crombie
Bonnington
Arbroath
Petterden
CARROT HILL
Monikie
Todhills
Affleck
Kirkton of Monikie
B9128
Newbigging
Monikie
Craigton
Bucklerheads
Wellbank
Muirdrum
17
Burnside of Duntrune
Kellas
Newbigging
Upper Victoria
East Haven
9
Murroes
Barry
Panbride
Douglas nd Angus
B961
11
West Haven
Baldovie
Carnoustie
A92
A930
Monifieth
Buddon
DUNDEE
Barnhill
Broughty Ferry
BUDDON NESS
Scotscraig
Tayport
Newport on-Tay
NO
B945
13
A919
Leuchars
ST ANDREWS BAY
Earlshall
Balmullo
13
10
Guardbridge
River Eden
Kincaple
A91
St Andrews
Strathkinness
Brownhills
Botanic Gardens
B939
Boarhills
Blebocraigs
Craigtoun
B9131
10
Denhead
Stravithie
Pitscottie
Cameron Reservoir
Kingsbarns
Baldinnie
A915
Dunino
B940
Radernie
A917
12
10
Peat Inn
Balcomie Links
FIFE NESS
Kingsmuir
B9171
Largoward
Lochty
Crail
Carnbee
A917
Easter Pitkierie
Kellie Castle NT
B9131
4
Wester Pitkierie
Kilrenny
Upper Largo
Arncroach
Fisheries Museum
Anstruther Easter
Colinsburgh
B942
Abercrombie
Anstruther
Drumeldrie
Kilconquhar
B942
6
Pittenweem
A917
St Monans
ARGO BAY
118
Earlsferry
Elie
5
6
Isle of May
7
119
8

SCALE
0   1   2   3   4   5 miles

0   1   2   3   4   5 kilometres

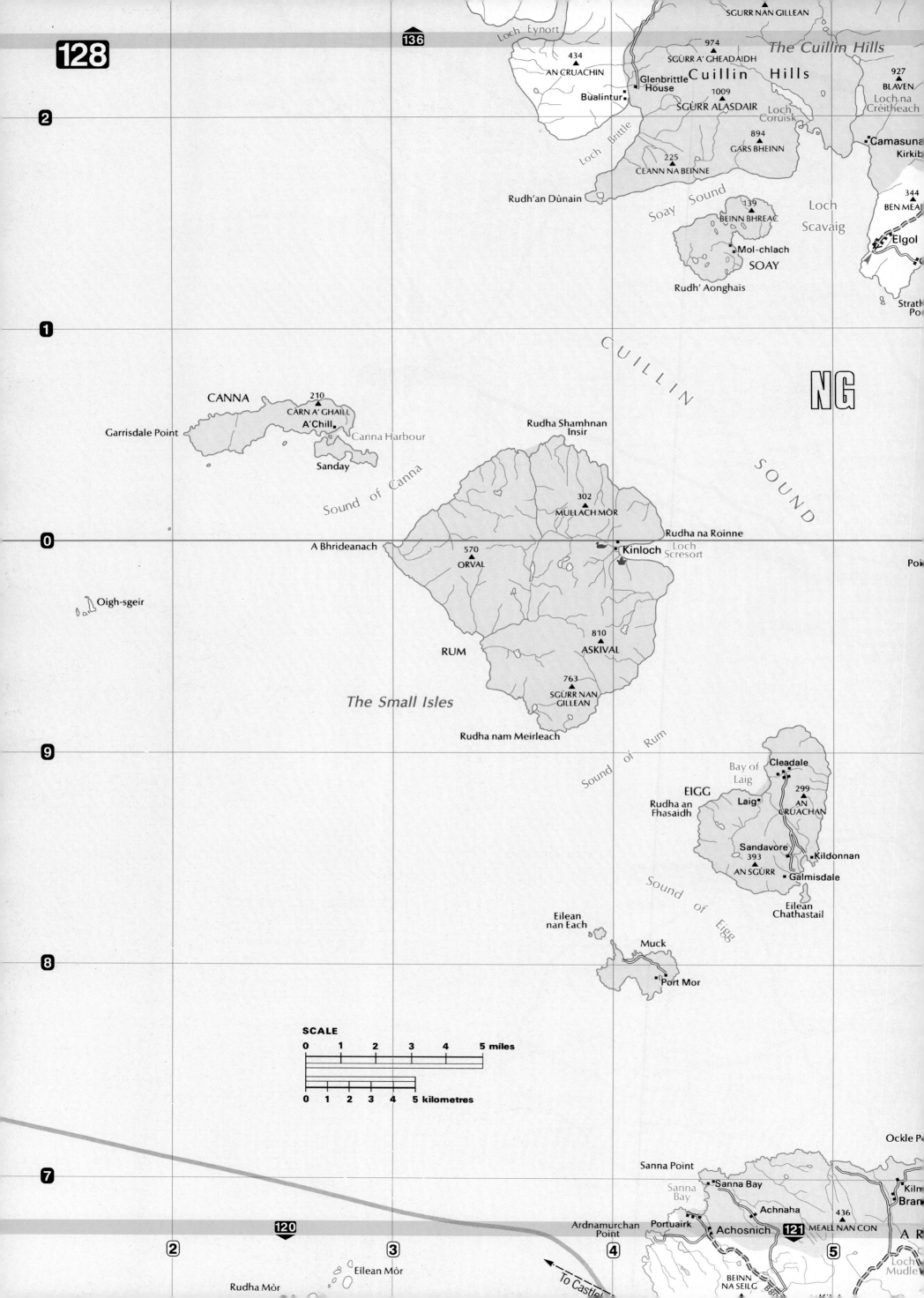

2

136

SGURR NAN GILLEAN

974
SGURR A' GHEADAIDH   The Cuillin Hills

AN CRUACHIN   Cuillin Hills
Glenbrittle
House   927
Bualintur   BLAVEN
                              1009   Loch.na
                    SGURR ALASDAIR   Loch   Crèitheach
                                        Coruisk
                              894
                         GARS BHEINN   Camasuna
                                                      Kirkib
            225
       CEANN NA BEINNE   344
Rudh'an Dùnain   BEN MEA

                                        Soay
                   139   Sound   Loch
              BEINN BHREAC   Scavaig
                                                              Elgol
                    Mol-chlach
              SOAY

         Rudh' Aonghais   Strath
                                                              Po

1

                                        C U I L L I N   NG

CANNA   210
           CÀRN A' GHAILL
           A'Chill   Rudha Shamhnan
                                         Insir
Garrisdale Point   Canna Harbour
                                                            S O U N D
              Sanday

         Sound of Canna
                                        302
                                    MULLACH MÒR

0   Rudha na Roinne
A Bhrideanach   570   Kinloch Loch
                                  ORVAL   Scresort   Poi

Oigh-sgeir

                                        810
                                    ASKIVAL
              RUM

                              763
                         SGURR NAN
                          GILLEAN
         The Small Isles

         Rudha nam Meirleach

9   Cleadale
                                   Sound   Bay of
                                    of   Laig
                                    Rum   299
                                         EIGG   AN
                              Rudha an   CRUACHAN
                              Fhasaidh Laig

                                         Sandavore
                                         393   Kildonnan
                                         AN SGÙRR   Galmisdale

                                                      Eilean
                                                      Chathastail
         Eilean
         nan Each
                                                 Sound
8   Muck   of Eigg
                                    Port Mor

SCALE
0   1   2   3   4   5 miles

0 1 2 3 4 5 kilometres

7   Sanna Point
                                             Sanna Bay
                                   Sanna   Kilm
                                   Bay   Achnaha   Bran
120   436
                                   Ardnamurchan   MEALL NAN CON
                                   Point   Portuairk   Achosnich 121   AR

2   3   4   5
         Eilean Mòr   To Castl   Loch
Rudha Mòr   Mudle
                         BEINN
                         NA SEILG

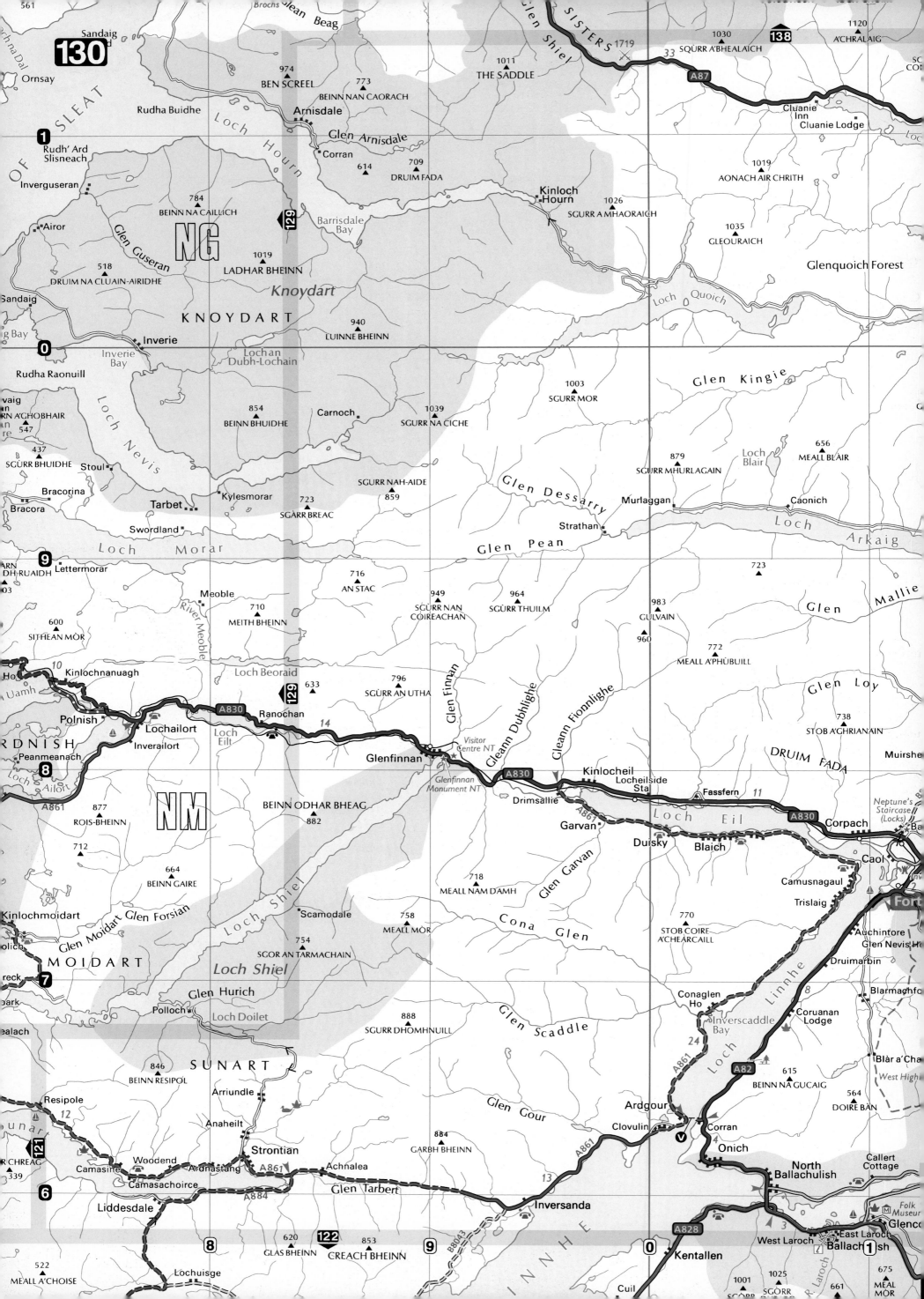

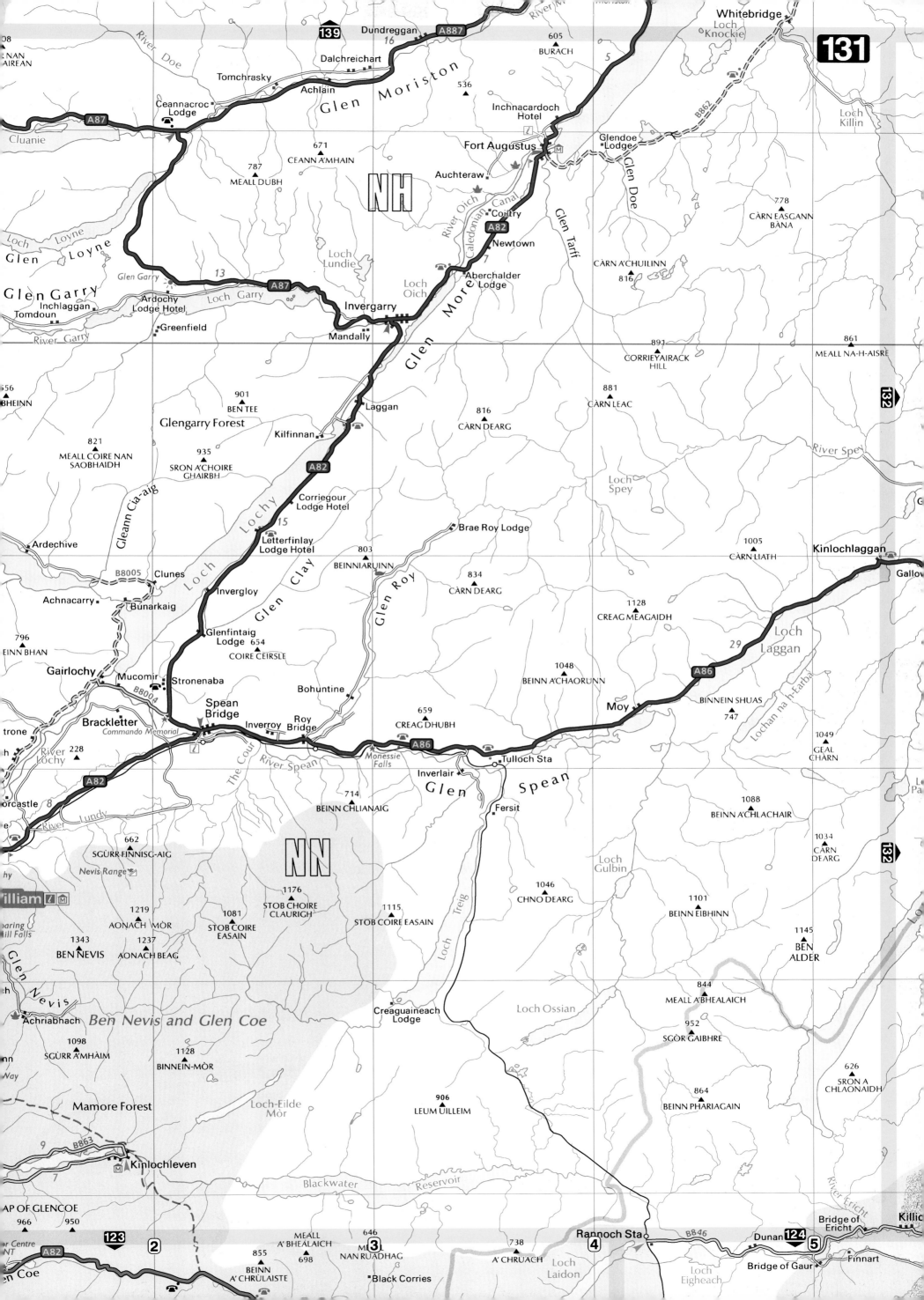

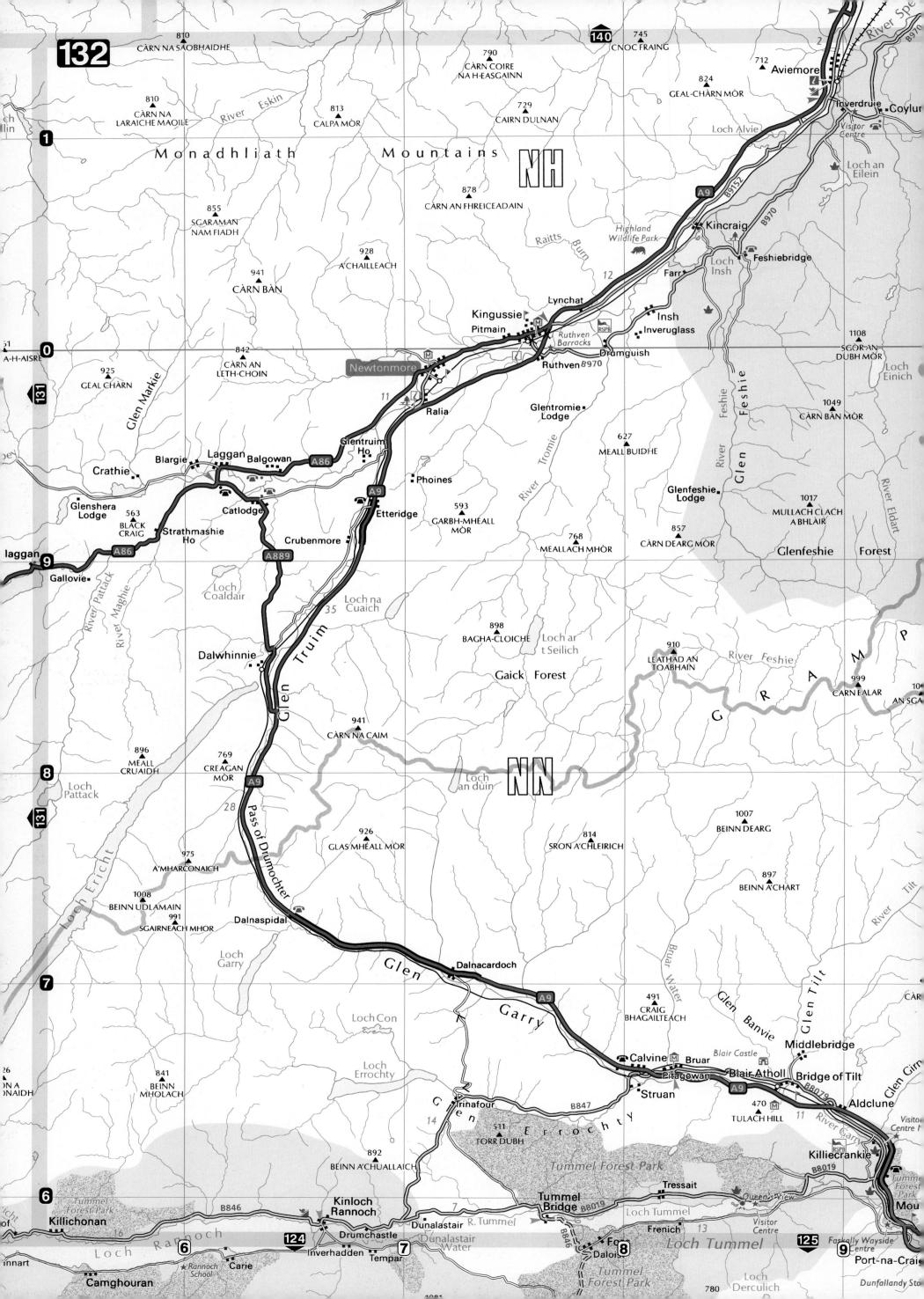

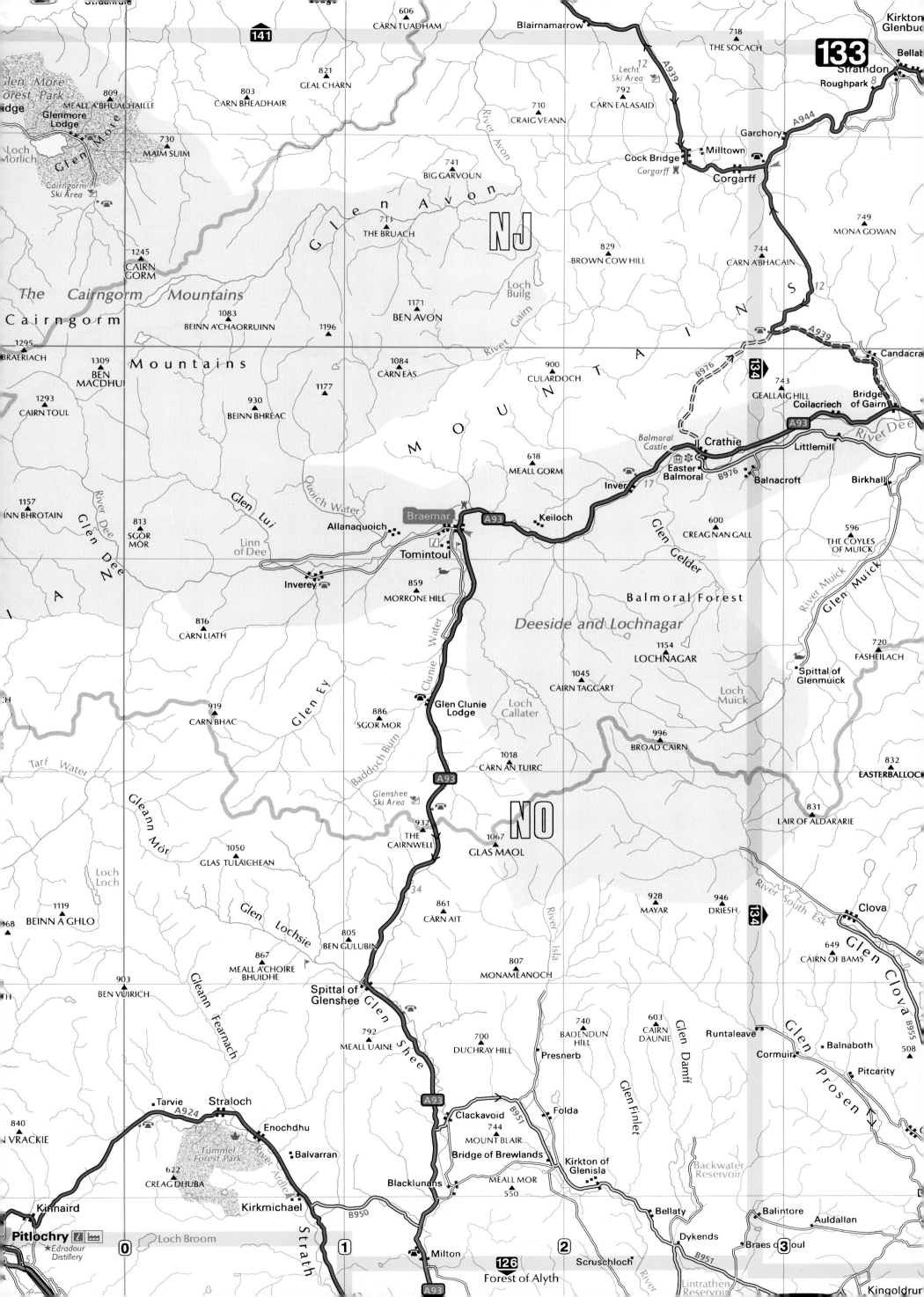

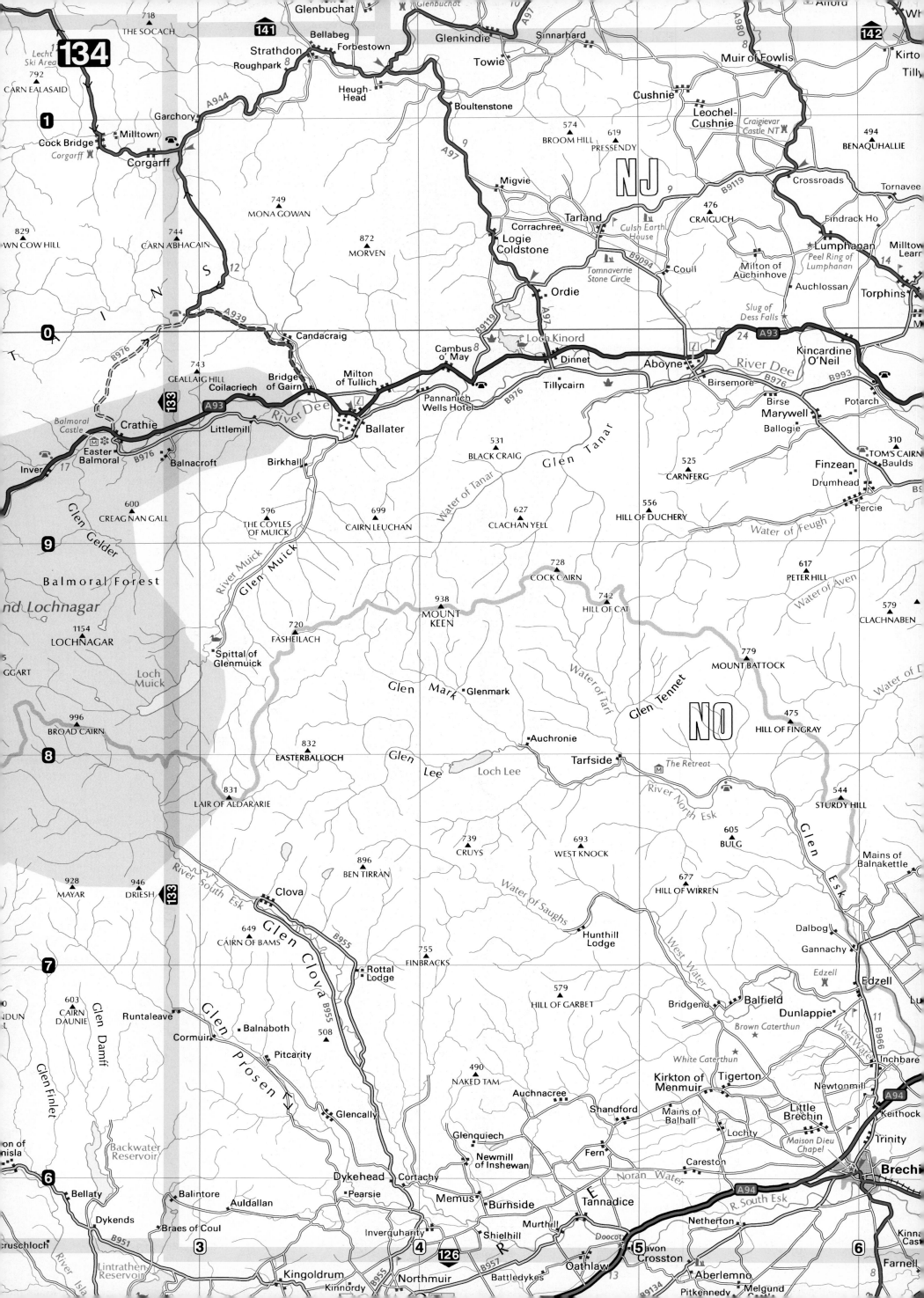

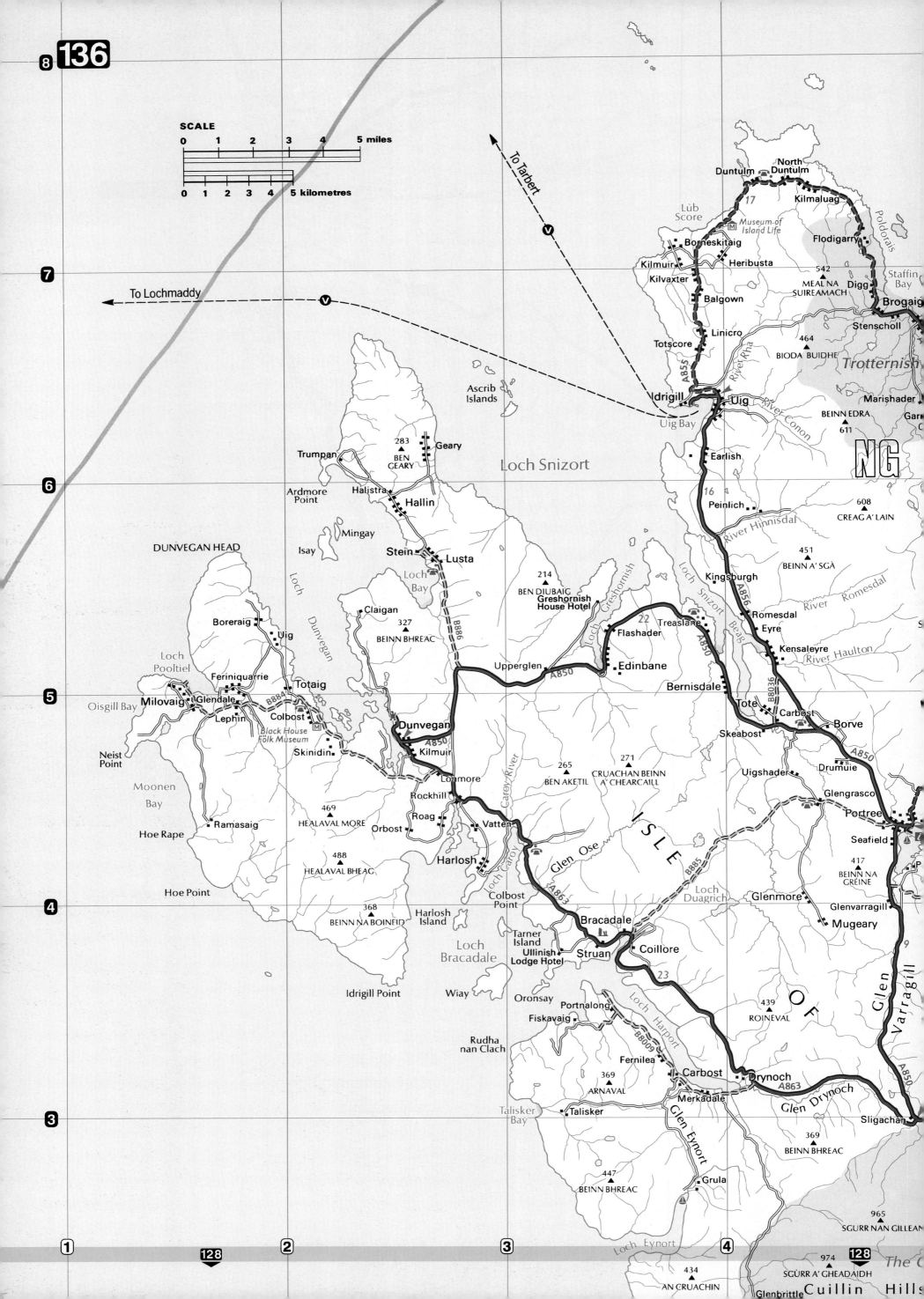

North Erradale
B8021
Big Sand
Longa Island
Strath Smithstown
A832
Poolewe
Londubh
MEALL NA MEIN
250
Inverewe Gardens NT
13
Loch Gairloch
Auchtercairn
Gairloch
Heritage Museum
Eilean Horrisdale
Charlestown
421
MEALL AN DOIREIN
Port Henderson
144
B8056
Badachro
Opinan
South Erradale
Loch Maree
20
Red Point
Tallada
619
BEINN BHREAC
Craig
River
985
BEINN ALLIGIN
138
Loch Torridon
Rudha na Fearn
Fearnmore
Lower Diabaig
Loch Diabaig
Fearnbeg
Arrina
Allig in Shuas
Inveralligin
Torridon Ho
1024
LIATHACH
Cuaig
Kenmore
Upper Loch Torridon
Torridon
19
RONA
Ardheslaig
Loch Shieldaig
Shieldaig
Torridon Cen
Callakille
Shieldaig Island
Wester Ross
Lonbain
492
AN GARBH-MHEALL
493
CRÒIC-BHEINN
Loch Damph
Glenshieldaig
Forest
902
BEINN DAMH
MAOL CH
Eilean Tigh
Loch Lundie
Umachan
Manish Point
Eilean Fladday
Loch Arnish
Torran
Arnish
River Applecross
895
BEINN BHAN
Loch Coultrie
730
SGURR A GHARAIDH
14
312
Brochel
RAASAY
SOUND OF RAASAY
Applecross Bay
Applecross
Milton
SGÙRR A'CHAORACHAIN
774
Camusteel
Camusterrach
Bealach-Na-Ba
Kishorn
Kirkton
412
N TIANAVAIG
DUN CAAN
444
Rudha na' Leac
Ardarroch
Lochcarron
INNER SOUND
Toscaig
River Toscaig
Slumbay
Camastianavaig
Tianavaig Bay
Ollach
Oskaig
310
BEINN NA LEAC
Kishorn Island
138
BAD A CHREAMHA
394
Clachan
Inverarish
Loch Kishorn
Loch Carron
B883
The Braes
LEE
Eyre Point
Eilean Meadhonach
Eilean Mòr
CROWLIN ISLANDS
Achmore
Stromeferry
Strome NT
Ardnarff
A890
einchorran
Suisnish Point
Plockton
15
Sconser
67
Longay
SCALPAY
Port-an-Eorna
Duirinish
BEINN RAIMH
447
773
GLAMAIG
Drumbuie
KYE
Loch Ainort
Dunan
Luib
396
MULLACH NA CARN
27
Pabay
Badicaul
Balmacara
Auchtertyre
Nostie
Conchra
Bundalloch
17
Kyle of Lochalsh
A87
Kirkton
Carndu
564
GLAS BHEINN MHÒR
Caolas Scalpay
Lochalsh House NT
Kyleakin
Ardelve
Dornie
Eilean Donan
BEINN NA CAILLICH
6
Corry
Broadford Bay
Lower Breakish
7
Upper Breakish
129
8
Keppoch
9
n Hills
927
708
732
Broadford
Waterloo
Harrapool
Skulamus
Kyle Rhea
732
SGURR NA
603
BEINN MCAU/RN
Letterfearn
A87
BEINN DEORG MHÒR
15
A850

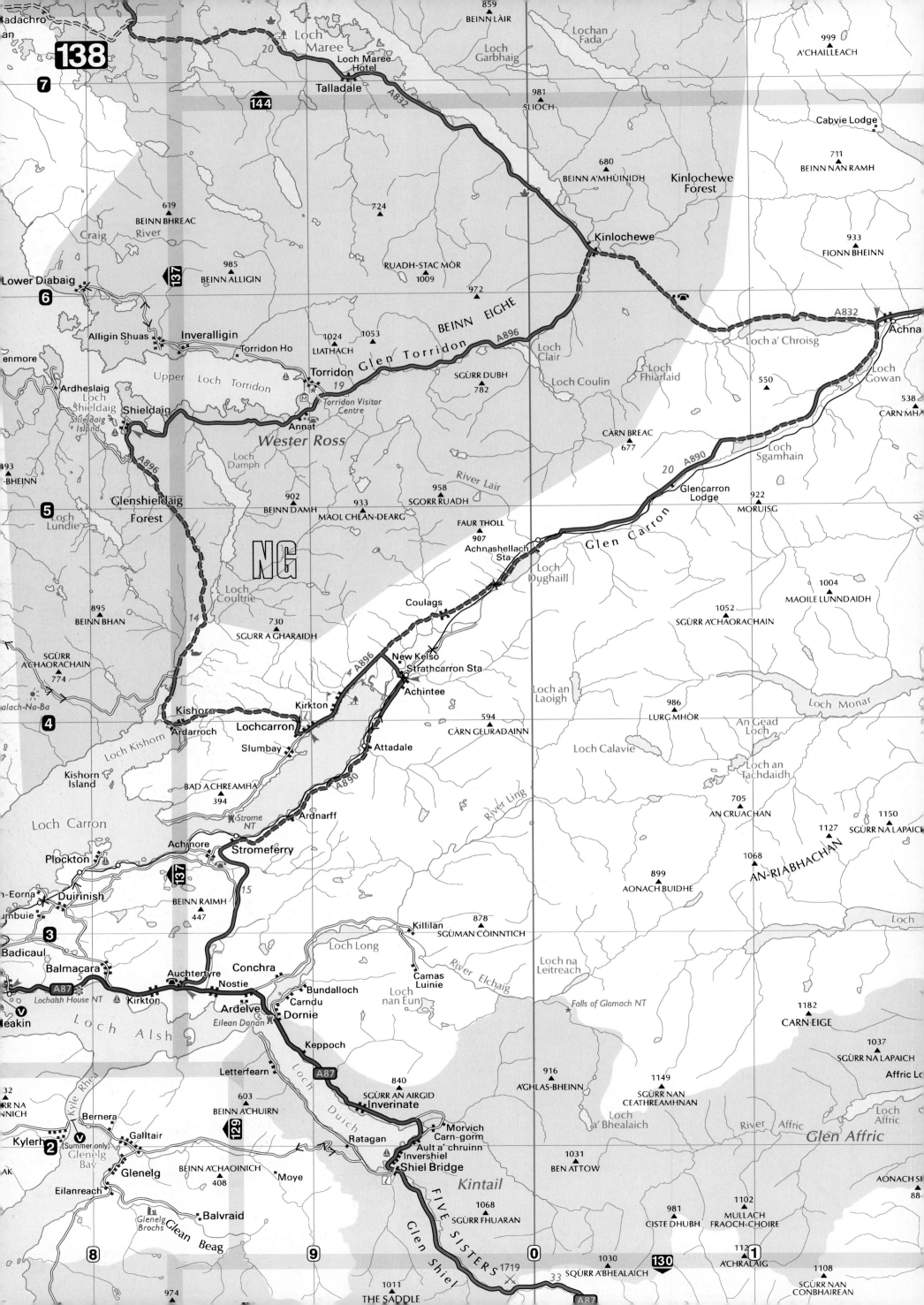

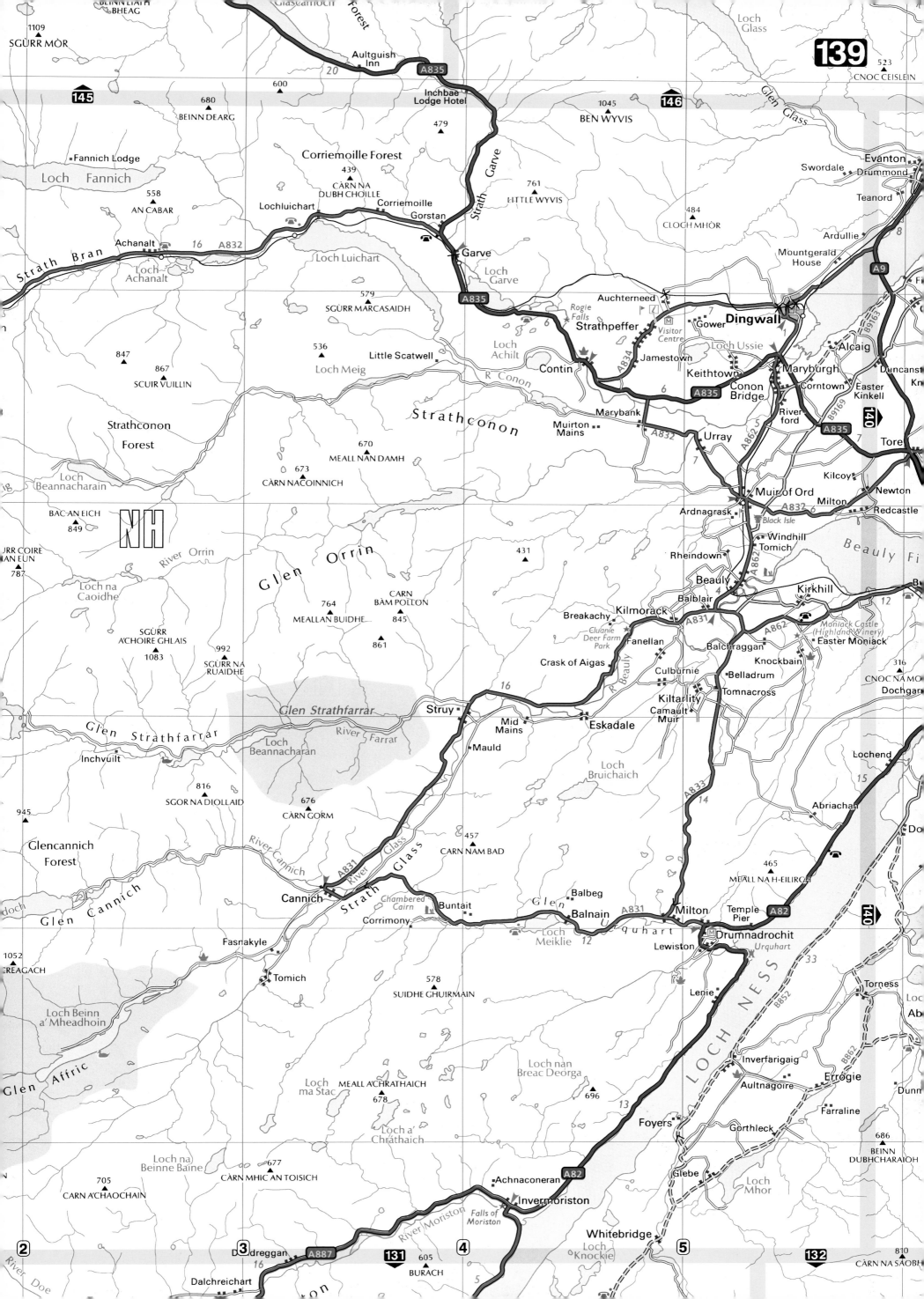

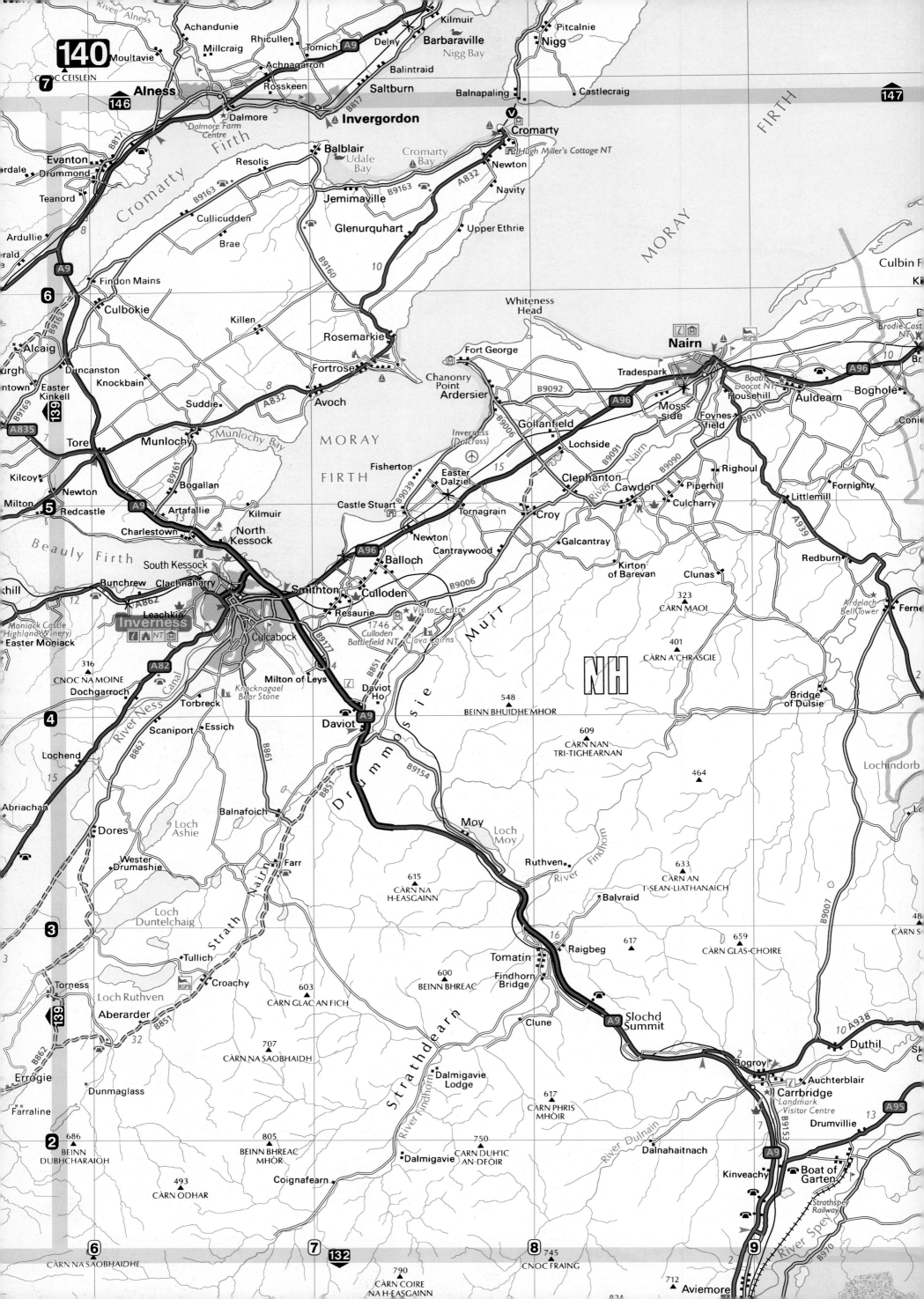

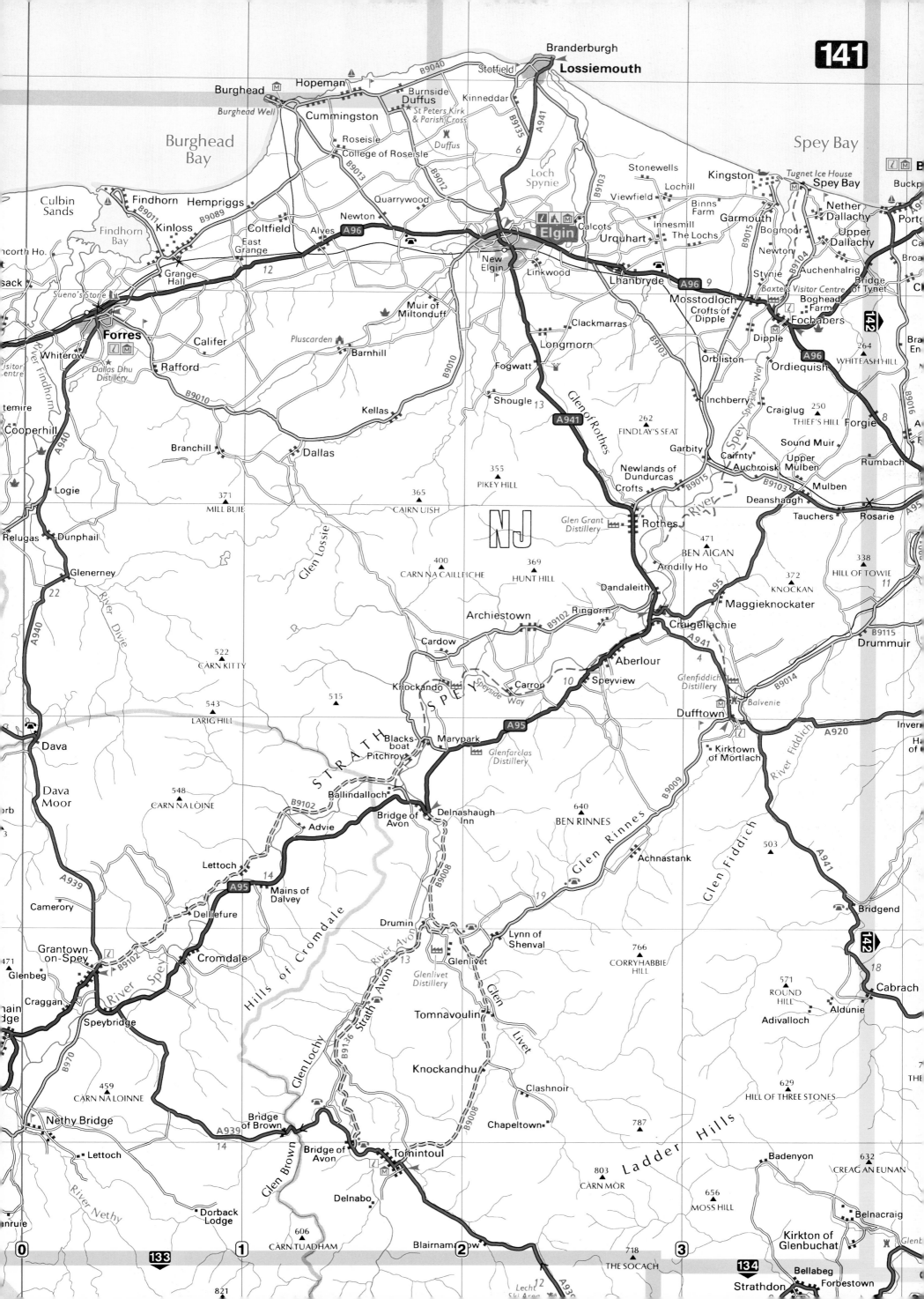

Troup Head
Cullykhan Bay
Aberdour Bay
nrie Bay
Crovie
Pennan
Protstonhill
own
ford
Rosehearty
Sandhaven
Kinnaird
Pittulie
Fraserburgh
Craigiefold
Peathill
Fraserburgh Bay
Coburby
Percyhorner
Pitblae
Kirktown
Cairnbulg
Whitelink Bay
Inverallochy
St Combs
B9031
Mid Ardlaw
Memsie
A92
Boyndlie
B9032
New Aberdour
A98
Rathen
B9033
Netherbrae
221
BRACKLAMORE HILL
Newburgh
Lonmay
Crofts of Savoch
B9027
New Byth
New Pitsligo
B9030
234
WAUGHTON HILL
Strichen
Crimonmogate
RSPB
Loch of Strathbeg
Crimond
Rattray Head
Bonnykelly
Oldwhat
12
12
Blackhill
18
Garmond
5
New Leeds
B9093
St Fergus
uminestown
13
A950
A981
Denhead
Leys
Backfolds
Kirktown
Rora
B9170
Fetterangus
6
Deer Abbey
Dunshillock
Mintlaw
River Ugie
Inverugie
Buchanhaven
Peterhead
Maud
B9106
A92
Aden Visitor Centre
Longside
A950
Peterhead Bay
New Deer
B9029
Old Deer
Inverquhomery
9
Hillhead of Cocklaw
Maryhill
A948
Blackhill of Clackriach
Bulwark
Stuartfield
Millbreck
Nether Kinmundy
Burnhaven
Slacks of Cairnbanno
Drymuir
Little Dens
Boddam
Millbrex
Nethermuir
B9030
Clola
Blackhill
Stirling
Buchan Ness
Kirkton
Knaven
Kinnadie
Lendrum Terrace
Cottown
Cairnorrie
12
Kinknockie
Coldwells
ethenty
B9005
Brownhill
Inkhorn
Blackhill
NK
odhead
Haddo
Haddo
Coldwells
Muirtack
Hatton
Auchiries
Bullers of Buchan
Methlick
14
B9005
Arthrath
14
A92
17
North Haven
R Ythan
Bogbrae
Chapel Hill
Cruden Bay
Barthol Chapel
Haddo House NT
Birness
Whinnyfold
Bay of Cruden
Earlsford
Auchedly
A948
A975
The Skares
Wedderlairs
Medieval Tomb
Kinharrachie
Artrochie
Tulloch
Ythsie
Tarves
Ellon
Kirkton of Slains
Collieston
Craigdam
Tolquhon
Esslemont
Kirkton of Logie Buchan
heldrum
A920
Pitmedden Garden NT
Pitmedden
B9999
32
Kirktown of Bourtie
Carnbrogie
Udny Green
Housieside
B9000
Whiterashes
Woodland
Udny Station
Newburgh
A947
Pettymuk
Cultercullen
Foveran
rurie
Nether Crimond
Tillygreig
B999
B993
Straloch
Reisque
Delfrigs
Kinmuck
Newmachar
Causeyend
Balmedie
17
kell Church
B979
Whitecairns
Balmedie
B977
Kinmundy
Belhelvie
Hatton of Fintray
Dyce Symbol Stones
18
B977
Potterton
8
135
9
Parkhill
Overton
Blackdog
0
1
Dyce
Aberdeen
A92
Blackburn

SCALE
0 1 2 3 4 5 miles
0 1 2 3 4 5 kilometres

2

1

SCALE

0   1   2   3   4   5 miles

0   1   2   3   4   5 kilometres

NB

Rhu Coigach

Rhu More
Reiff
Achnahaird

Eilean
Mullagrach
Isle Ristol

Altandhu

Polbain

Glas-leac Mòr
SUMMER ISLES

Tanera
Beg

Badentarbat
Bay

To Stornoway

Tanera More

Horse
Island

Glas-leac
Beag

Priest
Island

Eilean
Dubh

V

0

Greenstone Point

Cailleach Head

Leac Dh

Rudha Beag

Mellon
Udrigle

Stattic Point

Scoraig

Little

Slaggan

Gruinard
Island

Badluachrach

Foura

Mellon
Charles

Laide

Gruinard Bay

A832

Rudha
Reidh

Ormiscaig

Badcaul

Cove

B8057

Aultbea

Gruinard

9

296
AN CUAIDH

NG

Loch Ewe

Loch
Fada

347
CREAG-MHEAL BEAG

Little Gruinard River

Gruinard River

Loch
Gaineam

Melvaig

Aultgrishin

Midtown
Brae

Isle of Ewe

293
CNOC BREAC

Naast

Inverewe
Gardens NT

13

250
MEALL NA MEINE

681
BEINN A'
CHAISGEIN BEAG

Loch m
Sheall

North Erradale

B8021

Londubh

Poolewe

8

Big Sand

Longa Island

Strath
Smithstown

A832

Wester Ross

Fionn
Loch

Dubh
Loch

BEINN D

BEINN

Auchtercairn

Gairloch

Heritage
Museum

791
BEINN
AIRIDH CHARR

Loch
Gairloch

Eilean
Horrisdale

Charlestown

421
MEALL AN DOIREIN

Port
Henderson

B8056

859
BEINN LÀIR

Loch
Fa

137

Badachro

Opinan

Loch
Maree

20

Loch
Garbhaig

South Erradale

Loch Maree
Hotel

7

Talladale

A832

981
SLIOCH

Red Point

619

7

8

9

0

BEINN

724

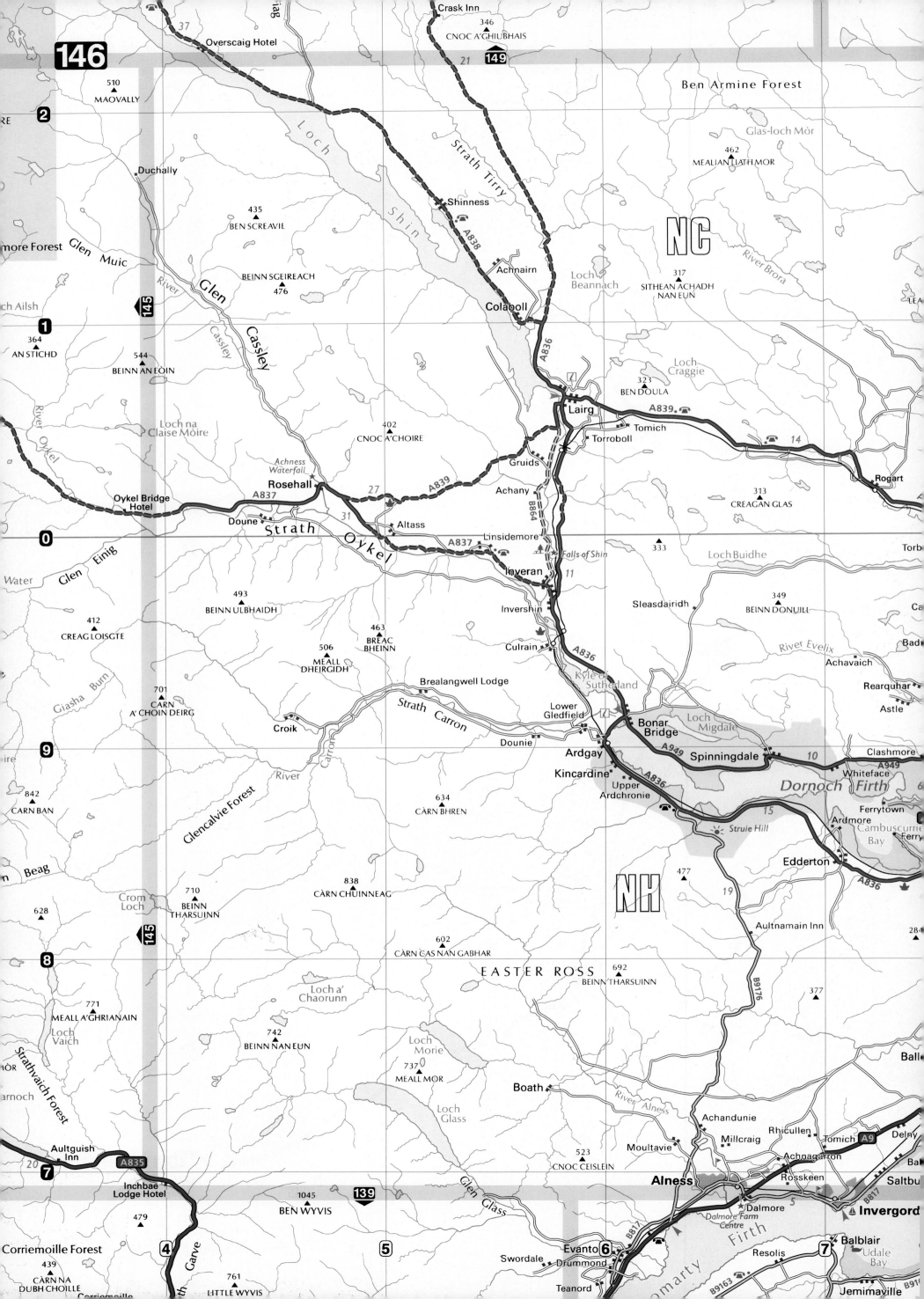

CNOC NA
BREUN-CHOILLE

Learable Hill
Cairns, Stone Rows
& Stone-Circle

Newport

554

CREAG SCALABSDALE

Langwell
Ho.

151

147

388
CREAG NAM FIADH

150

Kildonan
Lodge

Kildonan

416
BEINN DUBHAIN

401
CNOC NA MAOILE

A9

337
CNOC NA
H-INNSE MOIRE

Strath Skinsdale

Torrish

A897

River Helmsdale

17

404

Ord of Caithness

421
CNOC NAN
CRUBAG MOR

624
BEINN DHORAIN

591
BEINN NA MEILICH

West
Helmsdale

Navidale House
Hotel

East Helmsdale

ND

Balnacoil Lodge

Glen Loth

Gartymore

Helmsdale

Portgower

NACHD

Strath Brora

River Brora

Dalreavoch Lodge

Loch
Brora

539
COL-BHEINN

Lothmore

Lothbeg

A9

520
BEN HORN

Loch
Horn

Dalchalm

378
CAGAR FEOSAIG

Doll

Brora

Backies

446
BEINN LUNDIE

Golspie Burn

Cairn Liath

Rhives

Dunrobin Castle

A9

Golspie

Loch
Fleet

savie
form

Skelbo

Skelbo Street

Fourpenny

SCALE

0   1   2   3   4   5 miles

0   1   2   3   4   5 kilometres

Birichin

B9168

Embo

Embo Street

Pitgrudy

Evelix

A949

Camore

Dornoch

NJ

Cuthill

Tarbat Ness

Innis Mhor

Brucefield

Wilkhaven

Dornoch Firth

Portmahomack

Rockfield

Inver

Arboll

B9165

Tain

Toulvaddie

A9

Loch
Eye

Rhynie

B9165

Fearn

Balmuchy

11

Hill of Fearn

Newfield

B9166

Tullich

Hilton of Cadboll Chapel

B9175

Hilton of
Cadboll

Milton

Ankerville

Shandwick

Balintore

Shandwick Bay

Kilmuir

Pitcalnie

Barbaraville

Nigg

Nigg Bay

Balnapaling

Castlecraig

140

Burghead

141

Hopeman

Burghead Well

Cummingston

FIRTH

Burghead
Bay

Roseisle

Cromarty

V M

College of Ros

Miller's Cottage NT

A832

Newton

Navity

8

9

0

Culbin

Findhorn

Hemprigg

B9013

1

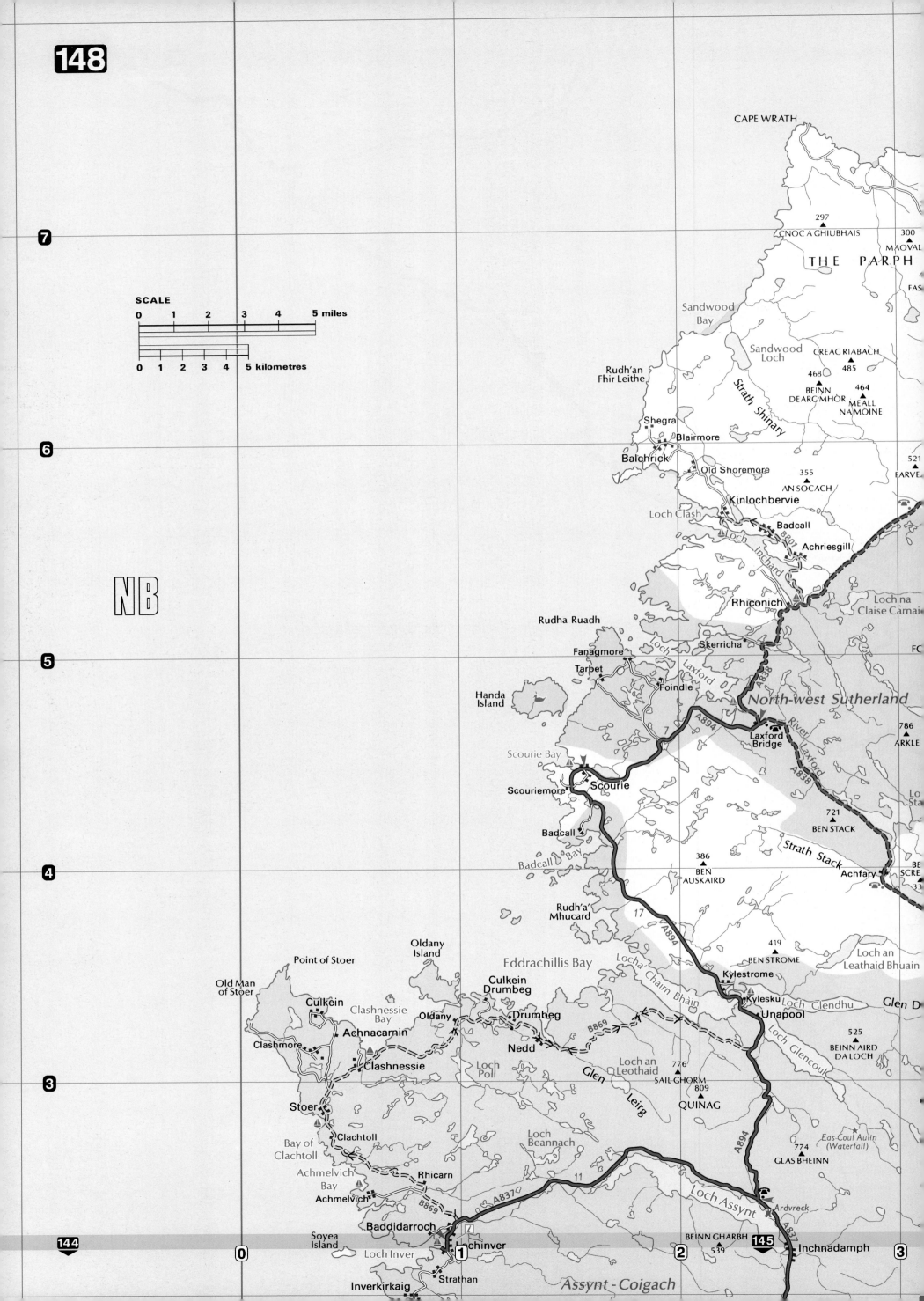

NB

SCALE

0 1 2 3 4 5 miles

0 1 2 3 4 5 kilometres

CAPE WRATH

THE PARPH

297
CNOC A GHIUBHAIS
300
MAOVAL

FAS

Sandwood
Bay

Sandwood
Loch

CREAG RIABACH
468
485

Rudh'an
Fhir Leithe

BEINN
DEARG MHÒR
464
MEALL
NA MÒINE

Strath Shinary

Shegra
Blairmore
Balchrick
355
AN SOCACH
Old Shoremore
521
FARVE

Kinlochbervie
Loch Clash
Badcall
Achriesgill

Loch Inchard
B801

Rhiconich
Loch na
Claise Carnai

FO

Rudha Ruadh
Skerricha

Fanagmore
Tarbet
Foindle

Loch Laxford
A838

North-west Sutherland

786
ARKLE

Handa
Island

Laxford
Bridge
River Laxford

Scourie Bay
7
A894

A838

Scouriemore
Scourie
721
BEN STACK

Badcall
Strath Stack

Badcall Bay
386
BEN
AUSKAIRD
Achfary
BE
SCRE
33

Rudh'a'
Mhucard

419
BEN STROME
Loch an
Leathaid Bhuain

17
A894
Kylestrome

Oldany
Island
Eddrachillis Bay
Locha Chàirn Bhàin
Kylesku
Loch Glendhu
Glen D

Point of Stoer

Culkein
Drumbeg
Unapool

Old Man
of Stoer
Culkein
Clashnessie
Bay
Oldany
Drumbeg
B869
Nedd
525
BEINN AIRD
DA LOCH

Achnacarnin
Loch
Poll
Glen
Loch an
Leothaid
776
SAIL GHORM
Loch Glencoul

Clashmore
Clashnessie
Leirg
809
QUINAG

Stoer
Loch
Beannach
Eas-Coul Aulin
(Waterfall)

Clachtoll
774
GLAS BHEINN

Bay of
Clachtoll
A894

Achmelvich
Bay
Rhicarn
11
A837
Loch Assynt
Ardvreck

Achmelvich
B869

Baddidarroch
Soyea
Island
chinver
BEINN GHARBH
539
Inchnadamph

Loch Inver
Strathan
Assynt - Coigach

Inverkirkaig

0
1
2
3

NC

Faraid Head

Balnakeil
Bay
Balnakeil
Durness
Sangomore
Keoldale
Smoo
Cave
Eilean
Hoan
Smoo
Sangobeg

Whiten Head

Loch Airigh
na Beinne

Loch
Meadaidh

408
BEN HUTIG

Strathan

Talmine

Eilean Nan Ròn

Neave Island

Farr Point

Kirtomy

Rabbit
Islands

Tongue
Bay

Skerray

Torrisdale
Bay

Farr
Bay

Farr

Sword

331
GHLAS-BHEINN

A838

423
MEALL MEADHONACH

Melness
Midtown

Scullomie

Torrisdale

Achtoty

Bettyhill

19

489
MEALL NA CRÀ

Laid

A838

230
BEN
ARNABOLL

A838

Kyle of Tongue

Coldbackie

A836

Borgie

13

773
BEINN SPIONNAIDH

262
DRUIM NAN
CLIAR

Tongue

310
MEALL LEATHAD
NA CRAOIBHE

River Borgie

Skelpic

Strath Naver

801
CRANSTACKIE

Strath Beag

31

520
AN LEAN-CHÀRN

Loch na
Seilg
927
BEN HOPE

Kyle of Tongue

Kinloch

318
CNOC
CRAGGIE

Loch
Craggie

12

River Dionard

598
MEALLAN LIATH

527
BEINN
STUMANADH

213
CNOC
MALPELLY

B871

WEN

NC

na Tuadh

River Hope

463
FEINNE--BHEINN NHOR

Strath More

Loch
an Deerie

BEN LOYAL

Loyal Lodge
557
CNOC
NAN CUILEAN

Loch
Loyal

17

Loch Syre

Syre

River Naver

Dun Dornaigil
Broch

Glen Golly

729
SÀBHAL BEAG

656
CNOC AN
DAIMH MÒR

294
POLE HILL

259
BEINN ROSAIL

800

796
CARN
DEARG

757
CARN
AN
TIONAIL

Loch Meadie

A836

Strath Naver

12

B873

River Mallart

Loch
More

Kinloch

A838

Loch Coire na
Saidhe Duibhe

873
BEN HEE

680
MEALL AN
LIATH MOR

Loch a'
Ghorm-choire

230
MEALL
A'BHROLLAICH

Strath Naver

Loch Naver

Altnaharra

270
BEADAIG

150

Loch
Rimsdale

613
MEALL AN
FHEUR LOCH

472
MEALL AN FHUARAIN

Strath Bagastie

721
BEN KLIBRECK

Loch Choire Forest

Loch
Truderscaig

92

LEOID

Loch Fiag

959
MEALL NAN CON

694
CREAG N-IOLAIRE

Fiag Lodge

Loch
Choire

713
CREAG MHOR

372
CNOC A'
GHRIAMA

Glen Fiag

A836

Loch
a'Bhealaich

Loch
Alltan

37

Overscaig Hotel

Crask Inn

346
CNOC A'GHILBHAIS

21

146

510
MAOVALLY

Ben Armine Forest

4

5

6

7

8

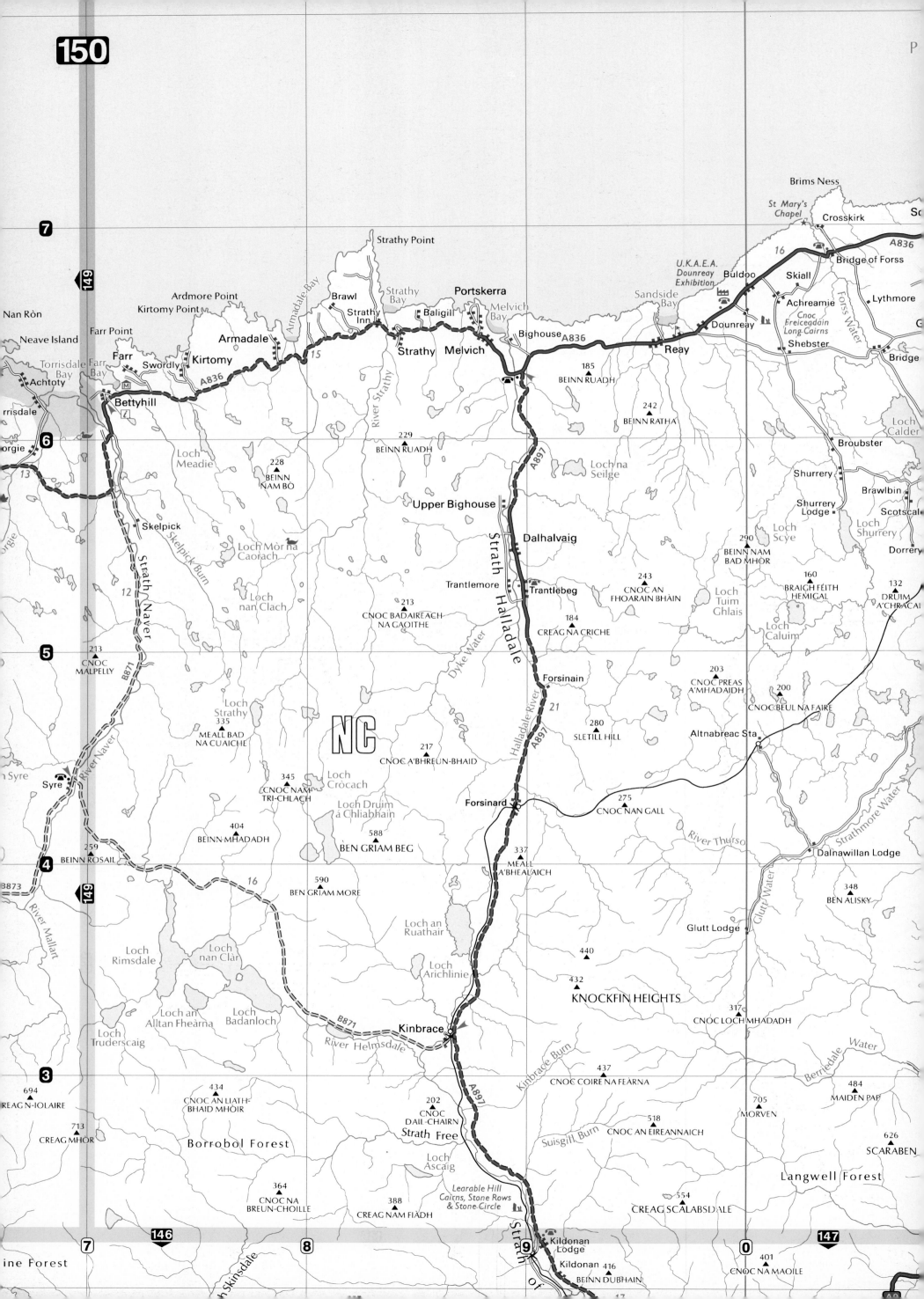

PENTLAND FIRTH

To Stromness

Langaton Point
Nethertown
Island of Stroma
Mell Head
Uppertown

DUNNET HEAD

Briga Head

Scarfskerry
St John's Point
Inner Sound

Brough
DUNNET HILL
121
Castle of Mey
15
Gills Bay
Kirkstyle
Huna
DUNCANSBY HEAD

West Dunnet
St John's Loch
Rattar
Mey
Gills
Canisbay
John O'Groats
Muckle Stack

A836
Barrock
Dunnet
Stacks of Duncansby

Dunnet Bay
Inkstack
Brabstermire
Tofts
Skirza

Thurso Bay
Murkle
Castlehill
Greenland
Loch Heilen
Slickly
Freswick
Freswick Bay

Thurso
5
Castletown
Thurdistoft
Ness Head
Bucholie

Olrig Ho
Tain
Bowermadden
Auckengill
A9

A882
Weydale
Hilliclay
Bower
Lyth
Sortat
Nybster

Westfield
B874
Sordale
Roadside
Knockdee
Howe
Keiss
17
Brough Head

B870
Halkirk
Clayock
Gillock
Halcro
Kirk
16

A895
A882
21
B874
B870
Loch of Wester
Sinclairs Bay

Harpsdale
176
SPITTAL HILL
Loch Watten
B876

Spittal
Watten
Reiss
Castle Girnigoe & Sinclair
Noss Head

Backlass
Bilbster
Winless
Sibster

Mybster
B870
Strath
A882
Haster
Milton
Wick

Westerdale
Loch of Toftingall
Janets-town
Staxigoe
Papigoe

23
Badlipster
Newton Row
Old Wick
South Head
Castle of Old Wick

136
BEINN CHAITEAG
Loch Hempriggs
Whiterow

ND
Tannach

145
BALLHARN HILL
Grey Cairns of Camster
Thrumster

Loch Ruard
212
HILL OF YARROWS
Loch of Yarrows
17
Sarclet

Achavanich
248
STERNSTER HILL
Camster
Ulbster

226
COIRE-NA-BEINN
Loch Rangag
Hill O'Many Stones

A895
Roster
Whaligoe
Whaligoe Steps
Bruan

287
BEN-A-CHIELT
Upper Lybster

264
CNOCAN CONACHREAG
Cairn O'Get
Mid Clyth
Halberry Head

Houstry
Swiney
Clyth
Clyth Ness

Landhallow
Forse House
Invershore
Lybster
Lybster Bay

Smerral
Forse

Latheron
Latheronwheel
Janetstown

Laidhay Croft Museum

Braemore
Dunbeath

Knockally

Ramscraigs
A9

Borgue

Newport
20

Langwell Ho.
Berriedale

SCALE

0 1 2 3 4 5 miles

0 1 2 3 4 5 kilometres

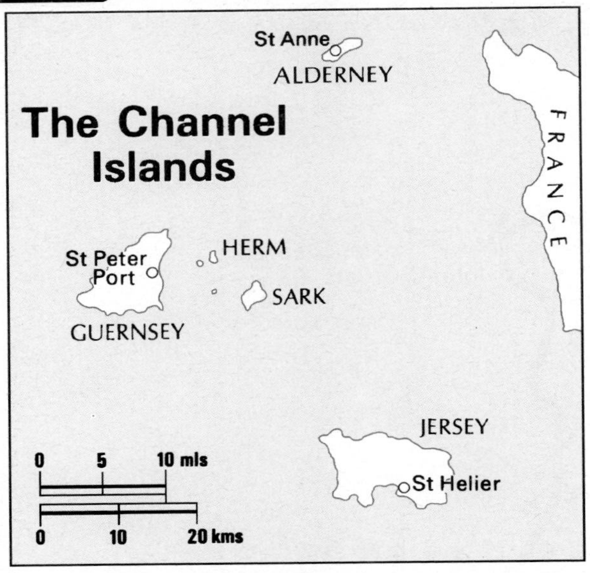

The Channel Islands

St Anne
ALDERNEY

FRANCE

St Peter Port
HERM
SARK
GUERNSEY

JERSEY
St Helier

SCALE
0   5   10 mls
0   10   20 kms

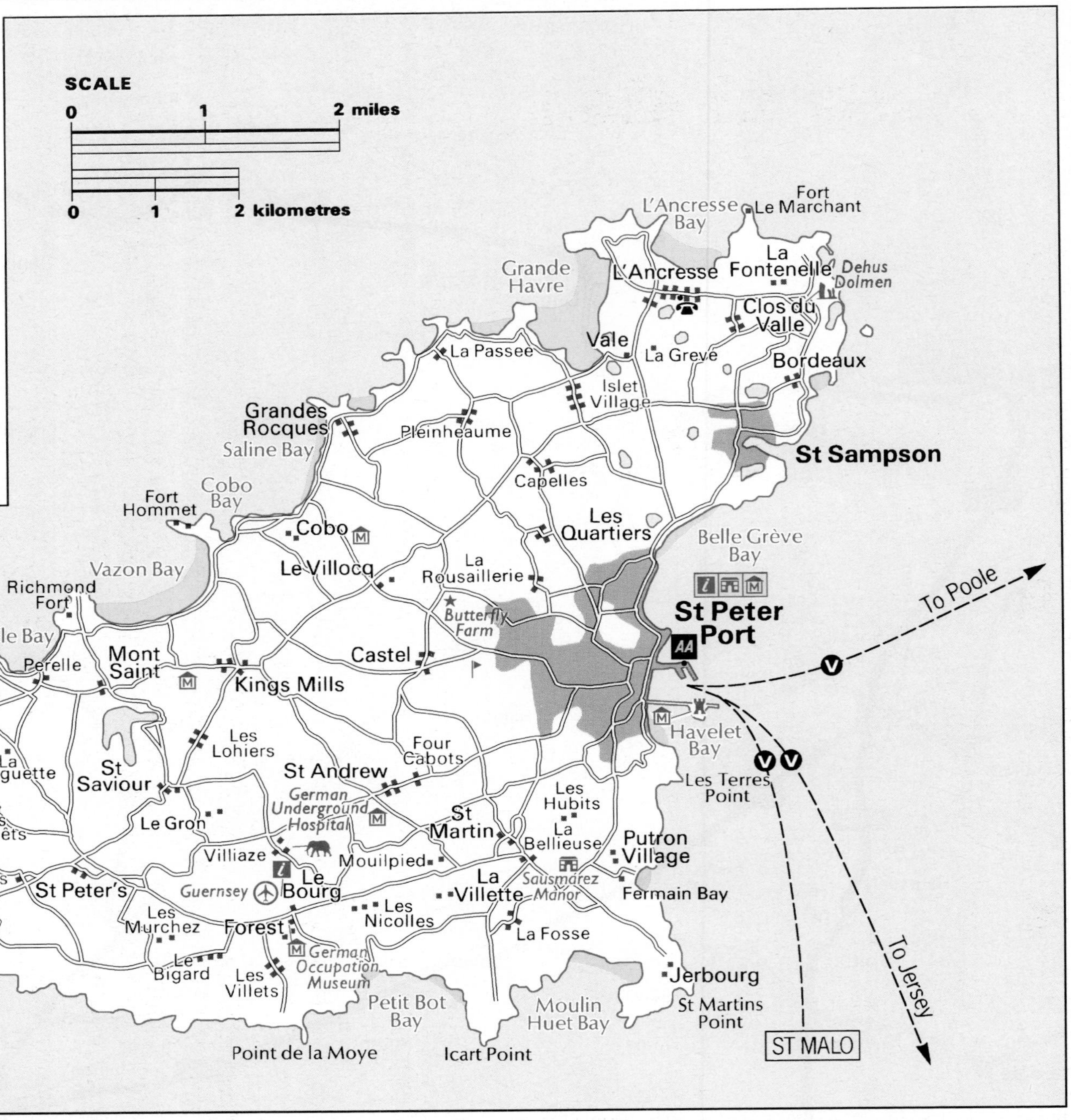

SCALE
0   1   2 miles
0   1   2 kilometres

Guernsey

L'Ancresse Bay
Fort Le Marchant
Grande Havre
L'Ancresse
La Fontenelle
Dehus Dolmen
Clos du Valle
Vale
La Greve
Bordeaux
La Passee
Islet Village
St Sampson
Grandes Rocques
Pleinheaume
Capelles
Les Quartiers
Belle Grève Bay
Saline Bay
Cobo Bay
Cobo
Le Villocq
La Rousaillerie
St Peter Port
Vazon Bay
Butterfly Farm
Havelet Bay
Richmond Fort
Castel
To Poole
Lihou Island
Perelle Bay
Mont Saint
Kings Mills
Les Terres Point
Perelle
L'Erée
Four Cabots
Les Lohiers
St Andrew
German Underground Hospital
St Martin
Les Hubits
La Bellieuse
Putron Village
To Jersey
Roquaine Bay
La Houguette
St Saviour
Le Gron
Villiaze
Mouilpied
Sausmarez Manor
Fermain Bay
Fort Grey Maritime Museum
Les Arquets
Les Sages
St Peter's
Le Bourg
Guernsey
La Villette
Les Nicolles
La Fosse
Pleinmont Point
Les Murchez
Forest
Le Bigard
Les Villets
German Occupation Museum
Jerbourg
St Martins Point
Torteval
Petit Bot Bay
Moulin Huet Bay
ST MALO
Point de la Moye
Icart Point

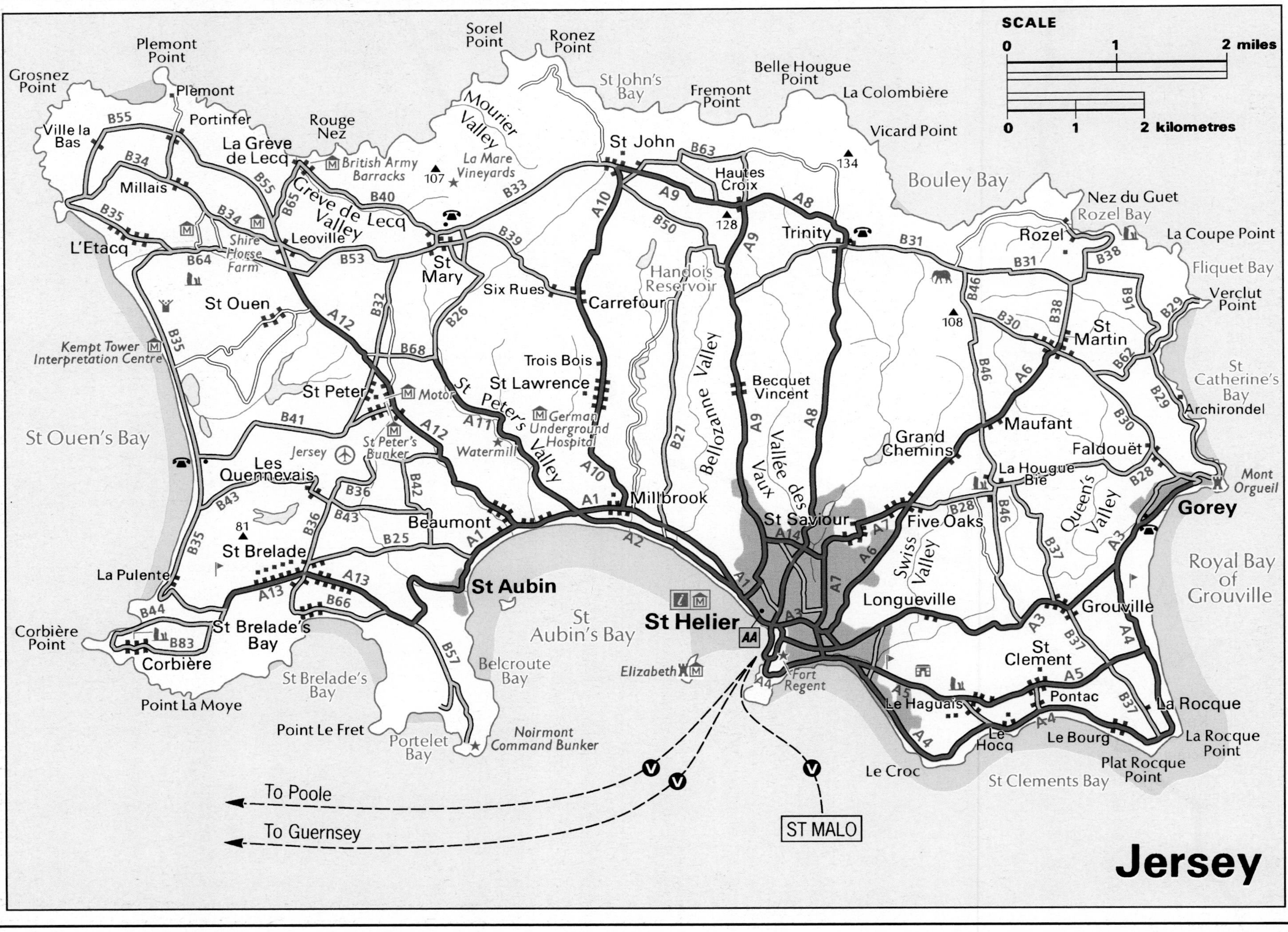

Jersey

Plemont Point
Sorel Point
Ronez Point
Grosnez Point
Plemont
Belle Hougue Point
St John's Bay
Fremont Point
La Colombière
Vicard Point
Ville la Bas
B55
Portinfer
La Greve de Lecq
Rouge Nez
Mourier Valley
St John
Hautes Croix
134
Bouley Bay
Nez du Guet
Rozel Bay
Millais
B34
B65
Greve de Lecq Valley
British Army Barracks
107
La Mare Vineyards
B33
A10
A9
B50
128
A9
Trinity
B31
Rozel
La Coupe Point
B35
Leoville
B40
B53
St Mary
B39
Handois Reservoir
Belfozanne Valley
B38
Fliquet Bay
L'Etacq
B64
Shire Horse Farm
B26
Six Rues
Carrefour
108
B30
St Martin
B91
B29
Verclut Point
Kempt Tower Interpretation Centre
St Ouen
A12
B32
B68
Trois Bois
St Lawrence
Becquet Vincent
A8
B46
A6
Maufant
B30
St Catherine's Bay
Archirondel
St Peter
Motor
German Underground Hospital
Vallée des Vaux
Grand Chemins
Faldouët
B37
B35
St Peter's Bunker
Watermill
B27
La Hougue Bie
B28
Mont Orgueil
Les Quennevais
Jersey
A11
A10
Millbrook
St Saviour
Five Oaks
Queen's Valley
Gorey
St Ouen's Bay
B41
B42
B36
A1
A14
A7
B28
B46
A3
Royal Bay of Grouville
Beaumont
A1
A2
A6
Swiss Valley
Longueville
Grouville
A5
81
B43
B25
St Brelade
Elizabeth
A1
A3
St Clement
La Pulente
B44
A13
B66
St Aubin
A4
Fort Regent
Le Haguais
Pontac
La Rocque
Corbière Point
B83
St Brelade's Bay
St Aubin's Bay
St Helier
Le Bourg
La Rocque Point
Corbière
Belcroute Bay
Le Hocq
Plat Rocque Point
Point La Moye
St Brelade's Bay
Elizabeth
To Poole
To Guernsey
ST MALO
Le Croc
St Clements Bay
Point Le Fret
Portelet Bay
Noirmont Command Bunker

Isle of Man

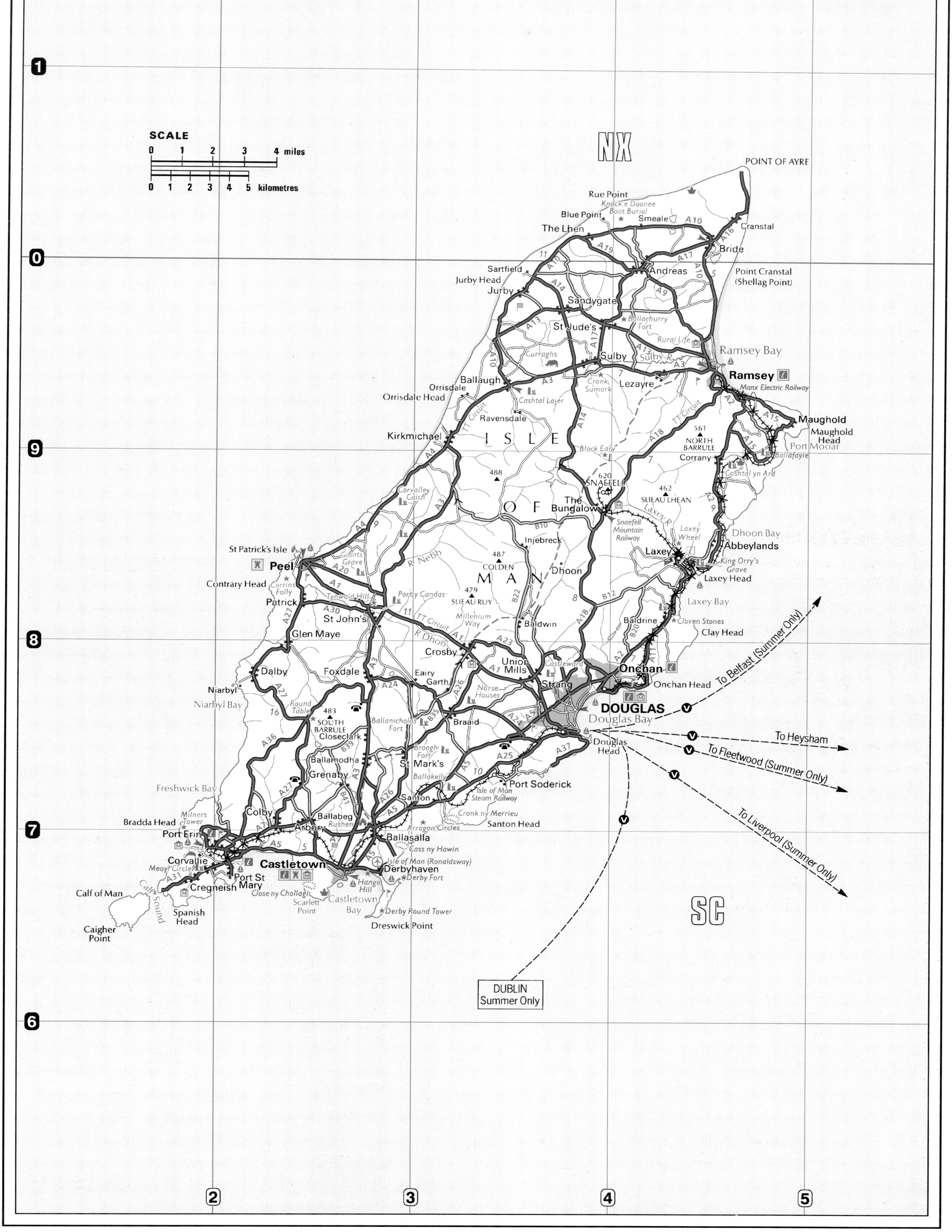

SCALE

0 1 2 3 4 miles

0 1 2 3 4 5 kilometres

NX

POINT OF AYRE

Rue Point
Knock e Doonee Boot Burial
Blue Point
Smeale
The Lhen
Cranstal
Bride
Sartfield
Jurby Head
Jurby
Andreas
Point Cranstal (Shellag Point)
Sandygate
St Jude's
Ballachurry Fort
Rural Life
Sulby
Sulby R.
Ramsey Bay
Curraghs
Lezayre
Ramsey
Manx Electric Railway
Ballaugh
Cronk Sumark
Orrisdale
Cashtal Lajer
Maughold
Maughold Head
Orrisdale Head
Port Mooar
Ravensdale
NORTH BARRULE
Ballafayle
561
Kirkmichael
ISLE
Corrany
Block Eary
Cashtal yn Ard
488
620
SNAEFELL
462
SLIEAU LHEAN
OF
St Patrick's Isle
Corvalley Cairn
The Bungalow
Snaefell Mountain Railway
Laxey Wheel
Dhoon Bay
Peel
Giants Grave
R Nebb
487
Injebreck
Laxey
Abbeylands
Contrary Head
Corrins Folly
MAN
COLDEN
Dhoon
King Orry's Grave
Patrick
Tynwald Hill
Port y Candas
479
SLIEAU RUY
Laxey Head
St John's
Millenium Way
Baldwin
Laxey Bay
Glen Maye
R Dhoo
Baldrine
Cloven Stones
Dalby
Foxdale
Crosby
Eairy Garth
Union Mills
Clay Head
Niarbyl
Norse Houses
Castleward
Onchan
Niarbyl Bay
Round Table
483
Strang
Onchan Head
To Belfast (Summer Only)
SOUTH BARRULE
Closeclark
Ballanicholas Fort
Braaid
DOUGLAS
Douglas Bay
Freshwick Bay
Ballamodha
Grenaby
Brooghy Fort
St Mark's
Ballakelly
Douglas Head
To Heysham
Milners Tower
Colby
Isle of Man Steam Railway
Port Soderick
To Fleetwood (Summer Only)
Bradda Head
Arbory
Ballabeg Rushen
Santon
Cronk ny Merriu
Santon Head
Port Erin
Ballasalla
Cass ny Hawin
Arragon Circles
To Liverpool (Summer Only)
Corvalljie
Castletown
Derbyhaven
Isle of Man (Ronaldsway)
Meayll Circle
Port St Mary
Derby Fort
Cregneish
Hango Hill
Close ny Chollagh
Castletown Bay
Calf of Man
Scarlett Point
Derby Round Tower
Spanish Head
Dreswick Point
Caigher Point

SC

DUBLIN
Summer Only

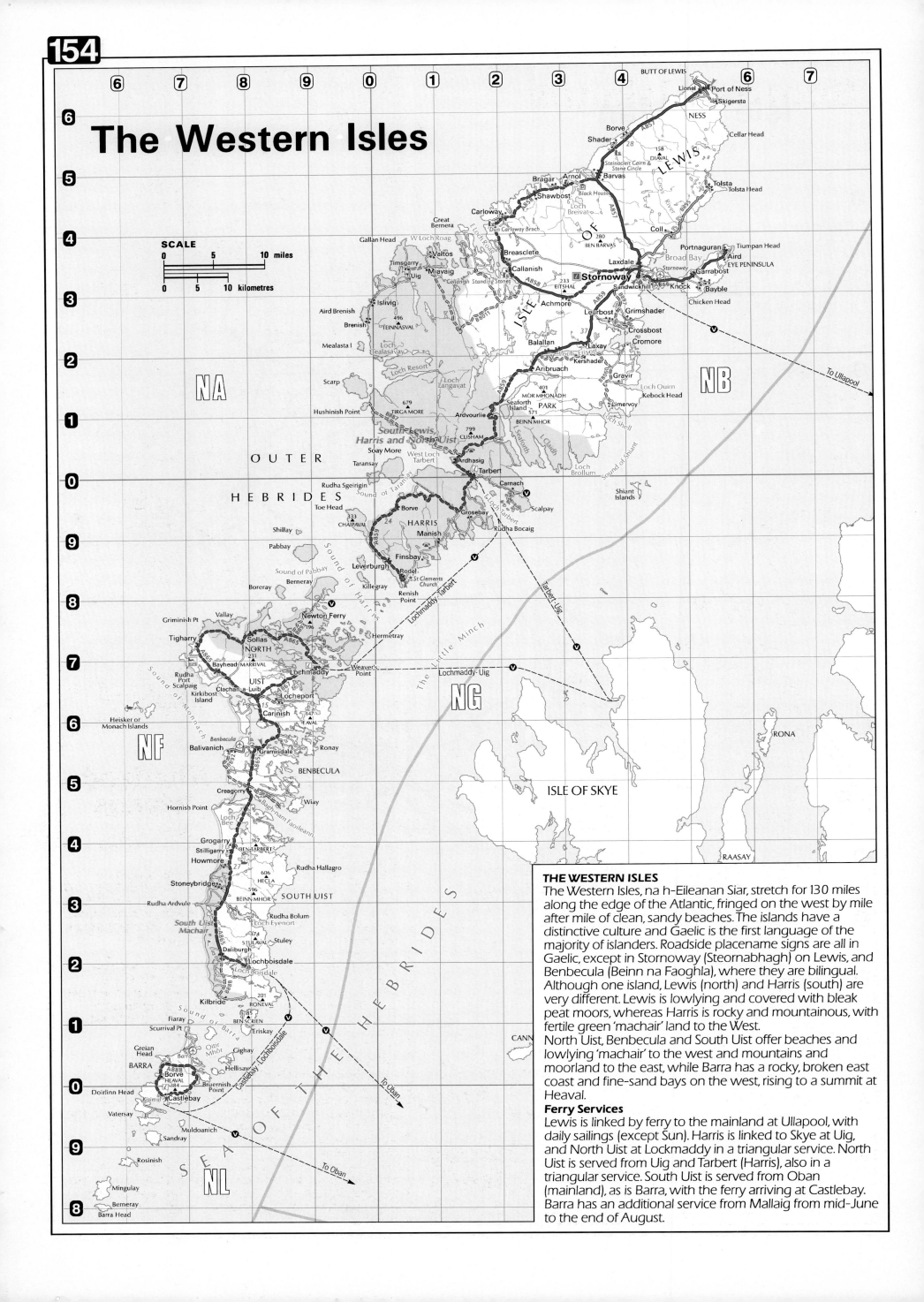

The Western Isles

SCALE

0   5   10 miles

0   5   10 kilometres

NA

OUTER

HEBRIDES

NB

To Ullapool

NF

NG

ISLE OF SKYE

RONA

RAASAY

CANN

NL

SEA OF THE HEBRIDES

To Oban

To Oban

THE WESTERN ISLES

The Western Isles, na h-Eileanan Siar, stretch for 130 miles along the edge of the Atlantic, fringed on the west by mile after mile of clean, sandy beaches. The islands have a distinctive culture and Gaelic is the first language of the majority of islanders. Roadside placename signs are all in Gaelic, except in Stornoway (Steòrnabhagh) on Lewis, and Benbecula (Beinn na Faoghla), where they are bilingual. Although one island, Lewis (north) and Harris (south) are very different. Lewis is lowlying and covered with bleak peat moors, whereas Harris is rocky and mountainous, with fertile green 'machair' land to the West.

North Uist, Benbecula and South Uist offer beaches and lowlying 'machair' to the west and mountains and moorland to the east, while Barra has a rocky, broken east coast and fine-sand bays on the west, rising to a summit at Heaval.

Ferry Services

Lewis is linked by ferry to the mainland at Ullapool, with daily sailings (except Sun). Harris is linked to Skye at Uig, and North Uist at Lockmaddy in a triangular service. North Uist is served from Uig and Tarbert (Harris), also in a triangular service. South Uist is served from Oban (mainland), as is Barra, with the ferry arriving at Castlebay. Barra has an additional service from Mallaig from mid-June to the end of August.

Scottish Islands

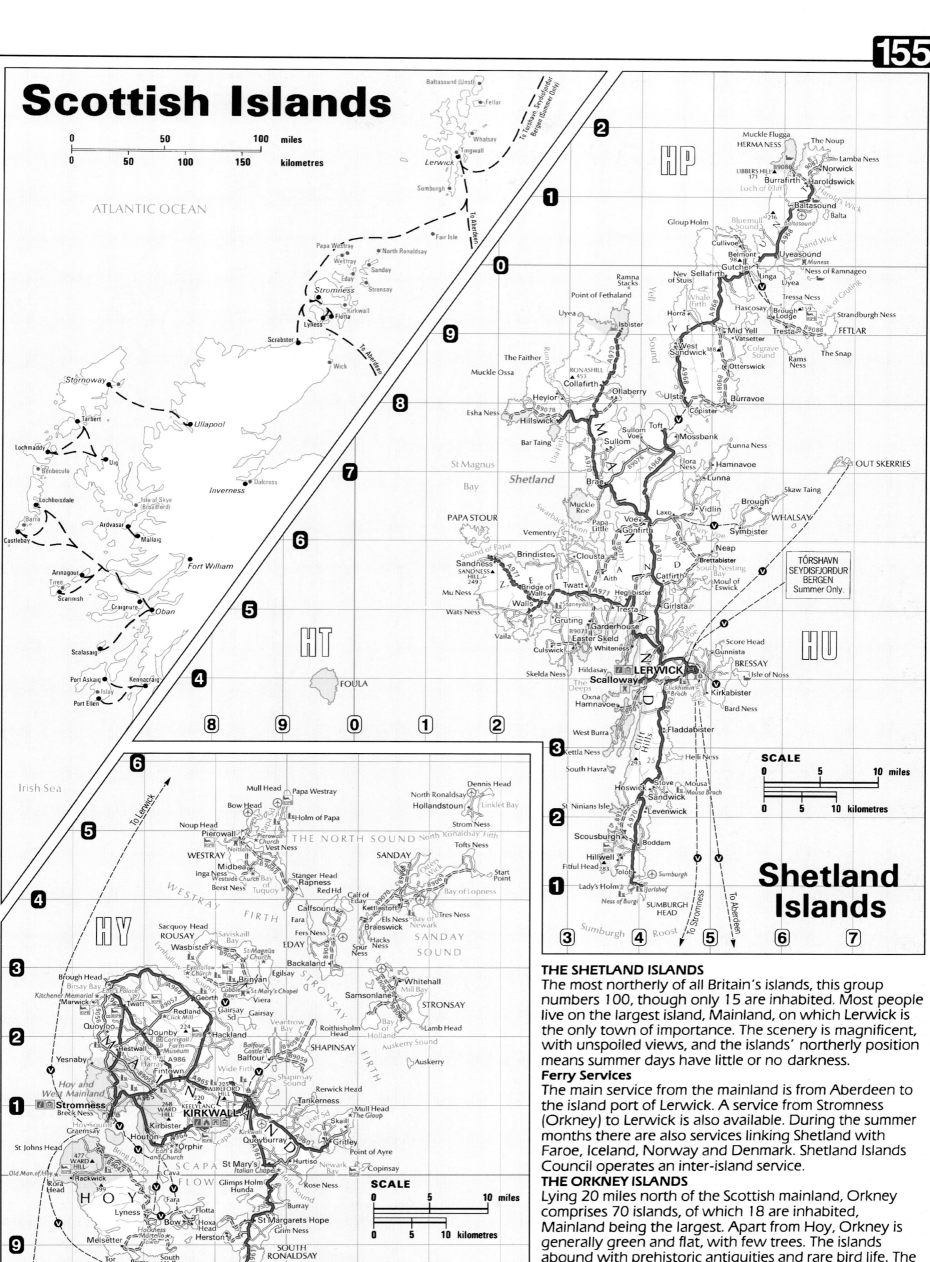

SCALE

0   50   100 miles

0   50   100   150 kilometres

ATLANTIC OCEAN

HP

HT

HU

FOULA

Irish Sea

HY

ND

SCALE

0   5   10 miles

0   5   10 kilometres

Shetland Islands

SCALE

0   5   10 miles

0   5   10 kilometres

Orkney Islands

THE SHETLAND ISLANDS

The most northerly of all Britain's islands, this group numbers 100, though only 15 are inhabited. Most people live on the largest island, Mainland, on which Lerwick is the only town of importance. The scenery is magnificent, with unspoiled views, and the islands' northerly position means summer days have little or no darkness.

Ferry Services

The main service from the mainland is from Aberdeen to the island port of Lerwick. A service from Stromness (Orkney) to Lerwick is also available. During the summer months there are also services linking Shetland with Faroe, Iceland, Norway and Denmark. Shetland Islands Council operates an inter-island service.

THE ORKNEY ISLANDS

Lying 20 miles north of the Scottish mainland, Orkney comprises 70 islands, of which 18 are inhabited, Mainland being the largest. Apart from Hoy, Orkney is generally green and flat, with few trees. The islands abound with prehistoric antiquities and rare bird life. The climate is one of even temperatures and 'twilight' summer nights but with violent winds at times.

Ferry Services

The main service is from Scrabster on Caithness coast to the island port of Stromness. A service from Aberdeen to Stromness provides a link to Shetland at Lerwick. Inter-island services are also operated (advance reservations necessary).

Ireland

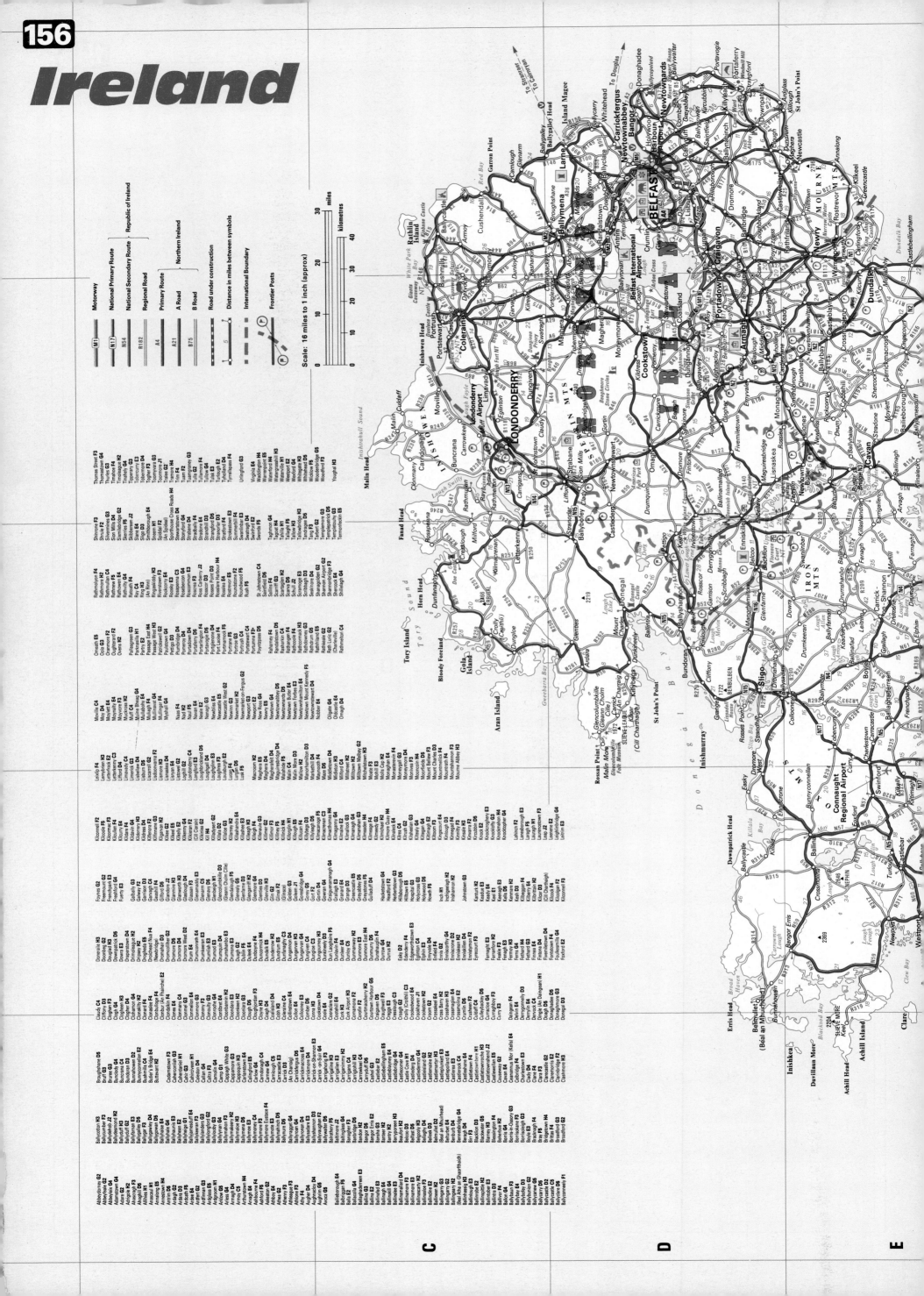

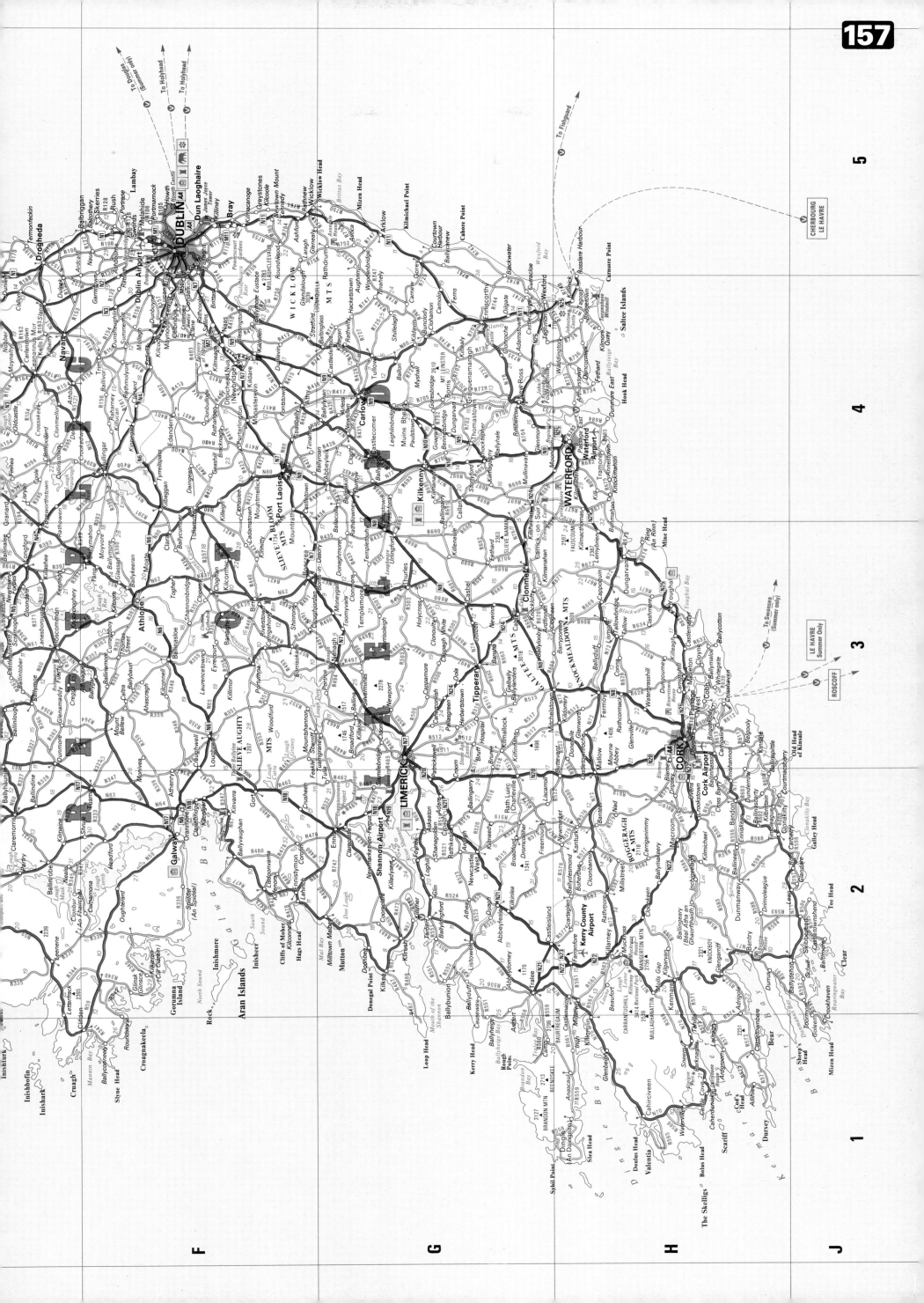

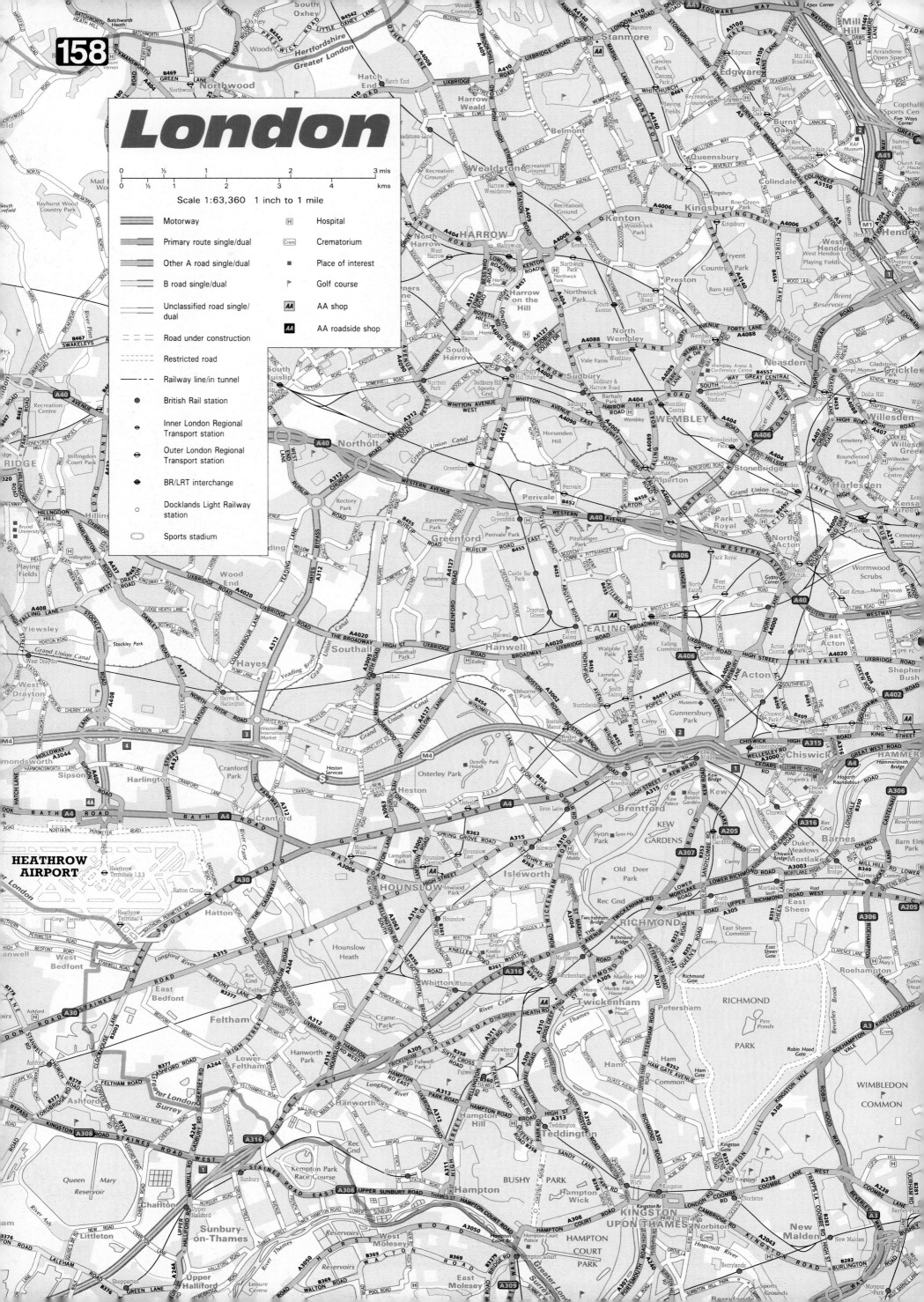

Index to place names

To locate a place in the atlas, first look up the name in the index. Turn to the page number indicated in bold type, then find the location using the last four numbers. (See page 1 for an explanation of the use of the 4-figure National Grid reference system.)

A

A'Chill *Highld* **128** NG2705
Ab Kettleby *Leics* **63** SK7223
Ab Lench *H & W* **47** SP0151
Abbas Combe *Somset* **22** ST7022
Abberley *H & W* **47** SO7567
Abberley Common *H & W* **47** SO7467
Abberton *Essex* **41** TM0019
Abberton *H & W* **47** SO9953
Abberwick *Nthumb* **111** NU1313
Abbess Roding *Essex* **40** TL5711
Abbey *Devon* **9** ST1410
Abbey Dore *H & W* **46** SO3830
Abbey Green *Staffs* **72** SJ9757
Abbey Hill *Somset* **10** ST2718
Abbey St Bathans *Border* **119** NT7661
Abbey Town *Cumb* **93** NY1750
Abbey Village *Lancs* **81** SD6422
Abbey Wood *Gt Lon* **27** TQ4779
Abbeycwmhir *Powys* **45** SO0571
Abbeydale *S York* **74** SK3281
Abbeylands *IOM* **153** SC4585
Abbeystead *Lancs* **81** SD5654
Abbot's Chair *Derbys* **74** SK0290
Abbot's Salford *Warwks* **48** SP0650
Abbotrule *Border* **110** NT6113
Abbots Bickington *Devon* **18** SS3813
Abbots Bromley *Staffs* **73** SK0724
Abbots Deuglie *Tays* **126** NO1111
Abbots Langley *Herts* **26** TL0901
Abbots Leigh *Avon* **34** ST5474
Abbots Morton *H & W* **48** SP0255
Abbots Ripton *Cambs* **52** TL2377
Abbots Worthy *Hants* **24** SU4932
Abbotsbury *Dorset* **10** SY5785
Abbotsford *Border* **109** NT5034
Abbotsham *Devon* **18** SS4226
Abbotskerswell *Devon* **7** SX8568
Abbotsleigh *Devon* **7** SX8048
Abbotsley *Cambs* **52** TL2256
Abbotstone *Hants* **24** SU5634
Abbotswood *Hants* **23** SU3623
Abbott Street *Dorset* **11** ST9800
Abbotts Ann *Hants* **23** SU3243
Abcott *Shrops* **46** SO3978
Abdon *Shrops* **59** SO5786
Abenhall *Gloucs* **35** SO6717
Aber *Gwynd* **69** SH6572
Aber Clydach *Powys* **33** SO1021
Aber-arad *Dyfed* **31** SN3140
Aber-banc *Dyfed* **31** SN3541
Aber-giar *Dyfed* **44** SN5040
Aber-Magwr *Dyfed* **43** SN6673
Aber-meurig *Dyfed* **44** SN5656
Aber-nant *M Glam* **33** SO0103
Aberaeron *Dyfed* **42** SN4562
Aberaman *M Glam* **33** SO0100
Aberangell *Powys* **57** SH8410
Aberarder *Highld* **140** NH6225
Aberargie *Tays* **126** NO1615
Aberarth *Dyfed* **42** SN4763
Aberavon *W Glam* **32** SS7489
Aberbargoed *M Glam* **33** SO1500
Aberbeeg *Gwent* **33** SO2002
Abercairny *Tays* **125** NN9222
Abercanaid *M Glam* **33** SO0503
Abercarn *Gwent* **33** ST2194
Abercastle *Dyfed* **30** SM8533
Abercegir *Powys* **57** SH8001
Aberchalder Lodge *Highld* **131** NH3403
Aberchirder *Gramp* **142** NJ6252
Abercraf *Powys* **33** SN8212
Abercregan *W Glam* **33** SS8496
Abercrombie *Fife* **127** NO5102
Abercwmboi *M Glam* **33** ST0299
Abercych *Dyfed* **31** SN2441
Abercynon *M Glam* **33** ST0794
Aberdalgie *Tays* **125** NO0720
Aberdare *Powys* **33** SO0002
Aberdaron *Gwynd* **56** SH1726
Aberdeen *Gramp* **135** NJ9306
Aberdesach *Gwynd* **68** SH4251
Aberdour *Fife* **117** NT1985
Aberdovey *Gwynd* **43** SN6196
Aberdulais *W Glam* **32** SS7799
Aberedw *Powys* **45** SO0847
Abereiddy *Dyfed* **30** SM7931
Abererch *Gwynd* **56** SH3936
Aberfan *M Glam* **33** SO0700
Aberfeldy *Tays* **125** NN8549
Aberffraw *Gwynd* **68** SH3569
Aberffrwd *Dyfed* **43** SN6878
Aberford *W York* **83** SE4337
Aberfoyle *Cent* **115** NN5200
Abergarw *M Glam* **33** SS9184
Abergarwed *W Glam* **33** SN8102
Abergavenny *Gwent* **34** SO2914
Abergele *Clwyd* **70** SH9477
Abergorlech *Dyfed* **44** SN5833
Abergwesyn *Powys* **45** SN8552
Abergwili *Dyfed* **31** SN4320
Abergwydol *Powys* **57** SH7903
Abergwynfi *W Glam* **33** SS8995
Abergynolwyn *Gwynd* **57** SH6806
Aberhosan *Powys* **43** SN8197
Aberkenfig *M Glam* **33** SS8984
Aberlady *Loth* **118** NT4679
Aberlemno *Tays* **127** NO5255
Aberllefenni *Gwynd* **57** SH7609
Aberllynfi *Powys* **45** SO1737
Aberlour *Gramp* **141** NJ2642
Abermorddu *Clwyd* **71** SJ3056
Abermule *Powys* **58** SO1694
Abernant *Dyfed* **31** SN3323
Abernethy *Tays* **126** NO1816
Abernyte *Tays* **126** NO2531
Aberporth *Dyfed* **42** SN2651
Aberriw *Powys* **58** SJ1801
Abersoch *Gwynd* **56** SH3127
Abersychan *Gwent* **34** SO2603
Aberthin *S Glam* **33** ST0074
Abertillery *Gwent* **33** SO2104
Abertridwr *M Glam* **33** ST1289
Abertridwr *Powys* **58** SJ0319
Abertysswg *M Glam* **33** SO1305
Aberuthven *Tays* **125** NN9815
Aberyscir *Powys* **45** SN9929
Aberystwyth *Dyfed* **43** SN5881
Abingdon *Oxon* **37** SU4997
Abinger *Surrey* **14** TQ1145
Abinger Hammer *Surrey* **14** TQ0947
Abington *Nhants* **50** SP7861
Abington *Strath* **108** NS9323
Abington Pigotts *Cambs* **39** TL3044
Ablington *Gloucs* **36** SP1007
Ablington *Wilts* **23** SU1546
Abney *Derbys* **74** SK1980
Above Church *Staffs* **73** SK0150
Aboyne *Gramp* **134** NO5298
Abram *Gt Man* **78** SD6001
Abriachan *Highld* **139** NH5535
Abridge *Essex* **27** TQ4696
Abson *Avon* **35** ST7074
Abthorpe *Nhants* **49** SP6446
Aby *Lincs* **77** TF4078
Acaster Malbis *N York* **83** SE5845
Acaster Selby *N York* **83** SE5741
Accott *Devon* **19** SS6432
Accrington *Lancs* **81** SD7628
Acha *Strath* **120** NM1854
Achahoish *Strath* **113** NR7877
Achalader *Tays* **126** NO1245
Achaleven *Strath* **122** NM9233
Achanalt *Highld* **139** NH2661
Achandunie *Highld* **146** NH6472
Achany *Highld* **146** NC5602
Acharacle *Highld* **121** NM6767
Acharn *Tays* **124** NN7543
Achavanich *Highld* **151** ND1842
Achduart *Highld* **145** NC0403
Achfary *Highld* **148** NC2939
Achiltibuie *Highld* **144** NC0208
Achinhoan *Strath* **105** NR7516
Achintee *Highld* **138** NG9441
Achlain *Highld* **131** NH2812
Achmelvich *Highld* **148** NC0524
Achmore *Highld* **138** NG8533
Achmore *W Isls* **154** NB3029
Achnacarnin *Highld* **148** NC0432
Achnacarry *Highld* **131** NN1787
Achnacloich *Highld* **129** NG5908
Achnaconeran *Highld* **139** NH4118
Achnacroish *Strath* **122** NM8541
Achnadrish Lodge *Strath* **121** NM4652
Achnafauld *Tays* **125** NN8736
Achnagarron *Highld* **146** NH6870
Achnaha *Highld* **128** NM4668
Achnahaird *Highld* **144** NC0013
Achnairn *Highld* **146** NC5512
Achnalea *Highld* **130** NM8561
Achnamara *Strath* **113** NR7887
Achnasheen *Highld* **138** NH1658
Achnashellach Station *Highld* **138** NH0048
Achnastank *Gramp* **141** NJ2733
Achosnich *Highld* **121** NM4467
Achranich *Highld* **122** NM7047
Achreamie *Highld* **150** ND0166
Achriabhach *Highld* **131** NN1468
Achriesgill *Highld* **148** NC2554
Achtoty *Highld* **149** NC6762
Achurch *Nhants* **51** TL0283
Achvaich *Highld* **146** NH7194
Ackenthwaite *Cumb* **87** SD5081
Acklam *Cleve* **97** NZ4817
Acklam *N York* **90** SE7861
Ackleton *Shrops* **60** SO7698
Acklington *Nthumb* **103** NU2301
Ackton *W York* **83** SE4121
Ackworth Moor Top *W York* **83** SE4316
Acle *Norfk* **67** TG4010
Acock's Green *W Mids* **61** SP1283
Acol *Kent* **29** TR3067
Acomb *N York* **83** SE5651
Acomb *Nthumb* **102** NY9366
Acombe *Somset* **9** ST1914
Aconbury *H & W* **46** SO5133
Acre *Lancs* **81** SD7924
Acrefair *Clwyd* **70** SJ2743
Acresford *Derbys* **61** SK2913
Acton *Ches* **71** SJ6352
Acton *Dorset* **11** SY9978
Acton *Gt Lon* **26** TQ2080
Acton *H & W* **47** SO8467
Acton *Shrops* **59** SO3185
Acton *Staffs* **72** SJ8241
Acton *Suffk* **54** TL8945
Acton Beauchamp *H & W* **47** SO6850
Acton Bridge *Ches* **71** SJ6075
Acton Burnell *Shrops* **59** SJ5302
Acton Green *H & W* **47** SO6950
Acton Park *Clwyd* **71** SJ3451
Acton Pigott *Shrops* **59** SJ5402
Acton Round *Shrops* **59** SO6395
Acton Scott *Shrops* **59** SO4589
Acton Trussell *Staffs* **72** SJ9318
Acton Turville *Avon* **35** ST8080
Adbaston *Staffs* **72** SJ7627
Adber *Dorset* **21** ST5920
Adbolton *Notts* **62** SK5938
Adderbury *Oxon* **49** SP4735
Adderley *Shrops* **72** SJ6640
Adderstone *Nthumb* **111** NU1330
Addiewell *Loth* **117** NS9962
Addingham *W York* **82** SE0749
Addington *Bucks* **49** SP7428
Addington *Gt Lon* **27** TQ3664
Addington *Kent* **28** TQ6559
Addiscombe *Gt Lon* **27** TQ3366
Addlestone *Surrey* **26** TQ0564
Addlestonemore *Surrey* **26** TQ0565
Addlethorpe *Lincs* **77** TF5468
Adeney *Shrops* **72** SJ6918
Adeyfield *Herts* **38** TL0708
Adfa *Powys* **58** SJ0601
Adforton *H & W* **46** SO4071
Adisham *Kent* **29** TR2253
Adlestrop *Gloucs* **48** SP2426
Adlingfleet *Humb* **84** SE8421
Adlington *Ches* **79** SJ9180
Adlington *Lancs* **81** SD6013
Admaston *Shrops* **59** SJ6313
Admaston *Staffs* **73** SK0423
Admington *Warwks* **48** SP2045
Adsborough *Somset* **20** ST2729
Adscombe *Somset* **20** ST1837
Adstock *Bucks* **49** SP7329
Adstone *Nhants* **49** SP5951
Adswood *Gt Man* **79** SJ8888
Adversane *W Susx* **14** TQ0723
Advie *Highld* **141** NJ1234
Adwalton *W York* **82** SE2328
Adwell *Oxon* **37** SU6999
Adwick Le Street *S York* **83** SE5308
Adwick upon Dearne *S York* **83** SE4701
Ae *D & G* **100** NX9889
Ae Bridgend *D & G* **100** NY0186
Affetside *Gt Man* **81** SD7513
Affleck *Gramp* **142** NJ5540
Affpuddle *Dorset* **11** SY8093
Affric Lodge *Highld* **138** NH1822
Afon-wen *Clwyd* **70** SJ1371
Afton *Devon* **7** SX8462
Afton *IOW* **12** SZ3486
Afton Bridgend *Strath* **107** NS6213
Agglethorpe *N York* **89** SE0885
Aigburth *Mersyd* **78** SJ3886
Aike *Humb* **84** TA0446
Aiketgate *Cumb* **94** NY4846
Aikhead *Cumb* **93** NY2349
Aikton *Cumb* **93** NY2753
Ailby *Lincs* **77** TF4376
Ailey *H & W* **46** SO3348
Ailsworth *Cambs* **64** TL1198
Ainderby Quernhow *N York* **89** SE3480
Ainderby Steeple *N York* **89** SE3392
Aingers Green *Essex* **41** TM1120
Ainsdale *Mersyd* **80** SD3112
Ainsdale-on-Sea *Mersyd* **80** SD2912
Ainstable *Cumb* **94** NY5246
Ainsworth *Gt Man* **79** SD7610
Ainthorpe *N York* **90** NZ7007
Aintree *Mersyd* **78** SJ3898
Aird *D & G* **98** NX0960
Aird *Strath* **113** NM7600
Aird *W Isls* **154** NB5635
Aird of Kinloch *Strath* **121** NM5228
Aird of Sleat *Highld* **129** NG5900
Airdeny *Strath* **122** NM9929
Airdrie *Strath* **116** NS7565
Airdriehill *Strath* **116** NS7867
Airds Bay *Strath* **122** NM9932
Airds of Kells *D & G* **99** NX6770
Airieland *D & G* **99** NX7556
Airmyn *Humb* **84** SE7224
Airntully *Tays* **125** NO0935
Airor *Highld* **129** NG7205
Airth *Cent* **116** NS9087
Airton *N York* **88** SD9059
Aisby *Lincs* **76** SK8692
Aisby *Lincs* **64** TF0138
Aisgill *Cumb* **88** SD7797
Aish *Devon* **7** SX6960
Aish *Devon* **7** SX8458
Aiskew *N York* **89** SE2788
Aislaby *Cleve* **89** NZ4012
Aislaby *N York* **90** NZ8608
Aislaby *N York* **90** SE7785
Aisthorpe *Lincs* **76** SK9480
Aith *Shet* **155** HU3455
Akeld *Nthumb* **111** NT9529
Akeley *Bucks* **49** SP7037
Akenham *Suffk* **54** TM1449
Albaston *Devon* **6** SX4270
Alberbury *Shrops* **59** SJ3614
Albert Street *Clwyd* **70** SJ2660
Albourne *W Susx* **15** TQ2516
Albourne Green *W Susx* **15** TQ2616
Albrighton *Shrops* **59** SJ4918
Albrighton *Shrops* **60** SJ8004
Alburgh *Norfk* **55** TM2687
Albury *Herts* **39** TL4324
Albury *Oxon* **37** SP6505
Albury *Surrey* **14** TQ0447
Albury End *Herts* **39** TL4223
Albury Heath *Surrey* **14** TQ0646
Alby Hill *Norfk* **67** TG1934
Alcaig *Highld* **139** NH5657
Alcaston *Shrops* **59** SO4587
Alcester *Warwks* **48** SP0857
Alcester Lane End *W Mids* **61** SP0780
Alciston *E Susx* **16** TQ5005
Alcombe *Wilts* **35** ST8169
Alconbury *Cambs* **52** TL1875
Alconbury Weston *Cambs* **52** TL1777
Aldborough *N York* **89** SE4066
Aldborough *Norfk* **66** TG1834
Aldbourne *Wilts* **36** SU2676
Aldbrough *Humb* **85** TA2438
Aldbury *Herts* **38** SP9612
Aldcliffe *Lancs* **87** SD4660
Aldclune *Tays* **132** NN8964
Aldeburgh *Suffk* **55** TM4656
Aldeby *Norfk* **67** TM4493
Aldenham *Herts* **26** TQ1498
Alder Moor *Staffs* **73** SK2226
Alderbury *Wilts* **23** SU1827
Aldercar *Derbys* **62** SK4447
Alderford *Norfk* **66** TG1218
Alderholt *Dorset* **12** SU1212
Alderley *Gloucs* **35** ST7690
Alderley Edge *Ches* **79** SJ8478
Aldermans Green *W Mids* **61** SP3683
Aldermaston *Berks* **24** SU5965
Alderminster *Warwks* **48** SP2348
Aldershot *Hants* **25** SU8650
Alderton *Gloucs* **47** SP0033
Alderton *Nhants* **49** SP7446
Alderton *Shrops* **59** SJ4924
Alderton *Suffk* **55** TM3441
Alderton *Wilts* **35** ST8482
Alderwasley *Derbys* **73** SK3053
Aldfield *N York* **89** SE2669
Aldford *Ches* **71** SJ4159
Aldgate *Leics* **63** SK9804
Aldham *Essex* **40** TL9126
Aldham *Suffk* **54** TM0545
Aldingbourne *W Susx* **14** SU9205
Aldingham *Cumb* **86** SD2870
Aldington *H & W* **48** SP0644
Aldington *Kent* **29** TR0736
Aldington Corner *Kent* **29** TR0636
Aldivalloch *Gramp* **141** NJ3526
Aldochlay *Strath* **115** NS3591
Aldon *Shrops* **46** SO4379
Aldoth *Cumb* **92** NY1448
Aldreth *Cambs* **53** TL4473
Aldridge *W Mids* **61** SK0500
Aldringham *Suffk* **55** TM4461
Aldro *N York* **90** SE8162
Aldsworth *Gloucs* **36** SP1509
Aldsworth *W Susx* **14** SU7608
Aldunie *Gramp* **141** NJ3626
Aldwark *Derbys* **74** SK2257
Aldwark *N York* **89** SE4663
Aldwick *W Susx* **14** SZ9198
Aldwincle *Nhants* **51** TL0081
Aldworth *Berks* **37** SU5579
Alexandria *Strath* **115** NS3979
Aley *Somset* **20** ST1838
Alfardisworthy *Devon* **18** SS2911
Alfington *Devon* **9** SY1197
Alfold *Surrey* **14** TQ0333
Alfold Bars *W Susx* **14** TQ0333
Alfold Crossways *Surrey* **14** TQ0335
Alford *Gramp* **142** NJ5715
Alford *Lincs* **77** TF4575
Alford *Somset* **21** ST6032
Alfreton *Derbys* **74** SK4155
Alfrick *H & W* **47** SO7453
Alfrick Pound *H & W* **47** SO7452
Alfriston *E Susx* **16** TQ5103
Algarkirk *Lincs* **64** TF2935
Alhampton *Somset* **21** ST6234
Alkborough *Humb* **84** SE8821
Alkerton *Gloucs* **35** SO7705
Alkerton *Oxon* **48** SP3743
Alkham *Kent* **29** TR2542
Alkington *Shrops* **71** SJ5339
Alkmonton *Derbys* **73** SK1838
All Cannings *Wilts* **23** SU0661
All Saints South Elmham *Suffk* **55** TM3482
All Stretton *Shrops* **59** SO4595
Allaleigh *Devon* **7** SX8053
Allanaquoich *Gramp* **133** NO1291
Allanbank *Strath* **116** NS8458
Allanton *Border* **119** NT8654
Allanton *Strath* **116** NS7454
Allanton *Strath* **116** NS8457
Allaston *Gloucs* **35** SO6304
Allbrook *Hants* **13** SU4521
Allen End *Warwks* **61** SP1696
Allen's Green *Herts* **39** TL4516
Allendale *Nthumb* **95** NY8355
Allenheads *Nthumb* **95** NY8645
Allensford *Dur* **95** NZ0750
Allensmore *H & W* **46** SO4635
Allenton *Derbys* **62** SK3732
Aller *Devon* **19** SS7625
Aller *Somset* **21** ST4029
Allerby *Cumb* **92** NY0839
Allercombe *Devon* **9** SY0494
Allerford *Somset* **20** SS9046
Allerston *N York* **90** SE8782
Allerthorpe *Humb* **84** SE7847
Allerton *Mersyd* **78** SJ3987
Allerton *W York* **82** SE1234
Allerton Bywater *W York* **83** SE4227
Allerton Mauleverer *N York* **89** SE4157
Allesley *W Mids* **61** SP3080
Allestree *Derbys* **62** SK3439
Allet Common *Cnwll* **3** SW7948
Allexton *Leics* **51** SK8100
Allgreave *Ches* **72** SJ9767
Allhallows *Kent* **28** TQ8377
Allhallows-on-Sea *Kent* **40** TQ8478
Alligin Shuas *Highld* **137** NG8357
Allimore Green *Staffs* **72** SJ8519
Allington *Dorset* **10** SY4693
Allington *Kent* **28** TQ7557
Allington *Lincs* **63** SK8540
Allington *Wilts* **35** ST8975
Allington *Wilts* **23** SU0663
Allington *Wilts* **23** SU2039
Allithwaite *Cumb* **87** SD3876
Alloa *Cent* **116** NS8892
Allonby *Cumb* **92** NY0842
Alloway *Strath* **106** NS3318
Allowenshay *Somset* **10** ST3913
Allscott *Shrops* **59** SJ6113
Allscott *Shrops* **60** SO7396
Alltami *Clwyd* **70** SJ2665
Alltchaorunn *Highld* **123** NN1951
Alltmawr *Powys* **45** SO0746
Alltwalis *Dyfed* **31** SN4431
Alltwen *W Glam* **32** SN7303
Alltyblaca *Dyfed* **44** SN5245
Allweston *Dorset* **11** ST6614
Allwood Green *Suffk* **54** TM0472
Almeley *H & W* **46** SO3351
Almeley Wooton *H & W* **46** SO3352
Almer *Dorset* **11** SY9199
Almholme *S York* **83** SE5808
Almington *Staffs* **72** SJ7034
Almodington *W Susx* **14** SZ8297
Almondbank *Tays* **125** NO0625
Almondbury *W York* **82** SE1614
Almondsbury *Avon* **34** ST6084
Alne *N York* **90** SE4965
Alnesbourn Priory *Suffk* **55** TM1940
Alness *Highld* **146** NH6569
Alnham *Nthumb* **111** NT9810
Alnmouth *Nthumb* **111** NU2410
Alnwick *Nthumb* **111** NU1813
Alperton *Gt Lon* **26** TQ1883
Alphamstone *Essex* **54** TL8735
Alpheton *Suffk* **54** TL8750
Alphington *Devon* **9** SX9190
Alpington *Norfk* **67** TG2901
Alport *Derbys* **74** SK2264
Alpraham *Ches* **71** SJ5859
Alresford *Essex* **41** TM0621
Alrewas *Staffs* **61** SK1614
Alsager *Ches* **72** SJ7955
Alsagers Bank *Staffs* **72** SJ7948
Alshot *Somset* **20** ST1935
Alsop en le Dale *Derbys* **73** SK1554
Alston *Cumb* **94** NY7146
Alston *Devon* **10** ST3002
Alston Sutton *Somset* **21** ST4151
Alstone *Gloucs* **47** SO9832
Alstone *Somset* **21** ST3146
Alstone Green *Staffs* **72** SJ8518
Alstonefield *Staffs* **73** SK1355
Alswear *Devon* **19** SS7222
Alt *Gt Man* **79** SD9403
Altandhu *Highld* **144** NB9812
Altarnun *Cnwll* **5** SX2281
Altass *Highld* **146** NC5000
Altcreich *Strath* **122** NM6938
Altgaltraig *Strath* **114** NS0473
Altham *Lancs* **81** SD7732
Althorne *Essex* **40** TQ9198
Althorpe *Humb* **84** SE8309
Altnabreac Station *Highld* **150** ND0045
Altnacraig *Strath* **122** NM8429
Altnaharra *Highld* **149** NC5635
Altofts *W York* **83** SE3823
Alton *Derbys* **74** SK3664
Alton *Hants* **24** SU7139
Alton *Staffs* **73** SK0741
Alton *Wilts* **23** SU1546
Alton Barnes *Wilts* **23** SU1062
Alton Pancras *Dorset* **11** ST7002
Alton Priors *Wilts* **23** SU1162
Altrincham *Gt Man* **79** SJ7687
Alva *Cent* **116** NS8897
Alvah *Gramp* **142** NJ6760
Alvanley *Ches* **71** SJ4974
Alvaston *Derbys* **62** SK3833
Alvechurch *H & W* **60** SP0272
Alvecote *Warwks* **61** SK2404
Alvediston *Wilts* **22** ST9723
Alveley *Shrops* **60** SO7584
Alverdiscott *Devon* **19** SS5225
Alverstoke *Hants* **13** SZ6098
Alverstone *IOW* **13** SZ5785
Alverthorpe *W York* **82** SE3121
Alverton *Notts* **63** SK7942
Alves *Gramp* **141** NJ1362
Alvescot *Oxon* **36** SP2704
Alveston *Avon* **35** ST6388
Alveston *Warwks* **48** SP2356
Alvingham *Lincs* **77** TF3691
Alvington *Gloucs* **34** SO6000
Alwalton *Cambs* **64** TL1396
Alwinton *Nthumb* **110** NT9106
Alwoodley *W York* **82** SE2840
Alwoodley Gates *W York* **82** SE3140
Alyth *Tays* **126** NO2448
Amber Hill *Lincs* **76** TF2346
Amber Row *Derbys* **74** SK3856
Ambergate *Derbys* **74** SK3451
Amberley *Gloucs* **35** SO8501
Amberley *W Susx* **14** TQ0213
Ambirstone *E Susx* **16** TQ5911
Amble *Nthumb* **103** NU2604
Amblecote *W Mids* **60** SO8985
Ambler Thorn *W York* **82** SE0929
Ambleside *Cumb* **87** NY3704
Ambleston *Dyfed* **30** SN0025
Ambrosden *Oxon* **37** SP6019
Amcotts *Humb* **84** SE8514
America *Cambs* **53** TL4378
Amersham *Bucks* **26** SU9597
Amersham on the Hill *Bucks* **26** SU9798
Amerton *Staffs* **73** SJ9927
Amesbury *Wilts* **23** SU1541
Amington *Staffs* **61** SK2304
Amisfield Town *D & G* **100** NY0082
Amlwch *Gwynd* **68** SH4492
Ammanford *Dyfed* **32** SN6212
Amotherby *N York* **90** SE7473
Ampfield *Hants* **13** SU4023
Ampleforth *N York* **90** SE5878
Ampney Crucis *Gloucs* **36** SP0601
Ampney St Mary *Gloucs* **36** SP0802
Ampney St Peter *Gloucs* **36** SP0801
Amport *Hants* **23** SU3044
Ampthill *Beds* **38** TL0337
Ampton *Suffk* **54** TL8671
Amroth *Dyfed* **31** SN1608
Amwell *Herts* **39** TL1613
Anaheilt *Highld* **130** NM8162
Ancaster *Lincs* **63** SK9843
Anchor *Shrops* **58** SO1785
Ancroft *Nthumb* **111** NT9945
Ancrum *Border* **110** NT6224
Ancton *W Susx* **14** SU9800
Anderby *Lincs* **77** TF5275
Andersea *Somset* **21** ST3333
Andersfield *Somset* **20** ST2434
Anderson *Dorset* **11** SY8897
Anderton *Ches* **79** SJ6475
Anderton *Cnwll* **6** SX4351
Andover *Hants* **23** SU3645
Andoversford *Gloucs* **35** SP0219
Andreas *IOM* **153** SC4199
Anelog *Gwynd* **56** SH1527
Anerley *Gt Lon* **27** TQ3369
Anfield *Mersyd* **78** SJ3692
Angarrack *Cnwll* **2** SW5838
Angarrick *Cnwll* **3** SW7937
Angelbank *Shrops* **46** SO5776
Angersleigh *Somset* **20** ST1918
Angerton *Cumb* **93** NY2257
Angle *Dyfed* **30** SM8603
Angmering *W Susx* **14** TQ0604
Angram *N York* **88** SD8899
Angram *N York* **83** SE5248
Angrouse *Cnwll* **2** SW6619
Anick *Nthumb* **102** NY9465
Ankerville *Highld* **147** NH8174
Ankle Hill *Leics* **63** SK7518
Anlaby *Humb* **84** TA0328
Anmer *Norfk* **65** TF7429
Anmore *Hants* **13** SU6611
Anna Valley *Hants* **23** SU3543
Annan *D & G* **101** NY1966
Annaside *Cumb* **86** SD0986
Annat *Highld* **138** NG8954
Annat *Strath* **122** NN0322
Annathill *Strath* **116** NS7270
Annbank *Strath* **106** NS4023
Annesley *Notts* **75** SK5053
Annesley Woodhouse *Notts* **75** SK4953
Annfield Plain *Dur* **96** NZ1651
Anniesland *Strath* **115** NS5368
Annitsford *T & W* **103** NZ2674
Annscroft *Shrops* **59** SJ4507
Ansdell *Lancs* **80** SD3428
Ansford *Somset* **21** ST6433
Ansley *Warwks* **61** SP3091
Anslow *Staffs* **73** SK2125
Anslow Gate *Staffs* **73** SK1924
Anslow Lees *Staffs* **73** SK2024
Ansteadbrook *Surrey* **14** SU9332
Anstey *Hants* **24** SU7240
Anstey *Herts* **39** TL4033
Anstey *Leics* **62** SK5508
Anstruther *Fife* **127** NO5703
Anstruther Easter *Fife* **127** NO5704
Ansty *W Susx* **15** TQ2923
Ansty *Warwks* **61** SP4083
Ansty *Wilts* **22** ST9526
Ansty Cross *Dorset* **11** ST7603
Anthill Common *Hants* **13** SU6312
Anthony's *Surrey* **26** TQ0161
Anthorn *Cumb* **93** NY1958
Antingham *Norfk* **67** TG2533
Antony *Cnwll* **5** SX4054
Antrobus *Ches* **79** SJ6480
Antron *Cnwll* **2** SW6327
Anvil Corner *Devon* **18** SS3704
Anvil Green *Kent* **29** TR1049
Anwick *Lincs* **76** TF1150
Anwoth *D & G* **99** NX5856
Aperfield *Gt Lon* **27** TQ4158
Apes Dale *H & W* **60** SO9972
Apethorpe *Nhants* **51** TL0295
Apeton *Staffs* **72** SJ8518
Apley *Lincs* **76** TF1075
Apperknowle *Derbys* **74** SK3878
Apperley *Gloucs* **47** SO8628
Apperley Bridge *W York* **82** SE1937
Apperley Dene *Nthumb* **95** NZ0558
Appersett *N York* **88** SD8690
Appin *Strath* **122** NM9346
Appleby *Humb* **84** SE9514
Appleby Magna *Leics* **61** SK3109
Appleby Parva *Leics* **61** SK3008
Appleby Street *Herts* **39** TL3304
Appleby-in-Westmorland *Cumb* **94** NY6820
Applecross *Highld* **137** NG7144
Appledore *Devon* **18** SS4630
Appledore *Devon* **9** ST0614
Appledore *Kent* **17** TQ9529
Appledore Heath *Kent* **17** TQ9530
Appleford *Oxon* **37** SU5293
Applegarth Town *D & G* **100** NY1084
Applehaigh *S York* **83** SE3512
Appleshaw *Hants* **23** SU3048
Applethwaite *Cumb* **93** NY2625
Appleton *Ches* **78** SJ5186
Appleton *Oxon* **37** SP4401
Appleton Roebuck *N York* **83** SE5542
Appleton Wiske *N York* **89** NZ3804
Appleton-le-Moors *N York* **90** SE7387
Appleton-le-Street *N York* **90** SE7373
Appletreehall *Border* **109** NT5117
Appletreewick *N York* **88** SE0560
Appley *Somset* **20** ST0721
Appley Bridge *Lancs* **78** SD5209
Apse Heath *IOW* **13** SZ5683
Apsley End *Beds* **38** TL1232
Apsley Heath *Warwks* **61** SP0970
Apuldram *W Susx* **14** SU8403
Arbirlot *Tays* **127** NO6040
Arboll *Highld* **147** NH8781
Arborfield *Berks* **24** SU7567
Arborfield Cross *Berks* **24** SU7666
Arbory *IOM* **153** SC2470
Arbourthorne *S York* **74** SK3785
Arbroath *Tays* **127** NO6441
Arbuthnott *Gramp* **135** NO8074
Arcadia *Kent* **28** TQ8836
Archddu *Dyfed* **32** SN4401
Archdeacon Newton *Dur* **96** NZ2517
Archencarroch *Strath* **115** NS4182
Archiestown *Gramp* **141** NJ2244
Archirondel *Jersey* **152** JS2111
Arclid Green *Ches* **72** SJ7861
Ard a'Chapuill *Strath* **114** NS0179
Ardaily *Strath* **104** NR6450
Ardalanish *Strath* **121** NM3619
Ardanaiseig Hotel *Strath* **123** NN0824
Ardarroch *Highld* **137** NG8339
Ardarroch *Strath* **114** NS2494
Ardbeg *Strath* **104** NR4146
Ardbeg *Strath* **114** NS0766
Ardbeg *Strath* **114** NS1583
Ardcharnich *Highld* **145** NH1788
Ardchiavaig *Strath* **121** NM3818
Ardchonnel *Strath* **122** NM9812
Ardchullarie More *Cent* **124** NN5813
Arddleen *Powys* **58** SJ2616
Ardechive *Highld* **131** NN1490
Ardeer *Strath* **106** NS2740
Ardeley *Herts* **39** TL3027
Ardelve *Highld* **138** NG8627
Arden *Strath* **115** NS3684
Ardens Grafton *Warwks* **48** SP1154
Ardentinny *Strath* **114** NS1887
Ardeonaig Hotel *Cent* **124** NN6735
Ardersier *Highld* **140** NH7855
Ardessie *Highld* **145** NH0689
Ardfern *Strath* **122** NM8004
Ardgay *Highld* **146** NH5990
Ardgour *Highld* **130** NN0163
Ardgowan *Strath* **114** NS2073
Ardhallow *Strath* **114** NS1674
Ardhasig *W Isls* **154** NB1202
Ardheslaig *Highld* **137** NG7855
Ardindrean *Highld* **145** NH1588
Ardingly *W Susx* **15** TQ3429
Ardington *Oxon* **36** SU4388
Ardington Wick *Oxon* **36** SU4389
Ardlamont *Strath* **114** NR9865
Ardleigh *Essex* **41** TM0529
Ardleigh Heath *Essex* **41** TM0430
Ardler *Tays* **126** NO2642
Ardley *Oxon* **49** SP5427
Ardley End *Essex* **39** TL5214
Ardlui *Strath* **123** NN3115
Ardlussa *Strath* **113** NR6487
Ardmaddy *Strath* **123** NN0837
Ardmair *Highld* **145** NH1097
Ardmaleish *Strath* **114** NS0768
Ardminish *Strath* **104** NR6448
Ardmolich *Highld* **129** NM7172
Ardmore *Highld* **146** NH7086
Ardmore *Strath* **115** NS3178
Ardnadam *Strath* **114** NS1780
Ardnagrask *Highld* **139** NH5249
Ardnarff *Highld* **138** NG8935
Ardnastang *Highld* **130** NM8061
Ardno *Strath* **123** NN1508
Ardochy Lodge Hotel *Highld* **131** NH2002
Ardpatrick *Strath* **113** NR7660
Ardpeaton *Strath* **114** NS2185
Ardrishaig *Strath* **113** NR8585
Ardrossan *Strath* **106** NS2342
Ardshealach *Highld* **121** NM6867
Ardsley *S York* **83** SE3805
Ardsley East *W York* **82** SE3025
Ardslignish *Highld* **121** NM5661
Ardtalla *Strath* **112** NR4654
Ardtoe *Highld* **129** NM6270
Arduaine *Strath* **122** NM7910
Ardvasar *Highld* **129** NG6303
Ardvorlich *Tays* **124** NN6322
Ardvourlie *W Isls* **154** NB1810
Ardwell *D & G* **98** NX1045
Ardwick *Gt Man* **79** SJ8597
Areley Kings *H & W* **60** SO7970
Arevegaig *Highld* **129** NM6568
Arford *Hants* **14** SU8236
Argoed *Gwent* **33** ST1799
Argoed *Shrops* **59** SJ3220
Argoed Mill *Powys* **45** SN9963
Argos Hill *E Susx* **16** TQ5728
Aribrauch *W Isls* **154** NB2417
Aridhglas *Strath* **120** NM3123
Arileod *Strath* **120** NM1655
Arinagour *Strath* **120** NM2257
Ariogan *Strath* **122** NM8627
Arisaig *Highld* **129** NM6586
Arisaig House *Highld* **129** NM6984
Arkendale *N York* **89** SE3861
Arkesden *Essex* **39** TL4834
Arkholme *Lancs* **87** SD5871
Arkleby *Cumb* **92** NY1439
Arkleton *D & G* **101** NY3791
Arkley *Gt Lon* **26** TQ2295
Arksey *S York* **83** SE5807
Arkwright Town *Derbys* **74** SK4270
Arle *Gloucs* **47** SO9223
Arlecdon *Cumb* **92** NY0419
Arlescote *Warwks* **48** SP3848
Arlesey *Beds* **39** TL1936
Arleston *Shrops* **60** SJ6609
Arley *Ches* **79** SJ6680
Arley *Warwks* **61** SP2890
Arlingham *Gloucs* **35** SO7010
Arlington *Devon* **19** SS6140
Arlington *E Susx* **16** TQ5407
Arlington *Gloucs* **36** SP1006
Arlington Beccott *Devon* **19** SS6241
Armadale *Highld* **150** NC7864
Armadale *Loth* **116** NS9368
Armaside *Cumb* **92** NY1527
Armathwaite *Cumb* **94** NY5046
Arminghall *Norfk* **67** TG2504
Armitage *Staffs* **73** SK0715
Armitage Bridge *W York* **82** SE1313
Armley *W York* **82** SE2833
Armshead *Staffs* **72** SJ9348
Armston *Nhants* **51** TL0685
Armthorpe *S York* **83** SE6204
Arnabost *Strath* **120** NM2159
Arnaby *Cumb* **86** SD1884
Arncliffe *N York* **88** SD9371
Arncliffe Cote *N York* **88** SD9470
Arncroach *Fife* **127** NO5105
Arndilly House *Gramp* **141** NJ2847
Arne *Dorset* **11** SY9788
Arnesby *Leics* **50** SP6192
Arnfield *Derbys* **79** SK0197
Arngask *Tays* **126** NO1410
Arnicle *Strath* **105** NR7138
Arnisdale *Highld* **130** NG8410
Arnish *Highld* **137** NG5948
Arniston *Loth* **118** NT3362
Arnol *W Isls* **154** NB3148
Arnold *Humb* **85** TA1241
Arnold *Notts* **62** SK5845
Arnprior *Cent* **116** NS6194
Arnside *Cumb* **87** SD4578
Aros *Strath* **121** NM5645
Arowry *Clwyd* **71** SJ4639
Arrad Foot *Cumb* **86** SD3080
Arram *Humb* **84** TA0344
Arrathorne *N York* **89** SE2093
Arreton *IOW* **13** SZ5386
Arrina *Highld* **137** NG7458
Arrington *Cambs* **52** TL3250
Arriundle *Highld* **130** NM8264
Arrochar *Strath* **123** NN2904
Arrow *Warwks* **48** SP0856
Arrowfield Top *H & W* **61** SP0374
Arscott *Shrops* **59** SJ4307
Artafallie *Highld* **140** NH6349
Arthington *W York* **82** SE2644
Arthingworth *Nhants* **50** SP7581
Arthog *Gwynd* **57** SH6414
Arthrath *Gramp* **143** NJ9636
Arthursdale *W York* **83** SE3737
Artrochie *Gramp* **143** NK0031
Arundel *W Susx* **14** TQ0106
Asby *Cumb* **92** NY0620
Ascog *Strath* **114** NS1062
Ascot *Berks* **25** SU9268
Ascott *Warwks* **48** SP3234
Ascott Earl *Oxon* **36** SP3018
Ascott-under-Wychwood *Oxon* **36** SP3018
Asenby *N York* **89** SE3975
Asfordby *Leics* **63** SK7019
Asfordby Hill *Leics* **63** SK7219
Asgarby *Lincs* **64** TF1145
Asgarby *Lincs* **77** TF3366
Ash *Devon* **19** SS5208
Ash *Devon* **7** SX8349
Ash *Dorset* **11** ST8610
Ash *Kent* **27** TQ6064
Ash *Kent* **29** TR2858
Ash *Somset* **20** ST2822
Ash *Somset* **21** ST4720
Ash *Surrey* **25** SU9051
Ash Green *Surrey* **25** SU9049
Ash Green *Warwks* **61** SP3384
Ash Magna *Shrops* **71** SJ5739
Ash Mill *Devon* **19** SS7823
Ash Parva *Shrops* **71** SJ5739
Ash Priors *Somset* **20** ST1529
Ash Street *Suffk* **54** TM0146
Ash Thomas *Devon* **9** ST0010
Ash Vale *Surrey* **25** SU8951
Ashampstead *Berks* **37** SU5676
Ashampstead Green *Berks* **37** SU5677
Ashbocking *Suffk* **54** TM1754
Ashbocking Green *Suffk* **54** TM1854
Ashbourne *Derbys* **73** SK1746
Ashbourne Green *Derbys* **73** SK1948
Ashbrittle *Somset* **20** ST0521
Ashburnham Place *E Susx* **16** TQ6814
Ashburton *Devon* **7** SX7570
Ashbury *Devon* **5** SX5098
Ashbury *Oxon* **36** SU2685
Ashby *Humb* **84** SE8908
Ashby by Partney *Lincs* **77** TF4266
Ashby cum Fenby *Humb* **77** TA2500
Ashby de la Launde *Lincs* **76** TF0555
Ashby Folville *Leics* **63** SK7012
Ashby Magna *Leics* **50** SP5690
Ashby Parva *Leics* **50** SP5288
Ashby Puerorum *Lincs* **77** TF3271
Ashby St Ledgers *Nhants* **50** SP5768
Ashby St Mary *Norfk* **67** TG3202
Ashby-de-la-Zouch *Leics* **62** SK3516
Ashchurch *Gloucs* **47** SO9233
Ashcombe *Avon* **21** ST3361
Ashcombe *Devon* **9** SX9179
Ashcott *Somset* **21** ST4336
Ashdon *Essex* **53** TL5842
Ashe *Hants* **24** SU5350
Asheldham *Essex* **41** TL9701
Ashen *Essex* **53** TL7442
Ashendon *Bucks* **37** SP7014
Asheridge *Bucks* **38** SP9304
Ashfield *Cent* **124** NN7803
Ashfield *Hants* **12** SU3619
Ashfield *Suffk* **55** TM2062
Ashfield Green *Suffk* **53** TL7655
Ashfield Green *Suffk* **55** TM2573
Ashfields *Shrops* **72** SJ7026
Ashfold Crossways *W Susx* **15** TQ2328
Ashford *Devon* **19** SS5335
Ashford *Devon* **7** SX6948
Ashford *Kent* **28** TR0142
Ashford *Surrey* **26** TQ0771
Ashford Bowdler *Shrops* **46** SO5170
Ashford Carbonel *Shrops* **46** SO5270
Ashford Hill *Hants* **24** SU5562
Ashford in the Water *Derbys* **74** SK1969
Ashgill *Strath* **116** NS7850
Ashill *Devon* **9** ST0811
Ashill *Norfk* **66** TF8804
Ashill *Somset* **10** ST3217
Ashingdon *Essex* **40** TQ8693
Ashington *Nthumb* **103** NZ2687
Ashington *Somset* **21** ST5621
Ashington *W Susx* **15** TQ1315
Ashkirk *Border* **109** NT4722
Ashlett *Hants* **13** SU4603
Ashleworth *Gloucs* **47** SO8125
Ashleworth Quay *Gloucs* **47** SO8125
Ashley *Cambs* **53** TL6961

Beeston Bouth

Beeston Beds 52 TL1648
Beeston Ches 71 SJ5358
Beeston Norfk 66 TF9015
Beeston Notts 62 SK5236
Beeston W York 82 SE2830
Beeston Regis Norfk 66 TG1642
Beeswing D & G 100 NX8969
Beetham Cumb 87 SD4979
Beetham Somset 10 ST2712
Beetley Norfk 66 TF9718
Began S Glam 34 ST2283
Begbroke Oxon 37 SP4614
Begdale Cambs 65 TF4506
Begelly Dyfed 31 SN1107
Beggar's Bush Powys 46 SO2664
Beggarinton Hill W York 82 SE2724
Beguildy Powys 45 SO1979
Beighton Norfk 67 TG3808
Beighton S York 75 SK4483
Beighton Hill Derbys 73 SK2951
Bein Inn Tays 126 NO1513
Beith Strath 115 NS3553
Bekesbourne Kent 29 TR1955
Bekesbourne Hill Kent 29 TR1856
Belaugh Norfk 67 TG2818
Belbroughton H & W 60 SO9277
Belchalwell Dorset 11 ST7909
Belchalwell Street Dorset 11 ST7909
Belchamp Otten Essex 54 TL8041
Belchamp St Paul Essex 53 TL7942
Belchamp Walter Essex 54 TL8240
Belchford Lincs 77 TF2975
Belford Nthumb 111 NU1034
Belgrave Leics 62 SK5906
Belhelvie Gramp 143 NJ9417
Belhinnie Gramp 142 NJ4627
Bell Bar Herts 39 TL2505
Bell Busk N York 81 SD9056
Bell End H & W 60 SO9477
Bell Heath H & W 60 SO9477
Bell Hill Hants 13 SU7324
Bell o' th'Hill Ches 71 SJ5245
Bellabeg Gramp 134 NJ3513
Belladrum Highld 139 NH5142
Bellanoch Strath 113 NR7992
Bellasize Humb 84 SE8227
Bellaty Tays 133 NO2359
Belle Vue Cumb 92 NY1131
Belle Vue Cumb 93 NY3756
Belle Vue W York 83 SE3419
Belleau Lincs 77 TF4078
Bellerby N York 89 SE1192
Bellever Devon 8 SX6577
Bellfield Strath 108 NS8234
Bellfield Strath 108 NS9620
Bellimoor H & W 46 SO3840
Bellingdon Bucks 38 SP9405
Bellingham Nthumb 102 NY8383
Belloch Strath 105 NR6737
Bellochantuy Strath 104 NR6632
Bellows Cross Dorset 12 SU0613
Bells Cross Suffk 54 TM1552
Bells Yew Green E Susx 16 TQ6135
Bellshill Nthumb 111 NU1230
Bellshill Strath 116 NS7360
Bellside Strath 116 NS8058
Bellsquarry Loth 117 NT0465
Belluton Avon 21 ST6164
Belmesthorpe Leics 64 TF0410
Belmont Gt Lon 27 TQ2562
Belmont Lancs 81 SD6715
Belmont Shet 155 HP5600
Belmont Strath 106 NS3419
Belnacraig Gramp 141 NJ3716
Belowda Cnwll 4 SW9661
Belper Derbys 62 SK3447
Belper Lane End Derbys 74 SK3349
Belsay Nthumb 103 NZ0978
Belsay Castle Nthumb 103 NZ0878
Belses Border 110 NT5725
Belsford Devon 7 SX7659
Belsize Herts 26 TL0300
Belstead Suffk 54 TM1241
Belstone Devon 8 SX6293
Belthorn Lancs 81 SD7124
Beltinge Kent 29 TR1967
Beltingham Nthumb 102 NY7863
Beltoft Humb 84 SE8006
Belton Humb 84 SE7806
Belton Leics 62 SK4420
Belton Leics 63 SK8101
Belton Lincs 63 SK9339
Belton Norfk 67 TG4802
Beltring Kent 28 TQ6747
Belvedere Gt Lon 27 TQ4978
Belvoir Leics 63 SK8133
Bembridge IOW 13 SZ6488
Bemersley Green Staffs 72 SJ8854
Bemerton Wilts 23 SU1230
Bempton Humb 91 TA1972
Ben Rhydding W York 82 SE1347
Benacre Suffk 55 TM5184
Benbuie D & G 107 NX7196
Benderloch Strath 122 NM9038
Benenden Kent 17 TQ8033
Benfield D & G 99 NX3763
Benfieldside Dur 95 NZ0952
Bengates Norfk 67 TG3027
Bengeworth H & W 48 SP0443
Benhall Green Suffk 55 TM3961
Benhall Street Suffk 55 TM3561
Benholm Gramp 135 NO8069
Beningbrough N York 90 SE5257
Benington Herts 39 TL2923
Benington Lincs 77 TF3946
Benllech Gwynd 68 SH5182
Benmore Strath 114 NS1385
Bennacott Cnwll 5 SX2992
Bennan Strath 105 NR9921
Bennet Head Cumb 93 NY4423
Bennetland Humb 84 SE8228
Bennett End Bucks 37 SU7897
Bennington Sea End Lincs 65 TF4145
Benniworth Lincs 76 TF2081
Benny Cnwll 4 SX1192
Benover Kent 28 TQ7048
Benson Oxon 37 SU6291
Bentfield Green Essex 39 TL5025
Benthall Shrops 60 SJ6602
Bentham Gloucs 35 SO9116
Benthoul Gramp 135 NJ8003
Bentlawn Shrops 59 SJ3301
Bentley Hants 25 SU7844
Bentley Humb 84 TA0136
Bentley S York 83 SE5605
Bentley Suffk 54 TM1138
Bentley Warwks 61 SP2895
Bentley Heath W Mids 61 SP1675
Bentley Rise S York 83 SE5604
Benton Devon 19 SS6536
Bentpath D & G 101 NY3190
Bentwichen Devon 19 SS7333
Bentworth Hants 24 SU6640
Benvie Tays 126 NO3231
Benville Dorset 10 ST5303
Benwick Cambs 52 TL3490
Beoley H & W 48 SP0669
Beoraidbeg Highld 129 NM6793
Bepton W Susx 14 SU8618
Berden Essex 39 TL4629
Bere Alston Devon 6 SX4466
Bere Ferrers Devon 6 SX4563
Bere Regis Dorset 11 SY8494
Berea Dyfed 30 SM7930
Berepper Cnwll 2 SW6523
Bergh Apton Norfk 67 TG3001
Berhill Somset 21 ST4436
Berinsfield Oxon 37 SU5696
Berkeley Gloucs 35 ST6899
Berkeley Heath Gloucs 35 ST6999
Berkeley Road Gloucs 35 SO7200
Berkhamsted Herts 38 SP9907
Berkley Somset 22 ST8049
Berkswell W Mids 61 SP2479
Bermondsey Gt Lon 27 TQ3479
Bernera Highld 129 NG8020
Bernice Strath 114 NS1391
Bernisdale Highld 136 NG4050
Berrick Prior Oxon 37 SU6294
Berrick Salome Oxon 37 SU6293
Berriedale Highld 147 ND1222
Berrier Cumb 93 NY3929
Berrington H & W 46 SO5767
Berrington Nthumb 111 NU0043
Berrington Shrops 59 SJ5206
Berrington Green H & W 46 SO5766
Berrow Somset 20 ST2951
Berry Brow W York 82 SE1314
Berry Cross Devon 18 SS4714
Berry Down Cross Devon 19 SS5743
Berry Hill Dyfed 30 SN0640
Berry Hill Gloucs 34 SO5712
Berry Pomeroy Devon 7 SX8261
Berry's Green Gt Lon 27 TQ4359
Berryhillock Gramp 142 NJ5054
Berryhillock Gramp 142 NJ5060
Berrynarbor Devon 19 SS5646
Bersham Clwyd 71 SJ3049
Berthengam Clwyd 70 SJ1179
Berwick E Susx 16 TQ5105
Berwick Bassett Wilts 36 SU0973
Berwick Hill Nthumb 103 NZ1775
Berwick St James Wilts 23 SU0739
Berwick St John Wilts 22 ST9422
Berwick St Leonard Wilts 22 ST9233
Berwick-upon-Tweed Nthumb 119 NT9953
Bescaby Leics 63 SK8126
Bescar Cumb 80 SD3913
Besford H & W 47 SO9144
Besford Shrops 59 SJ5525
Besom Hill Gt Man 79 SD9508
Bessacarr S York 75 SE6100
Bessels Leigh Oxon 37 SP4501
Besses o' th' Barn Gt Man 79 SD8005
Bessingby Humb 91 TA1566
Bessingham Norfk 66 TG1636
Bestbeech Hill E Susx 16 TQ6231
Besthorpe Norfk 66 TM0595
Besthorpe Notts 75 SK8264
Beswick Humb 84 TA0147
Betchworth Surrey 26 TQ2150
Bethania Dyfed 43 SN5763
Bethania Gwynd 57 SH7044
Bethel Gwynd 68 SH3970
Bethel Gwynd 68 SH5265
Bethel Gwynd 70 SH9839
Bethel Powys 58 SJ1021
Bethersden Kent 28 TQ9240
Bethesda Dyfed 31 SN0918
Bethesda Gwynd 69 SH6266
Bethlehem Dyfed 44 SN6825
Bethnal Green Gt Lon 27 TQ3482
Betley Staffs 72 SJ7548
Betsham Kent 27 TQ6071
Betteshanger Kent 29 TR3152
Bettisfield Clwyd 59 SJ4635
Betton Shrops 72 SJ6936
Betton Strange Shrops 59 SJ5009
Bettws Gwent 34 ST2890
Bettws Bledrws Dyfed 44 SN5952
Bettws Cedewain Powys 58 SO1296
Bettws Evan Dyfed 42 SN3047
Bettws-Newydd Gwent 34 SO3606
Bettyhill Highld 150 NC7061
Betws Dyfed 32 SN6311
Betws M Glam 33 SS9086
Betws Garmon Gwynd 69 SH5357
Betws Gwerfil Goch Clwyd 70 SJ0346
Betws-y-coed Gwynd 69 SH7956
Betws-yn-Rhos Clwyd 69 SH9073
Beulah Dyfed 42 SN2846
Beulah Powys 45 SN9251
Bevendean E Susx 15 TQ3306
Bevercotes Notts 75 SK6972
Beverley Humb 84 TA0339
Beverstone Gloucs 35 ST8694
Bevington Gloucs 35 ST6596
Bewaldeth Cumb 93 NY2034
Bewcastle Cumb 101 NY5674
Bewdley H & W 60 SO7875
Bewerley N York 89 SE1565
Bewholme Humb 85 TA1649
Bewlbridge Kent 16 TQ6834
Bexhill E Susx 17 TQ7407
Bexley Gt Lon 27 TQ4973
Bexley Heath Gt Lon 27 TQ4875
Bexleyhill W Susx 14 SU9125
Bexwell Norfk 65 TF6303
Beyton Suffk 54 TL9363
Beyton Green Suffk 54 TL9363
Bibstone Avon 35 ST6991
Bibury Gloucs 36 SP1106
Bicester Oxon 49 SP5823
Bickenhill W Mids 61 SP1882
Bicker Lincs 64 TF2237
Bicker Bar Lincs 64 TF2438
Bicker Gauntlet Lincs 64 TF2139
Bickershaw Gt Man 79 SD6201
Bickerstaffe Lancs 78 SD4404
Bickerton Ches 71 SJ5052
Bickerton Devon 7 SX8139
Bickerton N York 83 SE4550
Bickerton Nthumb 103 NT9900
Bickford Staffs 60 SJ8814
Bickington Devon 19 SS5332
Bickington Devon 7 SX8072
Bickleigh Devon 9 SS9407
Bickleigh Devon 6 SX5262
Bickleton Devon 19 SS5030
Bickley Ches 71 SJ5348
Bickley Gt Lon 27 TQ4268
Bickley H & W 47 SO6371
Bickley N York 91 SE9191
Bickley Moss Ches 71 SJ5448
Bicknacre Essex 40 TL7802
Bicknoller Somset 20 ST1139
Bicknor Kent 28 TQ8658
Bickton Hants 12 SU1412
Bicton H & W 46 SO4764
Bicton Shrops 59 SJ4415
Bicton Shrops 59 SO2983
Bidborough Kent 16 TQ5643
Bidden Hants 24 SU7049
Biddenden Kent 28 TQ8538
Biddenden Green Kent 28 TQ8842
Biddenham Beds 38 TL0250
Biddestone Wilts 35 ST8673
Biddisham Somset 21 ST3853
Biddlesden Bucks 49 SP6340
Biddlestone Nthumb 111 NT9508
Biddulph Staffs 72 SJ8858
Biddulph Moor Staffs 72 SJ9058
Bideford Devon 18 SS4526
Bidford-on-Avon Warwks 48 SP1052
Bidston Mersyd 78 SJ2890
Bielby Humb 84 SE7843
Bieldside Gramp 135 NJ8702
Bierley IOW 13 SZ5078
Bierton Bucks 38 SP8415
Big Balcraig D & G 99 NX3843
Big Carlae D & G 107 NX6597
Big Sand Highld 144 NG7578
Bigbury Devon 7 SX6646
Bigbury-on-Sea Devon 7 SX6544
Bigby Lincs 84 TA0507
Biggar Cumb 86 SD1966
Biggar Strath 108 NT0437
Biggin Derbys 74 SK1559
Biggin Derbys 73 SK2549
Biggin N York 83 SE5434
Biggin Hill Gt Lon 27 TQ4159
Biggleswade Beds 39 TL1944
Bigholms D & G 101 NY3180
Bighouse Highld 150 NC8964
Bighton Hants 24 SU6134
Bigland Hall Cumb 87 SD3583
Biglands Cumb 93 NY2553
Bignor W Susx 14 SU9814
Bigrigg Cumb 92 NY0013
Bilborough Notts 62 SK5241
Bilbrook Somset 20 ST0341
Bilbrook Staffs 60 SJ8703
Bilbrough N York 83 SE5346
Bilbster Highld 151 ND2853
Bildershaw Dur 96 NZ2024
Bildeston Suffk 54 TL9949
Billacott Cnwll 5 SX2690
Billericay Essex 40 TQ6794
Billesdon Leics 63 SK7202
Billesley Warwks 48 SP1456
Billingborough Lincs 64 TF1133
Billinge Mersyd 78 SD5200
Billingford Norfk 66 TG0120
Billingford Norfk 54 TM1678
Billingham Cleve 97 NZ4624
Billinghay Lincs 76 TF1554
Billingley S York 83 SE4304
Billingshurst W Susx 14 TQ0825
Billingsley Shrops 60 SO7085
Billington Beds 38 SP9422
Billington Lancs 81 SD7235
Billington Staffs 72 SJ8820
Billockby Norfk 67 TG4313
Billy Row Dur 96 NZ1637
Bilsborrow Lancs 80 SD5139
Bilsby Lincs 77 TF4776
Bilsham W Susx 14 SU9702
Bilsington Kent 17 TR0434
Bilsthorpe Notts 75 SK6460
Bilsthorpe Moor Notts 75 SK6560
Bilston Loth 117 NT2664
Bilston W Mids 60 SO9596
Bilstone Leics 62 SK3605
Bilting Kent 28 TR0549
Bilton Humb 85 TA1632
Bilton N York 83 SE4749
Bilton Nthumb 111 NU2210
Bilton Warwks 50 SP4873
Bilton Banks Nthumb 111 NU2010
Binbrook Lincs 76 TF2093
Binchester Blocks Dur 96 NZ2232
Bincombe Dorset 11 SY6884
Binegar Somset 21 ST6149
Bines Green W Susx 15 TQ1817
Binfield Berks 25 SU8471
Binfield Heath Oxon 37 SU7477
Bingfield Nthumb 102 NY9772
Bingham Notts 63 SK7039
Bingham's Melcombe Dorset 11 ST7702
Bingley W York 82 SE1039
Bings Shrops 59 SJ5318
Binham Norfk 66 TF9839
Binley Hants 24 SU4253
Binley W Mids 61 SP3778
Binnegar Dorset 11 SY8887
Binniehill Cent 116 NS8572
Binns Farm Gramp 141 NJ3164
Binscombe Surrey 25 SU9645
Binsey Oxon 37 SP4907
Binstead Hants 25 SU7740
Binstead IOW 13 SZ5892
Binsted W Susx 14 SU9806
Binton Warwks 48 SP1454
Bintree Norfk 66 TG0123
Binweston Shrops 59 SJ3004
Birch Essex 40 TL9419
Birch Gt Man 79 SD8507
Birch Close Dorset 11 ST8803
Birch Cross Staffs 73 SK1230
Birch Green Essex 40 TL9418
Birch Green Herts 39 TL2911
Birch Heath Ches 71 SJ5461
Birch Hill Ches 71 SJ5173
Birch Vale Derbys 74 SK0286
Birch Wood Somset 9 ST2414
Bircham Newton Norfk 65 TF7733
Bircham Tofts Norfk 65 TF7732
Birchanger Essex 39 TL5122
Birchencliffe W York 82 SE1218
Bircher H & W 46 SO4765
Birchfield W Mids 61 SP0790
Birchgrove E Susx 15 TQ4029
Birchgrove S Glam 33 ST1679
Birchgrove W Glam 32 SS7098
Birchington Kent 29 TR3069
Birchley Heath Warwks 61 SP2894
Birchmoor Green Beds 38 SP9534
Birchover Derbys 74 SK2362
Birchyfield H & W 47 SO6453
Bircotes Notts 75 SK6391
Bird End W Mids 60 SP0194
Bird Street Suffk 54 TM0052
Birdbrook Essex 53 TL7041
Birdforth N York 90 SE4875
Birdham W Susx 14 SU8200
Birdingbury Warwks 50 SP4368
Birdlip Gloucs 35 SO9214
Birdoswald Cumb 102 NY6166
Birds Edge W York 82 SE2007
Birds Green Essex 40 TL5808
Birdsall N York 90 SE8165
Birdsgreen Shrops 60 SO7785
Birdsmoorgate Dorset 10 ST3900
Birdwell S York 83 SE3401
Birdwood Gloucs 35 SO7418
Birgham Border 110 NT7939
Birichin Highld 147 NH7592
Birkacre Lancs 81 SD5714
Birkby N York 89 NZ3202
Birkdale Mersyd 80 SD3214
Birkenbog Gramp 142 NJ5365
Birkenhead Mersyd 78 SJ3288
Birkenhills Gramp 142 NJ7445
Birkenshaw W York 82 SE2028
Birkhall Gramp 134 NO3493
Birkhill D & G 109 NT2015
Birkhill Tays 126 NO3534
Birkholme Lincs 63 SK9623
Birkin N York 83 SE5326
Birks W York 82 SE2626
Birkshaw Nthumb 102 NY7765
Birley H & W 46 SO4553
Birley Carr S York 74 SK3392
Birling Kent 28 TQ6860
Birling Nthumb 111 NU2406
Birling Gap E Susx 16 TV5596
Birlingham H & W 47 SO9343
Birmingham W Mids 61 SP0786
Birnam Tays 125 NO0341
Birness Gramp 143 NJ9933
Birse Gramp 134 NO5697
Birsemore Gramp 134 NO5297
Birstall Leics 62 SK5909
Birstall W York 82 SE2225
Birstwith N York 89 SE2359
Birthorpe Lincs 64 TF1033
Birtley H & W 46 SO3669
Birtley Nthumb 102 NY8778
Birtley T & W 96 NZ2756
Birts Street H & W 47 SO7836
Bisbrooke Leics 51 SP8899
Biscathorpe Lincs 76 TF2284
Biscovey Cnwll 3 SX0552
Bish Mill Devon 19 SS7425
Bisham Berks 26 SU8485
Bishampton H & W 47 SO9951
Bishop Auckland Dur 96 NZ2028
Bishop Burton Humb 84 SE9839
Bishop Middleham Dur 96 NZ3231
Bishop Monkton N York 89 SE3266
Bishop Norton Lincs 76 SK9892
Bishop Sutton Avon 21 ST5859
Bishop Thornton N York 89 SE2563
Bishop Wilton Humb 84 SE7955
Bishop's Castle Shrops 59 SO3288
Bishop's Cleeve Gloucs 47 SO9627
Bishop's Frome H & W 47 SO6648
Bishop's Green Essex 40 TL6217
Bishop's Green Hants 24 SU5063
Bishop's Itchington Warwks 48 SP3857
Bishop's Norton Gloucs 47 SO8424
Bishop's Nympton Devon 19 SS7523
Bishop's Offley Staffs 72 SJ7729
Bishop's Stortford Herts 39 TL4821
Bishop's Sutton Hants 24 SU6032
Bishop's Tachbrook Warwks 48 SP3161
Bishop's Tawton Devon 19 SS5729
Bishop's Waltham Hants 13 SU5517
Bishop's Wood Staffs 60 SJ8309
Bishop's Caundle Dorset 11 ST6913
Bishopbridge Lincs 76 TF0391
Bishopbriggs Strath 116 NS6070
Bishops Cannings Wilts 23 SU0364
Bishops Gate Surrey 25 SU9871
Bishops Hull Somset 20 ST2024
Bishops Lydeard Somset 20 ST1729
Bishopsbourne Kent 29 TR1852
Bishopsteignton Devon 7 SX9073
Bishopstoke Hants 13 SU4619
Bishopston W Glam 32 SS5789
Bishopstone Bucks 38 SP8010
Bishopstone E Susx 16 TQ4701
Bishopstone H & W 46 SO4143
Bishopstone Kent 26 TQ2068
Bishopstone Wilts 23 SU0625
Bishopstone Wilts 36 SU2483
Bishopstrow Wilts 22 ST8943
Bishopswood Somset 10 ST2612
Bishopsworth Avon 21 ST5768
Bishopthorpe N York 83 SE5947
Bishopton Dur 96 NZ3621
Bishopton Strath 115 NS4371
Bishopton Warwks 48 SP1956
Bishton Gwent 34 ST3887
Bishton Staffs 73 SK0220
Bisley Gloucs 35 SO9005
Bisley Surrey 25 SU9559
Bisley Camp Surrey 25 SU9357
Bispham Lancs 80 SD3140
Bispham Green Lancs 80 SD4813
Bissoe Cnwll 3 SW7741
Bisterne Hants 12 SU1401
Bitchet Green Kent 27 TQ5654
Bitchfield Lincs 63 SK9828
Bittadon Devon 19 SS5441
Bittaford Devon 7 SX6656
Bittering Norfk 66 TF9417
Bitterley Shrops 46 SO5677
Bitterne Hants 13 SU4513
Bitteswell Leics 50 SP5385
Bitton Avon 35 ST6869
Bix Oxon 37 SU7284
Blaby Leics 50 SP5697
Black Bourton Oxon 36 SP2804
Black Callerton T & W 103 NZ1769
Black Car Norfk 66 TM0995
Black Corner W Susx 15 TQ2939
Black Corries Highld 123 NN2956
Black Crofts Strath 122 NM9234
Black Cross Cnwll 4 SW9060
Black Dog Devon 19 SS8009
Black Heddon Nthumb 103 NZ0775
Black Lane Gt Man 79 SD7708
Black Lane Ends Lancs 81 SD9243
Black Moor W York 82 SE2939
Black Notley Essex 40 TL7620
Black Street Suffk 55 TM5186
Black Tar Dyfed 30 SM9909
Black Torrington Devon 18 SS4605
Blackadder Border 119 NT8452
Blackawton Devon 7 SX8051
Blackbank Warwks 61 SP3586
Blackbeck Cumb 86 NY0207
Blackborough Devon 9 ST0909
Blackborough End Norfk 65 TF6615
Blackboys E Susx 16 TQ5220
Blackbrook Derbys 62 SK3347
Blackbrook Staffs 72 SJ7638
Blackbrook Surrey 15 TQ1846
Blackburn Gramp 135 NJ8212
Blackburn Lancs 81 SD6827
Blackburn Loth 117 NS9865
Blackcraig Strath 107 NS6308
Blackden Heath Ches 79 SJ7871
Blackdog Gramp 135 NJ9513
Blackdown Devon 5 SX5079
Blackdown Dorset 10 ST3903
Blackdyke Cumb 92 NY1452
Blackenall Heath W Mids 60 SK0002
Blacker S York 83 SE3309
Blacker Hill S York 83 SE3602
Blackfield Hants 13 SU4402
Blackford Cumb 101 NY3961
Blackford Somset 21 ST4147
Blackford Somset 21 ST6526
Blackford Tays 125 NN8908
Blackford Bridge Gt Man 79 SD8007
Blackfordby Leics 62 SK3217
Blackgang IOW 13 SZ4876
Blackhall Colliery Dur 97 NZ4539
Blackhaugh Border 109 NT4238
Blackheath Gt Lon 27 TQ3876
Blackheath Suffk 55 TM4274
Blackheath Surrey 14 TQ0346
Blackheath W Mids 60 SO9786
Blackhill Dur 95 NZ0851
Blackhill Gramp 143 NK0039
Blackhill Gramp 143 NK0755
Blackhorse Devon 9 SX9893
Blackhorse Hill E Susx 17 TQ7714
Blackjack Lincs 64 TF2639
Blackland Somset 19 SS8336
Blackland Wilts 22 SU0168
Blacklaw D & G 108 NT0408
Blackley Gt Man 79 SD8502
Blacklunans Tays 133 NO1460
Blackmarstone H & W 46 SO5038
Blackmill M Glam 33 SS9386
Blackmoor Avon 21 ST4661
Blackmoor Hants 14 SU7733
Blackmoorfoot W York 82 SE0913
Blackmore Essex 40 TL6001
Blackmore End Essex 40 TL7430
Blackmore End Herts 39 TL1716
Blackness Loth 117 NT0579
Blacknest Berks 25 SU9568
Blacknest Hants 25 SU7941
Blacko Lancs 81 SD8541
Blackpark D & G 100 NX9281
Blackpill W Glam 32 SS6190
Blackpool Devon 7 SX8547
Blackpool Devon 7 SX8174
Blackpool Lancs 80 SD3036
Blackpool Gate Cumb 101 NY5377
Blackridge Loth 116 NS8967
Blackrock Cnwll 2 SW6534
Blackrock Gwent 33 SO2112
Blackrock Gwent 34 ST5188
Blackrod Gt Man 78 SD6110
Blacksboat Gramp 141 NJ1838
Blackshaw D & G 100 NY0465
Blackshaw Head W York 82 SD9527
Blacksmith's Green Suffk 54 TM1465
Blacksnape Lancs 81 SD7121
Blackstone W Susx 15 TQ2316
Blackthorn Oxon 37 SP6219
Blackthorpe Suffk 54 TL9063
Blacktoft Humb 84 SE8324
Blacktop Gramp 135 NJ8604
Blackwall Derbys 73 SK2548
Blackwater Cnwll 3 SW7346
Blackwater Hants 25 SU8459
Blackwater IOW 13 SZ5086
Blackwater Somset 10 ST2615
Blackwaterfoot Strath 105 NR9028
Blackwell Cumb 93 NY4053
Blackwell Derbys 74 SK1272
Blackwell Derbys 75 SK4458
Blackwell Dur 89 NZ2713
Blackwell H & W 60 SO9972
Blackwell Warwks 48 SP2443
Blackwellsend Green Gloucs 47 SO7825
Blackwood D & G 100 NX9087
Blackwood Gwent 33 ST1797
Blackwood Strath 116 NS7844
Blackwood Hill Staffs 72 SJ9255
Blacon Ches 71 SJ3868
Bladbean Kent 29 TR1847
Bladnoch D & G 99 NX4254
Bladon Oxon 37 SP4514
Bladon Somset 21 ST4220
Blaen Dyryn Powys 45 SN9336
Blaen-y-Coed Dyfed 31 SN3427
Blaen-y-cwm Gwent 33 SO1311
Blaen-y-cwm M Glam 33 SS9298
Blaenannerch Dyfed 42 SN2448
Blaenau Ffestiniog Gwynd 57 SH7045
Blaenavon Gwent 34 SO2508
Blaenawey Gwent 34 SO2919
Blaenffos Dyfed 31 SN1937
Blaengarw M Glam 33 SS9092
Blaengeuffardd Dyfed 43 SN6480
Blaengwrach W Glam 33 SN8605
Blaengwynfi W Glam 33 SS8996
Blaenllechau M Glam 33 ST0097
Blaenpennal Dyfed 43 SN6264
Blaenplwyf Dyfed 43 SN5775
Blaenporth Dyfed 42 SN2648
Blaenrhondda M Glam 33 SS9299
Blaenwaun Dyfed 31 SN2327
Blaenycwm Dyfed 43 SN8275
Blagdon Avon 21 ST5059
Blagdon Devon 7 SX8561
Blagdon Somset 20 ST2118
Blagdon Hill Somset 9 ST2117
Blagill Cumb 94 NY7347
Blaguegate Lancs 78 SD4506
Blaich Highld 130 NN0376
Blain Highld 129 NM6769
Blaina Gwent 33 SO2008
Blair Atholl Tays 132 NN8665
Blair Drummond Cent 116 NS7399
Blairgowrie Tays 126 NO1745
Blairingone Fife 117 NS9896
Blairlogie Cent 116 NS8396
Blairmore Highld 148 NC1959
Blairmore Strath 114 NS1983
Blairnamarrow Gramp 141 NJ2015
Blairs Ferry Strath 114 NR9869
Blaisdon Gloucs 35 SO7017
Blake End Essex 40 TL7023
Blakebrook H & W 60 SO8276
Blakedown H & W 60 SO8878
Blakeley Lane Staffs 72 SJ9746
Blakemere Ches 71 SJ5571
Blakemere H & W 46 SO3641
Blakemore Devon 7 SX7660
Blakeney Gloucs 35 SO6707
Blakeney Norfk 66 TG0243
Blakenhall Ches 72 SJ7247
Blakenhall W Mids 60 SO9197
Blakeshall H & W 60 SO8381
Blakesley Nhants 49 SP6250
Blanchland Nthumb 95 NY9650
Bland Hill N York 82 SE2053
Blandford Camp Dorset 11 ST9107
Blandford Forum Dorset 11 ST8806
Blandford St Mary Dorset 11 ST8805
Blankney Lincs 76 TF0660
Blantyre Strath 116 NS6957
Blar a' Chaorainn Highld 130 NN1066
Blargie Highld 132 NN6094
Blarmachfoldach Highld 130 NN0969
Blashford Hants 12 SU1506
Blaston Leics 51 SP8095
Blatherwycke Nhants 51 SP9795
Blawith Cumb 86 SD2888
Blawquhairn D & G 99 NX6282
Blaxhall Suffk 55 TM3656
Blaxton S York 75 SE6700
Blaydon T & W 103 NZ1863
Bleadney Somset 21 ST4845
Bleadon Somset 21 ST3456
Bleak Street Somset 22 ST7631
Blean Kent 29 TR1260
Bleasby Lincs 75 SK7149
Bleasby Lincs 76 TF1384
Bleasdale Lancs 81 SD5745
Bleatarn Cumb 94 NY7313
Bleathwood H & W 46 SO5570
Blebocraigs Fife 127 NO4214
Bleddfa Powys 45 SO2068
Bledington Gloucs 36 SP2422
Bledlow Bucks 37 SP7702
Bledlow Ridge Bucks 37 SU7997
Bleet Wilts 22 ST8958
Blegbie Loth 118 NT4861
Blencarn Cumb 94 NY6331
Blencogo Cumb 93 NY1947
Blendworth Hants 13 SU7113
Blennerhasset Cumb 93 NY1741
Bletchingdon Oxon 37 SP5018
Bletchingley Surrey 27 TQ3250
Bletchley Bucks 38 SP8633
Bletchley Shrops 59 SJ6233
Bletherston Dyfed 31 SN0721
Bletsoe Beds 51 TL0258
Blewbury Oxon 37 SU5385
Blickling Norfk 66 TG1728
Blidworth Notts 75 SK5956
Blidworth Bottoms Notts 75 SK5954
Blindburn Nthumb 110 NT8210
Blindcrake Cumb 92 NY1434
Blindley Heath Surrey 15 TQ3645
Blisland Cnwll 4 SX1073
Bliss Gate H & W 60 SO7472
Blissford Hants 12 SU1713
Blisworth Nhants 49 SP7253
Blithbury Staffs 73 SK0819
Blitterlees Cumb 92 NY1052
Blo Norton Norfk 54 TM0179
Blockley Gloucs 48 SP1634
Blofield Norfk 67 TG3309
Bloomfield Border 110 NT5824
Blore Staffs 72 SJ7234
Blore Staffs 73 SK1349
Blounts Green Staffs 73 SK0732
Blowick Mersyd 80 SD3516
Bloxham Oxon 49 SP4336
Bloxwith W Mids 60 SJ9902
Bloxworth Dorset 11 SY8894
Blubberhouses N York 82 SE1655
Blue Anchor Cnwll 4 SW9157
Blue Anchor Somset 20 ST0243
Blue Bell Hill Kent 28 TQ7462
Blue Point IOM 153 NX3902
Blundellsands Mersyd 78 SJ3099
Blundeston Suffk 67 TM5297
Blunham Beds 52 TL1551
Blunsdon St Andrew Wilts 36 SU1389
Bluntington H & W 60 SO9074
Bluntisham Cambs 52 TL3674
Blunts Cnwll 5 SX3463
Blunts Green Warwks 48 SP1468
Blurton Staffs 72 SJ8941
Blyborough Lincs 76 SK9394
Blyford Suffk 55 TM4276
Blymhill Staffs 60 SJ8112
Blymhill Lawn Staffs 60 SJ8211
Blyth Notts 75 SK6287
Blyth Nthumb 103 NZ3181
Blyth Bridge Border 117 NT1345
Blythburgh Suffk 55 TM4475
Blythe Border 110 NT5849
Blythe Bridge Staffs 72 SJ9541
Blythe End Warwks 61 SP2190
Blyton Lincs 76 SK8594
Bo'Ness Cent 117 NT0081
Boar's Head Gt Man 78 SD5708
Boarhills Fife 127 NO5613
Boarhunt Hants 13 SU6008
Boarley Kent 28 TQ7659
Boars Hill Oxon 37 SP4902
Boarsgreave Lancs 81 SD8420
Boarshead E Susx 16 TQ5332
Boarstall Bucks 37 SP6214
Boasley Cross Devon 5 SX5093
Boat of Garten Highld 140 NH9319
Boath Highld 146 NH5774
Bobbing Kent 28 TQ8865
Bobbington Staffs 60 SO8090
Bobbingworth Essex 39 TL5305
Bocaddon Cnwll 4 SX1858
Bochym Cnwll 2 SW6920
Bocking Essex 40 TL7623
Bocking Churchstreet Essex 40 TL7525
Bockleton H & W 46 SO5961
Boconnoc Cnwll 4 SX1460
Boddam Gramp 143 NK1342
Boddam Shet 155 HU3915
Boddington Gloucs 47 SO8925
Bodedern Gwynd 68 SH3380
Bodelwyddan Clwyd 70 SJ0075
Bodenham H & W 46 SO5350
Bodenham Wilts 23 SU1626
Bodenham Moor H & W 46 SO5450
Bodewryd Gwynd 68 SH4090
Bodfari Clwyd 70 SJ0970
Bodffordd Gwynd 68 SH4277
Bodfuan Gwynd 56 SH3237
Bodham Street Norfk 66 TG1240
Bodiam E Susx 17 TQ7825
Bodicote Oxon 49 SP4538
Bodieve Cnwll 4 SW9973
Bodinnick Cnwll 3 SX1352
Bodle Street Green E Susx 16 TQ6514
Bodmin Cnwll 4 SX0667
Bodney Norfk 66 TL8298
Bodorgan Gwynd 68 SH3867
Bodrean Cnwll 3 SW8448
Bodsham Green Kent 29 TR1045
Bodwen Cnwll 4 SX0360
Bodymoor Heath Warwks 61 SP1996
Bogallan Highld 140 NH6350
Bogbrae Gramp 143 NK0335
Boghall Loth 117 NS9867
Boghall Loth 117 NT2465
Boghead Strath 107 NS7742
Boghead Farm Gramp 141 NJ3559
Boghole Highld 140 NH9655
Bogmoor Gramp 141 NJ3563
Bogmuir Gramp 135 NO6471
Bogniebrae Gramp 142 NJ5945
Bognor Regis W Susx 14 SZ9399
Bogroy Highld 140 NH9022
Bogue D & G 99 NX6481
Bohetherick Devon 5 SX4167
Bohortha Cnwll 3 SW8532
Bohuntine Highld 133 NN9983
Bojewyan Cnwll 2 SW3934
Bokiddick Cnwll 4 SX0562
Bolam Dur 96 NZ1922
Bolam Nthumb 103 NZ1082
Bolberry Devon 7 SX6939
Bold Heath Mersyd 78 SJ5389
Boldmere W Mids 61 SP1194
Boldon T & W 96 NZ3461
Boldon Colliery T & W 96 NZ3462
Boldre Hants 12 SZ3198
Boldron Dur 95 NZ0314
Bole Notts 75 SK7987
Bole Hill Derbys 74 SK3374
Bolehill Derbys 73 SK2955
Bolenowe Cnwll 2 SW6738
Bolfracks Tays 125 NN8248
Bolham Devon 9 SS9515
Bolham Water Devon 9 ST1612
Bolingey Cnwll 3 SW7653
Bollington Ches 79 SJ7286
Bollington Ches 79 SJ9377
Bollington Cross Ches 79 SJ9277
Bollow Gloucs 35 SO7413
Bolney W Susx 15 TQ2622
Bolnhurst Beds 51 TL0859
Bolshan Tays 127 NO6252
Bolsover Derbys 75 SK4770
Bolster Moor W York 82 SE0815
Bolsterstone S York 74 SK2696
Boltby N York 90 SE4886
Boltenstone Gramp 134 NJ4110
Bolter End Bucks 37 SU7992
Bolton Cumb 94 NY6323
Bolton Gt Man 79 SD7108
Bolton Humb 84 SE7752
Bolton Loth 118 NT5070
Bolton Nthumb 111 NU1013
Bolton Abbey N York 82 SE0754
Bolton Bridge N York 82 SE0653
Bolton by Bowland Lancs 81 SD7849
Bolton Hall N York 88 SE0789
Bolton Low Houses Cumb 93 NY2344
Bolton le Sands Lancs 87 SD4867
Bolton New Houses Cumb 93 NY2444
Bolton Percy N York 83 SE5341
Bolton Town End Lancs 87 SD4867
Bolton Upon Dearne S York 83 SE4502
Bolton-on-Swale N York 89 SE2599
Boltonfellend Cumb 101 NY4768
Boltongate Cumb 93 NY2340
Bolventor Cnwll 4 SX1876
Bomere Heath Shrops 59 SJ4719
Bonar Bridge Highld 146 NH6191
Bonawe Strath 122 NN0131
Bonawe Quarries Strath 122 NN0033
Bonby Humb 84 TA0015
Boncath Dyfed 31 SN2038
Bonchester Bridge Border 110 NT5812
Bonchurch IOW 13 SZ5778
Bond's Green H & W 46 SO3554
Bondleigh Devon 8 SS6505
Bonds Lancs 80 SD4944
Bone Cnwll 2 SW4632
Bonehill Staffs 61 SK1902
Boney Hay Staffs 61 SK0410
Bonhill Strath 115 NS3979
Boningale Shrops 60 SJ8202
Bonjedward Border 110 NT6522
Bonnington Kent 17 TR0535
Bonnington Loth 117 NT1269
Bonnington Tays 127 NO5739
Bonnybridge Cent 116 NS8279
Bonnykelly Gramp 143 NJ8653
Bonnyrigg Loth 117 NT3065
Bonnyton Tays 126 NO3338
Bonsall Derbys 74 SK2758
Bonshaw Tower D & G 101 NY2472
Bont Gwent 34 SO3819
Bont-Dolgadfan Powys 57 SH8800
Bontddu Gwynd 57 SH6718
Bonthorpe Lincs 77 TF4872
Bontnewydd Dyfed 43 SN6165
Bontnewydd Gwynd 68 SH4859
Bontuchel Clwyd 70 SJ0857
Bonvilston S Glam 33 ST0673
Bonwm Clwyd 70 SJ1042
Bonymaen W Glam 32 SS6795
Boode Devon 19 SS5037
Boohay Devon 7 SX8952
Booker Bucks 37 SU8391
Booley Shrops 59 SJ5625
Boon Hill Staffs 72 SJ8150
Boorley Green Hants 13 SU5014
Boosbeck Cleve 97 NZ6617
Boose's Green Essex 40 TL8431
Boot Cnwll 5 SX2697
Boot Cumb 86 NY1700
Booth Humb 84 SE7326
Booth W York 82 SE0427
Booth Green Ches 79 SJ9280
Booth Town W York 82 SE0926
Boothby Graffoe Lincs 76 SK9859
Boothby Pagnell Lincs 63 SK9730
Boothstown Gt Man 79 SD7200
Boothville Nhants 50 SP7864
Bootle Cumb 86 SD1088
Bootle Mersyd 78 SJ3495
Boots Green Ches 79 SJ7572
Booze N York 88 NZ0102
Boquhan Cent 115 NS5387
Boraston Shrops 46 SO6169
Bordeaux Guern 152 GN5512
Borden Kent 28 TQ8862
Borden W Susx 14 SU8324
Border Cumb 92 NY1654
Bordley N York 88 SD9465
Bordon Hants 14 SU8035
Bordon Camp Hants 14 SU7936
Boreham Essex 40 TL7609
Boreham Wilts 22 ST8944
Boreham Street E Susx 16 TQ6611
Borehamwood Herts 26 TQ1996
Boreland D & G 100 NY1691
Boreraig Highld 136 NG1853
Boreston Devon 7 SX7653
Boreton Ches 59 SJ5106
Borgie Highld 149 NC6759
Borgue D & G 99 NX6248
Borgue Highld 151 ND1326
Borley Essex 54 TL8443
Borley Green Essex 54 TL8442
Borley Green Suffk 54 TL9960
Borneskitaig Highld 136 NG3770
Borness D & G 99 NX6145
Borough Green Kent 27 TQ6157
Boroughbridge N York 89 SE3966
Borras Head Clwyd 71 SJ3653
Borrowash Derbys 62 SK4234
Borrowby N York 97 NZ7715
Borrowby N York 89 SE4289
Borrowdale Cumb 93 NY2514
Borrowstoun Cent 117 NS9980
Borstal Kent 28 TQ7366
Borth Dyfed 43 SN6090
Borth-y-Gest Gwynd 57 SH5637
Borthwick Loth 118 NT3659
Borthwickbrae Border 109 NT4113
Borthwickshiels Border 109 NT4315
Borve Highld 136 NG4448
Borve W Isls 154 NB4055
Borve W Isls 154 NF6501
Borwick Lancs 87 SD5272
Borwick Lodge Cumb 87 SD3499
Borwick Rails Cumb 86 SD1879
Bosavern Cnwll 2 SW3730
Bosbury H & W 47 SO6943
Boscarne Cnwll 4 SX0367
Boscastle Cnwll 4 SX0990
Boscombe Dorset 12 SZ1191
Boscombe Wilts 23 SU2038
Boscoppa Cnwll 3 SX0353
Bosham W Susx 14 SU8003
Bosham Hoe W Susx 14 SU8102
Bosherston Dyfed 30 SR9694
Boskednan Cnwll 2 SW4434
Boskennal Cnwll 2 SW4223
Bosley Ches 72 SJ9165
Bosoughan Cnwll 4 SW8760
Bossall N York 90 SE7160
Bossiney Cnwll 4 SX0688
Bossingham Kent 29 TR1548
Bossington Somset 19 SS8947
Bostock Green Ches 79 SJ6769
Boston Lincs 64 TF3343
Boston Spa W York 83 SE4245
Boswarthan Cnwll 2 SW4433
Boswinger Cnwll 3 SW9841
Botallack Cnwll 2 SW3732
Botany Bay Gt Lon 27 TQ2999
Botcheston Leics 62 SK4804
Botesdale Suffk 54 TM0475
Bothal Nthumb 103 NZ2386
Bothampstead Berks 37 SU5076
Bothamsall Notts 75 SK6773
Bothel Cumb 93 NY1838
Bothenhampton Dorset 10 SY4791
Bothwell Strath 116 NS7058
Botley Bucks 26 SP9802
Botley Hants 13 SU5113
Botley Oxon 37 SP4806
Botolph Claydon Bucks 49 SP7324
Botolph's Bridge Kent 17 TR1233
Botolphs W Susx 15 TQ1909
Bottesford Humb 84 SE8906
Bottesford Leics 63 SK8038
Bottisham Cambs 53 TL5460
Bottom o' th' Moor Gt Man 81 SD6511
Bottom of Hutton Lancs 80 SD4827
Bottomcraig Fife 126 NO3724
Bottoms Cnwll 2 SW3824
Bottoms W York 81 SD9321
Botts Green Warwks 61 SP2492
Botusfleming Cnwll 5 SX4061
Botwnnog Gwynd 56 SH2631
Bough Beech Kent 16 TQ4847
Boughrood Powys 45 SO1239
Boughspring Gloucs 34 ST5597
Boughton Cambs 52 TL1965
Boughton Nhants 50 SP7565
Boughton Norfk 65 TF7002
Boughton Notts 75 SK6768
Boughton Aluph Kent 28 TR0348
Boughton End Beds 38 SP9838
Boughton Green Kent 28 TQ7650
Boughton Lees Kent 28 TR0246
Boughton Malherbe Kent 28 TQ8849
Boughton Monchelsea Kent 28 TQ7749
Boughton Street Kent 28 TR0559
Boulby Cleve 97 NZ7618
Boulder Clough W York 82 SE0323
Bouldnor IOW 12 SZ3789
Bouldon Shrops 59 SO5485
Boulge Suffk 55 TM2552
Boulmer Nthumb 111 NU2614
Boulston Dyfed 30 SM9712
Boultham Lincs 76 SK9669
Bourn Cambs 52 TL3256
Bourne Lincs 64 TF0920
Bourne End Beds 38 SP9644
Bourne End Beds 51 TL0160
Bourne End Bucks 26 SU8987
Bourne End Herts 38 TL0206
Bournebridge Essex 27 TQ5094
Bournebrook W Mids 61 SP0483
Bournemouth Dorset 12 SZ0890
Bournes Green Essex 40 TQ9186
Bournes Green Gloucs 35 SO9104
Bournheath H & W 60 SO9574
Bournmoor T & W 96 NZ3150
Bournstream Gloucs 35 ST7494
Bournville W Mids 61 SP0481
Bourton Avon 21 ST3864
Bourton Dorset 22 ST7630
Bourton Oxon 36 SU2386
Bourton Shrops 59 SO5996
Bourton Wilts 23 SU0464
Bourton on Dunsmore Warwks 50 SP4370
Bourton-on-the- Hill Gloucs 48 SP1732
Bourton-on-the-Water Gloucs 36 SP1620
Bousd Strath 120 NM2563
Boustead Hill Cumb 93 NY2959
Bouth Cumb 86 SD3285

Bouthwaite
Bunnahabhainn

Bouthwaite N York 89 SE1271
Bouts H & W 48 SP0359
Bovain Cent 124 NN5430
Boveney Berks 26 SU9377
Boveridge Dorset 12 SU0514
Bovey Tracey Devon 8 SX8178
Bovingdon Herts 38 TL0103
Bovingdon Green Bucks 37 SU8386
Bovinger Essex 39 TL5205
Bovington Camp Dorset 11 SY8389
Bow Cumb 93 NY3356
Bow Devon 8 SS7201
Bow Devon 7 SX8156
Bow Ork 155 ND3693
Bow Brickhill Bucks 38 SP9034
Bow of Fife Fife 126 NO3212
Bow Street Dyfed 43 SN6285
Bow Street Norfk 66 TM0198
Bowbank Dur 95 NY9423
Bowbridge Gloucs 35 SO8505
Bowburn Dur 96 NZ3037
Bowcombe IOW 13 SZ4786
Bowd Devon 9 SY1090
Bowden Border 109 NT5530
Bowden Devon 7 SX8449
Bowden Hill Wilts 22 ST9367
Bowdon Gt Man 79 SJ7686
Bower Highld 151 ND2362
Bower Ashton Avon 34 ST5671
Bower Hinton Somset 10 ST4517
Bower House Tye Suffk 54 TL9840
Bower's Row W York 83 SE4028
Bowerchalke Wilts 23 SU0223
Bowerhill Wilts 22 ST9162
Bowermadden Highld 151 ND2464
Bowers Staffs 72 SJ8135
Bowers Gifford Essex 40 TQ7588
Bowershall Fife 117 NT0991
Bowes Dur 95 NY9913
Bowgreave Lancs 80 SD4943
Bowhill Border 109 NT4227
Bowhouse D & G 100 NY0165
Bowithick Cnwll 4 SX1882
Bowker's Green Lancs 78 SD4004
Bowland Border 109 NT4540
Bowland Bridge Cumb 87 SD4189
Bowlee Gt Man 79 SD8406
Bowley H & W 46 SO5452
Bowley Town H & W 46 SO5352
Bowlhead Green Surrey 25 SU9138
Bowling Strath 115 NS4373
Bowling W York 82 SE1731
Bowling Bank Clwyd 71 SJ3948
Bowling Green H & W 47 SO8251
Bowmanstead Cumb 86 SD3096
Bowmore Strath 112 NR3159
Bowness-on-Solway Cumb 101 NY2262
Bowness-on-Windermere Cumb 87 SD4097
Bowscale Cumb 93 NY3531
Bowsden Nthumb 111 NT9941
Bowthorpe Norfk 66 TG1709
Box Gloucs 35 SO8600
Box Wilts 22 ST8268
Box End Beds 38 TL0049
Box Hill Surrey 26 TQ1951
Box's Shop Cnwll 18 SS2101
Boxbush Gloucs 35 SO6720
Boxbush Gloucs 35 SO7413
Boxford Berks 24 SU4271
Boxford Suffk 54 TL9640
Boxgrove W Susx 14 SU9007
Boxholme Lincs 76 TF0653
Boxley Kent 28 TQ7758
Boxmoor Herts 38 TL0406
Boxted Essex 41 TL9933
Boxted Suffk 54 TL8251
Boxted Cross Essex 41 TM0032
Boxted Heath Essex 41 TM0031
Boxwell Gloucs 35 ST8192
Boxworth Cambs 52 TL3464
Boxworth End Cambs 52 TL3667
Boyden End Suffk 53 TL7355
Boyden Gate Kent 29 TR2265
Boylestone Derbys 73 SK1835
Boyndie Gramp 142 NJ6463
Boyndlie Gramp 143 NJ9162
Boynton Humb 91 TA1367
Boys Hill Dorset 11 ST6710
Boysack Tays 127 NO6249
Boythorpe Derbys 74 SK3869
Boyton Cnwll 5 SX3292
Boyton Suffk 55 TM3747
Boyton Wilts 22 ST9539
Boyton Cross Essex 40 TL6409
Boyton End Suffk 53 TL7244
Bozeat Nhants 51 SP9058
Braaid IOM 153 SC3276
Brabling Green Suffk 55 TM2964
Brabourne Kent 29 TR1041
Brabourne Lees Kent 29 TR0840
Brabstermire Highld 151 ND3169
Bracadale Highld 136 NG3538
Braceborough Lincs 64 TF0713
Bracebridge Heath Lincs 76 SK9867
Bracebridge Low Fields Lincs 76 SK9666
Braceby Lincs 64 TF0135
Bracewell Lancs 81 SD8648
Brackenfield Derbys 74 SK3759
Brackenhurst Strath 116 NS7468
Brackenthwaite Cumb 93 NY2946
Brackenthwaite N York 82 SE2851
Bracklesham W Susx 14 SZ8096
Brackletter Highld 131 NN1882
Brackley Nhants 49 SP5837
Brackley Hatch Nhants 49 SP6441
Bracknell Berks 25 SU8769
Braco Tays 125 NN8309
Bracobrae Gramp 142 NJ5053
Bracon Humb 84 SE7807
Bracon Ash Norfk 66 TM1899
Bracora Highld 129 NM7192
Bracorina Highld 129 NM7292
Bradaford Devon 5 SX3994
Bradbourne Derbys 73 SK2052
Bradbury Dur 96 NZ3128
Bradden Nhants 49 SP6448
Braddock Cnwll 4 SX1662
Bradeley Staffs 72 SJ8851
Bradenham Bucks 37 SU8297
Bradenstoke Wilts 35 SU0079
Bradfield Berks 24 SU6072
Bradfield Devon 9 ST0509
Bradfield Essex 41 TM1430
Bradfield Norfk 67 TG2733
Bradfield S York 74 SK2692
Bradfield Combust Suffk 54 TL8957
Bradfield Green Ches 72 SJ6859
Bradfield Heath Essex 41 TM1430
Bradfield St Clare Suffk 54 TL9057
Bradfield St George Suffk 54 TL9059
Bradford Cnwll 4 SX1175
Bradford Devon 18 SS4207
Bradford Nthumb 111 NU1532
Bradford Nthumb 103 NZ0679
Bradford W York 82 SE1632
Bradford Abbas Dorset 10 ST5813
Bradford Leigh Wilts 22 ST8362
Bradford Peverell Dorset 11 SY6593
Bradford-on-Avon Wilts 22 ST8261
Bradford-on-Tone Somset 20 ST1722
Brading IOW 13 SZ6087
Bradley Ches 71 SJ5377
Bradley Clwyd 71 SJ3253
Bradley Derbys 73 SK2246
Bradley H & W 47 SO9860
Bradley Hants 24 SU6341
Bradley Humb 85 TA2406
Bradley N York 88 SE0380
Bradley Staffs 72 SJ8717
Bradley W Mids 60 SO9595
Bradley W York 82 SE1720
Bradley Green Ches 71 SJ5045
Bradley Green H & W 47 SO9862
Bradley Green Somset 20 ST2538
Bradley Green Warwks 61 SK2800
Bradley in the Moors Staffs 73 SK0541
Bradley Stoke Avon 34 ST6181
Bradmore Notts 62 SK5830
Bradney Somset 21 ST3338
Bradninch Devon 19 SS6133
Bradninch Devon 9 SS9904
Bradnop Staffs 73 SK0155
Bradnor Green H & W 46 SO2957
Bradpole Dorset 10 SY4894
Bradshaw Gt Man 81 SD7312
Bradshaw W York 82 SE0514
Bradshaw W York 82 SE0729
Bradstone Devon 5 SX3880
Bradwall Green Ches 72 SJ7563
Bradwell Bucks 38 SP8340
Bradwell Derbys 74 SK1781
Bradwell Devon 19 SS5042
Bradwell Essex 40 TL8122
Bradwell Norfk 67 TG5003
Bradwell Waterside Essex 41 TL9907
Bradwell-on-Sea Essex 41 TM0006
Bradworthy Devon 18 SS3214
Brae Highld 140 NH6662
Brae Shet 155 HU3568
Brae Roy Lodge Highld 131 NN3391
Braeface Cent 116 NS7880
Braegrum Tays 125 NO0025
Braehead D & G 99 NX4152
Braehead Strath 117 NS9550
Braehead Tays 127 NO6952
Braelangwell Lodge Highld 146 NH5192
Braemar Gramp 133 NO1591
Braemore Highld 150 ND0829
Braemore Highld 145 NH2079
Braes of Coul Tays 133 NO2857
Braes of Enzie Gramp 142 NJ3957
Braeside Strath 114 NS2374
Braeswick Ork 155 HY6137
Braevallich Strath 122 NM9507
Brafferton Dur 96 NZ2921
Brafferton N York 89 SE4370
Brafield-on-the-Green Nhants 51 SP8258
Bragar W Isls 154 NB2947
Bragbury End Herts 39 TL2621
Braidwood Strath 116 NS8448
Brailsford Derbys 73 SK2541
Brailsford Green Derbys 73 SK2541
Brain's Green Gloucs 35 SO6609
Braintree Essex 40 TL7523
Braiseworth Suffk 54 TM1371
Braishfield Hants 23 SU3725
Braithwaite Cumb 93 NY2323
Braithwaite W York 82 SE0341
Braithwell S York 75 SK5394
Braken Hill W York 83 SE4216
Bramber W Susx 15 TQ1810
Brambridge Hants 13 SU4721
Bramcote Notts 62 SK5037
Bramcote Warwks 61 SP4088
Bramdean Hants 24 SU6128
Bramerton Norfk 67 TG2904
Bramfield Herts 39 TL2915
Bramfield Suffk 55 TM3973
Bramford Suffk 54 TM1246
Bramhall Gt Man 79 SJ8984
Bramham W York 83 SE4242
Bramhope W York 82 SE2543
Bramley Derbys 74 SK3978
Bramley Hants 24 SU6458
Bramley S York 75 SK4892
Bramley Surrey 25 TQ0044
Bramley W York 82 SE2435
Bramley Corner Hants 24 SU6359
Bramley Green Hants 24 SU6658
Bramley Head N York 89 SE1258
Bramling Kent 29 TR2256
Brampford Speke Devon 9 SX9298
Brampton Cambs 52 TL2170
Brampton Cumb 101 NY5361
Brampton Cumb 94 NY6723
Brampton Lincs 76 SK8479
Brampton Norfk 67 TG2223
Brampton S York 83 SE4101
Brampton Suffk 55 TM4381
Brampton Abbotts H & W 46 SO6026
Brampton Ash Nhants 50 SP7987
Brampton Bryan H & W 46 SO3772
Brampton-en-le-Morthen S York 75 SK4887
Bramshall Staffs 73 SK0532
Bramshaw Hants 12 SU2615
Bramshill Hants 24 SU7461
Bramshott Hants 14 SU8432
Bramwell Somset 21 ST4329
Bran End Essex 40 TL6525
Branault Highld 128 NM5269
Brancaster Norfk 65 TF7743
Brancaster Staithe Norfk 66 TF7944
Brancepeth Dur 96 NZ2237
Branch End Nthumb 103 NZ0661
Branchill Gramp 141 NJ0852
Brand End Lincs 64 TF3745
Brand Green Gloucs 47 SO7328
Branderburgh Gramp 141 NJ2371
Brandesburton Humb 85 TA1147
Brandeston Suffk 55 TM2460
Brandis Corner Devon 18 SS4104
Brandiston Norfk 66 TG1421
Brandon Dur 96 NZ2340
Brandon Lincs 76 SK9048
Brandon Nthumb 111 NU0417
Brandon Suffk 53 TL7886
Brandon Warwks 50 SP4176
Brandon Bank Cambs 53 TL6288
Brandon Creek Norfk 65 TL6091
Brandon Parva Norfk 66 TG0708
Brandsby N York 90 SE5872
Brandy Wharf Lincs 76 TF0196
Brane Cnwll 2 SW4028
Branksome Dorset 12 SZ0492
Branksome Park Dorset 12 SZ0590
Bransbury Hants 24 SU4242
Bransby Lincs 76 SK8978
Branscombe Devon 9 SY1988
Bransford H & W 47 SO7952
Bransgore Hants 12 SZ1897
Bransley Shrops 47 SO6575
Branson's Cross H & W 61 SP0970
Branston Leics 63 SK8129
Branston Lincs 76 TF0166
Branston Staffs 73 SK2221
Branston Booths Lincs 76 TF0668
Branstone IOW 13 SZ5583
Brant Broughton Lincs 76 SK9154
Brantham Suffk 54 TM1034
Branthwaite Cumb 92 NY0525
Branthwaite Cumb 93 NY2937
Brantingham Humb 84 SE9429
Branton Nthumb 111 NU0416
Branton S York 83 SE6401
Branton Green N York 89 SE4362
Branxton Nthumb 110 NT8937
Brassey Green Ches 71 SJ5260
Brassington Derbys 73 SK2254
Brasted Kent 27 TQ4755
Brasted Chart Gt Lon 27 TQ4653
Brathens Gramp 135 NO6798
Bratoft Lincs 77 TF4764
Brattleby Lincs 76 SK9481
Bratton Shrops 59 SJ6413
Bratton Somset 20 SS9446
Bratton Wilts 22 ST9152
Bratton Clovelly Devon 5 SX4691
Bratton Fleming Devon 19 SS6437
Bratton Seymour Somset 22 ST6729
Braughing Herts 39 TL3925
Braughing Friars Herts 39 TL4124
Braunston Leics 63 SK8306
Braunston Nhants 50 SP5466
Braunstone Leics 62 SK5502
Braunton Devon 18 SS4836
Brawby N York 90 SE7378
Brawdy Dyfed 30 SM8524
Brawl Highld 150 NC8166
Brawlbin Highld 150 ND0757
Braworth N York 90 NZ5007
Bray Berks 26 SU9079
Bray Shop Cnwll 5 SX3374
Bray's Hill E Susx 16 TQ6714
Braybrooke Nhants 50 SP7684
Braydon Wilts 36 SU0488
Braydon Brook Wilts 35 ST9891
Braydon Side Wilts 35 SU0185
Brayford Devon 19 SS6834
Braystones Cumb 86 NY0106
Braythorn N York 82 SE2449
Brayton N York 83 SE6030
Braywick Berks 26 SU8979
Braywoodside Berks 26 SU8775
Brazacott Cnwll 5 SX2691
Breach Kent 28 TQ8465
Breach Kent 29 TR1947
Breachwood Green Herts 39 TL1522
Breaden Heath Shrops 59 SJ4436
Breadsall Derbys 62 SK3639
Breadstone Gloucs 35 SO7000
Breadward H & W 46 SO2854
Breage Cnwll 2 SW6128
Breakachy Highld 139 NH4644
Bream Gloucs 34 SO6005
Breamore Hants 12 SU1517
Brean Somset 20 ST2956
Brearley W York 82 SE0225
Brearton N York 89 SE3261
Breasclete W Isls 154 NB2135
Breaston Derbys 62 SK4533
Brechfa Dyfed 44 SN5230
Brechin Tays 134 NO6060
Breckles Norfk 66 TL9594
Breckonside D & G 100 NX8489
Brecon Powys 45 SO0428
Bredbury Gt Man 79 SJ9291
Brede E Susx 17 TQ8218
Bredenbury H & W 46 SO6056
Bredfield Suffk 55 TM2653
Bredgar Kent 28 TQ8860
Bredhurst Kent 28 TQ7962
Bredon H & W 47 SO9236
Bredon's Hardwick H & W 47 SO9135
Bredon's Norton H & W 47 SO9339
Bredwardine H & W 46 SO3344
Breedon on the Hill Leics 62 SK4022
Breich Loth 117 NS9560
Breightmet Gt Man 79 SD7409
Breighton Humb 84 SE7033
Breinton H & W 46 SO4739
Bremhill Wilts 35 ST9773
Bremridge Devon 19 SS6929
Brenchley Kent 28 TQ6741
Brendon Devon 18 SS3607
Brendon Devon 19 SS7748
Brenfield Strath 113 NR8482
Brenish W Isls 154 NA9925
Brenkley T & W 103 NZ2175
Brent Eleigh Suffk 54 TL9448
Brent Knoll Somset 21 ST3350
Brent Mill Devon 7 SX6959
Brent Pelham Herts 39 TL4330
Brentford Gt Lon 26 TQ1777
Brentingby Leics 63 SK7818
Brentwood Essex 27 TQ5993
Brenzett Kent 17 TR0027
Brenzett Green Kent 17 TR0128
Brereton Staffs 73 SK0516
Brereton Cross Staffs 73 SK0615
Brereton Green Ches 72 SJ7764
Brereton Heath Ches 72 SJ8065
Brereton Hill Staffs 73 SK0515
Bressingham Norfk 54 TM0780
Bressingham Common Norfk 54 TM0981
Bretby Derbys 73 SK2922
Bretford Warwks 50 SP4377
Bretforton H & W 48 SP0944
Bretherdale Head Cumb 87 NY5705
Bretherton Lancs 80 SD4720
Brettabister Shet 155 HU4857
Brettenham Norfk 54 TL9383
Brettenham Suffk 54 TL9654
Bretton Clwyd 71 SJ3563
Bretton Derbys 74 SK2078
Brewer Street Surrey 27 TQ3251
Brewers End Essex 39 TL5521
Brewood Staffs 60 SJ8808
Briantspuddle Dorset 11 SY8193
Brick End Essex 40 TL5725
Brick Houses S York 74 SK3081
Bricket Wood Herts 26 TL1202
Brickkiln Green Essex 40 TL7331
Bricklehampton H & W 47 SO9742
Bride IOM 153 NX4401
Bridekirk Cumb 92 NY1133
Bridell Dyfed 31 SN1742
Bridestowe Devon 5 SX5189
Brideswell Gramp 142 NJ5738
Bridford Devon 8 SX8186
Bridge Cnwll 2 SW6744
Bridge Kent 29 TR1854
Bridge End Beds 38 TL0050
Bridge End Cumb 93 NY3748
Bridge End Cumb 86 SD1884
Bridge End Devon 7 SX6946
Bridge End Dur 95 NZ0236
Bridge End Essex 40 TL6731
Bridge End Lincs 64 TF1436
Bridge End Nthumb 102 NY8965
Bridge End Surrey 26 TQ0756
Bridge Fields Leics 62 SK4827
Bridge Green Essex 39 TL4636
Bridge Hewick N York 89 SE3370
Bridge of Alford Gramp 142 NJ5617
Bridge of Avon Gramp 141 NJ1835
Bridge of Avon Gramp 141 NJ1520
Bridge of Balgie Tays 124 NN5746
Bridge of Brewlands Tays 133 NO1961
Bridge of Brown Highld 141 NJ1120
Bridge of Cally Tays 126 NO1351
Bridge of Canny Gramp 135 NO6597
Bridge of Craigisla Tays 126 NO2553
Bridge of Dee D & G 99 NX7359
Bridge of Don Gramp 135 NJ9409
Bridge of Dulsie Highld 140 NH9341
Bridge of Dye Gramp 135 NO6586
Bridge of Earn Tays 126 NO1318
Bridge of Ericht Tays 131 NN5258
Bridge of Feugh Gramp 135 NO7094
Bridge of Forss Highld 150 ND0368
Bridge of Gairn Gramp 134 NO3597
Bridge of Gaur Tays 124 NN5056
Bridge of Marnoch Gramp 142 NJ5950
Bridge of Orchy Strath 123 NN2939
Bridge of Tilt Tays 132 NN8765
Bridge of Tynet Gramp 141 NJ3861
Bridge of Walls Shet 155 HU2752
Bridge of Weir Strath 115 NS3965
Bridge of Westfield Highld 150 ND0664
Bridge Reeve Devon 19 SS6613
Bridge Sollers H & W 46 SO4142
Bridge Street Suffk 54 TL8749
Bridge Trafford Ches 71 SJ4571
Bridgefoot Cumb 92 NY0529
Bridgehampton Somset 21 ST5624
Bridgehill Dur 95 NZ0951
Bridgehouse Gate N York 89 SE1565
Bridgemary Hants 13 SU5803
Bridgend Border 109 NT5235
Bridgend Cumb 93 NY4014
Bridgend D & G 108 NT0708
Bridgend Devon 6 SX5548
Bridgend Dyfed 42 SN1745
Bridgend Fife 126 NO3911
Bridgend Gramp 141 NJ3731
Bridgend Gramp 142 NJ5135
Bridgend Loth 117 NT0475
Bridgend M Glam 33 SS9079
Bridgend Strath 112 NR3362
Bridgend Tays 126 NO1224
Bridgend Tays 134 NO5368
Bridgend of Lintrathen Tays 126 NO2854
Bridgerule Devon 18 SS2702
Bridges Shrops 59 SO3996
Bridgetown Devon 5 SX3389
Bridgetown Somset 20 SS9233
Bridgeyate Avon 35 ST6872
Bridgham Norfk 54 TL9685
Bridgnorth Shrops 60 SO7193
Bridgtown Staffs 60 SJ9808
Bridgwater Somset 20 ST2937
Bridlington Humb 91 TA1866
Bridport Dorset 10 SY4692
Bridstow H & W 46 SO5824
Brierfield Lancs 81 SD8436
Brierley Gloucs 35 SO6215
Brierley H & W 46 SO4955
Brierley W York 83 SE4010
Brierley Hill W Mids 47 SO9169
Brierton Cleve 97 NZ4730
Briery Cumb 93 NY2824
Brig o'Turk Cent 124 NN5306
Brigg Humb 84 TA0007
Briggate Norfk 67 TG3127
Briggswath N York 90 NZ8608
Brigham Cumb 92 NY0830
Brigham Cumb 93 NY2823
Brigham Humb 85 TA0753
Brighouse W York 82 SE1422
Brighstone IOW 13 SZ4282
Brightgate Derbys 74 SK2659
Brighthampton Oxon 36 SP3803
Brightholmlee Derbys 74 SK2895
Brightley Devon 8 SX6097
Brightling E Susx 16 TQ6820
Brightlingsea Essex 41 TM0817
Brighton Cnwll 3 SW9054
Brighton E Susx 15 TQ3104
Brighton le Sands Mersyd 78 SJ3098
Brightons Cent 116 NS9277
Brightor Cnwll 5 SX3561
Brightwalton Berks 36 SU4279
Brightwalton Green Berks 36 SU4278
Brightwalton Holt Berks 36 SU4377
Brightwell Oxon 37 SU5790
Brightwell Suffk 55 TM2543
Brightwell Baldwin Oxon 37 SU6595
Brightwell Upperton Oxon 37 SU6594
Brignall Dur 95 NZ0712
Brigsley Humb 85 TA2501
Brigsteer Cumb 87 SD4889
Brigstock Nhants 51 SP9485
Brill Bucks 37 SP6513
Brill Cnwll 3 SW7229
Brilley H & W 46 SO2648
Brimfield H & W 46 SO5267
Brimfield Cross H & W 46 SO5368
Brimington Derbys 74 SK4073
Brimley Devon 8 SX8077
Brimpsfield Gloucs 35 SO9312
Brimpton Berks 24 SU5564
Brimscombe Gloucs 35 SO8702
Brimstage Mersyd 78 SJ3082
Brincliffe S York 74 SK3284
Brind Humb 84 SE7430
Brindham Somset 21 ST5139
Brindister Shet 155 HU2857
Brindle Lancs 81 SD5924
Brineton Staffs 60 SJ8013
Bringhurst Leics 51 SP8492
Brington Cambs 51 TL0875
Briningham Norfk 66 TG0434
Brinkely Notts 75 SK7153
Brinkhill Lincs 77 TF3773
Brinkley Cambs 53 TL6354
Brinklow Warwks 50 SP4379
Brinkworth Wilts 35 SU0184
Brinscall Lancs 81 SD6221
Brinscombe Somset 21 ST4251
Brinsea Avon 21 ST4461
Brinsley Notts 75 SK4548
Brinsop H & W 46 SO4444
Brinsworth S York 74 SK4289
Brinton Norfk 66 TG0335
Brinyan Ork 155 HY4327
Brisco Cumb 93 NY4252
Brisley Norfk 66 TF9421
Brislington Avon 35 ST6270
Brissenden Green Kent 28 TQ9439
Bristol Avon 34 ST5972
Briston Norfk 66 TG0632
Brisworthy Devon 6 SX5665
Britannia Lancs 81 SD8821
Britford Wilts 23 SU1627
Brithdir Gwynd 57 SH7618
Brithdir M Glam 33 SO1401
British Gwent 34 SO2503
British Legion Village Kent 28 TQ7257
Briton Ferry W Glam 32 SS7394
Britwell Salome Oxon 37 SU6792
Brixham Devon 7 SX9255
Brixton Devon 6 SX5552
Brixton Gt Lon 27 TQ3175
Brixton Deverill Wilts 22 ST8638
Brixworth Nhants 50 SP7470
Brize Norton Oxon 36 SP2907
Broad Alley H & W 47 SO8867
Broad Blunsdon Wilts 36 SU1491
Broad Campden Gloucs 48 SP1537
Broad Carr W York 82 SE0919
Broad Chalke Wilts 23 SU0325
Broad Clough Lancs 81 SD8623
Broad Ford Kent 28 TQ7139
Broad Green Cambs 53 TL6859
Broad Green Essex 40 TL8823
Broad Green H & W 47 SO7756
Broad Green H & W 60 SO9970
Broad Green Suffk 53 TL7859
Broad Haven Dyfed 30 SM8613
Broad Hill Cambs 53 TL5976
Broad Hinton Wilts 36 SU1075
Broad Laying Hants 24 SU4362
Broad Marston H & W 48 SP1446
Broad Meadow Staffs 72 SJ8348
Broad Oak Cumb 86 SD1194
Broad Oak Dyfed 44 SN5722
Broad Oak E Susx 17 TQ8219
Broad Oak H & W 34 SO4821
Broad Oak Hants 24 SU7551
Broad Oak Mersyd 78 SJ5395
Broad Road Suffk 55 TM2676
Broad Street E Susx 17 TQ8616
Broad Street Essex 39 TL5516
Broad Street Kent 28 TQ7672
Broad Street Kent 28 TR1139
Broad Street Wilts 23 SU1059
Broad Street Green Essex 40 TL8509
Broad Town Wilts 36 SU0977
Broad's Green Essex 40 TL6912
Broadbottom Gt Man 79 SJ9993
Broadbridge W Susx 14 SU8105
Broadbridge Heath W Susx 15 TQ1431
Broadclyst Devon 9 SX9897
Broadfield Dyfed 31 SN1303
Broadfield Strath 115 NS3373
Broadford Highld 129 NG6423
Broadford Bridge W Susx 14 TQ0921
Broadgairhill Border 109 NT2010
Broadgate Lincs 64 TF3610
Broadgrass Green Suffk 54 TL9663
Broadhaugh Border 119 NT8655
Broadheath Gt Man 79 SJ7689
Broadheath H & W 47 SO6665
Broadhembury Devon 9 ST1004
Broadhempston Devon 7 SX8066
Broadholme Notts 76 SK8874
Broadland Row E Susx 17 TQ8319
Broadlay Dyfed 31 SN3709
Broadley Gramp 142 NJ3961
Broadley Gt Man 81 SD8816
Broadley Common Essex 39 TL4206
Broadmayne Dorset 11 SY7286
Broadmere Hants 24 SU6247
Broadmoor Dyfed 31 SN0906
Broadmoor Gloucs 35 SO6415
Broadnymett Devon 8 SS7001
Broadoak Clwyd 71 SJ3658
Broadoak Dorset 10 SY4396
Broadoak E Susx 16 TQ6022
Broadoak Gloucs 35 SO6912
Broadoak Kent 29 TR1761
Broadstairs Kent 29 TR3967
Broadstone Dorset 11 SZ0095
Broadstone Gwent 34 SO5102
Broadstone Shrops 59 SO5489
Broadwas H & W 47 SO7555
Broadwater Herts 39 TL2422
Broadwater W Susx 15 TQ1404
Broadwaters H & W 60 SO8477
Broadway Dyfed 31 SN2910
Broadway Dyfed 31 SN3808
Broadway H & W 48 SP0937
Broadway Somset 10 ST3215
Broadway Suffk 55 TM3979
Broadwell Gloucs 34 SO5811
Broadwell Gloucs 48 SP2027
Broadwell Oxon 36 SP2504
Broadwell Warwks 50 SP4565
Broadwey Dorset 11 SY6683
Broadwindsor Dorset 10 ST4302
Broadwood Kelly Devon 8 SS6106
Broadwoodwidger Devon 5 SX4189
Brobury H & W 46 SO3444
Brochel Highld 137 NG5846
Brock Lancs 80 SD5140
Brock's Green Hants 24 SU5061
Brockamin H & W 47 SO7753
Brockbridge Hants 13 SU6118
Brockdish Norfk 55 TM2179
Brockencote H & W 60 SO8873
Brockenhurst Hants 12 SU3002
Brocketsbrae Strath 108 NS8239
Brockford Green Suffk 54 TM1265
Brockford Street Suffk 54 TM1167
Brockhall Nhants 49 SP6362
Brockham Surrey 15 TQ1949
Brockhampton Gloucs 47 SO9326
Brockhampton Gloucs 36 SP0322
Brockhampton H & W 46 SO5931
Brockhampton Green Dorset 11 ST7106
Brockholes W York 82 SE1510
Brockhurst Derbys 74 SK3364
Brockhurst Warwks 50 SP4683
Brocklebank Cumb 93 NY3042
Brocklesby Lincs 85 TA1311
Brockley Avon 21 ST4666
Brockley Suffk 54 TL8371
Brockley Green Suffk 53 TL7247
Brockley Green Suffk 54 TL8254
Brockleymoor Cumb 94 NY4937
Brockmoor W Mids 60 SO9088
Brockscombe Devon 5 SX4695
Brockton Shrops 59 SJ3104
Brockton Shrops 60 SJ7103
Brockton Shrops 59 SO3285
Brockton Shrops 59 SO5794
Brockton Staffs 72 SJ8131
Brockweir Gwent 34 SO5401
Brockwood Park Hants 13 SU6226
Brockworth Gloucs 35 SO8916
Brocton Cnwll 4 SX0168
Brocton Staffs 72 SJ9619
Brodick Strath 105 NS0135
Brodie Gramp 140 NH9757
Brodsworth S York 83 SE5007
Brogaig Highld 136 NG4767
Brogborough Beds 38 SP9638
Broken Cross Ches 79 SJ6873
Broken Cross Ches 79 SJ8973
Brokenborough Wilts 35 ST9189
Brokerswood Wilts 22 ST8352
Bromborough Mersyd 78 SJ3582
Brome Suffk 54 TM1376
Brome Street Suffk 54 TM1576
Bromeswell Suffk 55 TM3050
Bromfield Cumb 93 NY1746
Bromfield Shrops 46 SO4876
Bromham Beds 38 TL0051
Bromham Wilts 22 ST9665
Bromley Gt Lon 27 TQ4069
Bromley S York 74 SK3298
Bromley Shrops 60 SO7395
Bromley W Mids 60 SO9088
Bromley Common Gt Lon 27 TQ4266
Bromley Cross Essex 41 TM0627
Bromlow Shrops 59 SJ3201
Brompton Kent 28 TQ7668
Brompton N York 89 SE3796
Brompton N York 91 SE9482
Brompton Shrops 59 SJ5408
Brompton Ralph Somset 20 ST0832
Brompton Regis Somset 20 SS9531
Brompton-on-Swale N York 89 SE2199
Bromsash H & W 47 SO6524
Bromsberrow Gloucs 47 SO7433
Bromsberrow Heath Gloucs 47 SO7333
Bromsgrove H & W 60 SO9670
Bromstead Heath Staffs 72 SJ7917
Bromyard H & W 47 SO6554
Bromyard Downs H & W 47 SO6655
Bronaber Gwynd 57 SH7131
Bronant Dyfed 43 SN6467
Broncroft Shrops 59 SO5486
Brongest Dyfed 42 SN3245
Bronington Clwyd 71 SJ4839
Bronllys Powys 45 SO1434
Bronwydd Arms Dyfed 31 SN4123
Bronygarth Shrops 58 SJ2637
Brook Dyfed 31 SN2609
Brook Hants 12 SU2714
Brook Hants 23 SU3429
Brook IOW 13 SZ3983
Brook Kent 29 TR0644
Brook Surrey 14 SU9237
Brook Surrey 14 TQ0546
Brook End Beds 51 TL0773
Brook End Beds 52 TL1547
Brook End Bucks 38 SP9244
Brook Hill Hants 12 SU2714
Brook Street Essex 27 TQ5793
Brook Street Kent 17 TQ9333
Brook Street Suffk 54 TL8248
Brook Street W Susx 15 TQ3026
Brooke Leics 63 SK8405
Brooke Norfk 67 TM2899
Brookfield Strath 115 NS4164
Brookhampton Hants 13 SU7106
Brookhampton Oxon 37 SU6098
Brookhampton Somset 21 ST6327
Brookhouse Lancs 87 SD5464
Brookhouse S York 75 SK5188
Brookhouse Green Ches 72 SJ8161
Brookhouses Derbys 74 SK0388
Brookland Kent 17 TQ9926
Brooklands Gt Man 79 SJ7890
Brookmans Park Herts 39 TL2404
Brooks Powys 58 SO1499
Brooks End Kent 29 TR2967
Brooks Green W Susx 14 TQ1224
Brooksby Leics 63 SK6715
Brookthorpe Gloucs 35 SO8312
Brookville Norfk 65 TL7396
Brookwood Surrey 25 SU9557
Broom Beds 39 TL1742
Broom S York 75 SK4491
Broom Warwks 48 SP0853
Broom Green Norfk 66 TF9823
Broom Hill Dorset 12 SU0302
Broom Hill H & W 60 SO9175
Broom Hill Notts 62 SK5447
Broom Hill S York 83 SE4102
Broom Street Kent 28 TR0462
Broom's Green H & W 47 SO7132
Broome H & W 60 SO9078
Broome Norfk 67 TM3591
Broome Shrops 59 SO4080
Broome Park Nthumb 111 NU1012
Broomedge Ches 79 SJ7085
Broomer's Corner W Susx 14 TQ1220
Broomershill W Susx 14 TQ0619
Broomfield Essex 40 TL7010
Broomfield Kent 28 TQ8452
Broomfield Kent 29 TR1966
Broomfield Somset 20 ST2232
Broomfields Shrops 59 SJ4217
Broomfleet Humb 84 SE8727
Broomhall Surrey 25 SU9566
Broomhaugh Nthumb 103 NZ0261
Broomhill Nthumb 103 NU2401
Broomhill Green Ches 71 SJ6247
Broomley Nthumb 103 NZ0360
Broomsthorpe Norfk 66 TF8428
Brora Highld 147 NC9103
Broseley Shrops 60 SJ6701
Brotherhouse Bar Lincs 64 TF2614
Brotherlee Dur 95 NY9237
Brothertoft Lincs 77 TF2746
Brotherton N York 83 SE4825
Brotton Cleve 97 NZ6819
Broubster Highld 150 ND0359
Brough Cumb 95 NY7914
Brough Derbys 74 SK1882
Brough Highld 151 ND2273
Brough Humb 84 SE9326
Brough Notts 76 SK8458
Brough Shet 155 HU5665
Brough Lodge Shet 155 HU5892
Brough Sowerby Cumb 95 NY7912
Broughall Shrops 71 SJ5741
Broughton Border 108 NT1136
Broughton Bucks 38 SP8413
Broughton Bucks 38 SP8939
Broughton Cambs 52 TL2878
Broughton Clwyd 71 SJ3363
Broughton Gt Man 79 SD8201
Broughton Hants 23 SU3033
Broughton Humb 84 SE9608
Broughton Lancs 80 SD5234
Broughton N York 82 SD9451
Broughton N York 90 SE7673
Broughton Nhants 51 SP8375
Broughton Oxon 49 SP4138
Broughton S Glam 33 SS9270
Broughton Staffs 72 SJ7634
Broughton Astley Leics 50 SP5292
Broughton Beck Cumb 86 SD2882
Broughton Gifford Wilts 22 ST8763
Broughton Green H & W 47 SO9561
Broughton Hackett H & W 47 SO9254
Broughton Mains D & G 99 NX4545
Broughton Mills Cumb 86 SD2290
Broughton Moor Cumb 92 NY0533
Broughton Poggs Oxon 36 SP2303
Broughton Tower Cumb 86 SD2187
Broughton-in-Furness Cumb 86 SD2187
Broughty Ferry Tays 127 NO4630
Brow End Cumb 86 SD2674
Brow-of-the-Hill Norfk 65 TF6819
Brown Candover Hants 24 SU5739
Brown Edge Lancs 80 SD3614
Brown Edge Staffs 72 SJ9053
Brown Heath Ches 71 SJ4564
Brown Lees Staffs 72 SJ8756
Brown Street Suffk 54 TM0663
Brown's Green W Mids 61 SP0591
Brownber Cumb 87 NY7005
Brownheath Shrops 59 SJ4629
Brownhill Gramp 143 NJ8640
Brownhills Fife 127 NO5215
Brownhills W Mids 61 SK0405
Browninghill Green Hants 24 SU5859
Brownlow Heath Ches 72 SJ8360
Brownrigg Cumb 92 NY0420
Brownrigg Cumb 92 NY1652
Brownsham Devon 18 SS2826
Brownsover Warwks 50 SP5177
Brownston Devon 7 SX6952
Brownstone Devon 7 SX9050
Browston Green Norfk 67 TG4901
Brox Surrey 26 TQ0263
Broxa N York 91 SE9491
Broxbourne Herts 39 TL3606
Broxburn Loth 117 NT0872
Broxburn Loth 119 NT6977
Broxfield Nthumb 111 NU2016
Broxted Essex 40 TL5727
Broxton Ches 71 SJ4754
Broxwood H & W 46 SO3654
Broyle Side E Susx 16 TQ4513
Bruan Highld 151 ND3139
Bruar Tays 132 NN8265
Brucefield Highld 147 NH9386
Bruchag Strath 114 NS1157
Bruera Ches 71 SJ4360
Bruern Abbey Oxon 36 SP2620
Bruisyard Suffk 55 TM3266
Bruisyard Street Suffk 55 TM3365
Brumby Humb 84 SE8909
Brund Staffs 74 SK1061
Brundall Norfk 67 TG3308
Brundish Suffk 55 TM2769
Brundish Street Suffk 55 TM2671
Brunnian Cnwll 2 SW5036
Brunslow Shrops 59 SO3684
Bruntcliffe W York 82 SE2526
Brunthwaite W York 82 SE0546
Bruntingthorpe Leics 50 SP6089
Brunton Fife 126 NO3220
Brunton Nthumb 111 NU2024
Brunton Wilts 23 SU2456
Brushford Somset 20 SS9225
Brushford Barton Devon 8 SS6707
Bruton Somset 22 ST6835
Bryan's Green H & W 47 SO8868
Bryanston Dorset 11 ST8607
Bryant's Bottom Bucks 26 SU8599
Brydekirk D & G 101 NY1870
Brymbo Clwyd 71 SJ2953
Brympton Somset 10 ST5115
Bryn Ches 71 SJ6072
Bryn Gt Man 78 SD5600
Bryn Shrops 59 SO2985
Bryn W Glam 33 SS8192
Bryn Du Gwynd 68 SH3472
Bryn Gates Lancs 78 SD5901
Bryn Golau M Glam 33 ST0088
Bryn Saith Marchog Clwyd 70 SJ0750
Bryn-bwbach Gwynd 57 SH6236
Bryn-coch W Glam 32 SS7499
Bryn-Eden Gwynd 57 SH7129
Bryn-henllan Dyfed 30 SN0139
Bryn-mawr Gwynd 56 SH2433
Bryn-newydd Clwyd 70 SJ1842
Bryn-penarth Powys 58 SJ1004
Bryn-y-bal Clwyd 70 SJ2564
Bryn-y-maen Clwyd 69 SH8376
Bryn-yr-Eos Clwyd 70 SJ2840
Brynaman Dyfed 32 SN7114
Brynberian Dyfed 31 SN1035
Brynbryddan W Glam 32 SS7792
Bryncae M Glam 33 SS9982
Bryncethin M Glam 33 SS9183
Bryncir Gwynd 56 SH4844
Bryncroes Gwynd 56 SH2231
Bryncrug Gwynd 57 SH6103
Bryneglwys Clwyd 70 SJ1447
Brynfields Clwyd 71 SJ3044
Brynford Clwyd 70 SJ1774
Bryngwran Gwynd 68 SH3577
Bryngwyn Gwent 34 SO3909
Bryngwyn Powys 45 SO1849
Brynhoffnant Dyfed 42 SN3351
Bryning Lancs 80 SD4029
Brynithel Gwent 33 SO2101
Brynmawr Gwent 33 SO1911
Brynmenyn M Glam 33 SS9084
Brynmill W Glam 32 SS6392
Brynna M Glam 33 SS9883
Brynrefail Gwynd 68 SH4886
Brynrefail Gwynd 69 SH5562
Brynsadler M Glam 33 ST0280
Brynsiencyn Gwynd 68 SH4867
Brynteg Gwynd 68 SH4982
Bualintur Highld 128 NG4020
Buarth-draw Clwyd 70 SJ1779
Bubbenhall Warwks 61 SP3672
Bubwith Humb 84 SE7136
Buchanan Smithy Cent 115 NS4689
Buchanhaven Gramp 143 NK1247
Buchanty Tays 125 NN9328
Buchany Cent 124 NN7102
Buchlyvie Cent 115 NS5793
Buck's Cross Devon 18 SS3522
Buck's Mills Devon 18 SS3523
Buckabank Cumb 93 NY3749
Buckden Cambs 52 TL1967
Buckden N York 88 SD9477
Buckenham Norfk 67 TG3505
Buckerell Devon 9 ST1200
Buckfast Devon 7 SX7467
Buckfastleigh Devon 7 SX7366
Buckhaven Fife 118 NT3598
Buckholm Border 109 NT4738
Buckholt Gwent 34 SO5016
Buckhorn Weston Dorset 22 ST7524
Buckhurst Hill Essex 27 TQ4194
Buckie Gramp 142 NJ4265
Buckingham Bucks 49 SP6933
Buckland Bucks 38 SP8812
Buckland Devon 7 SX6743
Buckland Gloucs 48 SP0835
Buckland Hants 12 SZ3196
Buckland Herts 39 TL3533
Buckland Kent 29 TR3042
Buckland Oxon 36 SU3498
Buckland Surrey 26 TQ2150
Buckland Brewer Devon 18 SS4220
Buckland Common Bucks 38 SP9207
Buckland Dinham Somset 22 ST7551
Buckland Filleigh Devon 18 SS4609
Buckland in the Moor Devon 7 SX7273
Buckland Monachorum Devon 6 SX4968
Buckland Newton Dorset 11 ST6805
Buckland Ripers Dorset 11 SY6582
Buckland St Mary Somset 10 ST2613
Buckland-Tout-Saints Devon 7 SX7645
Bucklebury Berks 24 SU5570
Bucklerheads Tays 127 NO4636
Bucklers Hard Hants 13 SU4000
Bucklesham Suffk 55 TM2441
Buckley Clwyd 70 SJ2763
Buckley Green Warwks 48 SP1567
Buckley Mountain Clwyd 70 SJ2765
Bucklow Hill Ches 79 SJ7383
Buckminster Leics 63 SK8722
Bucknall Lincs 76 TF1668
Bucknall Staffs 72 SJ9047
Bucknell Oxon 49 SP5625
Bucknell Shrops 46 SO3574
Buckpool Gramp 142 NJ4165
Bucks Green W Susx 14 TQ0833
Bucks Hill Herts 26 TL0500
Bucks Horn Oak Hants 25 SU8041
Bucksburn Gramp 135 NJ8909
Buckshead Cnwll 3 SW8346
Buckton H & W 46 SO3873
Buckton Humb 91 TA1872
Buckton Nthumb 111 NU0838
Buckworth Cambs 52 TL1476
Budbrooke Warwks 48 SP2665
Budby Notts 75 SK6169
Budd's Titson Cnwll 18 SS2401
Buddileigh Staffs 72 SJ7449
Buddon Tays 127 NO5232
Bude Cnwll 18 SS2105
Budge's Shop Cnwll 5 SX3259
Budlake Devon 9 SS9800
Budle Nthumb 111 NU1535
Budleigh Salterton Devon 9 SY0682
Budlett's Common E Susx 16 TQ4723
Budock Water Cnwll 3 SW7831
Buerton Ches 72 SJ6843
Bugbrooke Nhants 49 SP6757
Bugford Devon 7 SX8350
Buglawton Ches 72 SJ8763
Bugle Cnwll 4 SX0158
Bugley Dorset 22 ST7824
Bugthorpe Humb 90 SE7757
Buildwas Shrops 59 SJ6204
Builth Road Powys 45 SO0353
Builth Wells Powys 45 SO0350
Bulbourne Herts 38 SP9313
Bulbridge Wilts 23 SU0830
Bulby Lincs 64 TF0526
Buldoo Highld 150 ND0067
Bulford Wilts 23 SU1643
Bulford Barracks Wilts 23 SU1843
Bulkeley Ches 71 SJ5354
Bulkington Warwks 61 SP3986
Bulkington Wilts 22 ST9458
Bulkworthy Devon 18 SS3914
Bull Bay Gwynd 68 SH4294
Bull's Green Herts 39 TL2717
Bull's Green Norfk 67 TM4194
Bullamore N York 89 SE3994
Bullbridge Derbys 74 SK3552
Bullbrook Berks 25 SU8869
Bullen's Green Herts 39 TL2105
Bulley Gloucs 35 SO7619
Bullgill Cumb 92 NY0938
Bullinghope H & W 46 SO5136
Bullington Hants 24 SU4541
Bullington Lincs 76 TF0877
Bullington End Bucks 38 SP8145
Bullockstone Kent 29 TR1665
Bulmer Essex 54 TL8440
Bulmer N York 90 SE6967
Bulmer Tye Essex 54 TL8438
Bulphan Essex 40 TQ6385
Bulstone Devon 9 SY1789
Bulstrode Herts 26 TL0302
Bulstrode Park Bucks 26 SU9888
Bulterley Heath Staffs 72 SJ7450
Bulverhythe E Susx 17 TQ7708
Bulwark Gramp 143 NJ9345
Bulwell Notts 62 SK5343
Bulwick Nhants 51 SP9694
Bumble's Green Essex 39 TL4005
Bunacaimb Highld 129 NM6588
Bunarkaig Highld 131 NN1887
Bunbury Ches 71 SJ5657
Bunbury Heath Ches 71 SJ5558
Bunchrew Highld 140 NH6246
Buncton W Susx 15 TQ1413
Bundalloch Highld 138 NG8927
Bunessan Strath 121 NM3821
Bungay Suffk 55 TM3389
Bunker's Hill Lincs 77 TF2653
Bunnahabhainn Strath 112 NR4173

Bunny
Chapel Row

Bunny Notts 62 SK5829
Buntait Highld 139 NH4030
Buntingford Herts 39 TL3629
Bunwell Norfk 66 TM1292
Bunwell Street Norfk 66 TM1193
Bupton Derbys 73 SK2237
Burbage Derbys 74 SK0472
Burbage Leics 50 SP4492
Burbage Wilts 23 SU2261
Burcher H & W 46 SO3360
Burchett's Green Berks 26 SU8481
Burchett's Green E Susx 16 TQ6631
Burcombe Wilts 23 SU0730
Burcot H & W 60 SO9871
Burcot Oxon 37 SU5695
Burcote Shrops 60 SO7495
Burcott Bucks 38 SP8415
Burcott Bucks 38 SP8823
Burdale N York 90 SE8762
Bures Suffk 54 TL9034
Burford H & W 46 SO5868
Burford Oxon 36 SP2512
Burg Strath 121 NM3845
Burgates Hants 14 SU7728
Burge End Herts 38 TL1432
Burgess Hill W Susx 15 TQ3218
Burgh Suffk 55 TM2351
Burgh by Sands Cumb 93 NY3259
Burgh Castle Norfk 67 TG4805
Burgh Heath Surrey 26 TQ2457
Burgh Hill E Susx 17 TQ7226
Burgh Le Marsh Lincs 77 TF5065
Burgh next Aylsham Norfk 67 TG2125
Burgh on Bain Lincs 76 TF2186
Burgh St Margaret Norfk 67 TG4413
Burgh St Peter Norfk 67 TM4693
Burghclere Hants 24 SU4761
Burghead Gramp 141 NJ1168
Burghfield Berks 24 SU6668
Burghfield Common Berks 24 SU6566
Burghill H & W 46 SO4844
Burghwallis S York 83 SE5311
Burham Kent 28 TQ7262
Buriton Hants 13 SU7419
Burland Ches 71 SJ6153
Burlawn Cnwll 4 SW9970
Burleigh Berks 25 SU9169
Burleigh Gloucs 35 SO8601
Burlescombe Devon 9 ST0716
Burleston Dorset 11 SY7794
Burlestone Devon 7 SX8248
Burley Hants 12 SU2102
Burley Leics 63 SK8810
Burley Shrops 59 SO4881
Burley Gate H & W 46 SO5947
Burley in Wharfedale W York 82 SE1646
Burley Lawn Hants 12 SU2103
Burley Street Hants 12 SU2004
Burley Wood Head W York 82 SE1544
Burleydam Ches 71 SJ6042
Burlingham Green Norfk 67 TG3610
Burlingjobb Powys 46 SO2558
Burlington Shrops 60 SJ7711
Burlton Shrops 59 SJ4526
Burmarsh Kent 17 TR1032
Burmington Warwks 48 SP2637
Burn N York 83 SE5928
Burn Cross S York 74 SK3496
Burn Naze Lancs 80 SD3443
Burn of Cambus Cent 124 NN7102
Burnage Gt Man 79 SJ8692
Burnaston Derbys 73 SK2832
Burnbanks Cumb 94 NY5016
Burnbrae Strath 116 NS8759
Burnby Humb 84 SE8346
Burndell W Susx 14 SU9802
Burnden Gt Man 79 SD7207
Burnedge Gt Man 79 SD9110
Burneside Cumb 87 SD5095
Burneston N York 89 SE3084
Burnett Avon 22 ST6665
Burnfoot Border 109 NT4113
Burnfoot Border 109 NT5116
Burnfoot D & G 100 NX9791
Burnfoot D & G 101 NY3388
Burnfoot D & G 101 NY3996
Burnfoot Tays 125 NN9904
Burnham Bucks 26 SU9282
Burnham Humb 84 TA0516
Burnham Deepdale Norfk 66 TF8044
Burnham Green Herts 39 TL2616
Burnham Market Norfk 66 TF8342
Burnham Norton Norfk 66 TF8343
Burnham Overy Norfk 66 TF8442
Burnham Thorpe Norfk 66 TF8541
Burnham-on-Crouch Essex 40 TQ9496
Burnham-on-Sea Somset 20 ST3049
Burnhaven Gramp 143 NK1244
Burnhead D & G 100 NX8695
Burnhervie Gramp 142 NJ7319
Burnhill Green Staffs 60 SJ7800
Burnhope Dur 96 NZ1948
Burnhouse Strath 115 NS3850
Burniston N York 91 TA0193
Burnley Lancs 81 SD8432
Burnmouth Border 119 NT9560
Burnopfield Dur 96 NZ1757
Burnrigg Cumb 94 NY4856
Burnsall N York 88 SE0361
Burnside Fife 126 NO1608
Burnside Fife 117 NT0575
Burnside Gramp 147 NJ1769
Burnside Tays 134 NO4259
Burnside Tays 127 NO5050
Burnside of Duntrune Tays 127 NO4434
Burnt Heath Essex 41 TM0627
Burnt Hill Berks 24 SU5774
Burnt Houses Dur 96 NZ1223
Burnt Oak E Susx 16 TQ5126
Burnt Yates N York 89 SE2561
Burntcommon Surrey 26 TQ0354
Burntheath Derbys 73 SK2431
Burnthouse Cnwll 3 SW7636
Burntisland Fife 117 NT2385
Burntwood Staffs 61 SK0509
Burntwood Green Staffs 61 SK0608
Burnville Devon 5 SX4982
Burnworthy Somset 9 ST1915
Burpham Surrey 26 TQ0152
Burpham W Susx 14 TQ0308
Burradon Nthumb 111 NT9806
Burradon T & W 103 NZ2772
Burrafirth Shet 155 HP6113
Burras Cnwll 2 SW6734
Burraton Cnwll 5 SX4167
Burraton Devon 6 SX6153
Burravoe Shet 155 HU5180
Burrells Cumb 94 NY6718
Burrelton Tays 126 NO2037
Burridge Devon 10 ST3106
Burridge Hants 13 SU5110
Burrill N York 89 SE2387
Burringham Humb 84 SE8309
Burrington Avon 21 ST4859
Burrington Devon 19 SS6416
Burrington H & W 46 SO4472
Burrough End Cambs 53 TL6255
Burrough Green Cambs 53 TL6355
Burrough on the Hill Leics 63 SK7510
Burrow Somset 20 SS9342
Burrow Bridge Somset 21 ST3530
Burrowhill Surrey 25 SU9762
Burrows Cross Surrey 14 TQ0846
Burry W Glam 32 SS4590
Burry Port Dyfed 32 SN4400
Burrygreen W Glam 32 SS4591
Burscough Lancs 78 SD4310
Burscough Bridge Lancs 80 SD4412
Bursea Humb 84 SE8033
Burshill Humb 85 TA0948
Bursledon Hants 13 SU4809
Burslem Staffs 72 SJ8649
Burstall Suffk 54 TM0944
Burstock Dorset 10 ST4202
Burston Norfk 54 TM1383
Burston Staffs 72 SJ9330
Burstow Surrey 15 TQ3141
Burstwick Humb 85 TA2227
Burtersett N York 88 SD8989
Burtholme Cumb 101 NY5463
Burthorpe Green Suffk 53 TL7764
Burthwaite Cumb 93 NY4149
Burthy Cnwll 3 SW9155
Burtle Hill Somset 21 ST3843
Burtoft Lincs 64 TF2635
Burton Ches 71 SJ3174
Burton Ches 71 SJ5063
Burton Dorset 11 SY6891
Burton Dorset 12 SZ1694
Burton Dyfed 30 SM9805
Burton Lincs 76 SK9574
Burton Nthumb 111 NU1833
Burton Somset 20 ST1944
Burton Somset 10 ST5313
Burton Wilts 35 ST8179
Burton Wilts 22 ST8232
Burton Agnes Humb 91 TA1062
Burton Bradstock Dorset 10 SY4889
Burton Coggles Lincs 63 SK9725
Burton Dassett Warwks 48 SP3951
Burton End Essex 39 TL5323
Burton End Suffk 53 TL6645
Burton Fleming Humb 91 TA0871
Burton Green Clwyd 71 SJ3458
Burton Green Warwks 61 SP2675
Burton Hastings Warwks 50 SP4189
Burton in Lonsdale N York 87 SD6572
Burton Joyce Notts 63 SK6443
Burton Latimer Nhants 51 SP9074
Burton Lazars Leics 63 SK7716
Burton Leonard N York 89 SE3263
Burton Overy Leics 50 SP6798
Burton on the Wolds Leics 62 SK5821
Burton Pedwardine Lincs 64 TF1142
Burton Pidsea Humb 85 TA2431
Burton Salmon N York 83 SE4927
Burton upon Stather Humb 84 SE8717
Burton upon Trent Staffs 73 SK2323
Burton's Green Essex 40 TL8226
Burton-in-Kendal Cumb 87 SD5376
Burtonwood Ches 78 SJ5692
Burwardsley Ches 71 SJ5156
Burwarton Shrops 59 SO6185
Burwash E Susx 16 TQ6724
Burwash Common E Susx 16 TQ6323
Burwash Weald E Susx 16 TQ6523
Burwell Cambs 53 TL5866
Burwell Lincs 77 TF3579
Burwen Gwynd 68 SH4293
Burwick Ork 155 ND4484
Bury Cambs 52 TL2883
Bury Gt Man 81 SD8011
Bury Somset 20 SS9427
Bury W Susx 14 TQ0113
Bury End Beds 38 TL1235
Bury End Bucks 26 SU9697
Bury Green Herts 39 TL4521
Bury St Edmunds Suffk 54 TL8564
Burythorpe N York 90 SE7964
Busby Strath 115 NS5756
Buscot Wilts 36 SU2298
Bush Cnwll 18 SS2307
Bush Gramp 135 NO7565
Bush Bank H & W 46 SO4551
Bush Green Norfk 55 TM2187
Bush Green Suffk 54 TL9157
Bush Hill Park Gt Lon 27 TQ3395
Bushbury W Mids 60 SJ9202
Bushby Leics 63 SK6503
Bushey Herts 26 TQ1395
Bushey Heath Herts 26 TQ1494
Bushley H & W 47 SO8734
Bushley Green H & W 47 SO8634
Bushmead Beds 52 TL1160
Bushton Wilts 36 SU0677
Busk Cumb 94 NY6042
Buslingthorpe Lincs 76 TF0785
Bussage Gloucs 35 SO8803
Bussex Somset 21 ST3535
Butcher Hill W York 81 SD9322
Butcher's Cross E Susx 16 TQ5525
Butcher's Pasture Essex 40 TL6024
Butcombe Avon 21 ST5161
Butleigh Somset 21 ST5233
Butleigh Wootton Somset 21 ST5035
Butler's Cross Bucks 38 SP8407
Butler's Hill Notts 75 SK5448
Butlers Green Staffs 72 SJ8150
Butlers Marston Warwks 48 SP3250
Butley Suffk 55 TM3650
Butley Corner Suffk 55 TM3849
Butt Green Ches 72 SJ6651
Butt Lane Staffs 72 SJ8253
Butt's Green Essex 40 TL7603
Buttercrambe N York 90 SE7358
Butterdean Border 119 NT7964
Butterhill Bank Staffs 72 SJ9330
Butterknowle Dur 95 NZ1025
Butterleigh Devon 9 SS9708
Butterley Derbys 74 SK4051
Buttermere Cumb 93 NY1717
Buttermere Wilts 23 SU3461
Buttershaw W York 82 SE1329
Butterstone Tays 125 NO0645
Butterton Staffs 72 SJ8242
Butterton Staffs 73 SK0756
Butterwick Dur 96 NZ3830
Butterwick Lincs 64 TF3845
Butterwick N York 90 SE7277
Butterwick N York 91 SE9871
Buttington Powys 58 SJ2408
Buttonbridge Shrops 60 SO7379
Buttonoak Shrops 60 SO7578
Buttsash Hants 13 SU4206
Buttsbear Cross Cnwll 18 SS2604
Buxhall Suffk 54 TM0057
Buxhall Fen Street Suffk 54 TM0059
Buxted E Susx 16 TQ4923
Buxton Derbys 74 SK0572
Buxton Norfk 67 TG2322
Buxton Heath Norfk 66 TG1821
Bwlch Powys 33 SO1522
Bwlch-y-cibau Powys 58 SJ1717
Bwlch-y-ffridd Powys 58 SO0795
Bwlch-y-groes Dyfed 31 SN2436
Bwlch-y-sarnau Powys 45 SO0374
Bwlchgwyn Clwyd 70 SJ2653
Bwlchllan Dyfed 44 SN5758
Bwlchnewydd Dyfed 31 SN3624
Bwlchtocyn Gwynd 56 SH3125
Bwlchyddar Clwyd 58 SJ1722
Bwlchyfadfa Dyfed 42 SN4349
Bwlchymyrdd W Glam 32 SS5798
Byermoor T & W 96 NZ1857
Byers Garth Dur 96 NZ3140
Byers Green Dur 96 NZ2233
Byfield Nhants 49 SP5152
Byfleet Surrey 26 TQ0661
Byford H & W 46 SO3942
Byker T & W 103 NZ2764
Bylchau Clwyd 70 SH9762
Byley Ches 79 SJ7269
Bynea Dyfed 32 SS5499
Byrewalls Border 110 NT6642
Byrness Nthumb 102 NT7602
Bystock Devon 9 SY0283
Bythorn Cambs 51 TL0575
Byton H & W 46 SO3764
Bywell Nthumb 103 NZ0461
Byworth W Susx 14 SU9821

C

Cabourne Lincs 85 TA1401
Cabrach Gramp 141 NJ3826
Cabrach Strath 112 NR4964
Cabus Lancs 80 SD4948
Cabvie Lodge Highld 138 NH1567
Cackle Street E Susx 16 TQ4526
Cackle Street E Susx 16 TQ6919
Cackle Street E Susx 17 TQ8218
Cadbury Devon 9 SS9105
Cadbury Barton Devon 19 SS6917
Cadder Strath 116 NS6072
Caddington Beds 38 TL0619
Caddonfoot Border 109 NT4535
Cade Street E Susx 16 TQ6020
Cadeby Leics 62 SK4202
Cadeby S York 75 SE5100
Cadeleigh Devon 9 SS9108
Cadgwith Cnwll 3 SW7214
Cadham Fife 126 NO2801
Cadishead Gt Man 79 SJ7091
Cadle W Glam 32 SS6296
Cadley Lancs 80 SD5231
Cadley Wilts 23 SU2066
Cadley Wilts 23 SU2453
Cadmore End Bucks 37 SU7892
Cadnam Hants 12 SU3013
Cadney Humb 84 TA0103
Cadole Clwyd 70 SJ2062
Cadoxton S Glam 20 ST1269
Cadoxton Juxta-Neath W Glam 32 SS7598
Cadsden Bucks 38 SP8204
Cadwst Clwyd 58 SJ0235
Cae'r bryn Dyfed 32 SN5913
Cae'r-bont Powys 32 SN8011
Caeathro Gwynd 68 SH5061
Caehopkin Powys 33 SN8212
Caenby Lincs 76 SK9989
Caenby Corner Lincs 76 SK9689
Caeo Dyfed 44 SN6740
Caer Farchell Dyfed 30 SM7927
Caerau M Glam 33 SS8694
Caerau S Glam 33 ST1375
Caerdeon Gwynd 57 SH6518
Caergeiliog Gwynd 68 SH3178
Caergwrle Clwyd 71 SJ3057
Caerhun Gwynd 69 SH7770
Caerlanrig Border 109 NT3904
Caerleon Gwent 34 ST3490
Caernarfon Gwynd 68 SH4862
Caerphilly M Glam 33 ST1587
Caersws Powys 58 SO0392
Caerwedros Dyfed 42 SN3755
Caerwent Gwent 34 ST4790
Caerwys Clwyd 70 SJ1272
Caerynwch Gwynd 57 SH7617
Caggle Street Gwent 34 SO3717
Caim Gwynd 69 SH6280
Cairnbaan Strath 113 NR8390
Cairnbrogie Gramp 143 NJ8527
Cairnbulg Gramp 143 NK0365
Cairncross Border 119 NT8963
Cairncurran Strath 115 NS3170
Cairndow Strath 123 NN1810
Cairneyhill Fife 117 NT0486
Cairnfield House Gramp 142 NJ4162
Cairngarroch D & G 98 NX0549
Cairngrassie Gramp 135 NO9095
Cairnhall D & G 100 NX9086
Cairnie Gramp 142 NJ4844
Cairnorrie Gramp 143 NJ8641
Cairnryan D & G 98 NX0668
Cairnty Gramp 141 NJ3352
Caister-on-Sea Norfk 67 TG5112
Caistor Lincs 85 TA1101
Caistor St Edmund Norfk 67 TG2303
Cake Street Norfk 54 TM0690
Cakebole H & W 60 SO8772
Calais Street Suffk 54 TL9739
Calbourne IOW 13 SZ4286
Calceby Lincs 77 TF3875
Calcot Berks 24 SU6671
Calcot Clwyd 70 SJ1674
Calcot Gloucs 36 SP0810
Calcot Row Berks 24 SU6771
Calcots Gramp 141 NJ2563
Calcott Kent 29 TR1762
Calcott Shrops 59 SJ4413
Calcutt Wilts 36 SU1193
Caldbeck Cumb 93 NY3240
Caldbergh N York 89 SE0985
Caldecote Cambs 52 TL1488
Caldecote Cambs 52 TL3456
Caldecote Herts 39 TL2338
Caldecote Nhants 49 SP6851
Caldecote Highfields Cambs 52 TL3559
Caldecott Leics 51 SP8693
Caldecott Nhants 51 SP9868
Caldecott Oxon 37 SU4996
Calder Bridge Cumb 86 NY0306
Calder Grove W York 82 SE3016
Calder Vale Lancs 80 SD5345
Calderbank Strath 116 NS7663
Calderbrook Gt Man 82 SD9418
Caldercote Bucks 38 SP8935
Caldercruix Strath 116 NS8167
Caldermill Strath 107 NS6641
Caldermore Gt Man 81 SD9316
Caldicot Gwent 34 ST4888
Caldwell N York 89 NZ1613
Caldy Mersyd 78 SJ2285
Calendra Cnwll 3 SW9240
Calenick Cnwll 3 SW8243
Calford Green Suffk 53 TL7045
Calfsound Ork 155 HY5738
Calgary Strath 121 NM3751
Califer Gramp 141 NJ0857
California Cent 116 NS9076
California Derbys 62 SK3335
California Norfk 67 TG5115
California Suffk 54 TM0641
California Cross Devon 7 SX7053
Calke Derbys 62 SK3721
Callakille Highld 137 NG6955
Callaly Nthumb 111 NU0509
Callander Cent 124 NN6207
Callanish W Isls 154 NB2133
Callaughton Shrops 59 SO6197
Callert Cottage Highld 130 NN1060
Callestick Cnwll 3 SW7750
Calligarry Highld 129 NG6203
Callington Cnwll 5 SX3669
Callingwood Staffs 73 SK1823
Callow H & W 46 SO4934
Callow End H & W 47 SO8350
Callow Hill H & W 60 SO7573
Callow Hill H & W 47 SP0164
Callow Hill Wilts 36 SU0384
Callows Grave H & W 46 SO5967
Calmore Hants 12 SU3414
Calmsden Gloucs 36 SP0508
Calne Wilts 35 ST9971
Calow Derbys 74 SK4071
Calshot Hants 13 SU4701
Calstock Cnwll 6 SX4368
Calstone Wellington Wilts 23 SU0268
Calthorpe Norfk 66 TG1831
Calthorpe Street Norfk 67 TG4025
Calthwaite Cumb 93 NY4640
Calton N York 88 SD9059
Calton Staffs 73 SK1049
Calton Green Staffs 73 SK1049
Calveley Ches 71 SJ5958
Calver Derbys 74 SK2374
Calver Hill H & W 46 SO3748
Calver Sough Derbys 74 SK2374
Calverhall Shrops 59 SJ6037
Calverleigh Devon 9 SS9214
Calverley W York 82 SE2036
Calvert Bucks 49 SP6824
Calverton Bucks 38 SP7939
Calverton Notts 75 SK6149
Calvine Tays 132 NN8065
Calvo Cumb 92 NY1453
Calzeat Border 108 NT1135
Cam Gloucs 35 ST7599
Camas Luinie Highld 138 NG9428
Camasachoirce Highld 130 NM7660
Camasine Highld 130 NM7561
Camastianavaig Highld 137 NG5039
Camasunary Highld 128 NG5118
Camault Muir Highld 139 NH5040
Camber E Susx 17 TQ9618
Camberley Surrey 25 SU8860
Camberwell Gt Lon 27 TQ3276
Camblesforth N York 83 SE6425
Cambo Nthumb 103 NZ0285
Cambois Nthumb 103 NZ3083
Camborne Cnwll 2 SW6440
Cambridge Cambs 53 TL4558
Cambridge Gloucs 35 SO7403
Cambrose Cnwll 2 SW6845
Cambus Cent 116 NS8594
Cambus O' May Gramp 134 NO4198
Cambusavie Platform Highld 147 NH7696
Cambusbarron Cent 116 NS7792
Cambuskenneth Cent 116 NS8094
Cambusmoon Strath 115 NS4285
Cambuswallace Strath 108 NT0438
Camden Town Gt Lon 27 TQ2883
Cameley Avon 21 ST6157
Camelford Cnwll 4 SX1083
Camelon Cent 116 NS8680
Camer's Green H & W 47 SO7735
Camerory Highld 141 NJ0131
Camerton Avon 22 ST6857
Camerton Cumb 92 NY0330
Camghouran Tays 124 NN5556
Cammachmore Gramp 135 NO9195
Cammeringham Lincs 76 SK9482
Camore Highld 147 NH7889
Camp The Gloucs 35 SO9109
Campbeltown Strath 105 NR7120
Camperdown T & W 103 NZ2772
Cample D & G 100 NX8993
Campmuir Tays 126 NO2137
Camps Loth 117 NT0968
Camps End Cambs 53 TL6142
Campsall S York 83 SE5413
Campsie Strath 116 NS6079
Campsie Ash Suffk 55 TM3356
Campton Beds 38 TL1238
Camptown Border 110 NT6813
Camrose Dyfed 30 SM9220
Camserney Tays 125 NN8149
Camster Highld 151 ND2642
Camusnagaul Highld 145 NH0589
Camusnagaul Highld 130 NN0874
Camusteel Highld 137 NG7042
Camusterrach Highld 137 NG7141
Canada Hants 12 SU2818
Canal Foot Cumb 86 SD3177
Canaston Bridge Dyfed 30 SN0615
Candacraig Gramp 134 NO3499
Candle Street Suffk 54 TM0374
Candlesby Lincs 77 TF4567
Candover Green Shrops 59 SJ5005
Candyburn Strath 108 NT0741
Cane End Oxon 37 SU6779
Canewdon Essex 40 TQ9094
Canfield End Essex 40 TL5821
Canfold Bottom Dorset 12 SU0305
Canford Cliffs Dorset 12 SZ0589
Canford Magna Dorset 12 SZ0398
Canhams Green Suffk 54 TM0565
Canisbay Highld 151 ND3472
Canklow S York 74 SK4291
Canley W Mids 61 SP3077
Cann Dorset 22 ST8721
Cannich Highld 139 NH3331
Canning Town Gt Lon 27 TQ4081
Cannington Somset 20 ST2539
Cannock Staffs 60 SJ9810
Cannock Wood Staffs 61 SK0412
Cannon Bridge H & W 46 SO4340
Canon Frome H & W 47 SO6443
Canon Pyon H & W 46 SO4548
Canonbie D & G 101 NY3976
Canons Ashby Nhants 49 SP5750
Canonstown Cnwll 2 SW5335
Canterbury Kent 29 TR1457
Cantley Norfk 67 TG3704
Cantley S York 83 SE6202
Cantlop Shrops 59 SJ5205
Canton S Glam 33 ST1676
Cantraywood Highld 140 NH7847
Cantsfield Lancs 87 SD6272
Canvey Island Essex 40 TQ7983
Canwick Lincs 76 SK9869
Canworthy Water Cnwll 5 SX2291
Caol Highld 130 NN1175
Caoles Strath 120 NM0848
Caonich Highld 130 NN0692
Capel Kent 16 TQ6344
Capel Surrey 15 TQ1740
Capel Bangor Dyfed 43 SN6580
Capel Betws Lleucu Dyfed 44 SN6058
Capel Coch Gwynd 68 SH4682
Capel Curig Gwynd 69 SH7258
Capel Cynon Dyfed 42 SN3849
Capel Dewi Dyfed 31 SN4542
Capel Dewi Dyfed 32 SN4720
Capel Garmon Gwynd 69 SH8155
Capel Green Suffk 55 TM3649
Capel Gwyn Dyfed 32 SN4622
Capel Gwyn Gwynd 68 SH3475
Capel Gwynfe Dyfed 32 SN7222
Capel Hendre Dyfed 32 SN5911
Capel Isaac Dyfed 44 SN5926
Capel Iwan Dyfed 31 SN2936
Capel Llanilltern M Glam 33 ST0979
Capel le Ferne Kent 29 TR2539
Capel Mawr Gwynd 68 SH4171
Capel Seion Dyfed 43 SN6379
Capel St Andrew Suffk 55 TM3748
Capel St Mary Suffk 54 TM0838
Capel Trisant Dyfed 43 SN7175
Capel-Dewi Dyfed 43 SN6282
Capel-y-ffin Powys 46 SO2531
Capel-y-graig Gwynd 69 SH5469
Capelles Guern 152 GN5211
Capelulo Gwynd 69 SH7476
Capenhurst Ches 71 SJ3673
Capernwray Lancs 87 SD5371
Capheaton Nthumb 103 NZ0380
Caplaw Strath 115 NS4458
Capon's Green Suffk 55 TM2867
Cappercleuch Border 109 NT2423
Capstone Kent 28 TQ7865
Capton Devon 7 SX8353
Capton Somset 20 ST0839
Caputh Tays 125 NO0840
Car Colston Notts 63 SK7142
Caradon Town Cnwll 5 SX2971
Carbeth Inn Cent 115 NS5279
Carbis Cnwll 4 SX0059
Carbis Bay Cnwll 2 SW5238
Carbost Highld 136 NG3731
Carbost Highld 136 NG4248
Carbrook S York 74 SK3889
Carbrooke Norfk 66 TF9402
Carburton Notts 75 SK6172
Carclaze Cnwll 3 SX0254
Carclew Cnwll 3 SW7838
Carcroft S York 83 SE5409
Cardenden Fife 117 NT2195
Cardeston Shrops 59 SJ3912
Cardewlees Cumb 93 NY3551
Cardiff S Glam 33 ST1876
Cardigan Dyfed 42 SN1746
Cardinal's Green Cambs 53 TL6146
Cardington Beds 38 TL0847
Cardington Shrops 59 SO5095
Cardinham Cnwll 4 SX1268
Cardow Gramp 141 NJ1943
Cardrain D & G 98 NX1231
Cardrona Border 109 NT3038
Cardross Strath 115 NS3477
Cardryne D & G 98 NX1132
Cardurnock Cumb 93 NY1758
Careby Lincs 64 TF0216
Careston Tays 134 NO5260
Carew Dyfed 30 SN0403
Carew Cheriton Dyfed 30 SN0402
Carew Newton Dyfed 30 SN0404
Carey H & W 46 SO5730
Carfin Strath 116 NS7759
Carfraemill Border 118 NT5053
Cargate Green Norfk 67 TG3912
Cargen D & G 100 NX9672
Cargenbridge D & G 100 NX9575
Cargill Tays 126 NO1536
Cargo Cumb 93 NY3659
Cargreen Cnwll 6 SX4362
Cargurrel Cnwll 3 SW8737
Carham Nthumb 110 NT7938
Carhampton Somset 20 ST0042
Carharrack Cnwll 3 SW7341
Carie Tays 124 NN6257
Carinish W Isls 154 NF8260
Carisbrooke IOW 13 SZ4888
Cark Cumb 87 SD3676
Carkeel Cnwll 5 SX4160
Carland Cross Cnwll 3 SW8554
Carlbury Dur 96 NZ2115
Carlby Lincs 64 TF0413
Carlcroft Nthumb 110 NT8311
Carlecotes S York 82 SE1703
Carleen Cnwll 2 SW6130
Carlesmoor N York 89 SE2073
Carleton Cumb 93 NY4252
Carleton Cumb 94 NY5329
Carleton Lancs 80 SD3339
Carleton N York 82 SD9749
Carleton N York 89 SE3959
Carleton W York 83 SE4620
Carleton Forehoe Norfk 66 TG0905
Carleton Rode Norfk 66 TM1093
Carleton St Peter Norfk 67 TG3402
Carlidnack Cnwll 3 SW7729
Carlin How Cleve 97 NZ7019
Carlincraig Gramp 142 NJ6743
Carlingcott Avon 22 ST6958
Carlisle Cumb 93 NY3956
Carloggas Cnwll 4 SW8765
Carlops Border 117 NT1656
Carloway W Isls 154 NB2043
Carlton Beds 51 SP9555
Carlton Cambs 53 TL6452
Carlton Cleve 96 NZ3921
Carlton Cumb 86 NY0109
Carlton Leics 62 SK3904
Carlton N York 90 NZ5004
Carlton N York 88 SE0684
Carlton N York 90 SE6086
Carlton N York 83 SE6423
Carlton Notts 62 SK6041
Carlton S York 83 SE3610
Carlton Suffk 55 TM3764
Carlton W York 83 SE3327
Carlton Colville Suffk 55 TM5189
Carlton Curlieu Leics 50 SP6997
Carlton Green Cambs 53 TL6451
Carlton Husthwaite N York 90 SE4976
Carlton in Lindrick Notts 75 SK5883
Carlton Miniott N York 89 SE3981
Carlton Scroop Lincs 63 SK9445
Carlton-le-Moorland Lincs 76 SK9058
Carlton-on-Trent Notts 75 SK7963
Carluddon Cnwll 3 SX0255
Carluke Strath 116 NS8450
Carmacoup Strath 107 NS7927
Carmarthen Dyfed 31 SN3919
Carmel Clwyd 70 SJ1676
Carmel Dyfed 32 SN5816
Carmel Gwynd 68 SH4954
Carmichael Strath 108 NS9238
Carminowe Cnwll 2 SW6623
Carmunnock Strath 115 NS5957
Carmyle Strath 116 NS6462
Carmyllie Tays 127 NO5442
Carn Brea Cnwll 2 SW6841
Carn-gorm Highld 138 NG9520
Carnaby Humb 91 TA1465
Carnach W Isls 154 NG2297
Carnbee Fife 127 NO5206
Carnbo Tays 125 NO0503
Carndu Highld 138 NG8827
Carnduff Strath 116 NS6646
Carne Cnwll 3 SW7724
Carne Cnwll 3 SW9138
Carne Cnwll 4 SW9558
Carnell Strath 107 NS4731
Carnewas Cnwll 4 SW8569
Carnforth Lancs 87 SD4970
Carnhell Green Cnwll 2 SW6137
Carnie Gramp 135 NJ8005
Carnkie Cnwll 2 SW7134
Carnkiet Cnwll 3 SW7852
Carnmenellis Cnwll 2 SW7035
Carno Powys 58 SN9696
Carnoch Highld 130 NM8696
Carnock Fife 117 NT0489
Carnon Downs Cnwll 3 SW7940
Carnousie Gramp 142 NJ6650
Carnoustie Tays 127 NO5534
Carnwath Strath 117 NS9846
Carnyorth Cnwll 2 SW3733
Carol Green W Mids 61 SP2577
Carpalla Cnwll 3 SW9654
Carperby N York 88 SE0089
Carr Gt Man 81 SD7816
Carr S York 75 SK5090
Carr Gate W York 82 SE3123
Carr Shield Nthumb 95 NY8047
Carr Vale Derbys 75 SK4669
Carradale Strath 105 NR8138
Carrbridge Highld 140 NH9022
Carrbrook Gt Man 79 SD9800
Carrefour Jersey 152 JS1213
Carreglefn Gwynd 68 SH3889
Carrhouse Humb 84 SE7706
Carrick Strath 114 NR9086
Carrick Castle Strath 114 NS1994
Carriden Cent 117 NT0181
Carrington Gt Man 79 SJ7492
Carrington Lincs 77 TF3155
Carrington Loth 117 NT3160
Carrismerry Cnwll 4 SX0158
Carrog Clwyd 70 SJ1043
Carrog Gwynd 69 SH7647
Carron Cent 116 NS8882
Carron Gramp 141 NJ2241
Carron Bridge Cent 116 NS7483
Carronbridge D & G 100 NX8698
Carronshore Cent 116 NS8983
Carrow Hill Gwent 34 ST4390
Carruth House Strath 115 NS3566
Carrutherstown D & G 100 NY1071
Carrville Dur 96 NZ3043
Carrycoats Hall Nthumb 102 NY9279
Carsaig Strath 121 NM5421
Carscreugh D & G 98 NX2260
Carse Gray Tays 127 NO4553
Carseriggan D & G 98 NX3167
Carsethorn D & G 92 NX9959
Carshalton Gt Lon 27 TQ2764
Carsington Derbys 73 SK2553
Carskey Strath 104 NR6508
Carsluith D & G 99 NX4854
Carsphairn D & G 107 NX5693
Carstairs Strath 116 NS9345
Carstairs Junction Strath 117 NS9545
Carswell Marsh Oxon 36 SU3299
Carter's Clay Hants 23 SU3024
Carters Green Essex 39 TL5110
Carterton Oxon 36 SP2806
Carterway Heads Nthumb 95 NZ0451
Carthew Cnwll 3 SX0056
Carthorpe N York 89 SE3083
Cartington Nthumb 103 NU0204
Cartland Strath 116 NS8646
Cartledge Derbys 74 SK3276
Cartmel Cumb 87 SD3878
Cartmel Fell Cumb 87 SD4188
Carway Dyfed 32 SN4606
Carwinley Cumb 101 NY4072
Cashe's Green Gloucs 35 SO8205
Cashmoor Dorset 11 ST9713
Cassington Oxon 37 SP4511
Cassop Colliery Dur 96 NZ3438
Castel Guern 152 GN5108
Castell Gwynd 69 SH7669
Castell-y-bwch Gwent 34 ST2792
Casterton Lancs 87 SD6279
Castle Cnwll 4 SX0958
Castle Acre Norfk 66 TF8115
Castle Ashby Nhants 51 SP8659
Castle Bolton N York 88 SE0391
Castle Bromwich W Mids 61 SP1489
Castle Bytham Lincs 63 SK9818
Castle Caereinion Powys 58 SJ1605
Castle Camps Cambs 53 TL6242
Castle Carrock Cumb 94 NY5455
Castle Cary Somset 21 ST6432
Castle Combe Wilts 35 ST8477
Castle Donington Leics 62 SK4427
Castle Douglas D & G 99 NX7662
Castle Eaton Wilts 36 SU1496
Castle Eden Dur 96 NZ4238
Castle End Cambs 64 TF1208
Castle Frome H & W 47 SO6645
Castle Gate Cnwll 2 SW4934
Castle Green Cumb 87 SD5392
Castle Green Surrey 25 SU9761
Castle Gresley Derbys 73 SK2717
Castle Hedingham Essex 53 TL7835
Castle Hill Kent 28 TQ6942
Castle Hill Suffk 54 TM1446
Castle Kennedy D & G 98 NX1159
Castle Lachlan Strath 114 NS0195
Castle Morris Dyfed 30 SM9031
Castle O'er D & G 101 NY2492
Castle Pulverbatch Shrops 59 SJ4202
Castle Rising Norfk 65 TF6624
Castle Street W York 82 SD9524
Castle Stuart Highld 140 NH7449
Castlebay W Isls 154 NL6698
Castlebythe Dyfed 30 SN0229
Castlecary Strath 116 NS7878
Castlecraig Highld 147 NH8269
Castlecroft W Mids 60 SO8797
Castleford W York 83 SE4225
Castlehill Border 109 NT2135
Castlehill Highld 151 ND1968
Castlemartin Dyfed 30 SR9198
Castlemorton H & W 47 SO7937
Castleside Dur 95 NZ0748
Castlethorpe Bucks 38 SP8044
Castlethorpe Humb 84 SE9807
Castleton Border 101 NY5189
Castleton Derbys 74 SK1582
Castleton Gt Man 79 SD8810
Castleton Gwent 34 ST2583
Castleton N York 90 NZ6807
Castletown Dorset 11 SY6874
Castletown Highld 151 ND1967
Castletown IOM 153 SC2667
Castletown T & W 96 NZ3658
Castley N York 82 SE2646
Caston Norfk 66 TL9597
Castor Cambs 64 TL1298
Caswell Bay W Glam 32 SS5987
Cat's Ash Gwent 34 ST3790
Catacol Strath 105 NR9149
Catbrook Gwent 34 SO5102
Catch Clwyd 70 SJ2070
Catchall Cnwll 2 SW4228
Catchem's Corner W Mids 61 SP2576
Catchgate Dur 96 NZ1652
Catcliffe S York 74 SK4288
Catcomb Wilts 35 SU0076
Catcott Somset 21 ST3939
Catcott Burtle Somset 21 ST4043
Caterham Surrey 27 TQ3455
Catfield Norfk 67 TG3821
Catfield Common Norfk 67 TG4021
Catfirth Shet 155 HU4354
Catford Gt Lon 27 TQ3773
Catforth Lancs 80 SD4735
Cathcart Strath 115 NS5860
Cathedine Powys 45 SO1425
Catherine Slack W York 82 SE0928
Catherine-de-Barnes W Mids 61 SP1780
Catherington Hants 13 SU6914
Catherston Leweston Dorset 10 SY3694
Catherton Shrops 47 SO6578
Cathpair Border 118 NT4646
Catisfield Hants 13 SU5506
Catley Lane Head Gt Man 81 SD8715
Catley Southfield H & W 47 SO6844
Catlodge Highld 132 NN6392
Catlow Lancs 81 SD8836
Catlowdy Cumb 101 NY4576
Catmere End Essex 39 TL4939
Catmore Berks 37 SU4580
Caton Devon 7 SX7872
Caton Lancs 87 SD5364
Caton Green Lancs 87 SD5565
Cator Court Devon 8 SX6877
Catrine Strath 107 NS5225
Catsfield E Susx 17 TQ7213
Catsfield Stream E Susx 17 TQ7113
Catsham Somset 21 ST5533
Catshill H & W 60 SO9573
Catstree Shrops 60 SO7496
Cattadale Strath 105 NR6710
Cattal N York 83 SE4454
Cattawade Suffk 41 TM1033
Catterall Lancs 80 SD4942
Catteralslane Shrops 71 SJ5640
Catterick N York 89 SE2397
Catterick Bridge N York 89 SE2299
Catterick Camp N York 89 SE1897
Catterlen Cumb 94 NY4833
Catterton N York 83 SE5145
Catteshall Surrey 25 SU9844
Catthorpe Leics 50 SP5578
Cattishall Suffk 54 TL8865
Cattistock Dorset 10 SY5999
Catton Cumb 95 NY8257
Catton N York 89 SE3678
Catton Norfk 67 TG2312
Catwick Humb 85 TA1345
Catworth Cambs 51 TL0873
Caudle Green Gloucs 35 SO9410
Caulcott Beds 38 TL0042
Caulcott Oxon 49 SP5024
Cauldcots Tays 127 NO6547
Cauldhame Cent 116 NS6493
Cauldmill Border 109 NT5315
Cauldon Staffs 73 SK0749
Cauldon Lowe Staffs 73 SK0747
Cauldwell Derbys 73 SK2517
Caulkerbush D & G 92 NX9257
Caulside D & G 101 NY4480
Caundle Marsh Dorset 11 ST6713
Caunsall H & W 60 SO8581
Caunton Notts 75 SK7460
Causeway Hants 13 SU7422
Causeway End Cumb 87 SD4885
Causeway End D & G 99 NX4260
Causeway End Essex 40 TL6819
Causewayend Strath 108 NT0336
Causewayhead Cent 116 NS8095
Causewayhead Cumb 92 NY1253
Causey Park Nthumb 103 NZ1794
Causeyend Gramp 143 NJ9419
Cavendish Suffk 54 TL8046
Cavenham Suffk 53 TL7670
Caversfield Oxon 49 SP5825
Caversham Berks 24 SU7274
Caverswall Staffs 72 SJ9542
Caverton Mill Border 110 NT7425
Cavil Humb 84 SE7730
Cawdor Highld 140 NH8450
Cawkwell Lincs 77 TF2879
Cawood N York 83 SE5737
Cawsand Cnwll 6 SX4350
Cawston Norfk 66 TG1323
Cawston Warwks 50 SP4773
Cawthorn N York 90 SE7788
Cawthorne S York 82 SE2808
Caxton Cambs 52 TL3058
Caxton End Cambs 52 TL2759
Caxton End Cambs 52 TL3157
Caxton Gibbet Cambs 52 TL2960
Caynham Shrops 46 SO5573
Caythorpe Lincs 76 SK9348
Caythorpe Notts 63 SK6845
Cayton N York 91 TA0583
Ceannacroc Lodge Highld 131 NH2211
Ceciliford Gwent 34 SO5003
Cefn Gwent 34 ST2788
Cefn Berain Clwyd 70 SH9969
Cefn Byrle Powys 33 SN8311
Cefn Canel Clwyd 58 SJ2331
Cefn Coch Powys 58 SJ1026
Cefn Cribwr M Glam 33 SS8582
Cefn Cross M Glam 33 SS8682
Cefn Mably M Glam 34 ST2283
Cefn-brith Clwyd 70 SH9350
Cefn-bryn-brain Dyfed 32 SN7413
Cefn-coed-y-cymmer M Glam 33 SO0308
Cefn-ddwysarn Gwynd 70 SH9638
Cefn-Einion Shrops 58 SO2886
Cefn-mawr Clwyd 70 SJ2842
Cefn-y-bedd Clwyd 71 SJ3156
Cefn-y-pant Dyfed 31 SN1925
Cefneithin Dyfed 32 SN5513
Cefngorwydd Powys 45 SN9045
Cefnpennar M Glam 33 SO0300
Ceint Gwynd 68 SH4875
Cellan Dyfed 44 SN6149
Cellarhead Staffs 72 SJ9547
Cellerton Cumb 94 NY4925
Celynen Gwent 33 ST2195
Cemaes Gwynd 68 SH3793
Cemmaes Powys 57 SH8406
Cemmaes Road Powys 57 SH8104
Cenarth Dyfed 31 SN2641
Cerbyd Dyfed 30 SM8227
Ceres Fife 126 NO4011
Cerne Abbas Dorset 11 ST6601
Cerney Wick Gloucs 36 SU0796
Cerrigceinwen Gwynd 68 SH4274
Cerrigydrudion Clwyd 70 SH9548
Cess Norfk 67 TG4417
Ceunant Gwynd 69 SH5361
Chaceley Gloucs 47 SO8530
Chacewater Cnwll 3 SW7544
Chackmore Bucks 49 SP6835
Chacombe Nhants 49 SP4944
Chadbury H & W 47 SP0146
Chadderton Gt Man 79 SD9005
Chadderton Fold Gt Man 79 SD9006
Chaddesden Derbys 62 SK3836
Chaddesley Corbett H & W 60 SO8973
Chaddlehanger Devon 5 SX4678
Chaddleworth Berks 36 SU4178
Chadlington Oxon 36 SP3321
Chadshunt Warwks 48 SP3453
Chadwell Leics 63 SK7824
Chadwell Shrops 60 SJ7814
Chadwell End Beds 51 TL0865
Chadwell Heath Gt Lon 27 TQ4888
Chadwell St Mary Essex 40 TQ6478
Chadwick H & W 47 SO8369
Chadwick End W Mids 61 SP2073
Chadwick Green Mersyd 78 SJ5299
Chaffcombe Somset 10 ST3510
Chafford Hundred Essex 40 TQ6079
Chagford Devon 8 SX7087
Chailey E Susx 15 TQ3919
Chainbridge Cambs 27 TL4200
Chainhurst Kent 28 TQ7248
Chalbury Common Dorset 12 SU0206
Chaldon Surrey 27 TQ3155
Chaldon Herring or East Chaldon Dorset 11 SY7983
Chale IOW 13 SZ4877
Chale Green IOW 13 SZ4879
Chalfont Common Bucks 26 TQ0092
Chalfont St Giles Bucks 26 SU9893
Chalfont St Peter Bucks 26 TQ0090
Chalford Gloucs 35 SO8802
Chalford Oxon 37 SP7200
Chalford Wilts 22 ST8650
Chalgrove Beds 38 TL0127
Chalgrove Oxon 37 SU6396
Chalk Kent 28 TQ6773
Chalk End Essex 40 TL6310
Chalkhouse Green Berks 37 SU7178
Chalkway Somset 10 ST3707
Chalkwell Kent 28 TQ8963
Challaborough Devon 7 SX6544
Challacombe Devon 19 SS6940
Challock Lees Kent 28 TR0050
Chalmington Dorset 10 ST5900
Chalton Beds 38 TL0326
Chalton Beds 52 TL1450
Chalton Hants 13 SU7315
Chalvey Berks 26 SU9679
Chalvington E Susx 16 TQ5109
Chambers Green Kent 28 TQ9243
Chandler's Cross Herts 26 TQ0698
Chandler's Ford Hants 13 SU4319
Chandlers Cross H & W 47 SO7738
Channel's End Beds 51 TL1056
Chantry Somset 22 ST7146
Chantry Suffk 54 TM1443
Chapel Cumb 93 NY2231
Chapel Fife 117 NT2593
Chapel Allerton Somset 21 ST4050
Chapel Allerton W York 82 SE3037
Chapel Amble Cnwll 4 SW9975
Chapel Brampton Nhants 50 SP7266
Chapel Chorlton Staffs 72 SJ8137
Chapel Cross E Susx 16 TQ6120
Chapel End Beds 38 TL0542
Chapel End Beds 51 TL1058
Chapel End Cambs 52 TL1282
Chapel End Warwks 61 SP3393
Chapel Field Gt Man 79 SD7906
Chapel Green Warwks 61 SP2785
Chapel Green Warwks 49 SP4660
Chapel Haddlesey N York 83 SE5826
Chapel Hill Gramp 143 NK0635
Chapel Hill Gwent 59 SO5399
Chapel Hill Lincs 76 TF2054
Chapel Hill N York 83 SE3446
Chapel Lawn Shrops 46 SO3176
Chapel Leigh Somset 20 ST1229
Chapel le Dale N York 88 SD7377
Chapel Milton Derbys 74 SK0581
Chapel of Garioch Gramp 142 NJ7124
Chapel Rossan D & G 98 NX1044
Chapel Row Berks 24 SU5769

Chapel Row
Comhampton

Chapel Row *E Susx* 16 TQ6312
Chapel Row *Essex* 40 TL7900
Chapel St Leonards *Lincs* 77 TF5672
Chapel Stile *Cumb* 86 NY3205
Chapel Town *Cnwll* 3 SW8855
Chapel-en-le-Frith *Derbys* 74 SK0580
Chapelbridge *Cambs* 64 TL2993
Chapelend Way *Essex* 53 TL7039
Chapelgate *Lincs* 65 TF4124
Chapelhall *Strath* 116 NS7862
Chapelknowe *D & G* 101 NY3173
Chapels *Cumb* 86 SD2383
Chapelton *Devon* 19 SS5726
Chapelton *Strath* 116 NS6848
Chapelton *Tays* 127 NO6247
Chapeltown *Gramp* 141 NJ2320
Chapeltown *Lancs* 81 SD7315
Chapeltown *S York* 74 SK3596
Chapmans Well *Devon* 5 SX3593
Chapmanslade *Wilts* 22 ST8247
Chapmore End *Herts* 39 TL3216
Chappel *Essex* 40 TL8928
Charaton *Cnwll* 5 SX3069
Chard *Somset* 10 ST3208
Chard Junction *Somset* 10 ST3404
Chardleigh Green *Somset* 10 ST3110
Chardstock *Devon* 10 ST3004
Charfield *Avon* 35 ST7292
Chargrove *Gloucs* 35 SO9219
Charing *Kent* 28 TQ9549
Charing Heath *Kent* 28 TQ9249
Charing Hill *Kent* 28 TQ9550
Charingworth *Gloucs* 48 SP1939
Charlbury *Oxon* 36 SP3519
Charlcombe *Avon* 22 ST7467
Charlcutt *Wilts* 35 ST9875
Charlecote *Warwks* 48 SP2656
Charles *Devon* 19 SS6832
Charles Tye *Suffk* 54 TM0252
Charleshill *Surrey* 25 SU8944
Charleston *Tays* 126 NO3845
Charlestown *Cnwll* 3 SX0351
Charlestown *Derbys* 74 SK0392
Charlestown *Dorset* 11 SY6579
Charlestown *Fife* 117 NT0683
Charlestown *Gramp* 135 NJ9300
Charlestown *Gt Man* 79 SD8100
Charlestown *Highld* 144 NG8174
Charlestown *Highld* 140 NH6448
Charlestown *Lincs* 63 SK9844
Charlestown *W York* 82 SD9726
Charlestown *W York* 82 SE1638
Charlesworth *Derbys* 79 SK0092
Charlinch *Somset* 20 ST2338
Charlton *Gt Lon* 27 TQ4178
Charlton *H & W* 60 SO8371
Charlton *H & W* 47 SP0045
Charlton *Hants* 23 SU3547
Charlton *Herts* 39 TL1728
Charlton *Nhants* 49 SP5335
Charlton *Nthumb* 102 NY8184
Charlton *Oxon* 36 SU4088
Charlton *Shrops* 59 SJ5911
Charlton *Somset* 20 ST2926
Charlton *Somset* 21 ST6343
Charlton *W Susx* 14 SU8812
Charlton *Wilts* 22 ST9022
Charlton *Wilts* 35 ST9588
Charlton *Wilts* 23 SU1156
Charlton *Wilts* 23 SU1723
Charlton Abbots *Gloucs* 48 SP0324
Charlton Adam *Somset* 21 ST5328
Charlton Hill *Shrops* 59 SJ5807
Charlton Horethorne *Somset* 22 ST6623
Charlton Kings *Gloucs* 35 SO9621
Charlton Mackrell *Somset* 21 ST5328
Charlton Marshall *Dorset* 11 ST9004
Charlton Musgrove *Somset* 22 ST7229
Charlton on the Hill *Dorset* 11 ST8903
Charlton-on-Otmoor *Oxon* 37 SP5616
Charlwood *Hants* 24 SU6731
Charlwood *Surrey* 15 TQ2441
Charminster *Dorset* 11 SY6792
Charmouth *Dorset* 10 SY3693
Charndon *Bucks* 49 SP6724
Charney Bassett *Oxon* 36 SU3894
Charnock Green *Lancs* 81 SD5516
Charnock Richard *Lancs* 81 SD5515
Charsfield *Suffk* 55 TM2556
Chart Corner *Kent* 28 TQ7950
Chart Hill *Kent* 28 TQ7949
Chart Sutton *Kent* 28 TQ8049
Charter Alley *Hants* 24 SU5958
Charterhall *Border* 110 NT7647
Charterhouse *Somset* 21 ST4955
Chartershall *Cent* 116 NS7990
Charterville Allotments *Oxon* 36 SP3110
Chartham *Kent* 29 TR1054
Chartham Hatch *Kent* 29 TR1056
Charton *Surrey* 26 TQ0869
Chartridge *Bucks* 38 SP9303
Chartway Street *Kent* 28 TQ8350
Charwelton *Nhants* 49 SP5356
Chase Terrace *Staffs* 61 SK0309
Chasetown *Staffs* 61 SK0408
Chastleton *Oxon* 48 SP2429
Chasty *Devon* 18 SS3402
Chatburn *Lancs* 81 SD7644
Chatcull *Staffs* 72 SJ7934
Chatham *Gwent* 33 ST2188
Chatham *Kent* 28 TQ7567
Chatham Green *Essex* 40 TL7115
Chathill *Nthumb* 111 NU1827
Chatley *H & W* 47 SO8561
Chattenden *Kent* 28 TQ7572
Chatter End *Essex* 39 TL4725
Chatteris *Cambs* 52 TL3985
Chatterton *Lancs* 81 SD7918
Chattisham *Suffk* 54 TM0942
Chatto *Border* 110 NT7717
Chatton *Nthumb* 111 NU0528
Chawleigh *Devon* 19 SS7112
Chawley *Oxon* 37 SP4604
Chawston *Beds* 52 TL1556
Chawton *Hants* 24 SU7037
Chaxhill *Gloucs* 35 SO7414
Chazey Heath *Oxon* 37 SU6977
Cheadle *Gt Man* 79 SJ8688
Cheadle *Staffs* 73 SK0043
Cheadle Heath *Gt Man* 79 SJ8789
Cheadle Hulme *Gt Man* 79 SJ8786
Cheam *Gt Lon* 26 TQ2463
Cheapside *Berks* 25 SU9469
Chearsley *Bucks* 37 SP7110
Chebsey *Staffs* 72 SJ8528
Checkendon *Oxon* 37 SU6683
Checkley *Ches* 72 SJ7346
Checkley *Staffs* 73 SK0237
Checkley Green *Ches* 72 SJ7245
Chedburgh *Suffk* 53 TL7957
Cheddar *Somset* 21 ST4553
Cheddington *Bucks* 38 SP9217
Cheddleton *Staffs* 72 SJ9752
Cheddleton Heath *Staffs* 72 SJ9853
Cheddon Fitzpaine *Somset* 20 ST2427
Chedglow *Wilts* 35 ST9493
Chedgrave *Norfk* 67 TM3699
Chedington *Dorset* 10 ST4805
Chediston *Suffk* 55 TM3577
Chediston Green *Suffk* 55 TM3578
Chedworth *Gloucs* 36 SP0512
Chedzoy *Somset* 21 ST3437
Cheesden *Gt Man* 81 SD8216
Cheeseman's Green *Kent* 28 TR0338
Cheetham Hill *Gt Man* 79 SD8401
Cheetwood *Gt Man* 79 SJ8399
Cheldon *Devon* 19 SS7313
Chelford *Ches* 79 SJ8174
Chellaston *Derbys* 62 SK3730
Chellington *Beds* 51 SP9555
Chelmarsh *Shrops* 60 SO7288
Chelmick *Shrops* 59 SO4791
Chelmondiston *Suffk* 55 TM2037
Chelmorton *Derbys* 74 SK1169
Chelmsford *Essex* 40 TL7007
Chelmsley Wood *W Mids* 61 SP1887
Chelsea *Gt Lon* 27 TQ2778
Chelsfield *Gt Lon* 27 TQ4864
Chelsham *Surrey* 27 TQ3758
Chelston *Somset* 20 ST1521
Chelsworth *Suffk* 54 TL9748
Cheltenham *Gloucs* 35 SO9422
Chelveston *Nhants* 51 SP9969
Chelvey *Avon* 21 ST4668
Chelwood *Avon* 21 ST6361
Chelwood Common *E Susx* 15 TQ4128
Chelwood Gate *E Susx* 15 TQ4130
Chelworth *Wilts* 35 ST9694
Chelworth Lower Green *Wilts* 36 SU0892
Chelworth Upper Green *Wilts* 36 SU0893
Cheney Longville *Shrops* 59 SO4284
Chenies *Bucks* 26 TQ0198
Chepstow *Gwent* 34 ST5393
Chequerbent *Gt Man* 79 SD6706
Chequers Corner *Norfk* 65 TF4908
Cherhill *Wilts* 36 SU0370
Cherington *Gloucs* 35 ST9098
Cherington *Warwks* 48 SP2936
Cheriton *Devon* 19 SS7346
Cheriton *Hants* 24 SU5828
Cheriton *Kent* 29 TR2037
Cheriton *W Glam* 32 SS4593
Cheriton Bishop *Devon* 8 SX7793
Cheriton Fitzpaine *Devon* 9 SS8606
Cheriton or Stackpole Elidor *Dyfed* 30 SR9897
Cherrington *Shrops* 72 SJ6619
Cherry Burton *Humb* 84 SE9841
Cherry Hinton *Cambs* 53 TL4856
Cherry Orchard *H & W* 47 SO8553
Cherry Willingham *Lincs* 76 TF0272
Chertsey *Surrey* 26 TQ0466
Cheselbourne *Dorset* 11 SY7699
Chesham *Bucks* 26 SP9601
Chesham *Gt Man* 81 SD8012
Chesham Bois *Bucks* 26 SU9699
Cheshunt *Herts* 27 TL3502
Chesley *Kent* 28 TQ8563
Cheslyn Hay *Staffs* 60 SJ9707
Chessetts Wood *Warwks* 61 SP1873
Chessington *Surrey* 26 TQ1863
Chester *Ches* 71 SJ4066
Chester Moor *Dur* 96 NZ2649
Chester-le-Street *T & W* 96 NZ2751
Chesterblade *Somset* 22 ST6641
Chesterfield *Derbys* 74 SK3871
Chesterfield *Staffs* 61 SK0905
Chesterhill *Loth* 118 NT3764
Chesters *Border* 110 NT6022
Chesters *Border* 110 NT6210
Chesterton *Cambs* 64 TL1295
Chesterton *Cambs* 53 TL4660
Chesterton *Gloucs* 35 SP0100
Chesterton *Oxon* 37 SP5621
Chesterton *Shrops* 60 SO7897
Chesterton *Staffs* 72 SJ8349
Chesterton Green *Warwks* 48 SP3558
Chesterwood *Nthumb* 102 NY8364
Chestfield *Kent* 29 TR1365
Chestnut Street *Kent* 28 TQ8763
Cheston *Devon* 7 SX6858
Cheswardine *Shrops* 72 SJ7130
Cheswell *Shrops* 72 SJ7116
Cheswick *Nthumb* 111 NU0346
Cheswick Green *W Mids* 61 SP1376
Chetnote *Dorset* 10 ST6008
Chettiscombe *Devon* 9 SS9614
Chettisham *Cambs* 53 TL5483
Chettle *Dorset* 11 ST9513
Chetton *Shrops* 60 SO6690
Chetwode *Bucks* 49 SP6429
Chetwynd *Shrops* 72 SJ7321
Chetwynd Aston *Shrops* 72 SJ7517
Cheveley *Cambs* 53 TL6861
Chevening *Kent* 27 TQ4857
Cheverton *IOW* 13 SZ4583
Chevington *Suffk* 53 TL7859
Chevington Drift *Nthumb* 103 NZ2598
Chevithorne *Devon* 9 SS9715
Chew Magna *Avon* 21 ST5763
Chew Moor *Gt Man* 79 SD6607
Chew Stoke *Avon* 21 ST5561
Chewton Keynsham *Avon* 21 ST6566
Chewton Mendip *Somset* 21 ST5953
Chichacott *Devon* 8 SX6096
Chicheley *Bucks* 38 SP9046
Chichester *W Susx* 14 SU8604
Chickerell *Dorset* 11 SY6480
Chickering *Suffk* 55 TM2176
Chicklade *Wilts* 22 ST9134
Chickward *H & W* 46 SO2853
Chidden *Hants* 13 SU6517
Chiddingfold *Surrey* 14 SU9635
Chiddingly *E Susx* 16 TQ5414
Chiddingstone *Kent* 16 TQ5045
Chiddingstone Causeway *Kent* 16 TQ5246
Chideock *Dorset* 10 SY4292
Chidham *W Susx* 14 SU7903
Chidswell *W York* 82 SE2623
Chieveley *Berks* 24 SU4774
Chignall Smealy *Essex* 40 TL6611
Chignall St James *Essex* 40 TL6610
Chigwell *Essex* 27 TQ4494
Chigwell Row *Essex* 27 TQ4693
Chilbolton *Hants* 23 SU3940
Chilcomb *Hants* 24 SU5028
Chilcombe *Dorset* 10 SY5291
Chilcompton *Somset* 21 ST6451
Chilcote *Leics* 61 SK2811
Child Okeford *Dorset* 11 ST8312
Child's Ercall *Shrops* 72 SJ6625
Childer Thornton *Ches* 71 SJ3677
Childrey *Oxon* 36 SU3687
Childswickham *H & W* 48 SP0738
Childwall *Mersyd* 78 SJ4189
Childwick Bury *Herts* 38 TL1410
Childwick Green *Herts* 38 TL1410
Chilfrome *Dorset* 10 SY5898
Chilgrove *W Susx* 14 SU8314
Chilham *Kent* 29 TR0653
Chilhampton *Wilts* 23 SU0933
Chilla *Devon* 18 SS4402
Chillaton *Devon* 5 SX4381
Chillenden *Kent* 29 TR2753
Chillerton *IOW* 13 SZ4883
Chillesford *Suffk* 55 TM3852
Chillingham *Nthumb* 111 NU0525
Chillington *Devon* 7 SX7942
Chillington *Somset* 10 ST3811
Chilmark *Wilts* 22 ST9732
Chilmington Green *Kent* 28 TQ9840
Chilson *Oxon* 36 SP3119
Chilsworthy *Cnwll* 5 SX4172
Chilsworthy *Devon* 18 SS3206
Chiltern Green *Beds* 38 TL1319
Chilthorne Domer *Somset* 21 ST5219
Chilton *Bucks* 37 SP6811
Chilton *Devon* 9 SS8604
Chilton *Kent* 29 TR2743
Chilton *Oxon* 37 SU4885
Chilton *Suffk* 54 TL8842
Chilton Candover *Hants* 24 SU5940
Chilton Cantelo *Somset* 21 ST5722
Chilton Foliat *Wilts* 36 SU3170
Chilton Polden *Somset* 21 ST3740
Chilton Street *Suffk* 53 TL7546
Chilton Trinity *Somset* 20 ST2939
Chilwell *Notts* 62 SK5135
Chilworth *Hants* 13 SU4018
Chilworth *Surrey* 14 TQ0347
Chimney *Oxon* 36 SP3501
Chineham *Hants* 24 SU6555
Chingford *Gt Lon* 27 TQ3894
Chinley *Derbys* 74 SK0482
Chinnor *Oxon* 37 SP7501
Chipchase Castle *Nthumb* 102 NY8775
Chipnall *Shrops* 72 SJ7231
Chippenham *Cambs* 53 TL6669
Chippenham *Wilts* 35 ST9173
Chipperfield *Herts* 26 TL0401
Chipping *Herts* 39 TL3531
Chipping *Lancs* 81 SD6243
Chipping Campden *Gloucs* 48 SP1539
Chipping Hill *Essex* 40 TL8215
Chipping Norton *Oxon* 48 SP3127
Chipping Ongar *Essex* 39 TL5503
Chipping Sodbury *Avon* 35 ST7282
Chipping Warden *Nhants* 49 SP4948
Chipstable *Somset* 20 ST0427
Chipstead *Kent* 27 TQ5056
Chipstead *Surrey* 27 TQ2756
Chirbury *Shrops* 58 SO2698
Chirk *Clwyd* 58 SJ2837
Chirnside *Border* 119 NT8756
Chirnsidebridge *Border* 119 NT8556
Chirton *Wilts* 23 SU0757
Chisbury *Wilts* 23 SU2766
Chiselborough *Somset* 10 ST4614
Chiseldon *Wilts* 36 SU1880
Chisholme *Border* 109 NT4112
Chislehampton *Oxon* 37 SU5999
Chislehurst *Gt Lon* 27 TQ4470
Chislet *Kent* 29 TR2264
Chisley *W York* 82 SE0028
Chiswellgreen *Herts* 38 TL1304
Chiswick *Gt Lon* 26 TQ2078
Chiswick End *Cambs* 52 TL3745
Chisworth *Derbys* 79 SJ9991
Chitcombe *E Susx* 17 TQ8120
Chithurst *W Susx* 14 SU8423
Chittering *Cambs* 53 TL4969
Chitterne *Wilts* 22 ST9843
Chittlehamholt *Devon* 19 SS6520
Chittlehampton *Devon* 19 SS6325
Chittlehampton *Devon* 19 SS6511
Chittoe *Wilts* 22 ST9566
Chivelstone *Devon* 7 SX7838
Chivenor *Devon* 19 SS5034
Chlenry *D & G* 98 NX1260
Chobham *Surrey* 25 SU9762
Cholderton *Wilts* 23 SU2242
Cholesbury *Bucks* 38 SP9307
Chollerford *Nthumb* 102 NY9170
Chollerton *Nthumb* 102 NY9372
Cholsey *Oxon* 37 SU5886
Cholstrey *H & W* 46 SO4659
Chop Gate *N York* 90 SE5599
Choppington *T & W* 103 NZ2484
Chopwell *T & W* 95 NZ1158
Chorley *Ches* 71 SJ5751
Chorley *Lancs* 81 SD5817
Chorley *Shrops* 60 SO6983
Chorley *Staffs* 61 SK0710
Chorleywood *Herts* 26 TQ0396
Chorleywood West *Herts* 26 TQ0296
Chorlton *Ches* 72 SJ7250
Chorlton Lane *Ches* 71 SJ4547
Chorlton-cum-Hardy *Gt Man* 79 SJ8193
Choulton *Shrops* 59 SO3788
Chowley *Ches* 71 SJ4756
Chrishall *Essex* 39 TL4439
Chrisswell *Strath* 114 NS2274
Christchurch *Cambs* 65 TL4996
Christchurch *Dorset* 12 SZ1592
Christian Malford *Wilts* 35 ST9678
Christleton *Ches* 71 SJ4465
Christmas Common *Oxon* 37 SU7193
Christon *Avon* 21 ST3757
Christon Bank *Nthumb* 111 NU2123
Christow *Devon* 8 SX8385
Christskirk *Gramp* 142 NJ6027
Chuck Hatch *E Susx* 16 TQ4733
Chudleigh *Devon* 9 SX8679
Chudleigh Knighton *Devon* 8 SX8477
Chulmleigh *Devon* 19 SS6814
Chunal *Derbys* 74 SK0390
Church *Lancs* 81 SD7429
Church Ashton *Shrops* 72 SJ7317
Church Brampton *Nhants* 50 SP7165
Church Brough *Cumb* 95 NY7913
Church Broughton *Derbys* 73 SK2033
Church Crookham *Hants* 25 SU8051
Church Eaton *Staffs* 72 SJ8417
Church End *Beds* 38 SP9832
Church End *Beds* 38 SP9921
Church End *Beds* 38 TL0334
Church End *Beds* 51 TL0558
Church End *Beds* 51 TL1058
Church End *Beds* 39 TL1937
Church End *Cambs* 51 TL0873
Church End *Cambs* 52 TL2082
Church End *Cambs* 52 TL3278
Church End *Cambs* 53 TL4857
Church End *Essex* 40 TL6223
Church End *Essex* 40 TL7228
Church End *Essex* 40 TL7316
Church End *Gt Lon* 26 TQ2490
Church End *Hants* 24 SU6756
Church End *Herts* 38 TL1011
Church End *Herts* 39 TL2630
Church End *Herts* 39 TL4422
Church End *Lincs* 64 TF2234
Church End *Lincs* 77 TF4295
Church End *Warwks* 61 SP2490
Church End *Warwks* 61 SP2992
Church Enstone *Oxon* 48 SP3725
Church Fenton *N York* 83 SE5136
Church Green *Devon* 9 SY1796
Church Gresley *Derbys* 73 SK2918
Church Hanborough *Oxon* 36 SP4213
Church Hill *Ches* 72 SJ6465
Church Hill *Staffs* 60 SK0011
Church Houses *N York* 90 SE6697
Church Knowle *Dorset* 11 SY9481
Church Laneham *Notts* 75 SK8176
Church Langton *Leics* 50 SP7293
Church Lawford *Warwks* 50 SP4576
Church Lawton *Staffs* 72 SJ8255
Church Leigh *Staffs* 73 SK0235
Church Lench *H & W* 48 SP0251
Church Mayfield *Staffs* 73 SK1544
Church Minshull *Ches* 72 SJ6660
Church Norton *W Susx* 14 SZ8795
Church Preen *Shrops* 59 SO5498
Church Pulverbatch *Shrops* 59 SJ4303
Church Stoke *Powys* 58 SO2794
Church Stowe *Nhants* 49 SP6357
Church Street *Essex* 53 TL7943
Church Street *Kent* 28 TQ7174
Church Street *Suffk* 55 TM4883
Church Stretton *Shrops* 59 SO4593
Church Town *Humb* 84 SE7806
Church Village *M Glam* 33 ST0885
Church Warsop *Notts* 75 SK5668
Church Wilne *Derbys* 62 SK4431
Churcham *Gloucs* 35 SO7618
Churchbridge *Staffs* 60 SJ9808
Churchdown *Gloucs* 35 SO8819
Churchend *Essex* 41 TR0093
Churchfield *W Mids* 60 SP0192
Churchgate *Herts* 27 TL3402
Churchgate Street *Essex* 39 TL4811
Churchill *Avon* 21 ST4459
Churchill *Devon* 19 SS5940
Churchill *Devon* 10 ST2902
Churchill *H & W* 60 SO8879
Churchill *H & W* 47 SO9253
Churchill *Oxon* 48 SP2824
Churchinford *Devon* 9 ST2112
Churchover *Warwks* 50 SP5180
Churchstanton *Somset* 9 ST1914
Churchstow *Devon* 7 SX7145
Churchthorpe *Lincs* 77 TF3297
Churchtown *Derbys* 74 SK2662
Churchtown *Devon* 19 SS6744
Churchtown *Lancs* 80 SD3240
Churchtown *Lancs* 80 SD4843
Churchtown *Mersyd* 80 SD3618
Churnsike Lodge *Nthumb* 102 NY6677
Churston Ferrers *Devon* 7 SX9056
Churt *Surrey* 25 SU8538
Churton *Ches* 71 SJ4156
Churwell *W York* 82 SE2729
Chute Lodge *Wilts* 23 SU3051
Chwilog *Gwynd* 56 SH4338
Chyandour *Cnwll* 2 SW4731
Chyanvounder *Cnwll* 2 SW6522
Chyeowling *Cnwll* 3 SW7941
Chyvarloe *Cnwll* 2 SW6523
Cil *Powys* 58 SJ1701
Cilcain *Clwyd* 70 SJ1765
Cilcennin *Dyfed* 44 SN5260
Cilcewydd *Powys* 58 SJ2204
Cilfrew *W Glam* 32 SN7700
Cilfynydd *M Glam* 33 ST0891
Cilgerran *Dyfed* 31 SN1942
Cilgwyn *Dyfed* 44 SN7429
Ciliau-Aeron *Dyfed* 44 SN5057
Cilmaengwyn *W Glam* 32 SN7405
Cilmery *Powys* 45 SO0051
Cilrhedyn *Dyfed* 31 SN2834
Cilsan *Dyfed* 32 SN5922
Ciltalgarth *Gwynd* 57 SH8940
Cilycwm *Dyfed* 44 SN7539
Cimla *W Glam* 32 SS7696
Cinder Hill *W Mids* 60 SO9294
Cinderford *Gloucs* 35 SO6514
Cippenham *Bucks* 26 SU9480
Cirencester *Gloucs* 35 SP0201
Citadilla *N York* 89 SE2299
City *S Glam* 33 SS9878
City Dulas *Gwynd* 68 SH4687
Clabhach *Strath* 120 NM1858
Clachaig *Strath* 114 NS1181
Clachan *Highld* 137 NG5436
Clachan *S Glam* 113 NR7656
Clachan *Strath* 122 NM7819
Clachan *Strath* 122 NM8543
Clachan Mor *Strath* 120 NL9847
Clachan-a-Luib *W Isls* 154 NF8163
Clachan-Seil *Strath* 122 NM7718
Clachaneasy *D & G* 98 NX3574
Clachnaharry *Highld* 140 NH6446
Clachtoll *Highld* 148 NC0427
Clackavoid *Tays* 133 NO1463
Clackmannan *Cent* 116 NS9191
Clackmarass *Gramp* 141 NJ2458
Clacton-on-Sea *Essex* 41 TM1715
Cladich *Strath* 123 NN0921
Cladswell *H & W* 48 SP0558
Claggan *Highld* 122 NM7049
Claigan *Highld* 136 NG2354
Clandown *Avon* 22 ST6855
Clanfield *Hants* 13 SU6916
Clanfield *Oxon* 36 SP2801
Clannaborough *Devon* 8 SS7402
Clanville *Hants* 23 SU3148
Clanville *Somset* 21 ST6233
Claonaig *Strath* 113 NR8656
Clap Hill *Kent* 28 TR0537
Clapgate *Dorset* 11 SU0102
Clapgate *Herts* 39 TL4424
Clapham *Beds* 38 TL0352
Clapham *Devon* 9 SX8987
Clapham *Gt Lon* 27 TQ2975
Clapham *N York* 88 SD7469
Clapham *W Susx* 14 TQ0906
Clapham Folly *Beds* 38 TL0252
Clappersgate *Cumb* 87 NY3603
Clapton *Somset* 10 ST4106
Clapton *Somset* 21 ST6453
Clapton *Somset* 22 ST6852
Clapton-in-Gordano *Avon* 34 ST4773
Clapton-on-the-Hill *Gloucs* 36 SP1617
Clapworthy *Devon* 19 SS6724
Clarach *Dyfed* 43 SN6084
Claravale *T & W* 103 NZ1364
Clarbeston *Dyfed* 30 SN0521
Clarbeston Road *Dyfed* 30 SN0121
Clarborough *Notts* 75 SK7383
Clare *Suffk* 53 TL7745
Clarebrand *D & G* 99 NX7665
Claredon Park *Leics* 62 SK6002
Clarencefield *D & G* 100 NY0968
Clarewood *Nthumb* 103 NZ0169
Clarilaw *Border* 109 NT5218
Clark's Green *Surrey* 15 TQ1739
Clarken Green *Hants* 24 SU5651
Clarkston *Strath* 115 NS5757
Clashmore *Highld* 148 NC0331
Clashmore *Highld* 146 NH7489
Clashnessie *Highld* 148 NC0530
Clashnoir *Gramp* 141 NJ2222
Clathy *Tays* 125 NN9920
Clathymore *Tays* 125 NO0121
Clatt *Gramp* 142 NJ5326
Clatter *Powys* 58 SN9994
Clatterford End *Essex* 40 TL6113
Clatworthy *Somset* 20 ST0531
Claughton *Lancs* 80 SD5342
Claughton *Lancs* 87 SD5566
Claughton *Mersyd* 78 SJ3088
Clavelshay *Somset* 20 ST2531
Claverdon *Warwks* 48 SP1965
Claverham *Avon* 21 ST4566
Clavering *Essex* 39 TL4731
Claverley *Shrops* 60 SO7993
Claverton *Avon* 22 ST7864
Claverton Down *Avon* 22 ST7763
Clawdd-coch *S Glam* 33 ST0577
Clawdd-newydd *Clwyd* 70 SJ0852
Clawthorpe *Cumb* 87 SD5377
Clawton *Devon* 18 SX3599
Claxby *Lincs* 76 TF1194
Claxby *Lincs* 77 TF4571
Claxton *N York* 90 SE6959
Claxton *Norfk* 67 TG3303
Clay Common *Suffk* 55 TM4681
Clay Coton *Nhants* 50 SP5976
Clay Cross *Derbys* 74 SK3963
Clay End *Herts* 39 TL3024
Claybrooke Magna *Leics* 50 SP4988
Claydon *Oxon* 49 SP4549
Claydon *Suffk* 54 TM1349
Claygate *D & G* 101 NY3979
Claygate *Kent* 28 TQ7144
Claygate *Surrey* 26 TQ1563
Claygate Cross *Kent* 27 TQ6155
Clayhanger *Devon* 20 ST0222
Clayhanger *W Mids* 61 SK0404
Clayhidon *Devon* 9 ST1615
Clayhill *E Susx* 17 TQ8323
Clayhill *Hants* 12 SU3006
Clayhithe *Cambs* 53 TL5064
Clayock *Highld* 151 ND1659
Claypit Hill *Cambs* 52 TL3554
Claypits *Gloucs* 35 SO7606
Claypole *Lincs* 76 SK8449
Claythorpe *Lincs* 77 TF4178
Clayton *S York* 83 SE4507
Clayton *W Susx* 15 TQ2914
Clayton *W York* 82 SE1231
Clayton Green *Lancs* 81 SD5723
Clayton West *W York* 82 SE2510
Clayton-le-Moors *Lancs* 81 SD7530
Clayton-le-Woods *Lancs* 81 SD5622
Clayworth *Notts* 75 SK7387
Cleadale *Highld* 128 NM4789
Cleadon *T & W* 96 NZ3862
Clearbrook *Devon* 6 SX5265
Clearwell *Gloucs* 34 SO5608
Clearwell Meend *Gloucs* 34 SO5808
Cleasby *N York* 89 NZ2512
Cleat *Ork* 155 ND4584
Cleatlam *Dur* 95 NZ1118
Cleator *Cumb* 92 NY0113
Cleator Moor *Cumb* 92 NY0115
Cleckheaton *W York* 82 SE1825
Clee St Margaret *Shrops* 59 SO5684
Cleedownton *Shrops* 59 SO5880
Cleehill *Shrops* 46 SO5975
Cleekhimin *Strath* 116 NS7658
Cleestanton *Shrops* 46 SO5779
Cleethorpes *Humb* 85 TA3008
Cleeton St Mary *Shrops* 46 SO6178
Cleeve *Avon* 21 ST4666
Cleeve *Oxon* 37 SU6081
Cleeve Hill *Gloucs* 47 SO9827
Cleeve Prior *H & W* 48 SP0849
Cleghornie *Loth* 118 NT5983
Clehonger *H & W* 46 SO4637
Cleish *Tays* 117 NT0998
Cleland *Strath* 116 NS7958
Clement Street *Kent* 27 TQ5370
Clement's End *Beds* 38 TL0214
Clenamacrie *Strath* 122 NM9228
Clench Common *Wilts* 23 SU1765
Clenchwarton *Norfk* 65 TF5920
Clent *H & W* 60 SO9279
Clenterty *Gramp* 142 NJ7760
Cleobury Mortimer *Shrops* 60 SO6775
Cleobury North *Shrops* 59 SO6286
Cleongart *Strath* 105 NR6734
Clephanton *Highld* 140 NH8150
Clerkhill *D & G* 101 NY2697
Cleuch Head *Border* 110 NT5910
Cleuch-head *D & G* 108 NS8200
Clevancy *Wilts* 36 SU0575
Clevedon *Avon* 34 ST4171
Cleveleys *Lancs* 80 SD3143
Clevelode *H & W* 47 SO8347
Cleverton *Wilts* 35 ST9785
Clewer *Somset* 21 ST4351
Cley next the Sea *Norfk* 66 TG0444
Cliburn *Cumb* 94 NY5824
Cliddesden *Hants* 24 SU6349
Cliff *Warwks* 61 SP2197
Cliff End *E Susx* 17 TQ8813
Cliffe *Dur* 96 NZ2115
Cliffe *Kent* 28 TQ7376
Cliffe *Lancs* 81 SD7333
Cliffe *N York* 83 SE6631
Cliffe Woods *Kent* 28 TQ7373
Clifford *H & W* 46 SO2445
Clifford *W York* 83 SE4344
Clifford Chambers *Warwks* 48 SP1952
Clifford's Mesne *Gloucs* 47 SO7023
Cliffsend *Kent* 29 TR3464
Clifton *Avon* 34 ST5773
Clifton *Beds* 39 TL1639
Clifton *Cent* 123 NN3231
Clifton *Cumb* 94 NY5326
Clifton *Derbys* 73 SK1644
Clifton *Gt Man* 79 SD7703
Clifton *H & W* 47 SO8446
Clifton *Lancs* 80 SD4630
Clifton *N York* 83 SE5953
Clifton *Notts* 62 SK5434
Clifton *Nthumb* 103 NZ2082
Clifton *Oxon* 49 SP4931
Clifton *S York* 75 SK5296
Clifton *W York* 82 SE1622
Clifton *W York* 82 SE1948
Clifton Campville *Staffs* 61 SK2510
Clifton Hampden *Oxon* 37 SU5495
Clifton Reynes *Bucks* 38 SP9051
Clifton upon Dunsmore *Warwks* 50 SP5376
Clifton upon Teme *H & W* 47 SO7161
Cliftonville *Kent* 29 TR3771
Climping *W Susx* 14 SU9902
Clink *Somset* 22 ST7948
Clint *N York* 89 SE2659
Clint Green *Norfk* 66 TG0210
Clinterty *Gramp* 135 NJ8311
Clintmains *Border* 110 NT6132
Clipiau *Gwynd* 57 SH8410
Clippesby *Norfk* 67 TG4214
Clipsham *Leics* 63 SK9716
Clipston *Nhants* 50 SP7181
Clipston *Notts* 63 SK6334
Clipstone *Beds* 38 SP9426
Clitheroe *Lancs* 81 SD7441
Clive *Shrops* 59 SJ5124
Cloatley *Wilts* 35 ST9890
Clocaenog *Clwyd* 70 SJ0854
Clochan *Gramp* 142 NJ4060
Clochtow *Tays* 127 NO4852
Clock Face *Mersyd* 78 SJ5291
Cloddiau *Powys* 58 SJ2009
Clodock *H & W* 46 SO3227
Cloford *Somset* 22 ST7244
Clola *Gramp* 143 NK0043
Clophill *Beds* 38 TL0838
Clopton *Nhants* 51 TL0680
Clopton *Suffk* 55 TM2253
Clopton Corner *Suffk* 55 TM2254
Clopton Green *Suffk* 53 TL7655
Clopton Green *Suffk* 54 TL9759
Clos du Valle *Guern* 152 GN5412
Closeburn *D & G* 100 NX8992
Closeburnmill *D & G* 100 NX9094
Closeclark *IOM* 153 SC2775
Closworth *Somset* 10 ST5610
Clothall *Herts* 39 TL2731
Clotton *Ches* 71 SJ5264
Cloudesley Bush *Warwks* 50 SP4686
Clough *Gt Man* 79 SD9408
Clough Foot *W York* 81 SD9123
Clough Head *W York* 82 SE0918
Cloughton *N York* 91 TA0194
Cloughton Newlands *N York* 91 TA0096
Clousta *Shet* 155 HU3057
Clova *Tays* 134 NO3273
Clovelly *Devon* 18 SS3124
Clovenfords *Border* 109 NT4536
Clovulin *Highld* 130 NN0063
Clow Bridge *Lancs* 81 SD8228
Clowne *Derbys* 75 SK4875
Clows Top *H & W* 60 SO7172
Cloy *Clwyd* 71 SJ3943
Cluanie Inn *Highld* 130 NH0711
Cluanie Lodge *Highld* 130 NH0910
Clubworthy *Cnwll* 5 SX2792
Clugston *D & G* 98 NX3557
Clun *Shrops* 59 SO3080
Clunas *Highld* 140 NH8846
Clunbury *Shrops* 59 SO3780
Clune *Highld* 140 NH7925
Clunes *Highld* 131 NN1988
Clungunford *Shrops* 46 SO3978
Clunie *Gramp* 142 NJ6350
Clunie *Tays* 126 NO1043
Clunton *Shrops* 59 SO3381
Clutton *Avon* 21 ST6259
Clutton *Ches* 71 SJ4654
Clutton Hill *Avon* 21 ST6359
Clwt-y-bont *Gwynd* 69 SH5762
Clydach *Gwent* 34 SO2213
Clydach *W Glam* 32 SN6800
Clydach Vale *M Glam* 33 SS9792
Clydebank *Strath* 115 NS4970
Clydey *Dyfed* 31 SN2535
Clyffe Pypard *Wilts* 36 SU0777
Clynder *Strath* 114 NS2484
Clynderwen *Dyfed* 31 SN1219
Clyne *W Glam* 32 SN8000
Clynnog-fawr *Gwynd* 68 SH4149
Clyro *Powys* 45 SO2143
Clyst Honiton *Devon* 9 SX9893
Clyst Hydon *Devon* 9 ST0301
Clyst St George *Devon* 9 SX9888
Clyst St Lawrence *Devon* 9 ST0200
Clyst St Mary *Devon* 9 SX9791
Clyth *Highld* 151 ND2835
Cnwch Coch *Dyfed* 43 SN6774
Coad's Green *Cnwll* 5 SX2976
Coal Aston *Derbys* 74 SK3679
Coal Pool *W Mids* 60 SP0199
Coal Street *Suffk* 55 TM2371
Coalbrookdale *Shrops* 60 SJ6604
Coalbrookvale *Gwent* 33 SO1909
Coalburn *Strath* 108 NS8134
Coalburns *T & W* 96 NZ1260
Coalcleugh *Nthumb* 95 NY8045
Coaley *Gloucs* 35 SO7701
Coalfell *Cumb* 94 NY5959
Coalhill *Essex* 40 TQ7597
Coalmoor *Shrops* 60 SJ6607
Coalpit Heath *Avon* 35 ST6780
Coalport *Shrops* 60 SJ6902
Coalsnaughton *Cent* 116 NS9195
Coaltown of Balgonie *Fife* 117 NT2999
Coaltown of Wemyss *Fife* 118 NT3295
Coalville *Leics* 62 SK4214
Coanwood *Nthumb* 94 NY6859
Coat *Somset* 21 ST4520
Coatbridge *Strath* 116 NS7365
Coatdyke *Strath* 116 NS7465
Coate *Wilts* 23 SU0462
Coate *Wilts* 36 SU1882
Coates *Cambs* 64 TL3097
Coates *Gloucs* 35 SO9701
Coates *Lincs* 75 SK8181
Coates *Lincs* 76 SK9083
Coates *W Susx* 14 SU9917
Coatham *Cleve* 97 NZ5925
Coatham Mundeville *Dur* 96 NZ2820
Cobbaton *Devon* 19 SS6126
Coberley *Gloucs* 35 SO9616
Cobhall Common *H & W* 46 SO4535
Cobham *Kent* 28 TQ6768
Cobham *Surrey* 26 TQ1060
Coblers Green *Essex* 40 TL6819
Cobley *Dorset* 12 SU0220
Cobnash *H & W* 46 SO4560
Cobo *Guern* 152 GN4910
Cobridge *Staffs* 72 SJ8747
Coburby *Gramp* 143 NJ9164
Cock Alley *Derbys* 74 SK4170
Cock Bank *Clwyd* 71 SJ3545
Cock Bevington *Warwks* 48 SP0552
Cock Bridge *Gramp* 133 NJ2509
Cock Clarks *Essex* 40 TL8102
Cock End *Suffk* 53 TL7253
Cock Green *Essex* 40 TL6919
Cock Marling *E Susx* 17 TQ8718
Cock Street *Kent* 28 TQ7850
Cockayne *N York* 90 SE6198
Cockayne Hatley *Beds* 52 TL2649
Cockburnspath *Border* 119 NT7770
Cockenzie and Port Seton *Loth* 118 NT4075
Cocker Bar *Lancs* 80 SD5022
Cocker Brook *Lancs* 81 SD7425
Cockerdale *W York* 82 SE2329
Cockerham *Lancs* 80 SD4651
Cockermouth *Cumb* 92 NY1230
Cockernhoe Green *Herts* 38 TL1223
Cockett *W Glam* 32 SS6394
Cockfield *Dur* 96 NZ1224
Cockfield *Suffk* 54 TL9054
Cockfosters *Gt Lon* 27 TQ2796
Cocking *W Susx* 14 SU8717
Cocking Causeway *W Susx* 14 SU8819
Cockington *Devon* 7 SX8963
Cocklake *Somset* 21 ST4449
Cockley Beck *Cumb* 86 NY2501
Cockley Cley *Norfk* 66 TF7904
Cockpole Green *Berks* 37 SU7981
Cocks *Cnwll* 3 SW7652
Cockshutford *Shrops* 59 SO5885
Cockshutt *Shrops* 59 SJ4328
Cockthorpe *Norfk* 66 TF9842
Cockwells *Cnwll* 2 SW5234
Cockwood *Devon* 9 SX9780
Cockwood *Somset* 20 ST2242
Cockyard *Derbys* 74 SK0479
Cockyard *H & W* 46 SO4133
Coddenham *Suffk* 54 TM1354
Coddington *Ches* 71 SJ4555
Coddington *H & W* 47 SO7142
Coddington *Notts* 76 SK8354
Codford St Mary *Wilts* 22 ST9739
Codford St Peter *Wilts* 22 ST9639
Codicote *Herts* 39 TL2118
Codmore Hill *W Susx* 14 TQ0520
Codnor *Derbys* 74 SK4149
Codrington *Avon* 35 ST7278
Codsall *Staffs* 60 SJ8603
Codsall Wood *Staffs* 60 SJ8404
Coed Morgan *Gwent* 34 SO3511
Coed Talon *Clwyd* 70 SJ2659
Coed Ystumgwern *Gwynd* 57 SH5824
Coed-y-caerau *Gwent* 34 ST3891
Coed-y-paen *Gwent* 34 ST3398
Coed-yr-ynys *Powys* 33 SO1520
Coedana *Gwynd* 68 SH4382
Coedely *M Glam* 33 ST0285
Coedkernew *Gwent* 34 ST2783
Coedpoeth *Clwyd* 70 SJ2851
Coedway *Powys* 59 SJ3315
Coelbren *Powys* 33 SN8511
Coffinswell *Devon* 7 SX8968
Coffle End *Beds* 51 TL0159
Cofton Hackett *H & W* 60 SP0075
Cogan *S Glam* 33 ST1771
Cogenhoe *Nhants* 51 SP8260
Cogges *Oxon* 36 SP3609
Coggeshall *Essex* 40 TL8522
Coggin's Mill *E Susx* 16 TQ5927
Coignafearn *Highld* 140 NH7018
Coilacriech *Gramp* 134 NO3296
Coilantogle *Cent* 124 NN5907
Coillore *Highld* 136 NG3537
Coiltry *Highld* 131 NH3506
Coity *M Glam* 33 SS9281
Col *W Isls* 154 NB4739
Colaboll *Highld* 146 NC5610
Colan *Cnwll* 4 SW8661
Colaton Raleigh *Devon* 9 SY0787
Colbost *Highld* 136 NG2148
Colburn *N York* 89 SE1999
Colbury *Hants* 12 SU3410
Colby *Cumb* 94 NY6620
Colby *IOM* 153 SC2370
Colby *Norfk* 67 TG2231
Colchester *Essex* 41 TL9925
Cold Ash *Berks* 24 SU5169
Cold Ashby *Nhants* 50 SP6576
Cold Ashton *Avon* 35 ST7572
Cold Aston *Gloucs* 36 SP1219
Cold Blow *Dyfed* 31 SN1212
Cold Brayfield *Bucks* 38 SP9252
Cold Cotes *N York* 88 SD7171
Cold Green *H & W* 47 SO6842
Cold Hanworth *Lincs* 76 TF0383
Cold Harbour *Herts* 38 TL1415
Cold Harbour *Oxon* 37 SU6379
Cold Harbour *Wilts* 22 ST8645
Cold Hatton *Shrops* 59 SJ6221
Cold Hatton Heath *Shrops* 59 SJ6321
Cold Hesledon *Dur* 96 NZ4146
Cold Hiendley *W York* 83 SE3714
Cold Higham *Nhants* 49 SP6653
Cold Kirby *N York* 90 SE5384
Cold Newton *Leics* 63 SK7106
Cold Northcott *Cnwll* 5 SX2086
Cold Norton *Essex* 40 TL8500
Cold Overton *Leics* 63 SK8010
Cold Weston *Shrops* 59 SO5583
Coldbackie *Highld* 149 NC6160
Coldbeck *Cumb* 88 NY7204
Coldblow *Gt Lon* 27 TQ5073
Coldean *E Susx* 15 TQ3308
Coldeast *Devon* 7 SX8174
Colden *W York* 82 SD9628
Colden Common *Hants* 13 SU4822
Coldfair Green *Suffk* 55 TM4360
Coldham *Cambs* 65 TF4303
Coldharbour *Cnwll* 3 SW7548
Coldharbour *Gloucs* 34 SO5503
Coldharbour *Surrey* 15 TQ1443
Coldingham *Border* 119 NT9065
Coldmeece *Staffs* 72 SJ8532
Coldred *Kent* 29 TR2747
Coldridge *Devon* 8 SS6907
Coldstream *Border* 110 NT8439
Coldwaltham *W Susx* 14 TQ0216
Coldwell *H & W* 46 SO4235
Coldwells *Gramp* 143 NJ9538
Coldwells *Gramp* 143 NK1039
Cole *Somset* 22 ST6733
Cole End *Warwks* 61 SP2089
Cole Green *Herts* 39 TL2811
Cole Green *Herts* 39 TL4330
Cole Henley *Hants* 24 SU4651
Cole's Cross *Devon* 7 SX7746
Colebatch *Shrops* 59 SO3187
Colebrook *Devon* 9 ST0006
Colebrook *Devon* 6 SX5457
Colebrooke *Devon* 8 SX7699
Coleby *Humb* 84 SE8919
Coleby *Lincs* 76 SK9760
Coleford *Devon* 8 SS7701
Coleford *Gloucs* 34 SO5710
Coleford *Somset* 22 ST6848
Coleford Water *Somset* 20 ST1133
Colegate End *Norfk* 55 TM1987
Colehill *Dorset* 12 SU0201
Coleman Green *Herts* 39 TL1812
Coleman's Hatch *E Susx* 16 TQ4433
Colemere *Shrops* 59 SJ4332
Colemore *Hants* 24 SU7030
Colemore Green *Shrops* 60 SO7197
Colenden *Tays* 126 NO1029
Coleorton *Leics* 62 SK4017
Colerne *Wilts* 35 ST8271
Coles Cross *Dorset* 10 ST3902
Coles Green *Suffk* 54 TM1041
Colesbourne *Gloucs* 35 SP0013
Colesden *Beds* 52 TL1255
Coleshill *Bucks* 26 SU9495
Coleshill *Oxon* 36 SU2393
Coleshill *Warwks* 61 SP2089
Colestocks *Devon* 9 ST0900
Coleton *Devon* 7 SX9051
Coley *Avon* 21 ST5855
Colgate *W Susx* 15 TQ2332
Colgrain *Strath* 115 NS3280
Colinsburgh *Fife* 127 NO4703
Colinton *Loth* 117 NT2168
Colintraive *Strath* 114 NS0374
Colkirk *Norfk* 66 TF9126
Collace *Tays* 126 NO2032
Collafirth *Shet* 155 HU3482
Collaton *Devon* 7 SX7139
Collaton *Devon* 7 SX7952
Collaton St Mary *Devon* 7 SX8660
College Green *Somset* 21 ST5736
College of Roseisle *Gramp* 141 NJ1466
College Town *Berks* 25 SU8560
Collessie *Fife* 126 NO2813
Colleton Mills *Devon* 19 SS6615
Collier Row *Gt Lon* 27 TQ5091
Collier Street *Kent* 28 TQ7145
Collier's End *Herts* 39 TL3720
Collier's Green *Kent* 17 TQ7822
Colliers Green *Kent* 28 TQ7538
Colliery Row *T & W* 96 NZ3249
Collieston *Gramp* 143 NK0328
Collin *D & G* 100 NY0276
Collingbourne Ducis *Wilts* 23 SU2453
Collingbourne Kingston *Wilts* 23 SU2355
Collingham *W York* 83 SE3945
Collington *H & W* 47 SO6460
Collingtree *Nhants* 49 SP7555
Collins Green *Ches* 78 SJ5594
Collins Green *H & W* 47 SO7457
Colliston *Tays* 127 NO6045
Colliton *Devon* 9 ST0804
Collyweston *Nhants* 63 SK9902
Colmonell *Strath* 98 NX1485
Colmworth *Beds* 51 TL1058
Coln Rogers *Gloucs* 36 SP0809
Coln St Aldwyns *Gloucs* 36 SP1405
Coln St Dennis *Gloucs* 36 SP0810
Colnbrook *Gt Lon* 26 TQ0277
Colne *Cambs* 52 TL3775
Colne *Lancs* 81 SD8939
Colne Bridge *W York* 82 SE1720
Colne Edge *Lancs* 81 SD8841
Colne Engaine *Essex* 40 TL8430
Colney *Norfk* 66 TG1807
Colney Heath *Herts* 39 TL2005
Colney Street *Herts* 26 TL1502
Colpy *Gramp* 142 NJ6432
Colquhar *Border* 109 NT3341
Colquite *Cnwll* 4 SX0570
Colscott *Devon* 18 SS3614
Colsterdale *N York* 89 SE1381
Colsterworth *Lincs* 63 SK9324
Colston Bassett *Notts* 63 SK7033
Colt Hill *Hants* 24 SU7551
Colt's Hill *Kent* 16 TQ6443
Coltfield *Gramp* 141 NJ1163
Coltishall *Norfk* 67 TG2719
Colton *Cumb* 86 SD3185
Colton *N York* 83 SE5444
Colton *Norfk* 66 TG1009
Colton *Staffs* 73 SK0420
Colton *W York* 83 SE3732
Columbjohn *Devon* 9 SX9699
Colva *Powys* 45 SO1952
Colvend *D & G* 92 NX8654
Colwall *H & W* 47 SO7542
Colwell *Nthumb* 102 NY9575
Colwich *Staffs* 73 SK0121
Colwick *Notts* 62 SK6140
Colwinston *S Glam* 33 SS9375
Colworth *W Susx* 14 SU9103
Colwyn Bay *Clwyd* 69 SH8578
Colyford *Devon* 10 SY2592
Colyton *Devon* 9 SY2494
Combe *Berks* 23 SU3760
Combe *Devon* 7 SX7238
Combe *Devon* 7 SX8448
Combe *H & W* 46 SO3463
Combe *Oxon* 36 SP4116
Combe Almer *Dorset* 11 SY9597
Combe Common *Surrey* 14 SU9436
Combe Fishacre *Devon* 7 SX8465
Combe Florey *Somset* 20 ST1531
Combe Hay *Avon* 22 ST7359
Combe Martin *Devon* 19 SS5846
Combe Moor *H & W* 46 SO3663
Combe Raleigh *Devon* 9 ST1502
Combe St Nicholas *Somset* 10 ST3011
Combeinteignhead *Devon* 7 SX9071
Comberbach *Ches* 79 SJ6477
Comberford *Staffs* 61 SK1907
Comberton *Cambs* 52 TL3856
Comberton *H & W* 46 SO4968
Combridge *Staffs* 73 SK0937
Combrook *Warwks* 48 SP3051
Combs *Derbys* 74 SK0478
Combs *Suffk* 54 TM0456
Combs Ford *Suffk* 54 TM0457
Combwich *Somset* 20 ST2542
Comers *Gramp* 135 NJ6707
Comhampton *H & W* 47 SO8367

Commercial Dyfed 31 SN1416
Commercial End Cambs 53 TL5563
Commins Coch Powys 57 SH8402
Common Edge Lancs 80 SD3232
Common End Cumb 92 NY0022
Common Moor Cnwll 5 SX2469
Common Platt Wilts 36 SU1186
Common Side Derbys 74 SK3375
Common The Wilts 23 SU2432
Commondale N York 90 NZ6610
Commonside Ches 71 SJ5473
Commonside Derbys 73 SK2441
Commonwood Clwyd 71 SJ3753
Commonwood Shrops 59 SJ4828
Compass Somset 20 ST2934
Compstall Gt Man 79 SJ9690
Compstonend D & G 99 NX6652
Compton Berks 37 SU5280
Compton Devon 7 SX8664
Compton Hants 23 SU3529
Compton Hants 13 SU4625
Compton Staffs 60 SO8284
Compton Surrey 25 SU9546
Compton W Susx 14 SU7714
Compton Wilts 23 SU1351
Compton Abbas Dorset 22 ST8618
Compton Abdale Gloucs 36 SP0516
Compton Bassett Wilts 36 SU0372
Compton Beauchamp Oxon 36 SU2786
Compton Bishop Somset 21 ST3955
Compton Chamberlayne Wilts 23 SU0229
Compton Dando Avon 21 ST6464
Compton Dundon Somset 21 ST4932
Compton Durville Somset 10 ST4117
Compton Greenfield Avon 34 ST5681
Compton Martin Avon 21 ST5457
Compton Pauncefoot Somset 21 ST6426
Compton Valence Dorset 10 SY5993
Compton Verney Warwks 48 SP3152
Comrie Fife 117 NT0289
Comrie Tays 124 NN7722
Conaglen House Highld 130 NN0268
Conchra Highld 138 NG8827
Concraigie Tays 125 NO0944
Conderton H & W 47 SO9637
Condicote Gloucs 48 SP1528
Condorrat Strath 116 NS7373
Condover Shrops 59 SJ4905
Coney Hill Gloucs 35 SO8517
Coney Weston Suffk 54 TL9578
Coneyhurst Common W Susx 14 TQ1023
Coneysthorpe N York 90 SE7171
Conford Hants 14 SU8233
Congdon's Shop Cnwll 5 SX2878
Congerstone Leics 62 SK3605
Congham Norfk 65 TF7123
Conghurst Kent 17 TQ7628
Congl-y-wal Gwynd 57 SH7044
Congleton Ches 72 SJ8562
Congresbury Avon 21 ST4363
Congreve Staffs 60 SJ9013
Conheath D & G 100 NX9969
Conicavel Gramp 140 NH9853
Coningsby Lincs 76 TF2257
Conington Cambs 52 TL1885
Conington Cambs 52 TL3266
Conisbrough S York 75 SK5098
Conisholme Lincs 77 TF4095
Coniston Cumb 86 SD3097
Coniston Humb 85 TA1434
Coniston Cold N York 81 SD9054
Conistone N York 88 SD9867
Connah's Quay Clwyd 71 SJ2969
Connel Strath 122 NM9134
Connel Park Strath 107 NS6012
Connor Downs Cnwll 2 SW5939
Conon Bridge Highld 139 NH5455
Cononley N York 82 SD9846
Consall Staffs 72 SJ9848
Consett Dur 95 NZ1051
Constable Burton N York 89 SE1690
Constable Lee Lancs 81 SD8123
Constantine Cnwll 3 SW7329
Contin Highld 139 NH4556
Conwy Gwynd 69 SH7877
Conyer Kent 28 TQ9664
Conyer's Green Suffk 54 TL8867
Cooden E Susx 17 TQ7107
Cook's Green Essex 41 TM1818
Cookbury Devon 18 SS4006
Cookbury Wick Devon 18 SS3905
Cookham Berks 26 SU8985
Cookham Dean Berks 26 SU8685
Cookham Rise Berks 26 SU8885
Cookhill Warwks 48 SP0558
Cookley H & W 60 SO8480
Cookley Suffk 55 TM3475
Cookley Green Oxon 37 SU6990
Cookney Gramp 135 NO8693
Cooks Green Suffk 54 TL9753
Cooksbridge E Susx 15 TQ4013
Cooksey Green H & W 47 SO9069
Cookshill Staffs 72 SJ9443
Cooksland Cnwll 4 SX0867
Cooksmill Green Essex 40 TL6306
Cookson Green Ches 71 SJ5774
Cookson's Green Dur 96 NZ2933
Coolham W Susx 14 TQ1122
Cooling Kent 28 TQ7575
Cooling Street Kent 28 TQ7474
Coombe Cnwll 2 SW6242
Coombe Cnwll 3 SW8340
Coombe Devon 7 SX9373
Coombe Devon 9 SY1091
Coombe Gloucs 35 ST7694
Coombe Hants 13 SU6620
Coombe Wilts 23 SU1450
Coombe Bissett Wilts 23 SU1026
Coombe Cellars Devon 7 SX9072
Coombe Cross Hants 13 SU6620
Coombe End Somset 20 ST0329
Coombe Hill Gloucs 47 SO8826
Coombe Keynes Dorset 11 SY8484
Coombe Pafford Devon 7 SX9166
Coombe Street Somset 22 ST7631
Coombes W Susx 15 TQ1808
Coombeswood W Mids 60 SO9785
Cooper Street Kent 29 TR3060
Cooper Turning Gt Man 79 SD6308
Cooper's Corner Kent 16 TQ4849
Cooperhill Gramp 141 NH9953
Coopers Green E Susx 16 TQ4723
Coopersale Common Essex 27 TL4702
Coopersale Street Essex 27 TL4701
Cootham W Susx 14 TQ0714
Cop Street Kent 27 TQ2959
Copdock Suffk 54 TM1242
Copford Green Essex 40 TL9222
Copgrove N York 89 SE3463
Copister Shet 155 HU4879
Cople Beds 38 TL1048
Copley Dur 95 NZ0825
Copley Gt Man 79 SJ9798
Copley W York 82 SE0822
Coplow Dale Derbys 74 SK1679
Copmanthorpe N York 83 SE5646
Copmere End Staffs 72 SJ8029
Copp Lancs 80 SD4239
Coppathorne Cnwll 18 SS2000
Coppenhall Staffs 72 SJ9019
Coppenhall Moss Ches 72 SJ7058
Copperhouse Cnwll 2 SW5637
Coppers Green Herts 39 TL1909
Coppicegate Shrops 60 SO7379
Coppingford Cambs 52 TL1679
Coppins Corner Kent 28 TQ9448
Copplestone Devon 8 SS7702
Coppull Lancs 81 SD5614
Coppull Moor Lancs 81 SD5512
Copsale W Susx 15 TQ1724
Copster Green Lancs 81 SD6733
Copston Magna Warwks 50 SP4588
Copt Heath W Mids 61 SP1777
Copt Hewick N York 89 SE3471
Copthall Green Essex 27 TL4201
Copthorne Cnwll 5 SX2692
Copthorne W Susx 15 TQ3139
Copy's Green Norfk 66 TF9439
Copythorne Hants 12 SU3014
Coram Street Suffk 54 TM0042
Corbets Tay Gt Lon 27 TQ5685
Corbiere Jersey 152 JS0508
Corbridge Nthumb 103 NY9964
Corby Nhants 51 SP8988
Corby Glen Lincs 63 TF0024
Corby Hill Cumb 94 NY4857
Cordon Strath 105 NS0230
Cordwell Derbys 74 SK3176
Coreley Shrops 46 SO6173
Cores End Bucks 26 SU9087
Corfe Somset 20 ST2319
Corfe Castle Dorset 11 SY9681
Corfe Mullen Dorset 11 SY9798
Corfton Shrops 59 SO4985
Corgarff Gramp 133 NJ2708
Corhampton Hants 13 SU6120
Corks Pond Kent 28 TQ6540
Corley Warwks 61 SP3085
Corley Ash Warwks 61 SP2986
Corley Moor Warwks 61 SP2884
Cormuir Tays 134 NO3066
Cornard Tye Suffk 54 TL9041
Corndon Devon 8 SX6985
Corner Row Lancs 80 SD4134
Corney Cumb 86 SD1191
Cornforth Dur 96 NZ3134
Cornhill Gramp 142 NJ5858
Cornhill-on-Tweed Nthumb 110 NT8639
Cornholme W York 81 SD9126
Cornish Hall End Essex 53 TL6836
Cornoigmore Strath 120 NL9846
Cornriggs Dur 95 NY8441
Cornsay Dur 96 NZ1443
Cornsay Colliery Dur 96 NZ1643
Corntown Highld 139 NH5556
Corntown M Glam 33 SS9177
Cornwell Oxon 48 SP2727
Cornwood Devon 6 SX6059
Cornworthy Devon 7 SX8255
Corpach Highld 130 NN0976
Corpusty Norfk 66 TG1129
Corrachree Gramp 134 NJ4604
Corran Cnwll 3 SW9946
Corran Highld 130 NG8409
Corran Highld 130 NN0263
Corrany IOM 153 SC4589
Corrie D & G 101 NY2086
Corrie Strath 105 NS0242
Corriecravie Strath 105 NR9223
Corriegour Lodge Hotel Highld 131 NN2692
Corriemoille Highld 139 NH3663
Corrimony Highld 139 NH3730
Corringham Essex 40 TQ7083
Corringham Lincs 76 SK8691
Corris Gwynd 57 SH7508
Corris Uchaf Gwynd 57 SH7408
Corrow Strath 114 NN1800
Corry Highld 137 NG6424
Corrygills Strath 105 NS0335
Cors-y-Gedol Gwynd 57 SH6022
Corscombe Devon 8 SX6296
Corscombe Dorset 10 ST5105
Corse Gloucs 47 SO7826
Corse Lawn Gloucs 47 SO8330
Corsham Wilts 35 ST8770
Corsindae Gramp 135 NJ6808
Corsley Wilts 22 ST8246
Corsley Heath Wilts 22 ST8245
Corsock D & G 99 NX7675
Corston Avon 22 ST6965
Corston Wilts 35 ST9283
Corstorphine Loth 117 NT1972
Cortachy Tays 134 NO3959
Corton Suffk 67 TM5497
Corton Wilts 22 ST9340
Corton Denham Somset 21 ST6322
Coruanan Lodge Highld 130 NN0668
Corvallie IOM 153 SC1968
Corwar Strath 98 NX2780
Corwen Clwyd 70 SJ0743
Coryates Dorset 10 SY6285
Coryton Devon 5 SX4583
Coryton Essex 40 TQ7382
Cosby Leics 50 SP5495
Coseley W Mids 60 SO9494
Cosford Shrops 60 SJ8005
Cosgrove Nhants 38 SP7942
Cosham Hants 13 SU6505
Cosheston Dyfed 30 SN0003
Coshieville Tays 124 NN7749
Cossall Notts 62 SK4842
Cossall Marsh Notts 62 SK4842
Cossington Leics 62 SK6013
Cossington Somset 21 ST3540
Costallack Cnwll 2 SW4525
Costessey Norfk 66 TG1711
Costock Notts 62 SK5726
Coston Leics 63 SK8422
Coston Norfk 66 TG0506
Cote Oxon 36 SP3502
Cote Somset 21 ST3444
Cotebrook Ches 71 SJ5765
Cotehill Cumb 93 NY4650
Cotes Cumb 87 SD4886
Cotes Leics 62 SK5520
Cotes Staffs 72 SJ8434
Cotes Heath Staffs 72 SJ8334
Cotesbach Leics 50 SP5382
Cotgrave Notts 63 SK6435
Cotham Notts 63 SK7947
Cothelstone Somset 20 ST1831
Cotherstone Dur 95 NZ0119
Cothill Oxon 37 SU4699
Cotleigh Devon 9 ST2002
Cotmanhay Derbys 62 SK4543
Coton Cambs 52 TL4058
Coton Nhants 50 SP6771
Coton Shrops 59 SJ5334
Coton Staffs 72 SJ8120
Coton Staffs 72 SJ9731
Coton Staffs 61 SK1804
Coton Clanford Staffs 72 SJ8723
Coton Hayes Staffs 72 SJ9832
Coton Hill Shrops 59 SJ4813
Coton in the Clay Staffs 73 SK1628
Coton in the Elms Derbys 73 SK2415
Coton Park Derbys 73 SK2617
Cott Devon 7 SX7861
Cottage End Hants 24 SU4143
Cottam Humb 91 SE9964
Cottam Lancs 80 SD5032
Cottam Notts 75 SK8179
Cottenham Cambs 53 TL4467
Cotterdale N York 88 SD8393
Cottered Herts 39 TL3129
Cotteridge W Mids 61 SP0480
Cotterstock Nhants 51 TL0490
Cottesbrooke Nhants 50 SP7173
Cottesmore Leics 63 SK9013
Cottingham Humb 84 TA0432
Cottingham Nhants 51 SP8490
Cottingley W York 82 SE1137
Cottisford Oxon 49 SP5831
Cottivett Cnwll 5 SX3662
Cotton Suffk 54 TM0666
Cotton End Beds 38 TL0845
Cotton Tree Lancs 81 SD9039
Cottown Gramp 142 NJ5026
Cottown Gramp 142 NJ7615
Cottown Gramp 143 NJ8140
Cottrell S Glam 33 ST0774
Cotts Devon 6 SX4365
Cotwall Shrops 59 SJ6017
Cotwalton Staffs 72 SJ9234
Couch's Mill Cnwll 4 SX1459
Coughton H & W 34 SO5921
Coughton Warwks 48 SP0860
Coulaghailtro Strath 113 NR7165
Coulags Highld 138 NG9645
Coulderton Cumb 86 NX9808
Coull Gramp 134 NJ5102
Coulport Strath 114 NS2187
Coulsdon Gt Lon 27 TQ2959
Coulston Wilts 22 ST9554
Coulter Strath 108 NT0234
Coultershaw Bridge W Susx 14 SU9719
Coultings Somset 20 ST2241
Coulton N York 90 SE6373
Coultra Fife 126 NO3523
Cound Shrops 59 SJ5505
Coundlane Shrops 59 SJ5705
Coundon Dur 96 NZ2329
Coundon Grange Dur 96 NZ2228
Countersett N York 88 SD9187
Countess Wilts 23 SU1542
Countess Cross Essex 40 TL8631
Countess Wear Devon 9 SX9489
Countesthorpe Leics 50 SP5895
Countisbury Devon 19 SS7449
Coup Green Lancs 81 SD5927
Coupar Angus Tays 126 NO2239
Coupland Cumb 94 NY7118
Coupland Nthumb 110 NT9330
Cour Strath 105 NR8248
Courance D & G 100 NY0590
Court Henry Dyfed 32 SN5522
Court-at-Street Kent 17 TR0935
Courteachan Highld 129 NM6897
Courteenhall Nhants 49 SP7653
Courtsend Essex 41 TR0293
Courtway Somset 20 ST2033
Cousland Loth 118 NT3768
Cousley Wood E Susx 16 TQ6533
Cove Devon 20 SS9619
Cove Gramp 135 NJ9501
Cove Hants 25 SU8555
Cove Highld 144 NG8191
Cove Strath 114 NS2282
Cove Bottom Suffk 55 TM4979
Covehithe Suffk 55 TM5282
Coven Staffs 60 SJ9106
Coven Lawn Staffs 60 SJ9005
Coveney Cambs 53 TL4882
Covenham St Bartholomew Lincs 77 TF3394
Covenham St Mary Lincs 77 TF3394
Coventry W Mids 61 SP3378
Coverack Cnwll 3 SW7818
Coverack Bridges Cnwll 2 SW6630
Coverham N York 89 SE1086
Covington Cambs 51 TL0570
Cow Green Suffk 54 TM0565
Cow Honeybourne H & W 48 SP1143
Cowan Bridge Lancs 87 SD6376
Cowbeech E Susx 16 TQ6114
Cowbit Lincs 64 TF2518
Cowbridge S Glam 33 SS9974
Cowdale Derbys 74 SK0771
Cowden Kent 16 TQ4640
Cowden Pound Kent 16 TQ4642
Cowden Station Kent 16 TQ4741
Cowdenbeath Fife 117 NT1691
Cowers Lane Derbys 73 SK3046
Cowes IOW 13 SZ4996
Cowesby N York 89 SE4689
Cowesfield Green Wilts 23 SU2523
Cowfold W Susx 15 TQ2122
Cowgill Cumb 88 SD7586
Cowhill Avon 34 ST6091
Cowie Cent 116 NS8389
Cowley Derbys 74 SK3376
Cowley Devon 9 SX9095
Cowley Gloucs 35 SO9614
Cowley Gt Lon 26 TQ0582
Cowley Oxon 37 SP5304
Cowley Oxon 49 SP6628
Cowling Lancs 81 SD5917
Cowling N York 82 SD9643
Cowling N York 89 SE2387
Cowlinge Suffk 53 TL7154
Cowmes W York 82 SE1815
Cowpe Lancs 81 SD8320
Cowpen Nthumb 103 NZ2981
Cowpen Bewley Cleve 97 NZ4824
Cowplain Hants 13 SU6810
Cowshill Dur 95 NY8540
Cowslip Green Avon 21 ST4861
Cowthorpe N York 83 SE4252
Cox Common Suffk 55 TM4082
Coxall Shrops 46 SO3774
Coxbank Ches 72 SJ6541
Coxbench Derbys 62 SK3743
Coxbridge Somset 21 ST5436
Coxford Cnwll 4 SX1696
Coxford Norfk 66 TF8529
Coxgreen Staffs 60 SO8086
Coxheath Kent 28 TQ7451
Coxhoe Dur 96 NZ3136
Coxley Somset 21 ST5343
Coxley W York 82 SE2717
Coxley Wick Somset 21 ST5243
Coxpark Cnwll 5 SX4072
Coxtie Green Essex 27 TQ5696
Coxwold N York 90 SE5377
Coychurch M Glam 33 SS9379
Coylton Strath 107 NS4219
Coylumbridge Highld 132 NH9111
Coytrahen M Glam 33 SS8885
Crab Orchard Dorset 12 SU0806
Crabbs Cross H & W 48 SP0465
Crabtree W Susx 15 TQ2125
Crabtree Green Clwyd 71 SJ3344
Crackenthorpe Cumb 94 NY6622
Crackington Haven Cnwll 4 SX1496
Crackley Staffs 72 SJ8350
Crackley Warwks 61 SP2973
Crackleybank Shrops 60 SJ7611
Crackpot N York 88 SD9796
Cracoe N York 88 SD9760
Craddock Devon 9 ST0812
Cradle End Herts 39 TL4521
Cradley H & W 47 SO7347
Cradoc Powys 45 SO0130
Crafthole Cnwll 5 SX3654
Crafton Bucks 38 SP8819
Crag Foot Lancs 87 SD4873
Cragg W York 82 SE0023
Cragg Hill W York 82 SE2437
Craggan Highld 141 NJ0226
Craghead Dur 96 NZ2150
Crai Powys 45 SN8924
Craibstone Gramp 142 NJ4959
Craibstone Gramp 135 NJ8710
Craichie Tays 127 NO5047
Craig Tays 127 NO6956
Craig Llangiwg W Glam 32 SN7204
Craig Penllyn S Glam 33 SS9777
Craig's End Essex 53 TL7137
Craig-y-Duke W Glam 32 SN7002
Craig-y-nos Powys 33 SN8415
Craigburn Border 117 NT2354
Craigcefnparc W Glam 32 SN6702
Craigcleuch D & G 101 NY3486
Craigdam Gramp 143 NJ8430
Craigdarroch D & G 107 NX7391
Craigdhu Strath 122 NM8205
Craigearn Gramp 142 NJ7214
Craigellachie Gramp 141 NJ2844
Craigend Strath 115 NS4670
Craigend Tays 126 NO1120
Craigendoran Strath 115 NS3181
Craigengillan Strath 107 NS4702
Craighlaw D & G 98 NX3061
Craigie Strath 107 NS4232
Craigie Tays 126 NO1143
Craigiefold Gramp 143 NJ9165
Craigley D & G 99 NX7658
Craiglockhart Fife 117 NT2271
Craiglug Gramp 141 NJ3355
Craigmillar Loth 117 NT3071
Craignant Shrops 58 SJ2535
Craigneston D & G 107 NX7587
Craigneuk Strath 116 NS7765
Craignure Strath 122 NM7236
Craigo Tays 135 NO6864
Craigrothie Fife 126 NO3810
Craigruie Cent 124 NN4920
Craigton Gramp 135 NJ8301
Craigton Strath 115 NS4954
Craigton Tays 127 NO5138
Craigton of Airlie Tays 126 NO3250
Craik Border 109 NT3408
Crail Fife 127 NO6107
Crailing Border 110 NT6824
Crakehall N York 89 SE2489
Crakehill N York 89 SE4273
Crakemarsh Staffs 73 SK0936
Crambe N York 90 SE7364
Cramlington Nthumb 103 NZ2676
Cramond Loth 117 NT1976
Cramond Bridge Loth 117 NT1775
Cranage Ches 79 SJ7568
Cranberry Staffs 72 SJ8235
Cranborne Dorset 12 SU0513
Cranbrook Kent 28 TQ7736
Cranbrook Common Kent 28 TQ7838
Crane Moor S York 82 SE3001
Crane's Corner Norfk 66 TF9113
Cranfield Beds 38 SP9542
Cranford Devon 18 SS3421
Cranford Gt Lon 26 TQ1076
Cranford St Andrew Nhants 51 SP9277
Cranford St John Nhants 51 SP9276
Cranham Gloucs 35 SO8913
Cranham Gt Lon 27 TQ5786
Cranhill Warwks 48 SP1253
Crank Mersyd 78 SJ5099
Cranleigh Surrey 14 TQ0539
Cranmer Green Suffk 54 TM0171
Cranmore IOW 13 SZ3990
Cranmore Somset 22 ST6643
Cranoe Leics 50 SP7695
Cransford Suffk 55 TM3164
Cranshaws Border 118 NT6861
Cranstal IOM 153 NX4602
Cranswick Humb 84 TA0252
Crantock Cnwll 4 SW7960
Cranwell Lincs 76 TF0349
Cranwich Norfk 65 TL7794
Cranworth Norfk 66 TF9804
Craobh Haven Strath 122 NM7907
Crapstone Devon 6 SX5067
Crarae Strath 114 NR9897
Crask Inn Highld 149 NC5224
Crask of Aigas Highld 139 NH4642
Craster Nthumb 111 NU2519
Craswall H & W 46 SO2735
Crateford Staffs 60 SJ9009
Cratfield Suffk 55 TM3175
Crathes Gramp 135 NO7596
Crathie Gramp 133 NO2695
Crathie Highld 132 NN5793
Crathorne N York 89 NZ4407
Craven Arms Shrops 59 SO4382
Crawcrook T & W 103 NZ1363
Crawford Lancs 78 SD4902
Crawford Strath 108 NS9520
Crawfordjohn Strath 108 NS8823
Crawick D & G 107 NS7811
Crawley Hants 24 SU4235
Crawley Oxon 36 SP3412
Crawley W Susx 15 TQ2636
Crawley Down W Susx 15 TQ3437
Crawley Side Dur 95 NY9940
Crawshawbooth Lancs 81 SD8125
Crawton Gramp 135 NO8779
Cray N York 88 SD9479
Cray's Pond Oxon 37 SU6380
Crayford Gt Lon 27 TQ5175
Crayke N York 90 SE5670
Craymere Beck Norfk 66 TG0631
Crays Hill Essex 40 TQ7192
Craythorne Staffs 73 SK2426
Craze Lowman Devon 9 SS9814
Crazies Hill Oxon 37 SU7980
Creacombe Devon 18 SS3219
Creagan Inn Strath 122 NM9744
Creagorry W Isls 154 NF7948
Creaguaineach Lodge Highld 131 NN3068
Creamore Bank Shrops 59 SJ5130
Creaton Nhants 50 SP7071
Creca D & G 101 NY2270
Credenhill H & W 46 SO4543
Crediton Devon 8 SS8300
Creebank D & G 98 NX3477
Creebridge D & G 99 NX4165
Creech Heathfield Somset 20 ST2727
Creech St Michael Somset 20 ST2725
Creed Cnwll 3 SW9347
Creedy Park Devon 8 SS8301
Creekmouth Gt Lon 27 TQ4581
Creeting St Mary Suffk 54 TM0956
Creeton Lincs 64 TF0120
Creetown D & G 99 NX4759
Creggans Inn Strath 123 NN0902
Cregneish IOM 153 SC1867
Cregrina Powys 45 SO1252
Creich Fife 126 NO3221
Creigiau M Glam 33 ST0781
Crelly Cnwll 2 SW6732
Cremyll Cnwll 6 SX4553
Cressage Shrops 59 SJ5904
Cressbrook Derbys 74 SK1673
Cresselly Dyfed 30 SN0606
Cressex Bucks 26 SU8492
Cressing Essex 40 TL7920
Cresswell Dyfed 30 SN0506
Cresswell Nthumb 103 NZ2993
Cresswell Staffs 72 SJ9739
Creswell Derbys 75 SK5274
Creswell Green Staffs 61 SK0710
Cretingham Suffk 55 TM2260
Cretshengan Strath 113 NR7166
Crew Green Powys 59 SJ3215
Crewe Ches 71 SJ4253
Crewe Ches 72 SJ7056
Crewe Green Ches 72 SJ7255
Crewkerne Somset 10 ST4409
Crews Hill H & W 35 SO6722
Crews Hill Station Herts 27 TL3000
Crewton Derbys 62 SK3733
Crianlarich Strath 123 NN3825
Cribbs Causeway Avon 34 ST5780
Cribyn Dyfed 44 SN5250
Criccieth Gwynd 56 SH4938
Crich Derbys 74 SK3454
Crich Carr Derbys 74 SK3354
Crich Common Derbys 74 SK3553
Crichton Loth 118 NT3862
Crick Gwent 34 ST4890
Crick Nhants 50 SP5872
Crickadarn Powys 45 SO0942
Cricket St Thomas Somset 10 ST3708
Crickheath Shrops 59 SJ2922
Crickhowell Powys 33 SO2118
Cricklade Wilts 36 SU0993
Cricklewood Gt Lon 26 TQ2385
Cridling Stubbs N York 83 SE5221
Crieff Tays 125 NN8621
Criggan Cnwll 4 SX0160
Criggion Powys 59 SJ2915
Crigglestone W York 82 SE3116
Crimble Gt Man 81 SD8611
Crimond Gramp 143 NK0556
Crimonmogate Gramp 143 NK0358
Crimplesham Norfk 65 TF6503
Crimscote Warwks 48 SP2347
Crinan Strath 113 NR7894
Crindledyke Strath 116 NS8356
Cringleford Norfk 67 TG1905
Cringles N York 82 SE0448
Crinow Dyfed 31 SN1214
Cripp's Corner E Susx 17 TQ7721
Cripplesease Cnwll 2 SW5036
Cripplestyle Dorset 12 SU0812
Crizeley H & W 46 SO4532
Croachy Highld 140 NH6527
Croanford Cnwll 4 SX0371
Crochmare House D & G 100 NX8977
Crock Street Somset 10 ST3213
Crockenhill Kent 27 TQ5067
Crocker End Oxon 37 SU7086
Crocker's Ash H & W 34 SO5316
Crockerhill W Susx 14 SU9206
Crockernwell Devon 8 SX7592
Crockerton Wilts 22 ST8642
Crocketford D & G 100 NX8372
Crockey Hill N York 83 SE6246
Crockham Hill Kent 27 TQ4450
Crockhurst Street Kent 16 TQ6245
Crockleford Heath Essex 41 TM0426
Croes-lan Dyfed 42 SN3844
Croes-y-mwyalch Gwent 34 ST3092
Croes-y-pant Gwent 34 SO3104
Croeserw W Glam 33 SS8795
Croesgoch Dyfed 30 SM8330
Croesor Gwynd 57 SH6344
Croesyceiliog Dyfed 31 SN4016
Croesyceiliog Gwent 34 ST3096
Croft Ches 79 SJ6393
Croft Devon 5 SX5296
Croft Leics 50 SP5195
Croft Lincs 77 TF5061
Croft Michael Cnwll 2 SW6637
Croft-on-Tees N York 89 NZ2809
Croftamie Cent 115 NS4785
Crofton Cumb 93 NY3050
Crofton Devon 9 SX9680
Crofton W York 83 SE3817
Crofton Wilts 23 SU2562
Crofts D & G 99 NX7365
Crofts Gramp 141 NJ2850
Crofts of Dipple Gramp 141 NJ3259
Crofts of Savoch Gramp 143 NK0460
Crofty W Glam 32 SS5294
Crogen Gwynd 58 SJ0036
Croggan Strath 122 NM7027
Croglin Cumb 94 NY5747
Crogo D & G 99 NX7576
Croik Highld 146 NH4591
Cromarty Highld 140 NH7867
Crombie Fife 117 NT0584
Cromdale Highld 141 NJ0728
Cromer Herts 39 TL2928
Cromer Norfk 67 TG2242
Cromford Derbys 73 SK2956
Cromhall Avon 35 ST6990
Cromhall Common Avon 35 ST6989
Cromore W Isls 154 NB4021
Crompton Fold Gt Man 79 SD9409
Cromwell Notts 75 SK7961
Cronberry Strath 107 NS6022
Crondall Hants 25 SU7948
Cronton Mersyd 78 SJ4988
Crook Cumb 87 SD4695
Crook Dur 96 NZ1635
Crook Inn Border 108 NT1026
Crook of Devon Tays 117 NO0400
Crookdake Cumb 93 NY1943
Crooke Gt Man 78 SD5507
Crooked End Gloucs 35 SO6217
Crooked Holme Cumb 101 NY5161
Crooked Soley Wilts 36 SU3172
Crookedholm Strath 107 NS4537
Crookes S York 74 SK3287
Crookhall Dur 95 NZ1150
Crookham Berks 24 SU5464
Crookham Nthumb 110 NT9138
Crookham Village Hants 25 SU7952
Crooklands Cumb 87 SD5383
Cropper Derbys 73 SK2335
Cropredy Oxon 49 SP4646
Cropston Leics 62 SK5510
Cropthorne H & W 47 SO9945
Cropton N York 90 SE7589
Cropwell Bishop Notts 63 SK6835
Cropwell Butler Notts 63 SK6837
Crosbie Strath 114 NS2149
Crosby Cumb 92 NY0738
Crosby Humb 84 SE8912
Crosby IOM 153 SC3279
Crosby Mersyd 78 SJ3198
Crosby Garret Cumb 88 NY7209
Crosby on Eden Cumb 93 NY4459
Crosby Ravensworth Cumb 94 NY6214
Crosby Villa Cumb 92 NY0939
Croscombe Somset 21 ST5944
Crosemere Shrops 59 SJ4329
Cross Somset 21 ST4154
Cross Ash Gwent 34 SO4019
Cross Bush W Susx 14 TQ0306
Cross Coombe Cnwll 3 SW7251
Cross End Beds 51 TL0658
Cross End Essex 54 TL8534
Cross Flatts W York 82 SE1040
Cross Gates W York 83 SE3534
Cross Green Devon 5 SX3888
Cross Green Staffs 60 SJ9105
Cross Green Suffk 54 TL8353
Cross Green Suffk 54 TL8955
Cross Green Suffk 54 TL9852
Cross Hands Dyfed 31 SN0712
Cross Hands Dyfed 32 SN5612
Cross Hill Derbys 74 SK4148
Cross Hills N York 82 SE0145
Cross Houses Shrops 59 SJ5307
Cross Houses Shrops 60 SO6991
Cross Inn Dyfed 42 SN3957
Cross Inn Dyfed 43 SN5464
Cross Inn M Glam 33 ST0582
Cross in Hand E Susx 16 TQ5521
Cross Keys Wilts 35 ST8771
Cross Lane IOW 13 SZ5089
Cross Lane Head Shrops 60 SO7195
Cross Lanes Clwyd 71 SJ3746
Cross Lanes Cnwll 2 SW6921
Cross Lanes Cnwll 3 SW7642
Cross Lanes N York 90 SE5364
Cross Oak Powys 45 SO1023
Cross o' th' hands Derbys 73 SK2846
Cross of Jackston Gramp 142 NJ7432
Cross Roads Powys 45 SN9756
Cross Street Suffk 54 TM1876
Cross Town Ches 79 SJ7578
Cross Ways Dorset 11 SY7788
Cross-at-Hand Kent 28 TQ7846
Crossaig Strath 113 NR8351
Crossapoll Strath 120 NL9943
Crossbost W Isls 154 NB3924
Crosscanonby Cumb 92 NY0739
Crossdale Street Norfk 67 TG2239
Crossens Mersyd 80 SD3720
Crossford Fife 117 NT0786
Crossford Strath 116 NS8246
Crossgate Cnwll 5 SX3488
Crossgate Lincs 64 TF2426
Crossgate Staffs 72 SJ9437
Crossgatehall Loth 118 NT3669
Crossgates Fife 117 NT1488
Crossgates Powys 45 SO0864
Crossgates Strath 115 NS3744
Crossgill Lancs 87 SD5563
Crosshands Dyfed 31 SN1923
Crosshands Strath 107 NS4830
Crosshill Fife 117 NT1796
Crosshill Strath 106 NS3206
Crosshouse Strath 106 NS3938
Crosskeys Gwent 34 ST2292
Crosskeys Strath 115 NS3385
Crosskirk Highld 150 ND0369
Crossland Edge W York 82 SE1012
Crossland Hill W York 82 SE1114
Crosslands Cumb 87 SD3489
Crosslanes Shrops 59 SJ3218
Crosslee Border 109 NT3018
Crosslee Strath 115 NS4066
Crossley W York 82 SE2021
Crossmichael D & G 99 NX7366
Crosspost W Susx 15 TQ2522
Crossroads Gramp 134 NJ5607
Crossroads Gramp 135 NO7594
Crosston Tays 127 NO5256
Crossway Dyfed 31 SN1542
Crossway Gwent 34 SO4419
Crossway Powys 45 SO0558
Crossway Green Gwent 34 ST5294
Crossway Green H & W 47 SO8468
Crosswell Dyfed 31 SN1236
Crosthwaite Cumb 87 SD4391
Croston Lancs 80 SD4818
Crostwick Norfk 67 TG2515
Crostwight Norfk 67 TG3429
Crouch Kent 28 TR0558
Crouch End Gt Lon 27 TQ3088
Crouch Hill Dorset 11 ST7010
Croucheston Wilts 23 SU0625
Crough House Green Kent 16 TQ4346
Croughton Nhants 49 SP5433
Crovie Gramp 143 NJ8065
Crow Hants 12 SU1604
Crow Edge S York 82 SE1804
Crow End Cambs 52 TL3257
Crow Green Essex 27 TQ5796
Crow Hill H & W 47 SO6326
Crow's Green Essex 40 TL6926
Crow's Nest Cnwll 5 SX2669
Crowan Cnwll 2 SW6434
Crowborough E Susx 16 TQ5131
Crowborough Town E Susx 16 TQ5031
Crowcombe Somset 20 ST1436
Crowdecote Derbys 74 SK1065
Crowden Derbys 74 SK0699
Crowden Devon 18 SX4999
Crowdhill Hants 13 SU4920
Crowdleham Kent 27 TQ5659
Crowell Oxon 37 SU7499
Crowfield Nhants 49 SP6141
Crowfield Suffk 54 TM1457
Crowfield Green Suffk 54 TM1458
Crowgate Street Norfk 67 TG3121
Crowhill Loth 119 NT7374
Crowhole Derbys 74 SK3375
Crowhurst E Susx 17 TQ7512
Crowhurst Surrey 15 TQ3847
Crowhurst Lane End Surrey 15 TQ3747
Crowland Lincs 64 TF2410
Crowland Suffk 54 TM0170
Crowlas Cnwll 2 SW5133
Crowle H & W 47 SO9256
Crowle Humb 84 SE7712
Crowle Green H & W 47 SO9156
Crowmarsh Gifford Oxon 37 SU6189
Crown Corner Suffk 55 TM2570
Crownhill Devon 6 SX4858
Crownpits Surrey 25 SU9743
Crownthorpe Norfk 66 TG0803
Crowntown Cnwll 2 SW6330
Crows-an-Wra Cnwll 2 SW3927
Crowshill Norfk 66 TF9506
Crowsnest Shrops 59 SJ3601
Crowthorne Berks 25 SU8464
Crowton Ches 71 SJ5774
Croxall Staffs 61 SK1913
Croxby Lincs 76 TF1898
Croxdale Dur 96 NZ2636
Croxden Staffs 73 SK0639
Croxley Green Herts 26 TQ0795
Croxton Cambs 52 TL2460
Croxton Humb 85 TA0912
Croxton Norfk 66 TF9831
Croxton Norfk 54 TL8786
Croxton Staffs 72 SJ7832
Croxton Green Ches 71 SJ5552
Croxton Kerrial Leics 63 SK8329
Croxtonbank Staffs 72 SJ7832
Croy Highld 140 NH7949
Croy Strath 116 NS7275
Croyde Devon 18 SS4439
Croyde Bay Devon 18 SS4339
Croydon Cambs 52 TL3149
Croydon Gt Lon 27 TQ3265
Crubenmore Highld 132 NN6790
Cruckmeole Shrops 59 SJ4309
Cruckton Shrops 59 SJ4310
Cruden Bay Gramp 143 NK0836
Crudgington Shrops 59 SJ6318
Crudwell Wilts 35 ST9593
Crug Powys 45 SO1972
Crug-y-byddar Powys 58 SO1682
Crugmeer Cnwll 4 SW9076
Crugybar Dyfed 44 SN6537
Crumlin Gwent 33 ST2197
Crumplehorn Cnwll 5 SX2051
Crumpsall Gt Man 79 SD8402
Crumstane Border 119 NT8053
Crundale Dyfed 30 SM9718
Crundale Kent 29 TR0749
Crunwear Dyfed 31 SN1810
Cruwys Morchard Devon 19 SS8712
Crux Easton Hants 24 SU4256
Cruxton Dorset 10 SY6096
Crwbin Dyfed 32 SN4713
Cryers Hill Bucks 26 SU8796
Crymmych Dyfed 31 SN1834
Crynant W Glam 32 SN7904
Crystal Palace Gt Lon 27 TQ3371
Cuaig Highld 137 NG7057
Cubbington Warwks 48 SP3468
Cubert Cnwll 4 SW7857
Cubley S York 82 SE2401
Cublington Bucks 38 SP8422
Cublington H & W 46 SO4038
Cuckfield W Susx 15 TQ3025
Cucklington Somset 22 ST7527
Cuckney Notts 75 SK5671
Cuckold's Green Kent 28 TQ8276
Cuckoo Bridge Lincs 64 TF2020
Cuckoo's Corner Hants 24 SU7441
Cuckoo's Nest Ches 71 SJ3860
Cuddesdon Oxon 37 SP5903
Cuddington Bucks 37 SP7311
Cuddington Ches 71 SJ5971
Cuddington Heath Ches 71 SJ4746
Cuddy Hill Lancs 80 SD4937
Cudham Gt Lon 27 TQ4459
Cudliptown Devon 5 SX5279
Cudnell Dorset 12 SZ0696
Cudworth S York 83 SE3808
Cudworth Somset 10 ST3810
Cudworth Common S York 83 SE4007
Cuerden Green Lancs 81 SD5525
Cuerdley Cross Ches 78 SJ5486
Cufaude Hants 24 SU6557
Cuffley Herts 39 TL3003
Culbokie Highld 140 NH6059
Culbone Somset 19 SS8448
Culburnie Highld 139 NH4941
Culcabock Highld 140 NH6844
Culcharry Highld 140 NH8650
Culcheth Ches 79 SJ6694
Culdrain Gramp 142 NJ5134
Culford Suffk 54 TL8370
Culgaith Cumb 94 NY6029
Culham Oxon 37 SU5095
Culkein Highld 148 NC0333
Culkein Drumbeg Highld 148 NC1133
Culkerton Gloucs 35 ST9395
Cullen Gramp 142 NJ5167
Cullercoats T & W 103 NZ3570
Cullerlie Gramp 135 NJ7603
Cullicudden Highld 140 NH6463
Cullingworth W York 82 SE0636
Cullipool Strath 122 NM7413
Cullivoe Shet 155 HP5402
Culloden Highld 140 NH7246
Cullompton Devon 9 ST0207
Culm Davy Devon 9 ST1215
Culmalzie D & G 99 NX3753
Culmington Shrops 59 SO4982
Culmstock Devon 9 ST1013
Culnacraig Highld 145 NC0603
Culnaightrie D & G 92 NX7750
Culnaknock Highld 137 NG5162
Culpho Suffk 55 TM2149
Culrain Highld 146 NH5794
Culross Fife 117 NS9886
Culroy Strath 106 NS3114
Culsalmond Gramp 142 NJ6532
Culscadden D & G 99 NX4748
Culshabbin D & G 98 NX3051
Culswick Shet 155 HU2745
Cultercullen Gramp 143 NJ9223
Cults Gramp 135 NJ8903
Culverstone Green Kent 27 TQ6362
Culverthorpe Lincs 64 TF0240
Culworth Nhants 49 SP5446
Cum brwyno Dyfed 43 SN7180
Cumbernauld Strath 116 NS7674
Cumberworth Lincs 77 TF5073
Cumdivock Cumb 93 NY3448
Cuminestown Gramp 143 NJ8050
Cummersdale Cumb 93 NY3953
Cummertrees D & G 100 NY1366
Cummingston Gramp 141 NJ1368
Cumnor Oxon 37 SP4504
Cumrew Cumb 94 NY5550
Cumwhinton Cumb 93 NY4552
Cumwhitton Cumb 94 NY5052
Cundall N York 89 SE4272
Cunninghamhead Strath 106 NS3741
Cupar Fife 126 NO3714
Cupar Muir Fife 126 NO3613
Cupernham Hants 23 SU3622
Curbar Derbys 74 SK2574
Curbridge Hants 13 SU5211
Curbridge Oxon 36 SP3308
Curdridge Hants 13 SU5213
Curdworth Warwks 61 SP1792
Curland Somset 10 ST2717
Curridge Berks 24 SU4972
Currie Loth 117 NT1867
Curry Mallet Somset 21 ST3221
Curry Rivel Somset 21 ST3925
Curteis Corner Kent 28 TQ8539
Curtisden Green Kent 28 TQ7440
Curtisknowle Devon 7 SX7353
Cury Cnwll 2 SW6721
Cusgarne Cnwll 3 SW7540
Cushnie Gramp 134 NJ5211
Cushuish Somset 20 ST1930
Cusop H & W 46 SO2441
Cutcloy D & G 99 NX4534
Cutcombe Somset 20 SS9339
Cutgate Gt Man 81 SD8614
Cuthill Highld 147 NH7587
Cutiau Gwynd 57 SH6317
Cutler's Green Essex 40 TL5930
Cutmadoc Cnwll 4 SX0963
Cutmere Cnwll 5 SX3260
Cutnall Green H & W 47 SO8868
Cutsdean Gloucs 48 SP0830
Cutsyke W York 83 SE4224
Cutthorpe Derbys 74 SK3473
Cuxham Oxon 37 SU6695
Cuxton Kent 28 TQ7066
Cuxwold Lincs 85 TA1701
Cwm Clwyd 70 SJ0677
Cwm Gwent 33 SO1805
Cwm Capel Dyfed 32 SN4502
Cwm Irfon Powys 45 SN8549
Cwm Morgan Dyfed 31 SN2934
Cwm Penmachno Gwynd 69 SH7547
Cwm-bach Dyfed 32 SN4801
Cwm-Cewydd Gwynd 57 SH8713
Cwm-Crownon Powys 33 SO1419
Cwm-celyn Gwent 33 SO2008
Cwm-Llinau Powys 57 SH8408
Cwm-y-glo Dyfed 32 SN5513
Cwm-y-glo Gwynd 69 SH5562
Cwmafan W Glam 32 SS7791
Cwmaman M Glam 33 ST0099
Cwmann Dyfed 44 SN5847
Cwmavon Gwent 34 SO2706
Cwmbach Dyfed 31 SN2526
Cwmbach M Glam 33 SO0201
Cwmbach Powys 45 SO1639
Cwmbach Llechrhyd Powys 45 SO0254
Cwmbelan Powys 58 SN9481
Cwmbran Gwent 34 ST2994
Cwmcarn Gwent 34 ST2293
Cwmcarvan Gwent 34 SO4707
Cwmcoy Dyfed 31 SN2942
Cwmdare M Glam 33 SN9803
Cwmdu Dyfed 44 SN6330
Cwmdu Powys 45 SO1823
Cwmdu W Glam 32 SS6494
Cwmduad Dyfed 31 SN3731
Cwmdwr Dyfed 44 SN7132
Cwmergyr Dyfed 43 SN7982
Cwmfelin M Glam 33 SO0901
Cwmfelin M Glam 33 SS8589
Cwmfelin Boeth Dyfed 31 SN1919
Cwmfelin Mynach Dyfed 31 SN2224
Cwmfelinfach Gwent 33 ST1891
Cwmffrwd Dyfed 31 SN4217
Cwmgiedd Powys 32 SN7911
Cwmgorse W Glam 32 SN7010
Cwmgwili Dyfed 32 SN5710
Cwmgwrach W Glam 33 SN8604
Cwmhiraeth Dyfed 31 SN3437
Cwmisfael Dyfed 32 SN4915
Cwmllynfell Dyfed 32 SN7412
Cwmparc M Glam 33 SS9495
Cwmpengraig Dyfed 31 SN3536
Cwmpennar M Glam 33 SO0300
Cwmrhydyceirw W Glam 32 SS6699
Cwmsychpant Dyfed 44 SN4746
Cwmtillery Gwent 33 SO2105
Cwmyoy Gwent 46 SO2923
Cwmystwyth Dyfed 43 SN7874
Cwrt Gwynd 32 SN6800
Cwrt-newydd Dyfed 44 SN4947
Cwrt-y-gollen Powys 34 SO2317
Cyfronydd Powys 58 SJ1408
Cylibebyll W Glam 32 SN7404
Cymer W Glam 33 SS8695
Cymmer M Glam 33 ST0290
Cynghordy Dyfed 44 SN8040
Cynheidre Dyfed 32 SN4907
Cynonville W Glam 33 SS8395
Cynwyd Clwyd 70 SJ0541
Cynwyl Elfed Dyfed 31 SN3727

D

Daccombe Devon 7 SX9068
Dacre Cumb 93 NY4526
Dacre N York 89 SE1960
Dacre Banks N York 89 SE1962
Daddry Shield Dur 95 NY8937

Dadford
Easington

Dadford *Bucks* 49 SP6638
Dadlington *Leics* 61 SP4097
Dafen *Dyfed* 32 SN5201
Daffy Green *Norfk* 66 TF9609
Dagenham *Gt Lon* 27 TQ5084
Daglingworth *Gloucs* 35 SO9905
Dagnall *Bucks* 38 SP9916
Dagworth *Suffk* 54 TM0361
Dailly *Strath* 106 NS2701
Dainton *Devon* 7 SX8566
Dairsie *Fife* 126 NO4117
Daisy Hill *Gt Man* 79 SD6504
Daisy Hill *W York* 82 SE2728
Dalavich *Strath* 122 NM9612
Dalbeattie *D & G* 100 NX8361
Dalblair *Strath* 107 NS6419
Dalbog *Tays* 134 NO5871
Dalbury *Derbys* 73 SK2634
Dalby *IOM* 153 SC2178
Dalby *Lincs* 77 TF4169
Dalby *N York* 90 SE6371
Dalcapon *Tays* 125 NN9754
Dalchalm *Highld* 147 NC9105
Dalchenna *Strath* 123 NN0706
Dalchreichart *Highld* 131 NH2812
Dalchruin *Tays* 124 NN7116
Dalcrue *Tays* 125 NO0427
Dalderby *Lincs* 77 TF2565
Dale *Cumb* 94 NY5443
Dale *Derbys* 62 SK4338
Dale *Dyfed* 30 SM8005
Dale Bottom *Cumb* 93 NY2921
Dale End *Derbys* 74 SK2161
Dale End *N York* 82 SD9645
Dale Hill *E Susx* 16 TQ7030
Dalehouse *N York* 97 NZ7717
Dalgarven *Strath* 115 NS2846
Dalgety Bay *Fife* 117 NT1683
Dalgig *Strath* 107 NS5512
Dalginross *Tays* 124 NN7721
Dalguise *Tays* 125 NN9847
Dalhalvaig *Highld* 150 NC8954
Dalham *Suffk* 53 TL7261
Daliburgh *W Isls* 154 NF7421
Dalkeith *Loth* 118 NT3367
Dallas *Gramp* 141 NJ1252
Dallinghoo *Suffk* 55 TM2655
Dallington *E Susx* 16 TQ6519
Dallow *N York* 89 SE1971
Dalmally *Strath* 123 NN1627
Dalmary *Cent* 115 NS5195
Dalmellington *Strath* 107 NS4705
Dalmeny *Loth* 117 NT1477
Dalmigavie *Highld* 140 NH7319
Dalmigavie Lodge *Highld* 140 NH7523
Dalmore *Highld* 140 NH6668
Dalnabreck *Highld* 129 NM7069
Dalnacardoch *Tays* 132 NN7270
Dalnahaitnach *Highld* 140 NH8519
Dalnaspidal *Tays* 132 NN6473
Dalnawillan Lodge *Highld* 150 ND0340
Daloist *Tays* 124 NN7857
Dalquhairn *Strath* 106 NX3296
Dalreavoch Lodge *Highld* 147 NC7508
Dalry *Strath* 115 NS2949
Dalrymple *Strath* 106 NS3514
Dalserf *Strath* 116 NS7950
Dalsmeran *Strath* 104 NR6413
Dalston *Cumb* 93 NY3650
Dalston *Gt Lon* 27 TQ3384
Dalswinton *D & G* 100 NX9385
Dalton *Cumb* 87 SD5476
Dalton *D & G* 100 NY1173
Dalton *Lancs* 78 SD4908
Dalton *N York* 89 NZ1108
Dalton *N York* 89 SE4376
Dalton *Nthumb* 103 NZ1172
Dalton *S York* 75 SK4594
Dalton in Furness *Cumb* 86 SD2274
Dalton Magna *S York* 75 SK4692
Dalton Parva *S York* 75 SK4593
Dalton Piercy *Cleve* 97 NZ4631
Dalton-le-Dale *Dur* 96 NZ4048
Dalton-on-Tees *N York* 89 NZ2907
Dalveen *D & G* 108 NS8806
Dalveich *Cent* 124 NN6124
Dalwhinnie *Highld* 132 NN6384
Dalwood *Devon* 9 ST2400
Dam Green *Norfk* 54 TM0485
Damask Green *Herts* 39 TL2529
Damerham *Hants* 12 SU1016
Damgate *Norfk* 67 TG4009
Dan's Castle *Dur* 95 NZ1139
Dan-y-Parc *Powys* 34 SO2217
Danaway *Kent* 28 TQ8663
Danbury *Essex* 40 TL7805
Danby *N York* 90 NZ7008
Danby Bottom *N York* 90 NZ6904
Danby Wiske *N York* 89 SE3398
Dandaleith *Gramp* 141 NJ2846
Danderhall *Loth* 117 NT3069
Dane End *Herts* 39 TL3321
Dane Hills *Leics* 62 SK5604
Dane Street *Kent* 28 TR0552
Danebridge *Ches* 72 SJ9665
Danegate *E Susx* 16 TQ5633
Danehill *E Susx* 15 TQ4027
Danemoor Green *Norfk* 66 TG0505
Danesford *Shrops* 60 SO7391
Danesmoor *Derbys* 74 SK4063
Daniel's Water *Kent* 28 TQ9541
Danshillock *Gramp* 142 NJ7157
Danskine *Loth* 118 NT5667
Danthorpe *Humb* 85 TA2532
Danzey Green *Warwks* 48 SP1269
Dapple Heath *Staffs* 73 SK0425
Darby Green *Hants* 25 SU8360
Darcy Lever *Gt Man* 79 SD7308
Daren-felen *Gwent* 34 SO2212
Darenth *Kent* 27 TQ5671
Daresbury *Ches* 78 SJ5882
Darfield *S York* 83 SE4104
Dargate *Kent* 29 TR0861
Darite *Cnwll* 5 SX2569
Darland *Clwyd* 71 SJ3757
Darland *Kent* 28 TQ7865
Darlaston *Staffs* 72 SJ8835
Darlaston *W Mids* 60 SO9796
Darlaston Green *W Mids* 60 SO9797
Darley *N York* 89 SE2059
Darley Abbey *Derbys* 62 SK3538
Darley Bridge *Derbys* 74 SK2661
Darley Dale *Derbys* 74 SK2663
Darley Green *Warwks* 61 SP1874
Darley Head *N York* 89 SE1959
Darleyhall *Herts* 38 TL1422
Darlingscott *Warwks* 48 SP2342
Darlington *Dur* 89 NZ2814
Darliston *Shrops* 59 SJ5733
Darlton *Notts* 75 SK7773
Darnford *Staffs* 61 SK1308
Darnick *Border* 109 NT5334
Darowen *Powys* 57 SH8201
Darra *Gramp* 142 NJ7447
Darracot *Cnwll* 18 SS2811
Darracott *Devon* 18 SS2317
Darracott *Devon* 18 SS4739
Darras Hall *T & W* 103 NZ1570
Darrington *W York* 83 SE4820
Darsham *Suffk* 55 TM4169
Dartford *Kent* 27 TQ5474
Dartington *Devon* 7 SX7862
Dartmeet *Devon* 7 SX6773
Dartmouth *Devon* 7 SX8751
Darton *S York* 82 SE3110
Darvel *Strath* 107 NS5637
Darwell Hole *E Susx* 16 TQ6919
Darwen *Lancs* 81 SD6922
Datchet *Berks* 26 SU9877
Datchworth *Herts* 39 TL2619
Datchworth Green *Herts* 39 TL2718
Daubhill *Gt Man* 79 SD7007
Dauntsey *Wilts* 35 ST9782
Dauntsey Green *Wilts* 35 ST9981
Dava *Highld* 141 NJ0038
Davenham *Ches* 79 SJ6571
Davenport *Gt Man* 79 SJ9088
Davenport Green *Ches* 79 SJ8379
Davenport Green *Gt Man* 79 SJ8086
Daventry *Nhants* 49 SP5762
David Street *Kent* 27 TQ6464
Davidson's Mains *Loth* 117 NT2175
Davidstow *Cnwll* 4 SX1587
Davington *D & G* 109 NT2302
Davington Hill *Kent* 28 TR0161
Daviot *Gramp* 142 NJ7428
Daviot *Highld* 140 NH7239
Daviot House *Highld* 140 NH7240
Davis's Town *E Susx* 16 TQ5217
Davoch of Grange *Gramp* 142 NJ4751
Daw End *W Mids* 61 SK0300
Daw's House *Cnwll* 5 SX3182
Dawesgreen *Surrey* 15 TQ2147
Dawley *Shrops* 60 SJ6808
Dawlish *Devon* 9 SX9576
Dawlish Warren *Devon* 9 SX9778
Dawn *Clwyd* 69 SH8672
Daws Green *Somset* 20 ST1921
Daws Heath *Essex* 40 TQ8188
Dawsmere *Lincs* 65 TF4430
Day Green *Ches* 72 SJ7757
Daybrook *Notts* 62 SK5744
Dayhills *Staffs* 72 SJ9532
Dayhouse Bank *H & W* 60 SO9678
Daylesford *Gloucs* 48 SP2425
Ddol *Clwyd* 70 SJ1471
Ddol-Cownwy *Powys* 58 SJ0117
Deal *Kent* 29 TR3752
Dean *Cumb* 92 NY0725
Dean *Devon* 19 SS6245
Dean *Devon* 19 SS7048
Dean *Devon* 7 SX7364
Dean *Dorset* 11 ST9715
Dean *Hants* 24 SU4431
Dean *Hants* 13 SU5619
Dean *Lancs* 81 SD8525
Dean *Oxon* 36 SP3422
Dean *Somset* 22 ST6743
Dean Bottom *Kent* 27 TQ5868
Dean Court *Oxon* 37 SP4705
Dean End *Dorset* 11 ST9717
Dean Head *S York* 74 SE2600
Dean Prior *Devon* 7 SX7363
Dean Row *Ches* 79 SJ8781
Dean Street *Kent* 28 TQ7453
Deanburnhaugh *Border* 109 NT3911
Deancombe *Devon* 7 SX7264
Deane *Gt Man* 79 SD6907
Deane *Hants* 24 SU5450
Deanhead *W York* 82 SE0415
Deanland *Dorset* 22 ST9918
Deanlane End *W Susx* 13 SU7412
Deanraw *Nthumb* 102 NY8162
Deanscales *Cumb* 92 NY0926
Deanshanger *Nhants* 49 SP7639
Deanshaugh *Gramp* 141 NJ3550
Deanston *Cent* 116 NN7101
Dearham *Cumb* 92 NY0736
Dearnley *Gt Man* 81 SD9215
Debach *Suffk* 55 TM2454
Debden *Essex* 53 TL5533
Debden *Essex* 27 TQ4496
Debden Green *Essex* 40 TL5831
Debenham *Suffk* 54 TM1763
Deblin's Green *H & W* 47 SO8148
Dechmont *Loth* 117 NT0370
Dechmont Road *Loth* 117 NT0269
Deddington *Oxon* 49 SP4631
Dedham *Essex* 41 TM0533
Dedham Heath *Essex* 41 TM0531
Dedworth *Berks* 26 SU9476
Deene *Nhants* 51 SP9492
Deenethorpe *Nhants* 51 SP9591
Deepcar *S York* 74 SK2897
Deepcut *Surrey* 25 SU9057
Deepdale *Cumb* 88 SD7184
Deepdale *N York* 88 SD8979
Deeping Gate *Lincs* 64 TF1509
Deeping St James *Lincs* 64 TF1609
Deeping St Nicholas *Lincs* 64 TF2115
Deerhurst *Gloucs* 47 SO8730
Deerhurst Walton *Gloucs* 47 SO8828
Deerton Street *Kent* 28 TQ9762
Defford *H & W* 47 SO9143
Defynnog *Powys* 45 SN9227
Deganwy *Gwynd* 69 SH7779
Degnish *Strath* 122 NM7812
Deighton *N York* 89 NZ3801
Deighton *N York* 83 SE6244
Deighton *W York* 82 SE1519
Deiniolen *Gwynd* 69 SH5763
Delabole *Cnwll* 4 SX0683
Delamere *Ches* 71 SJ5668
Delfrigs *Gramp* 143 NJ9620
Dell Quay *W Susx* 14 SU8302
Delley *Devon* 19 SS5424
Delliefure *Highld* 141 NJ0730
Delly End *Oxon* 36 SP3513
Delmonden Green *Kent* 17 TQ7330
Delnabo *Gramp* 141 NJ1517
Delnashaugh Inn *Gramp* 141 NJ1835
Delny *Highld* 146 NH7372
Delph *Gt Man* 82 SD9807
Delves *Dur* 95 NZ1149
Delvine *Tays* 126 NO1240
Dembleby *Lincs* 64 TF0437
Demelza *Cnwll* 4 SW9763
Denaby *S York* 75 SK4899
Denaby Main *S York* 75 SK4999
Denbies *Surrey* 26 TQ1450
Denbigh *Clwyd* 70 SJ0566
Denbrae *Fife* 126 NO3818
Denbury *Devon* 7 SX8268
Denby *Derbys* 62 SK3946
Denby Bottles *Derbys* 62 SK3846
Denby Dale *W York* 82 SE2208
Denchworth *Oxon* 36 SU3891
Dendron *Cumb* 86 SD2470
Denel End *Beds* 38 TL0335
Denfield *Tays* 125 NN9517
Denford *Nhants* 51 SP9976
Dengie *Essex* 41 TL9802
Denham *Bucks* 26 TQ0487
Denham *Suffk* 53 TL7561
Denham *Suffk* 55 TM1974
Denham End *Suffk* 53 TL7663
Denham Green *Bucks* 26 TQ0488
Denham Green *Suffk* 55 TM1974
Denhead *Fife* 127 NO4613
Denhead *Gramp* 143 NJ9952
Denhead of Gray *Tays* 126 NO3531
Denholm *Border* 110 NT5718
Denholme *W York* 82 SE0734
Denholme Clough *W York* 82 SE0732
Denio *Gwynd* 56 SH3635
Denmead *Hants* 13 SU6512
Denmore *Gramp* 135 NJ9411
Denne Park *W Susx* 15 TQ1628
Dennington *Suffk* 55 TM2867
Denny *Cent* 116 NS8082
Dennyloanhead *Cent* 116 NS8080
Denshaw *Gt Man* 82 SD9710
Denside *Gramp* 135 NO8095
Densole *Kent* 29 TR2141
Denston *Suffk* 53 TL7652
Denstone *Staffs* 73 SK0940
Denstroude *Kent* 29 TR1061
Dent *Cumb* 87 SD7086
Dent-de-Lion *Kent* 29 TR3269
Denton *Cambs* 52 TL1587
Denton *Dur* 96 NZ2118
Denton *E Susx* 16 TQ4502
Denton *Gt Man* 79 SJ9295
Denton *Kent* 28 TQ6673
Denton *Kent* 29 TR2147
Denton *Lincs* 63 SK8632
Denton *N York* 82 SE1448
Denton *Nhants* 51 SP8358
Denton *Norfk* 55 TM2788
Denton *Oxon* 37 SP5902
Denver *Norfk* 65 TF6001
Denwick *Nthumb* 111 NU2014
Deopham *Norfk* 66 TG0400
Deopham Green *Norfk* 66 TM0499
Depden *Suffk* 53 TL7857
Depden Green *Suffk* 53 TL7756
Deptford *Gt Lon* 27 TQ3777
Deptford *Wilts* 22 SU0138
Derby *Derbys* 62 SK3536
Derbyhaven *IOM* 153 SC2867
Derculich *Tays* 125 NN8852
Deri *M Glam* 33 SO1201
Derril *Devon* 18 SS3003
Derringstone *Kent* 29 TR2049
Derrington *Staffs* 72 SJ8922
Derriton *Devon* 18 SS3303
Derry Hill *Wilts* 35 ST9670
Derrythorpe *Humb* 84 SE8208
Dersingham *Norfk* 65 TF6830
Dervaig *Strath* 121 NM4352
Derwen *Clwyd* 70 SJ0750
Derwenlas *Powys* 57 SN7298
Desborough *Nhants* 51 SP8083
Desford *Leics* 62 SK4703
Deskford *Gramp* 142 NJ5061
Detchant *Nthumb* 111 NU0836
Detling *Kent* 28 TQ7958
Deuxhill *Shrops* 60 SO6987
Devauden *Gwent* 34 ST4898
Devil's Bridge *Dyfed* 43 SN7376
Deviock *Cnwll* 5 SX3155
Devitts Green *Warwks* 61 SP2790
Devizes *Wilts* 22 SU0061
Devonport *Devon* 6 SX4554
Devonside *Cent* 116 NS9196
Devoran *Cnwll* 3 SW7939
Dewarton *Loth* 118 NT3763
Dewlish *Dorset* 11 SY7798
Dewsbury *W York* 82 SE2421
Dewsbury Moor *W York* 82 SE2321
Deytheur *Powys* 58 SJ2317
Dhoon *IOM* 153 SC3784
Dial *Avon* 21 ST5366
Dial Green *W Susx* 14 SU9227
Dial Post *W Susx* 15 TQ1519
Dibberford *Dorset* 10 ST4504
Dibden *Hants* 13 SU4008
Dibden Purlieu *Hants* 13 SU4106
Dickens Heath *W Mids* 61 SP1176
Dickleburgh *Norfk* 54 TM1682
Didbrook *Gloucs* 48 SP0531
Didcot *Oxon* 37 SU5290
Diddington *Cambs* 52 TL1965
Diddlebury *Shrops* 59 SO5085
Didley *H & W* 46 SO4532
Didling *W Susx* 14 SU8318
Didmarton *Gloucs* 35 ST8287
Didsbury *Gt Man* 79 SJ8491
Didworthy *Devon* 7 SX6862
Digby *Lincs* 76 TF0854
Digg *Highld* 136 NG4668
Diggle *Gt Man* 82 SE0007
Digmore *Lancs* 78 SD4905
Digswell *Herts* 39 TL2415
Digswell Water *Herts* 39 TL2514
Dihewyd *Dyfed* 44 SN4855
Dilham *Norfk* 67 TG3325
Dilhorne *Staffs* 72 SJ9743
Dillington *Cambs* 52 TL1365
Dilston *Nthumb* 102 NY9763
Dilton *Wilts* 22 ST8548
Dilton Marsh *Wilts* 22 ST8449
Dilwyn *H & W* 46 SO4154
Dimma *Cnwll* 5 SX1997
Dimple *Gt Man* 81 SD7015
Dinas *Cnwll* 4 SW9274
Dinas *Dyfed* 30 SN0138
Dinas *Dyfed* 31 SN2730
Dinas *Gwynd* 56 SH2735
Dinas *M Glam* 33 ST0091
Dinas Dinlle *Gwynd* 68 SH4455
Dinas Powys *S Glam* 33 ST1571
Dinas-Mawddwy *Gwynd* 57 SH8515
Dinder *Somset* 21 ST5744
Dinedor *H & W* 46 SO5336
Dingestow *Gwent* 34 SO4510
Dingle *Mersyd* 78 SJ3687
Dingleden *Kent* 17 TQ8131
Dingley *Nhants* 50 SP7787
Dingwall *Highld* 139 NH5458
Dinham *Gwent* 34 ST4792
Dinmael *Clwyd* 70 SJ0044
Dinnet *Gramp* 134 NO4598
Dinnington *S York* 75 SK5285
Dinnington *Somset* 10 ST4012
Dinnington *T & W* 103 NZ2073
Dinorwic *Gwynd* 69 SH5961
Dinton *Bucks* 37 SP7610
Dinton *Wilts* 22 SU0131
Dinwoodie *D & G* 100 NY1190
Dinworthy *Devon* 18 SS3015
Dipford *Somset* 20 ST2021
Dipley *Hants* 24 SU7457
Dippen *Strath* 105 NR7937
Dippenhall *Surrey* 25 SU8146
Dippermill *Devon* 18 SS4406
Dippertown *Devon* 5 SX4284
Dippin *Strath* 105 NS0422
Dipple *Gramp* 141 NJ3258
Dipple *Strath* 106 NS2002
Diptford *Devon* 7 SX7256
Dipton *Dur* 96 NZ1554
Diptonmill *Nthumb* 102 NY9361
Dirleton *Loth* 118 NT5184
Dirt Pot *Nthumb* 95 NY8545
Discoed *Powys* 46 SO2764
Diseworth *Leics* 62 SK4524
Dishforth *N York* 89 SE3873
Disley *Ches* 79 SJ9784
Diss *Norfk* 54 TM1180
Disserth *Powys* 45 SO0358
Distington *Cumb* 92 NY0023
Ditchampton *Wilts* 23 SU0831
Ditchburn *Nthumb* 111 NU1320
Ditcheat *Somset* 21 ST6236
Ditchingham *Norfk* 67 TM3391
Ditchley *Oxon* 36 SP3820
Ditchling *E Susx* 15 TQ3215
Ditherington *Shrops* 59 SJ5014
Ditteridge *Wilts* 35 ST8169
Dittisham *Devon* 6 SX5370
Dittisham *Devon* 7 SX8655
Ditton *Ches* 78 SJ4986
Ditton *Kent* 28 TQ7158
Ditton Green *Cambs* 53 TL6558
Ditton Priors *Shrops* 59 SO6089
Dixton *Gloucs* 47 SO9830
Dixton *Gwent* 34 SO5113
Dizzard *Cnwll* 4 SX1698
Dobcross *Gt Man* 82 SD9906
Dobroyd Castle *W York* 81 SD9323
Dobwalls *Cnwll* 5 SX2165
Doccombe *Devon* 8 SX7786
Dochgarroch *Highld* 140 NH6140
Docker *Lancs* 87 SD5774
Docking *Norfk* 65 TF7636
Docklow *H & W* 46 SO5657
Dockray *Cumb* 93 NY2649
Dockray *Cumb* 93 NY3921
Dod's Leigh *Staffs* 73 SK0134
Dodbrooke *Devon* 7 SX7444
Dodd's Green *Ches* 71 SJ6043
Doddinghurst *Essex* 27 TQ5999
Doddington *Cambs* 52 TL4090
Doddington *Kent* 28 TQ9357
Doddington *Lincs* 76 SK8970
Doddington *Nthumb* 111 NT9932
Doddington *Shrops* 46 SO6176
Doddiscombsleigh *Devon* 8 SX8586
Doddshill *Norfk* 65 TF6930
Doddy Cross *Cnwll* 5 SX3062
Dodford *H & W* 60 SO9373
Dodford *Nhants* 49 SP6160
Dodington *Avon* 35 ST7580
Dodington *Somset* 20 ST1740
Dodleston *Ches* 71 SJ3661
Dodscott *Devon* 19 SS5419
Dodside *Strath* 115 NS5053
Dodworth *S York* 82 SE3105
Dodworth Bottom *S York* 83 SE3204
Dodworth Green *S York* 82 SE3004
Doe Bank *W Mids* 61 SP1197
Doe Lea *Derbys* 75 SK4666
Dog Village *Devon* 9 SX9896
Dogdyke *Lincs* 76 TF2055
Dogley Lane *W York* 82 SE1813
Dogmersfield *Hants* 25 SU7852
Dogridge *Wilts* 36 SU0887
Dogsthorpe *Cambs* 64 TF1901
Dol-for *Powys* 57 SH8106
Dol-gran *Dyfed* 31 SN4334
Dolanog *Powys* 58 SJ0612
Dolau *Powys* 45 SO1467
Dolbenmaen *Gwynd* 56 SH5043
Doley *Shrops* 72 SJ7429
Dolfor *Powys* 58 SO1087
Dolgarrog *Gwynd* 69 SH7767
Dolgellau *Gwynd* 57 SH7217
Dolgoch *Gwynd* 57 SH6504
Doll *Highld* 147 NC8803
Dollar *Cent* 117 NS9698
Dollarfield *Cent* 117 NS9697
Dolley Green *Powys* 46 SO2865
Dollwen *Dyfed* 43 SN6881
Dolphin *Clwyd* 70 SJ1973
Dolphinholme *Lancs* 80 SD5253
Dolphinston *Border* 110 NT6815
Dolphinton *Strath* 117 NT1046
Dolton *Devon* 19 SS5712
Dolwen *Clwyd* 69 SH8874
Dolwyddelan *Gwynd* 69 SH7352
Dolybont *Dyfed* 43 SN6288
Dolyhir *Powys* 46 SO2457
Domgay *Powys* 58 SJ2818
Doncaster *S York* 83 SE5703
Doncaster Carr *S York* 83 SE5801
Donehill *Devon* 8 SX7277
Donhead St Andrew *Wilts* 22 ST9124
Donhead St Mary *Wilts* 22 ST9024
Donibristle *Fife* 117 NT1688
Doniford *Somset* 20 ST0842
Donington *Lincs* 64 TF2035
Donington on Bain *Lincs* 76 TF2382
Donington Southing *Lincs* 64 TF2034
Donisthorpe *Leics* 61 SK3113
Donkey Street *Kent* 17 TR1032
Donkey Town *Surrey* 25 SU9360
Donnington *Berks* 24 SU4668
Donnington *Gloucs* 48 SP1928
Donnington *H & W* 47 SO7034
Donnington *Shrops* 59 SJ5708
Donnington *Shrops* 60 SJ7114
Donnington *W Susx* 14 SU8501
Donnington Wood *Shrops* 60 SJ7012
Donyatt *Somset* 10 ST3314
Doomsday Green *W Susx* 15 TQ1929
Doonfoot *Strath* 106 NS3219
Doonholm *Strath* 106 NS3317
Dorback Lodge *Highld* 141 NJ0716
Dorchester *Dorset* 11 SY6990
Dorchester *Oxon* 37 SU5794
Dordon *Warwks* 61 SK2500
Dore *S York* 74 SK3181
Dores *Highld* 140 NH5934
Dorking *Surrey* 15 TQ1649
Dormans Land *Surrey* 15 TQ4041
Dormans Park *Surrey* 15 TQ3940
Dormington *H & W* 46 SO5840
Dormston *H & W* 47 SO9857
Dorn *Gloucs* 48 SP2034
Dorney *Berks* 26 SU9378
Dornie *Highld* 138 NG8826
Dornoch *Highld* 147 NH7989
Dornock *D & G* 101 NY2366
Dorrery *Highld* 150 ND0754
Dorridge *W Mids* 61 SP1775
Dorrington *Lincs* 76 TF0852
Dorrington *Shrops* 59 SJ4702
Dorrington *Shrops* 72 SJ7340
Dorsington *Warwks* 48 SP1349
Dorstone *H & W* 46 SO3141
Dorton *Bucks* 37 SP6814
Dosthill *Staffs* 61 SP2199
Dottery *Dorset* 10 SY4595
Doublebois *Cnwll* 5 SX1964
Douganhill *D & G* 92 NX8155
Dougarie *Strath* 105 NR8837
Doughton *Gloucs* 35 ST8791
Douglas *IOM* 153 SC3775
Douglas *Strath* 108 NS8330
Douglas and Angus *Tays* 127 NO4233
Douglas Castle *Strath* 108 NS8431
Douglas Hill *Gwynd* 69 SH6065
Douglas Pier *Strath* 114 NS1999
Douglas Water *Strath* 108 NS8736
Douglas West *Strath* 108 NS8231
Douglastown *Tays* 126 NO4147
Dounby *Ork* 155 HY2920
Doune *Cent* 116 NN7201
Doune *Highld* 146 NC4400
Dounepark *Strath* 106 NX1897
Dounie *Highld* 146 NH5690
Dounreay *Highld* 150 ND0065
Dousland *Devon* 6 SX5369
Dovaston *Shrops* 59 SJ3521
Dove Green *Notts* 75 SK4652
Dove Holes *Derbys* 74 SK0777
Dovenby *Cumb* 92 NY0933
Dover *Gt Man* 78 SD6000
Dover *Kent* 29 TR3141
Dovercourt *Essex* 41 TM2431
Doverdale *H & W* 47 SO8666
Doveridge *Derbys* 73 SK1133
Doversgreen *Surrey* 15 TQ2548
Dowally *Tays* 125 NO0048
Dowbridge *Lancs* 80 SD4331
Dowdeswell *Gloucs* 35 SP0019
Dowhill *Strath* 106 NS2003
Dowlais *M Glam* 33 SO0607
Dowland *Devon* 19 SS5610
Dowlish Ford *Somset* 10 ST3513
Dowlish Wake *Somset* 10 ST3712
Down Ampney *Gloucs* 36 SU0996
Down Hatherley *Gloucs* 35 SO8622
Down St Mary *Devon* 8 SS7404
Down Thomas *Devon* 6 SX5050
Downacarey *Devon* 5 SX3790
Downderry *Cnwll* 5 SX3154
Downe *Gt Lon* 27 TQ4361
Downend *Avon* 35 ST6577
Downend *Berks* 37 SU4775
Downend *Gloucs* 35 ST8398
Downend *IOW* 13 SZ5387
Downfield *Tays* 126 NO3932
Downgate *Cnwll* 5 SX2871
Downgate *Cnwll* 5 SX3672
Downham *Cambs* 53 TL5284
Downham *Essex* 40 TQ7296
Downham *Gt Lon* 27 TQ3871
Downham *Lancs* 81 SD7844
Downham *Nthumb* 110 NT8633
Downham Market *Norfk* 65 TF6103
Downhead *Somset* 21 ST5625
Downhead *Somset* 22 ST6945
Downhill *Cnwll* 4 SW8669
Downhill *Tays* 125 NO0930
Downholland Cross *Lancs* 78 SD3606
Downholme *N York* 89 SE1197
Downies *Gramp* 135 NO9294
Downing *Clwyd* 70 SJ1578
Downley *Bucks* 26 SU8495
Downside *Somset* 21 ST6244
Downside *Somset* 21 ST6450
Downside *Surrey* 26 TQ1057
Downton *Hants* 12 SZ2693
Downton *Wilts* 12 SU1821
Downton on the Rock *H & W* 46 SO4273
Dowsby *Lincs* 64 TF1129
Dowsdale *Lincs* 64 TF2810
Dowsland Green *Essex* 40 TL8724
Doxey *Staffs* 72 SJ8923
Doxford *Nthumb* 111 NU1823
Doynton *Avon* 35 ST7274
Draethen *M Glam* 34 ST2287
Draffan *Strath* 116 NS7945
Dragonby *Humb* 84 SE9014
Dragons Green *W Susx* 15 TQ1423
Drakeholes *Notts* 75 SK7090
Drakelow *H & W* 60 SO8180
Drakemyre *Strath* 115 NS2950
Drakes Broughton *H & W* 47 SO9248
Drakes Cross *H & W* 61 SP0876
Drakewalls *Cnwll* 6 SX4270
Draughton *N York* 82 SE0352
Draughton *Nhants* 50 SP7676
Drax *N York* 83 SE6726
Drax Hales *N York* 83 SE6725
Draycot Foliat *Wilts* 36 SU1777
Draycote *Warwks* 50 SP4470
Draycott *Derbys* 62 SK4433
Draycott *Gloucs* 48 SP1835
Draycott *H & W* 47 SO8548
Draycott *Shrops* 60 SO8093
Draycott *Somset* 21 ST4751
Draycott *Somset* 21 ST5521
Draycott in the Clay *Staffs* 73 SK1528
Draycott in the Moors *Staffs* 72 SJ9840
Drayford *Devon* 19 SS7813
Draynes *Cnwll* 5 SX2169
Drayton *H & W* 60 SO8975
Drayton *Hants* 13 SU6705
Drayton *Leics* 51 SP8392
Drayton *Lincs* 64 TF2439
Drayton *Norfk* 66 TG1813
Drayton *Oxon* 49 SP4241
Drayton *Oxon* 37 SU4894
Drayton *Somset* 21 ST4024
Drayton Bassett *Staffs* 61 SK1900
Drayton Beauchamp *Bucks* 38 SP9011
Drayton Parslow *Bucks* 38 SP8328
Drayton St Leonard *Oxon* 37 SU5996
Drebley *N York* 88 SE0559
Dreenhill *Dyfed* 30 SM9214
Drefach *Dyfed* 31 SN3538
Drefach *Dyfed* 44 SN4945
Drefach *Dyfed* 32 SN5213
Drefelin *Dyfed* 31 SN3637
Dreghorn *Strath* 106 NS3538
Drellingore *Kent* 29 TR2441
Drem *Loth* 118 NT5079
Dresden *Staffs* 72 SJ9142
Drewsteignton *Devon* 8 SX7391
Driffield *Gloucs* 36 SU0799
Driffield *Humb* 91 TA0257
Driffield Cross Roads *Gloucs* 36 SU0698
Drift *Cnwll* 2 SW4328
Drigg *Cumb* 86 SD0699
Drighlington *W York* 82 SE2228
Drimnin *Highld* 121 NM5554
Drimpton *Dorset* 10 ST4104
Drimsallie *Highld* 130 NM9578
Dringhoe *Humb* 85 TA1454
Dringhouses *N York* 83 SE5849
Drinkstone *Suffk* 54 TL9561
Drinkstone Green *Suffk* 54 TL9660
Drinsey Nook *Notts* 76 SK8773
Drive End *Dorset* 10 ST5808
Driver's End *Herts* 39 TL2220
Drointon *Staffs* 73 SK0226
Droitwich *H & W* 47 SO8963
Dron *Tays* 126 NO1416
Dronfield *Derbys* 74 SK3578
Dronfield Woodhouse *Derbys* 74 SK3378
Drongan *Strath* 107 NS4418
Dronley *Tays* 126 NO3435
Droop *Dorset* 11 ST7508
Dropping Well *S York* 74 SK3994
Droxford *Hants* 13 SU6018
Droylsden *Gt Man* 79 SJ9097
Druid *Clwyd* 70 SJ0443
Druids Heath *W Mids* 61 SK0502
Druidston *Dyfed* 30 SM8616
Druimachoish *Highld* 123 NN1246
Druimarbin *Highld* 130 NN0770
Druimdrishaig *Strath* 113 NR7370
Druimindarroch *Highld* 129 NM6884
Drum *Strath* 114 NR9276
Drum *Tays* 117 NO0400
Drumalbin *Strath* 108 NS9038
Drumbeg *Highld* 148 NC1232
Drumblade *Gramp* 142 NJ5840
Drumblair House *Gramp* 142 NJ6343
Drumbreddon *D & G* 98 NX0843
Drumbuie *Highld* 137 NG7730
Drumburgh *Cumb* 93 NY2659
Drumburn *D & G* 92 NX8854
Drumchapel *Strath* 115 NS5270
Drumchastle *Tays* 132 NN6858
Drumclog *Strath* 107 NS6438
Drumeldrie *Fife* 127 NO4403
Drumelzier *Border* 108 NT1334
Drumfearn *Highld* 129 NG6716
Drumfrennie *Gramp* 135 NO7298
Drumhead *Gramp* 134 NO6092
Drumin *Gramp* 141 NJ1830
Drumjohn *D & G* 107 NX5297
Drumlamford *Strath* 98 NX2876
Drumlasie *Gramp* 135 NJ6405
Drumleaning *Cumb* 93 NY2751
Drumlemble *Strath* 104 NR6619
Drumlithie *Gramp* 135 NO7880
Drummoddie *D & G* 99 NX3845
Drummond *Highld* 140 NH6065
Drummore *D & G* 98 NX1336
Drummore *D & G* 100 NX9074
Drummuir *Gramp* 141 NJ3843
Drumnadrochit *Highld* 139 NH5030
Drumnagorrach *Gramp* 142 NJ5252
Drumore *Strath* 105 NR7022
Drumpark *D & G* 100 NX8779
Drumrunie Lodge *Highld* 145 NC1604
Drumshang *Strath* 106 NS2514
Drumuie *Highld* 136 NG4546
Drumvaich *Cent* 124 NN6704
Drumvillie *Highld* 140 NH9420
Drumwalt *D & G* 98 NX3053
Drumwhirn *D & G* 99 NX7480
Drunzie *Tays* 126 NO1308
Druridge *Nthumb* 103 NZ2796
Drury *Clwyd* 71 SJ2964
Dry Doddington *Lincs* 63 SK8546
Dry Drayton *Cambs* 52 TL3861
Dry Sandford *Oxon* 37 SP4600
Dry Street *Essex* 40 TQ6986
Drybeck *Cumb* 94 NY6615
Drybridge *Gramp* 142 NJ4362
Drybridge *Strath* 106 NS3536
Drybrook *Gloucs* 35 SO6417
Dryburgh *Border* 110 NT5932
Dryhope *Border* 109 NT2624
Drym *Cnwll* 2 SW6133
Drymen *Cent* 115 NS4788
Drymuir *Gramp* 143 NJ9046
Drynoch *Highld* 136 NG4031
Dryslwyn *Dyfed* 32 SN5520
Dryton *Shrops* 59 SJ5905
Dubford *Gramp* 143 NJ7963
Dublin *Suffk* 54 TM1669
Duchally *Highld* 145 NC3817
Duck End *Beds* 38 TL0544
Duck End *Cambs* 52 TL2464
Duck End *Essex* 40 TL6526
Duck's Cross *Beds* 52 TL1156
Duckend Green *Essex* 40 TL7223
Duckington *Ches* 71 SJ4851
Ducklington *Oxon* 36 SP3507
Duddingston *Loth* 117 NT2872
Duddington *Nhants* 51 SK9800
Duddlestone *Somset* 20 ST2321
Duddleswell *E Susx* 16 TQ4628
Duddlewick *Shrops* 59 SO6583
Duddo *Nthumb* 110 NT9342
Duddon *Ches* 71 SJ5164
Duddon Bridge *Cumb* 86 SD1988
Dudleston *Shrops* 71 SJ3438
Dudleston Heath *Shrops* 59 SJ3736
Dudley *T & W* 103 NZ2573
Dudley *W Mids* 60 SO9490
Dudley Hill *W York* 82 SE1830
Dudley Port *W Mids* 60 SO9691
Dudnill *Shrops* 47 SO6474
Dudsbury *Dorset* 12 SZ0798
Dudswell *Herts* 38 SP9609
Duffield *Derbys* 62 SK3443
Duffryn *M Glam* 33 SS8495
Dufftown *Gramp* 141 NJ3240
Duffus *Gramp* 141 NJ1668
Dufton *Cumb* 94 NY6825
Duggleby *N York* 90 SE8767
Duirinish *Highld* 137 NG7831
Duisdalemore *Highld* 129 NG7013
Duisky *Highld* 130 NN0076
Duke Street *Suffk* 54 TM0742
Dukestown *Gwent* 33 SO1410
Dukinfield *Gt Man* 79 SJ9397
Dulas *Gwynd* 68 SH4789
Dulcote *Somset* 21 ST5644
Dulford *Devon* 9 ST0706
Dull *Tays* 125 NN8049
Dullatur *Strath* 116 NS7476
Dullingham *Cambs* 53 TL6357
Dullingham Ley *Cambs* 53 TL6456
Dulnain Bridge *Highld* 141 NH9925
Duloe *Beds* 52 TL1560
Duloe *Cnwll* 5 SX2358
Dulverton *Somset* 20 SS9127
Dulwich *Gt Lon* 27 TQ3373
Dumbarton *Strath* 115 NS3975
Dumbleton *Gloucs* 47 SP0135
Dumcrieff *D & G* 108 NT1003
Dumfries *D & G* 100 NX9776
Dumgoyne *Cent* 115 NS5283
Dummer *Hants* 24 SU5846
Dumpton *Kent* 29 TR3966
Dun *Tays* 135 NO6659
Dunalastair *Tays* 132 NN7158
Dunan *Highld* 137 NG5828
Dunan *Strath* 114 NS1571
Dunan *Tays* 124 NN4757
Dunans *Strath* 114 NS0491
Dunaverty *Strath* 105 NR6807
Dunball *Somset* 21 ST3141
Dunbar *Loth* 118 NT6778
Dunbeath *Highld* 151 ND1629
Dunbeg *Strath* 122 NM8833
Dunblane *Cent* 116 NN7801
Dunbog *Fife* 126 NO2817
Dunbridge *Hants* 23 SU3226
Duncanston *Highld* 139 NH5856
Duncanstone *Gramp* 142 NJ5726
Dunchideock *Devon* 9 SX8787
Dunchurch *Warwks* 50 SP4871
Duncote *Nhants* 49 SP6750
Duncow *D & G* 100 NX9683
Duncrievie *Tays* 126 NO1309
Duncton *W Susx* 14 SU9617
Dundee *Tays* 126 NO4030
Dundon *Somset* 21 ST4832
Dundonald *Strath* 106 NS3634
Dundonnell *Highld* 145 NH0987
Dundraw *Cumb* 93 NY2149
Dundreggan *Highld* 131 NH3214
Dundrennan *D & G* 99 NX7447
Dundry *Avon* 21 ST5666
Dunecht *Gramp* 135 NJ7509
Dunfermline *Fife* 117 NT0987
Dunfield *Gloucs* 36 SU1497
Dunford Bridge *S York* 82 SE1502
Dungate *Kent* 28 TQ9159
Dungavel *Strath* 107 NS6537
Dunge *Wilts* 22 ST8954
Dunglass *Loth* 119 NT7671
Dungworth *S York* 74 SK2789
Dunham *Notts* 75 SK8074
Dunham Town *Gt Man* 79 SJ7387
Dunham Woodhouses *Gt Man* 79 SJ7287
Dunham-on-the-Hill *Ches* 71 SJ4772
Dunhampstead *H & W* 47 SO9160
Dunhampton *H & W* 47 SO8466
Dunholme *Lincs* 76 TF0279
Dunino *Fife* 127 NO5311
Dunipace *Cent* 116 NS8083
Dunk's Green *Kent* 27 TQ6152
Dunkeld *Tays* 125 NO0242
Dunkerton *Avon* 22 ST7159
Dunkeswell *Devon* 9 ST1407
Dunkeswick *W York* 82 SE3047
Dunkirk *Avon* 35 ST7885
Dunkirk *Ches* 71 SJ3872
Dunkirk *Kent* 29 TR0759
Dunkirk *Staffs* 72 SJ8152
Dunkirk *Wilts* 22 ST9962
Dunlappie *Tays* 134 NO5867
Dunley *H & W* 47 SO7869
Dunley *Hants* 24 SU4553
Dunlop *Strath* 115 NS4049
Dunmaglass *Highld* 140 NH5922
Dunmere *Cnwll* 4 SX0467
Dunmore *Cent* 116 NS8989
Dunmore *Strath* 113 NR7961
Dunn Street *Kent* 28 TQ7961
Dunnet *Highld* 151 ND2171
Dunnichen *Tays* 127 NO5048
Dunning *Tays* 125 NO0114
Dunnington *Humb* 85 TA1551
Dunnington *N York* 83 SE6652
Dunnington *Warwks* 48 SP0654
Dunnockshaw *Lancs* 81 SD8127
Dunoon *Strath* 114 NS1776
Dunphail *Gramp* 141 NJ0048
Dunragit *D & G* 98 NX1557
Duns *Border* 119 NT7853
Duns Tew *Oxon* 49 SP4528
Dunsa *Derbys* 74 SK2470
Dunsby *Lincs* 64 TF1026
Dunscar *Gt Man* 81 SD7113
Dunscore *D & G* 100 NX8684
Dunscroft *S York* 83 SE6409
Dunsdale *Cleve* 97 NZ6019
Dunsden Green *Oxon* 37 SU7377
Dunsdon *Devon* 18 SS3008
Dunsfold *Surrey* 14 TQ0035
Dunsford *Devon* 8 SX8189
Dunshelt *Fife* 126 NO2410
Dunshillock *Gramp* 143 NJ9848
Dunsill *Notts* 75 SK4661
Dunsley *N York* 90 NZ8511
Dunsley *Staffs* 60 SO8583
Dunsmore *Bucks* 38 SP8605
Dunsop Bridge *Lancs* 81 SD6649
Dunstable *Beds* 38 TL0122
Dunstall *Staffs* 73 SK1820
Dunstall Common *H & W* 47 SO8843
Dunstall Green *Suffk* 53 TL7460
Dunstan *Nthumb* 111 NU2419
Dunstan Steads *Nthumb* 111 NU2422
Dunster *Somset* 20 SS9943
Dunston *Lincs* 76 TF0662
Dunston *Norfk* 67 TG2202
Dunston *Staffs* 72 SJ9217
Dunston *T & W* 96 NZ2362
Dunston Heath *Staffs* 72 SJ9017
Dunstone *Devon* 6 SX5951
Dunstone *Devon* 7 SX7175
Dunsville *S York* 83 SE6407
Dunswell *Humb* 85 TA0735
Dunsyre *Strath* 117 NT0748
Dunterton *Devon* 5 SX3779
Dunthrop *Oxon* 48 SP3528
Duntisbourne Abbots *Gloucs* 35 SO9607
Duntisbourne Rouse *Gloucs* 35 SO9805
Duntish *Dorset* 11 ST6906
Duntocher *Strath* 115 NS4872
Dunton *Beds* 39 TL2344
Dunton *Bucks* 38 SP8224
Dunton *Norfk* 66 TF8830
Dunton Bassett *Leics* 50 SP5490
Dunton Green *Kent* 27 TQ5157
Dunton Wayletts *Essex* 40 TQ6590
Duntulm *Highld* 136 NG4174
Dunure *Strath* 106 NS2515
Dunvant *W Glam* 32 SS5993
Dunvegan *Highld* 136 NG2547
Dunwich *Suffk* 55 TM4770
Dunwood *Staffs* 72 SJ9455
Durdar *Cumb* 93 NY4051
Durgan *Cnwll* 3 SW7727
Durham *Dur* 96 NZ2742
Durisdeer *D & G* 108 NS8903
Durisdeermill *D & G* 108 NS8804
Durkar *W York* 82 SE3116
Durleigh *Somset* 20 ST2736
Durley *Hants* 13 SU5116
Durley *Wilts* 23 SU2364
Durley Street *Hants* 13 SU5217
Durlock *Kent* 29 TR2757
Durlock *Kent* 29 TR3164
Durlow Common *H & W* 47 SO6339
Durmgley *Tays* 127 NO4250
Durn *Gt Man* 82 SD9416
Durness *Highld* 149 NC4068
Duror *Highld* 122 NM9754
Durran *Highld* 151 ND1963
Durrington *W Susx* 14 TQ1105
Durrington *Wilts* 23 SU1544
Durris *Gramp* 135 NO7796
Dursley *Gloucs* 35 ST7598
Dursley Cross *Gloucs* 35 SO6920
Durston *Somset* 20 ST2928
Durweston *Dorset* 11 ST8508
Duston *Nhants* 49 SP7261
Duthil *Highld* 140 NH9324
Dutlas *Powys* 45 SO2177
Dutson *Cnwll* 5 SX3485
Dutton *Ches* 71 SJ5779
Duxford *Cambs* 53 TL4846
Duxford *Oxon* 36 SP3600
Dwygyfylchi *Gwynd* 69 SH7376
Dwyran *Gwynd* 68 SH4465
Dyce *Gramp* 135 NJ8812
Dye House *Nthumb* 95 NY9358
Dyer's End *Essex* 53 TL7238
Dyfatty *Dyfed* 32 SN4401
Dyffryn *M Glam* 33 SO0603
Dyffryn *S Glam* 33 ST0971
Dyffryn Ardudwy *Gwynd* 57 SH5823
Dyffryn Castell *Dyfed* 43 SN7782
Dyffryn Cellwen *W Glam* 33 SN8510
Dyke *Devon* 18 SS3123
Dyke *Gramp* 140 NH9858
Dyke *Lincs* 64 TF1022
Dykehead *Cent* 115 NS5997
Dykehead *Strath* 116 NS8759
Dykehead *Tays* 126 NO2453
Dykehead *Tays* 134 NO3859
Dykelands *Gramp* 135 NO7068
Dykends *Tays* 133 NO2557
Dykeside *Gramp* 142 NJ7243
Dylife *Powys* 43 SN8694
Dymchurch *Kent* 17 TR1029
Dymock *Gloucs* 47 SO7031
Dyrham *Avon* 35 ST7475
Dysart *Fife* 117 NT3093
Dyserth *Clwyd* 70 SJ0578

E

Eachway *H & W* 60 SO9876
Eachwick *Nthumb* 103 NZ1171
Eagland Hill *Lancs* 80 SD4345
Eagle *Lincs* 76 SK8766
Eagle Barnsdale *Lincs* 76 SK8865
Eagle Manor *Lincs* 76 SK8868
Eaglescliffe *Cleve* 96 NZ4215
Eaglesfield *Cumb* 92 NY0928
Eaglesfield *D & G* 101 NY2374
Eaglesham *Strath* 115 NS5751
Eagley *Gt Man* 81 SD7112
Eairy *IOM* 153 SC2977
Eakring *Notts* 75 SK6762
Ealand *Humb* 84 SE7811
Ealing *Gt Lon* 26 TQ1780
Eals *Nthumb* 94 NY6756
Eamont Bridge *Cumb* 94 NY5228
Earby *Lancs* 81 SD9046
Earcroft *Lancs* 81 SD6823
Eardington *Shrops* 60 SO7290
Eardisland *H & W* 46 SO4158
Eardisley *H & W* 46 SO3149
Eardiston *H & W* 47 SO6968
Eardiston *Shrops* 59 SJ3725
Earith *Cambs* 52 TL3875
Earl Shilton *Leics* 50 SP4697
Earl Soham *Suffk* 55 TM2363
Earl Sterndale *Derbys* 74 SK0966
Earl Stonham *Suffk* 54 TM1059
Earl's Croome *H & W* 47 SO8642
Earl's Down *E Susx* 16 TQ6419
Earl's Green *Suffk* 54 TM0366
Earle *Nthumb* 111 NT9826
Earlestown *Mersyd* 78 SJ5795
Earley *Berks* 24 SU7472
Earlham *Norfk* 67 TG1908
Earlish *Highld* 136 NG3861
Earls Barton *Nhants* 51 SP8563
Earls Colne *Essex* 40 TL8528
Earls Common *H & W* 47 SO9559
Earlsditton *Shrops* 47 SO6275
Earlsdon *W Mids* 61 SP3278
Earlsferry *Fife* 118 NO4800
Earlsfield *Gt Lon* 27 TQ2573
Earlsford *Gramp* 143 NJ8334
Earlsheaton *W York* 82 SE2621
Earlston *Border* 110 NT5738
Earlston *Strath* 106 NS4035
Earlswood *Surrey* 15 TQ2749
Earlswood *Warwks* 61 SP1174
Earlswood Common *Gwent* 34 ST4594
Earnley *W Susx* 14 SZ8196
Earnshaw Bridge *Lancs* 80 SD5222
Earsdon *Nthumb* 103 NZ1993
Earsdon *T & W* 103 NZ3272
Earsham *Norfk* 55 TM3288
Earswick *N York* 90 SE6157
Eartham *W Susx* 14 SU9309
Easby *N York* 90 NZ5708
Easebourne *W Susx* 14 SU9023
Easenhall *Warwks* 50 SP4679
Eashing *Surrey* 25 SU9443
Easington *Bucks* 37 SP6810

F

Glanaman
Hallow

Glanaman *Dyfed* 32 SN6713
Glandford *Norfk* 66 TG0441
Glandwr *Dyfed* 31 SN1928
Glandyfi *Dyfed* 43 SN6996
Glangrwyne *Powys* 34 SO2416
Glanrhyd *Dyfed* 31 SN1442
Glanton *Nthumb* 111 NU0714
Glanton Pike *Nthumb* 111 NU0514
Glanvilles Wootton *Dorset* 11 ST6708
Glapthorn *Nhants* 51 TL0290
Glapwell *Derbys* 75 SK4766
Glasbury *Powys* 45 SO1739
Glascoed *Clwyd* 70 SH9973
Glascoed *Gwent* 34 SO3301
Glascote *Staffs* 61 SK2203
Glascwm *Powys* 45 SO1552
Glasfryn *Clwyd* 70 SH9250
Glasgow *Strath* 115 NS5865
Glasinfryn *Gwynd* 69 SH5868
Glasnacardoch Bay *Highld* 129 NM6795
Glasnakille *Highld* 128 NG5313
Glaspwll *Powys* 43 SN7397
Glass Houghton *W York* 83 SE4324
Glassenbury *Kent* 28 TQ7536
Glasserton *D & G* 99 NX4237
Glassford *Strath* 116 NS7247
Glasshouse *Gloucs* 35 SO7021
Glasshouse Hill *Gloucs* 35 SO7020
Glasshouses *N York* 89 SE1764
Glasson *Cumb* 101 NY2560
Glasson *Lancs* 80 SD4456
Glassonby *Cumb* 94 NY5738
Glasterlaw *Tays* 127 NO5951
Glaston *Leics* 51 SK8900
Glastonbury *Somset* 21 ST5038
Glatton *Cambs* 52 TL1586
Glazebrook *Ches* 79 SJ6992
Glazebury *Ches* 79 SJ6797
Glazeley *Shrops* 60 SO7088
Gleadsmoss *Ches* 79 SJ8168
Gleaston *Cumb* 86 SD2570
Gledhow *W York* 82 SE3137
Gledpark *D & G* 99 NX6250
Gledrid *Shrops* 59 SJ3036
Glemsford *Suffk* 54 TL8348
Glen *D & G* 99 NX5457
Glen Clunie Lodge *Gramp* 133 NO1383
Glen Maye *IOM* 153 SC2379
Glen Nevis House *Highld* 130 NN1272
Glen Parva *Leics* 50 SP5798
Glen Trool Lodge *D & G* 99 NX4080
Glenancross *Highld* 129 NM6691
Glenaros House *Strath* 121 NM5544
Glenbarr *Strath* 105 NR6736
Glenbeg *Highld* 121 NM5862
Glenboig *Strath* 116 NS7268
Glenborrodale *Highld* 121 NM6061
Glenbranter *Strath* 114 NS1197
Glenbreck *Border* 108 NT0521
Glenbrittle House *Highld* 128 NG4121
Glenbuck *Strath* 107 NS7429
Glencally *Tays* 134 NO3562
Glencaple *D & G* 100 NX9968
Glencarron Lodge *Highld* 138 NH0650
Glencarse *Tays* 126 NO1921
Glenceitlein *Highld* 123 NN1548
Glencoe *Highld* 130 NN1058
Glencothe *Border* 108 NT0829
Glencraig *Fife* 117 NT1894
Glencrosh *D & G* 107 NX7689
Glendale *Highld* 136 NG1749
Glendaruel *Strath* 114 NR9983
Glendevon *Tays* 125 NN9904
Glendoe Lodge *Highld* 131 NH4009
Glendoick *Tays* 126 NO2022
Glenduckie *Fife* 126 NO2818
Gleneagles *Tays* 125 NN9208
Glenegedale *Strath* 112 NR3351
Glenelg *Highld* 129 NG8119
Glenerney *Gramp* 141 NJ0146
Glenfarg *Tays* 126 NO1310
Glenfeshie Lodge *Highld* 132 NN8493
Glenfield *Leics* 62 SK5406
Glenfinnan *Highld* 130 NM9080
Glenfinntaig Lodge *Highld* 131 NN2286
Glenfoot *Tays* 126 NO1815
Glenfyne Lodge *Strath* 123 NN2215
Glengarnock *Strath* 115 NS3252
Glengolly *Highld* 151 ND1065
Glengorm Castle *Strath* 121 NM4457
Glengrasco *Highld* 136 NG4444
Glenholm *Border* 108 NT1033
Glenhoul *D & G* 107 NX6187
Glenkerry *Border* 109 NT2710
Glenkin *Strath* 114 NS1280
Glenkindie *Gramp* 142 NJ4314
Glenlee *D & G* 99 NX6080
Glenlivet *Gramp* 141 NJ1929
Glenlochar *D & G* 99 NX7364
Glenloig *Strath* 105 NR9435
Glenlomond *Tays* 126 NO1704
Glenluce *D & G* 98 NX1957
Glenmark *Tays* 134 NO4183
Glenmassen *Strath* 114 NS1088
Glenmavis *Strath* 116 NS7467
Glenmore *Highld* 136 NG4340
Glenmore Lodge *Highld* 133 NH9709
Glenquiech *Tays* 134 NO4261
Glenralloch *Strath* 113 NR8569
Glenridding *Cumb* 93 NY3817
Glenrothes *Fife* 117 NO2700
Glenshero Lodge *Highld* 132 NN5592
Glenstriven *Strath* 114 NS0878
Glentham *Lincs* 76 TF0090
Glentromie Lodge *Highld* 132 NN7897
Glentrool Village *D & G* 98 NX3578
Glentruim House *Highld* 132 NN6894
Glentworth *Lincs* 76 SK9488
Glenuig *Highld* 129 NM6677
Glenure *Strath* 123 NN0448
Glenurquhart *Highld* 140 NH7462
Glenvarragill *Highld* 136 NG4739
Glenwhilly *D & G* 98 NX1771
Glespin *Strath* 108 NS8127
Glewstone *H & W* 34 SO5521
Glinton *Cambs* 64 TF1505
Glooston *Leics* 50 SP7595
Glororum *Nthumb* 111 NU1633
Glossop *Derbys* 74 SK0393
Gloster Hill *Nthumb* 103 NU2504
Gloucester *Gloucs* 35 SO8318
Glover's Hill *Staffs* 73 SK0516
Glusburn *N York* 82 SE0045
Glutt Lodge *Highld* 150 ND0036
Gluvian *Cnwll* 4 SW9164
Glympton *Oxon* 36 SP4221
Glyn Ceiriog *Clwyd* 70 SJ2038
Glyn-Neath *W Glam* 33 SN8806
Glynarthen *Dyfed* 42 SN3148
Glyncorrwg *W Glam* 33 SS8798
Glynde *E Susx* 16 TQ4509
Glyndebourne *E Susx* 16 TQ4510
Glyndyfrdwy *Clwyd* 70 SJ1442
Glynn *Cnwll* 4 SX1165
Glyntaff *M Glam* 33 ST0889
Glyntawe *Powys* 33 SN8416
Glynteg *Dyfed* 31 SN3538
Gnosall *Staffs* 72 SJ8220
Gnosall Heath *Staffs* 72 SJ8220
Goadby *Leics* 50 SP7598
Goadby Marwood *Leics* 63 SK7726
Goat Lees *Kent* 28 TR0145
Goatacre *Wilts* 35 SU0276
Goatfield *Strath* 114 NN0100
Goatham Green *E Susx* 17 TQ8120
Goathill *Dorset* 11 ST6717
Goathland *N York* 90 NZ8301
Goathurst *Somset* 20 ST2534
Goathurst Common *Kent* 27 TQ4952
Gobowen *Shrops* 59 SJ3033
Godalming *Surrey* 25 SU9643
Godameavy *Devon* 6 SX5364
Goddard's Corner *Suffk* 55 TM2868
Goddard's Green *Kent* 17 TQ8134
Godford Cross *Devon* 9 ST1302
Godington *Bucks* 49 SP6427
Godley *Gt Man* 79 SJ9595
Godmanchester *Cambs* 52 TL2470
Godmanstone *Dorset* 11 SY6697
Godmersham *Kent* 28 TR0550
Godney *Somset* 21 ST4842
Godolphin Cross *Cnwll* 2 SW6031
Godre'r-graig *W Glam* 32 SN7506
Godshill *Hants* 12 SU1715
Godshill *IOW* 13 SZ5281
Godstone *Staffs* 73 SK0134
Godstone *Surrey* 27 TQ3551
Godsworthy *Devon* 5 SX5277
Godwinscroft *Hants* 12 SZ1996
Goetre *Gwent* 34 SO3206
Goff's Oak *Herts* 27 TL3202
Gofilon *Gwent* 34 SO2613
Gogar *Loth* 117 NT1672
Goginan *Dyfed* 43 SN6881
Golan *Gwynd* 57 SH5242
Golant *Cnwll* 3 SX1254
Golberdon *Cnwll* 5 SX3271
Golborne *Gt Man* 78 SJ6097
Golcar *W York* 82 SE0915
Gold Hill *Cambs* 65 TL5392
Gold Hill *Dorset* 11 ST8213
Goldcliff *Gwent* 34 ST3683
Golden Cross *E Susx* 16 TQ5312
Golden Green *Kent* 16 TQ6348
Golden Grove *Dyfed* 32 SN5919
Golden Hill *Dyfed* 30 SM9802
Golden Pot *Hants* 24 SU7143
Golden Valley *Derbys* 74 SK4251
Goldenhill *Staffs* 72 SJ8553
Golders Green *Gt Lon* 26 TQ2487
Goldfinch Bottom *Berks* 24 SU5063
Goldhanger *Essex* 40 TL9008
Golding *Shrops* 59 SJ5403
Goldington *Beds* 38 TL0750
Golds Green *W Mids* 60 SO9893
Goldsborough *N York* 90 NZ8314
Goldsborough *N York* 83 SE3856
Goldsithney *Cnwll* 2 SW5430
Goldstone *Kent* 29 TR2961
Goldstone *Shrops* 72 SJ7028
Goldsworth *Surrey* 25 SU9958
Goldthorpe *S York* 83 SE4604
Goldworthy *Devon* 18 SS3922
Golford *Kent* 28 TQ7936
Golford Green *Kent* 28 TQ7936
Gollanfield *Highld* 140 NH8053
Gollinglith Foot *N York* 89 SE1481
Golly *Clwyd* 71 SJ3358
Golsoncott *Somset* 20 ST0239
Golspie *Highld* 147 NC8300
Gomeldon *Wilts* 23 SU1835
Gomersal *W York* 82 SE2026
Gomshall *Surrey* 14 TQ0847
Gonalston *Notts* 63 SK6747
Gonerby Hill Foot *Lincs* 63 SK9037
Gonfirth *Shet* 155 HU3661
Good Easter *Essex* 40 TL6212
Gooderstone *Norfk* 65 TF7602
Goodleigh *Devon* 19 SS6034
Goodmanham *Humb* 84 SE8843
Goodnestone *Kent* 28 TR0461
Goodnestone *Kent* 29 TR2554
Goodrich *H & W* 34 SO5719
Goodrington *Devon* 7 SX8958
Goodshaw *Lancs* 81 SD8125
Goodshaw Fold *Lancs* 81 SD8026
Goodstone *Devon* 7 SX7872
Goodwick *Dyfed* 30 SM9438
Goodworth Clatford *Hants* 23 SU3642
Goodyers End *Warwks* 61 SP3385
Goole *Humb* 84 SE7423
Goolefields *Humb* 84 SE7520
Goom's Hill *H & W* 47 SP0154
Goonbell *Cnwll* 3 SW7249
Goonhavern *Cnwll* 3 SW7853
Goonvrea *Cnwll* 2 SW7149
Goose Green *Avon* 35 ST6774
Goose Green *Essex* 41 TM1327
Goose Green *Gt Man* 78 SD5603
Goose Green *Kent* 27 TQ6451
Goose Green *Kent* 28 TQ8437
Goose Green *W Susx* 14 TQ1118
Goose Pool *H & W* 46 SO4636
Goosecruives *Gramp* 135 NO7583
Gooseford *Devon* 8 SX6792
Gooseham *Cnwll* 18 SS2316
Goosehill Green *H & W* 47 SO9361
Goosemoor *Somset* 20 SS9635
Goosey *Oxon* 36 SU3591
Goosnargh *Lancs* 81 SD5536
Goostrey *Ches* 79 SJ7770
Gorddinog *Gwynd* 69 SH6773
Gordon *Border* 110 NT6443
Gordon Arms Hotel *Border* 109 NT3025
Gordonstown *Gramp* 142 NJ5656
Gordonstown *Gramp* 142 NJ7138
Gore *Powys* 46 SO2558
Gore Pit *Essex* 40 TL8719
Gore Street *Kent* 29 TR2765
Gorebridge *Loth* 118 NT3461
Gorefield *Cambs* 65 TF4112
Gores *Wilts* 23 SU1158
Gorey *Jersey* 152 SY2110
Goring *Oxon* 37 SU6080
Goring Heath *Oxon* 37 SU6579
Goring-by-Sea *W Susx* 14 TQ1102
Gorleston on Sea *Norfk* 67 TG5204
Gorrachie *Gramp* 142 NJ7358
Gorran *Cnwll* 3 SW9942
Gorran Haven *Cnwll* 3 SX0141
Gorran High Lanes *Cnwll* 3 SW9843
Gors *Dyfed* 43 SN6277
Gorse Hill *Wilts* 36 SU1586
Gorsedd *Clwyd* 70 SJ1576
Gorseinon *W Glam* 32 SS5998
Gorseybank *Derbys* 73 SK2953
Gorsgoch *Dyfed* 44 SN4850
Gorslas *Dyfed* 32 SN5713
Gorsley *Gloucs* 47 SO6925
Gorsley Common *Gloucs* 47 SO6825
Gorsley Green *Ches* 79 SJ8469
Gorst Hill *H & W* 60 SO7373
Gorstage *Ches* 71 SJ6172
Gorstan *Highld* 139 NH3862
Gorstello *Ches* 71 SJ3562
Gorsty Common *H & W* 46 SO4437
Gorsty Hill *Staffs* 73 SK1028
Gorten *Strath* 122 NM7432
Gorthleck *Highld* 139 NH5420
Gorton *Gt Man* 79 SJ8896
Gosbeck *Suffk* 54 TM1555
Gosberton *Lincs* 64 TF2331
Gosberton Clough *Lincs* 64 TF1929
Gosfield *Essex* 40 TL7829
Gosforth *Cumb* 86 NY0603
Gosforth *T & W* 103 NZ2368
Gosland Green *Ches* 71 SJ5758
Gosling Street *Somset* 21 ST5433
Gosmore *Herts* 39 TL1827
Gospel End *Staffs* 60 SO8993
Gospel Green *W Susx* 14 SU9431
Gosport *Hants* 13 SZ6099
Gossard Green *Beds* 38 SP9643
Goswick *Nthumb* 111 NU0644
Gotham *Notts* 62 SK5330
Gotherington *Gloucs* 47 SO9529
Gotton *Somset* 20 ST2428
Goudhurst *Kent* 28 TQ7237
Goulceby *Lincs* 77 TF2579
Gourdas *Gramp* 142 NJ7741
Gourdie *Tays* 126 NO3532
Gourdon *Gramp* 135 NO8270
Gourock *Strath* 114 NS2477
Govan *Strath* 115 NS5465
Goveton *Devon* 7 SX7546
Gowdall *Humb* 83 SE6222
Gower *Highld* 139 NH5058
Gowerton *W Glam* 32 SS5896
Gowkhall *Fife* 117 NT0589
Gowthorpe *Humb* 84 SE7654
Goxhill *Humb* 85 TA1021
Goxhill *Humb* 85 TA1844
Graby *Lincs* 64 TF0929
Grade *Cnwll* 2 SW7114
Gradeley Green *Ches* 71 SJ5851
Graffham *W Susx* 14 SU9217
Grafham *Cambs* 52 TL1669
Grafham *Surrey* 14 TQ0241
Grafton *H & W* 46 SO4936
Grafton *H & W* 46 SO5761
Grafton *H & W* 47 SO9837
Grafton *N York* 89 SE4163
Grafton *Oxon* 36 SP2600
Grafton *Shrops* 59 SJ4319
Grafton Flyford *H & W* 47 SO9655
Grafton Regis *Nhants* 49 SP7546
Grafton Underwood *Nhants* 51 SP9280
Grafty Green *Kent* 28 TQ8748
Graianrhyd *Clwyd* 70 SJ2156
Graig *Clwyd* 70 SJ0872
Graig *Gwynd* 69 SH8071
Graig-fechan *Clwyd* 70 SJ1454
Grain *Kent* 28 TQ8876
Grains Bar *Gt Man* 79 SD9608
Grainsby *Lincs* 77 TF2799
Grainthorpe *Lincs* 77 TF3896
Graizelound *Humb* 75 SK7698
Gramisdale *W Isls* 154 NF8155
Grampound *Cnwll* 3 SW9348
Grampound Road *Cnwll* 3 SW9150
Granborough *Bucks* 49 SP7625
Granby *Notts* 63 SK7536
Grand Chemins *Jersey* 152 JS1710
Grandborough *Warwks* 50 SP4966
Grandes Rocques *Guern* 152 GN5011
Grandtully *Tays* 125 NN9153
Grange *Cumb* 93 NY2517
Grange *Kent* 28 TQ7968
Grange *Mersyd* 78 SJ2286
Grange *Tays* 126 NO2625
Grange Crossroads *Gramp* 142 NJ4754
Grange Gate *Dorset* 11 SY9182
Grange Hall *Gramp* 141 NJ0660
Grange Hill *Gt Lon* 27 TQ4492
Grange Lindores *Fife* 126 NO2516
Grange Moor *W York* 82 SE2215
Grange Villa *Dur* 96 NZ2352
Grange-over-Sands *Cumb* 87 SD4077
Grangehall *Strath* 108 NS9642
Grangemill *Derbys* 74 SK2457
Grangemouth *Cent* 116 NS9281
Grangepans *Cent* 117 NT0181
Grangetown *Cleve* 97 NZ5420
Gransmoor *Humb* 91 TA1259
Gransmore Green *Essex* 40 TL6922
Granston *Dyfed* 30 SM8934
Grantchester *Cambs* 53 TL4355
Grantham *Lincs* 63 SK9135
Granton *Fife* 117 NT2376
Grantown-on-Spey *Highld* 141 NJ0328
Grantsfield *H & W* 46 SO5260
Grantshouse *Border* 119 NT8065
Grappenhall *Ches* 79 SJ6486
Grasby *Lincs* 85 TA0804
Grasmere *Cumb* 86 NY3307
Grass Green *Essex* 53 TL7338
Grasscroft *Gt Man* 82 SD9704
Grassendale *Mersyd* 78 SJ3985
Grassgarth *Cumb* 93 NY3444
Grassington *N York* 88 SE0063
Grassmoor *Derbys* 74 SK4067
Grassthorpe *Notts* 75 SK7967
Grateley *Hants* 23 SU2741
Gratwich *Staffs* 73 SK0231
Graveley *Cambs* 52 TL2563
Graveley *Herts* 39 TL2327
Gravelly Hill *W Mids* 61 SP1090
Gravelsbank *Shrops* 59 SJ3300
Graveney *Kent* 28 TR0562
Gravesend *Kent* 28 TQ6574
Gravir *W Isls* 154 NB3915
Grayingham *Lincs* 76 SK9396
Grayrigg *Cumb* 87 SD5796
Grays *Essex* 27 TQ6177
Grayshott *Hants* 14 SU8735
Grayson Green *Cumb* 92 NX9925
Grayswood *Surrey* 14 SU9134
Graythorpe *Cleve* 97 NZ5227
Grazeley *Berks* 24 SU6966
Greasbrough *S York* 74 SK4195
Greasby *Mersyd* 78 SJ2587
Greasley *Notts* 62 SK4846
Great Abington *Cambs* 53 TL5348
Great Addington *Nhants* 51 SP9675
Great Alne *Warwks* 48 SP1259
Great Altcar *Lancs* 78 SD3305
Great Amwell *Herts* 39 TL3712
Great Asby *Cumb* 94 NY6713
Great Ashfield *Suffk* 54 TL9967
Great Ayton *N York* 90 NZ5610
Great Baddow *Essex* 40 TL7304
Great Badminton *Avon* 35 ST8082
Great Bardfield *Essex* 40 TL6730
Great Barford *Beds* 52 TL1351
Great Barr *W Mids* 61 SP0495
Great Barrington *Gloucs* 36 SP2113
Great Barrow *Ches* 71 SJ4768
Great Barton *Suffk* 54 TL8967
Great Barugh *N York* 90 SE7479
Great Bavington *Nthumb* 102 NY9880
Great Bealings *Suffk* 55 TM2348
Great Bedwyn *Wilts* 23 SU2764
Great Bentley *Essex* 41 TM1021
Great Billing *Nhants* 51 SP8162
Great Bircham *Norfk* 65 TF7732
Great Blakenham *Suffk* 54 TM1150
Great Blencow *Cumb* 93 NY4532
Great Bolas *Shrops* 72 SJ6421
Great Bookham *Surrey* 26 TQ1354
Great Bosullow *Cnwll* 2 SW4133
Great Bourton *Oxon* 49 SP4545
Great Bowden *Leics* 50 SP7488
Great Bradley *Suffk* 53 TL6753
Great Braxted *Essex* 40 TL8614
Great Bricett *Suffk* 54 TM0350
Great Brickhill *Bucks* 38 SP9030
Great Bridge *W Mids* 60 SO9892
Great Bridgeford *Staffs* 72 SJ8827
Great Brington *Nhants* 50 SP6665
Great Bromley *Essex* 41 TM0826
Great Broughton *Cumb* 92 NY0731
Great Broughton *N York* 90 NZ5405
Great Budworth *Ches* 79 SJ6677
Great Burdon *Dur* 96 NZ3116
Great Burstead *Essex* 40 TQ6892
Great Busby *N York* 90 NZ5205
Great Canfield *Essex* 40 TL5918
Great Carlton *Lincs* 77 TF4085
Great Casterton *Leics* 63 TF0008
Great Chart *Kent* 28 TQ9841
Great Chatfield *Wilts* 22 ST8563
Great Chatwell *Staffs* 60 SJ7914
Great Chell *Staffs* 72 SJ8652
Great Chesterford *Essex* 39 TL5042
Great Cheverell *Wilts* 22 ST9854
Great Chishill *Cambs* 39 TL4238
Great Clacton *Essex* 41 TM1716
Great Cliffe *W York* 82 SE3015
Great Clifton *Cumb* 92 NY0429
Great Coates *Humb* 85 TA2309
Great Comberton *H & W* 47 SO9542
Great Comp *Kent* 27 TQ6356
Great Corby *Cumb* 93 NY4754
Great Cornard *Suffk* 54 TL8840
Great Cowden *Humb* 85 TA2342
Great Coxwell *Oxon* 36 SU2693
Great Cransley *Nhants* 51 SP8376
Great Cressingham *Norfk* 66 TF8501
Great Crosthwaite *Cumb* 93 NY2524
Great Cubley *Derbys* 73 SK1638
Great Dalby *Leics* 63 SK7414
Great Doddington *Nhants* 51 SP8864
Great Doward *H & W* 34 SO5416
Great Dunham *Norfk* 66 TF8714
Great Dunmow *Essex* 40 TL6222
Great Durnford *Wilts* 23 SU1338
Great Easton *Essex* 40 TL6025
Great Easton *Leics* 51 SP8492
Great Eccleston *Lancs* 80 SD4240
Great Ellingham *Norfk* 66 TM0196
Great Elm *Somset* 22 ST7449
Great Englebourne *Devon* 7 SX7756
Great Everdon *Nhants* 49 SP5957
Great Eversden *Cambs* 52 TL3653
Great Finborough *Suffk* 54 TM0158
Great Fransham *Norfk* 66 TF8913
Great Gaddesden *Herts* 38 TL0211
Great Gidding *Cambs* 52 TL1183
Great Givendale *Humb* 84 SE8153
Great Glemham *Suffk* 55 TM3361
Great Glen *Leics* 50 SP6597
Great Gonerby *Lincs* 63 SK8938
Great Gransden *Cambs* 52 TL2655
Great Green *Cambs* 39 TL2844
Great Green *Norfk* 55 TM2889
Great Green *Suffk* 54 TL9155
Great Green *Suffk* 54 TL9365
Great Habton *N York* 90 SE7576
Great Hale *Lincs* 64 TF1442
Great Hallingbury *Essex* 39 TL5119
Great Hanwood *Shrops* 59 SJ4409
Great Harrowden *Nhants* 51 SP8770
Great Harwood *Lancs* 81 SD7332
Great Haseley *Oxon* 37 SP6401
Great Hatfield *Humb* 85 TA1842
Great Haywood *Staffs* 73 SJ9922
Great Heck *N York* 83 SE5920
Great Henny *Essex* 54 TL8637
Great Hinton *Wilts* 22 ST9059
Great Hockham *Norfk* 66 TL9592
Great Holland *Essex* 41 TM2019
Great Horkesley *Essex* 41 TL9731
Great Hormead *Herts* 39 TL4029
Great Horton *W York* 82 SE1431
Great Horwood *Bucks* 49 SP7731
Great Houghton *Nhants* 50 SP7958
Great Houghton *S York* 83 SE4206
Great Hucklow *Derbys* 74 SK1777
Great Kelk *Humb* 91 TA1058
Great Kimble *Bucks* 38 SP8205
Great Kingshill *Bucks* 26 SU8797
Great Langdale *Cumb* 86 NY2906
Great Langton *N York* 89 SE2996
Great Leighs *Essex* 40 TL7217
Great Limber *Lincs* 85 TA1308
Great Linford *Bucks* 38 SP8542
Great Livermere *Suffk* 54 TL8871
Great Longstone *Derbys* 74 SK2071
Great Lumley *T & W* 96 NZ2949
Great Lyth *Shrops* 59 SJ4507
Great Malvern *H & W* 47 SO7746
Great Maplestead *Essex* 54 TL8034
Great Marton *Lancs* 80 SD3235
Great Massingham *Norfk* 66 TF7922
Great Melton *Norfk* 66 TG1206
Great Meols *Mersyd* 78 SJ2390
Great Milton *Oxon* 37 SP6202
Great Missenden *Bucks* 26 SP8901
Great Mitton *Lancs* 81 SD7138
Great Mongeham *Kent* 29 TR3551
Great Moulton *Norfk* 54 TM1690
Great Munden *Herts* 39 TL3524
Great Musgrave *Cumb* 94 NY7613
Great Ness *Shrops* 59 SJ3919
Great Nurcott *Somset* 20 SS9036
Great Oak *Gwent* 34 SO3810
Great Oakley *Essex* 41 TM1927
Great Oakley *Nhants* 51 SP8785
Great Offley *Herts* 38 TL1427
Great Ormside *Cumb* 94 NY7017
Great Orton *Cumb* 93 NY3254
Great Ouseburn *N York* 89 SE4461
Great Oxendon *Nhants* 50 SP7383
Great Oxney Green *Essex* 40 TL6606
Great Pattenden *Kent* 28 TQ7344
Great Paxton *Cambs* 52 TL2063
Great Plumpton *Lancs* 80 SD3833
Great Plumstead *Norfk* 67 TG3010
Great Ponton *Lincs* 63 SK9230
Great Potheridge *Devon* 19 SS5114
Great Preston *W York* 83 SE4029
Great Purston *Nhants* 49 SP5139
Great Raveley *Cambs* 52 TL2581
Great Rissington *Gloucs* 36 SP1917
Great Rollright *Oxon* 48 SP3231
Great Rudbaxton *Dyfed* 30 SM9620
Great Ryburgh *Norfk* 66 TF9527
Great Ryle *Nthumb* 111 NU0212
Great Ryton *Shrops* 59 SJ4803
Great Saling *Essex* 40 TL6925
Great Salkeld *Cumb* 94 NY5536
Great Sampford *Essex* 53 TL6435
Great Sankey *Ches* 78 SJ5688
Great Saredon *Staffs* 60 SJ9508
Great Saughall *Ches* 71 SJ3669
Great Saxham *Suffk* 53 TL7862
Great Shefford *Berks* 36 SU3875
Great Shelford *Cambs* 53 TL4651
Great Smeaton *N York* 89 NZ3404
Great Snoring *Norfk* 66 TF9434
Great Somerford *Wilts* 35 ST9682
Great Soudley *Shrops* 72 SJ7229
Great Stainton *Dur* 96 NZ3322
Great Stambridge *Essex* 40 TQ8991
Great Staughton *Cambs* 52 TL1264
Great Steeping *Lincs* 77 TF4364
Great Stonar *Kent* 29 TR3359
Great Strickland *Cumb* 94 NY5522
Great Stukeley *Cambs* 52 TL2274
Great Sturton *Lincs* 76 TF2176
Great Sutton *Ches* 71 SJ3775
Great Sutton *Shrops* 59 SO5183
Great Swinburne *Nthumb* 102 NY9375
Great Tew *Oxon* 48 SP4028
Great Tey *Essex* 40 TL8925
Great Torrington *Devon* 18 SS4919
Great Tosson *Nthumb* 103 NU0200
Great Totham *Essex* 40 TL8611
Great Totham *Essex* 40 TL8713
Great Tows *Lincs* 76 TF2290
Great Urswick *Cumb* 86 SD2674
Great Wakering *Essex* 40 TQ9487
Great Waldingfield *Suffk* 54 TL9144
Great Walsingham *Norfk* 66 TF9437
Great Waltham *Essex* 40 TL6913
Great Warley *Essex* 27 TQ5890
Great Washbourne *Gloucs* 47 SO9834
Great Weeke *Devon* 8 SX7187
Great Weldon *Nhants* 51 SP9289
Great Welnetham *Suffk* 54 TL8759
Great Wenham *Suffk* 54 TM0738
Great Whittington *Nthumb* 103 NZ0070
Great Wigborough *Essex* 41 TL9615
Great Wilbraham *Cambs* 53 TL5557
Great Wishford *Wilts* 23 SU0735
Great Witchingham *Norfk* 66 TG1020
Great Witcombe *Gloucs* 35 SO9114
Great Witley *H & W* 47 SO7566
Great Wolford *Warwks* 48 SP2534
Great Wratting *Essex* 53 TL6848
Great Wymondley *Herts* 39 TL2128
Great Wyrley *Staffs* 60 SJ9907
Great Wytheford *Shrops* 59 SJ5719
Great Yarmouth *Norfk* 67 TG5207
Great Yeldham *Essex* 53 TL7638
Greatfield *Wilts* 36 SU0785
Greatford *Lincs* 64 TF0811
Greatgate *Staffs* 73 SK0539
Greatham *Cleve* 97 NZ4927
Greatham *Hants* 14 SU7730
Greatham *W Susx* 14 TQ0415
Greatstone-on-Sea *Kent* 17 TR0822
Greatworth *Nhants* 49 SP5542
Grebby *Lincs* 77 TF4368
Green Bank *Cumb* 87 SD3780
Green Cross *Surrey* 14 SU8637
Green Down *Somset* 21 ST5753
Green End *Beds* 38 TL0147
Green End *Beds* 51 TL0864
Green End *Beds* 51 TL1063
Green End *Beds* 52 TL1252
Green End *Cambs* 52 TL2274
Green End *Cambs* 52 TL3856
Green End *Cambs* 53 TL4668
Green End *Cambs* 53 TL4861
Green End *Herts* 39 TL2630
Green End *Herts* 39 TL3222
Green End *Herts* 39 TL3333
Green End *Warwks* 61 SP2686
Green Hammerton *N York* 83 SE4556
Green Head *Cumb* 93 NY3649
Green Heath *Staffs* 60 SJ9913
Green Hill *Wilts* 36 SU0686
Green Hills *Cambs* 53 TL6072
Green Lane *Devon* 8 SX7877
Green Lane *H & W* 48 SP0664
Green Moor *S York* 74 SK2899
Green Oak *Humb* 84 SE8127
Green Ore *Somset* 21 ST5750
Green Quarter *Cumb* 87 NY4603
Green Street *E Susx* 17 TQ7611
Green Street *Gloucs* 35 SO8915
Green Street *H & W* 47 SO8749
Green Street *Herts* 39 TL4521
Green Street *Herts* 26 TQ1998
Green Street Green *Gt Lon* 27 TQ4563
Green Street Green *Kent* 27 TQ5870
Green Tye *Herts* 39 TL4418
Greenburn *Loth* 116 NS9360
Greencroft *Norfk* 66 TG0243
Greencroft Hall *Dur* 96 NZ1549
Greenend *Oxon* 36 SP3221
Greenfield *Beds* 38 TL0534
Greenfield *Clwyd* 70 SJ1977
Greenfield *Gt Man* 82 SD9904
Greenfield *Highld* 131 NH2000
Greenfield *Oxon* 37 SU7191
Greenfield *Strath* 114 NS2490
Greenford *Gt Lon* 26 TQ1482
Greengairs *Strath* 116 NS7870
Greengates *W York* 82 SE1937
Greengill *Cumb* 92 NY1037
Greenhalgh *Lancs* 80 SD4035
Greenham *Berks* 24 SU4865
Greenham *Somset* 20 ST0820
Greenhaugh *Nthumb* 102 NY7987
Greenhead *Nthumb* 102 NY6565
Greenheys *Gt Man* 79 SD7104
Greenhill *Cent* 116 NS8279
Greenhill *D & G* 100 NY1079
Greenhill *H & W* 47 SO7248
Greenhill *Kent* 29 TR1666
Greenhill *Strath* 108 NS9332
Greenhillocks *Derbys* 74 SK4049
Greenhithe *Kent* 27 TQ5875
Greenholm *Strath* 107 NS5437
Greenholme *Cumb* 87 NY5905
Greenhouse *Border* 109 NT5523
Greenhow Hill *N York* 89 SE1164
Greenland *Highld* 151 ND2367
Greenland *S York* 74 SK3988
Greenlands *Bucks* 37 SU7785
Greenlaw *Border* 110 NT7146
Greenlea *D & G* 100 NY0375
Greenloaning *Tays* 125 NN8307
Greenmoor Hill *Oxon* 37 SU6481
Greenmount *Gt Man* 81 SD7714
Greenock *Strath* 115 NS2876
Greenodd *Cumb* 86 SD3182
Greens Norton *Nhants* 49 SP6649
Greensgate *Norfk* 66 TG1015
Greenside *T & W* 96 NZ1362
Greenside *W York* 82 SE1716
Greenstead *Essex* 41 TM0125
Greenstead Green *Essex* 40 TL8227
Greensted *Essex* 39 TL5403
Greenstreet Green *Suffk* 54 TM0349
Greenway *Gloucs* 47 SO7033
Greenway *H & W* 60 SO7470
Greenway *S Glam* 33 ST0573
Greenway *Somset* 21 ST3124
Greenwich *Gt Lon* 27 TQ3877
Greet *Gloucs* 48 SP0230
Greete *Shrops* 46 SO5770
Greetham *Leics* 63 SK9214
Greetham *Lincs* 77 TF3070
Greetland *W York* 82 SE0821
Gregson Lane *Lancs* 81 SD5926
Greinton *Somset* 21 ST4136
Grenaby *IOM* 153 SC2672
Grendon *Nhants* 51 SP8760
Grendon *Warwks* 61 SP2799
Grendon Green *H & W* 46 SO5957
Grendon Underwood *Bucks* 37 SP6820
Grenofen *Devon* 6 SX4971
Grenoside *S York* 74 SK3393
Gresford *Clwyd* 71 SJ3454
Gresham *Norfk* 66 TG1638
Greshornish House Hotel
Highld 136 NG3454
Gressenhall *Norfk* 66 TF9615
Gressenhall Green *Norfk* 66 TF9616
Gressingham *Lancs* 87 SD5769
Grestey Green *Ches* 72 SJ7053
Greta Bridge *Dur* 95 NZ0813
Gretna *D & G* 101 NY3167
Gretna Green *D & G* 101 NY3168
Gretton *Gloucs* 47 SP0030
Gretton *Nhants* 51 SP8994
Gretton *Shrops* 59 SO5195
Grewelthorpe *N York* 89 SE2376
Grey Friars *Suffk* 55 TM4770
Grey Green *Humb* 84 SE7807
Grey's Green *Oxon* 37 SU7182
Greygarth *N York* 89 SE1872
Greylake *Somset* 21 ST3833
Greyrigg *D & G* 100 NY0888
Greysouthern *Cumb* 92 NY0729
Greystoke *Cumb* 93 NY4430
Greystone *Tays* 127 NO5343
Greywell *Hants* 24 SU7151
Gribb *Dorset* 10 ST3703
Gribthorpe *Humb* 84 SE7635
Griff *Warwks* 61 SP3689
Griffithstown *Gwent* 34 ST2998
Griffydam *Leics* 62 SK4118
Griggs Green *Hants* 14 SU8231
Grimeford Village *Lancs* 81 SD6112
Grimesthorpe *S York* 74 SK3689
Grimethorpe *S York* 83 SE4109
Grimley *H & W* 47 SO8360
Grimmet *Strath* 106 NS3210
Grimoldby *Lincs* 77 TF3988
Grimpo *Shrops* 59 SJ3526
Grimsargh *Lancs* 81 SD5834
Grimsby *Humb* 85 TA2710
Grimscote *Nhants* 49 SP6553
Grimscott *Cnwll* 18 SS2606
Grimshader *W Isls* 154 NB4025
Grimshaw *Lancs* 81 SD7024
Grimshaw Green *Lancs* 80 SD4912
Grimsthorpe *Lincs* 64 TF0422
Grimston *Humb* 85 TA2735
Grimston *Leics* 63 SK6821
Grimston *Norfk* 65 TF7222
Grimston Hill *Notts* 75 SK6865
Grimstone *Dorset* 10 SY6394
Grimstone End *Suffk* 54 TL9368
Grinacombe Moor *Devon* 5 SX4191
Grindale *Humb* 91 TA1271
Grindle *Shrops* 60 SJ7503
Grindleford *Derbys* 74 SK2477
Grindleton *Lancs* 81 SD7545
Grindley Brook *Shrops* 71 SJ5242
Grindlow *Derbys* 74 SK1877
Grindon *Cleve* 96 NZ3925
Grindon *Nthumb* 110 NT9144
Grindon *Staffs* 73 SK0854
Grindon Hill *Nthumb* 102 NY8268
Grindonrigg *Nthumb* 110 NT9243
Gringley on the Hill *Notts* 75 SK7390
Grinsdale *Cumb* 93 NY3758
Grinshill *Shrops* 59 SJ5223
Grinton *N York* 88 SE0498
Grishipoll *Strath* 120 NM1859
Grisling Common *E Susx* 16 TQ4322
Gristhorpe *N York* 91 TA0981
Griston *Norfk* 66 TL9499
Gritley *Ork* 155 HY5504
Grittenham *Wilts* 36 SU0382
Grittleton *Wilts* 35 ST8580
Grizebeck *Cumb* 86 SD2384
Grizedale *Cumb* 86 SD3394
Groby *Leics* 62 SK5207
Groes *Clwyd* 70 SJ0064
Groes-faen *M Glam* 33 ST0680
Groes-Wen *M Glam* 33 ST1286
Groesffordd *Gwynd* 56 SH2739
Groesffordd Marli *Clwyd* 70 SJ0073
Groesllwyd *Powys* 58 SJ2111
Groeslon *Gwynd* 68 SH4755
Groeslon *Gwynd* 68 SH5260
Grogport *Strath* 105 NR8144
Gromford *Suffk* 55 TM3858
Gronant *Clwyd* 70 SJ0983
Groombridge *E Susx* 16 TQ5337
Grosebay *W Isls* 154 NG1593
Grosmont *Gwent* 46 SO4024
Grosmont *N York* 90 NZ8305
Grossington *Gloucs* 35 SO7302
Groton *Suffk* 54 TL9641
Grotton *Gt Man* 79 SD9604
Grouville *Jersey* 152 JS1908
Grove *Bucks* 38 SP9122
Grove *Dorset* 11 SY6972
Grove *Dyfed* 30 SM9900
Grove *Kent* 29 TR2362
Grove *Notts* 75 SK7479
Grove *Oxon* 36 SU4090
Grove Green *Kent* 28 TQ7856
Grove Park *Gt Lon* 27 TQ4072
Grove Vale *W Mids* 61 SP0394
Grovenhurst *Kent* 28 TQ7140
Grovesend *Avon* 35 ST6589
Grovesend *W Glam* 32 SN5900
Grubb Street *Kent* 27 TQ5869
Gruids *Highld* 146 NC5603
Gruinard *Highld* 144 NG9489
Gruinart *Strath* 112 NR2966
Grula *Highld* 136 NG3826
Gruline *Strath* 121 NM5440
Grumbla *Cnwll* 2 SW4029
Grundisburgh *Suffk* 55 TM2251
Gruting *Shet* 155 HU2749
Gualachulain *Highld* 123 NN1145
Guanockgate *Lincs* 64 TF3710
Guardbridge *Fife* 127 NO4518
Guarlford *H & W* 47 SO8145
Guay *Tays* 125 NN9948
Guestling Green *E Susx* 17 TQ8513
Guestling Thorn *E Susx* 17 TQ8516
Guestwick *Norfk* 66 TG0626
Guide *Lancs* 81 SD7025
Guide Bridge *Gt Man* 79 SJ9297
Guilden Down *Shrops* 59 SO3082
Guilden Morden *Cambs* 39 TL2744
Guilden Sutton *Ches* 71 SJ4468
Guildford *Surrey* 25 SU9949
Guildstead *Kent* 28 TQ8262
Guildtown *Tays* 126 NO1331
Guilsborough *Nhants* 50 SP6772
Guilsfield *Powys* 58 SJ2211
Guilton *Kent* 29 TR2858
Guiltreehill *Strath* 106 NS3610
Guineaford *Devon* 19 SS5537
Guisborough *Cleve* 97 NZ6015
Guiseley *W York* 82 SE1942
Guist *Norfk* 66 TG0025
Guiting Power *Gloucs* 48 SP0924
Gullane *Loth* 118 NT4882
Gulling Green *Suffk* 54 TL8256
Gulval *Cnwll* 2 SW4831
Gulworthy *Devon* 6 SX4572
Gumfreston *Dyfed* 31 SN1001
Gumley *Leics* 50 SP6889
Gummow's Shop *Cnwll* 4 SW8657
Gun Green *Kent* 17 TQ7731
Gun Hill *E Susx* 16 TQ5614
Gun Hill *Warwks* 61 SP2889
Gunby *Humb* 84 SE7035
Gunby *Lincs* 63 SK9121
Gunby *Lincs* 77 TF4666
Gundleton *Hants* 24 SU6133
Gunn *Devon* 19 SS6333
Gunnerside *N York* 88 SD9598
Gunnerton *Nthumb* 102 NY9074
Gunness *Humb* 84 SE8411
Gunnislake *Devon* 6 SX4371
Gunnista *Shet* 155 HU5043
Gunthorpe *Cambs* 64 TF1802
Gunthorpe *Norfk* 66 TG0134
Gunthorpe *Notts* 63 SK6844
Gunton *Suffk* 67 TM5395
Gunville *IOW* 13 SZ4788
Gunwalloe *Cnwll* 2 SW6522
Gupworthy *Somset* 20 SS9734
Gurnard *IOW* 13 SZ4795
Gurnett *Ches* 79 SJ9271
Gurney Slade *Somset* 21 ST6249
Gurnos *W Glam* 32 SN7709
Gushmere *Kent* 28 TR0457
Gussage All Saints *Dorset* 11 SU0010
Gussage St Michael *Dorset* 11 ST9811
Guston *Kent* 29 TR3244
Gutcher *Shet* 155 HU5499
Guthrie *Tays* 127 NO5650
Guy's Marsh *Dorset* 22 ST8420
Guyhirn *Cambs* 65 TF4003
Guyhirn Gull *Cambs* 65 TF3904
Guyzance *Nthumb* 103 NU2103
Gwaenysgor *Clwyd* 70 SJ0781
Gwalchmai *Gwynd* 68 SH3876
Gwastadnant *Gwynd* 69 SH6157
Gwaun-Cae-Gurwen *W Glam* 32 SN6911
Gwbert on Sea *Dyfed* 42 SN1650
Gwealavellan *Cnwll* 2 SW6041
Gwealeath *Cnwll* 2 SW6922
Gweek *Cnwll* 2 SW7026
Gwehelog *Gwent* 34 SO3804
Gwenddwr *Powys* 45 SO0643
Gwendreath *Cnwll* 3 SW7217
Gwennap *Cnwll* 3 SW7340
Gwenter *Cnwll* 3 SW7417
Gwernaffield *Clwyd* 70 SJ2065
Gwernesney *Gwent* 34 SO4101
Gwernogle *Dyfed* 44 SN5333
Gwernymynydd *Clwyd* 70 SJ2162
Gwersyllt *Clwyd* 71 SJ3153
Gwespyr *Clwyd* 70 SJ1183
Gwindra *Cnwll* 3 SW9552
Gwinear *Cnwll* 2 SW5937
Gwithian *Cnwll* 2 SW5841
Gwredog *Gwynd* 68 SH4085
Gwrhay *Gwent* 33 ST1899
Gwyddelwern *Clwyd* 70 SJ0746
Gwyddgrug *Dyfed* 44 SN4635
Gwynfryn *Clwyd* 70 SJ2552
Gwystre *Powys* 45 SO0665
Gwytherin *Clwyd* 69 SH8761
Gyfelia *Clwyd* 71 SJ3245
Gyrn-goch *Gwynd* 68 SH4048

H

Habberley *H & W* 60 SO8177
Habberley *Shrops* 59 SJ3903
Habergham *Lancs* 81 SD8033
Habertoft *Lincs* 77 TF5069
Habin *W Susx* 14 SU8022
Habrough *Humb* 85 TA1413
Hacconby *Lincs* 64 TF1025
Haceby *Lincs* 64 TF0236
Hacheston *Suffk* 55 TM3059
Hack Green *Ches* 72 SJ6448
Hackbridge *Gt Lon* 27 TQ2865
Hackenthorpe *S York* 74 SK4183
Hackford *Norfk* 66 TG0502
Hackforth *N York* 89 SE2492
Hackland *Ork* 155 HY3920
Hackleton *Nhants* 51 SP8055
Hacklinge *Kent* 29 TR3454
Hackman's Gate *H & W* 60 SO8978
Hackness *N York* 91 SE9790
Hackness *Somset* 21 ST3345
Hackney *Gt Lon* 27 TQ3484
Hackthorn *Lincs* 76 SK9982
Hackthorpe *Cumb* 94 NY5423
Hacton *Gt Lon* 27 TQ5585
Hadden *Border* 110 NT7836
Haddenham *Bucks* 37 SP7308
Haddenham *Cambs* 53 TL4675
Haddington *Lincs* 76 SK9162
Haddington *Loth* 118 NT5173
Haddiscoe *Norfk* 67 TM4497
Haddo *Gramp* 143 NJ8337
Haddon *Cambs* 64 TL1392
Hade Edge *W York* 82 SE1404
Hademore *Staffs* 61 SK1708
Hadfield *Derbys* 74 SK0296
Hadham Cross *Herts* 39 TL4218
Hadham Ford *Herts* 39 TL4321
Hadleigh *Essex* 40 TQ8187
Hadleigh *Suffk* 54 TM0242
Hadleigh Heath *Suffk* 54 TL9941
Hadley *H & W* 47 SO8564
Hadley *Shrops* 60 SJ6711
Hadley End *Staffs* 73 SK1320
Hadley Wood *Gt Lon* 27 TQ2698
Hadlow *Kent* 27 TQ6350
Hadlow Down *E Susx* 16 TQ5324
Hadnall *Shrops* 59 SJ5220
Hadstock *Essex* 53 TL5644
Hadzor *H & W* 47 SO9162
Haffenden Quarter *Kent* 28 TQ8840
Hafod-y-bwch *Clwyd* 71 SJ3147
Hafod-y-coed *Gwent* 34 SO2200
Hafodunos *Clwyd* 69 SH8666
Hafodyrynys *Gwent* 34 ST2298
Haggate *Lancs* 81 SD8735
Haggbeck *Cumb* 101 NY4773
Haggerston *Nthumb* 111 NU0443
Haggington Hill *Devon* 19 SS5547
Haggs *Cent* 116 NS7879
Hagley *H & W* 46 SO5641
Hagley *H & W* 60 SO9180
Hagnaby *Lincs* 77 TF3462
Hagworthingham *Lincs* 77 TF3469
Haigh *Gt Man* 78 SD6009
Haighton Green *Lancs* 81 SD5634
Hail Weston *Cambs* 52 TL1662
Haile *Cumb* 86 NY0308
Hailes *Gloucs* 48 SP0430
Hailey *Herts* 39 TL3710
Hailey *Oxon* 37 SU6485
Hailsham *E Susx* 16 TQ5909
Hainault *Gt Lon* 27 TQ4591
Haine *Kent* 29 TR3566
Hainford *Norfk* 67 TG2218
Hainton *Lincs* 76 TF1884
Hainworth *W York* 82 SE0638
Haisthorpe *Humb* 91 TA1264
Hakin *Dyfed* 30 SM8905
Halam *Notts* 75 SK6754
Halbeath *Fife* 117 NT1288
Halberton *Devon* 9 ST0112
Halcro *Highld* 151 ND2360
Hale *Ches* 78 SJ4782
Hale *Cumb* 87 SD5078
Hale *Gt Man* 79 SJ7786
Hale *Hants* 12 SU1818
Hale *Somset* 22 ST7427
Hale *Surrey* 25 SU8448
Hale Bank *Ches* 78 SJ4784
Hale Green *E Susx* 16 TQ5514
Hale Nook *Lancs* 80 SD3944
Hale Street *Kent* 28 TQ6749
Halebarns *Gt Man* 79 SJ7985
Hales *Norfk* 67 TM3797
Hales *Staffs* 72 SJ7134
Hales Green *Derbys* 73 SK1841
Hales Place *Kent* 29 TR1459
Halesgate *Lincs* 64 TF3226
Halesowen *W Mids* 60 SO9683
Halesworth *Suffk* 55 TM3877
Halewood *Mersyd* 78 SJ4585
Halewood Green *Mersyd* 78 SJ4486
Halford *Devon* 7 SX8174
Halford *Shrops* 59 SO4383
Halford *Warwks* 48 SP2645
Halfpenny *Cumb* 87 SD5387
Halfpenny Green *Staffs* 60 SO8291
Halfpenny Houses *N York* 89 SE2284
Halfway *Berks* 24 SU4068
Halfway *Dyfed* 44 SN6430
Halfway *Powys* 44 SN8232
Halfway *S York* 75 SK4381
Halfway Bridge *W Susx* 14 SU9321
Halfway House *Shrops* 59 SJ3411
Halfway Houses *Kent* 28 TQ9372
Halifax *W York* 82 SE0925
Halistra *Highld* 136 NG2459
Halket *Strath* 115 NS4252
Halkirk *Highld* 151 ND1359
Halkyn *Clwyd* 70 SJ2171
Hall *Strath* 115 NS4154
Hall Cliffe *W York* 82 SE2918
Hall Cross *Lancs* 80 SD4230
Hall Dunnerdale *Cumb* 86 SD2195
Hall End *Beds* 38 TL0045
Hall End *Beds* 38 TL0737
Hall End *W Mids* 60 SP0092
Hall Green *Ches* 72 SJ8356
Hall Green *W Mids* 61 SP1181
Hall's Green *Essex* 39 TL4108
Hall's Green *Herts* 39 TL2728
Hallam Fields *Derbys* 62 SK4739
Halland *E Susx* 16 TQ4916
Hallaton *Leics* 50 SP7896
Hallatrow *Avon* 21 ST6357
Hallbankgate *Cumb* 94 NY5859
Hallbeck *Cumb* 87 SD6288
Hallen *Avon* 34 ST5580
Hallfield Gate *Derbys* 74 SK3958
Hallgarth *Dur* 96 NZ3243
Hallin *Highld* 136 NG2558
Halling *Kent* 28 TQ7063
Hallington *Lincs* 77 TF3085
Hallington *Nthumb* 102 NY9875
Halliwell *Gt Man* 79 SD6910
Halloughton *Notts* 75 SK6951
Hallow *H & W* 47 SO8258

Hallow Heath
Highampton

Hallow Heath H & W 47 SO8259
Hallrule Border 110 NT5914
Hallsands Devon 7 SX8138
Hallthwaites Cumb 86 SD1885
Halltoft End Lincs 64 TF3645
Hallworthy Cnwll 4 SX1787
Hallyne Border 109 NT1940
Halmer End Staffs 72 SJ7948
Halmond's Frome H & W 47 SO6747
Halnaker W Susx 14 SU9007
Halsall Lancs 78 SD3710
Halse Nhants 49 SP5640
Halse Somset 20 ST1428
Halsetown Cnwll 2 SW5038
Halsham Humb 85 TA2727
Halsinger Devon 19 SS5138
Halstead Essex 40 TL8130
Halstead Kent 27 TQ4861
Halstead Leics 63 SK7505
Halstock Dorset 10 ST5308
Halsway Somset 20 ST1337
Haltcliff Bridge Cumb 93 NY3636
Haltham Lincs 77 TF2463
Halton Bucks 38 SP8710
Halton Ches 78 SJ5481
Halton Clwyd 71 SJ3039
Halton Lancs 87 SD5064
Halton Nthumb 103 NY9967
Halton W York 83 SE3533
Halton East N York 82 SE0454
Halton Fenside Lincs 77 TF4263
Halton Gill N York 88 SD8776
Halton Green Lancs 87 SD5165
Halton Holegate Lincs 77 TF4165
Halton Lea Gate Nthumb 94 NY6458
Halton Quay Cnwll 5 SX4165
Halton Shields Nthumb 103 NZ0168
Halton West N York 81 SD8454
Haltwhistle Nthumb 102 NY7064
Halvergate Norfk 67 TG4106
Halwell Devon 7 SX7753
Halwill Devon 18 SX4299
Halwill Junction Devon 18 SS4400
Ham Devon 9 ST2301
Ham Gloucs 35 SO9721
Ham Gloucs 35 ST6898
Ham Gt Lon 26 TQ1772
Ham Kent 29 TR3254
Ham Somset 20 ST2825
Ham Somset 22 ST6748
Ham Wilts 23 SU3262
Ham Common Dorset 22 ST8125
Ham Green Avon 34 ST5375
Ham Green H & W 47 SO7544
Ham Green H & W 47 SP0163
Ham Green Kent 28 TQ8468
Ham Green Kent 17 TQ8926
Ham Hill Kent 28 TQ6960
Ham Street Somset 21 ST5534
Hamble Hants 13 SU4806
Hambleden Bucks 37 SU7886
Hambledon Hants 13 SU6414
Hambledon Surrey 25 SU9638
Hambleton Lancs 80 SD3742
Hambleton N York 83 SE5530
Hambleton Moss Side Lancs 80 SD3842
Hambridge Somset 21 ST3921
Hambridge Somset 21 ST5936
Hambrook Avon 35 ST6478
Hambrook W Susx 14 SU7806
Hamels Herts 39 TL3724
Hameringham Lincs 77 TF3167
Hamerton Cambs 52 TL1379
Hamilton Strath 116 NS7255
Hamlet Dorset 10 ST5908
Hamlins E Susx 16 TQ5908
Hammerpot W Susx 14 TQ0605
Hammersmith Gt Lon 26 TQ2378
Hammerwich Staffs 61 SK0707
Hammerwood E Susx 16 TQ4339
Hammond Street Herts 39 TL3304
Hammoon Dorset 11 ST8114
Hamnavoe Shet 155 HU3735
Hamnavoe Shet 155 HU4971
Hampden Park E Susx 16 TQ6002
Hampden Row Bucks 26 SP8501
Hamperden End Essex 40 TL5730
Hampnett Gloucs 36 SP0915
Hampole S York 83 SE5010
Hampreston Dorset 12 SZ0598
Hampsfield Cumb 87 SD4080
Hampson Green Lancs 80 SD4954
Hampstead Gt Lon 27 TQ2685
Hampstead Norrey's Berks 37 SU5276
Hampsthwaite N York 89 SE2559
Hampt Cnwll 5 SX3874
Hampton Gt Lon 26 TQ1369
Hampton H & W 48 SP0243
Hampton Kent 29 TR1568
Hampton Shrops 60 SO7486
Hampton Wilts 36 SU1892
Hampton Bishop H & W 46 SO5637
Hampton Green Ches 71 SJ5149
Hampton Heath Ches 71 SJ5049
Hampton in Arden W Mids 61 SP2080
Hampton Loade Shrops 60 SO7486
Hampton Lovett H & W 47 SO8865
Hampton Lucy Warwks 48 SP2557
Hampton on the Hill Warwks 48 SP2564
Hampton Poyle Oxon 37 SP5015
Hampton Wick Gt Lon 26 TQ1769
Hamptworth Wilts 12 SU2419
Hamrow Norfk 66 TF9124
Hamsey E Susx 15 TQ4012
Hamsey Green Gt Lon 27 TQ3559
Hamstall Ridware Staffs 73 SK1019
Hamstead IOW 13 SZ4091
Hamstead W Mids 61 SP0592
Hamstead Marshall Berks 24 SU4165
Hamsterley Dur 95 NZ1156
Hamsterley Dur 96 NZ1231
Hamstreet Kent 17 TR0033
Hamwood Avon 21 ST3756
Hamworthy Dorset 11 SY9991
Hanbury H & W 47 SO9664
Hanbury Staffs 73 SK1727
Hanby Lincs 64 TF0231
Hanchet End Suffk 53 TL6446
Hanchurch Staffs 72 SJ8441
Hand and Pen Devon 9 SY0495
Hand Green Ches 71 SJ5460
Handale Cleve 97 NZ7215
Handbridge Ches 71 SJ4065
Handcross W Susx 15 TQ2629
Handforth Ches 79 SJ8583
Handley Ches 71 SJ4657
Handley Derbys 74 SK3761
Handley Green Essex 40 TL6501
Handsacre Staffs 73 SK0915
Handsworth S York 74 SK4186
Handsworth W Mids 61 SP0489
Handy Cross Bucks 26 SU8590
Hanford Dorset 11 ST8411
Hanford Staffs 72 SJ8741
Hanging Langford Wilts 23 SU0337
Hangleton E Susx 15 TQ2607
Hangleton W Susx 14 TQ0803
Hanham Avon 35 ST6472
Hankelow Ches 72 SJ6645
Hankerton Wilts 35 ST9790
Hankham E Susx 16 TQ6105
Hanley Staffs 72 SJ8847
Hanley Castle H & W 47 SO8442
Hanley Child H & W 47 SO6565
Hanley Swan H & W 47 SO8142
Hanley William H & W 47 SO6766
Hanlith N York 88 SD8961
Hanmer Clwyd 71 SJ4539
Hannaford Devon 19 SS6029
Hannah Lincs 77 TF4979
Hannington Hants 24 SU5355
Hannington Nhants 51 SP8170
Hannington Wilts 36 SU1793
Hannington Wick Wilts 36 SU1795
Hanscombe End Beds 38 TL1133
Hanslope Bucks 38 SP8046
Hanthorpe Lincs 64 TF0823
Hanwell Gt Lon 26 TQ1579
Hanwell Oxon 49 SP4343
Hanworth Gt Lon 26 TQ1271
Hanworth Norfk 67 TG1935
Happendon Strath 108 NS8533
Happisburgh Norfk 67 TG3831
Happisburgh Common Norfk 67 TG3728
Hapsford Ches 71 SJ4774
Hapton Lancs 81 SD7931
Hapton Norfk 66 TM1796
Harberton Devon 7 SX7758
Harbertonford Devon 7 SX7856
Harbledown Kent 29 TR1357
Harborne W Mids 60 SP0284
Harborough Magna Warwks 50 SP4778
Harborough Parva Warwks 50 SP4878
Harbottle Nthumb 102 NT9304
Harbourneford Devon 7 SX7162
Harbours Hill H & W 47 SO9565
Harbridge Hants 12 SU1410
Harbridge Green Hants 12 SU1410
Harbury Warwks 48 SP3759
Harby Leics 63 SK7431
Harby Notts 76 SK8770
Harcombe Devon 9 SX8881
Harcombe Devon 9 SY1590
Harcombe Bottom Devon 10 SY3395
Harden W Mids 60 SK0100
Harden W York 82 SE0838
Hardenhuish Wilts 35 ST9174
Hardgate D & G 100 NX8167
Hardgate Gramp 135 NJ7901
Hardgate N York 89 SE2662
Hardgate Strath 115 NS5072
Hardham W Susx 14 TQ0317
Hardhorn Lancs 80 SD3537
Hardingham Norfk 66 TG0403
Hardings Wood Staffs 72 SJ8254
Hardingstone Nhants 49 SP7657
Hardington Somset 22 ST7452
Hardington Mandeville Somset 10 ST5111
Hardington Marsh Somset 10 ST5009
Hardington Moor Somset 10 ST5112
Hardisworthy Devon 18 SS2320
Hardley Hants 13 SU4205
Hardley Street Norfk 67 TG3701
Hardmead Bucks 38 SP9347
Hardraw N York 88 SD8691
Hardsough Lancs 81 SD7920
Hardstoft Derbys 75 SK4363
Hardway Hants 13 SU6001
Hardway Somset 22 ST7234
Hardwick Bucks 38 SP8019
Hardwick Cambs 52 TL3758
Hardwick Lincs 76 SK8675
Hardwick Nhants 51 SP8469
Hardwick Norfk 55 TM2289
Hardwick Oxon 36 SP3806
Hardwick Oxon 49 SP5729
Hardwick S York 75 SK4885
Hardwick W Mids 61 SP0798
Hardwick Green H & W 47 SO8133
Hardwicke Gloucs 35 SO7912
Hardwicke Gloucs 47 SO9027
Hardy's Green Essex 40 TL9320
Hare Croft W York 82 SE0835
Hare Green Essex 41 TM1025
Hare Hatch Berks 37 SU8077
Hare Street Essex 39 TL4209
Hare Street Essex 27 TL5300
Hare Street Herts 39 TL3929
Harebeating E Susx 16 TQ5910
Hareby Lincs 77 TF3365
Harefield Gt Lon 26 TQ0590
Harehill Derbys 73 SK1735
Harehills W York 82 SE3135
Harehope Nthumb 111 NU0920
Harelaw Border 109 NT5323
Harelaw Dur 96 NZ1652
Hareplain Kent 28 TQ8339
Harescough Cumb 94 NY6042
Harescombe Gloucs 35 SO8310
Haresfield Gloucs 35 SO8010
Harestock Hants 24 SU4631
Harewood W York 83 SE3245
Harewood End H & W 46 SO5227
Harford Devon 6 SX6359
Hargate Norfk 66 TM1191
Hargrave Ches 71 SJ4862
Hargrave Nhants 51 TL0370
Hargrave Suffk 53 TL7760
Hargrave Green Suffk 53 TL7759
Harker Cumb 101 NY3960
Harkstead Suffk 54 TM1834
Harlaston Staffs 61 SK2110
Harlaxton Lincs 63 SK8832
Harle Syke Lancs 81 SD8635
Harlech Gwynd 57 SH5831
Harlescott Shrops 59 SJ4916
Harlesden Gt Lon 26 TQ2183
Harlesthorpe Derbys 75 SK4976
Harleston Devon 7 SX7945
Harleston Norfk 55 TM2483
Harleston Suffk 54 TM0160
Harlestone Nhants 49 SP7064
Harley S York 74 SK3698
Harley Shrops 59 SJ5901
Harlington Beds 38 TL0330
Harlington Gt Lon 26 TQ0877
Harlington S York 83 SE4802
Harlosh Highld 136 NG2841
Harlow Essex 39 TL4611
Harlow Hill Nthumb 103 NZ0768
Harlthorpe Humb 84 SE7337
Harlton Cambs 52 TL3852
Harlyn Bay Cnwll 4 SW8775
Harman's Cross Dorset 11 SY9880
Harmby N York 89 SE1289
Harmer Green Herts 39 TL2515
Harmer Hill Shrops 59 SJ4822
Harmondsworth Gt Lon 26 TQ0577
Harmston Lincs 76 SK9662
Harnage Shrops 59 SJ5604
Harnham Nthumb 103 NZ0781
Harnhill Gloucs 36 SP0600
Harold Hill Gt Lon 27 TQ5392
Harold Wood Gt Lon 27 TQ5590
Haroldston West Dyfed 30 SM8615
Haroldswick Shet 155 HP6312
Harome N York 90 SE6481
Harpenden Herts 38 TL1314
Harpford Devon 9 SY0990
Harpham Humb 91 TA0861
Harpley H & W 47 SO6861
Harpley Norfk 65 TF7825
Harpole Nhants 49 SP6961
Harpsdale Highld 151 ND1355
Harpsden Oxon 37 SU7680
Harpswell Lincs 76 SK9389
Harpur Hill Derbys 74 SK0671
Harpurhey Gt Man 79 SD8501
Harraby Cumb 93 NY4154
Harracott Devon 19 SS5527
Harrapool Highld 129 NG6523
Harrietfield Tays 125 NN9829
Harrietsham Kent 28 TQ8652
Harringay Gt Lon 27 TQ3188
Harrington Lincs 77 TF3671
Harrington Nhants 50 SP7780
Harringworth Nhants 51 SP9197
Harriseahead Staffs 72 SJ8655
Harriston Cumb 92 NY1541
Harrogate N York 82 SE3054
Harrold Beds 51 SP9457
Harrop Dale Gt Man 82 SE0008
Harrow Gt Lon 26 TQ1588
Harrow Green Suffk 54 TL8654
Harrow on the Hill Gt Lon 26 TQ1587
Harrow Weald Gt Lon 26 TQ1591
Harrowbarrow Cnwll 5 SX4070
Harrowden Beds 38 TL0647
Harrowgate Village Dur 96 NZ2917
Harston Cambs 53 TL4250
Harston Leics 63 SK8331
Harswell Humb 84 SE8240
Hart Cleve 97 NZ4734
Hart Station Cleve 97 NZ4836
Hartburn Nthumb 103 NZ0885
Hartest Suffk 54 TL8352
Hartfield E Susx 16 TQ4735
Hartford Cambs 52 TL2572
Hartford Ches 71 SJ6372
Hartford Somset 20 SS9529
Hartford End Essex 40 TL6817
Hartfordbridge Hants 25 SU7757
Hartforth N York 89 NZ1606
Harthill Ches 71 SJ4955
Harthill Loth 116 NS9064
Harthill S York 75 SK4980
Hartington Derbys 74 SK1260
Hartland Devon 18 SS2524
Hartland Quay Devon 18 SS2224
Hartlebury H & W 60 SO8471
Hartlepool Cleve 97 NZ5032
Hartley Cumb 88 NY7808
Hartley Kent 27 TQ6066
Hartley Kent 17 TQ7634
Hartley Nthumb 103 NZ3475
Hartley Green Kent 27 TQ6067
Hartley Green Staffs 72 SJ9829
Hartley Wespall Hants 24 SU6958
Hartley Wintney Hants 24 SU7656
Hartlip Kent 28 TQ8464
Hartoft End N York 90 SE7493
Harton N York 90 SE7061
Harton Shrops 59 SO4888
Harton T & W 103 NZ3765
Hartpury Gloucs 47 SO7924
Hartshead W York 82 SE1822
Hartshead Moor Side W York 82 SE1625
Hartshill Staffs 72 SJ8546
Hartshill Warwks 61 SP3194
Hartshorne Derbys 62 SK3221
Hartside Nthumb 111 NT9716
Hartsop Cumb 93 NY4013
Hartswell Somset 20 ST0827
Hartwell Nhants 38 SP7850
Hartwith N York 89 SE2161
Hartwood Strath 116 NS8459
Hartwoodmyres Border 109 NT4324
Harvel Kent 28 TQ6563
Harvington H & W 60 SO8775
Harvington H & W 48 SP0549
Harwell Notts 75 SK6891
Harwell Oxon 37 SU4989
Harwich Essex 41 TM2531
Harwood Gt Man 79 SD7410
Harwood Nthumb 95 NY8233
Harwood Nthumb 103 NZ0189
Harwood Dale N York 91 SE9695
Harwood Lee Gt Man 81 SD7411
Harworth Notts 75 SK6191
Hasbury W Mids 60 SO9582
Hascombe Surrey 25 TQ0039
Haselbeach Nhants 50 SP7177
Haselbury Plucknett Somset 10 ST4710
Haseley Warwks 48 SP2367
Haseley Green Warwks 48 SP2369
Haseley Knob Warwks 61 SP2371
Haselor Warwks 48 SP1257
Hasfield Gloucs 47 SO8227
Hasguard Dyfed 30 SM8509
Haskayne Lancs 78 SD3508
Hasketon Suffk 55 TM2450
Hasland Derbys 74 SK3969
Hasland Green Derbys 74 SK3968
Haslemere Surrey 14 SU9032
Haslingden Lancs 81 SD7823
Haslingden Grane Lancs 81 SD7522
Haslingfield Cambs 52 TL4052
Haslington Ches 72 SJ7355
Hassall Ches 72 SJ7657
Hassall Green Ches 72 SJ7858
Hassell Street Kent 29 TR0946
Hassingham Norfk 67 TG3605
Hassness Cumb 93 NY1816
Hassocks W Susx 15 TQ3015
Hassop Derbys 74 SK2272
Haste Hill Surrey 14 SU9032
Haster Highld 151 ND3251
Hasthorpe Lincs 77 TF4869
Hastingleigh Kent 29 TR0945
Hastings E Susx 17 TQ8209
Hastings Somset 10 ST3116
Hastingwood Essex 39 TL4807
Hastoe Herts 38 SP9209
Haswell Dur 96 NZ3743
Haswell Plough Dur 96 NZ3742
Hatch Beds 52 TL1547
Hatch Beauchamp Somset 20 ST3020
Hatch End Beds 51 TL0760
Hatch End Herts 26 TQ1390
Hatchet Gate Hants 12 SU3701
Hatching Green Herts 38 TL1312
Hatchmere Ches 71 SJ5571
Hatcliffe Humb 76 TA2100
Hatfield H & W 46 SO5959
Hatfield Herts 39 TL2308
Hatfield S York 83 SE6609
Hatfield Broad Oak Essex 39 TL5416
Hatfield Heath Essex 39 TL5215
Hatfield Peverel Essex 40 TL7911
Hatfield Woodhouse S York 83 SE6708
Hatford Oxon 36 SU3395
Hatherden Hants 23 SU3450
Hatherleigh Devon 8 SS5404
Hathern Leics 62 SK5022
Hatherop Gloucs 36 SP1505
Hathersage Derbys 74 SK2381
Hathersage Booths Derbys 74 SK2480
Hatherton Ches 72 SJ6847
Hatherton Staffs 60 SJ9510
Hatley St George Cambs 52 TL2751
Hatt Cnwll 5 SX4062
Hattingley Hants 24 SU6437
Hatton Ches 78 SJ5982
Hatton Derbys 73 SK2130
Hatton Gramp 143 NK0537
Hatton Gt Lon 26 TQ0975
Hatton Lincs 76 TF1776
Hatton Shrops 59 SO4790
Hatton Tays 127 NO4642
Hatton Warwks 48 SP2367
Hatton Heath Ches 71 SJ4561
Hatton of Fintray Gramp 143 NJ8316
Haugh Lincs 77 TF4175
Haugh Strath 107 NS4925
Haugh W York 81 SD9311
Haugh Head Nthumb 111 NU0026
Haugh of Glass Gramp 142 NJ4238
Haugh of Urr D & G 100 NX8066
Haugham Lincs 77 TF3381
Haughhead Inn Strath 116 NS6079
Haughley Suffk 54 TM0262
Haughley Green Suffk 54 TM0264
Haughton Notts 75 SK6872
Haughton Powys 59 SJ3018
Haughton Shrops 59 SJ3726
Haughton Shrops 59 SJ5516
Haughton Shrops 60 SJ7408
Haughton Shrops 60 SO6896
Haughton Staffs 72 SJ8620
Haughton Green Gt Man 79 SJ9393
Haughton le Skerne Dur 96 NZ3116
Haughton Moss Ches 71 SJ5756
Haultwick Herts 39 TL3323
Haunton Staffs 61 SK2310
Hautes Croix Jersey 152 JS1414
Hauxley Nthumb 103 NU2703
Hauxton Cambs 53 TL4452
Havannah Ches 72 SJ8664
Havant Hants 13 SU7106
Haven H & W 46 SO4054
Haven Bank Lincs 76 TF2352
Haven Side Humb 85 TA1827
Havenstreet IOW 13 SZ5690
Havercroft W York 83 SE3913
Haverfordwest Dyfed 30 SM9515
Haverhill Suffk 53 TL6745
Haverigg Cumb 86 SD1578
Havering-atte-Bower Essex 27 TQ5193
Haversham Bucks 38 SP8242
Haverthwaite Cumb 87 SD3483
Haverton Hill Cleve 97 NZ4822
Havyat Avon 21 ST4761
Havyatt Somset 21 ST5338
Hawarden Clwyd 71 SJ3165
Hawbridge H & W 47 SO9049
Hawbush Green Essex 40 TL7820
Hawcoat Cumb 86 SD2071
Hawe's Green Norfk 67 TM2399
Hawen Dyfed 42 SN3446
Hawes N York 88 SD8789
Hawford H & W 47 SO8460
Hawick Border 109 NT5014
Hawk Green Gt Man 79 SJ9687
Hawkchurch Devon 10 ST3400
Hawkedon Suffk 53 TL7953
Hawkenbury Kent 28 TQ8045
Hawkeridge Wilts 22 ST8653
Hawkerland Devon 9 SY0588
Hawkes End W Mids 61 SP2982
Hawkesbury Avon 35 ST7686
Hawkesbury Warwks 61 SP3784
Hawkesbury Upton Avon 35 ST7786
Hawkhill Nthumb 111 NU2212
Hawkhurst Kent 17 TQ7530
Hawkhurst Common E Susx 16 TQ5217
Hawkinge Kent 29 TR2139
Hawkley Hants 24 SU7429
Hawkridge Devon 19 SS8630
Hawksdale Cumb 93 NY3648
Hawkshaw Gt Man 81 SD7615
Hawkshead Cumb 87 SD3598
Hawkshead Hill Cumb 86 SD3398
Hawksland Strath 108 NS8439
Hawkspur Green Essex 40 TL6532
Hawkstone Shrops 59 SJ5830
Hawkswick N York 88 SD9570
Hawksworth Notts 63 SK7543
Hawksworth W York 82 SE1641
Hawkwell Essex 40 TQ8591
Hawley Hants 25 SU8657
Hawley Kent 27 TQ5471
Hawling Gloucs 36 SP0622
Hawnby N York 90 SE5489
Haworth W York 82 SE0337
Hawstead Suffk 54 TL8559
Hawstead Green Suffk 54 TL8658
Hawthorn Dur 96 NZ4145
Hawthorn Hants 24 SU6733
Hawthorn M Glam 33 ST0987
Hawthorn Hill Berks 25 SU8773
Hawthorn Hill Lincs 76 TF2155
Hawthorpe Lincs 64 TF0427
Hawton Notts 75 SK7851
Haxby N York 90 SE6058
Haxby Gates N York 83 SE6056
Haxey Humb 75 SK7799
Haxey Turbary Humb 84 SE7501
Haxted Surrey 16 TQ4245
Haxton Wilts 23 SU1449
Hay Cnwll 3 SW8651
Hay Cnwll 3 SW9243
Hay Cnwll 3 SW9552
Hay Cnwll 4 SW9770
Hay Green Norfk 65 TF5418
Hay Street Herts 39 TL3926
Hay-on-Wye Powys 45 SO2342
Haydock Mersyd 78 SJ5697
Haydon Dorset 11 ST6715
Haydon Somset 20 ST2523
Haydon Bridge Nthumb 102 NY8464
Haydon Wick Wilts 36 SU1387
Haye Cnwll 5 SX3570
Hayes Gt Lon 26 TQ0980
Hayes Gt Lon 27 TQ4066
Hayes End Gt Lon 26 TQ0882
Hayfield Derbys 74 SK0386
Hayfield Strath 123 NN0723
Haygate Shrops 59 SJ6410
Hayhillock Tays 127 NO5242
Hayle Cnwll 2 SW5537
Hayley Green W Mids 60 SO9582
Haymoor Green Ches 72 SJ6850
Hayne Devon 9 SS9515
Hayne Devon 8 SX7685
Haynes Beds 38 TL0740
Haynes West End Beds 38 TL0640
Hayscastle Dyfed 30 SM8925
Hayscastle Cross Dyfed 30 SM9125
Haysden Kent 16 TQ5745
Hayton Cumb 92 NY1041
Hayton Cumb 94 NY5157
Hayton Humb 84 SE8245
Hayton Notts 75 SK7284
Hayton's Bent Shrops 59 SO5280
Haytor Vale Devon 8 SX7777
Haytown Devon 18 SS3814
Haywards Heath W Susx 15 TQ3324
Haywood H & W 46 SO4834
Haywood S York 83 SE5812
Haywood Oaks Notts 75 SK6055
Hazards Green E Susx 16 TQ6812
Hazel Grove Gt Man 79 SJ9287
Hazel Street Kent 28 TQ6939
Hazel Stub Suffk 53 TL6544
Hazelbank Strath 116 NS8345
Hazelbury Bryan Dorset 11 ST7408
Hazeleigh Essex 40 TL8203
Hazeley Hants 24 SU7458
Hazelford Notts 75 SK7249
Hazelhurst Gt Man 79 SD9600
Hazelslade Staffs 60 SK0212
Hazelton Walls Fife 126 NO3322
Hazelwood Derbys 62 SK3245
Hazlemere Bucks 26 SU8895
Hazlerigg T & W 103 NZ2372
Hazles Staffs 73 SK0047
Hazleton Gloucs 36 SP0718
Heacham Norfk 65 TF6737
Headbourne Worthy Hants 24 SU4832
Headbrook H & W 46 SO2854
Headcorn Kent 28 TQ8344
Headingley W York 82 SE2836
Headington Oxon 37 SP5207
Headlam Dur 96 NZ1818
Headless Cross H & W 48 SP0365
Headlesscross Strath 116 NS9158
Headley Hants 24 SU5162
Headley Hants 14 SU8236
Headley Surrey 26 TQ2054
Headley Down Hants 14 SU8336
Headley Heath H & W 61 SP0676
Headon Notts 75 SK7476
Heads Strath 116 NS7247
Heads Nook Cumb 94 NY5054
Heage Derbys 74 SK3750
Healaugh N York 88 SE0199
Healaugh N York 83 SE5047
Heald Green Gt Man 79 SJ8485
Heale Devon 19 SS6446
Heale Somset 20 ST2420
Heale Somset 21 ST3825
Healey Lancs 81 SD8816
Healey N York 89 SE1780
Healey Nthumb 95 NZ0158
Healey W York 82 SE2719
Healeyfield Dur 95 NZ0648
Healing Humb 85 TA2110
Heamoor Cnwll 2 SW4631
Heanor Derbys 62 SK4346
Heanton Punchardon Devon 19 SS5035
Heapey Lancs 81 SD5920
Heapham Lincs 76 SK8788
Hearn Hants 14 SU8337
Hearts Delight Kent 28 TQ8862
Heasley Mill Devon 19 SS7332
Heast Highld 129 NG6417
Heath Derbys 75 SK4567
Heath W York 83 SE3520
Heath and Reach Beds 38 SP9228
Heath Common W Susx 14 TQ0915
Heath End Bucks 26 SU8898
Heath End Hants 24 SU4161
Heath End Hants 24 SU5862
Heath End Leics 62 SK3621
Heath End Surrey 25 SU8549
Heath End Warwks 48 SP2360
Heath Green H & W 61 SP0771
Heath Hayes Staffs 60 SK0110
Heath Hill Shrops 60 SJ7613
Heath House Somset 21 ST4146
Heath Town W Mids 60 SO9399
Heathall D & G 100 NX9979
Heathbrook Shrops 59 SJ6228
Heathcote Derbys 74 SK1460
Heathcote Shrops 72 SJ6528
Heathencote Nhants 49 SP7147
Heather Leics 62 SK3910
Heathfield Devon 8 SX8376
Heathfield E Susx 16 TQ5821
Heathfield N York 89 SE1367
Heathfield Somset 20 ST1626
Heathstock Devon 9 ST2402
Heathton Shrops 60 SO8192
Heatley Gt Man 79 SJ7088
Heatley Staffs 73 SK0626
Heaton Gt Man 79 SD6909
Heaton Lancs 87 SD4460
Heaton Staffs 72 SJ9562
Heaton T & W 103 NZ2666
Heaton W York 82 SE1335
Heaton Chapel Gt Man 79 SJ8891
Heaton Mersey Gt Man 79 SJ8690
Heaton Norris Gt Man 79 SJ8890
Heaton's Bridge Lancs 80 SD4011
Heaverham Kent 27 TQ5758
Heaviley Gt Man 79 SJ9088
Heavitree Devon 9 SX9492
Hebburn T & W 103 NZ3164
Hebden N York 88 SE0263
Hebden Bridge W York 82 SD9927
Hebden Green Ches 71 SJ6365
Hebing End Herts 39 TL3122
Hebron Dyfed 31 SN1827
Hebron Nthumb 103 NZ1989
Heckfield Hants 24 SU7160
Heckfield Green Suffk 54 TM1875
Heckfordbridge Essex 40 TL9421
Heckington Lincs 64 TF1444
Heckmondwike W York 82 SE1824
Heddington Wilts 22 ST9966
Heddon-on-the-Wall Nthumb 103 NZ1366
Hedenham Norfk 67 TM3193
Hedge End Hants 13 SU4912
Hedgerley Bucks 26 SU9687
Hedgerley Green Bucks 26 SU9787
Hedging Somset 20 ST3029
Hedley on the Hill Nthumb 95 NZ0759
Hednesford Staffs 60 SJ9912
Hedon Humb 85 TA1928
Hedsor Bucks 26 SU9086
Hegdon Hill H & W 46 SO5853
Heglibister Shet 155 HU3851
Heighington Dur 96 NZ2422
Heighington Lincs 76 TF0269
Heightington H & W 60 SO7671
Heiton Border 110 NT7130
Hele Cnwll 5 SX2198
Hele Devon 19 SS5347
Hele Devon 9 SS9902
Hele Devon 7 SX7470
Hele Somset 20 ST1824
Hele Lane Devon 19 SS7910
Helebridge Cnwll 18 SS2103
Helensburgh Strath 115 NS2982
Helenton Strath 106 NS3830
Helford Cnwll 3 SW7526
Helford Passage Cnwll 3 SW7626
Helhoughton Norfk 66 TF8626
Helions Bumpstead Essex 53 TL6541
Hell Corner Berks 23 SU3864
Hellaby S York 75 SK5092
Helland Cnwll 4 SX0771
Hellandbridge Cnwll 4 SX0671
Hellescott Cnwll 5 SX2888
Hellesdon Norfk 67 TG2010
Hellesvear Cnwll 2 SW5040
Hellidon Nhants 49 SP5158
Hellifield N York 81 SD8556
Hellingly E Susx 16 TQ5812
Hellington Norfk 67 TG3103
Helmdon Nhants 49 SP5943
Helme W York 82 SE0912
Helmingham Suffk 54 TM1857
Helmington Row Dur 96 NZ1835
Helmsdale Highld 147 ND0315
Helmshore Lancs 81 SD7821
Helmsley N York 90 SE6183
Helperby N York 89 SE4469
Helperthorpe N York 91 SE9570
Helpringham Lincs 64 TF1440
Helpston Cambs 64 TF1205
Helsby Ches 71 SJ4975
Helsey Lincs 77 TF5172
Helston Cnwll 2 SW6527
Helstone Cnwll 4 SX0881
Helton Cumb 94 NY5021
Helwith N York 88 NZ0702
Helwith Bridge N York 88 SD8069
Hemblington Norfk 67 TG3411
Hemel Hempstead Herts 38 TL0507
Hemerdon Devon 6 SX5657
Hemingbrough N York 83 SE6730
Hemingby Lincs 76 TF2374
Hemingfield S York 83 SE3801
Hemingford Abbots Cambs 52 TL2871
Hemingford Grey Cambs 52 TL2970
Hemingstone Suffk 54 TM1454
Hemington Nhants 51 TL0985
Hemington Somset 22 ST7253
Hemley Suffk 55 TM2842
Hemlington Cleve 90 NZ5014
Hemp Green Suffk 55 TM3769
Hempholme Humb 85 TA0850
Hempnall Norfk 67 TM2494
Hempnall Green Norfk 67 TM2493
Hempriggs Gramp 141 NJ1063
Hempstead Essex 53 TL6338
Hempstead Gloucs 35 SO8116
Hempstead Kent 28 TQ7964
Hempstead Norfk 66 TG1037
Hempstead Norfk 67 TG4028
Hempton Norfk 66 TF9129
Hempton Oxon 49 SP4431
Hemsby Norfk 67 TG4917
Hemswell Lincs 76 SK9290
Hemsworth W York 83 SE4213
Hemyock Devon 9 ST1313
Henbury Avon 34 ST5678
Henbury Ches 79 SJ8773
Hendersyde Park Border 110 NT7435
Hendham Devon 7 SX7450
Hendomen Powys 58 SO2197
Hendon Gt Lon 26 TQ2389
Hendra Cnwll 3 SW7237
Hendra Cnwll 4 SX0275
Hendre M Glam 33 SS9381
Hendy Dyfed 32 SN5803
Heneglwys Gwynd 68 SH4276
Henfield W Susx 15 TQ2115
Henford Devon 5 SX3794
Henghurst Kent 28 TQ9536
Hengoed M Glam 33 ST1494
Hengoed Powys 45 SO2253
Hengoed Shrops 58 SJ2833
Hengrave Suffk 54 TL8268
Henham Essex 39 TL5428
Henhurst Kent 28 TQ6669
Heniarth Powys 58 SJ1208
Henlade Somset 20 ST2623
Henley Dorset 11 ST6904
Henley Gloucs 35 SO9016
Henley Shrops 59 SO4588
Henley Shrops 46 SO5476
Henley Somset 21 ST4232
Henley Suffk 54 TM1551
Henley W Susx 14 SU8925
Henley Green W Mids 61 SP3681
Henley Park Surrey 25 SU9352
Henley Street Kent 28 TQ6667
Henley's Down E Susx 17 TQ7312
Henley-in-Arden Warwks 48 SP1566
Henley-on-Thames Oxon 37 SU7682
Henllan Clwyd 70 SJ0268
Henllan Dyfed 31 SN3540
Henllan Amgoed Dyfed 31 SN1819
Henllys Gwent 34 ST2691
Henlow Beds 39 TL1738
Hennock Devon 8 SX8381
Henny Street Essex 54 TL8738
Henry's Moat (Castell Hendre) Dyfed 30 SN0427
Henryd Gwynd 69 SH7774
Hensall N York 83 SE5923
Henshaw Nthumb 102 NY7664
Hensingham Cumb 92 NX9816
Henstead Suffk 55 TM4885
Hensting Hants 13 SU4922
Henstridge Somset 22 ST7219
Henstridge Ash Somset 22 ST7220
Henstridge Marsh Somset 22 ST7320
Henton Oxon 37 SP7602
Henton Somset 21 ST4945
Henwick H & W 47 SO8355
Henwood Cnwll 5 SX2673
Heol Senni Powys 45 SN9223
Heol-las W Glam 32 SS6998
Heol-y-Cyw M Glam 33 SS9484
Hepburn Nthumb 111 NU0624
Hepple Nthumb 103 NT9901
Hepscott Nthumb 103 NZ2284
Heptonstall W York 82 SD9828
Hepworth Suffk 54 TL9874
Hepworth W York 82 SE1606
Herbrandston Dyfed 30 SM8707
Hereford H & W 46 SO5139
Hereson Kent 29 TR3865
Heribusta Highld 136 NG3970
Heriot Loth 118 NT3953
Hermiston Loth 117 NT1870
Hermit Hill S York 74 SE3200
Hermitage Berks 24 SU5072
Hermitage Border 101 NY5095
Hermitage Dorset 11 ST6506
Hermitage Hants 13 SU7505
Hermon Dyfed 31 SN2031
Hermon Gwynd 68 SH3968
Herne Kent 29 TR1865
Herne Bay Kent 29 TR1768
Herne Common Kent 29 TR1765
Herne Pound Kent 28 TQ6654
Herner Devon 19 SS5826
Hernhill Kent 29 TR0660
Herodsfoot Cnwll 5 SX2160
Heronden Kent 29 TR2954
Herongate Essex 40 TQ6291
Heronsford Strath 98 NX1283
Heronsgate Herts 26 TQ0294
Herriard Hants 24 SU6646
Herring's Green Beds 38 TL0844
Herringfleet Suffk 67 TM4797
Herringswell Suffk 53 TL7270
Herringthorpe S York 75 SK4492
Herrington T & W 96 NZ3453
Hersden Kent 29 TR2062
Hersham Cnwll 18 SS2507
Hersham Surrey 26 TQ1164
Herstmonceux E Susx 16 TQ6312
Herston Dorset 11 SZ0178
Herston Ork 155 ND4191
Hertford Herts 39 TL3212
Hertford Heath Herts 39 TL3510
Hertingfordbury Herts 39 TL3012
Hesketh Bank Lancs 80 SD4423
Hesketh Lane Lancs 81 SD6141
Heskin Green Lancs 80 SD5315
Hesleden Dur 96 NZ4438
Hesleden N York 88 SD8874
Hesleyside Nthumb 102 NY8183
Heslington N York 83 SE6250
Hessay N York 83 SE5253
Hessenford Cnwll 5 SX3057
Hessett Suffk 54 TL9361
Hessle Humb 84 TA0326
Hessle W York 84 TA0326
Hest Bank Lancs 87 SD4666
Hestley Green Suffk 54 TM1567
Heston Gt Lon 26 TQ1277
Hestwall Ork 155 HY2618
Heswall Mersyd 78 SJ2681
Hethe Oxon 49 SP5929
Hethersett Norfk 66 TG1404
Hethersgill Cumb 101 NY4767
Hetherside Cumb 101 NY4366
Hetherson Green Ches 71 SJ5250
Hethpool Nthumb 110 NT8928
Hett Dur 96 NZ2836
Hetton N York 88 SD9658
Hetton Steads Nthumb 111 NU0335
Hetton-le-Hole T & W 96 NZ3547
Heugh Nthumb 103 NZ0873
Heugh Head Border 119 NT8762
Heugh-Head Gramp 134 NJ3811
Heveningham Suffk 55 TM3372
Hever Kent 16 TQ4745
Heversham Cumb 87 SD4983
Hevingham Norfk 67 TG1921
Hewas Water Cnwll 3 SW9649
Hewelsfield Gloucs 34 SO5602
Hewenden W York 82 SE0736
Hewish Avon 21 ST4064
Hewish Somset 10 ST4208
Hewood Dorset 10 ST3502
Hexham Nthumb 102 NY9364
Hextable Kent 27 TQ5170
Hexthorpe S York 83 SE5602
Hexton Herts 38 TL1030
Hexworthy Cnwll 5 SX3581
Hexworthy Devon 7 SX6572
Hey Lancs 81 SD8843
Hey Houses Lancs 80 SD3429
Heybridge Essex 40 TL8508
Heybridge Essex 40 TQ6398
Heybridge Basin Essex 40 TL8707
Heybrook Bay Devon 6 SX4949
Heydon Cambs 39 TL4339
Heydon Norfk 66 TG1127
Heydour Lincs 63 TF0039
Heyhead Gt Man 79 SJ8285
Heylipoll Strath 120 NL9743
Heylor Shet 155 HU2980
Heyrod Gt Man 79 SJ9799
Heysham Lancs 87 SD4160
Heyshaw N York 89 SE1761
Heyshott W Susx 14 SU8917
Heyside Gt Man 79 SD9307
Heytesbury Wilts 22 ST9242
Heythrop Oxon 48 SP3527
Heywood Gt Man 79 SD8510
Heywood Wilts 22 ST8753
Hibaldstow Humb 84 SE9702
Hickleton S York 83 SE4805
Hickling Norfk 67 TG4124
Hickling Notts 63 SK6928
Hickling Green Norfk 67 TG4123
Hickling Heath Norfk 67 TG4022
Hickmans Green Kent 29 TR0658
Hicks Forstal Kent 29 TR1863
Hickstead W Susx 15 TQ2620
Hidcote Bartrim Gloucs 48 SP1742
Hidcote Boyce Gloucs 48 SP1742
High Ackworth W York 83 SE4417
High Angerton Nthumb 103 NZ0985
High Ardwell D & G 98 NX0745
High Auldgirth D & G 100 NX9187
High Bankhill Cumb 94 NY5542
High Beach Essex 27 TQ4198
High Bentham N York 87 SD6669
High Bewaldeth Cumb 93 NY2234
High Bickington Devon 19 SS6020
High Bickwith N York 88 SD8076
High Biggins Cumb 87 SD6078
High Blantyre Strath 116 NS6756
High Bonnybridge Cent 116 NS8379
High Borrans Cumb 87 NY4300
High Bradley N York 82 SE0049
High Bray Devon 19 SS6934
High Brooms Kent 16 TQ5941
High Bullen Devon 19 SS5320
High Buston Nthumb 111 NU2308
High Callerton Nthumb 103 NZ1670
High Catton Humb 84 SE7153
High Close N York 96 NZ1715
High Cogges Oxon 36 SP3709
High Common Norfk 66 TF9905
High Coniscliffe Dur 96 NZ2215
High Crosby Cumb 93 NY4559
High Cross Cnwll 3 SW7429
High Cross Hants 13 SU7126
High Cross Herts 39 TL3618
High Cross Strath 115 NS4046
High Cross W Susx 15 TQ2417
High Cross Warwks 48 SP2067
High Cross Bank Derbys 73 SK2817
High Disley Ches 79 SJ9784
High Drummore D & G 98 NX1235
High Dubmire T & W 96 NZ3250
High Easter Essex 40 TL6214
High Eggborough N York 83 SE5721
High Ellington N York 89 SE2083
High Ercall Shrops 59 SJ5917
High Etherley Dur 96 NZ1728
High Ferry Lincs 77 TF3549
High Flats W York 82 SE2107
High Garrett Essex 40 TL7727
High Grange Dur 96 NZ1731
High Grantley N York 89 SE2369
High Green Cumb 87 NY4103
High Green H & W 47 SO8745
High Green Norfk 66 TG1305
High Green Norfk 54 TM1689
High Green Norfk 67 TM2898
High Green S York 74 SK3397
High Green Shrops 60 SO7083
High Green Suffk 54 TL8560
High Green W York 82 SE2014
High Halden Kent 28 TQ8937
High Halstow Kent 28 TQ7875
High Ham Somset 21 ST4231
High Harrington Cumb 92 NY0025
High Harrogate N York 82 SE3155
High Hartlington Nthumb 103 NZ0288
High Haswell Dur 96 NZ3643
High Hatton Shrops 59 SJ6124
High Hawsker N York 91 NZ9207
High Hesket Cumb 93 NY4744
High Hoyland S York 82 SE2710
High Hunsley Humb 84 SE9535
High Hurstwood E Susx 16 TQ4926
High Hutton N York 90 SE7568
High Ireby Cumb 93 NY2237
High Kilburn N York 90 SE5179
High Killerby N York 91 TA0683
High Knipe Cumb 94 NY5219
High Lands Dur 96 NZ1226
High Lane Ches 79 SJ8868
High Lane Gt Man 79 SJ9585
High Lane H & W 47 SO6760
High Lanes Cnwll 2 SW5637
High Laver Essex 39 TL5208
High Legh Ches 79 SJ7084
High Leven Cleve 89 NZ4512
High Littleton Avon 21 ST6458
High Lorton Cumb 92 NY1625
High Marnham Notts 75 SK8070
High Melton S York 83 SE5001
High Mickley Nthumb 103 NZ0761
High Moorsley T & W 96 NZ3345
High Newport T & W 96 NZ3754
High Newton Cumb 87 SD4082
High Newton by-the-Sea Nthumb 111 NU2325
High Nibthwaite Cumb 86 SD2989
High Offley Staffs 72 SJ7826
High Ongar Essex 40 TL5603
High Onn Staffs 72 SJ8216
High Park Corner Essex 41 TM0320
High Pennyvenie Strath 107 NS4907
High Post Wilts 23 SU1536
High Roding Essex 40 TL6017
High Row Cumb 93 NY3535
High Row Cumb 93 NY3821
High Salter Lancs 87 SD6062
High Salvington W Susx 14 TQ1206
High Scales Cumb 93 NY1845
High Seaton Cumb 92 NY0231
High Shaw N York 88 SD8691
High Side Cumb 93 NY2330
High Spen T & W 96 NZ1359
High Stoop Dur 95 NZ1040
High Street Cambs 52 TL3762
High Street Cnwll 3 SW9653
High Street Kent 17 TQ7430
High Street Kent 29 TR0862
High Street Suffk 55 TM4171
High Street Suffk 55 TM4355
High Throston Cleve 97 NZ4833
High Town Staffs 60 SJ9911
High Toynton Lincs 77 TF2869
High Trewhitt Nthumb 111 NU0105
High Urpeth Dur 96 NZ2354
High Valleyfield Fife 117 NT0086
High Warden Nthumb 102 NY9067
High Westwood Dur 95 NZ1155
High Woolaston Gloucs 34 ST5899
High Worsall Cleve 89 NZ3809
High Wray Cumb 87 SD3799
High Wych Herts 39 TL4614
High Wycombe Bucks 26 SU8693
Higham Derbys 74 SK3859
Higham Kent 16 TQ6048
Higham Kent 28 TQ7171
Higham Lancs 81 SD8136
Higham S York 82 SE3107
Higham Suffk 53 TL7465
Higham Suffk 54 TM0335
Higham Dykes Nthumb 103 NZ1375
Higham Ferrers Nhants 51 SP9668
Higham Gobion Beds 38 TL1032
Higham Hill Gt Lon 27 TQ3590
Higham on the Hill Leics 61 SP3895
Highampton Devon 18 SS4804

Highams Park
Inver-boyndie

Highams Park *Gt Lon* 27 TQ3891
Highbridge *Hants* 13 SU4621
Highbridge *Somset* 21 ST3247
Highbrook *W Susx* 15 TQ3630
Highburton *W York* 82 SE1813
Highbury *Gt Lon* 27 TQ3185
Highbury *Somset* 22 ST6949
Highclere *Hants* 24 SU4359
Highcliffe *Dorset* 12 SZ2193
Highclifflane *Derbys* 73 SK2947
Higher Alham *Somset* 22 ST6741
Higher Ansty *Dorset* 11 ST7604
Higher Ballam *Lancs* 80 SD3630
Higher Bartle *Lancs* 80 SD5033
Higher Berry End *Beds* 38 SP9834
Higher Bockhampton *Dorset* 11 SY7292
Higher Brixham *Devon* 7 SX9155
Higher Burrowton *Devon* 9 SY0097
Higher Burwardsley *Ches* 71 SJ5156
Higher Chillington *Somset* 10 ST3810
Higher Combe *Somset* 20 SS9030
Higher Coombe *Dorset* 10 SY5391
Higher Gabwell *Devon* 7 SX9169
Higher Halstock Leigh *Dorset* 10 ST5107
Higher Harpers *Lancs* 81 SD8237
Higher Heysham *Lancs* 87 SD4160
Higher Hurdsfield *Ches* 79 SJ9374
Higher Irlam *Gt Man* 79 SJ7295
Higher Kinnerton *Clwyd* 71 SJ3261
Higher Melcombe *Dorset* 11 ST7402
Higher Muddiford *Devon* 19 SS5638
Higher Nyland *Dorset* 22 ST7322
Higher Ogden *Gt Man* 82 SD9512
Higher Pentire *Cnwll* 2 SW6525
Higher Penwortham *Lancs* 80 SD5128
Higher Studfold *N York* 88 SD8170
Higher Town *Cnwll* 3 SW8044
Higher Town *Cnwll* 4 SX0061
Higher Town *IOS* 2 SV9215
Higher Tregantle *Cnwll* 5 SX4052
Higher Walton *Ches* 78 SJ5985
Higher Walton *Lancs* 81 SD5727
Higher Wambrook *Somset* 10 ST2908
Higher Waterston *Dorset* 11 SY7295
Higher Whatcombe *Dorset* 11 ST8301
Higher Wheelton *Lancs* 81 SD6022
Higher Whiteleigh *Cnwll* 5 SX2494
Higher Whitley *Ches* 78 SJ6180
Higher Wraxhall *Dorset* 10 ST5601
Higher Wych *Ches* 71 SJ4943
Higherford *Lancs* 81 SD8640
Highfield *Devon* 8 SX7097
Highfield *Humb* 84 SE7236
Highfield *Strath* 115 NS3150
Highfield *T & W* 96 NZ1458
Highfields *S York* 83 SE5406
Highgate *E Susx* 16 TQ4234
Highgate *Gt Lon* 27 TQ2887
Highgate *N York* 83 SE5918
Highgate Head *Derbys* 74 SK0486
Highgreen Manor *Nthumb* 102 NY8091
Highlane *S York* 74 SK4081
Highlaws *Cumb* 92 NY1449
Highleadon *Gloucs* 47 SO7623
Highleigh *W Susx* 14 SZ8498
Highley *Shrops* 60 SO7483
Highmoor *Cumb* 93 NY2647
Highmoor *Oxon* 37 SU7084
Highmoor Cross *Oxon* 37 SU7084
Highmoor Hill *Gwent* 34 ST4689
Highnam *Gloucs* 35 SO7817
Highnam Green *Gloucs* 35 SO7920
Highridge *Avon* 21 ST5567
Highstead *Kent* 29 TR2166
Highsted *Kent* 28 TQ9061
Highstreet Green *Essex* 53 TL7634
Highstreet Green *Surrey* 14 SU9835
Hightae *D & G* 100 NY0978
Highter's Heath *W Mids* 61 SP0879
Hightown *Ches* 72 SJ8762
Hightown *Hants* 12 SU1704
Hightown *Mersyd* 78 SD3003
Hightown Green *Suffk* 54 TL9756
Highway *H & W* 46 SO4549
Highway *Wilts* 36 SU0474
Highweek *Devon* 7 SX8472
Highwood *Staffs* 73 SK0931
Highwood Hill *Gt Lon* 26 TQ2193
Highworth *Wilts* 36 SU2092
Hilden Park *Kent* 16 TQ5747
Hildenborough *Kent* 16 TQ5648
Hildersham *Cambs* 53 TL5448
Hilderstone *Staffs* 72 SJ9534
Hilderthorpe *Humb* 91 TA1766
Hilfield *Dorset* 10 ST6305
Hilgay *Norfk* 65 TL6298
Hill *Avon* 35 ST6495
Hill *Warwks* 50 SP4566
Hill Brow *Hants* 14 SU7926
Hill Chorlton *Staffs* 72 SJ7939
Hill Cliff *Ches* 78 SJ6185
Hill Common *Norfk* 67 TG4122
Hill Common *Somset* 20 ST1426
Hill Deverill *Wilts* 22 ST8640
Hill Dyke *Lincs* 77 TF3447
Hill End *Dur* 95 NZ0136
Hill End *Fife* 117 NT0395
Hill End *Gloucs* 47 SO9037
Hill Green *Kent* 28 TQ8362
Hill Head *Hants* 13 SU5402
Hill of Beath *Fife* 117 NT1590
Hill of Fearn *Highld* 147 NH8377
Hill Ridware *Staffs* 73 SK0817
Hill Side *H & W* 47 SO7561
Hill Side *W York* 82 SE1717
Hill Top *Dur* 95 NY9924
Hill Top *Hants* 13 SU4003
Hill Top *S York* 74 SK3992
Hill Top *W Mids* 60 SO9993
Hill Top *W York* 82 SE0712
Hill Top *W York* 83 SE3315
Hillam *N York* 83 SE5028
Hillbeck *Cumb* 95 NY7915
Hillborough *Kent* 29 TR2168
Hillbutts *Dorset* 11 ST9901
Hillcott *Wilts* 23 SU1158
Hillend *Fife* 117 NT1483
Hillend *Loth* 117 NT2566
Hillend *Strath* 116 NS8267
Hillend *W Glam* 31 SS4190
Hillersland *Gloucs* 34 SO5614
Hillerton *Devon* 8 SX7298
Hillesden *Bucks* 49 SP6828
Hillesley *Avon* 35 ST7689
Hillfarrance *Somset* 20 ST1624
Hillfoot *Strath* 115 NS5472
Hillgrove *W Susx* 14 SU9428
Hillhampton *H & W* 46 SO5847
Hillhead *Devon* 7 SX9054
Hillhead *Strath* 108 NS9840
Hillhead of Cocklaw *Gramp* 143 NK0844
Hillhead of Durno *Gramp* 142 NJ7128
Hilliard's Cross *Staffs* 61 SK1511
Hilliclay *Highld* 151 ND1764
Hillingdon *Gt Lon* 26 TQ0782
Hillington *Norfk* 65 TF7225
Hillington *Strath* 115 NS5164
Hillis Corner *IOW* 13 SZ4793
Hillmorton *Warwks* 50 SP5373
Hillock Vale *Lancs* 81 SD7629
Hillowtan *D & G* 100 NX7763
Hillpool *H & W* 60 SO8976
Hillpound *Hants* 13 SU5715
Hills Town *Derbys* 75 SK4869
Hillside *Devon* 7 SX7060
Hillside *Gramp* 135 NO9197
Hillside *T & W* 135 NO6960
Hillstreet *Hants* 12 SU3416
Hillswick *Shet* 155 HU2877
Hilltown *Devon* 8 SX5380
Hillwell *Shet* 155 HU3714
Hilmarton *Wilts* 35 SU0175
Hilperton *Wilts* 22 ST8759
Hilperton Marsh *Wilts* 22 ST8659
Hilsea *Hants* 13 SU6503
Hilston *Humb* 85 TA2833
Hilston Park *Gwent* 34 SO4418
Hiltingbury *Hants* 13 SU4221
Hilton *Border* 119 NT8750
Hilton *Cambs* 52 TL2966
Hilton *Cleve* 89 NZ4611
Hilton *Cumb* 94 NY7320
Hilton *Derbys* 73 SK2430
Hilton *Dorset* 11 ST7802
Hilton *Dur* 96 NZ1622
Hilton *Shrops* 60 SO7795
Hilton of Cadboll *Highld* 147 NH8776
Himbleton *H & W* 47 SO9458
Himley *Staffs* 60 SO8891
Hincaster *Cumb* 87 SD5084
Hinckley *Leics* 50 SP4294
Hinderclay *Suffk* 54 TM0276
Hinderwell *N York* 97 NZ7916
Hindford *Shrops* 59 SJ3333
Hindhead *Surrey* 14 SU8835
Hindle Fold *Lancs* 81 SD7332
Hindley *Gt Man* 78 SD6104
Hindley *Nthumb* 95 NZ0459
Hindley Green *Gt Man* 79 SD6403
Hindlip *H & W* 47 SO8858
Hindolveston *Norfk* 66 TG0329
Hindon *Wilts* 22 ST9132
Hindringham *Norfk* 66 TF9836
Hingham *Norfk* 66 TG0202
Hinksford *Staffs* 60 SO8689
Hinnington *Shrops* 60 SJ7404
Hinstock *Shrops* 72 SJ6925
Hintlesham *Suffk* 54 TM0843
Hinton *Avon* 35 ST7376
Hinton *Gloucs* 35 SO6803
Hinton *H & W* 46 SO3338
Hinton *Hants* 12 SZ2195
Hinton *Shrops* 59 SJ4008
Hinton *Shrops* 59 SO6582
Hinton Admiral *Hants* 12 SZ2096
Hinton Ampner *Hants* 13 SU6027
Hinton Blewett *Somset* 21 ST5956
Hinton Charterhouse *Avon* 22 ST7758
Hinton Green *H & W* 48 SP0240
Hinton Marsh *Hants* 24 SU5828
Hinton Martell *Dorset* 11 SU0106
Hinton on the Green *H & W* 48 SP0240
Hinton Parva *Wilts* 36 SU2383
Hinton St George *Somset* 10 ST4212
Hinton St Mary *Dorset* 11 ST7816
Hinton Waldrist *Oxon* 36 SU3799
Hinton-in-the-Hedges *Nhants* 49 SP5636
Hints *Shrops* 46 SO6174
Hints *Staffs* 61 SK1502
Hinwick *Beds* 51 SP9361
Hinxhill *Kent* 28 TR0442
Hinxton *Cambs* 53 TL4945
Hinxworth *Herts* 39 TL2340
Hipperholme *W York* 82 SE1225
Hipswell *N York* 89 SE1898
Hirn *Gramp* 135 NJ7200
Hirnant *Powys* 58 SJ0422
Hirst *Nthumb* 103 NZ2787
Hirst Courtney *N York* 83 SE6124
Hirwaen *Clwyd* 70 SJ1361
Hirwaun *M Glam* 33 SN9505
Hiscott *Devon* 19 SS5426
Histon *Cambs* 53 TL4463
Hitcham *Suffk* 54 TL9851
Hitcham Causeway *Suffk* 54 TL9852
Hitcham Street *Suffk* 54 TL9851
Hitchin *Herts* 39 TL1829
Hither Green *Gt Lon* 27 TQ3874
Hittisleigh *Devon* 8 SX7395
Hittisleigh Cross *Devon* 8 SX7395
Hive *Humb* 84 SE8230
Hixon *Staffs* 73 SK0025
Hoaden *Kent* 29 TR2759
Hoar Cross *Staffs* 73 SK1323
Hoarwithy *H & W* 46 SO5429
Hoath *Kent* 29 TR2064
Hoathly *Kent* 28 TQ6536
Hobarris *Shrops* 46 SO3178
Hobbles Green *Suffk* 53 TL7053
Hobbs Cross *Essex* 27 TQ4799
Hobkirk *Border* 110 NT5811
Hobland Hall *Norfk* 67 TG5001
Hobsick *Notts* 75 SK4549
Hobson *Dur* 96 NZ1756
Hoby *Leics* 63 SK6617
Hockering *Norfk* 66 TG0713
Hockerton *Notts* 75 SK7156
Hockley *Ches* 79 SJ9383
Hockley *Essex* 40 TQ8392
Hockley *Staffs* 61 SK2200
Hockley *W Mids* 61 SP2779
Hockley Heath *W Mids* 61 SP1572
Hockliffe *Beds* 38 SP9726
Hockwold cum Wilton *Norfk* 53 TL7388
Hockworthy *Devon* 20 ST0319
Hoddesdon *Herts* 39 TL3708
Hoddleston *Lancs* 81 SD7122
Hoddom Cross *D & G* 101 NY1873
Hoddom Mains *D & G* 100 NY1572
Hodgehill *Ches* 79 SJ8269
Hodgeston *Dyfed* 30 SS0399
Hodnet *Shrops* 59 SJ6128
Hodsall Street *Kent* 27 TQ6263
Hodsock *Notts* 75 SK6185
Hodson *Wilts* 36 SU1780
Hodthorpe *Derbys* 75 SK5376
Hoe *Hants* 13 SU5617
Hoe *Norfk* 66 TF9916
Hoe Gate *Hants* 13 SU6213
Hoff *Cumb* 94 NY6717
Hog Hill *E Susx* 17 TQ8815
Hogben's Hill *Kent* 28 TR0356
Hoggards Green *Suffk* 54 TL8856
Hoggeston *Bucks* 38 SP8024
Hoghton *Lancs* 81 SD6125
Hoghton Bottoms *Lancs* 81 SD6227
Hognaston *Derbys* 73 SK2350
Hogrill's End *Warwks* 61 SP2292
Hogsthorpe *Lincs* 77 TF5372
Holbeach *Lincs* 64 TF3624
Holbeach Bank *Lincs* 64 TF3527
Holbeach Clough *Lincs* 64 TF3526
Holbeach Drove *Lincs* 64 TF3212
Holbeach Hurn *Lincs* 65 TF3926
Holbeach St Johns *Lincs* 64 TF3518
Holbeach St Mark's *Lincs* 64 TF3731
Holbeach St Matthew *Lincs* 65 TF4132
Holbeck *Notts* 75 SK5473
Holbeck Woodhouse *Notts* 75 SK5472
Holberrow Green *H & W* 48 SP0259
Holbeton *Devon* 6 SX6150
Holborn *Gt Lon* 27 TQ3181
Holborough *Kent* 28 TQ7062
Holbrook *Derbys* 62 SK3644
Holbrook *S York* 75 SK4481
Holbrook *Suffk* 54 TM1636
Holbrook Moor *Derbys* 62 SK3645
Holburn *Nthumb* 111 NU0436
Holbury *Hants* 13 SU4303
Holcombe *Devon* 7 SX9574
Holcombe *Gt Man* 81 SD7816
Holcombe *Somset* 20 ST1129
Holcombe *Somset* 22 ST6749
Holcombe Brook *Gt Man* 81 SD7815
Holcombe Rogus *Devon* 20 ST0518
Holcot *Nhants* 50 SP7969
Holden *Lancs* 81 SD7749
Holden *Lancs* 81 SD8833
Holden Gate *W York* 81 SD8923
Holdenby *Nhants* 50 SP6967
Holder's Green *Essex* 40 TL6328
Holdgate *Shrops* 59 SO5689
Holdingham *Lincs* 76 TF0547
Holditch *Dorset* 10 ST3402
Holdsworth *W York* 82 SE0829
Hole *Devon* 18 SS4206
Hole Street *W Susx* 15 TQ1314
Hole-in-the-Wall *H & W* 46 SO6128
Holehouse *Derbys* 79 SK0092
Holemoor *Devon* 18 SS4205
Holford *Somset* 20 ST1541
Holgate *N York* 83 SE5851
Holker *Cumb* 87 SD3676
Holkham *Norfk* 66 TF8943
Hollacombe *Devon* 18 SS3702
Hollam *Somset* 20 SS9232
Holland Fen *Lincs* 76 TF2349
Holland Lees *Lancs* 78 SD5208
Holland-on-Sea *Essex* 41 TM1916
Hollandstoun *Ork* 155 HY7553
Hollesley *Suffk* 55 TM3544
Hollicombe *Devon* 7 SX8962
Hollies Hill *H & W* 60 SO9377
Hollin Green *Ches* 71 SJ5952
Hollingbourne *Kent* 28 TQ8455
Hollingdon *Bucks* 38 SP8727
Hollingthorpe *W York* 83 SE3831
Hollington *Derbys* 73 SK2239
Hollington *Staffs* 73 SK0538
Hollingworth *Gt Man* 79 SK0096
Hollinlane *Ches* 79 SJ8384
Hollins *Derbys* 74 SK3271
Hollins *Gt Man* 79 SD8107
Hollins *Staffs* 73 SJ9947
Hollins End *S York* 74 SK3883
Hollins Green *Ches* 79 SJ6990
Hollins Lane *Lancs* 80 SD4951
Hollinsclough *Staffs* 74 SK0666
Hollinswood *Shrops* 60 SJ7008
Hollinwood *Shrops* 59 SJ5136
Holllingrove *E Susx* 16 TQ6821
Hollocombe *Devon* 19 SS6311
Holloway *Derbys* 74 SK3256
Holloway *Gt Lon* 27 TQ3086
Holloway *Wilts* 22 ST8730
Hollowell *Nhants* 50 SP6971
Hollowmoor Heath *Ches* 71 SJ4868
Holly End *Norfk* 65 TF4906
Holly Green *H & W* 47 SO8641
Hollybush *Gwent* 33 SO1603
Hollybush *H & W* 47 SO7536
Hollybush *Strath* 106 NS3915
Hollyhurst *Ches* 71 SJ5744
Hollym *Humb* 85 TA3425
Hollywood *H & W* 61 SP0877
Holmbridge *W York* 82 SE1206
Holmbury St Mary *Surrey* 14 TQ1143
Holmbush *Cnwll* 3 SX0352
Holmcroft *Staffs* 72 SJ9024
Holme *Cambs* 52 TL1987
Holme *Cumb* 87 SD5278
Holme *Humb* 84 SE9206
Holme *N York* 89 SE3582
Holme *Notts* 75 SK8059
Holme *W York* 82 SE1105
Holme Chapel *Lancs* 81 SD8728
Holme Green *N York* 83 SE5541
Holme Hale *Norfk* 66 TF8807
Holme Lacy *H & W* 46 SO5535
Holme Marsh *H & W* 46 SO3454
Holme next the Sea *Norfk* 65 TF7043
Holme on the Wolds *Humb* 84 SE9646
Holme Pierrepont *Notts* 62 SK6238
Holme St Cuthbert *Cumb* 92 NY1047
Holme upon Spalding Moor *Humb* 84 SE8038
Holmer *H & W* 46 SO5042
Holmer Green *Bucks* 26 SU9097
Holmes Chapel *Ches* 72 SJ7667
Holmes Hill *E Susx* 16 TQ5312
Holmesfield *Derbys* 74 SK3277
Holmeswood *Lancs* 80 SD4316
Holmethorpe *Surrey* 27 TQ2851
Holmewood *Derbys* 75 SK4365
Holmfield *W York* 82 SE0828
Holmfirth *W York* 82 SE1408
Holmgate *Derbys* 74 SK3763
Holmhead *Strath* 107 NS5620
Holmpton *Humb* 85 TA3623
Holmrook *Cumb* 86 SD0799
Holmsey Green *Suffk* 53 TL6978
Holmshurst *E Susx* 16 TQ6425
Holmside *Dur* 96 NZ2149
Holmwood *Surrey* 15 TQ1647
Holmwrangle *Cumb* 94 NY5148
Holne *Devon* 7 SX7069
Holnest *Dorset* 11 ST6510
Holnicote *Somset* 20 SS9146
Holsworthy *Devon* 18 SS3403
Holsworthy Beacon *Devon* 18 SS3608
Holt *Clwyd* 71 SJ4053
Holt *Dorset* 12 SU0303
Holt *H & W* 47 SO8362
Holt *Norfk* 66 TG0838
Holt *Wilts* 22 ST8661
Holt End *H & W* 48 SP0769
Holt Fleet *H & W* 47 SO8263
Holt Green *Lancs* 78 SD3905
Holt Heath *Dorset* 12 SU0504
Holt Heath *H & W* 47 SO8163
Holt Street *Kent* 29 TR2551
Holtby *N York* 83 SE6754
Holton *Oxon* 37 SP6006
Holton *Somset* 22 ST6826
Holton *Suffk* 55 TM4077
Holton cum Beckering *Lincs* 76 TF1181
Holton Heath *Dorset* 11 SY9490
Holton Hill *E Susx* 16 TQ6625
Holton le Clay *Lincs* 85 TA2802
Holton le Moor *Lincs* 76 TF0897
Holton St Mary *Suffk* 54 TM0536
Holtye *E Susx* 16 TQ4539
Holway *Clwyd* 70 SJ1876
Holwell *Dorset* 11 ST6911
Holwell *Herts* 39 TL1633
Holwell *Leics* 63 SK7323
Holwell *Oxon* 36 SP2309
Holwick *Dur* 95 NY9126
Holworth *Dorset* 11 SY7683
Holy Cross *H & W* 60 SO9278
Holy Island *Nthumb* 111 NU1241
Holybourne *Hants* 24 SU7340
Holyfield *Essex* 39 TL3803
Holyhead *Gwynd* 68 SH2482
Holymoorside *Derbys* 74 SK3369
Holyport *Berks* 26 SU8977
Holystone *Nthumb* 102 NT9502
Holytown *Strath* 116 NS7660
Holywell *Cambs* 52 TL3370
Holywell *Clwyd* 70 SJ1875
Holywell *Cnwll* 4 SW7659
Holywell *Dorset* 10 ST5904
Holywell Green *W York* 82 SE0819
Holywell Lake *Somset* 20 ST1020
Holywell Row *Suffk* 53 TL7177
Holywood *D & G* 100 NX9480
Hom Green *H & W* 34 SO5822
Homer *Shrops* 59 SJ6101
Homer Green *Mersyd* 78 SD3402
Homersfield *Suffk* 55 TM2885
Homescales *Cumb* 87 SD5587
Homington *Wilts* 23 SU1226
Honey Hill *Kent* 29 TR1161
Honey Tye *Suffk* 54 TL9535
Honeyborough *Dyfed* 30 SM9406
Honeybourne *H & W* 48 SP1144
Honeychurch *Devon* 8 SS6303
Honeystreet *Wilts* 23 SU1061
Honiley *Warwks* 61 SP2372
Honing *Norfk* 67 TG3227
Honingham *Norfk* 66 TG1011
Honington *Lincs* 63 SK9443
Honington *Suffk* 54 TL9174
Honington *Warwks* 48 SP2642
Honiton *Devon* 9 ST1600
Honley *W York* 82 SE1311
Honnington *Shrops* 72 SJ7215
Hoo *Kent* 27 TQ2964
Hoo *Kent* 28 TQ7872
Hoo End *Herts* 39 TL1820
Hoo Green *Ches* 79 SJ7182
Hoo Meavy *Devon* 6 SX5265
Hoobrook *H & W* 60 SO8374
Hood Green *S York* 82 SE3102
Hood Hill *S York* 74 SK3697
Hooe *Devon* 6 SX5052
Hooe *E Susx* 16 TQ6809
Hooe Common *E Susx* 16 TQ6910
Hoohill *Lancs* 80 SD3237
Hook *Cambs* 65 TL4293
Hook *Devon* 10 ST3005
Hook *Dyfed* 30 SM9711
Hook *Hants* 13 SU5105
Hook *Hants* 24 SU7254
Hook *Humb* 84 SE7625
Hook *Kent* 27 TQ6170
Hook *Surrey* 26 TQ1864
Hook *Wilts* 36 SU0784
Hook Bank *H & W* 47 SO8140
Hook Green *Kent* 16 TQ6535
Hook Norton *Oxon* 48 SP3533
Hook Street *Gloucs* 35 ST6799
Hook Street *Wilts* 36 SU0884
Hookagate *Shrops* 59 SJ4609
Hooke *Dorset* 10 ST5300
Hookgate *Staffs* 72 SJ7435
Hookway *Devon* 8 SX8598
Hookwood *Surrey* 15 TQ2643
Hooley *Surrey* 27 TQ2856
Hooley Bridge *Gt Man* 81 SD8511
Hooton *Ches* 71 SJ3678
Hooton Levitt *S York* 75 SK5291
Hooton Pagnell *S York* 83 SE4807
Hooton Roberts *S York* 75 SK4897
Hop Pole *Lincs* 64 TF1813
Hopcrofts Holt *Oxon* 49 SP4625
Hope *Clwyd* 71 SJ3058
Hope *Derbys* 74 SK1783
Hope *Devon* 7 SX6740
Hope *Powys* 58 SJ2507
Hope *Shrops* 59 SJ3401
Hope *Shrops* 46 SO5974
Hope *Staffs* 73 SK1254
Hope Bowdler *Shrops* 59 SO4792
Hope End Green *Essex* 40 TL5720
Hope Mansell *H & W* 35 SO6219
Hope under Dinmore *H & W* 46 SO5052
Hopehouse *Border* 109 NT2916
Hopeman *Gramp* 147 NJ1469
Hopesay *Shrops* 59 SO3983
Hopetown *W York* 83 SE3923
Hopperton *N York* 83 SE4256
Hopsford *Warwks* 50 SP4284
Hopstone *Shrops* 60 SO7894
Hopton *Derbys* 73 SK2653
Hopton *Shrops* 59 SJ3820
Hopton *Staffs* 72 SJ9426
Hopton *Suffk* 54 TL9979
Hopton Cangeford *Shrops* 59 SO5480
Hopton Castle *Shrops* 46 SO3678
Hopton on Sea *Norfk* 67 TM5299
Hopton Wafers *Shrops* 47 SO6376
Hoptonheath *Shrops* 46 SO3877
Hopwas *Staffs* 61 SK1804
Hopwood *Gt Man* 79 SD8609
Hopwood *H & W* 61 SP0375
Horam *E Susx* 16 TQ5717
Horbling *Lincs* 64 TF1135
Horbury *W York* 82 SE2918
Horcott *Gloucs* 36 SP1500
Horden *Dur* 96 NZ4440
Horderley *Shrops* 59 SO4086
Hordle *Hants* 12 SZ2795
Hordley *Shrops* 59 SJ3831
Horeb *Dyfed* 31 SN3942
Horeb *Dyfed* 32 SN4905
Horfield *Avon* 34 ST5976
Horham *Suffk* 55 TM2072
Horkesley Green *Essex* 41 TL9831
Horkesley Heath *Essex* 41 TL9829
Horkstow *Humb* 84 SE9817
Horley *Oxon* 49 SP4144
Horley *Surrey* 15 TQ2842
Horn Hill *Bucks* 26 TQ0192
Horn Street *Kent* 29 TR1836
Hornblotton Green *Somset* 21 ST5833
Hornby *Lancs* 87 SD5868
Hornby *N York* 89 NZ3605
Hornby *N York* 89 SE2293
Horncastle *Lincs* 77 TF2669
Hornchurch *Gt Lon* 27 TQ5387
Horndean *Border* 110 NT9049
Horndean *Hants* 13 SU7013
Horndon *Devon* 5 SX5280
Horndon on the Hill *Essex* 40 TQ6683
Horne *Surrey* 15 TQ3344
Horne Row *Essex* 40 TL7704
Horner *Somset* 20 SS9045
Horners Green *Suffk* 54 TL9641
Horney Common *E Susx* 16 TQ4525
Horning *Norfk* 67 TG3417
Horninghold *Leics* 51 SP8097
Horninglow *Staffs* 73 SK2425
Horningsea *Cambs* 53 TL4962
Horningsham *Wilts* 22 ST8141
Horningtoft *Norfk* 66 TF9323
Horningtops *Cnwll* 5 SX2760
Horns Cross *Devon* 18 SS3823
Horns Cross *E Susx* 17 TQ8222
Hornsby *Cumb* 94 NY5150
Hornsby *Somset* 10 ST3310
Hornsbygate *Cumb* 94 NY5250
Hornsea *Humb* 85 TA1947
Hornsey *Gt Lon* 27 TQ3089
Hornton *Oxon* 48 SP3945
Horpit *Wilts* 36 SU2183
Horra *Shet* 155 HU4693
Horrabridge *Devon* 6 SX5169
Horridge *Devon* 7 SX7674
Horringer *Suffk* 54 TL8261
Horringford *IOW* 13 SZ5485
Horrocks Fold *Gt Man* 81 SD7012
Horrocksford *Lancs* 81 SD7543
Horsacott *Devon* 19 SS5231
Horsebridge *Devon* 5 SX4075
Horsebridge *E Susx* 16 TQ5811
Horsebridge *Hants* 23 SU3430
Horsebridge *Shrops* 59 SJ3606
Horsebridge *Staffs* 72 SJ9553
Horsebrook *Staffs* 60 SJ8810
Horsecastle *Avon* 21 ST4265
Horsedown *Cnwll* 2 SW6134
Horsegate *Lincs* 64 TF1510
Horsehay *Shrops* 60 SJ6707
Horseheath *Cambs* 53 TL6147
Horsehouse *N York* 88 SE0480
Horsell *Surrey* 25 SU9959
Horseman's Green *Clwyd* 71 SJ4441
Horsenden *Bucks* 37 SP7902
Horsey *Norfk* 67 TG4622
Horsey *Somset* 21 ST3239
Horsey Corner *Norfk* 67 TG4523
Horsford *Norfk* 67 TG1916
Horsforth *W York* 82 SE2338
Horsham *H & W* 47 SO7358
Horsham *W Susx* 15 TQ1731
Horsham St Faith *Norfk* 67 TG2115
Horsington *Lincs* 76 TF1968
Horsington *Somset* 22 ST7023
Horsley *Derbys* 62 SK3744
Horsley *Gloucs* 35 ST8497
Horsley *Nthumb* 102 NY8496
Horsley *Nthumb* 103 NZ0965
Horsley Cross *Essex* 41 TM1227
Horsley Woodhouse *Derbys* 62 SK3944
Horsley's Green *Bucks* 37 SU7894
Horsley-Gate *Derbys* 74 SK3076
Horsleycross Street *Essex* 41 TM1228
Horsleyhill *Border* 109 NT5319
Horsmonden *Kent* 28 TQ7040
Horspath *Oxon* 37 SP5705
Horstead *Norfk* 67 TG2619
Horsted Keynes *W Susx* 15 TQ3828
Horton *Avon* 35 ST7584
Horton *Berks* 26 TQ0175
Horton *Bucks* 38 SP9219
Horton *Dorset* 12 SU0307
Horton *Lancs* 81 SD8550
Horton *Nhants* 51 SP8154
Horton *Shrops* 59 SJ4929
Horton *Shrops* 60 SJ6814
Horton *Somset* 10 ST3214
Horton *Staffs* 72 SJ9457
Horton *W Glam* 32 SS4785
Horton *Wilts* 23 SU0463
Horton Cross *Somset* 10 ST3315
Horton Green *Ches* 71 SJ4549
Horton Heath *Hants* 13 SU4916
Horton in Ribblesdale *N York* 88 SD8071
Horton Kirby *Kent* 27 TQ5668
Horton-cum-Studley *Oxon* 37 SP5912
Horwich *Gt Man* 81 SD6311
Horwich End *Derbys* 79 SK0080
Horwood *Devon* 19 SS5027
Hoscar *Lancs* 80 SD4611
Hoscote *Border* 109 NT3911
Hose *Leics* 63 SK7329
Hosey Hill *Kent* 27 TQ4553
Hosh *Tays* 125 NN8523
Hoswick *Shet* 155 HU4123
Hotham *Humb* 84 SE8934
Hothfield *Kent* 28 TQ9644
Hoton *Leics* 62 SK5722
Hott *Nthumb* 102 NY7785
Hough *Ches* 72 SJ7151
Hough *Ches* 79 SJ8578
Hough End *W York* 82 SE2433
Hough Green *Ches* 78 SJ4886
Hough-on-the-Hill *Lincs* 63 SK9246
Hougham *Lincs* 63 SK8844
Houghton *Cambs* 52 TL2872
Houghton *Cumb* 93 NY4159
Houghton *Dyfed* 30 SM9807
Houghton *Hants* 23 SU3432
Houghton *Nthumb* 103 NZ1266
Houghton *W Susx* 14 TQ0111
Houghton Conquest *Beds* 38 TL0441
Houghton Green *Ches* 79 SJ6291
Houghton Green *E Susx* 17 TQ9222
Houghton le Side *Dur* 96 NZ2221
Houghton le Spring *T & W* 96 NZ3449
Houghton on the Hill *Leics* 63 SK6703
Houghton Regis *Beds* 38 TL0123
Houghton St Giles *Norfk* 66 TF9235
Hound Green *Hants* 24 SU7359
Houndslow *Border* 110 NT6347
Houndsmoor *Somset* 20 ST1225
Houndwood *Border* 119 NT8463
Hounslow *Gt Lon* 26 TQ1375
Hounslow Green *Essex* 40 TL6518
Househill *Highld* 140 NH8855
Houses Hill *W York* 82 SE1916
Housieside *Gramp* 143 NJ8926
Houston *Strath* 115 NS4066
Houstry *Highld* 151 ND1534
Houton *Ork* 155 HY3104
Hove *E Susx* 15 TQ2804
Hove Edge *W York* 82 SE1324
Hoveringham *Notts* 63 SK6946
Hoveton *Norfk* 67 TG3018
Hovingham *N York* 90 SE6675
How *Cumb* 94 NY5056
How Caple *H & W* 46 SO6030
How End *Beds* 38 TL0340
Howbrook *S York* 74 SK3298
Howden *Humb* 84 SE7428
Howden-le-Wear *Dur* 96 NZ1633
Howe *Highld* 151 ND3061
Howe *N York* 89 SE3580
Howe *Norfk* 67 TM2799
Howe Bridge *Gt Man* 79 SD6602
Howe Green *Essex* 40 TL7403
Howe of Teuchar *Gramp* 143 NJ7946
Howe Street *Essex* 40 TL6914
Howe Street *Essex* 53 TL6934
Howegreen *Essex* 40 TL8301
Howell *Lincs* 76 TF1346
Howes *D & G* 101 NY1866
Howey *Powys* 45 SO0558
Howgate *Loth* 117 NT2457
Howgill *Lancs* 81 SD8246
Howick *Nthumb* 111 NU2517
Howle *Dur* 95 NZ0926
Howle *Shrops* 72 SJ6923
Howle Hill *H & W* 34 SO6020
Howlett End *Essex* 53 TL5834
Howley *Somset* 10 ST2609
Howmore *W Isls* 154 NF7536
Hownam *Border* 110 NT7719
Howrigg *Cumb* 93 NY3347
Howsham *Humb* 84 TA0404
Howsham *N York* 90 SE7362
Howt Green *Kent* 28 TQ8965
Howtel *Nthumb* 110 NT8934
Howton *Devon* 8 SX7487
Howton *H & W* 46 SO4129
Howtown *Cumb* 93 NY4419
Howwood *Strath* 115 NS3960
Hoxne *Suffk* 54 TM1777
Hoylake *Mersyd* 78 SJ2189
Hoyland Common *S York* 74 SE3600
Hoyland Nether *S York* 74 SE3700
Hoyland Swaine *S York* 82 SE2604
Hoyle *W Susx* 14 SU9018
Hoyle Mill *S York* 83 SE3506
Hubberholme *N York* 88 SD9278
Hubberston *Dyfed* 30 SM8906
Hubbert's Bridge *Lincs* 64 TF2643
Huby *N York* 82 SE2747
Huby *N York* 90 SE5665
Hucclecote *Gloucs* 35 SO8717
Hucking *Kent* 28 TQ8458
Hucknall *Notts* 75 SK5349
Huddersfield *W York* 82 SE1416
Huddington *H & W* 47 SO9457
Huddlesford *Staffs* 61 SK1509
Hudswell *N York* 89 NZ1400
Huggate *Humb* 84 SE8855
Hugglescote *Leics* 62 SK4212
Hugh Town *IOS* 2 SV9010
Hughenden Valley *Bucks* 26 SU8697
Hughley *Shrops* 59 SO5698
Huish *Devon* 19 SS5311
Huish *Wilts* 23 SU1463
Huish Champflower *Somset* 20 ST0529
Huish Episcopi *Somset* 21 ST4326
Hulberry *Kent* 27 TQ5265
Hulcote *Beds* 38 SP9438
Hulcott *Bucks* 38 SP8516
Hull *Humb* 85 TA0829
Hullaby *Devon* 7 SX6673
Hulland *Derbys* 73 SK2446
Hulland Ward *Derbys* 73 SK2546
Hullavington *Wilts* 35 ST8981
Hullbridge *Essex* 40 TQ8095
Hulme *Ches* 78 SJ6091
Hulme *Gt Man* 79 SJ8396
Hulme *Staffs* 72 SJ9345
Hulme End *Staffs* 74 SK1059
Hulme Walfield *Ches* 72 SJ8465
Hulse Heath *Ches* 79 SJ7283
Hulton Lane Ends *Gt Man* 79 SD6905
Hulver Street *Norfk* 66 TF9311
Hulver Street *Suffk* 55 TM4686
Hulverstone *IOW* 13 SZ3984
Humberston *Humb* 85 TA3105
Humberstone *Leics* 63 SK6305
Humberton *N York* 89 SE4168
Humbie *Loth* 118 NT4662
Humbleton *Humb* 85 TA2234
Humbleton *Nthumb* 111 NT9728
Humby *Lincs* 63 TF0032
Hume *Border* 110 NT7041
Humshaugh *Nthumb* 102 NY9171
Huna *Highld* 151 ND3573
Huncoat *Lancs* 81 SD7730
Huncote *Leics* 50 SP5197
Hundalee *Border* 110 NT6418
Hundall *Derbys* 74 SK3876
Hunderthwaite *Dur* 95 NY9821
Hundle Houses *Lincs* 77 TF2453
Hundleby *Lincs* 77 TF3966
Hundleton *Dyfed* 30 SM9600
Hundon *Suffk* 53 TL7348
Hundred Acres *Hants* 13 SU5911
Hundred End *Lancs* 80 SD4122
Hundred House *Powys* 45 SO1154
Hundred The *H & W* 46 SO5264
Hungarton *Leics* 63 SK6907
Hungate End *Bucks* 38 SP7946
Hunger Hill *Lancs* 80 SD5411
Hungerford *Berks* 23 SU3368
Hungerford *Hants* 12 SU1612
Hungerford *Somset* 20 ST0440
Hungerford Newtown *Berks* 36 SU3571
Hungerstone *H & W* 46 SO4435
Hungerton *Lincs* 63 SK8729
Hungryhatton *Shrops* 72 SJ6626
Hunmanby *N York* 91 TA0977
Hunningham *Warwks* 48 SP3767
Hunnington *H & W* 60 SO9681
Hunny Hill *IOW* 13 SZ4990
Hunsdon *Herts* 39 TL4114
Hunsingore *N York* 83 SE4253
Hunslet *W York* 82 SE3130
Hunsonby *Cumb* 94 NY5835
Hunstanton *Norfk* 65 TF6740
Hunstanworth *Dur* 95 NY9448
Hunston *Suffk* 54 TL9768
Hunston *W Susx* 14 SU8601
Hunston Green *Suffk* 54 TL9866
Hunstrete *Avon* 21 ST6462
Hunsworth *W York* 82 SE1827
Hunt End *H & W* 48 SP0364
Hunt's Corner *Norfk* 54 TM0588
Hunt's Cross *Mersyd* 78 SJ4385
Hunters Quay *Strath* 114 NS1879
Hunterston *Ches* 72 SJ6946
Huntham *Somset* 21 ST3426
Hunthill Lodge *Tays* 134 NO4771
Huntingdon *Cambs* 52 TL2471
Huntingdon *H & W* 46 SO2553
Huntingfield *Suffk* 55 TM3374
Huntingford *Dorset* 22 ST8030
Huntington *H & W* 46 SO4841
Huntington *Loth* 118 NT4874
Huntington *N York* 83 SE6156
Huntington *Staffs* 60 SJ9712
Huntley *Gloucs* 35 SO7219
Huntly *Gramp* 142 NJ5339
Hunton *Hants* 24 SU4840
Hunton *Kent* 28 TQ7149
Hunton *N York* 89 SE1892
Hunton Bridge *Herts* 26 TL0800
Hunts Green *Bucks* 38 SP8903
Hunts Green *Warwks* 61 SP1897
Huntscott *Somset* 20 SS9144
Huntsham *Devon* 20 ST0020
Huntshaw *Devon* 19 SS5023
Huntshaw Cross *Devon* 19 SS5222
Huntspill *Somset* 21 ST3145
Huntstile *Somset* 20 ST2633
Huntworth *Somset* 21 ST3134
Hunwick *Dur* 96 NZ1832
Hunworth *Norfk* 66 TG0635
Hurdcott *Wilts* 23 SU1733
Hurdsfield *Ches* 79 SJ9274
Hurley *Berks* 37 SU8283
Hurley *Warwks* 61 SP2495
Hurley Bottom *Berks* 37 SU8283
Hurley Common *Warwks* 61 SP2496
Hurlford *Strath* 107 NS4536
Hurlston Green *Lancs* 80 SD3911
Hurn *Dorset* 12 SZ1296
Hursley *Hants* 13 SU4225
Hurst *Berks* 25 SU7973
Hurst *Dorset* 11 SY7990
Hurst *N York* 88 NZ0402
Hurst *Somset* 10 ST4518
Hurst Green *E Susx* 17 TQ7327
Hurst Green *Lancs* 81 SD6838
Hurst Green *Surrey* 27 TQ3951
Hurst Hill *W Mids* 60 SO9393
Hurst Wickham *W Susx* 15 TQ2816
Hurstbourne Priors *Hants* 24 SU4346
Hurstbourne Tarrant *Hants* 23 SU3853
Hurstley *H & W* 46 SO3548
Hurstpierpoint *W Susx* 15 TQ2716
Hurstway Common *H & W* 46 SO2949
Hurstwood *Lancs* 81 SD8831
Hurtiso *Ork* 155 HY5001
Hurtmore *Surrey* 25 SU9445
Hurworth Burn *Dur* 96 NZ4033
Hurworth-on-Tees *Dur* 89 NZ3009
Hury *Dur* 95 NY9519
Husbands Bosworth *Leics* 50 SP6484
Husborne Crawley *Beds* 38 SP9635
Husthwaite *N York* 90 SE5175
Hut Green *N York* 83 SE5623
Hutcherleigh *Devon* 7 SX7850
Huthwaite *N York* 90 NZ4801
Huthwaite *Notts* 75 SK4659
Huttoft *Lincs* 77 TF5176
Hutton *Avon* 21 ST3558
Hutton *Border* 119 NT9053
Hutton *Cumb* 93 NY4326
Hutton *Essex* 40 TQ6395
Hutton *Humb* 84 TA0253
Hutton *Lancs* 80 SD4926
Hutton Bonville *N York* 89 NZ3300
Hutton Buscel *N York* 91 SE9784
Hutton Conyers *N York* 89 SE3273
Hutton Cranswick *Humb* 84 TA0252
Hutton End *Cumb* 93 NY4538
Hutton Hall *Cleve* 90 NZ6014
Hutton Hang *N York* 89 SE1788
Hutton Henry *Dur* 96 NZ4236
Hutton Lowcross *Cleve* 90 NZ5914
Hutton Magna *Dur* 89 NZ1212
Hutton Mulgrave *N York* 90 NZ8309
Hutton Roof *Cumb* 93 NY3734
Hutton Roof *Cumb* 87 SD5677
Hutton Rudby *N York* 89 NZ4606
Hutton Sessay *N York* 89 SE4776
Hutton Wandesley *N York* 83 SE5050
Hutton-le-Hole *N York* 90 SE7090
Huxham *Devon* 9 SX9497
Huxham Green *Somset* 21 ST5936
Huxley *Ches* 71 SJ5061
Huyton *Mersyd* 78 SJ4490
Hycemoor *Cumb* 86 SD0989
Hyde *Gloucs* 35 SO8801
Hyde *Gt Man* 79 SJ9494
Hyde *Hants* 12 SU1612
Hyde End *Berks* 24 SU7266
Hyde Heath *Bucks* 26 SP9300
Hyde Lea *Staffs* 72 SJ9120
Hyde Park Corner *Somset* 20 ST2832
Hydestile *Surrey* 25 SU9640
Hykeham Moor *Lincs* 76 SK9366
Hylands *Essex* 40 TL6704
Hynish *Strath* 120 NL9839
Hyssington *Powys* 59 SO3194
Hystfield *Gloucs* 35 ST6695
Hythe *Hants* 13 SU4207
Hythe *Kent* 29 TR1634
Hythe *Somset* 21 ST4452
Hythe End *Berks* 26 TQ0172
Hyton *Cumb* 86 SD0987

I

Ibberton *Dorset* 11 ST7807
Ible *Derbys* 74 SK2457
Ibsley *Hants* 12 SU1509
Ibstock *Leics* 62 SK4009
Ibstone *Bucks* 37 SU7593
Ibthorpe *Hants* 23 SU3753
Iburndale *N York* 90 NZ8707
Ibworth *Hants* 24 SU5654
Icelton *Avon* 21 ST3765
Ickburgh *Norfk* 66 TL8195
Ickenham *Gt Lon* 26 TQ0786
Ickford *Bucks* 37 SP6407
Ickham *Kent* 29 TR2258
Ickleford *Herts* 39 TL1831
Icklesham *E Susx* 17 TQ8716
Ickleton *Cambs* 39 TL4943
Icklingham *Suffk* 53 TL7772
Ickornshaw *N York* 82 SD9642
Ickwell Green *Beds* 52 TL1545
Icomb *Gloucs* 36 SP2122
Idbury *Oxon* 36 SP2319
Iddesleigh *Devon* 19 SS5708
Ide *Devon* 9 SX8990
Ide Hill *Kent* 27 TQ4851
Ideford *Devon* 9 SX8977
Iden *E Susx* 17 TQ9123
Iden Green *Kent* 28 TQ7437
Iden Green *Kent* 17 TQ8031
Idle *W York* 82 SE1737
Idless *Cnwll* 3 SW8147
Idlicote *Warwks* 48 SP2844
Idmiston *Wilts* 23 SU1937
Idridgehay *Derbys* 73 SK2849
Idrigill *Highld* 136 NG3863
Idstone *Oxon* 36 SU2584
Idvies *Tays* 127 NO5347
Iffley *Oxon* 37 SP5203
Ifield *W Susx* 15 TQ2537
Ifold *W Susx* 14 TQ0231
Iford *Dorset* 12 SZ1393
Iford *E Susx* 15 TQ4007
Ifton *Gwent* 34 ST4688
Ifton Heath *Shrops* 59 SJ3237
Ightam *Kent* 27 TQ5956
Ightfield *Shrops* 71 SJ5938
Iken *Suffk* 55 TM4155
Ilam *Staffs* 73 SK1350
Ilchester *Somset* 21 ST5222
Ilderton *Nthumb* 111 NU0121
Ilford *Gt Lon* 27 TQ4486
Ilford *Somset* 10 ST3617
Ilfracombe *Devon* 19 SS5247
Ilkeston *Derbys* 62 SK4641
Ilketshall St Andrew *Suffk* 55 TM3887
Ilketshall St Margaret *Suffk* 55 TM3485
Ilkley *W York* 82 SE1147
Illand *Cnwll* 5 SX2878
Illey *W Mids* 60 SO9881
Illidge Green *Ches* 72 SJ7963
Illingworth *W York* 82 SE0728
Illogan *Cnwll* 2 SW6743
Illston on the Hill *Leics* 50 SP7099
Ilmer *Bucks* 37 SP7605
Ilmington *Warwks* 48 SP2143
Ilminster *Somset* 10 ST3614
Ilsingston *Dorset* 11 SY7592
Ilsington *Devon* 7 SX7875
Ilston *W Glam* 32 SS5590
Ilton *N York* 89 SE1978
Ilton *Somset* 10 ST3517
Imachar *Strath* 105 NR8640
Immingham *Humb* 85 TA1814
Immingham Dock *Humb* 85 TA1916
Impington *Cambs* 53 TL4463
Ince *Ches* 71 SJ4576
Ince Blundell *Mersyd* 78 SD3203
Ince-in-Makerfield *Gt Man* 78 SD5904
Inchbae Lodge Hotel *Highld* 146 NH4069
Inchbare *Tays* 134 NO6065
Inchberry *Gramp* 141 NJ3055
Inchinnan *Strath* 115 NS4868
Inchlaggan *Highld* 131 NH1701
Inchmichael *Tays* 126 NO2425
Inchnacardoch Hotel *Highld* 131 NH3810
Inchnadamph *Highld* 145 NC2521
Inchture *Tays* 126 NO2728
Inchvuilt *Highld* 139 NH2438
Inchyra *Tays* 126 NO1820
Indian Queens *Cnwll* 4 SW9159
Ingate Place *Suffk* 55 TM4288
Ingatestone *Essex* 40 TQ6499
Ingbirchworth *S York* 82 SE2205
Ingerthorpe *N York* 89 SE2866
Ingestre *Staffs* 72 SJ9724
Ingham *Lincs* 76 SK9483
Ingham *Norfk* 67 TG3926
Ingham *Suffk* 54 TL8570
Ingham Corner *Norfk* 67 TG3927
Ingleborough *Norfk* 65 TF4715
Ingleby *Derbys* 62 SK3426
Ingleby Arncliffe *N York* 89 NZ4400
Ingleby Barwick *Cleve* 89 NZ4414
Ingleby Cross *N York* 89 NZ4500
Ingleby Greenhow *N York* 90 NZ5706
Ingleigh Green *Devon* 8 SS6007
Inglesbatch *Avon* 22 ST7061
Inglesham *Wilts* 36 SU2098
Ingleston *D & G* 99 NX6048
Ingleston *D & G* 100 NX9865
Ingleton *Dur* 96 NZ1720
Ingleton *N York* 87 SD6972
Inglewhite *Lancs* 80 SD5439
Ingmire Hall *Cumb* 87 SD6391
Ingoe *Nthumb* 103 NZ0374
Ingoldisthorpe *Norfk* 65 TF6832
Ingoldmells *Lincs* 77 TF5668
Ingoldsby *Lincs* 64 TF0129
Ingon *Warwks* 48 SP2157
Ingram *Nthumb* 111 NU0115
Ingrave *Essex* 40 TQ6291
Ingrow *W York* 82 SE0539
Ings *Cumb* 87 SD4498
Ingst *Avon* 34 ST5887
Ingthorpe *Leics* 63 SK9908
Ingworth *Norfk* 67 TG1929
Injebreck *IOM* 153 SC3585
Inkberrow *H & W* 47 SP0157
Inkerman *Dur* 95 NZ1139
Inkhorn *Gramp* 143 NJ9239
Inkpen *Berks* 23 SU3664
Inkstack *Highld* 151 ND2570
Inmarsh *Wilts* 22 ST9460
Innellan *Strath* 114 NS1570
Innerleithen *Border* 109 NT3336
Innerleven *Fife* 118 NO3700
Innermessan *D & G* 98 NX0862
Innerwick *Loth* 119 NT7273
Innesmill *Gramp* 141 NJ2863
Insch *Gramp* 142 NJ6228
Insh *Highld* 132 NH8101
Inskip *Lancs* 80 SD4637
Inskip Moss Side *Lancs* 80 SD4539
Instow *Devon* 18 SS4730
Insworke *Cnwll* 6 SX4252
Intake *S York* 74 SK3884
Inver *Gramp* 133 NO2293
Inver *Highld* 147 NH8682
Inver *Tays* 125 NO0142
Inver-boyndie *Gramp* 142 NJ6664

Inverailort Kyloe

Inverailort *Highld* 129 NM7681
Inveralligin *Highld* 138 NG8457
Inverallochy *Gramp* 143 NK0365
Inveran *Highld* 146 NH5797
Inveraray *Strath* 123 NN0908
Inverarish *Highld* 137 NG5535
Inverarity *Tays* 127 NO4544
Inverarnan *Cent* 123 NN3118
Inveravon *Cent* 117 NS9579
Inverawe *Strath* 122 NN0231
Inverbervie *Gramp* 135 NO8272
Inverbroom *Highld* 145 NH1883
Inverchaolain *Strath* 114 NS0975
Invercreran House Hotel *Strath* 122 NN0146
Inverdruie *Highld* 132 NH8911
Inveresk *Loth* 118 NT3471
Inveresragan *Strath* 122 NM9835
Inverey *Gramp* 133 NO0889
Inverfarigaig *Highld* 139 NH5123
Inverfolia *Strath* 122 NM9544
Invergarry *Highld* 131 NH3001
Invergeldie *Tays* 124 NN7327
Invergloy *Highld* 131 NN2288
Invergordon *Highld* 140 NH7068
Invergowrie *Tays* 126 NO3430
Inverguseran *Highld* 129 NG7407
Inverhadden *Tays* 124 NN6757
Inverherive Hotel *Cent* 123 NN3626
Inverie *Highld* 129 NG7600
Inverinan *Strath* 122 NM9917
Inverinate *Highld* 138 NG9221
Inverkeilor *Tays* 127 NO6649
Inverkeithing *Fife* 117 NT1383
Inverkeithny *Gramp* 142 NJ6247
Inverkip *Strath* 114 NS2072
Inverkirkaig *Highld* 145 NC0719
Inverlael *Highld* 145 NH1885
Inverlair *Highld* 131 NN3479
Inverliever Lodge *Strath* 122 NM8905
Inverlochlarig *Cent* 124 NN4318
Inverlochy *Strath* 123 NN1927
Invermarkie *Gramp* 142 NJ4239
Invermoriston *Highld* 139 NH4216
Inverneg *Strath* 115 NS3497
Inverness *Highld* 140 NH6645
Invernoaden *Strath* 114 NS1297
Inveroran Hotel *Strath* 123 NN2741
Inverquharity *Tays* 134 NO4057
Inverquhomery *Gramp* 143 NK0146
Inverroy *Highld* 131 NN2581
Inversanda *Highld* 130 NM9459
Invershiel *Highld* 138 NG9319
Invershin *Highld* 146 NH5796
Invershore *Highld* 151 ND2435
Inversnaid Hotel *Cent* 123 NN3308
Inverugie *Gramp* 143 NK0948
Inveruglas *Strath* 123 NN3109
Inveruglass *Highld* 132 NH8000
Inverurie *Gramp* 142 NJ7721
Inwardleigh *Devon* 8 SX5699
Inworth *Essex* 40 TL8717
Iping *W Susx* 14 SU8522
Ipplepen *Devon* 7 SX8366
Ipsden *Oxon* 37 SU6285
Ipstones *Staffs* 73 SK0149
Ipswich *Suffk* 54 TM1644
Irby *Mersyd* 78 SJ2584
Irby in the Marsh *Lincs* 77 TF4663
Irby upon Humber *Humb* 85 TA1904
Irchester *Nhants* 51 SP9265
Ireby *Cumb* 93 NY2338
Ireby *Lancs* 87 SD6575
Ireland *Beds* 38 TL1341
Irelands Cross *Shrops* 72 SJ7341
Ireleth *Cumb* 86 SD2277
Ireshopeburn *Dur* 95 NY8638
Ireton Wood *Derbys* 73 SK2847
Irlam *Gt Man* 79 SJ7294
Irnham *Lincs* 64 TF0226
Iron Acton *Avon* 35 ST6783
Iron Bridge *Cambs* 65 TL4898
Iron Cross *Warwks* 48 SP0552
Ironbridge *Shrops* 60 SJ6703
Ironmacannie *D & G* 99 NX6675
Irons Bottom *Surrey* 15 TQ2446
Ironville *Derbys* 75 SK4351
Irstead *Norfk* 67 TG3620
Irthington *Cumb* 101 NY4961
Irthlingborough *Nhants* 51 SP9470
Irton *N York* 91 TA0184
Irvine *Strath* 106 NS3238
Isbister *Shet* 155 HU3790
Isfield *E Susx* 16 TQ4417
Isham *Nhants* 51 SP8873
Isington *Hants* 25 SU7842
Islandpool *H & W* 60 SO8780
Isle Abbotts *Somset* 21 ST3520
Isle Brewers *Somset* 21 ST3621
Isle of Whithorn *D & G* 99 NX4736
Isleham *Cambs* 53 TL6474
Isleornsay *Highld* 129 NG7012
Islesteps *D & G* 100 NX9672
Islet Village *Guern* 152 GN5212
Isley Walton *Leics* 62 SK4224
Islington *Gt Lon* 27 TQ3184
Islip *Nhants* 51 SP9879
Islip *Oxon* 37 SP5214
Islivig *W Isls* 154 NB0029
Isombridge *Shrops* 59 SJ6113
Istead Rise *Kent* 27 TQ6370
Itchen Abbas *Hants* 24 SU5333
Itchen Stoke *Hants* 24 SU5532
Itchingfield *W Susx* 15 TQ1328
Itchington *Avon* 35 ST6587
Itteringham *Norfk* 66 TG1430
Itton *Devon* 8 SX6899
Itton *Gwent* 34 ST4995
Ivegill *Cumb* 93 NY4143
Ivelet *N York* 88 SD9398
Iver *Bucks* 26 TQ0381
Iver Heath *Bucks* 26 TQ0283
Iveston *Dur* 96 NZ1350
Ivinghoe *Bucks* 38 SP9416
Ivinghoe Aston *Bucks* 38 SP9517
Ivington *H & W* 46 SO4756
Ivington Green *H & W* 46 SO4656
Ivy Cross *Dorset* 22 ST8623
Ivy Hatch *Kent* 27 TQ5854
Ivy Todd *Norfk* 66 TF8909
Ivybridge *Devon* 6 SX6356
Ivychurch *Kent* 17 TR0327
Iwade *Kent* 28 TQ9067
Iwerne Courtney or Shroton *Dorset* 11 ST8512
Iwerne Minster *Dorset* 11 ST8614
Ixworth *Suffk* 54 TL9370
Ixworth Thorpe *Suffk* 54 TL9173

J

Jack Green *Lancs* 81 SD5925
Jack Hill *N York* 82 SE1951
Jack-in-the-Green *Devon* 9 SY0195
Jacksdale *Notts* 75 SK4451
Jackson Bridge *W York* 82 SE1607
Jackton *Strath* 115 NS5952
Jacobs Well *Surrey* 25 TQ0053
Jacobstow *Cnwll* 5 SX1995
Jacobstowe *Devon* 8 SS5801
Jameston *Dyfed* 30 SS0598
Jamestown *Highld* 139 NH4756
Jamestown *Strath* 115 NS3981
Janets-town *Highld* 151 ND3551
Janetstown *Highld* 151 ND1932
Jardine Hall *D & G* 100 NY1088
Jarrow *T & W* 103 NZ3364
Jarvis Brook *E Susx* 16 TQ5329
Jasper's Green *Essex* 40 TL7226
Jawcraig *Cent* 116 NS8475
Jaywick *Essex* 41 TM1413
Jealott's Hill *Berks* 25 SU8673
Jeator Houses *N York* 89 SE4394
Jedburgh *Border* 110 NT6420
Jeffreston *Dyfed* 31 SN0906
Jemimaville *Highld* 140 NH7165
Jerbourg *Guern* 152 GN5305
Jerusalem *Lincs* 76 SK9170
Jesmond *T & W* 103 NZ2566
Jevington *E Susx* 16 TQ5601
Jingle Street *Gwent* 34 SO4710
Jockey End *Herts* 38 TL0413
Jodrell Bank *Ches* 79 SJ7970
John O'Groats *Highld* 151 ND3872
John's Cross *E Susx* 17 TQ7421
Johnby *Cumb* 93 NY4332
Johnshaven *Gramp* 135 NO7967
Johnson's Street *Norfk* 67 TG3717
Johnston *Dyfed* 30 SM9310
Johnston *Dyfed* 31 SN3919
Johnstone *Strath* 115 NS4263
Johnstonebridge *D & G* 100 NY1092
Johnstown *Clwyd* 71 SJ3046
Joppa *Dyfed* 43 SN5666
Joppa *Strath* 106 NS4119
Jordans *Bucks* 26 SU9791
Jordanston *Dyfed* 30 SM9132
Jordanthorpe *S York* 74 SK3580
Jubilee Corner *Kent* 28 TQ8447
Jump *S York* 83 SE3801
Jumper's Town *E Susx* 16 TQ4632
Juniper Green *Loth* 117 NT1968
Jurby *IOM* 153 SC3598

K

Kaber *Cumb* 88 NY7911
Kames *Strath* 114 NR9771
Kames *Strath* 107 NS6926
Kea *Cnwll* 3 SW8142
Keadby *Humb* 84 SE8311
Keal Cotes *Lincs* 77 TF3660
Kearby Town End *N York* 83 SE3447
Kearsley *Gt Man* 79 SD7504
Kearsney *Kent* 29 TR2844
Kearstwick *Cumb* 87 SD6079
Kearton *N York* 88 SD9998
Keasden *N York* 88 SD7266
Keason *Cnwll* 5 SX3168
Keaton *Devon* 7 SX6454
Keckwick *Ches* 78 SJ5783
Keddington *Lincs* 77 TF3488
Keddington Corner *Lincs* 77 TF3589
Kedington *Suffk* 53 TL7046
Kedleston *Derbys* 73 SK3040
Keelby *Lincs* 85 TA1610
Keele *Staffs* 72 SJ8045
Keele University *Staffs* 72 SJ8144
Keeley Green *Beds* 38 TL0046
Keelham *W York* 82 SE0732
Keeston *Dyfed* 30 SM9019
Keevil *Wilts* 22 ST9258
Kegworth *Leics* 62 SK4826
Kehelland *Cnwll* 2 SW6241
Keig *Gramp* 142 NJ6119
Keighley *W York* 82 SE0541
Keillour *Tays* 125 NN9725
Keiloch *Gramp* 133 NO1891
Keils *Strath* 113 NR5268
Keinton Mandeville *Somset* 21 ST5430
Keir Mill *D & G* 100 NX8593
Keirsleywell Row *Nthumb* 94 NY7751
Keisby *Lincs* 64 TF0328
Keisley *Cumb* 94 NY7124
Keiss *Highld* 151 ND3461
Keith *Gramp* 142 NJ4250
Keithick *Tays* 126 NO2038
Keithock *Tays* 134 NO6063
Keithtown *Gramp* 139 NH5256
Kelbrook *Lancs* 81 SD9044
Kelburn *Strath* 114 NS2156
Kelby *Lincs* 63 TF0041
Keld *Cumb* 94 NY5514
Keld *N York* 88 NY8900
Keld Head *N York* 90 SE7884
Keldholme *N York* 90 SE7086
Kelfield *Humb* 84 SE8201
Kelfield *N York* 83 SE5938
Kelham *Notts* 75 SK7755
Kelhead *D & G* 100 NY1469
Kellacott *Devon* 5 SX4088
Kellamergh *Lancs* 80 SD4029
Kellas *Gramp* 141 NJ1654
Kellas *Tays* 127 NO4535
Kellaton *Devon* 7 SX8039
Kelleth *Cumb* 87 NY6605
Kelling *Norfk* 66 TG0942
Kellington *N York* 83 SE5524
Kelloe *Dur* 96 NZ3436
Kells *Cumb* 92 NX9616
Kelly *Devon* 5 SX3981
Kelly Bray *Cnwll* 5 SX3671
Kelmarsh *Nhants* 50 SP7379
Kelmscot *Oxon* 36 SU2499
Kelsale *Suffk* 55 TM3865
Kelsall *Ches* 71 SJ5268
Kelshall *Herts* 39 TL3336
Kelsick *Cumb* 93 NY1950
Kelso *Border* 110 NT7234
Kelstedge *Derbys* 74 SK3363
Kelstern *Lincs* 77 TF2489
Kelsterton *Clwyd* 70 SJ2770
Kelston *Avon* 22 ST7067
Keltneyburn *Tays* 124 NN7749
Kelty *Fife* 117 NT1494
Kelvedon *Essex* 40 TL8619
Kelvedon Hatch *Essex* 27 TQ5698
Kelynack *Cnwll* 2 SW3729
Kemacott *Devon* 19 SS6647
Kemback *Fife* 126 NO4115
Kemberton *Shrops* 60 SJ7204
Kemble *Wilts* 35 ST9897
Kemble Wick *Gloucs* 35 ST9895
Kemerton *H & W* 47 SO9536
Kemeys Commander *Gwent* 34 SO3404
Kemnay *Gramp* 142 NJ7316
Kemp Town *E Susx* 15 TQ3303
Kempe's Corner *Kent* 28 TR0346
Kempley *Gloucs* 47 SO6629
Kempley Green *Gloucs* 47 SO6728
Kemps Green *Warwks* 61 SP1470
Kempsey *H & W* 47 SO8549
Kempsford *Gloucs* 36 SU1696
Kempshott *Hants* 24 SU6050
Kempston *Beds* 38 TL0347
Kempston Hardwick *Beds* 38 TL0344
Kempton *Shrops* 59 SO3682
Kemsing *Kent* 27 TQ5558
Kemsley *Kent* 28 TQ9166
Kemsley Street *Kent* 28 TQ8062
Kenardington *Kent* 17 TQ9732
Kenchester *H & W* 46 SO4342
Kencot *Oxon* 36 SP2504
Kendal *Cumb* 87 SD5192
Kenderchurch *H & W* 46 SO4028
Kendleshire *Avon* 35 ST6679
Kenfig Hill *M Glam* 33 SS8382
Kenilworth *Warwks* 61 SP2871
Kenley *Gt Lon* 27 TQ3260
Kenley *Shrops* 59 SJ5500
Kenmore *Highld* 137 NG7557
Kenmore *Tays* 124 NN7745
Kenn *Avon* 21 ST4268
Kenn *Devon* 9 SX9285
Kennacraig *Strath* 113 NR8262
Kennards House *Cnwll* 5 SX2883
Kenneggy *Cnwll* 2 SW5628
Kennerleigh *Devon* 8 SS8107
Kennessee Green *Mersyd* 78 SD3801
Kennet *Cent* 116 NS9291
Kennethmont *Gramp* 142 NJ5428
Kennett *Cambs* 53 TL7068
Kennford *Devon* 9 SX9186
Kenninghall *Norfk* 54 TM0386
Kennington *Kent* 28 TR0245
Kennington *Oxon* 37 SP5201
Kennoway *Fife* 126 NO3502
Kenny *Somset* 10 ST3117
Kennyhill *Suffk* 53 TL6679
Kennythorpe *N York* 90 SE7865
Kenovay *Strath* 120 NL9946
Kensaleyre *Highld* 136 NG4151
Kensham Green *Kent* 17 TQ8229
Kensington *Gt Lon* 27 TQ2579
Kensworth *Beds* 38 TL0319
Kensworth Common *Beds* 38 TL0317
Kent End *Wilts* 36 SU0594
Kent Green *Ches* 72 SJ8458
Kent Street *E Susx* 17 TQ7816
Kent Street *Kent* 28 TQ6654
Kent's Green *Gloucs* 47 SO7423
Kent's Oak *Hants* 23 SU3224
Kentallen *Highld* 122 NN0057
Kentchurch *H & W* 46 SO4125
Kentford *Suffk* 53 TL7066
Kentisbeare *Devon* 9 ST0608
Kentisbury *Devon* 19 SS6243
Kentisbury Ford *Devon* 19 SS6242
Kentish Town *Gt Lon* 27 TQ2884
Kentmere *Cumb* 87 NY4504
Kenton *Devon* 9 SX9583
Kenton *Gt Lon* 26 TQ1788
Kenton *Suffk* 55 TM1965
Kenton *T & W* 103 NZ2267
Kenton Bank Foot *Nthumb* 103 NZ2069
Kentra *Highld* 129 NM6569
Kents Bank *Cumb* 87 SD3975
Kenwick *Shrops* 59 SJ4230
Kenwyn *Cnwll* 3 SW8145
Kenyon *Gt Man* 79 SJ6395
Keoldale *Highld* 149 NC3866
Keppoch *Highld* 138 NG8924
Kepwick *N York* 89 SE4690
Keresley *W Mids* 61 SP3282
Keresley Green *Warwks* 61 SP3283
Kergilliak *Cnwll* 3 SW7833
Kernborough *Devon* 7 SX7941
Kerne Bridge *H & W* 34 SO5818
Kerridge *Ches* 79 SJ9376
Kerridge-end *Ches* 79 SJ9475
Kerris *Cnwll* 2 SW4427
Kerry *Powys* 58 SO1490
Kerrycroy *Strath* 114 NS1061
Kersall *Notts* 75 SK7162
Kersbrook *Devon* 9 SY0683
Kerscott *Devon* 19 SS6329
Kersey *Suffk* 54 TM0044
Kersey Tye *Suffk* 54 TL9843
Kersey Upland *Suffk* 54 TL9942
Kershader *W Isls* 154 NB3320
Kershopefoot *D & G* 101 NY4782
Kersoe *H & W* 47 SO9940
Kerswell *Devon* 9 ST0806
Kerswell Green *H & W* 47 SO8646
Kerthen Wood *Cnwll* 2 SW5833
Kesgrave *Suffk* 55 TM2245
Kessingland *Suffk* 55 TM5286
Kessingland Beach *Suffk* 55 TM5385
Kestle *Cnwll* 3 SW9845
Kestle Mill *Cnwll* 4 SW8459
Keston *Gt Lon* 27 TQ4164
Keswick *Cumb* 93 NY2623
Keswick *Norfk* 67 TG2004
Ketsby *Lincs* 77 TF3676
Kettering *Nhants* 51 SP8678
Ketteringham *Norfk* 66 TG1603
Kettins *Tays* 126 NO2338
Kettle Green *Herts* 39 TL4118
Kettlebaston *Suffk* 54 TL9650
Kettlebridge *Fife* 126 NO3007
Kettlebrook *Staffs* 61 SK2103
Kettleburgh *Suffk* 55 TM2660
Kettleholm *D & G* 100 NY1577
Kettleshulme *Ches* 79 SJ9879
Kettlesing *N York* 82 SE2256
Kettlesing Bottom *N York* 89 SE2357
Kettlestoft *Ork* 155 HY6538
Kettlestone *Norfk* 66 TF9631
Kettlethorpe *Lincs* 76 SK8475
Kettlewell *N York* 88 SD9672
Ketton *Leics* 63 SK9704
Kew *Gt Lon* 26 TQ1876
Kexbrough *S York* 82 SE3009
Kexby *Lincs* 76 SK8785
Kexby *N York* 84 SE7050
Key Green *Ches* 72 SJ8963
Key Green *N York* 90 NZ8004
Key Street *Kent* 28 TQ8764
Key's Toft *Lincs* 77 TF4858
Keyham *Leics* 63 SK6706
Keyhaven *Hants* 12 SZ3091
Keyingham *Humb* 85 TA2425
Keymer *W Susx* 15 TQ3115
Keynsham *Avon* 21 ST6568
Keysoe *Beds* 51 TL0762
Keysoe Row *Beds* 51 TL0861
Keyston *Cambs* 51 TL0475
Keyworth *Notts* 62 SK6130
Kibbear *Somset* 20 ST2222
Kibblesworth *T & W* 96 NZ2456
Kibworth Beauchamp *Leics* 50 SP6893
Kibworth Harcourt *Leics* 50 SP6894
Kidbrooke *Gt Lon* 27 TQ4176
Kidburngill *Cumb* 92 NY0621
Kidd's Moor *Norfk* 66 TG1103
Kiddemore Green *Staffs* 60 SJ8509
Kidderminster *H & W* 60 SO8376
Kiddington *Oxon* 49 SP4123
Kidlington *Oxon* 37 SP4913
Kidmore End *Oxon* 37 SU6979
Kidsdale *D & G* 99 NX4336
Kidsgrove *Staffs* 72 SJ8454
Kidstones *N York* 88 SD9581
Kidwelly *Dyfed* 31 SN4006
Kiel Crofts *Strath* 122 NM9039
Kielder *Nthumb* 102 NY6293
Kiells *Strath* 112 NR4168
Kilbeg *Highld* 129 NG6506
Kilberry *Strath* 113 NR7164
Kilbirnie *Strath* 115 NS3154
Kilbride *Strath* 122 NM8525
Kilbride *Strath* 113 NR7279
Kilbride *Strath* 114 NS0367
Kilbride *W Isls* 154 NF7514
Kilburn *Derbys* 62 SK3845
Kilburn *Gt Lon* 26 TQ2483
Kilburn *N York* 90 SE5179
Kilby *Leics* 50 SP6295
Kilchamaig *Strath* 113 NR8060
Kilchattan *Strath* 112 NR3795
Kilchattan *Strath* 114 NS1054
Kilchenzie *Strath* 105 NR6724
Kilcheran *Strath* 122 NM8239
Kilchoan *Highld* 121 NM4863
Kilchrenan *Strath* 122 NN0322
Kilconquhar *Fife* 127 NO4802
Kilcot *Gloucs* 47 SO6925
Kilcoy *Highld* 139 NH5751
Kilcreggan *Strath* 114 NS2480
Kildale *N York* 90 NZ6009
Kildalloig *Strath* 105 NR7518
Kildary *Highld* 147 NH7674
Kildavanan *Strath* 114 NS0266
Kildonan *Highld* 147 NC9120
Kildonan *Strath* 105 NS0321
Kildonan Lodge *Highld* 147 NC9022
Kildonnan *Highld* 128 NM4885
Kildrochet House *D & G* 98 NX0856
Kildrummy *Gramp* 142 NJ4617
Kildwick *N York* 82 SE0046
Kilfinan *Strath* 114 NR9378
Kilfinnan *Highld* 131 NN2795
Kilgetty *Dyfed* 31 SN1207
Kilgrammie *Strath* 106 NS2502
Kilgwrrwg Common *Gwent* 34 ST4797
Kilham *Humb* 91 TA0664
Kilham *Nthumb* 110 NT8832
Kilkenneth *Strath* 120 NL9444
Kilkhampton *Cnwll* 18 SS2511
Killamarsh *Derbys* 75 SK4581
Killay *W Glam* 32 SS6092
Killearn *Cent* 115 NS5286
Killen *Highld* 140 NH6758
Killerby *Dur* 96 NZ1919
Killerton *Devon* 9 SS9700
Killichonan *Tays* 132 NN5458
Killiechronan *Strath* 121 NM5441
Killiecrankie *Tays* 132 NN9162
Killilan *Highld* 138 NG9430
Killin *Cent* 124 NN5733
Killinghall *N York* 89 SE2858
Killington *Cumb* 87 SD6188
Killington *Devon* 19 SS6646
Killingworth *T & W* 103 NZ2770
Killiow *Cnwll* 3 SW8042
Killivose *Cnwll* 3 SW8049
Killochyett *Border* 118 NT4545
Kilmacolm *Strath* 115 NS3567
Kilmahog *Cent* 124 NN6108
Kilmahumaig *Strath* 113 NR7893
Kilmaluag *Highld* 136 NG4374
Kilmany *Fife* 126 NO3821
Kilmarie *Highld* 129 NG5517
Kilmarnock *Strath* 107 NS4237
Kilmartin *Strath* 113 NR8398
Kilmaurs *Strath* 106 NS4141
Kilmelford *Strath* 122 NM8512
Kilmeny *Strath* 112 NR3965
Kilmersdon *Somset* 22 ST6952
Kilmeston *Hants* 13 SU5825
Kilmichael *Strath* 113 NR8593
Kilmichael of Inverlussa *Strath* 113 NR7786
Kilmington *Devon* 10 SY2797
Kilmington *Wilts* 22 ST7736
Kilmington Common *Wilts* 22 ST7735
Kilmington Street *Wilts* 22 ST7835
Kilmorack *Highld* 139 NH4944
Kilmore *Highld* 129 NG6507
Kilmory *Highld* 128 NM5270
Kilmory *Strath* 122 NM8825
Kilmory *Strath* 113 NR7074
Kilmuir *Highld* 136 NG2547
Kilmuir *Highld* 136 NG3770
Kilmuir *Highld* 140 NH6749
Kilmuir *Highld* 147 NH7573
Kilmun *Strath* 114 NS1781
Kiln Green *Berks* 37 SU8178
Kiln Pit Hill *Nthumb* 95 NZ0355
Kilnave *Strath* 112 NR2871
Kilncadzow *Strath* 116 NS8848
Kilndown *Kent* 16 TQ7035
Kilnhill *Cumb* 93 NY2132
Kilnhouses *Ches* 71 SJ6366
Kilnhurst *S York* 75 SK4597
Kilninver *Strath* 122 NM8221
Kilnsea *Humb* 85 TA4115
Kilnsey *N York* 88 SD9767
Kilnwick *Humb* 84 SE9949
Kilnwick Percy *Humb* 84 SE8249
Kiloran *Strath* 112 NR3996
Kilpeck *H & W* 46 SO4430
Kilpin *Humb* 84 SE7726
Kilpin Pike *Humb* 84 SE7626
Kilrie *Ches* 79 SJ7478
Kilsby *Nhants* 50 SP5671
Kilspindie *Tays* 126 NO2125
Kilstay *D & G* 98 NX1238
Kilsyth *Strath* 116 NS7178
Kiltarlity *Highld* 139 NH5041
Kilton *Cleve* 97 NZ7018
Kilton Thorpe *Cleve* 97 NZ6917
Kilvaxter *Highld* 136 NG3869
Kilve *Somset* 20 ST1442
Kilvington *Notts* 63 SK8042
Kilwinning *Strath* 106 NS3043
Kimberley *Norfk* 66 TG0603
Kimberley *Notts* 62 SK4944
Kimberworth *S York* 74 SK4093
Kimble Wick *Bucks* 38 SP8007
Kimblesworth *Dur* 96 NZ2547
Kimbolton *Cambs* 51 TL1067
Kimbolton *H & W* 46 SO5261
Kimcote *Leics* 50 SP5886
Kimmeridge *Dorset* 11 SY9179
Kimmerston *Nthumb* 111 NT9535
Kimpton *Hants* 23 SU2746
Kimpton *Herts* 39 TL1718
Kimworthy *Devon* 18 SS3112
Kinbrace *Highld* 150 NC8631
Kinbuck *Cent* 125 NN7905
Kincaple *Fife* 127 NO4618
Kincardine *Fife* 116 NS9387
Kincardine *Highld* 146 NH6089
Kincardine O'Neil *Tays* 134 NO5999
Kinclaven *Tays* 126 NO1538
Kincorth *Gramp* 135 NJ9403
Kincorth House *Gramp* 141 NJ0161
Kincraig *Highld* 132 NH8305
Kindallachan *Tays* 125 NN9949
Kinerarach *Strath* 113 NR6553
Kineton *Gloucs* 48 SP0926
Kineton *Warwks* 48 SP3350
Kinfauns *Tays* 126 NO1622
Kinfig *M Glam* 32 SS8081
King Sterndale *Derbys* 74 SK0972
King's Acre *H & W* 46 SO4841
King's Bromley *Staffs* 73 SK1216
King's Cliffe *Nhants* 51 TL0097
King's Coughton *Warwks* 48 SP0859
King's Heath *W Mids* 61 SP0781
King's Hill *Warwks* 61 SP3274
King's Lynn *Norfk* 65 TF6120
King's Mills *Guern* 152 GN4808
King's Moss *Lancs* 78 SD5000
King's Newton *Derbys* 62 SK3825
King's Norton *Leics* 50 SK6800
King's Norton *W Mids* 61 SP0579
King's Nympton *Devon* 19 SS6819
King's Pyon *H & W* 46 SO4450
King's Somborne *Hants* 23 SU3531
King's Stag *Dorset* 11 ST7210
King's Stanley *Gloucs* 35 SO8103
King's Sutton *Oxon* 49 SP4936
King's Walden *Herts* 39 TL1623
Kingarth *Strath* 114 NS0956
Kingcausie *Gramp* 135 NO8699
Kingcoed *Gwent* 34 SO4305
Kingerby *Lincs* 76 TF0592
Kingford *Devon* 18 SS2806
Kingham *Oxon* 48 SP2624
Kingholm Quay *D & G* 100 NX9773
Kinglassie *Loth* 117 NT2298
Kingoldrum *Tays* 126 NO3355
Kingoodie *Tays* 126 NO3329
Kings Bridge *W Glam* 32 SS5997
Kings Caple *H & W* 46 SO5528
Kings Green *Gloucs* 47 SO7734
Kings Hill *W Mids* 60 SO9896
Kings House Hotel *Highld* 123 NN2654
Kings Langley *Herts* 26 TL0702
Kings Meaburn *Cumb* 94 NY6221
Kings Muir *Border* 109 NT2539
Kings Newnham *Warwks* 50 SP4577
Kings Ripton *Cambs* 52 TL2676
Kings Weston *Avon* 34 ST5477
Kings Worthy *Hants* 24 SU4932
Kingsand *Cnwll* 6 SX4350
Kingsash *Bucks* 38 SP8805
Kingsbarns *Fife* 127 NO5912
Kingsbridge *Devon* 7 SX7344
Kingsbridge *Somset* 20 SS9837
Kingsburgh *Highld* 136 NG3955
Kingsbury *Gt Lon* 26 TQ1988
Kingsbury *Warwks* 61 SP2196
Kingsbury Episcopi *Somset* 21 ST4321
Kingsclere *Hants* 24 SU5258
Kingscote *Gloucs* 35 ST8196
Kingscott *Devon* 19 SS5318
Kingscross *Strath* 105 NS0428
Kingsdon *Somset* 21 ST5126
Kingsdown *Kent* 29 TR3748
Kingsdown *Wilts* 22 ST8167
Kingsdown *Wilts* 36 SU1688
Kingseat *Fife* 117 NT1290
Kingsey *Bucks* 37 SP7406
Kingsfold *W Susx* 15 TQ1636
Kingsford *H & W* 60 SO8181
Kingsford *Strath* 115 NS4447
Kingsgate *Kent* 29 TR3970
Kingshall Street *Suffk* 54 TL9161
Kingsheanton *Devon* 19 SS5537
Kingshouse Hotel *Cent* 124 NN5620
Kingshurst *W Mids* 61 SP1688
Kingside Hill *Cumb* 92 NY1551
Kingskerswell *Devon* 7 SX8767
Kingskettle *Fife* 126 NO3008
Kingsland *Dorset* 10 SY4597
Kingsland *H & W* 46 SO4461
Kingsley *Ches* 71 SJ5574
Kingsley *Hants* 25 SU7838
Kingsley *Staffs* 73 SK0146
Kingsley Green *W Susx* 14 SU8930
Kingsley Park *Nhants* 49 SP7762
Kingslow *Shrops* 60 SO7998
Kingsmead *Hants* 13 SU5813
Kingsmuir *Fife* 127 NO5308
Kingsmuir *Tays* 127 NO4849
Kingsnorth *Kent* 28 TR0039
Kingstanding *W Mids* 61 SP0794
Kingsteignton *Devon* 7 SX8773
Kingsthorne *H & W* 46 SO4931
Kingsthorpe *Nhants* 49 SP7563
Kingston *Cambs* 52 TL3455
Kingston *Cnwll* 5 SX3675
Kingston *Devon* 6 SX6347
Kingston *Dorset* 11 ST7509
Kingston *Dorset* 11 SY9579
Kingston *Gramp* 141 NJ3365
Kingston *Hants* 12 SU1401
Kingston *IOW* 13 SZ4781
Kingston *Kent* 29 TR1950
Kingston *Loth* 118 NT5482
Kingston *W Susx* 14 TQ0802
Kingston Bagpuize *Oxon* 36 SU4098
Kingston Blount *Oxon* 37 SU7399
Kingston by Sea *W Susx* 15 TQ2305
Kingston Deverill *Wilts* 22 ST8437
Kingston Lisle *Oxon* 36 SU3287
Kingston near Lewes *E Susx* 15 TQ3908
Kingston on Soar *Notts* 62 SK5027
Kingston Russell *Dorset* 10 SY5791
Kingston Seymour *Avon* 21 ST4066
Kingston St Mary *Somset* 20 ST2229
Kingston Stert *Oxon* 37 SP7200
Kingston upon Thames *Gt Lon* 26 TQ1869
Kingstone *H & W* 46 SO4235
Kingstone *Oxon* 36 SU2685
Kingstone *Somset* 10 ST3713
Kingstone *Staffs* 73 SK0629
Kingstown *Cumb* 93 NY3959
Kingswear *Devon* 7 SX8851
Kingswells *Gramp* 135 NJ8606
Kingswinford *W Mids* 60 SO8888
Kingswood *Avon* 35 ST6473
Kingswood *Bucks* 37 SP6919
Kingswood *Gloucs* 35 ST7491
Kingswood *Kent* 28 TQ8350
Kingswood *Powys* 58 SJ2302
Kingswood *Somset* 20 ST1037
Kingswood *Surrey* 26 TQ2455
Kingswood *Warwks* 61 SP1871
Kingswood Brook *Warwks* 61 SP1970
Kingswood Common *H & W* 46 SO2954
Kingswood Common *Staffs* 60 SJ8302
Kingthorpe *Lincs* 76 TF1275
Kington *Avon* 35 ST6290
Kington *H & W* 46 SO2956
Kington *H & W* 47 SO9956
Kington Langley *Wilts* 35 ST9276
Kington Magna *Dorset* 22 ST7622
Kington St Michael *Wilts* 35 ST9077
Kingussie *Highld* 132 NH7500
Kingweston *Somset* 21 ST5230
Kinharrachie *Gramp* 143 NJ9231
Kinharvie *D & G* 100 NX9266
Kinkell Bridge *Tays* 125 NN9316
Kinknockie *Gramp* 143 NK0041
Kinleith *Loth* 117 NT1866
Kinlet *Shrops* 60 SO7180
Kinloch *Highld* 149 NC3434
Kinloch *Highld* 149 NC5552
Kinloch *Highld* 128 NM4099
Kinloch *Tays* 126 NO1444
Kinloch *Tays* 126 NO2644
Kinloch Hourn *Highld* 130 NG9506
Kinloch Rannoch *Tays* 132 NN6658
Kinlochard *Cent* 124 NN4502
Kinlochbervie *Highld* 148 NC2256
Kinlocheil *Highld* 130 NM9779
Kinlochewe *Highld* 138 NH0261
Kinlochlaggan *Highld* 131 NN5289
Kinlochleven *Highld* 131 NN1861
Kinlochmoidart *Highld* 129 NM7072
Kinlochnanuagh *Highld* 129 NM7384
Kinloss *Gramp* 141 NJ0661
Kinmel Bay *Clwyd* 70 SH9880
Kinmount House *D & G* 100 NY1368
Kinmuck *Gramp* 143 NJ8119
Kinmundy *Gramp* 143 NJ8817
Kinnadie *Gramp* 143 NJ9743
Kinnaird *Tays* 133 NN9559
Kinnaird *Tays* 126 NO2428
Kinnaird Castle *Tays* 134 NO6357
Kinneddar *Gramp* 141 NJ2269
Kinneff *Gramp* 135 NO8574
Kinnelhead *D & G* 108 NT0201
Kinnell *Tays* 127 NO6150
Kinnerley *Shrops* 59 SJ3320
Kinnersley *H & W* 46 SO3449
Kinnersley *H & W* 47 SO8743
Kinnerton *Powys* 46 SO2463
Kinnerton *Shrops* 59 SO3796
Kinnerton Green *Clwyd* 71 SJ3361
Kinnesswood *Tays* 126 NO1702
Kinninvie *Dur* 95 NZ0521
Kinnordy *Tays* 126 NO3655
Kinoulton *Notts* 63 SK6730
Kinross *Tays* 126 NO1102
Kinrossie *Tays* 126 NO1832
Kinsbourne Green *Herts* 38 TL1016
Kinsey Heath *Ches* 72 SJ6642
Kinsham *H & W* 46 SO3665
Kinsham *H & W* 47 SO9335
Kinsley *W York* 83 SE4114
Kinson *Dorset* 12 SZ0796
Kintbury *Berks* 23 SU3866
Kintessack *Gramp* 141 NJ0060
Kintillo *Tays* 126 NO1317
Kinton *H & W* 46 SO4174
Kinton *Shrops* 59 SJ3719
Kintore *Gramp* 143 NJ7916
Kintour *Strath* 112 NR4551
Kintra *Strath* 120 NM3125
Kintraw *Strath* 122 NM8204
Kinveachy *Highld* 140 NH9018
Kinver *Staffs* 60 SO8483
Kiplin *N York* 89 SE2897
Kippax *W York* 83 SE4130
Kippen *Cent* 116 NS6494
Kippford or Scaur *D & G* 92 NX8354
Kipping's Cross *Kent* 16 TQ6440
Kirbister *Ork* 155 HY3607
Kirby Bedon *Norfk* 67 TG2705
Kirby Bellars *Leics* 63 SK7117
Kirby Cane *Norfk* 67 TM3794
Kirby Corner *W Mids* 61 SP2976
Kirby Cross *Essex* 41 TM2120
Kirby Fields *Leics* 62 SK5203
Kirby Grindalythe *N York* 91 SE9067
Kirby Hill *N York* 89 NZ1406
Kirby Hill *N York* 89 SE3968
Kirby Knowle *N York* 89 SE4687
Kirby le Soken *Essex* 41 TM2121
Kirby Misperton *N York* 90 SE7779
Kirby Muxloe *Leics* 62 SK5104
Kirby Row *Norfk* 67 TM3792
Kirby Sigston *N York* 89 SE4194
Kirby Underdale *Humb* 90 SE8058
Kirby Wiske *N York* 89 SE3784
Kirconnel *D & G* 100 NX9868
Kirdford *W Susx* 14 TQ0126
Kirk *Highld* 151 ND2859
Kirk Bramwith *S York* 83 SE6211
Kirk Deighton *N York* 83 SE3950
Kirk Ella *Humb* 84 TA0129
Kirk Hallam *Derbys* 62 SK4540
Kirk Hammerton *N York* 83 SE4655
Kirk Ireton *Derbys* 73 SK2650
Kirk Langley *Derbys* 73 SK2838
Kirk Merrington *Dur* 96 NZ2631
Kirk of Shotts *Strath* 116 NS8462
Kirk Sandall *S York* 83 SE6108
Kirk Smeaton *N York* 83 SE5216
Kirk Yetholm *Border* 110 NT8228
Kirkabister *Shet* 155 HU4938
Kirkandrews *D & G* 99 NX6048
Kirkandrews upon Eden *Cumb* 93 NY3558
Kirkbampton *Cumb* 93 NY3056
Kirkbean *D & G* 92 NX9759
Kirkbride *Cumb* 93 NY2256
Kirkbridge *N York* 89 SE2590
Kirkbuddo *Tays* 127 NO5043
Kirkburn *Border* 109 NT2938
Kirkburn *Humb* 84 SE9855
Kirkburton *W York* 82 SE1912
Kirkby *Lincs* 76 TF0592
Kirkby *Mersyd* 78 SJ4099
Kirkby *N York* 90 NZ5305
Kirkby Fleetham *N York* 89 SE2894
Kirkby Green *Lincs* 76 TF0857
Kirkby Hall *N York* 89 SE2795
Kirkby in Ashfield *Notts* 75 SK4856
Kirkby Lonsdale *Cumb* 87 SD6178
Kirkby la Thorpe *Lincs* 76 TF0946
Kirkby Malham *N York* 88 SD8960
Kirkby Mallory *Leics* 50 SK4500
Kirkby Malzeard *N York* 89 SE2374
Kirkby Mills *N York* 90 SE7085
Kirkby Overblow *N York* 83 SE3249
Kirkby on Bain *Lincs* 77 TF2462
Kirkby Stephen *Cumb* 88 NY7708
Kirkby Thore *Cumb* 94 NY6325
Kirkby Underwood *Lincs* 64 TF0727
Kirkby Wharf *N York* 83 SE5041
Kirkby Woodhouse *Notts* 75 SK4954
Kirkby-in-Furness *Cumb* 86 SD2282
Kirkbymoorside *N York* 90 SE6986
Kirkcaldy *Fife* 117 NT2892
Kirkcambeck *Cumb* 101 NY5368
Kirkchrist *D & G* 99 NX6751
Kirkcolm *D & G* 98 NX0268
Kirkconnel *D & G* 107 NS7311
Kirkconnell *D & G* 99 NX6760
Kirkcowan *D & G* 98 NX3260
Kirkcudbright *D & G* 99 NX6850
Kirkdale *Mersyd* 78 SJ3493
Kirkfieldbank *Strath* 108 NS8643
Kirkgunzeon *D & G* 100 NX8666
Kirkham *Lancs* 80 SD4232
Kirkham *N York* 90 SE7365
Kirkhamgate *W York* 82 SE2922
Kirkharle *Nthumb* 103 NZ0182
Kirkhaugh *Nthumb* 94 NY6949
Kirkheaton *Nthumb* 103 NZ0177
Kirkheaton *W York* 82 SE1818
Kirkhill *Highld* 139 NH5545
Kirkhope *Border* 109 NT3723
Kirkhope *Strath* 108 NS9606
Kirkhouse *Cumb* 94 NY5759
Kirkhouse Green *S York* 83 SE6213
Kirkibost *Highld* 129 NG5518
Kirkinch *Tays* 126 NO3044
Kirkinner *D & G* 99 NX4251
Kirkintilloch *Strath* 116 NS6573
Kirkland *Cumb* 92 NY0718
Kirkland *Cumb* 93 NY2648
Kirkland *Cumb* 94 NY6432
Kirkland *D & G* 107 NS7213
Kirkland *D & G* 99 NX4356
Kirkland *D & G* 100 NX8190
Kirkland *D & G* 100 NY0389
Kirkland Guards *Cumb* 93 NY1840
Kirkleatham *Cleve* 97 NZ5921
Kirklevington *Cleve* 89 NZ4309
Kirkley *Suffk* 67 TM5391
Kirklington *N York* 89 SE3181
Kirklington *Notts* 75 SK6757
Kirklinton *Cumb* 101 NY4367
Kirkliston *Loth* 117 NT1274
Kirkmabreck *D & G* 99 NX4856
Kirkmaiden *D & G* 98 NX1236
Kirkmichael *IOM* 153 SC3190
Kirkmichael *Strath* 106 NS3408
Kirkmichael *Tays* 133 NO0759
Kirkmuirhill *Strath* 107 NS7842
Kirknewton *Loth* 117 NT1166
Kirknewton *Nthumb* 110 NT9130
Kirkney *Gramp* 142 NJ5132
Kirkoswald *Cumb* 94 NY5541
Kirkoswald *Strath* 106 NS2407
Kirkpatrick *D & G* 100 NX9090
Kirkpatrick Durham *D & G* 100 NX7870
Kirkpatrick-Fleming *D & G* 101 NY2770
Kirksanton *Cumb* 86 SD1380
Kirkstall *W York* 82 SE2635
Kirkstead *Lincs* 76 TF1762
Kirkstile *D & G* 101 NY3690
Kirkstile *Gramp* 142 NJ5235
Kirkstone Pass Inn *Cumb* 87 NY4007
Kirkstyle *Highld* 151 ND3472
Kirkthorpe *W York* 83 SE3621
Kirkton *Border* 109 NT5413
Kirkton *D & G* 100 NX9781
Kirkton *Fife* 126 NO3625
Kirkton *Gramp* 142 NJ6425
Kirkton *Gramp* 143 NJ8243
Kirkton *Highld* 137 NG8227
Kirkton *Highld* 138 NG9141
Kirkton *Tays* 125 NN9618
Kirkton Manor *Border* 109 NT2238
Kirkton of Airlie *Tays* 126 NO3151
Kirkton of Auchterhouse *Tays* 126 NO3438
Kirkton of Barevan *Highld* 140 NH8347
Kirkton of Collace *Tays* 126 NO1931
Kirkton of Glenbuchat *Gramp* 141 NJ3715
Kirkton of Glenisla *Tays* 133 NO2160
Kirkton of Logie Buchan *Gramp* 143 NJ9829
Kirkton of Menmuir *Tays* 134 NO5364
Kirkton of Monikie *Tays* 127 NO5138
Kirkton of Rayne *Gramp* 142 NJ6930
Kirkton of Skene *Gramp* 135 NJ8007
Kirkton of Strathmartine *Tays* 126 NO3735
Kirkton of Tealing *Tays* 126 NO4038
Kirktown *Gramp* 143 NJ9965
Kirktown *Gramp* 143 NK0852
Kirktown of Bourtie *Gramp* 143 NJ8025
Kirktown of Fetteresso *Gramp* 135 NO8486
Kirktown of Mortlach *Gramp* 141 NJ3138
Kirktown of Slains *Gramp* 143 NK0329
Kirkwall *Ork* 155 HY4411
Kirkwhelpington *Nthumb* 103 NY9984
Kirmington *Humb* 85 TA1011
Kirmond le Mire *Lincs* 76 TF1892
Kirn *Strath* 114 NS1878
Kirriemuir *Tays* 126 NO3853
Kirstead Green *Norfk* 67 TM2997
Kirtlebridge *D & G* 101 NY2372
Kirtling *Cambs* 53 TL6857
Kirtling Green *Suffk* 53 TL6855
Kirtlington *Oxon* 37 SP4919
Kirtomy *Highld* 150 NC7463
Kirton *Gramp* 134 NJ6113
Kirton *Lincs* 64 TF3038
Kirton *Notts* 75 SK6969
Kirton *Suffk* 55 TM2740
Kirton End *Lincs* 64 TF2940
Kirton Holme *Lincs* 64 TF2642
Kirton in Lindsey *Lincs* 76 SK9398
Kirtonhill *Strath* 115 NS3875
Kirwaugh *D & G* 99 NX4054
Kishorn *Highld* 138 NG8440
Kislingbury *Nhants* 49 SP6959
Kite Green *Warwks* 48 SP1666
Kites Hardwick *Warwks* 50 SP4768
Kitleigh *Cnwll* 18 SX2499
Kitt Green *Gt Man* 78 SD5405
Kittisford *Somset* 20 ST0822
Kittle *W Glam* 32 SS5789
Kitts Green *W Mids* 61 SP1587
Kittybrewster *Gramp* 135 NJ9207
Kitwood *Hants* 24 SU6633
Kivernoll *H & W* 46 SO4632
Kiveton Park *S York* 75 SK4982
Knaith *Lincs* 75 SK8284
Knaith Park *Lincs* 76 SK8485
Knap Corner *Dorset* 22 ST8023
Knaphill *Surrey* 25 SU9658
Knaplock *Somset* 19 SS8633
Knapp *Somset* 20 ST3025
Knapp Hill *Hants* 13 SU4023
Knapthorpe *Notts* 75 SK7458
Knapton *N York* 83 SE5652
Knapton *N York* 90 SE8876
Knapton *Norfk* 67 TG3034
Knapton Green *H & W* 46 SO4452
Knapwell *Cambs* 52 TL3362
Knaresborough *N York* 89 SE3557
Knarsdale *Nthumb* 94 NY6754
Knaven *Gramp* 143 NJ8943
Knayton *N York* 89 SE4387
Knebworth *Herts* 39 TL2520
Knedlington *Humb* 84 SE7327
Kneesall *Notts* 75 SK7064
Kneesworth *Cambs* 39 TL3444
Kneeton *Notts* 63 SK7146
Knelston *W Glam* 32 SS4688
Knenhall *Staffs* 72 SJ9237
Knettishall *Suffk* 54 TL9780
Knightacott *Devon* 19 SS6539
Knightcote *Warwks* 48 SP4054
Knightley *Staffs* 72 SJ8125
Knightley Dale *Staffs* 72 SJ8123
Knighton *Devon* 6 SX5349
Knighton *Dorset* 10 ST6111
Knighton *Dorset* 12 SZ0497
Knighton *Leics* 62 SK6001
Knighton *Powys* 46 SO2872
Knighton *Somset* 20 ST1944
Knighton *Staffs* 72 SJ7240
Knighton *Staffs* 72 SJ7527
Knighton *Wilts* 36 SU2971
Knighton on Teme *H & W* 47 SO6369
Knightsmill *Cnwll* 4 SX0780
Knightwick *H & W* 47 SO7356
Knill *H & W* 46 SO2960
Knipton *Leics* 63 SK8231
Knitsley *Dur* 95 NZ1048
Kniveton *Derbys* 73 SK2050
Knock *Cumb* 94 NY6727
Knock *Gramp* 142 NJ5452
Knock *Highld* 129 NG6709
Knock *W Isls* 154 NB4931
Knock Castle *Strath* 114 NS1963
Knockally *Highld* 151 ND1429
Knockan *Highld* 145 NC2110
Knockandhu *Gramp* 141 NJ2023
Knockando *Gramp* 141 NJ1941
Knockbain *Highld* 139 NH5543
Knockbain *Highld* 140 NH6256
Knockdee *Highld* 151 ND1760
Knockdown *Wilts* 35 ST8388
Knockeen *Strath* 106 NX3195
Knockenkelly *Strath* 105 NS0427
Knockentiber *Strath* 106 NS4039
Knockespock House *Gramp* 142 NJ5423
Knockhall *Kent* 27 TQ5974
Knockholt *Kent* 27 TQ4658
Knockholt Pound *Kent* 27 TQ4859
Knockin *Shrops* 59 SJ3322
Knockinlaw *Strath* 107 NS4239
Knockmill *Kent* 27 TQ5761
Knocknain *D & G* 98 NW9764
Knocksheen *D & G* 99 NX5882
Knockvennie Smithy *D & G* 99 NX7571
Knodishall *Suffk* 55 TM4262
Knole *Somset* 21 ST4825
Knole Park *Avon* 34 ST5983
Knolls Green *Ches* 79 SJ8079
Knolton *Clwyd* 71 SJ3739
Knook *Wilts* 22 ST9341
Knossington *Leics* 63 SK8008
Knott End-on-Sea *Lancs* 80 SD3548
Knotting *Beds* 51 TL0063
Knotting Green *Beds* 51 TL0062
Knottingley *W York* 83 SE5023
Knotty Green *Bucks* 26 SU9392
Knowbury *Shrops* 46 SO5775
Knowe *D & G* 98 NX3171
Knowehead *D & G* 107 NX6090
Knoweside *Strath* 106 NS2512
Knowl Green *Essex* 53 TL7841
Knowl Hill *Berks* 37 SU8279
Knowle *Avon* 34 ST6070
Knowle *Devon* 18 SS4938
Knowle *Devon* 8 SS7801
Knowle *Devon* 9 ST0007
Knowle *Devon* 9 SY0582
Knowle *Shrops* 46 SO5973
Knowle *Somset* 20 SS9643
Knowle *W Mids* 61 SP1876
Knowle Cross *Devon* 9 SY0397
Knowle Green *Lancs* 81 SD6338
Knowle Hill *Surrey* 25 SU9966
Knowle St Giles *Somset* 10 ST3411
Knowlton *Dorset* 12 SU0209
Knowlton *Kent* 29 TR2853
Knowsley *Mersyd* 78 SJ4395
Knowstone *Devon* 19 SS8323
Knox *N York* 89 SE2957
Knox Bridge *Kent* 28 TQ7840
Knucklas *Powys* 46 SO2574
Knuston *Nhants* 51 SP9266
Knutsford *Ches* 79 SJ7578
Knutton *Staffs* 72 SJ8347
Knypersley *Staffs* 72 SJ8856
Krumlin *W York* 82 SE0518
Kuggar *Cnwll* 3 SW7216
Kyle of Lochalsh *Highld* 137 NG7627
Kyleakin *Highld* 137 NG7526
Kylerhea *Highld* 129 NG7820
Kylesku *Highld* 148 NC2233
Kylesmorar *Highld* 129 NM8093
Kylestrome *Highld* 148 NC2234
Kyloe *Nthumb* 111 NU0540

Kynaston Littleton

Kynaston *H & W* 47 SO6435
Kynaston *Shrops* 59 SJ3520
Kynnersley *Shrops* 72 SJ6716
Kyre Green *H & W* 46 SO6162
Kyre Park *H & W* 47 SO6263
Kyrewood *H & W* 46 SO5967
Kyrle *Somset* 20 ST0522

L

L'Ancresse *Guern* 152 GN5413
L'Eree *Guern* 152 GN4508
L'Etacq *Jersey* 152 JS0514
La Beilleuse *Guern* 152 GN5206
La Fontenelle *Guern* 152 GN5513
La Fosse *Guern* 152 GN5205
La Greve *Guern* 152 GN5312
La Greve de Lecq *Jersey* 152 JS0815
La Hougue Bie *Jersey* 152 JS1810
La Houguette *Guern* 152 GN4607
La Passee *Guern* 152 GN5112
La Pulente *Jersey* 152 JS0608
La Rocque *Jersey* 152 JS2007
La Rousaillerie *Guern* 152 GN5209
La Villette *Guern* 152 GN5105
Labbacott *Devon* 18 SS4021
Laceby *Humb* 85 TA2106
Lacey Green *Bucks* 37 SP8200
Lach Dennis *Ches* 79 SJ7071
Lackenby *Cleve* 97 NZ5619
Lackford *Suffk* 53 TL7970
Lackford Green *Suffk* 53 TL7970
Lacock *Wilts* 22 ST9168
Ladbroke *Warwks* 49 SP4158
Ladderedge *Staffs* 72 SJ9654
Laddingford *Kent* 28 TQ6948
Lade Bank *Lincs* 77 TF3954
Ladock *Cnwll* 3 SW8950
Lady Hall *Cumb* 86 SD1986
Lady's Green *Suffk* 53 TL7559
Ladybank *Fife* 126 NO3009
Ladycross *Cnwll* 5 SX3188
Ladygill *Strath* 108 NS9428
Ladykirk *Border* 110 NT8847
Ladykirk Ho *Border* 110 NT8845
Ladywood *H & W* 47 SO8661
Ladywood *W Mids* 61 SP0586
Lag *D & G* 100 NX8786
Lagavulin *Strath* 104 NR4045
Lagg *Strath* 105 NR9521
Laggan *Highld* 131 NN2997
Laggan *Highld* 132 NN6194
Laggan *Strath* 98 NX0982
Laid *Highld* 149 NC4159
Laide *Highld* 144 NG9091
Laig *Highld* 128 NM4687
Laigh Church *Strath* 115 NS4647
Laigh Fenwick *Strath* 107 NS4542
Laigh Glenmuir *Strath* 107 NS6120
Laighstonehall *Strath* 116 NS7054
Laindon *Essex* 40 TQ6889
Lairg *Highld* 146 NC5806
Laisterdyke *W York* 82 SE1932
Laithes *Cumb* 93 NY4633
Lake *Devon* 19 SS5531
Lake *Devon* 5 SX5289
Lake *Dorset* 11 SY9990
Lake *IOW* 13 SZ5883
Lake *Wilts* 23 SU1339
Lake Side *Cumb* 87 SD3787
Lakenheath *Suffk* 53 TL7182
Laker's Green *Surrey* 14 TQ0335
Lakesend *Norfk* 65 TL5196
Lakley Lanes *Bucks* 38 SP8250
Laleham *Surrey* 26 TQ0568
Laleston *M Glam* 33 SS8779
Lamancha *Border* 117 NT2052
Lamanva *Cnwll* 3 SW7631
Lamarsh *Essex* 54 TL8835
Lamas *Norfk* 67 TG2423
Lamb Roe *Lancs* 81 SD7337
Lambden *Border* 110 NT7443
Lamberhurst *Kent* 28 TQ6736
Lamberhurst Down *Kent* 16 TQ6735
Lamberton *Border* 119 NT9658
Lambfair Green *Suffk* 53 TL7153
Lambley *Notts* 63 SK6345
Lambley *Nthumb* 94 NY6658
Lambourn *Berks* 36 SU3278
Lambourne End *Essex* 27 TQ4794
Lambs Green *W Susx* 15 TQ2136
Lambston *Dyfed* 30 SM9016
Lamerton *Devon* 5 SX4577
Lamesley *T & W* 96 NZ2557
Lamington *Strath* 108 NS9731
Lamlash *Strath* 105 NS0231
Lamonby *Cumb* 93 NY4036
Lamorick *Cnwll* 4 SX0364
Lamorna *Cnwll* 2 SW4424
Lamorran *Cnwll* 3 SW8741
Lampen *Cnwll* 4 SX1867
Lampeter *Dyfed* 44 SN5747
Lampeter Velfrey *Dyfed* 31 SN1514
Lamphey *Dyfed* 30 SN0100
Lamplugh *Cumb* 92 NY0820
Lamport *Nhants* 50 SP7574
Lamyatt *Somset* 21 ST6536
Lana *Devon* 18 SS3007
Lana *Devon* 5 SX3496
Lanark *Strath* 108 NS8843
Lanarth *Cnwll* 3 SW7621
Lancaster *Lancs* 87 SD4761
Lancaut *Gloucs* 34 ST5396
Lanchester *Dur* 96 NZ1647
Lancing *W Susx* 15 TQ1804
Land-hallow *Highld* 151 ND1833
Landbeach *Cambs* 53 TL4765
Landcross *Devon* 18 SS4523
Landerberry *Gramp* 135 NJ7404
Landewednack *Cnwll* 2 SW7012
Landford *Wilts* 12 SU2519
Landimore *W Glam* 32 SS4692
Landkey *Devon* 19 SS6031
Landkey Town *Devon* 19 SS5931
Landore *W Glam* 32 SS6695
Landrake *Cnwll* 5 SX3760
Lands End *Cnwll* 2 SW3425
Landscove *Devon* 7 SX7766
Landshipping *Dyfed* 30 SN0211
Landue *Cnwll* 5 SX3579
Landulph *Cnwll* 6 SX4361
Landwade *Cambs* 53 TL6268
Landywood *Staffs* 60 SJ9805
Lane *Cnwll* 4 SW8260
Lane Bottom *Lancs* 81 SD8735
Lane End *Bucks* 37 SU8091
Lane End *Ches* 79 SJ6890
Lane End *Cnwll* 4 SX0369
Lane End *Cumb* 86 SD1093
Lane End *Hants* 13 SU5525
Lane End *Kent* 27 TQ5671
Lane End *Lancs* 81 SD8747
Lane End *Wilts* 22 ST8145
Lane Ends *Derbys* 73 SK2334
Lane Ends *Dur* 96 NZ1833
Lane Ends *Lancs* 81 SD7930
Lane Ends *N York* 82 SD9743
Lane Green *Staffs* 60 SJ8703
Lane Head *Dur* 89 NZ1211
Lane Head *Gt Man* 79 SJ6296
Lane Head *W Mids* 35 SO9700
Lane Heads *Lancs* 80 SD4339
Lane Side *Lancs* 81 SD7922
Laneast *Cnwll* 5 SX2283
Laneham *Notts* 75 SK8076
Lanehead *Dur* 95 NY8441
Laneshaw Bridge *Lancs* 81 SD9240
Langaford *Devon* 18 SX4199
Langaller *Somset* 20 ST2626
Langar *Notts* 63 SK7234
Langbank *Strath* 115 NS3873
Langbar *N York* 82 SE0951
Langbaurgh *N York* 90 NZ5511
Langcliffe *N York* 88 SD8264
Langdale End *N York* 91 SE9391
Langdon *Cnwll* 5 SX3089
Langdon Beck *Dur* 95 NY8531
Langdown *Hants* 13 SU4206
Langdyke *Fife* 126 NO3304
Langenhoe *Essex* 41 TM0018
Langford *Avon* 21 ST4560
Langford *Beds* 39 TL1841
Langford *Devon* 9 ST0203
Langford *Essex* 40 TL8309
Langford *Notts* 75 SK8258
Langford *Oxon* 36 SP2402
Langford Budville *Somset* 20 ST1122
Langford End *Beds* 52 TL1753
Langham *Dorset* 22 ST7725
Langham *Essex* 41 TM0333
Langham *Leics* 63 SK8411
Langham *Norfk* 66 TG0141
Langham *Suffk* 54 TL9769
Langham Moor *Essex* 41 TM0131
Langham Wick *Essex* 41 TM0231
Langho *Lancs* 81 SD7034
Langholm *D & G* 101 NY3684
Langland *W Glam* 32 SS6087
Langley *Berks* 26 TQ0178
Langley *Ches* 79 SJ9471
Langley *Derbys* 62 SK4445
Langley *Essex* 39 TL4334
Langley *Gloucs* 47 SP0028
Langley *Gt Man* 79 SD8506
Langley *Hants* 13 SU4401
Langley *Herts* 39 TL2122
Langley *Kent* 28 TQ8052
Langley *Nthumb* 102 NY8261
Langley *Oxon* 36 SP2915
Langley *Somset* 20 ST0828
Langley *W Susx* 14 SU8029
Langley *Warwks* 48 SP1962
Langley Burrell *Wilts* 35 ST9375
Langley Castle *Nthumb* 102 NY8362
Langley Common *Derbys* 73 SK2937
Langley Green *Derbys* 73 SK2738
Langley Green *Essex* 40 TL8722
Langley Green *Warwks* 48 SP1962
Langley Marsh *Somset* 20 ST0729
Langley Mill *Derbys* 62 SK4446
Langley Moor *Dur* 96 NZ2540
Langley Park *Dur* 96 NZ2145
Langley Street *Norfk* 67 TG3601
Langleybury *Herts* 26 TL0700
Langney *E Susx* 16 TQ6302
Langold *Notts* 75 SK5886
Langore *Cnwll* 5 SX2986
Langport *Somset* 21 ST4226
Langrick *Lincs* 77 TF2648
Langridge *Avon* 35 ST7469
Langridge Ford *Devon* 19 SS5722
Langrigg *Cumb* 92 NY1645
Langrish *Hants* 13 SU7023
Langsett *S York* 74 SE2100
Langshaw *Border* 109 NT5139
Langside *Tays* 125 NN7913
Langstone *Gwent* 34 ST3789
Langstone *Hants* 13 SU7204
Langthorne *N York* 89 SE2491
Langthorpe *N York* 89 SE3867
Langthwaite *N York* 88 NZ0001
Langtoft *Humb* 91 TA0066
Langtoft *Lincs* 64 TF1212
Langton *Dur* 96 NZ1619
Langton *Lincs* 76 TF2368
Langton *Lincs* 77 TF3970
Langton *N York* 90 SE7966
Langton by Wragby *Lincs* 76 TF1476
Langton Green *Kent* 16 TQ5439
Langton Green *Suffk* 54 TM1474
Langton Herring *Dorset* 10 SY6182
Langtree *Devon* 18 SS4515
Langwathby *Cumb* 94 NY5733
Langwell House *Highld* 147 ND1122
Langwith *Derbys* 75 SK5370
Langworth *Lincs* 76 TF0676
Langworthy *Devon* 5 SX4894
Lanieth *Cnwll* 3 SW9752
Lanivet *Cnwll* 4 SX0464
Lank *Cnwll* 4 SX0875
Lanlivery *Cnwll* 4 SX0759
Lanner *Cnwll* 2 SW7139
Lanoy *Cnwll* 5 SX2977
Lanreath *Cnwll* 4 SX1857
Lansallos *Cnwll* 4 SX1751
Lanteglos *Cnwll* 4 SX0882
Lanteglos Highway *Cnwll* 3 SX1453
Lantilio-Crossenny *Gwent* 34 SO3914
Lanton *Border* 110 NT6221
Lanton *Nthumb* 110 NT9231
Lapford *Devon* 19 SS7308
Laphroaig *Strath* 104 NR3845
Lapley *Staffs* 60 SJ8712
Lapworth *Warwks* 61 SP1671
Larachbeg *Highld* 122 NM6948
Larbert *Cent* 116 NS8582
Larbreck *Lancs* 80 SD4040
Largie *Gramp* 142 NJ6131
Largiemore *Strath* 114 NR9486
Largoward *Fife* 127 NO4607
Largs *Strath* 114 NS2059
Largybeg *Strath* 105 NS0423
Largymore *Strath* 105 NS0424
Larkfield *Kent* 28 TQ7058
Larkfield *Strath* 114 NS2475
Larkhall *Strath* 116 NS7651
Larkhill *Wilts* 23 SU1244
Larling *Norfk* 54 TL9889
Lartington *Dur* 95 NZ0117
Lasborough *Gloucs* 35 ST8294
Lasham *Hants* 24 SU6742
Lashbrook *Devon* 18 SS4305
Lashenden *Kent* 28 TQ8440
Lask Edge *Staffs* 72 SJ9156
Lassodie *Fife* 117 NT1292
Lasswade *Loth* 117 NT3065
Lastingham *N York* 90 SE7290
Latcham *Somset* 21 ST4447
Latchford *Herts* 39 TL3920
Latchford *Oxon* 37 SP6501
Latchingdon and Snoreham *Essex* 40 TL8800
Latchley *Cnwll* 5 SX4173
Latebrook *Staffs* 72 SJ8453
Lately Common *Gt Man* 79 SJ6797
Lathbury *Bucks* 38 SP8744
Latheron *Highld* 151 ND2033
Latheronwheel *Highld* 151 ND1832
Lathones *Fife* 127 NO4708
Latimer *Bucks* 26 TQ0099
Latteridge *Avon* 35 ST6684
Lattiford *Somset* 22 ST6926
Latton *Wilts* 36 SU0995
Lauder *Border* 118 NT5347
Laugharne *Dyfed* 31 SN3010
Laughterton *Lincs* 76 SK8375
Laughton *E Susx* 16 TQ4913
Laughton *Leics* 50 SP6688
Laughton *Lincs* 76 SK8497
Laughton *Lincs* 64 TF0731
Laughton-en-le-Morthen *S York* 75 SK5187
Launcells *Cnwll* 18 SS2405
Launcells Cross *Cnwll* 18 SS2605
Launceston *Cnwll* 5 SX3384
Launton *Oxon* 37 SP6022
Laurencekirk *Gramp* 135 NO7171
Laurieston *Cent* 116 NS9179
Laurieston *D & G* 99 NX6864
Lavendon *Bucks* 51 SP9153
Lavenham *Suffk* 54 TL9149
Lavernock *S Glam* 20 ST1868
Laversdale *Cumb* 101 NY4762
Laverstock *Wilts* 23 SU1630
Laverstoke *Hants* 24 SU4948
Laverton *Gloucs* 48 SP0735
Laverton *N York* 89 SE2273
Laverton *Somset* 22 ST7753
Lavister *Clwyd* 71 SJ3758
Law *Strath* 116 NS8252
Law Hill *Strath* 116 NS8251
Lawers *Tays* 124 NN6739
Lawford *Essex* 41 TM0831
Lawford *Somset* 20 ST1336
Lawgrove *Tays* 125 NO0926
Lawhitton *Cnwll* 5 SX3582
Lawkland *N York* 88 SD7766
Lawkland Green *N York* 88 SD7765
Lawley *Shrops* 60 SJ6608
Lawnhead *Staffs* 72 SJ8325
Lawrence End *Herts* 38 TL1419
Lawrenny *Dyfed* 30 SN0106
Lawshall *Suffk* 54 TL8654
Lawshall Green *Suffk* 54 TL8853
Lawton *H & W* 46 SO4459
Laxay *W Isls* 154 NB3321
Laxdale *W Isls* 154 NB4234
Laxey *IOM* 153 SC4384
Laxfield *Suffk* 55 TM2972
Laxford Bridge *Highld* 148 NC2346
Laxo *Shet* 155 HU4463
Laxton *Humb* 84 SE7925
Laxton *Nhants* 51 SP9596
Laxton *Notts* 75 SK7267
Laycock *W York* 82 SE0341
Layer Breton *Essex* 40 TL9417
Layer Marney *Essex* 40 TL9217
Layer-de-la-Haye *Essex* 41 TL9620
Layham *Suffk* 54 TM0240
Layland's Green *Berks* 23 SU3866
Laymore *Dorset* 10 ST3804
Layter's Green *Bucks* 26 SU9890
Laytham *Humb* 84 SE7439
Laythes *Cumb* 93 NY2455
Lazenby *Cleve* 97 NZ5719
Lazonby *Cumb* 94 NY5439
Le Bigard *Guern* 152 GN4805
Le Bourg *Guern* 152 GN4905
Le Bourg *Jersey* 152 JS2006
Le Gron *Guern* 152 GN4807
Le Haquais *Jersey* 152 JS1807
Le Hocq *Jersey* 152 JS1806
Le Villocq *Guern* 152 GN5009
Lea *Derbys* 74 SK3257
Lea *H & W* 35 SO6521
Lea *Lincs* 75 SK8286
Lea *Shrops* 59 SJ4108
Lea *Shrops* 59 SO3589
Lea *Wilts* 35 ST9586
Lea Bridge *Derbys* 74 SK3156
Lea Heath *Staffs* 73 SK0225
Lea Marston *Warwks* 61 SP2093
Lea Town *Lancs* 80 SD4730
Lea Yeat *Cumb* 88 SD7686
Leachkin *Highld* 140 NH6344
Leadburn *Loth* 117 NT2355
Leaden Roding *Essex* 40 TL5913
Leadenham *Lincs* 76 SK9452
Leadgate *Dur* 96 NZ1251
Leadgate *Nthumb* 95 NZ1159
Leadhills *Strath* 108 NS8815
Leadingcross Green *Kent* 28 TQ8951
Leadmill *Derbys* 74 SK2380
Leafield *Oxon* 36 SP3115
Leagrave *Beds* 38 TL0523
Leahead *Ches* 72 SJ6864
Leaholm Side *N York* 90 NZ7607
Leake *N York* 89 SE4390
Leake Common Side *Lincs* 77 TF3952
Lealholm *N York* 90 NZ7607
Lealt *Highld* 137 NG5060
Leam *Derbys* 74 SK2379
Leamington Hastings *Warwks* 50 SP4467
Leamington Spa *Warwks* 48 SP3265
Leamonsley *Staffs* 61 SK1009
Leap Cross *E Susx* 16 TQ5810
Leasgill *Cumb* 87 SD4983
Leasingham *Lincs* 76 TF0548
Leasingthorne *Dur* 96 NZ2530
Leatherhead *Surrey* 26 TQ1656
Leathley *N York* 82 SE2347
Leaths *D & G* 100 NX7862
Leaton *Shrops* 59 SJ4618
Leaton *Shrops* 59 SJ6111
Leaveland *Kent* 28 TR0053
Leavenheath *Suffk* 54 TL9537
Leavening *N York* 90 SE7863
Leaves Green *Gt Lon* 27 TQ4161
Lebberston *N York* 91 TA0782
Lechampstead Thicket *Berks* 36 SU4276
Lechlade *Wilts* 36 SU2199
Leck *Lancs* 87 SD6476
Leck Gruinart *Strath* 112 NR2768
Leckbuie *Tays* 124 NN7040
Leckford *Hants* 23 SU3737
Leckhampstead *Berks* 36 SU4375
Leckhampstead *Bucks* 49 SP7237
Leckhampton *Gloucs* 35 SO9419
Leckmelm *Highld* 145 NH1689
Leckwith *S Glam* 33 ST1574
Leconfield *Humb* 84 TA0143
Ledaig *Strath* 122 NM9037
Ledburn *Bucks* 38 SP9021
Ledbury *H & W* 47 SO7137
Leddington *Gloucs* 47 SO6834
Ledgemoor *H & W* 46 SO4150
Ledicot *H & W* 46 SO4162
Ledmore Junction *Highld* 145 NC2412
Ledsham *Ches* 71 SJ3574
Ledsham *W York* 83 SE4529
Ledston *W York* 83 SE4328
Ledstone *Devon* 7 SX7446
Ledwell *Oxon* 49 SP4128
Lee *Devon* 18 SS4846
Lee *Gt Lon* 27 TQ3875
Lee *Hants* 12 SU3617
Lee *Shrops* 59 SJ4032
Lee Brockhurst *Shrops* 59 SJ5427
Lee Chapel *Essex* 40 TQ6987
Lee Clump *Bucks* 38 SP9004
Lee Common *Bucks* 38 SP9103
Lee Green *Ches* 72 SJ6661
Lee Mill *Devon* 6 SX5955
Lee Moor *Devon* 6 SX5762
Lee Street *Surrey* 15 TQ2743
Lee-on-the-Solent *Hants* 13 SU5600
Leebotwood *Shrops* 59 SO4798
Leece *Cumb* 86 SD2469
Leedon *Beds* 38 SP9325
Leeds *Kent* 28 TQ8253
Leeds *W York* 82 SE2932
Leeds Beck *Lincs* 76 TF2065
Leedstown *Cnwll* 2 SW6034
Leek *Staffs* 72 SJ9856
Leek Wootton *Warwks* 48 SP2868
Leeming *N York* 89 SE2989
Leeming *W York* 82 SE0434
Leeming Bar *N York* 89 SE2889
Lees *Derbys* 73 SK2637
Lees *Gt Man* 79 SD9504
Lees *W York* 82 SE0437
Lees Green *Derbys* 73 SK2637
Lees Hill *Cumb* 101 NY5568
Leesthorpe *Leics* 63 SK7813
Leetown *Tays* 126 NO2121
Leftwich *Ches* 79 SJ6672
Legbourne *Lincs* 77 TF3784
Legburthwaite *Cumb* 93 NY3219
Legerwood *Border* 110 NT5843
Legsby *Lincs* 76 TF1385
Leicester *Leics* 62 SK5804
Leicester Forest East *Leics* 62 SK5202
Leigh *Dorset* 10 ST6108
Leigh *Gloucs* 47 SO8626
Leigh *Gt Man* 79 SJ6599
Leigh *H & W* 47 SO7853
Leigh *Kent* 16 TQ5446
Leigh *Shrops* 59 SJ3303
Leigh *Surrey* 15 TQ2246
Leigh *Wilts* 36 SU0692
Leigh Beck *Essex* 40 TQ8183
Leigh Delamere *Wilts* 35 ST8879
Leigh Green *Kent* 17 TQ9033
Leigh Knoweglass *Strath* 116 NS6350
Leigh Sinton *H & W* 47 SO7750
Leigh upon Mendip *Somset* 22 ST6947
Leigh Woods *Avon* 34 ST5672
Leigh-on-Sea *Essex* 40 TQ8286
Leighland Chapel *Somset* 20 ST0336
Leighterton *Gloucs* 35 ST8290
Leighton *N York* 89 SE1679
Leighton *Powys* 58 SJ2306
Leighton *Shrops* 59 SJ6105
Leighton *Somset* 22 ST7043
Leighton Bromswold *Cambs* 52 TL1175
Leighton Buzzard *Beds* 38 SP9225
Leinthall Earls *H & W* 46 SO4467
Leinthall Starkes *H & W* 46 SO4369
Leintwardine *H & W* 46 SO4074
Leire *Leics* 50 SP5290
Leiston *Suffk* 55 TM4462
Leitfie *Tays* 126 NO2545
Leith *Loth* 117 NT2776
Leitholm *Border* 110 NT7944
Lelant *Cnwll* 2 SW5437
Lelley *Humb* 85 TA2032
Lem Hill *H & W* 60 SO7275
Lemmington Hall *Nthumb* 111 NU1211
Lempitlaw *Border* 110 NT7832
Lemreway *W Isls* 154 NB3711
Lemsford *Herts* 39 TL2212
Lenchwick *H & W* 48 SP0347
Lendalfoot *Strath* 106 NX1390
Lendrick *Cent* 124 NN5506
Lendrum Terrace *Gramp* 143 NK1141
Lenham *Kent* 28 TQ8952
Lenham Heath *Kent* 28 TQ9149
Lenie *Highld* 139 NH5126
Lennel *Border* 110 NT8540
Lennox Plunton *D & G* 99 NX6051
Lennoxlove *Loth* 118 NT5172
Lennoxtown *Strath* 116 NS6277
Lent *Bucks* 26 SU9381
Lenton *Lincs* 64 TF0230
Lenton *Notts* 62 SK5539
Lenwade *Norfk* 66 TG0918
Lenzie *Strath* 116 NS6572
Leochel-Cushnie *Gramp* 134 NJ5210
Leominster *H & W* 46 SO4959
Leonard Stanley *Gloucs* 35 SO8003
Leoville *Jersey* 152 JS0813
Lepe *Hants* 13 SZ4498
Lephin *Highld* 136 NG1749
Leppington *N York* 90 SE7661
Lepton *W York* 82 SE2015
Lerags *Strath* 122 NM8324
Lerryn *Cnwll* 4 SX1457
Lerwick *Shet* 155 HU4741
Les Arquets *Guern* 152 GN4607
Les Hubits *Guern* 152 GN5206
Les Lohiers *Guern* 152 GN4807
Les Murchez *Guern* 152 GN4805
Les Nicolles *Guern* 152 GN5005
Les Quartiers *Guern* 152 GN5210
Les Quennevais *Jersey* 152 JS0810
Les Sages *Guern* 152 GN4606
Les Villets *Guern* 152 GN4905
Lesbury *Nthumb* 111 NU2311
Leslie *Fife* 126 NO2501
Leslie *Gramp* 142 NJ5924
Lesmahagow *Strath* 108 NS8139
Lesnewth *Cnwll* 4 SX1390
Lessingham *Norfk* 67 TG3928
Lessonhall *Cumb* 93 NY2250
Lestowder *Cnwll* 3 SW7924
Leswalt *D & G* 98 NX0163
Letchmore Heath *Herts* 26 TQ1597
Letchworth *Herts* 39 TL2232
Letcombe Bassett *Oxon* 36 SU3784
Letcombe Regis *Oxon* 36 SU3886
Letham *Border* 110 NT6709
Letham *Fife* 126 NO3014
Letham *Tays* 127 NO5348
Letham Grange *Tays* 127 NO6345
Lethenty *Gramp* 142 NJ5820
Lethenty *Gramp* 143 NJ8140
Letheringham *Suffk* 55 TM2757
Letheringsett *Norfk* 66 TG0638
Lett's Green *Kent* 27 TQ4559
Lettaford *Devon* 8 SX7084
Letterfearn *Highld* 138 NG8823
Letterfinlay Lodge Hotel *Highld* 131 NN2491
Lettermorar *Highld* 129 NM7389
Letters *Highld* 145 NH1687
Lettershaw *Strath* 108 NS8920
Letterston *Dyfed* 30 SM9429
Lettoch *Highld* 141 NJ0219
Lettoch *Highld* 141 NJ1032
Letton *H & W* 46 SO3346
Letton *H & W* 46 SO3770
Letty Green *Herts* 39 TL2810
Letwell *S York* 75 SK5686
Leuchars *Fife* 127 NO4521
Leurbost *W Isls* 154 NB3725
Levalsa Moor *Cnwll* 3 SX0049
Levedale *Staffs* 72 SJ8916
Level's Green *Essex* 39 TL4724
Leven *Fife* 118 NO3800
Leven *Humb* 85 TA1045
Levencorroch *Strath* 105 NS0021
Levens *Cumb* 87 SD4886
Levens Green *Herts* 39 TL3522
Levenshulme *Gt Man* 79 SJ8794
Levenwick *Shet* 155 HU4021
Leverburgh *W Isls* 154 NG0186
Leverington *Cambs* 65 TF4411
Leverstock Green *Herts* 38 TL0806
Leverton *Lincs* 77 TF4047
Levington *Suffk* 55 TM2339
Levisham *N York* 90 SE8390
Lew *Oxon* 36 SP3206
Lewannick *Cnwll* 5 SX2780
Lewdown *Devon* 5 SX4586
Lewes *E Susx* 15 TQ4110
Leweston *Dorset* 10 ST6312
Leweston *Dyfed* 30 SM9322
Lewis Wych *H & W* 46 SO3357
Lewisham *Gt Lon* 27 TQ3774
Lewiston *Highld* 139 NH5129
Lewknor *Oxon* 37 SU7197
Leworthy *Devon* 18 SS3201
Leworthy *Devon* 19 SS6738
Lewson Street *Kent* 28 TQ9661
Lewth *Lancs* 80 SD4836
Lewtrenchard *Devon* 5 SX4586
Lexden *Essex* 41 TL9625
Lexworthy *Somset* 20 ST2535
Ley *Cnwll* 4 SX1766
Leybourne *Kent* 28 TQ6858
Leyburn *N York* 89 SE1190
Leycett *Staffs* 72 SJ7946
Leygreen *Herts* 39 TL1624
Leyland *Lancs* 80 SD5422
Leyland Green *Mersyd* 78 SD5500
Leylodge *Gramp* 135 NJ7613
Leys *Gramp* 143 NK0052
Leys *Tays* 126 NO2537
Leys of Cossans *Tays* 126 NO3849
Leysdown-on-Sea *Kent* 28 TR0370
Leysmill *Tays* 127 NO6047
Leysters *H & W* 46 SO5664
Leyton *Gt Lon* 27 TQ3786
Leytonstone *Gt Lon* 27 TQ3987
Lezant *Cnwll* 5 SX3479
Lezayre *IOM* 153 SC4294
Lezerea *Cnwll* 2 SW6833
Lhanbryde *Gramp* 141 NJ2761
Libanus *Powys* 45 SN9925
Libberton *Strath* 108 NS9943
Liberton *Loth* 117 NT2769
Lichfield *Staffs* 61 SK1109
Lickey *H & W* 60 SO9975
Lickey End *H & W* 60 SO9772
Lickey Rock *H & W* 60 SO9774
Lickfold *W Susx* 14 SU9226
Liddaton Green *Devon* 5 SX4582
Liddesdale *Highld* 130 NM7759
Liddington *Wilts* 36 SU2081
Lidgate *Derbys* 74 SK3077
Lidgate *Suffk* 53 TL7258
Lidget *S York* 75 SE6500
Lidgett *Notts* 75 SK6365
Lidham Hill *E Susx* 17 TQ8316
Lidlington *Beds* 38 SP9939
Lidsing *Kent* 28 TQ7862
Liff *Tays* 126 NO3332
Lifford *W Mids* 61 SP0580
Lifton *Devon* 5 SX3885
Liftondown *Devon* 5 SX3685
Lighthazles *W York* 82 SE0220
Lighthorne *Warwks* 48 SP3355
Lightwater *Surrey* 25 SU9362
Lightwood *Staffs* 72 SJ9241
Lightwood Green *Ches* 71 SJ6342
Lightwood Green *Clwyd* 71 SJ3840
Lilbourne *Nhants* 50 SP5676
Lilburn Tower *Nthumb* 111 NU0224
Lilleshall *Shrops* 72 SJ7315
Lilley *Berks* 37 SU4479
Lilley *Herts* 38 TL1126
Lilliesleaf *Border* 109 NT5325
Lillingstone Dayrell *Bucks* 49 SP7039
Lillingstone Lovell *Bucks* 49 SP7140
Lillington *Dorset* 10 ST6212
Lilliput *Dorset* 12 SZ0489
Lilstock *Somset* 20 ST1645
Lilyhurst *Shrops* 60 SJ7413
Limbrick *Lancs* 81 SD6016
Limbury *Beds* 38 TL0724
Lime Street *H & W* 47 SO8130
Limebrook *H & W* 46 SO3766
Limefield *Gt Man* 81 SD8012
Limekilnburn *Strath* 116 NS7050
Limekilns *Fife* 117 NT0883
Limerigg *Cent* 116 NS8571
Limerstone *IOW* 13 SZ4482
Limestone Brae *Nthumb* 95 NY7949
Limington *Somset* 21 ST5422
Limmerhaugh *Strath* 107 NS6127
Limpenhoe *Norfk* 67 TG3903
Limpley Stoke *Wilts* 22 ST7860
Limpsfield *Surrey* 27 TQ4053
Limpsfield Chart *Surrey* 27 TQ4251
Linby *Notts* 75 SK5351
Linchmere *W Susx* 14 SU8630
Lincluden *D & G* 100 NX9677
Lincoln *Lincs* 76 SK9771
Lincomb *H & W* 47 SO8268
Lincombe *Devon* 7 SX7440
Lindal in Furness *Cumb* 86 SD2475
Lindale *Cumb* 87 SD4180
Lindfield *W Susx* 15 TQ3425
Lindford *Hants* 14 SU8036
Lindley *W York* 82 SE1217
Lindley Green *N York* 82 SE2248
Lindores *Fife* 126 NO2616
Lindow End *Ches* 79 SJ8178
Lindridge *H & W* 47 SO6769
Lindsell *Essex* 40 TL6427
Lindsey *Suffk* 54 TL9745
Lindsey Tye *Suffk* 54 TL9845
Liney *Somset* 21 ST3535
Linford *Essex* 40 TQ6779
Linford *Hants* 12 SU1806
Lingbob *W York* 82 SE0935
Lingdale *Cleve* 97 NZ6716
Lingen *H & W* 46 SO3667
Lingley Green *Ches* 78 SJ5588
Lingwood *Norfk* 67 TG3508
Linicro *Highld* 136 NG3966
Linkend *H & W* 47 SO8231
Linkenholt *Hants* 23 SU3657
Linkhill *Kent* 17 TQ8127
Linkinhorne *Cnwll* 5 SX3173
Linktown *Fife* 117 NT2790
Linkwood *Gramp* 141 NJ2361
Linley *Shrops* 59 SO3592
Linley Green *H & W* 47 SO6953
Linleygreen *Shrops* 60 SO6898
Linlithgow *Loth* 117 NS9977
Linshiels *Nthumb* 110 NT8906
Linsidemore *Highld* 146 NH5499
Linslade *Beds* 38 SP9125
Linstead Parva *Suffk* 55 TM3377
Linstock *Cumb* 93 NY4258
Linthurst *H & W* 60 SO9972
Linthwaite *W York* 82 SE1014
Lintlaw *Border* 119 NT8258
Lintmill *Gramp* 142 NJ5165
Linton *Border* 110 NT7726
Linton *Cambs* 53 TL5646
Linton *Derbys* 73 SK2716
Linton *H & W* 47 SO6625
Linton *Kent* 28 TQ7550
Linton *N York* 88 SD9962
Linton *W York* 83 SE3946
Linton Heath *Derbys* 73 SK2816
Linton Hill *Gloucs* 47 SO6624
Linton-on-Ouse *N York* 90 SE4860
Linwood *Hants* 12 SU1809
Linwood *Lincs* 76 TF1186
Linwood *Strath* 115 NS4464
Lionel *W Isls* 154 NB5263
Lions Green *E Susx* 16 TQ5518
Liphook *Hants* 14 SU8431
Lipley *Shrops* 72 SJ7330
Liscard *Mersyd* 78 SJ2991
Liscombe *Devon* 19 SS8732
Liskeard *Cnwll* 5 SX2564
Liss *Hants* 14 SU7727
Liss Forest *Hants* 14 SU7828
Lissett *Humb* 91 TA1458
Lissington *Lincs* 76 TF1083
Liston *Essex* 54 TL8544
Lisvane *S Glam* 33 ST1883
Litcham *Norfk* 66 TF8817
Litchard *M Glam* 33 SS9081
Litchborough *Nhants* 49 SP6354
Litchfield *Hants* 24 SU4653
Litherland *Mersyd* 78 SJ3397
Litlington *Cambs* 39 TL3142
Litlington *E Susx* 16 TQ5201
Little Abington *Cambs* 53 TL5349
Little Addington *Nhants* 51 SP9673
Little Airies *D & G* 99 NX4248
Little Almshoe *Herts* 39 TL2026
Little Alne *Warwks* 48 SP1461
Little Amwell *Herts* 39 TL3511
Little Asby *Cumb* 87 NY6909
Little Aston *Staffs* 61 SK0900
Little Atherfield *IOW* 13 SZ4679
Little Ayton *N York* 90 NZ5610
Little Baddow *Essex* 40 TL7707
Little Badminton *Avon* 35 ST8084
Little Bampton *Cumb* 93 NY2755
Little Bardfield *Essex* 40 TL6531
Little Barford *Beds* 52 TL1756
Little Barningham *Norfk* 66 TG1333
Little Barrington *Gloucs* 36 SP2012
Little Barrow *Ches* 71 SJ4769
Little Barugh *N York* 90 SE7679
Little Bavington *Nthumb* 102 NY9878
Little Bayton *Warwks* 61 SP3585
Little Bealings *Suffk* 55 TM2247
Little Bedwyn *Wilts* 23 SU2866
Little Bentley *Essex* 41 TM1125
Little Berkhamsted *Herts* 39 TL2907
Little Billing *Nhants* 51 SP8061
Little Billington *Beds* 38 SP9322
Little Birch *H & W* 46 SO5130
Little Bispham *Lancs* 80 SD3141
Little Blakenham *Suffk* 54 TM1048
Little Blencow *Cumb* 93 NY4532
Little Bloxwich *W Mids* 60 SK0003
Little Bognor *W Susx* 14 TQ0020
Little Bolehill *Derbys* 73 SK2954
Little Bookham *Surrey* 26 TQ1254
Little Bourton *Oxon* 49 SP4544
Little Bowden *Leics* 50 SP7487
Little Bradley *Suffk* 53 TL6852
Little Brampton *H & W* 46 SO3061
Little Braxted *Essex* 40 TL8314
Little Brechin *Tays* 134 NO5862
Little Brickhill *Bucks* 38 SP9132
Little Bridgeford *Staffs* 72 SJ8727
Little Brington *Nhants* 49 SP6663
Little Bromley *Essex* 41 TM0928
Little Broughton *Cumb* 92 NY0731
Little Budworth *Ches* 71 SJ5965
Little Burstead *Essex* 40 TQ6692
Little Bytham *Lincs* 64 TF0118
Little Carlton *Lincs* 77 TF3985
Little Carlton *Notts* 75 SK7757
Little Casterton *Leics* 64 TF0109
Little Catwick *Humb* 85 TA1244
Little Catworth *Cambs* 51 TL1072
Little Cawthorpe *Lincs* 77 TF3583
Little Chalfont *Bucks* 26 SU9997
Little Charlinch *Somset* 20 ST2437
Little Chart *Kent* 28 TQ9446
Little Chatfield *Wilts* 22 ST8563
Little Chesterford *Essex* 39 TL5141
Little Cheveney *Kent* 28 TQ7243
Little Cheverell *Wilts* 22 ST9953
Little Chishill *Cambs* 39 TL4137
Little Clacton *Essex* 41 TM1618
Little Clanfield *Oxon* 36 SP2701
Little Clifton *Cumb* 92 NY0528
Little Coates *Humb* 85 TA2408
Little Comberton *H & W* 47 SO9643
Little Common *E Susx* 17 TQ7107
Little Comp *Kent* 27 TQ6356
Little Compton *Warwks* 48 SP2630
Little Corby *Cumb* 93 NY4757
Little Cornard *Suffk* 54 TL9039
Little Cowarne *H & W* 46 SO6051
Little Coxwell *Oxon* 36 SU2893
Little Crakehall *N York* 89 SE2390
Little Cransley *Nhants* 51 SP8376
Little Cressingham *Norfk* 66 TF8700
Little Crosby *Mersyd* 78 SD3201
Little Crosthwaite *Cumb* 93 NY2327
Little Cubley *Derbys* 73 SK1537
Little Dalby *Leics* 63 SK7714
Little Dens *Gramp* 143 NK0643
Little Dewchurch *H & W* 46 SO5231
Little Ditton *Cambs* 53 TL6658
Little Doward *H & W* 34 SO5416
Little Driffield *Humb* 91 TA0058
Little Dunham *Norfk* 66 TF8612
Little Dunkeld *Tays* 125 NO0342
Little Dunmow *Essex* 40 TL6521
Little Durnford *Wilts* 23 SU1234
Little Eaton *Derbys* 62 SK3641
Little Ellingham *Norfk* 66 TM0099
Little Elm *Somset* 22 ST7146
Little Everdon *Nhants* 49 SP5957
Little Eversden *Cambs* 52 TL3753
Little Faringdon *S York* 36 SP2201
Little Fencote *N York* 89 SE2893
Little Fenton *N York* 83 SE5235
Little Fransham *Norfk* 66 TF9011
Little Gaddesden *Herts* 38 SP9913
Little Garway *H & W* 46 SO4424
Little Gidding *Cambs* 52 TL1282
Little Glemham *Suffk* 55 TM3458
Little Gorsley *H & W* 47 SO6924
Little Gransden *Cambs* 52 TL2755
Little Green *Notts* 63 SK7243
Little Green *Somset* 22 ST7248
Little Grimsby *Lincs* 77 TF3291
Little Gringley *Notts* 75 SK7380
Little Habton *N York* 90 SE7477
Little Hadham *Herts* 39 TL4322
Little Hale *Lincs* 64 TF1441
Little Hallam *Derbys* 62 SK4640
Little Hallingbury *Essex* 39 TL5017
Little Hanford *Dorset* 11 ST8411
Little Harrowden *Nhants* 51 SP8771
Little Hartlip *Kent* 28 TQ8464
Little Haseley *Oxon* 37 SP6400
Little Hatfield *Humb* 85 TA1743
Little Hautbois *Norfk* 67 TG2521
Little Haven *Dyfed* 30 SM8512
Little Hay *Staffs* 61 SK1102
Little Hayfield *Derbys* 74 SK0388
Little Haywood *Staffs* 73 SK0021
Little Heath *Staffs* 72 SJ8917
Little Heath *W Mids* 61 SP3482
Little Hereford *H & W* 46 SO5568
Little Hermitage *Kent* 28 TQ7170
Little Horkesley *Essex* 40 TL9532
Little Hormead *Herts* 39 TL4028
Little Horsted *E Susx* 16 TQ4718
Little Horton *W York* 82 SE1531
Little Horton *Wilts* 23 SU0462
Little Horwood *Bucks* 38 SP7930
Little Houghton *Nhants* 51 SP8059
Little Houghton *S York* 83 SE4205
Little Hucklow *Derbys* 74 SK1678
Little Hulton *Gt Man* 79 SD7203
Little Hungerford *Berks* 24 SU5173
Little Hutton *N York* 89 SE4576
Little Ingestre *Staffs* 72 SJ9824
Little Irchester *Nhants* 51 SP9066
Little Kelk *Humb* 91 TA0959
Little Keyford *Somset* 22 ST7746
Little Kimble *Bucks* 38 SP8207
Little Kineton *Warwks* 48 SP3350
Little Kingshill *Bucks* 26 SU8999
Little Knox *D & G* 100 NX8060
Little Langdale *Cumb* 86 NY3103
Little Langford *Wilts* 23 SU0436
Little Lashbrook *Devon* 18 SS4007
Little Laver *Essex* 39 TL5409
Little Leigh *Ches* 71 SJ6175
Little Leighs *Essex* 40 TL7117
Little Lever *Gt Man* 79 SD7507
Little Linford *Bucks* 38 SP8444
Little Linton *Cambs* 53 TL5547
Little Load *Somset* 21 ST4724
Little London *Cambs* 65 TL4196
Little London *E Susx* 16 TQ5620
Little London *Essex* 39 TL4729
Little London *Essex* 53 TL6835
Little London *Gloucs* 35 SO7018
Little London *Hants* 23 SU3749
Little London *Hants* 24 SU6259
Little London *Lincs* 64 TF2321
Little London *Lincs* 77 TF3374
Little London *Lincs* 65 TF4323
Little London *Norfk* 65 TF5621
Little London *Oxon* 37 SP6412
Little London *Powys* 58 SO0488
Little London *W York* 82 SE2039
Little Longstone *Derbys* 74 SK1871
Little Madeley *Staffs* 72 SJ7745
Little Malvern *H & W* 47 SO7640
Little Mancot *Clwyd* 71 SJ3266
Little Maplestead *Essex* 54 TL8234
Little Marcle *H & W* 47 SO6736
Little Marlow *Bucks* 26 SU8787
Little Massingham *Norfk* 65 TF7824
Little Melton *Norfk* 66 TG1607
Little Mill *Gwent* 34 SO3203
Little Milton *Oxon* 37 SP6100
Little Missenden *Bucks* 26 SU9299
Little Mongham *Kent* 29 TR3351
Little Moor *Somset* 21 ST3232
Little Musgrave *Cumb* 94 NY7612
Little Ness *Shrops* 59 SJ4019
Little Neston *Ches* 71 SJ2976
Little Newcastle *Dyfed* 30 SM9829
Little Newsham *Dur* 96 NZ1217
Little Norton *Somset* 10 ST4715
Little Norton *Staffs* 60 SK0207
Little Oakley *Essex* 41 TM2129
Little Oakley *Nhants* 51 SP8985
Little Odell *Beds* 51 SP9557
Little Offley *Herts* 38 TL1328
Little Onn *Staffs* 72 SJ8315
Little Ormside *Cumb* 94 NY7016
Little Orton *Cumb* 93 NY3555
Little Oxendon *Nhants* 50 SP7283
Little Packington *Warwks* 61 SP2184
Little Pannell *Wilts* 22 SU0053
Little Pattenden *Kent* 28 TQ7445
Little Paxton *Cambs* 52 TL1862
Little Petherick *Cnwll* 4 SW9172
Little Plumpton *Lancs* 80 SD3832
Little Plumstead *Norfk* 67 TG3112
Little Ponton *Lincs* 63 SK9232
Little Posbrook *Hants* 13 SU5304
Little Potheridge *Devon* 19 SS5214
Little Preston *Nhants* 49 SP5854
Little Preston *W York* 83 SE3930
Little Raveley *Cambs* 52 TL2579
Little Reedness *Humb* 84 SE8022
Little Ribston *N York* 83 SE3853
Little Rissington *Gloucs* 36 SP1819
Little Rollright *Oxon* 48 SP2930
Little Rowsley *Derbys* 74 SK2566
Little Ryburgh *Norfk* 66 TF9628
Little Ryle *Nthumb* 111 NU0111
Little Ryton *Shrops* 59 SJ4803
Little Salkeld *Cumb* 94 NY5636
Little Sampford *Essex* 40 TL6533
Little Sandhurst *Berks* 25 SU8262
Little Saredon *Staffs* 60 SJ9407
Little Saughall *Ches* 71 SJ3768
Little Saxham *Suffk* 54 TL8063
Little Scatwell *Highld* 139 NH3856
Little Sessay *N York* 89 SE4674
Little Shelford *Cambs* 53 TL4551
Little Silver *Devon* 9 SS8601
Little Silver *Devon* 9 SS9109
Little Singleton *Lancs* 80 SD3739
Little Skipwith *N York* 83 SE6538
Little Smeaton *N York* 83 SE5216
Little Snoring *Norfk* 66 TF9532
Little Sodbury *Avon* 35 ST7582
Little Sodbury End *Avon* 35 ST7483
Little Somborne *Hants* 23 SU3832
Little Somerford *Wilts* 35 ST9684
Little Soudley *Shrops* 72 SJ7128
Little Stainforth *N York* 88 SD8166
Little Stainton *Dur* 96 NZ3420
Little Stanney *Ches* 71 SJ4174
Little Staughton *Beds* 51 TL1062
Little Steeping *Lincs* 77 TF4362
Little Stoke *Staffs* 72 SJ9132
Little Stonham *Suffk* 54 TM1160
Little Stretton *Leics* 50 SK6600
Little Stretton *Shrops* 59 SO4491
Little Strickland *Cumb* 94 NY5619
Little Stukeley *Cambs* 52 TL2175
Little Sugnall *Staffs* 72 SJ8031
Little Sutton *Ches* 71 SJ3776
Little Sutton *Shrops* 59 SO5182
Little Sypland *D & G* 99 NX7253
Little Tew *Oxon* 48 SP3828
Little Tey *Essex* 40 TL8923
Little Thetford *Cambs* 53 TL5376
Little Thirkleby *N York* 89 SE4778
Little Thornage *Norfk* 66 TG0538
Little Thornton *Lancs* 80 SD3541
Little Thorpe *Dur* 96 NZ4242
Little Thurlow *Suffk* 53 TL6751
Little Thurlow Green *Suffk* 53 TL6851
Little Thurrock *Essex* 27 TQ6277
Little Torrington *Devon* 18 SS4916
Little Totham *Essex* 40 TL8811
Little Town *Ches* 79 SJ6494
Little Town *Cumb* 93 NY2319
Little Town *Lancs* 81 SD6635
Little Twycross *Leics* 62 SK3405
Little Wakering *Essex* 40 TQ9388
Little Walden *Essex* 39 TL5441
Little Waldingfield *Suffk* 54 TL9245
Little Walsingham *Norfk* 66 TF9337
Little Waltham *Essex* 40 TL7012
Little Warley *Essex* 40 TQ6090
Little Washbourne *Gloucs* 47 SO9833
Little Weighton *Humb* 84 SE9833
Little Weldon *Nhants* 51 SP9289
Little Welnetham *Suffk* 54 TL8859
Little Welton *Lincs* 77 TF3087
Little Wenham *Suffk* 54 TM0839
Little Wenlock *Shrops* 59 SJ6406
Little Weston *Somset* 21 ST6225
Little Whitefield *IOW* 13 SZ5889
Little Whittington *Nthumb* 102 NY9869
Little Wilbraham *Cambs* 53 TL5458
Little Witcombe *Gloucs* 35 SO9115
Little Witley *H & W* 47 SO7863
Little Wittenham *Oxon* 37 SU5693
Little Wolford *Warwks* 48 SP2635
Little Woodcote *Surrey* 27 TQ2861
Little Wratting *Suffk* 53 TL6847
Little Wymington *Beds* 51 SP9565
Little Wymondley *Herts* 39 TL2127
Little Wyrley *Staffs* 60 SK0105
Little Yeldham *Essex* 53 TL7839
Littlebeck *N York* 90 NZ8804
Littleborough *Devon* 19 SS8210
Littleborough *Gt Man* 81 SD9316
Littleborough *Notts* 75 SK8282
Littlebourne *Kent* 29 TR2057
Littlebredy *Dorset* 10 SY5889
Littlebury *Essex* 39 TL5139
Littlebury Green *Essex* 39 TL4838
Littlecott *Wilts* 23 SU1352
Littledean *Gloucs* 35 SO6713
Littledown *Hants* 23 SU3457
Littleham *Devon* 18 SS4323
Littleham *Devon* 9 SY0381
Littlehampton *W Susx* 14 TQ0201
Littleharle Tower *Nthumb* 103 NZ0183
Littlehempston *Devon* 7 SX8162
Littlehoughton *Nthumb* 111 NU2216
Littlemill *Gramp* 134 NO3295
Littlemill *Highld* 140 NH9150
Littlemoor *Derbys* 74 SK3663
Littlemore *Oxon* 37 SP5302
Littleover *Derbys* 62 SK3334
Littleport *Cambs* 53 TL5686
Littleport Bridge *Cambs* 53 TL5787
Littler *Ches* 71 SJ6366
Littlestone-on-Sea *Kent* 17 TR0824
Littlethorpe *Leics* 50 SP5496
Littlethorpe *N York* 89 SE3269
Littleton *Avon* 21 ST5563
Littleton *Ches* 71 SJ4466
Littleton *D & G* 99 NX6355
Littleton *Dorset* 11 ST8904
Littleton *Hants* 24 SU4532
Littleton *Somset* 21 ST4930
Littleton *Surrey* 25 SU9847
Littleton *Surrey* 26 TQ0668

Littleton Drew *Wilts* 35 ST8380
Littleton-on-Severn *Avon* 34 ST5989
Littletown *Dur* 96 NZ3343
Littletown *IOW* 13 SZ5390
Littlewick Green *Berks* 37 SU8379
Littlewindsor *Dorset* 10 ST4304
Littlewood *Staffs* 60 SJ9807
Littleworth *Bucks* 38 SP8823
Littleworth *H & W* 47 SO8850
Littleworth *H & W* 47 SO9962
Littleworth *Oxon* 36 SU3197
Littleworth *Staffs* 72 SJ9323
Littleworth *Staffs* 60 SK0111
Littleworth *W Susx* 15 TQ1920
Littleworth Common *Bucks* 26 SU9386
Littleworth End *Cambs* 52 TL2266
Littley Green *Essex* 40 TL6917
Litton *Derbys* 74 SK1675
Litton *N York* 88 SD9074
Litton *Somset* 21 ST5954
Litton Cheney *Dorset* 10 SY5490
Liverpool *Mersyd* 78 SJ3490
Liversedge *W York* 82 SE1923
Liverton *Cleve* 97 NZ7115
Liverton *Devon* 7 SX8075
Liverton Mines *Cleve* 97 NZ7117
Liverton Street *Kent* 28 TQ8750
Livesey Street *Kent* 28 TQ7054
Livingston *Loth* 117 NT0668
Livingston Village *Loth* 117 NT0366
Lixton *Devon* 7 SX6950
Lixwm *Clwyd* 70 SJ1671
Lizard *Cnwll* 2 SW7012
Llaingoch *Gwynd* 68 SH2382
Llaithddu *Powys* 58 SO0680
Llan-y-pwll *Clwyd* 71 SJ3752
Llanaber *Gwynd* 57 SH6018
Llanaelhaearn *Gwynd* 56 SH3844
Llanafan *Dyfed* 43 SN6872
Llanafan-fechan *Powys* 45 SN9750
Llanallgo *Gwynd* 68 SH5085
Llanarmon *Gwynd* 56 SH4239
Llanarmon Dyffryn Ceiriog *Clwyd* 58 SJ1532
Llanarmon-yn-Ial *Clwyd* 70 SJ1956
Llanarth *Dyfed* 42 SN4257
Llanarth *Gwent* 34 SO3710
Llanarthne *Dyfed* 32 SN5320
Llanasa *Clwyd* 70 SJ1081
Llanbabo *Gwynd* 68 SH3787
Llanbadarn Fawr *Dyfed* 43 SN6081
Llanbadarn Fynydd *Powys* 45 SO0977
Llanbadarn-y-garreg *Powys* 45 SO1148
Llanbadoc *Gwent* 34 ST3799
Llanbadrig *Gwynd* 68 SH3794
Llanbeder *Gwent* 34 ST3890
Llanbedr *Gwynd* 57 SH5826
Llanbedr *Powys* 45 SO1446
Llanbedr *Powys* 34 SO2320
Llanbedr-Dyffryn-Clwyd *Clwyd* 70 SJ1459
Llanbedr-y-cennin *Gwynd* 69 SH7669
Llanbedrgoch *Gwynd* 68 SH5180
Llanbedrog *Gwynd* 56 SH3231
Llanberis *Gwynd* 69 SH5760
Llanbethery *S Glam* 20 ST0369
Llanbister *Powys* 45 SO1173
Llanblethian *S Glam* 33 SS9873
Llanboidy *Dyfed* 31 SN2123
Llanbradach *M Glam* 33 ST1490
Llanbrynmair *Powys* 57 SH8902
Llancarfan *S Glam* 33 ST0470
Llancayo *Gwent* 34 SO3603
Llancillo *H & W* 46 SO3625
Llancloudy *H & W* 34 SO4921
Llancynfelyn *Dyfed* 43 SN6492
Llandaf *S Glam* 33 ST1577
Llandanwg *Gwynd* 57 SH5728
Llandawke *Dyfed* 31 SN2811
Llanddanielfab *Gwynd* 68 SH4970
Llanddarog *Dyfed* 32 SN5016
Llanddeiniol *Dyfed* 43 SN5571
Llanddeiniolen *Gwynd* 69 SH5465
Llandderfel *Gwynd* 58 SH9837
Llanddeusant *Dyfed* 44 SN7724
Llanddeusant *Gwynd* 68 SH3485
Llanddew *Powys* 45 SO0530
Llanddewi *W Glam* 32 SS4588
Llanddewi Brefi *Dyfed* 44 SN6655
Llanddewi Rhydderch *Gwent* 34 SO3512
Llanddewi Velfrey *Dyfed* 31 SN1415
Llanddewi Ystradenni *Powys* 45 SO1068
Llanddewi'r Cwm *Powys* 45 SO0348
Llanddoget *Gwynd* 69 SH8063
Llanddona *Gwynd* 69 SH5779
Llanddowror *Dyfed* 31 SN2514
Llanddulas *Clwyd* 70 SH9178
Llanddyfnan *Gwynd* 68 SH5078
Llandecwyn *Gwynd* 57 SH6337
Llandefaelog Fach *Powys* 45 SO0332
Llandefaelogtrer-graig *Powys* 45 SO1229
Llandefalle *Powys* 45 SO1035
Llandegai *Gwynd* 69 SH5971
Llandegfan *Gwynd* 69 SH5674
Llandegla *Clwyd* 70 SJ2051
Llandegley *Powys* 45 SO1463
Llandegveth *Gwent* 34 ST3395
Llandegwning *Gwynd* 56 SH2629
Llandeilo *Dyfed* 32 SN6222
Llandeilo Graban *Powys* 45 SO0944
Llandeilo'r Fan *Powys* 45 SN8934
Llandeloy *Dyfed* 30 SM8626
Llandenny *Gwent* 34 SO4104
Llandevaud *Gwent* 34 ST4090
Llandevenny *Gwent* 34 ST4186
Llandinabo *H & W* 46 SO5128
Llandinam *Powys* 58 SO0288
Llandissilio *Dyfed* 31 SN1221
Llandogo *Gwent* 34 SO5203
Llandough *S Glam* 33 SS9972
Llandough *S Glam* 33 ST1673
Llandovery *Dyfed* 44 SN7634
Llandow *S Glam* 33 SS9473
Llandre *Dyfed* 43 SN6286
Llandre *Dyfed* 44 SN6741
Llandre Isaf *Dyfed* 31 SN1328
Llandrillo *Clwyd* 58 SJ0337
Llandrillo-yn-Rhos *Clwyd* 69 SH8380
Llandrindod Wells *Powys* 45 SO0561
Llandrinio *Powys* 58 SJ2817
Llandudno *Gwynd* 69 SH7882
Llandudno Junction *Gwynd* 69 SH7977
Llandudwen *Gwynd* 56 SH2736
Llandulas *Powys* 45 SN8841
Llandwrog *Gwynd* 68 SH4555
Llandybie *Dyfed* 32 SN6115
Llandyfaelog *Dyfed* 31 SN4111
Llandyfan *Dyfed* 32 SN6417
Llandyfriog *Dyfed* 31 SN3341
Llandyfrydog *Gwynd* 68 SH4485
Llandygwydd *Dyfed* 31 SN2443
Llandyrnog *Clwyd* 70 SJ1065
Llandyssil *Powys* 58 SO1995
Llandysul *Dyfed* 31 SN4140
Llanedeyrn *S Glam* 33 ST2181
Llanedi *Dyfed* 32 SN5806
Llaneglwys *Powys* 45 SO0538
Llanegryn *Gwynd* 57 SH6005
Llanegwad *Dyfed* 32 SN5221
Llaneilian *Gwynd* 68 SH4692
Llanelian-yn-Rhos *Clwyd* 69 SH8676
Llanelidan *Clwyd* 70 SJ1150
Llanelieu *Powys* 45 SO1834
Llanellen *Gwent* 34 SO3010
Llanelli *Dyfed* 32 SN5000
Llanelltyd *Gwynd* 57 SH7119
Llanelly *Gwent* 34 SO2314
Llanelwedd *Powys* 45 SO0451
Llanenddwyn *Gwynd* 57 SH5823
Llanengan *Gwynd* 56 SH2926
Llanerch *Gwynd* 57 SH8816
Llanerch *Powys* 59 SO3093
Llanerchymedd *Gwynd* 68 SH4184
Llanerfyl *Powys* 58 SJ0309
Llanfachraeth *Gwynd* 68 SH3182
Llanfachreth *Gwynd* 57 SH7522
Llanfaelog *Gwynd* 68 SH3373
Llanfaelrhys *Gwynd* 56 SH2026
Llanfaenor *Gwent* 34 SO4317
Llanfaes *Gwynd* 69 SH6077
Llanfaes *Powys* 45 SO0328
Llanfaethlu *Gwynd* 68 SH3186
Llanfair *Gwynd* 57 SH5728
Llanfair Caereinion *Powys* 58 SJ1006
Llanfair Clydogau *Dyfed* 44 SN6251
Llanfair Dyffryn Clwyd *Clwyd* 70 SJ1355
Llanfair Kilgeddin *Gwent* 34 SO3506
Llanfair P G *Gwynd* 68 SH5271
Llanfair Talhaiarn *Clwyd* 70 SH9270
Llanfair Waterdine *Shrops* 45 SO2376
Llanfair-is-gaer *Gwynd* 68 SH5065
Llanfair-Nant-Gwyn *Dyfed* 31 SN1637
Llanfair-y-Cwmmwd *Gwynd* 68 SH4466
Llanfair-yn-Neubwll *Gwynd* 68 SH3076
Llanfairfechan *Gwynd* 69 SH6874
Llanfairynghornwy *Gwynd* 68 SH3290
Llanfallteg *Dyfed* 31 SN1520
Llanfallteg West *Dyfed* 31 SN1419
Llanfarian *Dyfed* 43 SN5877
Llanfechain *Powys* 58 SJ1920
Llanfechelli *Gwynd* 68 SH3791
Llanferres *Clwyd* 70 SJ1860
Llanfflewyn *Gwynd* 68 SH3588
Llanfihangel ar-Arth *Dyfed* 31 SN4540
Llanfihangel Glyn Myfyr *Clwyd* 70 SH9849
Llanfihangel Nant Bran *Powys* 45 SN9434
Llanfihangel Rhydithon *Powys* 45 SO1566
Llanfihangel Rogiet *Gwent* 34 ST4587
Llanfihangel Tal-y-llyn *Powys* 45 SO1128
Llanfihangel yn Nhowyn *Gwynd* 68 SH3277
Llanfihangel-nant-Melan *Powys* 45 SO1758
Llanfihangel-uwch-Gwili *Dyfed* 32 SN4922
Llanfihangel-y-Creuddyn *Dyfed* 43 SN6675
Llanfihangel-y-pennant *Gwynd* 57 SH5244
Llanfihangel-y-pennant *Gwynd* 57 SH6708
Llanfihangel-y-traethau *Gwynd* 57 SH5934
Llanfihangel-yng-Ngwynfa *Powys* 58 SJ0816
Llanfilo *Powys* 45 SO1132
Llanfoist *Gwent* 34 SO2813
Llanfor *Gwynd* 58 SH9336
Llanfrechfa *Gwent* 34 ST3293
Llanfrothen *Gwynd* 57 SH6241
Llanfrynach *Powys* 45 SO0725
Llanfwrog *Clwyd* 70 SJ1157
Llanfwrog *Gwynd* 68 SH3084
Llanfyllin *Powys* 58 SJ1419
Llanfynydd *Clwyd* 70 SJ2856
Llanfynydd *Dyfed* 44 SN5527
Llanfyrnach *Dyfed* 31 SN2231
Llangadfan *Powys* 58 SJ0110
Llangadog *Dyfed* 31 SN4207
Llangadog *Dyfed* 44 SN7028
Llangadwaladr *Clwyd* 58 SJ1830
Llangadwaladr *Gwynd* 68 SH3869
Llangaffo *Gwynd* 68 SH4468
Llangain *Dyfed* 31 SN3815
Llangammarch Wells *Powys* 45 SN9346
Llangan *S Glam* 33 SS9577
Llangarron *H & W* 34 SO5220
Llangasty-Talyllyn *Powys* 45 SO1326
Llangathen *Dyfed* 32 SN5822
Llangattock *Powys* 33 SO2117
Llangattock Lingoed *Gwent* 34 SO3620
Llangattock-Vibon-Avel *Gwent* 34 SO4515
Llangedwyn *Clwyd* 58 SJ1824
Llangefni *Gwynd* 68 SH4675
Llangeinor *M Glam* 33 SS9187
Llangeinwen *Gwynd* 68 SH4465
Llangeitho *Dyfed* 44 SN6259
Llangeler *Dyfed* 31 SN3739
Llangelynin *Gwynd* 57 SH5707
Llangendeirne *Dyfed* 32 SN4513
Llangennech *Dyfed* 32 SN5601
Llangennith *W Glam* 31 SS4291
Llangenny *Powys* 34 SO2417
Llangernyw *Clwyd* 69 SH8767
Llangian *Gwynd* 56 SH2928
Llangiwg *W Glam* 32 SN7205
Llangloffan *Dyfed* 30 SM9032
Llanglydwen *Dyfed* 31 SN1826
Llangoed *Gwynd* 69 SH6079
Llangoedmor *Dyfed* 42 SN2046
Llangollen *Clwyd* 70 SJ2141
Llangolman *Dyfed* 31 SN1127
Llangors *Powys* 45 SO1327
Llangovan *Gwent* 34 SO4505
Llangower *Gwynd* 58 SH9032
Llangranog *Dyfed* 42 SN3154
Llangristiolus *Gwynd* 68 SH4373
Llangrove *H & W* 34 SO5219
Llangua *Gwent* 46 SO3925
Llangunllo *Powys* 45 SO2171
Llangunnor *Dyfed* 31 SN4320
Llangurig *Powys* 43 SN9079
Llangwm *Clwyd* 70 SH9644
Llangwm *Dyfed* 30 SM9909
Llangwm *Gwent* 34 ST4299
Llangwm-isaf *Gwent* 34 SO4300
Llangwyfan *Clwyd* 70 SJ1166
Llangwyllog *Gwynd* 68 SH4379
Llangwyryfon *Dyfed* 43 SN5970
Llangybi *Dyfed* 44 SN6053
Llangybi *Gwent* 34 ST3796
Llangybi *Gwynd* 56 SH4341
Llangyfelach *W Glam* 32 SS6498
Llangynhafal *Clwyd* 70 SJ1263
Llangynidr *Powys* 33 SO1519
Llangynin *Dyfed* 31 SN2517
Llangynllo *Dyfed* 42 SN3544
Llangynog *Dyfed* 31 SN3314
Llangynog *Powys* 58 SJ0526
Llangynog *Powys* 45 SO0145
Llangynwyd *M Glam* 33 SS8588
Llanhamlach *Powys* 45 SO0926
Llanharan *M Glam* 33 ST0083
Llanharry *M Glam* 33 ST0080
Llanhennock *Gwent* 34 ST3592
Llanhilleth *Gwent* 33 SO2100
Llanidan *Gwynd* 68 SH4966
Llanidloes *Powys* 58 SN9584
Llaniestyn *Gwynd* 56 SH2733
Llanigon *Powys* 45 SO2139
Llanilar *Dyfed* 43 SN6275
Llanilid *M Glam* 33 SS9781
Llanina *Dyfed* 42 SN4059
Llanishen *Gwent* 34 SO4703
Llanishen *S Glam* 33 ST1781
Llanllechid *Gwynd* 69 SH6268
Llanlleonfel *Powys* 45 SN9350
Llanllowell *Gwent* 34 ST3998
Llanllugan *Powys* 58 SJ0502
Llanllwch *Dyfed* 31 SN3818
Llanllwchaiarn *Powys* 58 SO1292
Llanllwni *Dyfed* 44 SN4741
Llanllyfni *Gwynd* 68 SH4751
Llanmadoc *W Glam* 32 SS4493
Llanmaes *S Glam* 20 SS9769
Llanmartin *Gwent* 34 ST3989
Llanmerewig *Powys* 58 SO1593
Llanmihangel *S Glam* 33 SS9871
Llanmiloe *Dyfed* 31 SN2408
Llanmorlais *W Glam* 32 SS5294
Llannefydd *Clwyd* 70 SH9870
Llannon *Dyfed* 32 SN5308
Llannor *Gwynd* 56 SH3537
Llanon *Dyfed* 42 SN5166
Llanover *Gwent* 34 SO3109
Llanpumsaint *Dyfed* 31 SN4229
Llanrhaeadr-ym-Mochnant *Clwyd* 58 SJ1226
Llanrhidian *W Glam* 32 SS4992
Llanrhos *Gwynd* 69 SH7980
Llanrhychwyn *Gwynd* 69 SH7761
Llanrhyddlad *Gwynd* 68 SH3389
Llanrhystud *Dyfed* 43 SN5369
Llanrian *Dyfed* 30 SM8231
Llanrothal *H & W* 34 SO4718
Llanrug *Gwynd* 69 SH5363
Llanrumney *S Glam* 34 ST2280
Llanrwst *Gwynd* 69 SH8061
Llansadurnen *Dyfed* 31 SN2810
Llansadwrn *Dyfed* 44 SN6931
Llansadwrn *Gwynd* 69 SH5575
Llansaint *Dyfed* 31 SN3808
Llansamlet *W Glam* 32 SS6897
Llansanffraid Glan Conwy *Gwynd* 69 SH8076
Llansannan *Clwyd* 70 SH9365
Llansannor *S Glam* 33 SS9977
Llansantffraed *Powys* 45 SO1223
Llansantffraed-Cwmdeuddwr *Powys* 45 SN9667
Llansantffraed-in-Elvel *Powys* 45 SO0954
Llansantffraid *Dyfed* 42 SN5167
Llansantffraid-ym-Mechain *Powys* 58 SJ2220
Llansawel *Dyfed* 44 SN6136
Llansilin *Clwyd* 58 SJ2128
Llansoy *Gwent* 34 SO4402
Llanspyddid *Powys* 45 SO0128
Llanstadwell *Dyfed* 30 SM9404
Llansteffan *Dyfed* 31 SN3511
Llanstephan *Powys* 45 SO1141
Llantarnam *Gwent* 34 ST3093
Llanteg *Dyfed* 31 SN1810
Llanthewy Skirrid *Gwent* 34 SO3416
Llanthony *Gwent* 46 SO2827
Llantilio Pertholey *Gwent* 34 SO3116
Llantrisant *Gwent* 34 ST3996
Llantrisant *Gwynd* 68 SH3584
Llantrisant *M Glam* 33 ST0483
Llantrithyd *S Glam* 33 ST0472
Llantwit Fardre *M Glam* 33 ST0886
Llantwit Major *S Glam* 20 SS9668
Llantysilio *Clwyd* 70 SJ1943
Llanuwchllyn *Gwynd* 57 SH8730
Llanvaches *Gwent* 34 ST4391
Llanvair Discoed *Gwent* 34 ST4492
Llanvapley *Gwent* 34 SO3614
Llanvetherine *Gwent* 34 SO3617
Llanveynoe *H & W* 46 SO3031
Llanvihangel Crucorney *Gwent* 34 SO3220
Llanvihangel Gobion *Gwent* 34 SO3409
Llanvihangel-Ystern-Llewern *Gwent* 34 SO4313
Llanwarne *H & W* 46 SO5027
Llanwddyn *Powys* 58 SJ0219
Llanwenarth *Gwent* 34 SO2714
Llanwenog *Dyfed* 44 SN4945
Llanwern *Gwent* 34 ST3688
Llanwinio *Dyfed* 31 SN2626
Llanwnda *Dyfed* 30 SM9339
Llanwnda *Gwynd* 68 SH4758
Llanwnen *Dyfed* 44 SN5347
Llanwnog *Powys* 58 SO0293
Llanwonno *M Glam* 33 ST0395
Llanwrda *Dyfed* 44 SN7131
Llanwrin *Powys* 57 SH7803
Llanwrthwl *Powys* 45 SN9763
Llanwrtyd *Powys* 45 SN8647
Llanwrtyd Wells *Powys* 45 SN8846
Llanwyddelan *Powys* 58 SJ0801
Llanyblodwel *Shrops* 58 SJ2323
Llanybri *Dyfed* 31 SN3312
Llanybydder *Dyfed* 44 SN5244
Llanycefn *Dyfed* 31 SN0923
Llanychaer Bridge *Dyfed* 30 SM9835
Llanycrwys *Dyfed* 44 SN6445
Llanymawddwy *Gwynd* 58 SH9019
Llanymynech *Shrops* 58 SJ2621
Llanynghenedl *Gwynd* 68 SH3181
Llanynis *Powys* 45 SN9950
Llanynys *Clwyd* 70 SJ1062
Llanyre *Powys* 45 SO0462
Llanystumdwy *Gwynd* 56 SH4738
Llanywern *Powys* 45 SO1028
Llawhaden *Dyfed* 31 SN0717
Llawnt *Shrops* 58 SJ2430
Llawryglyn *Powys* 58 SN9291
Llay *Clwyd* 71 SJ3355
Llechcynfarwy *Gwynd* 68 SH3880
Llechfaen *Powys* 45 SO0828
Llechryd *Dyfed* 31 SN2143
Lledrod *Dyfed* 43 SN6470
Llidiadnenog *Dyfed* 44 SN5437
Llidiardau *Gwynd* 57 SH8738
Llidiart-y-parc *Clwyd* 70 SJ1143
Llithfaen *Gwynd* 56 SH3542
Llong *Clwyd* 70 SJ2662
Llowes *Powys* 45 SO1941
Llwydcoed *M Glam* 33 SN9904
Llwydiarth *Powys* 58 SJ0315
Llwyn-drain *Dyfed* 31 SN2634
Llwyn-du *Gwent* 34 SO2816
Llwyn-on *M Glam* 33 SO0111
Llwyn-y-brain *Dyfed* 31 SN1914
Llwyn-y-Groes *Dyfed* 44 SN5956
Llwyncelyn *Dyfed* 42 SN4459
Llwyndafydd *Dyfed* 42 SN3755
Llwynderw *Powys* 58 SJ2104
Llwyndyrys *Gwynd* 56 SH3740
Llwyngwril *Gwynd* 57 SH5909
Llwynhendy *Dyfed* 32 SS5399
Llwynmawr *Clwyd* 58 SJ2237
Llwynypia *M Glam* 33 SS9993
Llyn-y-pandy *Clwyd* 70 SJ2065
Llynclys *Shrops* 58 SJ2824
Llynfaes *Gwynd* 68 SH4178
Llys-y-fran *Dyfed* 30 SN0424
Llysfaen *Clwyd* 69 SH8977
Llyswen *Dyfed* 44 SN4661
Llyswen *Powys* 45 SO1337
Llysworney *S Glam* 33 SS9673
Llywel *Powys* 45 SN8630
Load Brook *S York* 74 SK2788
Loan *Cent* 117 NS9675
Loanend *Nthumb* 119 NT9450
Loanhead *Loth* 117 NT2865
Loaningfoot *D & G* 92 NX9655
Loans *Strath* 106 NS3431
Lobb *Devon* 18 SS4737
Lobhillcross *Devon* 5 SX4686
Loch Katrine Pier *Cent* 124 NN4907
Loch Loyal Lodge *Highld* 149 NC6146
Loch Maree Hotel *Highld* 144 NG9170
Lochailort *Highld* 129 NM7682
Lochans *D & G* 98 NX0656
Locharbriggs *D & G* 100 NX9980
Lochavich *Strath* 122 NM9415
Lochawe *Strath* 123 NN1227
Lochboisdale *W Isls* 154 NF7919
Lochbuie *Strath* 121 NM6025
Lochcarron *Highld* 138 NG8939
Lochdon *Strath* 122 NM7233
Lochead *Strath* 113 NR7778
Lochearnhead *Cent* 124 NN5823
Lochee *Tays* 126 NO3731
Locheilside Station *Highld* 130 NM9978
Lochend *Highld* 140 NH5937
Locheport *W Isls* 154 NF8563
Lochfoot *D & G* 100 NX8973
Lochgair *Strath* 114 NR9290
Lochgelly *Fife* 117 NT1893
Lochgilphead *Strath* 113 NR8688
Lochgoilhead *Strath* 114 NN2001
Lochieheads *Fife* 126 NO2513
Lochill *Gramp* 141 NJ2964
Lochindorb Lodge *Highld* 140 NH9635
Lochinver *Highld* 145 NC0922
Lochluichart *Highld* 139 NH3363
Lochmaben *D & G* 100 NY0882
Lochmaddy *W Isls* 154 NF9169
Lochore *Fife* 117 NT1796
Lochranza *Strath* 105 NR9350
Lochside *Gramp* 135 NO7364
Lochside *Highld* 140 NH8152
Lochton *Strath* 98 NX2579
Lochty *Fife* 127 NO5208
Lochty *Tays* 134 NO5362
Lochuisge *Highld* 122 NM7955
Lochwinnoch *Strath* 115 NS3559
Lochwood *D & G* 100 NY0896
Lockengate *Cnwll* 4 SX0361
Lockerbie *D & G* 100 NY1381
Lockeridge *Wilts* 23 SU1467
Lockerley *Hants* 23 SU3025
Locking *Avon* 21 ST3659
Lockington *Humb* 84 SE9947
Lockington *Leics* 62 SK4627
Lockleywood *Shrops* 72 SJ6928
Locks Heath *Hants* 13 SU5107
Locksbottom *Gt Lon* 27 TQ4265
Locksgreen *IOW* 13 SZ4490
Lockton *N York* 90 SE8489
Loddington *Leics* 63 SK7902
Loddington *Nhants* 51 SP8178
Loddiswell *Devon* 7 SX7248
Loddon *Norfk* 67 TM3698
Lode *Cambs* 53 TL5362
Lode Heath *W Mids* 61 SP1580
Loders *Dorset* 10 SY4994
Lodge Green *W Mids* 61 SP2583
Lodsworth *W Susx* 14 SU9223
Lofhouse Gate *W York* 83 SE3324
Lofthouse *N York* 89 SE1073
Lofthouse *W York* 83 SE3325
Loftus *Cleve* 97 NZ7218
Logan *Strath* 107 NS5820
Loganbeck *Cumb* 86 SD1890
Loganlea *Loth* 117 NS9762
Loggerheads *Staffs* 72 SJ7336
Logie *Fife* 126 NO4020
Logie *Gramp* 141 NJ0150
Logie *Tays* 135 NO6963
Logie Coldstone *Gramp* 134 NJ4304
Logie Pert *Tays* 135 NO6664
Logierait *Tays* 125 NN9752
Login *Dyfed* 31 SN1623
Lolworth *Cambs* 52 TL3664
Lon-las *W Glam* 32 SS7097
Lonbain *Highld* 137 NG6852
Londesborough *Humb* 84 SE8645
London *Gt Lon* 27 TQ2879
London Apprentice *Cnwll* 3 SX0049
London Beach *Kent* 28 TQ8836
London Colney *Herts* 39 TL1803
Londonderry *N York* 89 SE3087
Londonthorpe *Lincs* 63 SK9537
Londubh *Highld* 144 NG8680
Long Ashton *Avon* 34 ST5570
Long Bank *H & W* 60 SO7674
Long Bennington *Lincs* 63 SK8344
Long Bredy *Dorset* 10 SY5690
Long Buckby *Nhants* 50 SP6367
Long Cause *Devon* 7 SX7961
Long Clawson *Leics* 63 SK7227
Long Common *Hants* 13 SU5014
Long Compton *Staffs* 72 SJ8522
Long Compton *Warwks* 48 SP2832
Long Crendon *Bucks* 37 SP6908
Long Crichel *Dorset* 11 ST9710
Long Ditton *Surrey* 26 TQ1766
Long Drax *N York* 83 SE6828
Long Duckmanton *Derbys* 75 SK4471
Long Eaton *Derbys* 62 SK4833
Long Green *Ches* 71 SJ4770
Long Green *H & W* 47 SO8433
Long Hedges *Lincs* 77 TF3547
Long Itchington *Warwks* 50 SP4165
Long Lane *Shrops* 59 SJ6315
Long Lawford *Warwks* 50 SP4776
Long Load *Somset* 21 ST4623
Long Marston *Herts* 38 SP8915
Long Marston *N York* 83 SE5051
Long Marston *Warwks* 48 SP1548
Long Marton *Cumb* 94 NY6624
Long Meadowend *Shrops* 59 SO4181
Long Melford *Suffk* 54 TL8645
Long Newnton *Gloucs* 35 ST9192
Long Newton *Loth* 118 NT5164
Long Preston *N York* 88 SD8358
Long Riston *Humb* 85 TA1242
Long Sight *Gt Man* 79 SD9206
Long Stratton *Norfk* 67 TM1992
Long Street *Bucks* 38 SP7947
Long Sutton *Hants* 24 SU7347
Long Sutton *Lincs* 65 TF4322
Long Sutton *Somset* 21 ST4725
Long Thurlow *Suffk* 54 TM0068
Long Waste *Shrops* 59 SJ6115
Long Whatton *Leics* 62 SK4723
Long Wittenham *Oxon* 37 SU5493
Longbenton *T & W* 103 NZ2668
Longborough *Gloucs* 48 SP1729
Longbridge *W Mids* 60 SP0177
Longbridge *Warwks* 48 SP2762
Longbridge Deverill *Wilts* 22 ST8640
Longburgh *Cumb* 93 NY3058
Longburton *Dorset* 11 ST6412
Longcliffe *Derbys* 73 SK2255
Longcombe *Devon* 7 SX8359
Longcot *Oxon* 36 SU2790
Longcroft *Cumb* 93 NY2158
Longcross *Surrey* 25 SU9865
Longden *Shrops* 59 SJ4406
Longden Common *Shrops* 59 SJ4305
Longdon *H & W* 47 SO8336
Longdon *Staffs* 61 SK0714
Longdon Green *Staffs* 61 SK0813
Longdon Heath *H & W* 47 SO8338
Longdon upon Tern *Shrops* 59 SJ6115
Longdown *Devon* 9 SX8691
Longdowns *Cnwll* 3 SW7434
Longfield *Kent* 27 TQ6069
Longford *Derbys* 73 SK2137
Longford *Gloucs* 35 SO8320
Longford *Gt Lon* 26 TQ0576
Longford *Kent* 27 TQ5156
Longford *Shrops* 72 SJ6434
Longford *Shrops* 72 SJ7218
Longford *W Mids* 61 SP3583
Longforgan *Tays* 126 NO2929
Longformacus *Border* 119 NT6957
Longframlington *Nthumb* 103 NU1300
Longham *Dorset* 12 SZ0698
Longham *Norfk* 66 TF9416
Longhirst *Nthumb* 103 NZ2289
Longhope *Gloucs* 35 SO6918
Longhorsley *Nthumb* 103 NZ1494
Longhoughton *Nthumb* 111 NU2415
Longlands *Cumb* 93 NY2636
Longlane *Derbys* 73 SK2437
Longlevens *Gloucs* 35 SO8519
Longley *W York* 82 SE0522
Longley *W York* 82 SE1406
Longley Green *H & W* 47 SO7350
Longleys *Tays* 126 NO2643
Longmanhill *Gramp* 142 NJ7362
Longmoor Camp *Hants* 14 SU7931
Longmorn *Gramp* 141 NJ2358
Longmoss *Ches* 79 SJ8974
Longnewton *Border* 110 NT5827
Longnewton *Cleve* 96 NZ3816
Longney *Gloucs* 35 SO7612
Longniddry *Loth* 118 NT4476
Longnor *Shrops* 59 SJ4800
Longnor *Staffs* 74 SK0864
Longparish *Hants* 24 SU4345
Longpark *Cumb* 101 NY4362
Longridge *Lancs* 81 SD6037
Longridge *Loth* 116 NS9462
Longridge *Staffs* 72 SJ9015
Longriggend *Strath* 116 NS8270
Longrock *Cnwll* 2 SW5031
Longsdon *Staffs* 72 SJ9654
Longshaw Common *Gt Man* 78 SD5302
Longside *Gramp* 143 NK0347
Longslow *Shrops* 72 SJ6535
Longstanton *Cambs* 52 TL3966
Longstock *Hants* 23 SU3537
Longstone *Dyfed* 31 SN1409
Longstowe *Cambs* 52 TL3054
Longstreet *Wilts* 23 SU1451
Longthorpe *Cambs* 64 TL1698
Longthwaite *Cumb* 93 NY4323
Longton *Lancs* 80 SD4825
Longton *Staffs* 72 SJ9143
Longtown *Cumb* 101 NY3768
Longtown *H & W* 46 SO3229
Longueville *Jersey* 152 JS1708
Longville in the Dale *Shrops* 59 SO5393
Longwick *Bucks* 38 SP7905
Longwitton *Nthumb* 103 NZ0788
Longwood *D & G* 99 NX7060
Longwood *Shrops* 59 SJ6007
Longwood House *Hants* 13 SU5324
Longworth *Oxon* 36 SU3899
Longyester *Loth* 118 NT5465
Lonmay *Gramp* 143 NK0159
Lonmore *Highld* 136 NG2646
Looe *Cnwll* 5 SX2553
Loose *Kent* 28 TQ7552
Loosebeare *Devon* 8 SS7105
Loosegate *Lincs* 64 TF3125
Loosley Row *Bucks* 37 SP8100
Lootcherbrae *Gramp* 142 NJ6053
Lopcombe Corner *Wilts* 23 SU2535
Lopen *Somset* 10 ST4214
Loppington *Shrops* 59 SJ4629
Lorbottle *Nthumb* 111 NU0306
Lordington *W Susx* 14 SU7809
Lordsbridge *Norfk* 65 TF5712
Lornty *Tays* 126 NO1746
Loscoe *Derbys* 62 SK4247
Loscombe *Dorset* 10 SY4997
Lossiemouth *Gramp* 141 NJ2370
Lostford *Shrops* 59 SJ6231
Lostock Gralam *Ches* 79 SJ6974
Lostock Green *Ches* 79 SJ6973
Lostock Hall Fold *Gt Man* 79 SD6509
Lostock Junction *Gt Man* 79 SD6708
Lostwithiel *Cnwll* 4 SX1059
Lothbeg *Highld* 147 NC9410
Lothersdale *N York* 82 SD9545
Lothmore *Highld* 147 NC9611
Loudwater *Bucks* 26 SU9090
Loughborough *Leics* 62 SK5319
Loughor *W Glam* 32 SS5698
Loughton *Bucks* 38 SP8337
Loughton *Essex* 27 TQ4296
Loughton *Shrops* 59 SO6182
Lound *Lincs* 64 TF0618
Lound *Notts* 75 SK6986
Lound *Suffk* 67 TM5099
Lounston *Devon* 7 SX7875
Lount *Leics* 62 SK3819
Louth *Lincs* 77 TF3287
Love Clough *Lancs* 81 SD8127
Lovedean *Hants* 13 SU6812
Lover *Wilts* 12 SU2120
Loversall *S York* 75 SK5798
Loves Green *Essex* 40 TL6404
Lovesome Hill *N York* 89 SE3699
Loveston *Dyfed* 31 SN0808
Lovington *Somset* 21 ST5930
Low Ackworth *W York* 83 SE4517
Low Angerton *Nthumb* 103 NZ0984
Low Barbeth *D & G* 98 NX0166
Low Barlings *Lincs* 76 TF0873
Low Bell End *N York* 90 SE7197
Low Bentham *N York* 87 SD6469
Low Biggins *Cumb* 87 SD6077
Low Borrowbridge *Cumb* 87 NY6101
Low Bradfield *S York* 74 SK2691
Low Bradley *N York* 82 SE0048
Low Braithwaite *Cumb* 93 NY4242
Low Burnham *Humb* 84 SE7802
Low Buston *Nthumb* 111 NU2207
Low Catton *Humb* 84 SE7053
Low Coniscliffe *Dur* 89 NZ2513
Low Dinsdale *Dur* 89 NZ3411
Low Eggborough *N York* 83 SE5623
Low Ellington *N York* 89 SE1983
Low Fell *T & W* 96 NZ2559
Low Gartachorrans *Cent* 115 NS4685
Low Gettbridge *Cumb* 94 NY5259
Low Grantley *N York* 89 SE2370
Low Green *N York* 89 SE2059
Low Habberley *H & W* 60 SO8077
Low Ham *Somset* 21 ST4329
Low Harrogate *N York* 82 SE2955
Low Hawsker *N York* 91 NZ9207
Low Hesket *Cumb* 93 NY4646
Low Hill *H & W* 60 SO8473
Low Hutton *N York* 90 SE7667
Low Knipe *Cumb* 94 NY5119
Low Laithe *N York* 89 SE1963
Low Langton *Lincs* 76 TF1576
Low Leighton *Derbys* 79 SK0085
Low Lorton *Cumb* 92 NY1525
Low Marnham *Notts* 75 SK8069
Low Middleton *Nthumb* 111 NU1035
Low Mill *N York* 90 SE6795
Low Moor *Lancs* 81 SD7341
Low Moor *W York* 82 SE1628
Low Moorsley *T & W* 96 NZ3446
Low Mowthorpe *N York* 91 SE8966
Low Newton *Cumb* 87 SD4082
Low Rogerscales *Cumb* 92 NY1426
Low Row *Cumb* 93 NY1944
Low Row *Cumb* 93 NY3536
Low Row *Cumb* 102 NY5863
Low Row *N York* 88 SD9797
Low Salchrie *D & G* 98 NX0365
Low Santon *Humb* 84 SE9412
Low Skeog *D & G* 99 NX4540
Low Street *Essex* 28 TQ6677
Low Street *Norfk* 67 TG3423
Low Tharston *Norfk* 66 TM1895
Low Toynton *Lincs* 77 TF2770
Low Valley *S York* 83 SE4003
Low Walworth *Dur* 96 NZ2417
Low Wood *Cumb* 87 SD3483
Low Worsall *N York* 89 NZ3909
Low Wray *Cumb* 87 NY3701
Lowbands *H & W* 47 SO7731
Lowca *Cumb* 92 NX9821
Lowdham *Notts* 63 SK6646
Lowe *Shrops* 59 SJ4930
Lowe Hill *Staffs* 73 SJ9955
Lower Aisholt *Somset* 20 ST2035
Lower Ansty *Dorset* 11 ST7603
Lower Apperley *Gloucs* 47 SO8527
Lower Arncott *Oxon* 37 SP6019
Lower Ashton *Devon* 8 SX8484
Lower Assendon *Oxon* 37 SU7484
Lower Ballam *Lancs* 80 SD3631
Lower Barewood *H & W* 46 SO3956
Lower Bartle *Lancs* 80 SD4933
Lower Bayston *Shrops* 59 SJ4908
Lower Beeding *W Susx* 15 TQ2127
Lower Benefield *Nhants* 51 SP9988
Lower Bentley *H & W* 47 SO9865
Lower Beobridge *Shrops* 60 SO7891
Lower Berry Hill *Gloucs* 34 SO5711
Lower Birchwood *Derbys* 75 SK4354
Lower Boddington *Nhants* 49 SP4852
Lower Boscaswell *Cnwll* 2 SW3734
Lower Bourne *Surrey* 25 SU8444
Lower Brailes *Warwks* 48 SP3139
Lower Breakish *Highld* 129 NG6723
Lower Bredbury *Gt Man* 79 SJ9191
Lower Broadheath *H & W* 47 SO8157
Lower Buckenhill *H & W* 46 SO6033
Lower Bullingham *H & W* 46 SO5138
Lower Burgate *Hants* 12 SU1515
Lower Burrowton *Devon* 9 SY0097
Lower Burton *H & W* 46 SO4256
Lower Caldecote *Beds* 52 TL1746
Lower Cam *Gloucs* 35 SO7400
Lower Canada *Avon* 21 ST3558
Lower Catesby *Nhants* 49 SP5159
Lower Chapel *Powys* 45 SO0235
Lower Chicksgrove *Wilts* 22 ST9729
Lower Chute *Wilts* 23 SU3153
Lower Clapton *Gt Lon* 27 TQ3485
Lower Clent *H & W* 60 SO9279
Lower Creedy *Devon* 8 SS8402
Lower Crossings *Derbys* 74 SK0480
Lower Cumberworth *W York* 82 SE2209
Lower Cwmtwrch *Powys* 32 SN7610
Lower Darwen *Lancs* 81 SD6825
Lower Dean *Beds* 51 TL0569
Lower Denby *W York* 82 SE2307
Lower Diabaig *Highld* 137 NG7960
Lower Dicker *E Susx* 16 TQ5511
Lower Dinchope *Shrops* 59 SO4584
Lower Down *Shrops* 59 SO3484
Lower Dunsforth *N York* 89 SE4464
Lower Egleton *H & W* 47 SO6245
Lower Elkstone *Staffs* 74 SK0658
Lower Ellastone *Staffs* 73 SK1142
Lower End *Bucks* 37 SP6809
Lower End *Bucks* 38 SP9238
Lower End *Nhants* 51 SP8861
Lower Everleigh *Wilts* 23 SU1854
Lower Exbury *Hants* 13 SZ4299
Lower Eythorne *Kent* 29 TR2849
Lower Failand *Avon* 34 ST5173
Lower Farringdon *Hants* 24 SU7035
Lower Feltham *Gt Lon* 26 TQ0971
Lower Fittleworth *W Susx* 14 TQ0118
Lower Frankton *Shrops* 59 SJ3732
Lower Freystrop *Dyfed* 30 SM9512
Lower Froyle *Hants* 24 SU7544
Lower Gabwell *Devon* 7 SX9169
Lower Gledfield *Highld* 146 NH5890
Lower Godney *Somset* 21 ST4742
Lower Gornal *W Mids* 60 SO9191
Lower Gravenhurst *Beds* 38 TL1035
Lower Green *Essex* 39 TL4334
Lower Green *Gt Man* 79 SJ7098
Lower Green *Herts* 39 TL1832
Lower Green *Herts* 39 TL4233
Lower Green *Kent* 16 TQ5640
Lower Green *Kent* 16 TQ6341
Lower Green *Nhants* 51 SP8159
Lower Green *Norfk* 66 TF9837
Lower Green *Staffs* 60 SJ9007
Lower Green *Suffk* 53 TL7465
Lower Hacheston *Suffk* 55 TM3156
Lower Halliford *Surrey* 26 TQ0866
Lower Halstock Leigh *Dorset* 10 ST5207
Lower Halstow *Kent* 28 TQ8567
Lower Hamworthy *Dorset* 11 SY9990
Lower Hardres *Kent* 29 TR1553
Lower Harpton *H & W* 46 SO2760
Lower Hartshay *Derbys* 74 SK3851
Lower Hartwell *Bucks* 38 SP7912
Lower Hatton *Staffs* 72 SJ8236
Lower Hawthwaite *Cumb* 86 SD2189
Lower Hergest *H & W* 46 SO2755
Lower Heyford *Oxon* 49 SP4824
Lower Heysham *Lancs* 87 SD4160
Lower Higham *Kent* 28 TQ7172
Lower Holbrook *Suffk* 54 TM1834
Lower Hordley *Shrops* 59 SJ3929
Lower Horncroft *W Susx* 14 TQ0017
Lower Howsell *H & W* 47 SO7848
Lower Irlam *Gt Man* 79 SJ7193
Lower Kilburn *Derbys* 62 SK3744
Lower Kilcott *Avon* 35 ST7889
Lower Killeyan *Strath* 104 NR2742
Lower Kingcombe *Dorset* 10 SY5599
Lower Kingswood *Surrey* 26 TQ2453
Lower Kinnerton *Ches* 71 SJ3462
Lower Langford *Avon* 21 ST4560
Lower Largo *Fife* 126 NO4102
Lower Leigh *Staffs* 73 SK0135
Lower Lemington *Gloucs* 48 SP2134
Lower Llanfadog *Powys* 45 SN9567
Lower Lovacott *Devon* 19 SS5227
Lower Loxhore *Devon* 19 SS6137
Lower Lydbrook *Gloucs* 34 SO5916
Lower Lye *H & W* 46 SO4066
Lower Machen *Gwent* 34 ST2288
Lower Maes-coed *H & W* 46 SO3430
Lower Mannington *Dorset* 12 SU0604
Lower Marston *Somset* 22 ST7644
Lower Meend *Gloucs* 34 SO5504
Lower Middleton Cheney *Nhants* 49 SP5041
Lower Milton *Somset* 21 ST5347
Lower Moor *W Mids* 47 SO9747
Lower Morton *Avon* 35 ST6491
Lower Nazeing *Essex* 39 TL3906
Lower Norton *Warwks* 48 SP2363
Lower Nyland *Dorset* 22 ST7521
Lower Penarth *S Glam* 20 ST1869
Lower Penn *Staffs* 60 SO8796
Lower Pennington *Hants* 12 SZ3193
Lower Penwortham *Lancs* 80 SD5327
Lower Peover *Ches* 79 SJ7474
Lower Place *Gt Man* 81 SD9011
Lower Pollicott *Bucks* 37 SP7013
Lower Pond Street *Essex* 39 TL4537
Lower Quinton *Warwks* 48 SP1847
Lower Rainham *Kent* 28 TQ8167
Lower Raydon *Suffk* 54 TM0338
Lower Roadwater *Somset* 20 ST0339
Lower Salter *Lancs* 87 SD6063
Lower Seagry *Wilts* 35 ST9580
Lower Sheering *Essex* 39 TL4914
Lower Shelton *Beds* 38 SP9942
Lower Shiplake *Oxon* 37 SU7679
Lower Shuckburgh *Warwks* 49 SP4862
Lower Slaughter *Gloucs* 36 SP1622
Lower Soothill *W York* 82 SE2523
Lower Soudley *Gloucs* 35 SO6609
Lower Standen *Kent* 29 TR2340
Lower Stanton St Quintin *Wilts* 35 ST9180
Lower Stoke *Kent* 28 TQ8375
Lower Stone *Gloucs* 35 ST6794
Lower Stonnall *Staffs* 61 SK0803
Lower Stow Bedon *Norfk* 66 TL9694
Lower Street *Dorset* 11 SY8399
Lower Street *E Susx* 16 TQ7012
Lower Street *Norfk* 67 TG2635
Lower Street *Suffk* 53 TL7852
Lower Street *Suffk* 54 TM1052
Lower Stretton *Ches* 79 SJ6281
Lower Stroud *Dorset* 10 SY4598
Lower Sundon *Beds* 38 TL0526
Lower Swanwick *Hants* 13 SU4909
Lower Swell *Gloucs* 48 SP1725
Lower Tadmarton *Oxon* 48 SP4036
Lower Tale *Devon* 9 ST0601
Lower Tean *Staffs* 73 SK0138
Lower Thurlton *Norfk* 67 TM4299
Lower Town *Cnwll* 2 SW6528
Lower Town *Devon* 7 SX7172
Lower Town *Dyfed* 30 SM9637
Lower Town *H & W* 47 SO6342
Lower Tregantle *Cnwll* 5 SX3953
Lower Treluswell *Cnwll* 3 SW7735
Lower Tysoe *Warwks* 48 SP3445
Lower Ufford *Suffk* 55 TM2952
Lower Upcott *Devon* 9 SX8880
Lower Upham *Hants* 13 SU5219
Lower Upnor *Kent* 28 TQ7571
Lower Vexford *Somset* 20 ST1135
Lower Walton *Ches* 78 SJ6086
Lower Waterston *Dorset* 11 SY7395
Lower Weare *Somset* 21 ST4053
Lower Welson *H & W* 46 SO2950
Lower Westmancote *H & W* 47 SO9337
Lower Whatcombe *Dorset* 11 ST8401
Lower Whatley *Somset* 22 ST7447
Lower Whitley *Ches* 71 SJ6179
Lower Wick *Gloucs* 35 ST7096
Lower Wick *H & W* 47 SO8352
Lower Wield *Hants* 24 SU6340
Lower Wigginton *Herts* 38 SP9409
Lower Willingdon *E Susx* 16 TQ5803
Lower Winchendon *Bucks* 37 SP7312
Lower Woodend *Bucks* 37 SU8187
Lower Woodford *Wilts* 23 SU1235
Lower Wraxhall *Dorset* 10 ST5700
Lower Wyche *H & W* 47 SO7743
Lower Wyke *W York* 82 SE1525
Lowerhouse *Lancs* 81 SD8032
Lowesby *Leics* 63 SK7207
Lowestoft *Suffk* 67 TM5493
Loweswater *Cumb* 92 NY1421
Lowfield Heath *W Susx* 15 TQ2739
Lowgill *Cumb* 87 SD6297
Lowgill *Lancs* 87 SD6564
Lowick *Cumb* 86 SD2885
Lowick *Nhants* 51 SP9881
Lowick *Nthumb* 111 NU0139
Lowick Bridge *Cumb* 86 SD2986
Lowick Green *Cumb* 86 SD2985
Lowlands *Dur* 96 NZ1325
Lowlands *Gwent* 34 ST2996
Lowsonford *Warwks* 48 SP1868
Lowther *Cumb* 94 NY5323
Lowther Castle *Cumb* 94 NY5223
Lowtherton *D & G* 101 NY2466
Lowthorpe *Humb* 91 TA0860
Lowton *Devon* 8 SS6604
Lowton *Gt Man* 78 SJ6197
Lowton *Somset* 20 ST1918
Lowton Common *Gt Man* 79 SJ6397
Lowton St Mary's *Gt Man* 79 SJ6397
Loxbeare *Devon* 9 SS9116
Loxhill *Surrey* 25 TQ0038
Loxhore *Devon* 19 SS6138
Loxhore Cott *Devon* 19 SS6138
Loxley *Warwks* 48 SP2553
Loxley Green *Staffs* 73 SK0630
Loxter *H & W* 47 SO7140
Loxton *Avon* 21 ST3755
Loxwood *W Susx* 14 TQ0331
Lubenham *Nhants* 50 SP7087
Lucas Green *Surrey* 25 SU9460
Lucasgate *Lincs* 77 TF4147
Luccombe *Somset* 20 SS9243
Luccombe Village *IOW* 13 SZ5879
Lucker *Nthumb* 111 NU1530
Luckett *Cnwll* 5 SX3873
Lucking Street *Essex* 54 TL8134
Luckington *Wilts* 35 ST8383
Lucklawhill *Fife* 127 NO4221
Lucknam *Wilts* 35 ST8272
Luckwell Bridge *Somset* 20 SS9038
Lucott *Somset* 19 SS8645
Lucton *H & W* 46 SO4364
Lucy Cross *N York* 89 NZ2112
Ludborough *Lincs* 77 TF2995
Ludbrook *Devon* 7 SX6654
Ludchurch *Dyfed* 31 SN1411
Luddenden *W York* 82 SE0426
Luddenden Foot *W York* 82 SE0325
Luddenham Court *Kent* 28 TQ9963
Luddesdown *Kent* 28 TQ6666
Luddington *Humb* 84 SE8316
Luddington *Warwks* 48 SP1652
Luddington in the Brook *Nhants* 51 TL1083
Ludford *Lincs* 76 TF1989
Ludford *Shrops* 46 SO5174
Ludgershall *Bucks* 37 SP6517
Ludgershall *Wilts* 23 SU2650
Ludgvan *Cnwll* 2 SW5033
Ludham *Norfk* 67 TG3818
Ludlow *Shrops* 46 SO5175
Ludney *Somset* 10 ST3812
Ludwell *Wilts* 22 ST9122
Ludworth *Dur* 96 NZ3641
Luffincott *Devon* 5 SX3394
Luffness *Loth* 118 NT4780
Lugar *Strath* 107 NS5921
Lugg Green *H & W* 46 SO4462
Luggate Burn *Loth* 118 NT5974
Luggiebank *Strath* 116 NS7672
Lugsdale *Ches* 78 SJ5285
Lugton *Strath* 115 NS4152
Lugwardine *H & W* 46 SO5540
Luib *Highld* 137 NG5627
Lulham *H & W* 46 SO4141
Lullington *Derbys* 61 SK2412
Lullington *E Susx* 16 TQ5202
Lullington *Somset* 22 ST7851
Lulsgate Bottom *Avon* 21 ST5165
Lulsley *H & W* 47 SO7455
Lulworth Camp *Dorset* 11 SY8381
Lumb *Lancs* 81 SD8324
Lumb *W York* 82 SE0221
Lumbutts *W York* 82 SD9523
Lumby *N York* 83 SE4830
Lumloch *Strath* 116 NS6370
Lumphanan *Gramp* 134 NJ5804
Lumphinnans *Fife* 117 NT1792
Lumsden *Gramp* 142 NJ4722
Lunan *Tays* 127 NO6851
Lunanhead *Tays* 127 NO4752
Luncarty *Tays* 125 NO0929
Lund *Humb* 84 SE9647
Lund *N York* 83 SE6532
Lundford Magna *Lincs* 76 TF1989
Lundie *Cent* 124 NN7304
Lundie *Tays* 126 NO2836
Lundin Links *Fife* 126 NO4002
Lundy Green *Norfk* 67 TM2392
Lunna *Shet* 155 HU4869
Lunsford *Kent* 28 TQ6959
Lunsford's Cross *E Susx* 17 TQ7210
Lunt *Mersyd* 78 SD3402
Luntley *H & W* 46 SO3955
Luppitt *Devon* 9 ST1606
Lupridge *Devon* 7 SX7153
Lupset *W York* 82 SE3119
Lupton *Cumb* 87 SD5581
Lurgashall *W Susx* 14 SU9326
Lurley *Devon* 9 SS9215
Lusby *Lincs* 77 TF3467
Luscombe *Devon* 7 SX7957
Luson *Devon* 6 SX6050
Luss *Strath* 115 NS3692
Lusta *Highld* 136 NG2656
Lustleigh *Devon* 8 SX7881
Luston *H & W* 46 SO4863
Luthermuir *Gramp* 135 NO6568
Luthrie *Fife* 126 NO3319
Lutley *W Mids* 60 SO9382
Luton *Beds* 38 TL0921
Luton *Devon* 9 ST0802
Luton *Devon* 9 SX9076

Luton Minsterworth

Luton Kent 28 TQ7766
Lutterworth Leics 50 SP5484
Lutton Devon 6 SX5959
Lutton Dorset 11 SY8980
Lutton Lincs 65 TF4325
Lutton Nhants 52 TL1187
Luxborough Somset 20 SS9738
Luxulyan Cnwll 4 SX0558
Luzley Gt Man 79 SD9600
Lybster Highld 151 ND2435
Lydbury North Shrops 59 SO3486
Lydcott Devon 19 SS6936
Lydd Kent 17 TR0420
Lydden Kent 29 TR2645
Lydden Kent 29 TR3567
Lyddington Leics 51 SP8797
Lyde Green Hants 24 SU7057
Lydeard St Lawrence Somset 20 ST1332
Lydford Devon 5 SX5185
Lydford on Fosse Somset 21 ST5630
Lydgate Gt Man 82 SD9516
Lydgate W York 81 SD9225
Lydham Shrops 59 SO3391
Lydiard Green Wilts 36 SU0885
Lydiard Millicent Wilts 36 SU0986
Lydiard Tregoze Wilts 36 SU1085
Lydiate Mersyd 78 SD3604
Lydiate Ash H & W 60 SO9775
Lydlinch Dorset 11 ST7413
Lydney Gloucs 35 SO6303
Lydstep Dyfed 31 SS0898
Lye W Mids 60 SO9284
Lye Cross Avon 21 ST4962
Lye Green Bucks 38 SP9703
Lye Green E Susx 16 TQ5134
Lye Green Warwks 48 SP1965
Lye Head H & W 60 SO7573
Lye's Green Wilts 22 ST8146
Lyford Oxon 36 SU3994
Lymbridge Green Kent 29 TR1244
Lyme Border 109 NT2041
Lyme Regis Dorset 10 SY3492
Lyminge Kent 29 TR1641
Lymington Hants 12 SZ3295
Lyminster W Susx 14 TQ0204
Lymm Ches 79 SJ6887
Lympne Kent 17 TR1135
Lympsham Somset 21 ST3354
Lympstone Devon 9 SX9984
Lynbridge Devon 19 SS7248
Lynch Somset 20 SS9047
Lynch Green Norfk 66 TG1505
Lynchat Highld 132 NH7801
Lyndhurst Hants 12 SU3008
Lyndon Leics 63 SK9004
Lyndon Green W Mids 61 SP1485
Lyne Surrey 26 TQ0166
Lyne Down H & W 47 SO6431
Lyne Hill Staffs 60 SJ9212
Lyne of Skene Gramp 135 NJ7610
Lyneal Shrops 59 SJ4433
Lyneham Devon 8 SX8579
Lyneham Oxon 36 SP2720
Lyneham Wilts 35 SU0278
Lyneholmford Cumb 101 NY5172
Lynemouth Nthumb 103 NZ2991
Lyness Ork 155 ND3094
Lyng Norfk 66 TG0617
Lyng Somset 21 ST3329
Lynhales H & W 46 SO3255
Lynmouth Devon 19 SS7249
Lynn Shrops 72 SJ7815
Lynn of Shenval Gramp 141 NJ2129
Lynsted Kent 28 TQ9460
Lynstone Cnwll 18 SS2005
Lynton Devon 19 SS7249
Lyon's Gate Dorset 11 ST6505
Lyonshall H & W 46 SO3355
Lytchett Matravers Dorset 11 SY9495
Lytchett Minster Dorset 11 SY9693
Lyth Highld 151 ND2762
Lytham Lancs 80 SD3627
Lytham St Anne's Lancs 80 SD3427
Lythbank Shrops 59 SJ4607
Lythe N York 90 NZ8413
Lythmore Highld 150 ND0566

M

Mabe Burnthouse Cnwll 3 SW7634
Mabie D & G 100 NX9570
Mablethorpe Lincs 77 TF5085
Macclesfield Ches 79 SJ9173
Macclesfield Forest Ches 79 SJ9772
Macduff Gramp 142 NJ7064
Macharioch Strath 105 NR7309
Machen M Glam 33 ST2189
Machire Strath 112 NR2164
Machrie Farm Strath 105 NR9033
Machrihanish Strath 104 NR6320
Machrins Strath 112 NR3693
Machynlleth Powys 57 SH7400
Machynys Dyfed 32 SS5198
Mackworth Derbys 62 SK3137
Macmerry Loth 118 NT4372
Maddaford Devon 8 SX5494
Madderty Tays 125 NN9522
Maddington Wilts 23 SU0744
Maddiston Cent 116 NS9476
Madehurst W Susx 14 SU9810
Madeley Shrops 60 SJ6904
Madeley Staffs 72 SJ7744
Madeley Heath Staffs 72 SJ7845
Madford Devon 9 ST1411
Madingley Cambs 52 TL3960
Madley H & W 46 SO4238
Madresfield H & W 47 SO8047
Madron Cnwll 2 SW4531
Maen-y-groes Dyfed 42 SN3858
Maenaddwyn Gwynd 68 SH4684
Maenan Gwynd 69 SH7965
Maenclochog Dyfed 31 SN0827
Maendy S Glam 33 ST0076
Maenporth Cnwll 3 SW7829
Maentwrog Gwynd 57 SH6640
Maer Cnwll 18 SS2008
Maer Staffs 72 SJ7938
Maerdy M Glam 33 SS9798
Maes-glas Gwent 34 ST2985
Maesbrook Shrops 59 SJ3021
Maesbury Shrops 59 SJ3026
Maesbury Marsh Shrops 59 SJ3125
Maesgwynne Dyfed 31 SN2024
Maeshafn Clwyd 70 SJ2061
Maesllyn Dyfed 42 SN3644
Maesmynis Powys 45 SO0146
Maesmynis Powys 45 SO0349
Maesteg M Glam 33 SS8590
Maesybont Dyfed 32 SN5616
Maesycwmmer M Glam 33 ST1594
Magdalen Laver Essex 39 TL5108
Maggieknockater Gramp 141 NJ3145
Maggots End Essex 39 TL4827
Magham Down E Susx 16 TQ6011
Maghull Mersyd 78 SD3703
Magor Gwent 34 ST4286
Maiden Bradley Wilts 22 ST8038
Maiden Head Avon 21 ST5666
Maiden Law Dur 96 NZ1749
Maiden Newton Dorset 10 SY5997
Maiden Wells Dyfed 30 SR9799
Maidencombe Devon 7 SX9268
Maidenhayne Devon 10 SY2795
Maidenhead Berks 26 SU8980
Maidens Strath 106 NS2107
Maidens Green Berks 25 SU8972
Maidenwell Lincs 77 TF3179
Maidford Nhants 49 SP6052
Maids Moreton Bucks 49 SP7035
Maidstone Kent 28 TQ7555
Maidwell Nhants 50 SP7476
Mains of Bainakettle Gramp 134 NO6274
Mains of Balhall Tays 134 NO5163
Mains of Dalvey Highld 141 NJ1132
Mains of Haulkerton Gramp 135 NO7172
Mainsforth Dur 96 NZ3131
Mainsriddle D & G 92 NX9456
Mainstone Shrops 58 SO2787
Maisemore Gloucs 35 SO8121
Major's Green H & W 61 SP1077
Makeney Derbys 62 SK3544
Malborough Devon 7 SX7139
Malcoff Derbys 74 SK0782
Malden Surrey 26 TQ2166
Malden Rushett Gt Lon 26 TQ1761
Maldon Essex 40 TL8506
Malham N York 88 SD9063
Mallaig Highld 129 NM6796
Mallaigvaig Highld 129 NM6897
Malleny Mills Loth 117 NT1665
Mallows Green Essex 39 TL4726
Malltraeth Gwynd 68 SH4068
Mallwyd Gwynd 57 SH8612
Malmesbury Wilts 35 ST9387
Malmsmead Somset 19 SS7947
Malpas Ches 71 SJ4847
Malpas Cnwll 3 SW8442
Malpas Gwent 34 ST3090
Maltby Cleve 89 NZ4613
Maltby Lincs 77 TF3183
Maltby S York 75 SK5392
Maltby le Marsh Lincs 77 TF4681
Malting Green Essex 41 TL9720
Maltman's Hill Kent 28 TQ9043
Malton N York 90 SE7871
Malvern Link H & W 47 SO7947
Malvern Wells H & W 47 SO7742
Malzie D & G 99 NX3754
Mamble H & W 60 SO6871
Mamhilad Gwent 34 SO3003
Manaccan Cnwll 3 SW7624
Manafon Powys 58 SJ1102
Manaton Devon 8 SX7581
Manby Lincs 77 TF3986
Mancetter Warwks 61 SP3296
Manchester Gt Man 79 SJ8497
Mancot Clwyd 71 SJ3167
Mandally Highld 131 NH2900
Manea Cambs 53 TL4789
Maney W Mids 61 SP1195
Manfield N York 89 NZ2113
Mangerton Dorset 10 SY4995
Mangotsfield Avon 35 ST6676
Mangrove Green Herts 38 TL1224
Manhay Cnwll 2 SW6930
Manish W Isls 154 NG1089
Mankinholes W York 82 SD9523
Manley Ches 71 SJ5071
Manmoel Gwent 33 SO1803
Mannel Strath 120 NL9840
Manning's Heath W Susx 15 TQ2028
Manningford Bohune Wilts 23 SU1357
Manningford Bruce Wilts 23 SU1358
Manningham W York 82 SE1435
Mannington Dorset 12 SU0605
Manningtree Essex 41 TM1031
Mannofield Gramp 135 NJ9104
Manor Park Gt Lon 27 TQ4285
Manorbier Dyfed 30 SS0697
Manorbier Newton Dyfed 30 SN0400
Manordeilo Dyfed 44 SN6726
Manorhill Border 110 NT6632
Manorowen Dyfed 30 SM9336
Mansell Gamage H & W 46 SO3944
Mansell Lacy H & W 46 SO4245
Mansergh Cumb 87 SD6082
Mansfield Notts 75 SK5361
Mansfield Strath 107 NS6214
Mansfield Woodhouse Notts 75 SK5363
Mansriggs Cumb 86 SD2980
Manston Dorset 11 ST8115
Manston Kent 29 TR3466
Manston W York 83 SE3634
Manswood Dorset 11 ST9708
Manthorpe Lincs 63 SK9137
Manthorpe Lincs 64 TF0715
Manton Humb 84 SE9302
Manton Leics 63 SK8704
Manton Notts 75 SK6078
Manton Wilts 23 SU1768
Manuden Essex 39 TL4926
Manwood Green Essex 39 TL5412
Maolachy Strath 122 NM8913
Maperton Somset 22 ST6726
Maple Cross Herts 26 TQ0393
Maplebeck Notts 75 SK7060
Mapledurham Oxon 37 SU6776
Mapledurwell Hants 24 SU6851
Maplehurst W Susx 15 TQ1824
Maplescombe Kent 27 TQ5664
Mapleton Derbys 73 SK1647
Mapleton Kent 16 TQ4649
Mapperley Derbys 62 SK4342
Mapperley Park Notts 62 SK5842
Mapperton Dorset 10 SY5099
Mappleborough Green Warwks 48 SP0866
Mappleton Humb 85 TA2243
Mappowder Dorset 11 ST7306
Marazanvose Cnwll 3 SW7950
Marazion Cnwll 2 SW5130
Marbury Ches 71 SJ5645
March Cambs 65 TL4196
March Strath 108 NS9914
Marcham Oxon 37 SU4596
Marchamley Shrops 59 SJ5929
Marchamley Wood Shrops 59 SJ5831
Marchington Staffs 73 SK1330
Marchington Woodlands Staffs 73 SK1128
Marchros Gwynd 56 SH3125
Marchwiel Clwyd 71 SJ3547
Marchwood Hants 12 SU3810
Marcross S Glam 20 SS9269
Marden H & W 46 SO5146
Marden Kent 28 TQ7444
Marden Wilts 23 SU0857
Marden Ash Essex 27 TL5502
Marden Beech Kent 28 TQ7442
Marden Thorn Kent 28 TQ7642
Mardens Hill E Susx 16 TQ5032
Mardleybury Herts 39 TL2618
Mardy Gwent 34 SO3015
Mare Green Somset 21 ST3326
Marefield Leics 63 SK7407
Mareham le Fen Lincs 77 TF2761
Mareham on the Hill Lincs 77 TF2867
Marehay Derbys 62 SK3947
Marehill W Susx 14 TQ0618
Maresfield E Susx 16 TQ4624
Marfleet Humb 85 TA1429
Marford Clwyd 71 SJ3556
Margam W Glam 32 SS7887
Margaret Marsh Dorset 22 ST8218
Margaretting Essex 40 TL6701
Margaretting Tye Essex 40 TL6800
Margate Kent 29 TR3571
Margnaheglish Strath 105 NS0332
Margrie D & G 99 NX5950
Margrove Park Cleve 97 NZ6515
Marham Norfk 65 TF7009
Marhamchurch Cnwll 18 SS2203
Marholm Cambs 64 TF1401
Marian-glas Gwynd 68 SH5084
Mariansleigh Devon 19 SS7422
Marine Town Kent 28 TQ9274
Marionburgh Gramp 135 NJ7006
Marishader Highld 136 NG4963
Maristow Devon 6 SX4764
Marjoriebanks D & G 100 NY0883
Mark D & G 98 NX1157
Mark Somset 21 ST3847
Mark Causeway Somset 21 ST3547
Mark Cross E Susx 16 TQ5010
Mark Cross E Susx 16 TQ5831
Mark's Corner IOW 13 SZ4692
Markbeech Kent 16 TQ4742
Markby Lincs 77 TF4878
Markeaton Derbys 62 SK3237
Market Bosworth Leics 62 SK4002
Market Deeping Lincs 64 TF1310
Market Drayton Shrops 72 SJ6734
Market Harborough Leics 50 SP7387
Market Lavington Wilts 22 SU0154
Market Overton Leics 63 SK8816
Market Rasen Lincs 76 TF1089
Market Stainton Lincs 76 TF2279
Market Street Norfk 67 TG2921
Market Weighton Humb 84 SE8741
Market Weston Suffk 54 TL9877
Markfield Leics 62 SK4809
Markham Gwent 33 SO1601
Markham Moor Notts 75 SK7173
Markinch Fife 126 NO2901
Markington N York 89 SE2865
Marks Tey Essex 40 TL9023
Marksbury Avon 22 ST6662
Markshall Essex 40 TL8425
Markwell Cnwll 5 SX3758
Markyate Herts 38 TL0616
Marl Bank H & W 47 SO7840
Marlborough Wilts 23 SU1868
Marlbrook H & W 46 SO5154
Marlbrook H & W 60 SO9774
Marlcliff Warwks 48 SP0950
Marldon Devon 7 SX8663
Marle Green E Susx 16 TQ5816
Marlesford Suffk 55 TM3258
Marley Kent 29 TR1850
Marley Kent 29 TR3353
Marley Green Ches 71 SJ5845
Marley Hill T & W 96 NZ2058
Marlingford Norfk 66 TG1309
Marloes Dyfed 30 SM7908
Marlow Bucks 26 SU8486
Marlow H & W 46 SO4076
Marlpit Hill Kent 16 TQ4347
Marlpits E Susx 16 TQ4528
Marlpits E Susx 16 TQ7013
Marlpool Derbys 62 SK4345
Marnhull Dorset 22 ST7818
Marple Gt Man 79 SJ9588
Marple Bridge Gt Man 79 SJ9688
Marr S York 83 SE5105
Marrick N York 88 SE0798
Marros Dyfed 31 SN2008
Marsden T & W 103 NZ3964
Marsden W York 82 SE0411
Marsden Height Lancs 81 SD8636
Marsett N York 88 SD9085
Marsh Bucks 38 SP8109
Marsh Somset 10 ST2510
Marsh W York 82 SE0235
Marsh Baldon Oxon 37 SU5699
Marsh Gibbon Bucks 37 SP6422
Marsh Green Devon 9 SY0493
Marsh Green Kent 16 TQ4344
Marsh Green Shrops 59 SJ6014
Marsh Green Staffs 72 SJ8858
Marsh Lane Derbys 74 SK4079
Marsh Lane Gloucs 34 SO5807
Marsh Street Somset 20 SS9944
Marsh The Powys 59 SO3197
Marshall's Heath Herts 39 TL1614
Marshalswick Herts 39 TL1608
Marsham Norfk 67 TG1923
Marshborough Kent 29 TR3057
Marshbrook Shrops 59 SO4489
Marshchapel Lincs 77 TF3599
Marshfield Avon 35 ST7873
Marshfield Gwent 34 ST2582
Marshgate Cnwll 4 SX1592
Marshland Green Gt Man 79 SJ6899
Marshland St James Norfk 65 TF5209
Marshside Mersyd 80 SD3619
Marshwood Dorset 10 SY3899
Marske N York 89 NZ1000
Marske-by-the-Sea Cleve 97 NZ6322
Marston Ches 79 SJ6775
Marston H & W 46 SO3557
Marston Lincs 63 SK8943
Marston Oxon 37 SP5208
Marston Staffs 60 SJ8313
Marston Staffs 72 SJ9227
Marston Warwks 61 SP2094
Marston Wilts 22 ST9656
Marston Green W Mids 61 SP1785
Marston Jabbet Warwks 61 SP3788
Marston Magna Somset 21 ST5922
Marston Meysey Wilts 36 SU1297
Marston Montgomery Derbys 73 SK1337
Marston Moretaine Beds 38 SP9941
Marston on Dove Derbys 73 SK2329
Marston St Lawrence Nhants 49 SP5341
Marston Stannet H & W 46 SO5655
Marston Trussell Nhants 50 SP6985
Marstow H & W 34 SO5518
Marsworth Bucks 38 SP9114
Marten Wilts 23 SU2860
Marthall Ches 79 SJ7975
Martham Norfk 67 TG4518
Martin Hants 12 SU0619
Martin Kent 29 TR3447
Martin Lincs 76 TF1259
Martin Lincs 77 TF2466
Martin Dales Lincs 76 TF1762
Martin Drove End Hants 12 SU0520
Martin Hussingtree H & W 47 SO8860
Martindale Cumb 93 NY4319
Martinhoe Devon 19 SS6648
Martinscroft Ches 79 SJ6589
Martinstown Dorset 11 SY6489
Martlesham Suffk 55 TM2547
Martletwy Dyfed 30 SN0310
Martley H & W 47 SO7560
Martock Somset 21 ST4619
Marton Ches 71 SJ6267
Marton Ches 79 SJ8568
Marton Cleve 97 NZ5115
Marton Humb 85 TA1739
Marton Lincs 76 SK8381
Marton N York 89 SE4162
Marton N York 90 SE7383
Marton Shrops 58 SJ2802
Marton Warwks 48 SP4068
Marton-le-Moor N York 89 SE3770
Martyr Worthy Hants 24 SU5132
Martyr's Green Surrey 26 TQ0857
Marwick Ork 155 HY2324
Marwood Devon 19 SS5437
Mary Tavy Devon 5 SX5079
Marybank Highld 139 NH4853
Maryburgh Highld 139 NH5456
Maryculter Gramp 135 NO8599
Maryhill Gramp 143 NJ8245
Maryhill Strath 115 NS5669
Marykirk Gramp 135 NO6865
Maryland Gwent 34 SO5105
Marylebone Gt Man 78 SD5807
Marypark Gramp 141 NJ1938
Maryport Cumb 92 NY0336
Maryport D & G 98 NX1434
Marystow Devon 5 SX4382
Maryton Tays 127 NO6856
Marywell Gramp 135 NO9399
Marywell Tays 134 NO5895
Marywell Tays 127 NO6544
Masham N York 89 SE2280
Mashbury Essex 40 TL6511
Mason T & W 103 NZ2073
Masongill N York 87 SD6675
Mastin Moor Derbys 75 SK4575
Matching Essex 39 TL5212
Matching Green Essex 39 TL5311
Matching Tye Essex 39 TL5111
Matfen Nthumb 103 NZ0371
Matfield Kent 28 TQ6541
Mathern Gwent 34 ST5290
Mathon H & W 47 SO7346
Mathry Dyfed 30 SM8832
Matlaske Norfk 66 TG1534
Matlock Derbys 74 SK3059
Matlock Bank Derbys 74 SK3060
Matlock Bath Derbys 74 SK2958
Matlock Dale Derbys 74 SK2959
Matson Gloucs 35 SO8515
Matterdale End Cumb 93 NY3923
Mattersey Notts 75 SK6889
Mattersey Thorpe Notts 75 SK6889
Mattingley Hants 24 SU7357
Mattishall Norfk 66 TG0511
Mattishall Burgh Norfk 66 TG0512
Mauchline Strath 107 NS4927
Maud Gramp 143 NJ9148
Maufant Jersey 152 JS1811
Maugersbury Gloucs 48 SP2025
Maughold IOM 153 SC4991
Mauld Highld 139 NH4038
Maulden Beds 38 TL0538
Maulds Meaburn Cumb 94 NY6216
Maunby N York 89 SE3586
Maund Bryan H & W 46 SO5650
Maundown Somset 20 ST0628
Mautby Norfk 67 TG4812
Mavesyn Ridware Staffs 73 SK0816
Mavis Enderby Lincs 77 TF3666
Maw Green Ches 72 SJ7057
Maw Green W Mids 60 SP0196
Mawbray Cumb 92 NY0846
Mawdesley Lancs 80 SD4914
Mawdlam M Glam 32 SS8081
Mawgan Cnwll 2 SW7025
Mawgan Cross Cnwll 2 SW7024
Mawgan Porth Cnwll 4 SW8567
Mawla Cnwll 2 SW7045
Mawnan Cnwll 3 SW7827
Mawnan Smith Cnwll 3 SW7728
Mawthorpe Lincs 77 TF4672
Maxey Cambs 64 TF1208
Maxstoke Warwks 61 SP2386
Maxted Street Kent 29 TR1244
Maxton Border 110 NT6130
Maxton Kent 29 TR3041
Maxwell Town D & G 100 NX9676
Maxwellheugh Border 110 NT7333
Maxworthy Cnwll 5 SX2593
May Bank Staffs 72 SJ8547
May's Green Oxon 37 SU7480
May's Green Surrey 26 TQ0957
Mayals W Glam 32 SS6089
Maybole Strath 106 NS2909
Maybury Surrey 26 TQ0159
Mayes Green Surrey 14 TQ1239
Mayfield E Susx 16 TQ5826
Mayfield Loth 118 NT3565
Mayfield Staffs 73 SK1545
Mayford Surrey 25 SU9956
Mayland Essex 40 TL9201
Maynard's Green E Susx 16 TQ5818
Maypole Gwent 34 SO4716
Maypole Kent 29 TR2064
Maypole W Mids 61 SP0778
Maypole Green Norfk 67 TM4195
Maypole Green Suffk 54 TL9159
Maypole Green Suffk 55 TM2767
Mead Devon 18 SS2217
Meadgate Avon 22 ST6758
Meadle Bucks 38 SP8005
Meadowfield Dur 96 NZ2439
Meadowhall S York 74 SK3991
Meadowtown Shrops 59 SJ3001
Meadwell Devon 5 SX4081
Meal Bank Cumb 87 SD5495
Mealrigg Cumb 92 NY1345
Mealsgate Cumb 93 NY2042
Meamskirk Strath 115 NS5455
Meanwood W York 82 SE2837
Mearbeck N York 88 SD8160
Meare Somset 21 ST4541
Meare Green Somset 20 ST2922
Mears Ashby Nhants 51 SP8366
Measham Leics 62 SK3311
Meathop Cumb 87 SD4380
Meaux Humb 85 TA0839
Meavy Devon 6 SX5467
Medbourne Leics 51 SP8093
Meddon Devon 18 SS2717
Medlam Lincs 77 TF3156
Medlar Lancs 80 SD4135
Medmenham Berks 37 SU8084
Medomsley Dur 95 NZ1154
Medstead Hants 24 SU6537
Meer Common H & W 46 SO3652
Meer End W Mids 61 SP2474
Meerbrook Staffs 72 SJ9860
Meesden Herts 39 TL4332
Meeson Shrops 72 SJ6421
Meeth Devon 19 SS5408
Meeting Green Suffk 53 TL7455
Meeting House Hill Norfk 67 TG3028
Meidrim Dyfed 31 SN2920
Meifod Powys 58 SJ1513
Meigle Tays 126 NO2844
Meikle Carco D & G 107 NS7813
Meikle Earnock Strath 116 NS7053
Meikle Kilmory Strath 114 NS0560
Meikle Obney Tays 125 NO0337
Meikle Wartle Gramp 142 NJ7230
Meikleour Tays 126 NO1539
Meinciau Dyfed 32 SN4610
Meir Staffs 72 SJ9342
Meir Heath Staffs 72 SJ9240
Melbourn Cambs 39 TL3844
Melbourne Derbys 62 SK3825
Melbourne Humb 84 SE7543
Melbury Devon 18 SS3719
Melbury Abbas Dorset 22 ST8820
Melbury Bubb Dorset 10 ST5906
Melbury Osmond Dorset 10 ST5707
Melbury Sampford Dorset 10 ST5705
Melchbourne Beds 51 TL0265
Melcombe Bingham Dorset 11 ST7602
Meldon Devon 8 SX5692
Meldon Nthumb 103 NZ1183
Meldreth Cambs 52 TL3746
Meldrum Cent 116 NS7299
Meledor Cnwll 3 SW9254
Melfort Strath 122 NM8313
Melgund Castle Tays 127 NO5455
Meliden Clwyd 70 SJ0680
Melin Court W Glam 33 SN8201
Melin-byrhedyn Powys 57 SN8198
Melin-y-coed Gwynd 69 SH8160
Melin-y-ddol Powys 58 SJ0807
Melin-y-wig Clwyd 70 SJ0448
Melinau Dyfed 31 SN1613
Melkinthorpe Cumb 94 NY5525
Melkridge Nthumb 102 NY7364
Melksham Wilts 22 ST9063
Mell Green Berks 37 SU4577
Mellangoose Cnwll 2 SW6826
Melldalloch Strath 114 NR9374
Mellguards Cumb 93 NY4445
Melling Lancs 87 SD5970
Melling Mersyd 78 SD3800
Melling Mount Mersyd 78 SD4001
Mellis Suffk 54 TM0974
Mellon Charles Highld 144 NG8491
Mellon Udrigle Highld 144 NG8996
Mellor Gt Man 79 SJ9888
Mellor Lancs 81 SD6530
Mellor Brook Lancs 81 SD6431
Mells Somset 22 ST7248
Mells Suffk 55 TM4076
Melmerby Cumb 94 NY6137
Melmerby N York 88 SE0785
Melmerby N York 89 SE3376
Melness Highld 149 NC5861
Melon Green Suffk 54 TL8456
Melplash Dorset 10 SY4898
Melrose Border 109 NT5434
Melsetter Ork 155 ND2689
Melsonby N York 89 NZ1908
Meltham S York 82 SE1010
Meltham Mills W York 82 SE1110
Melton Humb 84 SE9726
Melton Suffk 55 TM2850
Melton Constable Norfk 66 TG0432
Melton Mowbray Leics 63 SK7518
Melton Ross Humb 84 TA0610
Meltonby Humb 84 SE7952
Melvaig Highld 144 NG7486
Melverley Shrops 59 SJ3316
Melverley Green Shrops 59 SJ3317
Melvich Highld 150 NC8764
Membury Devon 10 ST2803
Memsie Gramp 143 NJ9762
Menabilly Cnwll 3 SX0951
Menagissey Cnwll 2 SW7146
Menai Bridge Gwynd 69 SH5571
Mendham Suffk 55 TM2782
Mendlesham Suffk 54 TM1065
Mendlesham Green Suffk 54 TM0963
Menheniot Cnwll 5 SX2863
Menithwood H & W 47 SO7069
Mennock D & G 108 NS8107
Menston W York 82 SE1643
Menstrie Cent 116 NS8597
Menthorpe N York 84 SE7034
Mentmore Bucks 38 SP9019
Meoble Highld 129 NM7987
Meole Brace Shrops 59 SJ4810
Meonstoke Hants 13 SU6119
Meopham Kent 27 TQ6466
Meopham Green Kent 27 TQ6465
Meopham Station Kent 27 TQ6467
Mepal Cambs 53 TL4481
Meppershall Beds 38 TL1336
Mere Ches 79 SJ7281
Mere Wilts 22 ST8132
Mere Brow Lancs 80 SD4218
Mere Green H & W 47 SO9562
Mere Green W Mids 61 SP1198
Mere Heath Ches 79 SJ6670
Mereclough Lancs 81 SD8730
Meresborough Kent 28 TQ8264
Mereworth Kent 28 TQ6553
Meriden W Mids 61 SP2482
Merkadale Highld 136 NG3931
Merlin's Bridge Dyfed 30 SM9414
Merrifield Devon 7 SX8147
Merrington Shrops 59 SJ4720
Merrion Dyfed 30 SR9397
Merriott Somset 10 ST4412
Merrivale Devon 6 SX5475
Merrow Surrey 26 TQ0250
Merry Field Hill Dorset 12 SU0201
Merry Hill Herts 26 TQ1394
Merry Hill W Mids 60 SO9286
Merry Lees Leics 62 SK4705
Merryhill W Mids 60 SO8897
Merrymeet Cnwll 5 SX2766
Mersham Kent 28 TR0540
Merstham Surrey 27 TQ2853
Merston W Susx 14 SU8902
Merstone IOW 13 SZ5285
Merther Cnwll 3 SW8644
Merthyr Dyfed 31 SN3520
Merthyr Cynog Powys 45 SN9837
Merthyr Dyfan S Glam 20 ST1168
Merthyr Mawr M Glam 33 SS8877
Merthyr Tydfil M Glam 33 SO0406
Merthyr Vale M Glam 33 ST0799
Merton Devon 19 SS5212
Merton Gt Lon 27 TQ2570
Merton Norfk 66 TL9098
Merton Oxon 37 SP5717
Meshaw Devon 19 SS7619
Messing Essex 40 TL8918
Messingham Humb 84 SE8904
Metfield Suffk 55 TM2980
Metherell Cnwll 5 SX4069
Metherin Cnwll 4 SX1174
Metheringham Lincs 76 TF0661
Methil Fife 118 NT3799
Methleigh Cnwll 2 SW6226
Methley W York 83 SE3926
Methley Junction W York 83 SE3925
Methlick Gramp 143 NJ8537
Methven Tays 125 NO0225
Methwold Norfk 65 TL7394
Methwold Hythe Norfk 65 TL7194
Mettingham Suffk 55 TM3689
Metton Norfk 67 TG2037
Mevagissey Cnwll 3 SX0144
Mexborough S York 75 SE4700
Mey Highld 151 ND2872
Meyllteyrn Gwynd 56 SH2332
Meysey Hampton Gloucs 36 SP1100
Miavaig W Isls 154 NB0834
Michaelchurch H & W 46 SO5225
Michaelchurch Escley H & W 46 SO3134
Michaelchurch-on-Arrow Powys 46 SO2450
Michaelston-le-Pit S Glam 33 ST1572
Michaelstone-y-Fedw Gwent 34 ST2484
Michaelstow Cnwll 4 SX0778
Michelcombe Devon 7 SX6969
Micheldever Hants 24 SU5139
Micheldever Station Hants 24 SU5143
Michelmersh Hants 23 SU3426
Mickfield Suffk 54 TM1361
Mickle Trafford Ches 71 SJ4469
Micklebring S York 75 SK5194
Mickleby N York 90 NZ8012
Micklefield W York 83 SE4432
Micklefield Green Herts 26 TQ0498
Mickleham Surrey 26 TQ1653
Mickleover Derbys 73 SK3033
Micklethwaite Cumb 93 NY2850
Micklethwaite W York 82 SE1041
Mickleton Dur 95 NY9623
Mickleton Gloucs 48 SP1643
Mickletown W York 83 SE4027
Mickley Derbys 74 SK3279
Mickley N York 89 SE2576
Mickley Green Suffk 54 TL8457
Mickley Square Nthumb 103 NZ0762
Mid Ardlaw Gramp 143 NJ9463
Mid Beltie Gramp 134 NJ6200
Mid Bockhampton Hants 12 SZ1796
Mid Calder Loth 117 NT0767
Mid Clyth Highld 151 ND2937
Mid Lavant W Susx 14 SU8508
Mid Mains Highld 139 NH4239
Mid Sannox Strath 105 NS0145
Mid Thorpe Lincs 77 TF2672
Mid Yell Shet 155 HU5190
Midbea Ork 155 HY4444
Middle Assendon Oxon 37 SU7385
Middle Aston Oxon 49 SP4726
Middle Barton Oxon 49 SP4325
Middle Chinnock Somset 10 ST4713
Middle Claydon Bucks 49 SP7225
Middle Duntisbourne Gloucs 35 SO9806
Middle Handley Derbys 74 SK4077
Middle Harling Norfk 54 TL9885
Middle Kames Strath 114 NR9189
Middle Littleton H & W 48 SP0847
Middle Madeley Staffs 72 SJ7745
Middle Maes-coed H & W 46 SO3333
Middle Mayfield Staffs 73 SK1444
Middle Mill Dyfed 30 SM8026
Middle Quarter Kent 28 TQ8938
Middle Rasen Lincs 76 TF0889
Middle Rocombe Devon 7 SX9069
Middle Salter Lancs 87 SD6062
Middle Stoford Somset 20 ST1821
Middle Stoke Kent 28 TQ8275
Middle Stoughton Somset 21 ST4249
Middle Street Essex 39 TL4005
Middle Street Gloucs 35 SO7704
Middle Taphouse Cnwll 4 SX1763
Middle Town IOS 2 SV8808
Middle Tysoe Warwks 48 SP3444
Middle Wallop Hants 23 SU2937
Middle Winterslow Wilts 23 SU2333
Middle Woodford Wilts 23 SU1136
Middle Yard Gloucs 35 SO8203
Middlebie D & G 101 NY2176
Middlebridge Tays 132 NN8866
Middlecliffe S York 83 SE4204
Middlecott Devon 8 SX7186
Middlegill D & G 108 NT0406
Middleham N York 89 SE1287
Middlehill Cnwll 5 SX2869
Middlehill Wilts 22 ST8168
Middlehope Shrops 59 SO4988
Middlemarsh Dorset 11 ST6707
Middlemore Devon 6 SX4973
Middlesbrough Cleve 97 NZ4919
Middlesceugh Cumb 93 NY4041
Middleshaw Cumb 87 SD5588
Middlesmoor N York 89 SE0973
Middlestone Dur 96 NZ2531
Middlestone Moor Dur 96 NZ2432
Middlestown W York 82 SE2617
Middlethird Border 110 NT6843
Middleton Cleve 97 NZ5233
Middleton Cumb 87 SD6285
Middleton Derbys 74 SK1963
Middleton Derbys 73 SK2755
Middleton Essex 54 TL8639
Middleton Gt Man 79 SD8705
Middleton H & W 46 SO5469
Middleton Hants 24 SU4244
Middleton Lancs 87 SD4258
Middleton Loth 118 NT3758
Middleton N York 90 SE7885
Middleton Nhants 51 SP8489
Middleton Norfk 65 TF6616
Middleton Nthumb 111 NU1035
Middleton Nthumb 103 NZ0584
Middleton Shrops 59 SJ3129
Middleton Shrops 46 SO5477
Middleton Strath 120 NL9443
Middleton Strath 115 NS3952
Middleton Suffk 55 TM4267
Middleton Tays 126 NO1206
Middleton W Glam 31 SS4287
Middleton W York 82 SE1249
Middleton W York 82 SE3028
Middleton Warwks 61 SP1798
Middleton Cheney Nhants 49 SP4941
Middleton Green Staffs 73 SJ9935
Middleton Hall Nthumb 111 NT9825
Middleton Moor Suffk 55 TM4167
Middleton One Row Dur 89 NZ3512
Middleton on the Hill H & W 46 SO5364
Middleton Priors Shrops 59 SO6290
Middleton Quernhow N York 89 SE3378
Middleton Scriven Shrops 60 SO6887
Middleton St George Dur 89 NZ3412
Middleton Stoney Oxon 49 SP5323
Middleton Tyas N York 89 NZ2205
Middleton-in-Teesdale Dur 95 NY9425
Middleton-on-Leven N York 89 NZ4609
Middleton-on-Sea W Susx 14 SU9600
Middleton-on-the-Wolds Humb 84 SE9449
Middletown Avon 34 ST4571
Middletown Cumb 86 NX9908
Middletown Powys 59 SJ3012
Middlewich Ches 72 SJ7066
Middlewood Cnwll 5 SX2775
Middlewood H & W 46 SO2844
Middlewood Green Suffk 54 TM0961
Middleyard Strath 107 NS5132
Middlezoy Somset 21 ST3733
Middridge Dur 96 NZ2426
Midford Avon 22 ST7660
Midge Hall Lancs 80 SD5122
Midgeholme Cumb 94 NY6359
Midgham Berks 24 SU5567
Midgley W York 82 SE0226
Midgley W York 82 SE2714
Midhopestones S York 74 SK2399
Midhurst W Susx 14 SU8821
Midlem Border 109 NT5227
Midney Somset 21 ST4927
Midpark Strath 114 NS0259
Midsomer Norton Avon 22 ST6654
Midtown Highld 149 NC5861
Midtown Brae Highld 144 NG8284
Midville Lincs 77 TF3756
Midway Ches 79 SJ9182
Migvie Gramp 134 NJ4306
Milborne Port Somset 22 ST6718
Milborne St Andrew Dorset 11 SY8097
Milborne Wick Somset 22 ST6620
Milbourne Nthumb 103 NZ1175
Milbourne Wilts 35 ST9587
Milburn Cumb 94 NY6529
Milbury Heath Avon 35 ST6790
Milby N York 89 SE4067
Milcombe Oxon 49 SP4134
Milden Suffk 54 TL9546
Mildenhall Suffk 53 TL7174
Mildenhall Wilts 36 SU2069
Mile Elm Wilts 35 ST9969
Mile End Essex 41 TL9927
Mile End Gloucs 34 SO5811
Mile End Suffk 55 TM3489
Mile Oak E Susx 15 TQ2407
Mile Oak Kent 28 TQ6743
Mile Oak Staffs 61 SK1802
Mile Town Kent 28 TQ9274
Milebrook Powys 46 SO3172
Milebush Kent 28 TQ7545
Mileham Norfk 66 TF9119
Miles Hope H & W 46 SO5764
Miles Platting Gt Man 79 SJ8599
Milesmark Fife 117 NT0688
Milfield Nthumb 110 NT9333
Milford Derbys 62 SK3545
Milford Devon 18 SS2322
Milford Powys 58 SO0991
Milford Staffs 72 SJ9720
Milford Surrey 25 SU9442
Milford Haven Dyfed 30 SM9005
Milford on Sea Hants 12 SZ2891
Milkwall Gloucs 34 SO5809
Mill Bank W York 82 SE0321
Mill Brow Gt Man 79 SJ9789
Mill Common Norfk 67 TG3201
Mill Common Suffk 55 TM4081
Mill Cross Devon 7 SX7361
Mill End Bucks 37 SU7885
Mill End Cambs 52 TL3180
Mill End Herts 39 TL3332
Mill Green Cambs 53 TL6245
Mill Green Essex 40 TL6301
Mill Green Herts 39 TL2410
Mill Green Lincs 64 TF2223
Mill Green Norfk 54 TM1384
Mill Green Staffs 73 SK0821
Mill Green Suffk 54 TL9542
Mill Green Suffk 54 TL9957
Mill Green Suffk 54 TM1360
Mill Green Suffk 55 TM3161
Mill Green W Mids 61 SK0701
Mill Hill E Susx 16 TQ6205
Mill Hill Gt Lon 26 TQ2292
Mill Meece Staffs 72 SJ8333
Mill of Drummond Tays 125 NN8315
Mill of Haldane Strath 115 NS3982
Mill of Uras Gramp 135 NO8680
Mill Side Cumb 87 SD4484
Mill Street Kent 28 TQ6957
Mill Street Norfk 66 TG0118
Mill Street Suffk 54 TM0672
Millais Jersey 152 JS0615
Milland W Susx 14 SU8328
Milland Marsh W Susx 14 SU8326
Millbeck Cumb 93 NY2526
Millbreck Gramp 143 NK0044
Millbrex Gramp 143 NJ8144
Millbridge Surrey 25 SU8442
Millbrook Beds 38 TL0138
Millbrook Cnwll 6 SX4252
Millbrook Gt Man 79 SJ9799
Millbrook Hants 12 SU3813
Millbrook Jersey 152 JS1210
Millbuie Gramp 135 NJ7909
Millburn Strath 107 NS4429
Millcombe Devon 7 SX8049
Millcorner E Susx 17 TQ8223
Millcraig Highld 146 NH6571
Milldale Staffs 73 SK1354
Millend Gloucs 34 SO5609
Millend Gloucs 35 ST7496
Miller's Dale Derbys 74 SK1473
Miller's Green Essex 40 TL5808
Millerhill Loth 118 NT3269
Millers Green Derbys 73 SK2852
Millerston Strath 116 NS6467
Millgate Lancs 81 SD8819
Millgreen Shrops 72 SJ6828
Millhalf H & W 46 SO2747
Millhayes Devon 9 ST2303
Millhead Lancs 87 SD4971
Millhouse Cumb 93 NY3637
Millhouse Strath 114 NR9570
Millhouse Green S York 82 SE2203
Millhousebridge D & G 100 NY1085
Millhouses S York 83 SE4204
Millhouses S York 74 SK3484
Millikenpark Strath 115 NS4162
Millin Cross Dyfed 30 SM9914
Millington Humb 84 SE8351
Millisle D & G 99 NX4547
Millness Cumb 87 SD5382
Millom Cumb 86 SD1780
Millook Cnwll 18 SX1899
Millpool Cnwll 2 SW5730
Millpool Cnwll 4 SX1170
Millport Strath 114 NS1654
Millthorpe Derbys 74 SK3167
Millthrop Cumb 87 SD6591
Milltimber Gramp 135 NJ8501
Milltown D & G 101 NY3375
Milltown Derbys 74 SK3561
Milltown Devon 19 SS5538
Milltown Gramp 133 NJ2609
Milltown Gramp 142 NJ4716
Milltown of Campfield Gramp 135 NJ6500
Milltown of Learney Gramp 134 NJ6303
Milnathort Tays 126 NO1204
Milngavie Strath 115 NS5574
Milnmark D & G 99 NX6582
Milnrow Gt Man 81 SD9212
Milnthorpe Cumb 87 SD4981
Milnthorpe W York 83 SE3317
Milovaig Highld 136 NG1549
Milson Shrops 47 SO6472
Milsted Kent 28 TQ9058
Milston Wilts 23 SU1645
Milthorpe Lincs 64 TF1130
Milthorpe Nhants 49 SP5946
Milton Avon 21 ST3462
Milton Cambs 53 TL4762
Milton Cent 115 NN5001
Milton Cumb 101 NY5560
Milton D & G 98 NX2154
Milton D & G 100 NX8470
Milton Derbys 62 SK3126
Milton Dyfed 30 SN0403
Milton Gramp 142 NJ5163
Milton Gwent 34 ST3688
Milton Highld 151 ND3451
Milton Highld 137 NG7043
Milton Highld 139 NH4930
Milton Highld 139 NH5749
Milton Highld 147 NH7674
Milton Kent 28 TQ6674
Milton Notts 75 SK7173
Milton Oxon 49 SP4535
Milton Oxon 37 SU4892
Milton Somset 21 ST4621
Milton Staffs 72 SJ9050
Milton Strath 115 NS3569
Milton Strath 115 NS4274
Milton Tays 133 NO1357
Milton Abbas Dorset 11 ST8002
Milton Abbot Devon 5 SX4079
Milton Bridge Loth 117 NT2562
Milton Bryan Beds 38 SP9730
Milton Clevedon Somset 22 ST6637
Milton Combe Devon 6 SX4866
Milton Common Oxon 37 SP6503
Milton Damerel Devon 18 SS3810
Milton End Gloucs 35 SO7110
Milton End Gloucs 36 SP1400
Milton Ernest Beds 51 TL0156
Milton Green Ches 71 SJ4658
Milton Hill Oxon 37 SU4790
Milton Keynes Bucks 38 SP8537
Milton Lilbourne Wilts 23 SU1960
Milton Malsor Nhants 49 SP7355
Milton Morenish Tays 124 NN6135
Milton of Auchinhove Gramp 134 NJ5503
Milton of Balgonie Fife 118 NO3200
Milton of Buchanan Cent 115 NS4490
Milton of Campsie Strath 116 NS6576
Milton of Leys Highld 140 NH6942
Milton of Tullich Gramp 134 NO3897
Milton on Stour Dorset 22 ST7928
Milton Regis Kent 28 TQ9064
Milton Street E Susx 16 TQ5304
Milton-under-Wychwood Oxon 36 SP2618
Milverton Somset 20 ST1225
Milverton Warwks 48 SP3166
Milwich Staffs 72 SJ9632
Milwr Clwyd 70 SJ1974
Minard Strath 114 NR9796
Minchington Dorset 11 ST9614
Minchinhampton Gloucs 35 SO8700
Mindrum Nthumb 110 NT8432
Mindrummill Nthumb 110 NT8433
Minehead Somset 20 SS9646
Minera Clwyd 70 SJ2751
Minety Lower Moor Wilts 35 SU0291
Minffordd Gwynd 57 SH5938
Mingarry Park Highld 129 NM6869
Miningsby Lincs 77 TF3264
Minions Cnwll 5 SX2671
Minishant Strath 106 NS3314
Minllyn Gwynd 57 SH8514
Minnigaff D & G 99 NX4166
Minnis Bay Kent 29 TR2869
Minnonie Gramp 142 NJ7760
Minskip N York 89 SE3864
Minstead Hants 12 SU2811
Minsted W Susx 14 SU8520
Minster Kent 28 TQ9573
Minster Kent 29 TR3064
Minster Lovell Oxon 36 SP3111
Minsteracres Nthumb 95 NZ0156
Minsterley Shrops 59 SJ3705
Minsterworth Gloucs 35 SO7817

Minterne Magna Newton

Minterne Magna Dorset 11 ST6504
Minterne Parva Dorset 11 ST6603
Minting Lincs 76 TF1873
Mintlaw Gramp 143 NJ9948
Minto Border 109 NT5620
Minton Shrops 59 SO4390
Minwear Dyfed 30 SN0413
Minworth W Mids 61 SP1691
Mirehouse Cumb 92 NX9715
Mirfield W York 82 SE2019
Miserden Gloucs 35 SO9308
Miskin M Glam 33 ST0480
Miskin M Glam 33 ST0498
Misson Notts 75 SK6895
Misterton Leics 50 SP5583
Misterton Notts 75 SK7694
Misterton Somset 10 ST4508
Mistley Essex 41 TM1231
Mistley Heath Essex 41 TM1230
Mitcham Gt Lon 27 TQ2768
Mitchel Troy Gwent 34 SO4910
Mitcheldean Gloucs 35 SO6618
Mitchell Cnwll 3 SW8554
Mitchellslacks D & G 100 NX9696
Mitford Nthumb 103 NZ1786
Mithian Cnwll 3 SW7450
Mitton Staffs 72 SJ8815
Mixbury Oxon 49 SP6033
Mixenden W York 82 SE0629
Mixon Staffs 74 SK0457
Moats Tye Suffk 54 TM0455
Mobberley Ches 79 SJ7879
Mobberley Staffs 73 SK0041
Moccas H & W 46 SO3543
Mochdre Powys 69 SH8278
Mochdre Powys 58 SO0788
Mochrum D & G 98 NX3446
Mockbeggar Hants 12 SU1609
Mockbeggar Kent 28 TQ7146
Mockerkin Cumb 92 NY0923
Modbury Devon 7 SX6651
Moddershall Staffs 72 SJ9236
Moelfre Clwyd 58 SJ1828
Moelfre Gwynd 68 SH5186
Moffat D & G 108 NT0805
Mogerhanger Beds 52 TL1449
Moira Leics 62 SK3115
Mol-chlach Highld 128 NG4513
Molash Kent 28 TR0251
Mold Clwyd 70 SJ2363
Moldgreen W York 82 SE1516
Molehill Green Essex 40 TL5624
Molehill Green Essex 40 TL7120
Molescroft Humb 84 TA0140
Molesden Nthumb 103 NZ1484
Molesworth Cambs 51 TL0775
Molland Devon 19 SS8028
Mollington Ches 71 SJ3870
Mollington Oxon 49 SP4447
Mollinsburn Strath 116 NS7171
Monachty Dyfed 44 SN5061
Monachylemore Cent 124 NN4719
Monday Boys Kent 28 TQ9045
Mondynes Gramp 135 NO7779
Monewden Suffk 55 TM2358
Moneydie Tays 125 NO0629
Moneygrow Green Berks 26 SU8977
Moniaive D & G 107 NX7890
Monifieth Tays 127 NO4932
Monikie Tays 127 NO4938
Monimail Fife 126 NO2914
Monington Dyfed 42 SN1344
Monk Bretton S York 83 SE3607
Monk Fryston N York 83 SE5029
Monk Hesleden Dur 97 NZ4537
Monk Sherborne Hants 24 SU6056
Monk Soham Suffk 55 TM2165
Monk Soham Green Suffk 55 TM2066
Monk Street Essex 40 TL6128
Monk's Gate W Susx 15 TQ2027
Monken Hadley Gt Lon 26 TQ2497
Monkhide H & W 46 SO6144
Monkhill Cumb 93 NY3458
Monkhopton Shrops 59 SO6293
Monkland H & W 46 SO4557
Monkleigh Devon 18 SS4520
Monknash S Glam 33 SS9170
Monkokehampton Devon 8 SS5805
Monks Horton Kent 28 TQ8356
Monks Eleigh Suffk 54 TL9647
Monks Heath Ches 79 SJ8474
Monks Kirby Warwks 50 SP4683
Monks Risborough Bucks 38 SP8104
Monkseaton T & W 103 NZ3472
Monksilver Somset 20 ST0737
Monkspath Street W Mids 61 SP1376
Monksthorpe Lincs 77 TF4465
Monkswood Gwent 34 SO3402
Monkton E Susx 9 ST1803
Monkton Kent 29 TR2964
Monkton S Glam 33 SS9270
Monkton Strath 106 NS3527
Monkton T & W 103 NZ3363
Monkton Combe Avon 22 ST7762
Monkton Deverill Wilts 22 ST8537
Monkton Farleigh Wilts 22 ST8065
Monkton Heathfield Somset 20 ST2526
Monkton Up Wimborne Dorset 11 SU0113
Monkton Wyld Dorset 10 SY3396
Monkwearmouth T & W 96 NZ3958
Monkwood Hants 24 SU6630
Monmore Green W Mids 60 SO9297
Monmouth Gwent 34 SO5012
Monnington on Wye H & W 46 SO3743
Monreith D & G 98 NX3541
Mont Saint Guern 152 GN4708
Montacute Somset 10 ST4916
Montcliffe Gt Man 81 SD6611
Montford Shrops 59 SJ4114
Montford Bridge Shrops 59 SJ4215
Montgarrie Gramp 142 NJ5717
Montgarswood Strath 107 NS5227
Montgomery Powys 58 SO2296
Montgreenan Strath 106 NS3343
Monton Gt Man 79 SJ7699
Montrose Tays 135 NO7157
Monxton Hants 23 SU3144
Monyash Derbys 74 SK1566
Monymusk Gramp 142 NJ6815
Monzie Tays 125 NN8725
Moodiesburn Strath 116 NS6970
Moonzie Fife 126 NO3317
Moor Allerton W York 82 SE3038
Moor Crichel Dorset 11 ST9908
Moor End Beds 38 SP9719
Moor End Devon 19 SS6609
Moor End Humb 84 SE8137
Moor End Lancs 80 SD3744
Moor End N York 83 SE6038
Moor End W York 82 SE0528
Moor Green Herts 39 TL3226
Moor Head W York 82 SE1337
Moor Head W York 82 SE2329
Moor Monkton N York 83 SE5156
Moor Row Cumb 92 NY0014
Moor Row Cumb 93 NY2149
Moor Row Dur 96 NZ1515
Moor Side Lancs 80 SD4935
Moor Side Lincs 77 TF2557
Moor Street Kent 28 TQ8265
Moor Street W Mids 60 SO9982
Moorbath Dorset 10 SY4395
Moorby Lincs 77 TF2964
Moorcot H & W 46 SO3555
Moordown Dorset 12 SZ0994
Moore Ches 78 SJ5784
Moorend Gloucs 35 SO7303
Moorends S York 83 SE6915
Moorgreen Hants 13 SU4815
Moorgreen Notts 62 SK4847
Moorhall Derbys 74 SK3074
Moorhampton H & W 46 SO3746
Moorhouse Cumb 93 NY2551
Moorhouse Cumb 93 NY3356
Moorhouse Notts 75 SK7566
Moorhouse W York 83 SE4810
Moorhouse Bank Surrey 27 TQ4353
Moorland Somset 21 ST3332
Moorlinch Somset 21 ST3936
Moorsholm Cleve 90 NZ6814
Moorside Cumb 86 NY0701
Moorside Dorset 22 ST7919
Moorside Gt Man 79 SD9407
Moorstock Kent 29 TR1038
Moorswater Cnwll 5 SX2364
Moorthorpe W York 83 SE4611
Moortown Devon 6 SX5274
Moortown Hants 12 SU1503
Moortown IOW 13 SZ4283
Moortown Lincs 76 TF0798
Moortown Shrops 59 SJ6118
Moortown W York 82 SE2939
Morangie Highld 147 NH7683
Morar Highld 129 NM6793
Morborne Cambs 64 TL1391
Morchard Bishop Devon 8 SS7707
Morcombelake Dorset 10 SY4094
Morcott Leics 51 SK9200
Morda Shrops 58 SJ2827
Morden Dorset 11 SY9195
Morden Gt Lon 27 TQ2666
Mordiford H & W 46 SO5737
Mordon Dur 96 NZ3226
More Shrops 59 SO3491
Morebath Devon 20 SS9525
Morebattle Border 110 NT7724
Morecambe Lancs 87 SD4364
Moredon Wilts 36 SU1487
Morefield Highld 145 NH1195
Morehall Kent 29 TR2136
Moreleigh Devon 7 SX7652
Morenish Tays 124 NN6035
Moresby Cumb 92 NX9921
Moresby Parks Cumb 92 NX9919
Morestead Hants 13 SU5025
Moreton Dorset 11 SY8089
Moreton Essex 39 TL5307
Moreton H & W 46 SO5064
Moreton Mersyd 78 SJ2689
Moreton Oxon 37 SP6904
Moreton Staffs 72 SJ7817
Moreton Staffs 73 SK1429
Moreton Corbet Shrops 59 SJ5623
Moreton Jeffries H & W 46 SO6048
Moreton Mill Shrops 59 SJ5723
Moreton Morrell Warwks 48 SP3155
Moreton on Lugg H & W 46 SO5045
Moreton Paddox Warwks 48 SP3154
Moreton Pinkney Nhants 49 SP5749
Moreton Say Shrops 59 SJ6334
Moreton Valence Gloucs 35 SO7809
Moreton-in-Marsh Gloucs 48 SP2032
Moretonhampstead Devon 8 SX7586
Morfa Dyfed 42 SN3053
Morfa Bychan Gwynd 57 SH5437
Morfa Glas W Glam 33 SN8606
Morfa Nefyn Gwynd 56 SH2840
Morgan's Vale Wilts 12 SU1920
Morganstown S Glam 33 ST1281
Morham Loth 118 NT5571
Moriah Dyfed 43 SN6279
Morland Cumb 94 NY6022
Morley Ches 79 SJ8282
Morley Derbys 62 SK3940
Morley Dur 96 NZ1227
Morley W York 82 SE2627
Morley Green Ches 79 SJ8281
Morley St Botolph Norfk 66 TM0799
Mornick Cnwll 5 SX3272
Morningside Loth 117 NT2470
Morningside Strath 116 NS8355
Morningthorpe Norfk 67 TM2192
Morpeth Nthumb 103 NZ1986
Morphie Gramp 135 NO7164
Morrey Staffs 73 SK1218
Morridge Side Staffs 73 SK0254
Morridge Top Staffs 74 SK0365
Morriston W Glam 32 SS6697
Morston Norfk 66 TG0043
Mortehoe Devon 18 SS4545
Morthen S York 75 SK4788
Mortimer Berks 24 SU6564
Mortimer Common Berks 24 SU6565
Mortimer West End Hants 24 SU6363
Mortimer's Cross H & W 46 SO4263
Mortlake Gt Lon 26 TQ2075
Morton Cumb 93 NY3854
Morton Cumb 93 NY4539
Morton Derbys 74 SK4060
Morton IOW 13 SZ6085
Morton Lincs 75 SK8091
Morton Lincs 64 TF0923
Morton Norfk 66 TG1216
Morton Notts 75 SK7251
Morton Shrops 59 SJ2924
Morton Bagot Warwks 48 SP1164
Morton Hall Lincs 76 SK8863
Morton Tinmouth Dur 96 NZ1821
Morton-on-Swale N York 89 SE3291
Morvah Cnwll 2 SW4035
Morval Cnwll 5 SX2556
Morvich Highld 138 NG9621
Morville Shrops 60 SO6794
Morville Heath Shrops 60 SO6893
Morwenstow Cnwll 18 SS2015
Mosborough S York 74 SK4281
Moscow Strath 107 NS4840
Mose Shrops 60 SO7590
Mosedale Cumb 93 NY3532
Moseley H & W 47 SO8159
Moseley W Mids 60 SO9498
Moseley W Mids 61 SP0783
Moses Gate Gt Man 79 SD7306
Moss Clwyd 71 SJ3053
Moss S York 83 SE5914
Moss Strath 120 NL9544
Moss Bank Mersyd 78 SJ5197
Moss End Ches 79 SJ6778
Moss Side Cumb 93 NY1952
Moss Side Lancs 80 SD3730
Moss Side Mersyd 78 SD3802
Moss-side Highld 140 NH8555
Mossat Gramp 142 NJ4719
Mossbank Shet 155 HU4575
Mossbay Cumb 92 NX9927
Mossblown Strath 106 NS3925
Mossbrow Gt Man 79 SJ7089
Mossburnford Border 110 NT6616
Mossdale D & G 99 NX6670
Mossdale Strath 107 NS4904
Mossend Strath 116 NS7460
Mosser Mains Cumb 92 NY1125
Mossgiel Strath 107 NS4828
Mossknowe D & G 101 NY2769
Mossley Ches 72 SJ8861
Mossley Gt Man 82 SD9701
Mossley Staffs 73 SK0417
Mosspaul Hotel Border 109 NY3999
Mosstodloch Gramp 141 NJ3259
Mossy Lea Lancs 80 SD5312
Mossyard D & G 99 NX5451
Mosterton Dorset 10 ST4505
Moston Gt Man 79 SD8701
Moston Shrops 59 SJ5626
Moston Green Ches 72 SJ7261
Mostyn Clwyd 70 SJ1580
Motcombe Dorset 22 ST8525
Mothecombe Devon 6 SX6047
Motherby Cumb 93 NY4228
Motherwell Strath 116 NS7457
Motspur Park Gt Lon 26 TQ2267
Mottingham Gt Lon 27 TQ4272
Mottisfont Hants 23 SU3226
Mottistone IOW 13 SZ4083
Mottram in Longdendale Gt Man 79 SJ9995
Mottram St Andrew Ches 79 SJ8778
Mouilpied Guern 152 GN5106
Mouldsworth Ches 71 SJ5071
Moulin Tays 132 NN9459
Moulsecoomb E Susx 15 TQ3307
Moulsford Oxon 37 SU5883
Moulsoe Bucks 38 SP9141
Moultavie Highld 146 NH6371
Moulton Ches 79 SJ6569
Moulton Lincs 64 TF3023
Moulton N York 89 NZ2303
Moulton Nhants 50 SP7866
Moulton S Glam 33 ST0770
Moulton Suffk 53 TL6964
Moulton Chapel Lincs 64 TF2918
Moulton Seas End Lincs 64 TF3227
Moulton St Mary Norfk 67 TG3907
Mount Cnwll 3 SW7856
Mount Cnwll 4 SX1468
Mount W York 82 SE0917
Mount Ambrose Cnwll 2 SW7043
Mount Bures Essex 40 TL9032
Mount Hawke Cnwll 2 SW7147
Mount Hermon Cnwll 2 SW6915
Mount Lothian Loth 117 NT2757
Mount Pleasant Ches 72 SJ8456
Mount Pleasant Derbys 74 SK3448
Mount Pleasant Dur 96 NZ2634
Mount Pleasant E Susx 16 TQ4216
Mount Pleasant H & W 47 SP0064
Mount Pleasant Norfk 66 TL9994
Mount Pleasant Suffk 53 TL7347
Mount Sorrel Wilts 23 SU0324
Mount Tabor W York 82 SE0527
Mountain W York 82 SE0930
Mountain Ash M Glam 33 ST0499
Mountain Cross Border 117 NT1547
Mountain Street Kent 29 TR0652
Mountfield E Susx 17 TQ7320
Mountgerald House Highld 139 NH5661
Mountjoy Cnwll 4 SW8760
Mountnessing Essex 40 TQ6297
Mounton Gwent 34 ST5193
Mountsorrel Leics 62 SK5814
Mountstuart Strath 114 NS1159
Mousehill Surrey 25 SU9441
Mousehole Cnwll 2 SW4626
Mouswald D & G 100 NY0672
Mow Cop Ches 72 SJ8557
Mowhaugh Border 110 NT8120
Mowmacre Hill Leics 62 SK5807
Mowsley Leics 50 SP6489
Mowtie Gramp 135 NO8388
Moy Highld 140 NH7634
Moy Highld 131 NN4282
Moye Highld 138 NG8818
Moyles Court Hants 12 SU1608
Moylgrove Dyfed 42 SN1144
Muasdale Strath 105 NR6840
Much Birch H & W 46 SO5030
Much Cowarne H & W 46 SO6147
Much Dewchurch H & W 46 SO4831
Much Hadham Herts 39 TL4219
Much Hoole Lancs 80 SD4723
Much Hoole Town Lancs 80 SD4722
Much Marcle H & W 47 SO6532
Much Wenlock Shrops 59 SO6299
Muchalls Gramp 135 NO9092
Muchelney Somset 21 ST4224
Muchelney Ham Somset 21 ST4423
Muchlarnick Cnwll 5 SX2156
Mucking Essex 40 TQ6881
Muckingford Essex 40 TQ6779
Muckleford Dorset 10 SY6393
Mucklestone Staffs 72 SJ7237
Muckton Lincs 77 TF3781
Mucomir Highld 131 NN1884
Mud Row Kent 28 TR0072
Muddiford Devon 19 SS5638
Muddlebridge Devon 19 SS5232
Muddles Green E Susx 16 TQ5413
Mudeford Dorset 12 SZ1892
Mudford Somset 21 ST5719
Mudford Sock Somset 21 ST5519
Mudgley Somset 21 ST4545
Mugdock Cent 115 NS5577
Mugeary Highld 136 NG4439
Mugginton Derbys 73 SK2842
Muggintonlane End Derbys 73 SK2844
Muggleswick Dur 95 NZ0449
Muir of Fowlis Gramp 134 NJ5612
Muir of Miltonduff Gramp 141 NJ1859
Muir of Ord Highld 139 NH5250
Muir of Thorn Tays 125 NO0637
Muirden Gramp 142 NJ7054
Muirdrum Tays 127 NO5637
Muiresk Gramp 142 NJ6948
Muirhead Fife 126 NO2805
Muirhead Strath 116 NS6869
Muirhead Tays 126 NO3434
Muirhouselaw Border 110 NT6328
Muirhouses Cent 117 NT0180
Muirkirk Strath 107 NS6927
Muirmill Cent 116 NS7283
Muirshearlich Highld 131 NN1380
Muirtack Gramp 143 NJ9937
Muirton Tays 125 NN9211
Muirton Mains Highld 139 NH4553
Muirton of Ardblair Tays 126 NO1643
Muker N York 88 SD9097
Mulbarton Norfk 67 TG1901
Mulben Gramp 141 NJ3550
Mulfra Cnwll 2 SW4534
Mulindry Strath 112 NR3659
Mullacott Cross Devon 19 SS5144
Mullion Cnwll 2 SW6719
Mullion Cove Cnwll 2 SW6617
Mumby Lincs 77 TF5174
Muncher's Green Herts 39 TL3126
Munderfield Row H & W 47 SO6451
Munderfield Stocks H & W 47 SO6550
Mundesley Norfk 67 TG3136
Mundford Norfk 66 TL8093
Mundham Norfk 67 TM3397
Mundon Hill Essex 40 TL8602
Mungrisdale Cumb 93 NY3630
Munlochy Highld 140 NH6453
Munnoch Strath 114 NS2548
Munsley H & W 47 SO6640
Munslow Shrops 59 SO5287
Murchington Devon 8 SX6888
Murcot H & W 48 SP0640
Murcott Oxon 37 SP5815
Murcott Wilts 35 ST9591
Murkle Highld 151 ND1668
Murlaggan Highld 130 NN0192
Murrell Green Hants 24 SU7455
Murroes Tays 127 NO4635
Murrow Cambs 64 TF3707
Mursley Bucks 38 SP8128
Murston Kent 28 TQ9264
Murthill Tays 134 NO4657
Murthly Tays 126 NO1038
Murton Cumb 94 NY7221
Murton Dur 96 NZ3847
Murton N York 83 SE6452
Murton Nthumb 111 NT9748
Murton T & W 103 NZ3270
Musbury Devon 10 SY2794
Muscoates N York 90 SE6879
Musselburgh Loth 118 NT3472
Muston Leics 63 SK8237
Muston N York 91 TA0979
Mustow Green H & W 60 SO8774
Muswell Hill Gt Lon 27 TQ2889
Mutehill D & G 99 NX6848
Mutford Suffk 55 TM4888
Muthill Tays 125 NN8717
Mutterton Devon 9 ST0205
Muxton Shrops 60 SJ7114
Mybster Highld 151 ND1652
Myddfai Dyfed 44 SN7730
Myddle Shrops 59 SJ4623
Mydroilyn Dyfed 42 SN4555
Mylor Cnwll 3 SW8135
Mylor Bridge Cnwll 3 SW8036
Mynachlog ddu Dyfed 31 SN1430
Myndd-llan Clwyd 70 SJ1572
Myndtown Shrops 59 SO3989
Mynydd Buch Dyfed 43 SN7276
Mynydd Isa Clwyd 70 SJ2563
Mynydd-bach Gwent 34 ST4894
Mynydd-bach W Glam 32 SS6597
Mynyddgarreg Dyfed 31 SN4208
Mynytho Gwynd 56 SH3031
Myrebird Gramp 135 NO7398
Myredykes Border 102 NY5998
Mytchett Surrey 25 SU8855
Mytholm W York 82 SD9827
Mytholmroyd W York 82 SE0126
Mythop Lancs 80 SD3634
Myton-on-Swale N York 89 SE4366

N

Naast Highld 144 NG8283
Nab's Head Lancs 81 SD6229
Naburn N York 83 SE5945
Nackholt Kent 28 TR0543
Nackington Kent 29 TR1554
Nacton Suffk 55 TM2240
Nafferton Humb 91 TA0559
Nag's Head Gloucs 35 ST8898
Nailbridge Gloucs 35 SO6415
Nailsbourne Somset 20 ST2128
Nailsea Avon 34 ST4770
Nailstone Leics 62 SK4106
Nailsworth Gloucs 35 ST8499
Nairn Highld 140 NH8856
Nalderswood Surrey 15 TQ2445
Nancegollan Cnwll 2 SW6332
Nancledra Cnwll 2 SW4936
Nanhoron Gwynd 56 SH2731
Nannerch Clwyd 70 SJ1669
Nanpantan Leics 62 SK5017
Nanpean Cnwll 3 SW9556
Nanquidno Cnwll 2 SW3629
Nanstallon Cnwll 4 SX0367
Nant Gwynant Gwynd 69 SH6350
Nant Peris Gwynd 69 SH6058
Nant-ddu Powys 33 SO0014
Nant-glas Powys 45 SN9965
Nant-y-Bwch Gwent 33 SO1210
Nant-y-caws Dyfed 32 SN4518
Nant-y-derry Gwent 34 SO3306
Nant-y-gollen Shrops 58 SJ2428
Nant-y-moel M Glam 33 SS9392
Nant-y-pandy Gwynd 69 SH6973
Nanternis Dyfed 42 SN3756
Nantgaredig Dyfed 32 SN4921
Nantgarw M Glam 33 ST1285
Nantglyn Clwyd 70 SJ0061
Nantgwyn Powys 45 SN9776
Nantlle Gwynd 68 SH5153
Nantmawr Shrops 58 SJ2524
Nantmel Powys 45 SO0366
Nantmor Gwynd 57 SH6046
Nantwich Ches 72 SJ6552
Nantyffyllon M Glam 33 SS8492
Naphill Bucks 26 SU8496
Napleton H & W 47 SO8648
Nappa N York 81 SD8553
Napton on the Hill Warwks 49 SP4661
Narberth Dyfed 31 SN1015
Narborough Leics 50 SP5497
Narborough Norfk 65 TF7412
Narkurs Cnwll 5 SX3255
Nasareth Gwynd 68 SH4749
Naseby Nhants 50 SP6978
Nash Bucks 38 SP7833
Nash Gt Lon 27 TQ4063
Nash Gwent 34 ST3483
Nash H & W 46 SO3062
Nash Shrops 46 SO6071
Nash End H & W 60 SO7781
Nash Lee Bucks 38 SP8408
Nash Street Kent 27 TQ6469
Nash's Green Hants 24 SU6745
Nassington Nhants 51 TL0696
Nasty Herts 39 TL3524
Nateby Cumb 88 NY7706
Nateby Lancs 80 SD4644
Natland Cumb 87 SD5289
Naughton Suffk 54 TM0249
Naunton Gloucs 48 SP1123
Naunton H & W 47 SO8645
Naunton H & W 47 SO8739
Naunton Beauchamp H & W 47 SO9652
Navenby Lincs 76 SK9858
Navestock Essex 27 TQ5397
Navestock Side Essex 27 TQ5697
Navidale House Hotel Highld 147 ND0316
Navity Highld 140 NH7864
Nawton N York 90 SE6584
Nayland Suffk 54 TL9734
Nazeing Essex 39 TL4106
Nazeing Gate Essex 39 TL4105
Neacroft Hants 12 SZ1896
Neal's Green Warwks 61 SP3384
Nealhouse Cumb 93 NY3351
Neap Shet 155 HU5058
Near Cotton Staffs 73 SK0646
Near Sawry Cumb 87 SD3795
Neasden Gt Lon 26 TQ2185
Neasham Dur 89 NZ3210
Neath W Glam 32 SS7597
Neatham Hants 24 SU7440
Neatishead Norfk 67 TG3420
Nebo Dyfed 43 SN5465
Nebo Gwynd 68 SH4850
Nebo Gwynd 69 SH8355
Necton Norfk 66 TF8709
Nedd Highld 148 NC1331
Nedging Suffk 54 TL9948
Nedging Tye Suffk 54 TM0149
Needham Norfk 55 TM2281
Needham Market Suffk 54 TM0855
Needham Street Suffk 53 TL7265
Needingworth Cambs 52 TL3472
Neen Savage Shrops 60 SO6777
Neen Sollars Shrops 60 SO6672
Neenton Shrops 59 SO6387
Nefyn Gwynd 56 SH3040
Neilston Strath 115 NS4857
Nelson Lancs 81 SD8638
Nelson M Glam 33 ST1195
Nemphlar Strath 116 NS8544
Nempnett Thrubwell Avon 21 ST5260
Nenthall Cumb 94 NY7545
Nenthead Cumb 94 NY7743
Nenthorn Border 110 NT6837
Neopardy Devon 8 SX7999
Nep Town W Susx 15 TQ2115
Nercwys Clwyd 70 SJ2360
Nereabolls Strath 112 NR2255
Nerston Strath 116 NS6456
Nesbit Nthumb 111 NT9833
Nesfield N York 82 SE0949
Ness Ches 71 SJ3076
Nesscliffe Shrops 59 SJ3819
Neston Ches 71 SJ2977
Neston Wilts 22 ST8668
Netchwood Shrops 59 SO6291
Nether Alderley Ches 79 SJ8476
Nether Blainslie Border 109 NT5443
Nether Broughton Notts 63 SK6925
Nether Burrow Lancs 87 SD6174
Nether Cerne Dorset 11 SY6798
Nether Compton Dorset 10 ST5917
Nether Crimond Gramp 143 NJ8222
Nether Dallachy Gramp 141 NJ3563
Nether Exe Devon 9 SS9300
Nether Fingland Strath 108 NS9310
Nether Handley Derbys 74 SK4176
Nether Handwick Tays 126 NO3641
Nether Haugh S York 74 SK4196
Nether Headon Notts 75 SK7477
Nether Heage Derbys 74 SK3650
Nether Heyford Nhants 49 SP6658
Nether Howcleugh Strath 108 NT0312
Nether Kellet Lancs 87 SD5068
Nether Kinmundy Gramp 143 NK0543
Nether Moor Derbys 74 SK3866
Nether Padley Derbys 74 SK2478
Nether Poppleton N York 83 SE5654
Nether Row Cumb 93 NY3237
Nether Silton N York 89 SE4592
Nether Skyborry Shrops 46 SO2873
Nether Stowey Somset 20 ST1939
Nether Street Essex 40 TL5812
Nether Wallop Hants 23 SU3036
Nether Wasdale Cumb 86 NY1204
Nether Wellwood Strath 107 NS6526
Nether Welton Cumb 93 NY3545
Nether Westcote Oxon 36 SP2220
Nether Whitacre Warwks 61 SP2392
Nether Whitecleuch Strath 108 NS8319
Netheravon Wilts 23 SU1448
Netherbrae Gramp 143 NJ7959
Netherburn Strath 116 NS7947
Netherbury Dorset 10 SY4799
Netherby Cumb 101 NY3971
Netherby N York 83 SE3346
Nethercleuch D & G 100 NY1186
Nethercote Warwks 49 SP5164
Nethercott Devon 18 SS4839
Nethercott Devon 5 SX3596
Netherend Gloucs 34 SO5900
Netherfield E Susx 16 TQ7019
Netherfield Leics 62 SK5816
Netherfield Notts 62 SK6140
Netherfield Road E Susx 17 TQ7417
Nethergate Norfk 66 TG0529
Nethergate Notts 75 SK7599
Netherhampton Wilts 23 SU1029
Netherhay Dorset 10 ST4105
Netherland Green Staffs 73 SK1030
Netherlaw D & G 99 NX7444
Netherley Gramp 135 NO8593
Nethermill D & G 100 NY0487
Nethermuir Gramp 143 NJ9044
Netheroyd Hill W York 82 SE1419
Netherplace Strath 115 NS5255
Netherseal Derbys 61 SK2812
Netherstreet Wilts 22 ST9864
Netherthong W York 82 SE1309
Netherthorpe Derbys 75 SK4474
Netherton Cent 115 NS5579
Netherton Devon 7 SX8971
Netherton H & W 46 SO5226
Netherton H & W 47 SO9941
Netherton Hants 23 SU3757
Netherton Nthumb 111 NT9807
Netherton Nthumb 103 NZ2382
Netherton Oxon 36 SU4199
Netherton Shrops 60 SO7382
Netherton Strath 116 NS7854
Netherton Tays 126 NO1452
Netherton Tays 134 NO5457
Netherton W Mids 60 SO9488
Netherton W York 82 SE1213
Netherton W York 82 SE2816
Nethertown Cumb 86 NX9907
Nethertown Highld 151 ND3578
Nethertown Lancs 81 SD7236
Nethertown Staffs 73 SK1017
Netherwitton Nthumb 103 NZ0990
Nethy Bridge Highld 141 NJ0020
Netley Hants 13 SU4508
Netley Marsh Hants 12 SU3313
Nettacott Devon 9 SX8999
Nettlebed Oxon 37 SU6986
Nettlebridge Somset 21 ST6448
Nettlecombe Dorset 10 SY5195
Nettlecombe IOW 13 SZ5278
Nettleden Herts 38 TL0110
Nettleham Lincs 76 TF0075
Nettlestead Kent 28 TQ6852
Nettlestead Green Kent 28 TQ6850
Nettlestone IOW 13 SZ6290
Nettlesworth Dur 96 NZ2547
Nettleton Lincs 76 TA1100
Nettleton Wilts 35 ST8278
Nettleton Shrub Wilts 35 ST8277
Netton Devon 6 SX5546
Netton Wilts 23 SU1336
Neuadd Dyfed 32 SN7021
Neuadd Fawr Dyfed 44 SN7441
Neuadd-ddu Powys 45 SN9175
Nevendon Essex 40 TQ7591
Nevern Dyfed 31 SN0840
Nevill Holt Leics 51 SP8193
New Abbey D & G 100 NX9666
New Aberdour Gramp 143 NJ8863
New Addington Gt Lon 27 TQ3763
New Alresford Hants 24 SU5832
New Alyth Tays 126 NO2447
New Arram Humb 84 TA0344
New Ash Green Kent 27 TQ6065
New Balderton Notts 75 SK8152
New Barn Kent 27 TQ6169
New Barnet Gt Lon 27 TQ2695
New Barton Nhants 51 SP8564
New Bewick Nthumb 111 NU0620
New Bilton Warwks 50 SP4875
New Bolingbroke Lincs 77 TF3057
New Boultham Lincs 76 SK9670
New Bradwell Bucks 38 SP8341
New Brampton Derbys 74 SK3771
New Brancepeth Dur 96 NZ2241
New Bridge N York 90 SE8085
New Brighton Clwyd 70 SJ2565
New Brighton Mersyd 78 SJ3093
New Brinsley Notts 75 SK4550
New Brotton Cleve 97 NZ6920
New Broughton Clwyd 71 SJ3151
New Buckenham Norfk 54 TM0890
New Bury Gt Man 79 SD7304
New Byth Gramp 143 NJ8254
New Clipstone Notts 75 SK5963
New Costessey Norfk 66 TG1810
New Cowper Cumb 92 NY1245
New Crofton W York 83 SE3817
New Cross Dyfed 43 SN6376
New Cross Gt Lon 27 TQ3676
New Cross Somset 21 ST4119
New Cumnock Strath 107 NS6213
New Cut E Susx 17 TQ8115
New Deer Gramp 143 NJ8847
New Delaval Nthumb 103 NZ2979
New Delph Gt Man 82 SD9907
New Denham Bucks 26 TQ0484
New Duston Nhants 49 SP7162
New Earswick N York 83 SE6155
New Eastwood Notts 62 SK4646
New Edlington S York 75 SK5398
New Elgin Gramp 141 NJ2261
New Ellerby Humb 85 TA1639
New Eltham Gt Lon 27 TQ4472
New End H & W 48 SP0560
New Farnley W York 82 SE2531
New Ferry Mersyd 78 SJ3385
New Fletton Cambs 64 TL1997
New Fryston W York 83 SE4526
New Galloway D & G 99 NX6377
New Gilston Fife 127 NO4208
New Grimsby IOS 2 SV8815
New Hartley Nthumb 103 NZ3076
New Haw Surrey 26 TQ0563
New Hedges Dyfed 31 SN1202
New Herrington T & W 96 NZ3352
New Holkham Norfk 66 TF8839
New Holland Humb 85 TA0823
New Houghton Derbys 75 SK4965
New Houghton Norfk 66 TF7927
New Houses Gt Man 78 SD5502
New Houses N York 88 SD8073
New Hutton Cumb 87 SD5691
New Hythe Kent 28 TQ7159
New Inn Dyfed 44 SN4736
New Inn Gwent 34 ST3099
New Invention Shrops 46 SO2976
New Kelso Highld 138 NG9442
New Lakenham Norfk 67 TG2307
New Lambton Dur 96 NZ3051
New Lanark Strath 108 NS8842
New Lane Lancs 80 SD4212
New Lane End Ches 79 SJ6394
New Langholm D & G 101 NY3684
New Leake Lincs 77 TF4057
New Leeds Gramp 143 NJ9954
New Longton Lancs 80 SD5025
New Luce D & G 98 NX1764
New Malden Gt Lon 26 TQ2168
New Marston Oxon 37 SP5407
New Marton Shrops 59 SJ3334
New Mill Cnwll 2 SW4534
New Mill Gramp 135 NO7883
New Mill Herts 38 SP9212
New Mill W York 82 SE1609
New Mills Cnwll 3 SW8952
New Mills Derbys 79 SK0085
New Mills Powys 58 SJ0901
New Milton Hants 12 SZ2495
New Mistley Essex 41 TM1131
New Moat Dyfed 30 SN0625
New Ollerton Notts 75 SK6667
New Oscott W Mids 61 SP0994
New Oxted Surrey 27 TQ3952
New Pitsligo Gramp 143 NJ8855
New Polzeath Cnwll 4 SW9379
New Prestwick Strath 106 NS3424
New Quay Dyfed 42 SN3959
New Quay Essex 41 TM0223
New Rackheath Norfk 67 TG2812
New Radnor Powys 45 SO2161
New Rent Cumb 93 NY4536
New Ridley Nthumb 95 NZ0559
New Road Side N York 82 SD9743
New Romney Kent 17 TR0624
New Rossington Notts 75 SK6198
New Row Dyfed 43 SN7273
New Row Lancs 81 SD6438
New Scone Tays 126 NO1326
New Sharlston W York 83 SE3819
New Shoreston Nthumb 111 NU1932
New Silksworth T & W 96 NZ3853
New Skelton Cleve 97 NZ6618
New Somerby Lincs 63 SK9235
New Spilsby Lincs 77 TF4165
New Springs Gt Man 78 SD5906
New Stevenston Strath 116 NS7659
New Street H & W 46 SO3356
New Swannington Leics 62 SK4215
New Thundersley Essex 40 TQ7789
New Town Beds 52 TL1945
New Town Dorset 22 ST8318
New Town Dorset 11 ST9515
New Town Dorset 11 ST9907
New Town Dorset 22 ST9918
New Town E Susx 16 TQ4720
New Town Loth 118 NT4470
New Town Nhants 51 SP9677
New Town Somset 10 ST2712
New Town Wilts 36 SU2871
New Tredegar M Glam 33 SO1403
New Trows Strath 108 NS8038
New Tupton Derbys 74 SK3966
New Village Humb 84 SE8530
New Walsoken Cambs 65 TF4609
New Waltham Humb 85 TA2804
New Whittington Derbys 74 SK3975
New Wimpole Cambs 52 TL3549
New Winton Loth 118 NT4271
New Yatt Oxon 36 SP3713
New York Lincs 77 TF2455
New York N York 89 SE1963
New York T & W 103 NZ3270
New Zealand Derbys 62 SK3336
Newall W York 82 SE1946
Newark Cambs 64 TF2100
Newark D & G 107 NS7808
Newark-on-Trent Notts 75 SK7953
Newarthill Strath 116 NS7859
Newbarn Kent 29 TR1540
Newbattle Loth 118 NT3365
Newbie D & G 101 NY1764
Newbiggin Cumb 93 NY4729
Newbiggin Cumb 94 NY5549
Newbiggin Cumb 94 NY6228
Newbiggin Cumb 86 SD0994
Newbiggin Cumb 86 SD2669
Newbiggin Dur 95 NY9127
Newbiggin Dur 96 NZ1447
Newbiggin N York 88 SD9591
Newbiggin N York 88 SE0086
Newbiggin-by-the-Sea Nthumb 103 NZ3087
Newbiggin-on-Lune Cumb 87 NY7005
Newbigging Strath 117 NT0145
Newbigging Tays 126 NO2841
Newbigging Tays 127 NO4237
Newbold Derbys 74 SK3672
Newbold Leics 62 SK4019
Newbold on Avon Warwks 50 SP4877
Newbold on Stour Warwks 48 SP2446
Newbold Pacey Warwks 48 SP2957
Newbold Revel Warwks 50 SP4580
Newbold Verdon Leics 62 SK4403
Newborough Cambs 64 TF2005
Newborough Gwynd 68 SH4265
Newborough Staffs 73 SK1325
Newbottle Nhants 49 SP5236
Newbottle T & W 96 NZ3351
Newbourne Suffk 55 TM2743
Newbridge Clwyd 70 SJ2841
Newbridge Cnwll 2 SW4231
Newbridge Cnwll 3 SW7944
Newbridge D & G 100 NX9479
Newbridge Dyfed 30 SM9431
Newbridge Dyfed 44 SN5059
Newbridge Gwent 33 ST2097
Newbridge Hants 12 SU2915
Newbridge IOW 13 SZ4187
Newbridge Loth 117 NT1272
Newbridge Oxon 36 SP4001
Newbridge Green H & W 47 SO8439
Newbridge on Wye Powys 45 SO0158
Newbridge-on-Usk Gwent 34 ST3894
Newbrough Nthumb 102 NY8767
Newbuildings Devon 8 SS7903
Newburgh Fife 126 NO2318
Newburgh Gramp 143 NJ9659
Newburgh Gramp 143 NJ9925
Newburgh Lancs 78 SD4810
Newburgh Priory N York 90 SE5476
Newburn T & W 103 NZ1665
Newbury Berks 24 SU4766
Newbury Somset 22 ST6949
Newbury Wilts 22 ST8241
Newby Cumb 94 NY5921
Newby Lancs 81 SD8146
Newby N York 90 NZ5012
Newby N York 88 SD7269
Newby N York 91 TA0190
Newby Bridge Cumb 87 SD3686
Newby Cross Cumb 93 NY3653
Newby East Cumb 93 NY4758
Newby Head Cumb 94 NY5821
Newby West Cumb 93 NY3753
Newby Wiske N York 89 SE3687
Newcastle Gwent 34 SO4417
Newcastle Shrops 58 SO2582
Newcastle Emlyn Dyfed 31 SN3040
Newcastle upon Tyne T & W 103 NZ2464
Newcastle-under-Lyme Staffs 72 SJ8445
Newcastleton D & G 101 NY4887
Newchapel Dyfed 31 SN2239
Newchapel Staffs 72 SJ8654
Newchapel Surrey 15 TQ3641
Newchurch Gwent 33 SO1710
Newchurch Gwent 34 ST4597
Newchurch H & W 46 SO3550
Newchurch IOW 13 SZ5685
Newchurch Kent 17 TR0531
Newchurch Powys 45 SO2150
Newchurch Staffs 73 SK1423
Newchurch in Pendle Lancs 81 SD8239
Newcraighall Loth 118 NT3272
Newdigate Surrey 15 TQ1942
Newell Green Berks 25 SU8770
Newenden Kent 17 TQ8327
Newent Gloucs 47 SO7225
Newfield Dur 96 NZ2033
Newfield Dur 96 NZ2452
Newfield Highld 147 NH7877
Newfound Hants 24 SU5851
Newgale Dyfed 30 SM8522
Newgate Cambs 52 TL3990
Newgate Norfk 66 TG0443
Newgate Street Herts 39 TL3005
Newhall Ches 71 SJ6145
Newhall Derbys 73 SK2820
Newham Nthumb 111 NU1728
Newhaven Derbys 74 SK1660
Newhaven E Susx 16 TQ4401
Newhey Gt Man 82 SD9411
Newholm N York 90 NZ8610
Newhouse Strath 116 NS7961
Newick E Susx 15 TQ4121
Newingreen Kent 29 TR1236
Newington Kent 28 TQ8564
Newington Kent 29 TR1837
Newington Oxon 37 SU6096
Newington Shrops 59 SO4283
Newington Bagpath Gloucs 35 ST8194
Newland Cumb 86 SD3079
Newland Gloucs 34 SO5509
Newland H & W 47 SO7948
Newland Humb 84 SE8029
Newland Humb 84 TA0631
Newland N York 83 SE6824
Newland Oxon 36 SP3609
Newland Somset 19 SS8238
Newlandrig Loth 118 NT3762
Newlands Border 101 NY5094
Newlands Cumb 93 NY3439
Newlands Nthumb 95 NZ0855
Newlands of Dundurcas Gramp 141 NJ2951
Newlyn Cnwll 2 SW4628
Newmachar Gramp 143 NJ8919
Newmains Strath 116 NS8256
Newman's End Essex 39 TL5112
Newman's Green Suffk 54 TL8843
Newmarket Cumb 93 NY3438
Newmarket Suffk 53 TL6463
Newmill Border 109 NT4510
Newmill Gramp 142 NJ4352
Newmill of Inshewan Tays 134 NO4260
Newmillerdam W York 83 SE3215
Newmills Fife 117 NT0186
Newmills Gwent 34 SO5107
Newmills Loth 117 NT1667
Newmiln Tays 126 NO1230
Newmilns Strath 107 NS5337
Newnes Shrops 59 SJ3834
Newney Green Essex 40 TL6507
Newnham Gloucs 35 SO6911
Newnham H & W 47 SO6469
Newnham Hants 24 SU7053
Newnham Herts 39 TL2437
Newnham Kent 28 TQ9557
Newnham Nhants 49 SP5859
Newnham Paddox Warwks 50 SP4983
Newport Devon 19 SS5632
Newport Dorset 11 SY8895
Newport Dyfed 30 SN0539
Newport Essex 39 TL5234
Newport Gloucs 35 ST7097
Newport Gwent 34 ST3188
Newport Highld 151 ND1324
Newport Humb 84 SE8530
Newport IOW 13 SZ5089
Newport Norfk 67 TG5017
Newport Shrops 72 SJ7419
Newport Pagnell Bucks 38 SP8743
Newport-on-Tay Fife 127 NO4228
Newpound Common W Susx 14 TQ0627
Newquay Cnwll 4 SW8161
Newsam Green W York 83 SE3630
Newsbank Ches 72 SJ8366
Newseat Gramp 142 NJ7032
Newsham Lancs 80 SD5136
Newsham N York 89 NZ1010
Newsham N York 89 SE3784
Newsham Nthumb 103 NZ3080
Newsholme Humb 84 SE7129
Newsholme Lancs 81 SD8451
Newstead Border 109 NT5634
Newstead Notts 75 SK5152
Newstead Nthumb 111 NU1527
Newstead W York 83 SE4014
Newtack Gramp 142 NJ4446
Newthorpe N York 83 SE4632
Newtimber Place W Susx 15 TQ2613
Newton Beds 39 TL2344
Newton Border 110 NT6020
Newton Cambs 65 TF4314
Newton Cambs 53 TL4349
Newton Ches 71 SJ4167
Newton Ches 71 SJ5059
Newton Cumb 86 SD2271
Newton D & G 100 NY1195
Newton Derbys 75 SK4459
Newton Gramp 141 NJ1663
Newton Gramp 141 NJ3362
Newton H & W 46 SO3432
Newton H & W 46 SO3769
Newton H & W 46 SO5153
Newton Highld 139 NH5850
Newton Highld 140 NH7448
Newton Highld 140 NH7866
Newton Lancs 80 SD3436
Newton Lancs 80 SD4430
Newton Lancs 87 SD5974
Newton Lancs 81 SD6950
Newton Lincs 64 TF0436
Newton Loth 117 NT0977
Newton M Glam 33 SS8377
Newton N York 90 SE8872
Newton Nhants 51 SP8883
Newton Norfk 66 TF8315
Newton Notts 63 SK6841
Newton Nthumb 110 NT9406
Newton Nthumb 103 NZ0364
Newton Shrops 59 SJ4234
Newton Somset 20 ST1038
Newton Staffs 73 SK0325
Newton Strath 114 NS0498
Newton Strath 116 NS6760
Newton Strath 108 NS9331
Newton Suffk 54 TL9240
Newton W Mids 61 SP0393

Newton Paddolgreen

Newton W Mids 61 SP0393
Newton W York 83 SE4527
Newton Warwks 50 SP5378
Newton Wilts 23 SU2322
Newton Abbot Devon 7 SX8571
Newton Arlosh Cumb 93 NY2055
Newton Aycliffe Dur 96 NZ2724
Newton Bewley Cleve 97 NZ4626
Newton Blossomville Bucks 38 SP9251
Newton Bromswold Beds 51 SP9966
Newton Burgoland Leics 62 SK3708
Newton by Toft Lincs 76 TF0487
Newton Ferrers Cnwll 5 SX3466
Newton Ferrers Devon 6 SX5548
Newton Ferry W Isls 154 NF8978
Newton Flotman Norfk 67 TM2198
Newton Green Gwent 34 ST5191
Newton Harcourt Leics 50 SP6497
Newton Heath Gt Man 79 SD8700
Newton Hill W York 83 SE3222
Newton Kyme N York 83 SE4644
Newton Longville Bucks 38 SP8431
Newton Mearns Strath 115 NS5355
Newton Morrell N York 89 NZ2309
Newton Mountain Dyfed 30 SM9808
Newton Mulgrave N York 97 NZ7815
Newton of Balcanquhal Tays 126 NO1610
Newton on Ouse N York 90 SE5159
Newton on Trent Lincs 76 SK8373
Newton on the Hill Shrops 59 SJ4823
Newton Poppleford Devon 9 SY0889
Newton Purcell Oxon 49 SP6230
Newton Regis Warwks 61 SK2707
Newton Reigny Cumb 93 NY4731
Newton Row Highld 151 ND3449
Newton Solney Derbys 73 SK2825
Newton St Cyres Devon 9 SX8898
Newton St Faith Norfk 67 TG2217
Newton St Loe Avon 22 ST7064
Newton St Petrock Devon 18 SS4112
Newton Stacey Hants 24 SU4140
Newton Stewart D & G 99 NX4065
Newton Toney Wilts 23 SU2140
Newton Tracey Devon 19 SS5226
Newton Underwood Nthumb 103 NZ1486
Newton under Roseberry Cleve 90 NZ5713
Newton upon Derwent Humb 84 SE7149
Newton Valence Hants 24 SU7232
Newton-le-Willows Mersyd 78 SJ5995
Newton-le-Willows N York 89 SE2189
Newton-on-the-Moor Nthumb 111 NU1705
Newtongarry Croft Gramp 142 NJ5735
Newtongrange Loth 118 NT3364
Newtonhill Gramp 135 NO9193
Newtonloan Loth 118 NT3362
Newtonmill Tays 134 NO6064
Newtonmore Highld 132 NN7098
Newtown Ches 71 SJ5375
Newtown Ches 71 SJ6247
Newtown Ches 72 SJ9060
Newtown Cnwll 2 SW5729
Newtown Cnwll 3 SW7423
Newtown Cnwll 3 SX1052
Newtown Cnwll 5 SX2978
Newtown Cumb 92 NY1048
Newtown Cumb 101 NY5062
Newtown Cumb 94 NY5224
Newtown D & G 107 NS7710
Newtown Derbys 79 SJ9984
Newtown Devon 19 SS7625
Newtown Dorset 10 ST4802
Newtown Dorset 12 SZ0393
Newtown Gloucs 35 SO6702
Newtown Gt Man 78 SD5604
Newtown Gwent 33 SO1709
Newtown H & W 46 SO4757
Newtown H & W 46 SO5333
Newtown H & W 46 SO6145
Newtown H & W 47 SO7037
Newtown H & W 47 SO8755
Newtown H & W 60 SO9478
Newtown Hants 12 SU2710
Newtown Hants 24 SU4763
Newtown Hants 13 SU6013
Newtown Highld 131 NH3504
Newtown IOW 13 SZ4290
Newtown Lancs 80 SD5118
Newtown M Glam 33 ST0598
Newtown Nthumb 111 NT9631
Newtown Nthumb 103 NU0300
Newtown Powys 58 SO1091
Newtown Shrops 59 SJ4222
Newtown Shrops 59 SJ4731
Newtown Staffs 60 SJ9904
Newtown Wilts 22 ST9129
Newtown Wilts 23 SU2963
Newtown Linford Leics 62 SK5209
Newtown of Beltrees Strath 115 NS3758
Newtown St Boswells Border 110 NT5732
Newtown Unthank Leics 62 SK4904
Newtyle Tays 126 NO2941
Newyears Green Gt Lon 26 TQ0788
Newyork Strath 122 NM9611
Nextend H & W 46 SO3357
Neyland Dyfed 30 SM9605
Niarbyl IOM 153 SC2177
Nibley Avon 35 ST6982
Nibley Gloucs 35 SO6606
Nibley Green Gloucs 35 ST7396
Nicholashayne Devon 9 ST1016
Nicholaston W Glam 32 SS5288
Nickies Hill Cumb 101 NY5367
Nidd N York 89 SE3060
Nigg Gramp 135 NJ9402
Nigg Highld 147 NH8071
Nightcott Devon 19 SS8925
Nine Elms Wilts 36 SU1085
Nine Wells Dyfed 30 SM7924
Ninebanks Nthumb 94 NY7853
Nineveh H & W 47 SO6265
Ninfield E Susx 16 TQ7012
Ningwood IOW 13 SZ3989
Nisbet Border 110 NT6725
Nisbet Hill Border 119 NT7950
Niton IOW 13 SZ5076
Nitshill Strath 115 NS5260
No Man's Heath Ches 71 SJ5148
No Man's Heath Warwks 61 SK2808
No Man's Land Cnwll 4 SW9470
No Man's Land Cnwll 5 SX2756
Noah's Ark Kent 27 TQ5557
Noak Bridge Essex 40 TQ6990
Noak Hill Essex 27 TQ5494
Noblethorpe W York 82 SE2805
Nobold Shrops 59 SJ4609
Nobottle Nhants 49 SP6763
Nocton Lincs 76 TF0564
Nogdam End Norfk 67 TG3900
Noke Oxon 37 SP5413
Nolton Dyfed 30 SM8618
Nolton Haven Dyfed 30 SM8618
Nomansland Devon 19 SS8313
Nomansland Wilts 12 SU2517
Noneley Shrops 59 SJ4828
Nonington Kent 29 TR2552
Nook Cumb 101 NY4679
Nook Cumb 87 SD5481
Norbiton Common Gt Lon 26 TQ2067
Norbreck Lancs 80 SD3140
Norbridge H & W 47 SO7144
Norbury Ches 71 SJ5547
Norbury Derbys 73 SK1241
Norbury Gt Lon 27 TQ3069
Norbury Shrops 59 SO3692
Norbury Staffs 72 SJ7823
Norbury Common Ches 71 SJ5548
Norbury Junction Staffs 72 SJ7923
Norchard H & W 47 SO8568
Norcott Brook Ches 78 SJ6080
Norcross Lancs 80 SD3341
Nordam Humb 84 SE8932
Nordelph Norfk 65 TF5501
Norden Gt Man 81 SD8614
Nordley Shrops 60 SO6996
Norham Nthumb 110 NT9047
Norland Town W York 82 SE0622
Norley Ches 71 SJ5772
Norleywood Hants 12 SZ3597
Norlington E Susx 16 TQ4413
Norman Cross Cambs 52 TL1690
Norman's Bay E Susx 16 TQ6805
Norman's Green Devon 9 ST0503
Normanby Cleve 97 NZ5418
Normanby Humb 84 SE8816
Normanby Lincs 76 SK9988
Normanby N York 90 SE7381
Normanby le Wold Lincs 76 TF1295
Normandy Surrey 25 SU9351
Normanton Derbys 62 SK3433
Normanton Leics 63 SK8140
Normanton Leics 63 SK9305
Normanton Lincs 63 SK9446
Normanton Notts 75 SK7054
Normanton W York 83 SE3822
Normanton Wilts 23 SU1340
Normanton le Heath Leics 62 SK3712
Normanton on Soar Notts 62 SK5122
Normanton on Trent Notts 75 SK7868
Normanton on the Wolds Notts 62 SK6232
Normoss Lancs 80 SD3437
Norney Surrey 25 SU9444
Norrington Common Wilts 22 ST8864
Norris Green Cnwll 5 SX4169
Norristhorpe W York 82 SE2123
North Anston S York 75 SK5184
North Aston Oxon 49 SP4828
North Baddesley Hants 13 SU3920
North Ballachulish Highld 130 NN0560
North Barrow Somset 21 ST6129
North Barsham Norfk 66 TF9135
North Benfleet Essex 40 TQ7588
North Bersted W Susx 14 SU9201
North Berwick Loth 118 NT5485
North Biddick T & W 96 NZ3153
North Bitchburn Dur 96 NZ1732
North Boarhunt Hants 13 SU6010
North Bockhampton Hants 12 SZ1797
North Bovey Devon 8 SX7484
North Bradley Wilts 22 ST8555
North Brentor Devon 5 SX4881
North Brewham Somset 22 ST7236
North Bridge Surrey 14 SU9636
North Brook End Cambs 39 TL2944
North Buckland Devon 18 SS4840
North Burlingham Norfk 67 TG3609
North Cadbury Somset 21 ST6327
North Carlton Lincs 76 SK9477
North Carlton Notts 75 SK5984
North Cave Humb 84 SE8932
North Cerney Gloucs 35 SP0107
North Charford Hants 12 SU1919
North Charlton Nthumb 111 NU1622
North Cheam Gt Lon 26 TQ2365
North Cheriton Somset 22 ST6925
North Chideock Dorset 10 SY4294
North Cliffe Humb 84 SE8736
North Clifton Notts 75 SK8272
North Close Dur 96 NZ2532
North Cockerington Lincs 77 TF3790
North Collingham Notts 76 SK8362
North Common E Susx 15 TQ3921
North Connel Strath 122 NM9034
North Cornelly M Glam 33 SS8181
North Corner Cnwll 3 SW7818
North Corry Highld 122 NM8353
North Cotes Lincs 77 TA3400
North Country Cnwll 2 SW6943
North Cove Suffk 55 TM4689
North Cowton N York 89 NZ2803
North Crawley Bucks 38 SP9244
North Cray Gt Lon 27 TQ4872
North Creake Norfk 66 TF8538
North Curry Somset 21 ST3125
North Dalton Humb 84 SE9351
North Deighton N York 83 SE3951
North Duffield N York 83 SE6837
North Duntulm Highld 136 NG4274
North Elham Kent 29 TR1844
North Elkington Lincs 77 TF2890
North Elmham Norfk 66 TF9820
North Elmsall W York 83 SE4712
North End Avon 21 ST4266
North End Cumb 93 NY3259
North End Dorset 22 ST8427
North End Essex 40 TL6618
North End Hants 12 SU1016
North End Hants 24 SU5828
North End Hants 13 SU6502
North End Humb 85 TA1022
North End Humb 85 TA1941
North End Humb 85 TA2831
North End Humb 85 TA3101
North End Leics 62 SK5715
North End Lincs 76 TF0499
North End Lincs 64 TF2341
North End Lincs 77 TF4289
North End Mersyd 78 SD3004
North End Nhants 51 SP9668
North End Norfk 66 TL9992
North End W Susx 14 SU9703
North End W Susx 14 TQ1109
North Erradale Highld 144 NG7480
North Evington Leics 62 SK6204
North Fambridge Essex 40 TQ8597
North Feorline Strath 105 NR9029
North Ferriby Humb 84 SE9826
North Frodingham Humb 85 TA1053
North Gorley Hants 12 SU1611
North Green Norfk 55 TM2288
North Green Suffk 55 TM3162
North Green Suffk 55 TM3966
North Grimston N York 90 SE8467
North Halling Kent 28 TQ7065
North Hayling Hants 13 SU7303
North Hazelrigg Nthumb 111 NU0533
North Heasley Devon 19 SS7333
North Heath W Susx 14 TQ0621
North Hele Somset 20 ST0323
North Hill Cnwll 5 SX2776
North Hillingdon Gt Lon 26 TQ0784
North Hinksey Oxon 37 SP4905
North Huish Devon 7 SX7156
North Hykeham Lincs 76 SK9465
North Kelsey Humb 84 TA0401
North Kessock Highld 140 NH6548
North Killingholme Humb 85 TA1417
North Kilvington N York 89 SE4285
North Kilworth Leics 50 SP6183
North Kingston Hants 12 SU1603
North Kyme Lincs 76 TF1552
North Landing Humb 91 TA2471
North Lee Bucks 38 SP8308
North Lees N York 89 SE2973
North Leigh Kent 29 TR1347
North Leigh Oxon 36 SP3813
North Leverton with Habblesthorpe Notts 75 SK7882
North Littleton H & W 48 SP0847
North Lopham Norfk 54 TM0382
North Luffenham Leics 63 SK9303
North Marden W Susx 14 SU8016
North Marston Bucks 37 SP7722
North Middleton Loth 118 NT3559
North Middleton Nthumb 111 NT9924
North Milmain D & G 98 NX0852
North Molton Devon 19 SS7329
North Moreton Oxon 37 SU5689
North Mundham W Susx 14 SU8702
North Muskham Notts 75 SK7958
North Newbald Humb 84 SE9136
North Newington Oxon 49 SP4240
North Newnton Wilts 23 SU1257
North Newton Somset 20 ST3031
North Nibley Gloucs 35 ST7495
North Oakley Hants 24 SU5354
North Ockendon Gt Lon 27 TQ5985
North Ormsby Lincs 77 TF2893
North Otterington N York 89 SE3689
North Owersby Lincs 76 TF0594
North Perrott Somset 10 ST4709
North Petherton Somset 20 ST2833
North Petherwin Cnwll 5 SX2789
North Pickenham Norfk 66 TF8606
North Piddle H & W 47 SO9654
North Pool Devon 7 SX7741
North Poorton Dorset 10 SY5298
North Poulner Hants 12 SU1606
North Quarme Somset 20 SS9236
North Queensferry Fife 117 NT1380
North Radworthy Devon 19 SS7534
North Rauceby Lincs 76 TF0246
North Reston Lincs 77 TF3883
North Rigton N York 82 SE2749
North Ripley Hants 12 SZ1699
North Rode Ches 72 SJ8866
North Row Cumb 93 NY2232
North Runcton Norfk 65 TF6416
North Scale Cumb 86 SD1869
North Scarle Lincs 76 SK8466
North Seaton Nthumb 103 NZ2986
North Seaton Colliery Nthumb 103 NZ2985
North Shian Strath 122 NM9143
North Shields T & W 103 NZ3568
North Shoebury Essex 40 TQ9286
North Shore Lancs 80 SD3037
North Side Cambs 64 TL2799
North Side Cumb 92 NX9929
North Skelton Cleve 97 NZ6718
North Skirlaugh Humb 85 TA1439
North Somercotes Lincs 77 TF4296
North Stainley N York 89 SE2876
North Stainmore Cumb 95 NY8314
North Stifford Essex 40 TQ6080
North Stoke Avon 35 ST7069
North Stoke Oxon 37 SU6186
North Stoke W Susx 14 TQ0110
North Street Berks 24 SU6371
North Street Cambs 53 TL5868
North Street Hants 12 SU1518
North Street Hants 24 SU6433
North Street Kent 28 TQ8174
North Street Kent 28 TR0157
North Sunderland Nthumb 111 NU2131
North Tamerton Cnwll 5 SX3197
North Tawton Devon 8 SS6601
North Third Cent 116 NS7589
North Tidworth Wilts 23 SU2349
North Town Berks 26 SU8882
North Town Devon 19 SS5109
North Town Somset 21 ST5642
North Tuddenham Norfk 66 TG0314
North Walbottle T & W 103 NZ1767
North Walsham Norfk 67 TG2830
North Waltham Hants 24 SU5646
North Warnborough Hants 24 SU7351
North Weald Basset Essex 39 TL4904
North Wheatley Notts 75 SK7585
North Whilborough Devon 7 SX8766
North Wick Avon 21 ST5865
North Widcombe Somset 21 ST5758
North Willingham Lincs 76 TF1688
North Wingfield Derbys 74 SK4065
North Witham Lincs 63 SK9221
North Wootton Dorset 11 ST6514
North Wootton Norfk 65 TF6424
North Wootton Somset 21 ST5641
North Wraxall Wilts 35 ST8175
North Wroughton Wilts 36 SU1481
Northacre Norfk 66 TL9598
Northall Bucks 38 SP9520
Northall Green Norfk 66 TF9914
Northallerton N York 89 SE3694
Northam Devon 18 SS4529
Northam Hants 13 SU4312
Northampton H & W 47 SO8365
Northampton Nhants 49 SP7560
Northaw Herts 27 TL2702
Northay Somset 10 ST2811
Northborough Cambs 64 TF1507
Northbourne Kent 29 TR3352
Northbridge Street E Susx 17 TQ7324
Northbrook Hants 24 SU5139
Northbrook Oxon 37 SP4922
Northchapel W Susx 14 SU9529
Northchurch Herts 38 SP9708
Northcott Devon 9 ST0912
Northcott Devon 9 ST1209
Northcott Devon 5 SX3392
Northcourt Oxon 37 SU4998
Northdown Kent 29 TR3770
Northedge Derbys 74 SK3665
Northend Bucks 37 SU7392
Northend Warwks 48 SP3952
Northend Woods Bucks 26 SU9089
Northenden Gt Man 79 SJ8289
Northfield Gramp 135 NJ9008
Northfield Humb 84 TA0326
Northfield W Mids 60 SP0279
Northfields Lincs 64 TF0208
Northfleet Kent 27 TQ6374
Northiam E Susx 17 TQ8324
Northill Beds 52 TL1446
Northington Gloucs 35 SO7008
Northington Hants 24 SU5637
Northlands Lincs 77 TF3453
Northleach Gloucs 36 SP1114
Northleigh Devon 19 SS6034
Northleigh Devon 9 SY1995
Northlew Devon 19 SX5099
Northload Bridge Somset 21 ST4939
Northmooor Somset 20 SS9028
Northmoor Oxon 36 SP4202
Northmuir Tays 126 NO3854
Northney Hants 13 SU7303
Northolt Gt Lon 26 TQ1384
Northop Clwyd 70 SJ2468
Northop Hall Clwyd 70 SJ2667
Northorpe Lincs 76 SK8997
Northorpe Lincs 64 TF0917
Northorpe Lincs 64 TF2036
Northorpe W York 82 SE2221
Northover Somset 21 ST4838
Northover Somset 21 ST5223
Northowram W York 82 SE1126
Northport Dorset 11 SY9288
Northrepps Norfk 67 TG2439
Northway Somset 20 ST1329
Northway W Glam 32 SS5889
Northwich Ches 79 SJ6673
Northwick Avon 34 ST5686
Northwick H & W 47 SO8458
Northwick Somset 21 ST3548
Northwold Norfk 65 TL7597
Northwood Derbys 74 SK2664
Northwood Gt Lon 26 TQ0990
Northwood IOW 13 SZ4992
Northwood Shrops 59 SJ4633
Northwood Staffs 72 SJ8949
Northwood End Beds 38 TL0941
Northwood Green Gloucs 35 SO7216
Norton Avon 21 ST3463
Norton Ches 78 SJ5581
Norton Cleve 96 NZ4421
Norton Cnwll 4 SX0869
Norton E Susx 16 TQ4701
Norton Gloucs 47 SO8524
Norton Gwent 34 SO4420
Norton H & W 47 SO8751
Norton H & W 48 SP0447
Norton Herts 39 TL2334
Norton IOW 12 SZ3488
Norton N York 90 SE7971
Norton Nhants 49 SP5963
Norton Notts 75 SK5771
Norton Powys 46 SO3067
Norton S York 83 SE5415
Norton S York 74 SK3681
Norton Shrops 59 SJ5609
Norton Shrops 60 SJ7200
Norton Shrops 59 SO4681
Norton Shrops 59 SO6382
Norton Suffk 54 TL9565
Norton W Glam 32 SS6188
Norton W Susx 14 SU9206
Norton Wilts 35 ST8884
Norton Bavant Wilts 22 ST9043
Norton Bridge Staffs 72 SJ8630
Norton Canes Staffs 60 SK0107
Norton Canon H & W 46 SO3847
Norton Corner Norfk 66 TG0928
Norton Disney Lincs 76 SK8859
Norton Ferris Wilts 22 ST7936
Norton Fitzwarren Somset 20 ST1925
Norton Green IOW 12 SZ3488
Norton Green Staffs 60 SK0107
Norton Hawkfield Avon 21 ST5964
Norton Heath Essex 40 TL6004
Norton in Hales Shrops 72 SJ7038
Norton in the Moors Staffs 72 SJ8951
Norton Lindsey Warwks 48 SP2263
Norton Little Green Suffk 54 TL9766
Norton Malreward Avon 21 ST6064
Norton Mandeville Essex 40 TL5804
Norton St Philip Somset 22 ST7755
Norton Subcourse Norfk 67 TM4198
Norton sub Hamdon Somset 10 ST4615
Norton Wood H & W 46 SO3648
Norton-Juxta-Twycross Leics 61 SK3207
Norton-le-Clay N York 89 SE4071
Norwell Notts 75 SK7761
Norwell Woodhouse Notts 75 SK7362
Norwich Norfk 67 TG2308
Norwick Shet 155 HP6414
Norwood Cent 116 NS8793
Norwood Kent 17 TR0530
Norwood S York 75 SK4681
Norwood End Essex 40 TL5608
Norwood Green Gt Lon 26 TQ1378
Norwood Green W York 82 SE1326
Norwood Hill Surrey 15 TQ2343
Norwoodside Cambs 65 TL4197
Noseley Leics 50 SP7398
Noss Mayo Devon 6 SX5547
Nosterfield N York 89 SE2780
Nosterfield End Cambs 53 TL6344
Nostie Highld 138 NG8527
Notgrove Gloucs 36 SP1020
Nottage M Glam 33 SS8177
Notter Cnwll 5 SX3960
Nottingham Notts 62 SK5739
Nottington Dorset 11 SY6682
Notton W York 83 SE3413
Notton Wilts 35 ST9169
Nottswood Hill Gloucs 35 SO7018
Nounsley Essex 40 TL7910
Noutard's Green H & W 47 SO8066
Nox Shrops 59 SJ4110
Nuffield Oxon 37 SU6687
Nun Monkton N York 90 SE5057
Nunburnholme Humb 84 SE8447
Nuncargate Notts 75 SK5054
Nunclose Cumb 94 NY4945
Nuneaton Warwks 61 SP3691
Nuneham Courtenay Oxon 37 SU5599
Nunhead Gt Lon 27 TQ3475
Nunkeeling Humb 85 TA1449
Nunnerie Strath 108 NS9612
Nunney Somset 22 ST7345
Nunney Catch Somset 22 ST7344
Nunnington H & W 46 SO5543
Nunnington N York 90 SE6679
Nunnykirk Nthumb 103 NZ0793
Nuns Moor T & W 103 NZ2266
Nunsthorpe Humb 85 TA2607
Nunthorpe Cleve 97 NZ5314
Nunthorpe N York 83 SE6050
Nunthorpe Village Cleve 90 NZ5413
Nunton Wilts 23 SU1526
Nunwick N York 89 SE3274
Nunwick Nthumb 102 NY8774
Nup End Bucks 38 SP8619
Nupdown Avon 35 ST6395
Nupend Gloucs 35 SO7806
Nuptow Berks 25 SU8873
Nursling Hants 12 SU3716
Nursted Hants 13 SU7521
Nursteed Wilts 23 SU0260
Nurton Staffs 60 SO8399
Nutbourne W Susx 14 SU7705
Nutbourne W Susx 14 TQ0718
Nutfield Surrey 27 TQ3050
Nuthall Notts 62 SK5243
Nuthampstead Herts 39 TL4034
Nuthurst W Susx 15 TQ1925
Nutley E Susx 16 TQ4427
Nutley Hants 24 SU6044
Nuttal Lane Gt Man 81 SD7915
Nutwell S York 83 SE6304
Nybster Highld 151 ND3663
Nyetimber W Susx 14 SZ8998
Nyewood W Susx 14 SU8021
Nymet Rowland Devon 19 SS7108
Nymet Tracey Devon 8 SS7200
Nympsfield Gloucs 35 SO8000
Nynehead Somset 20 ST1422
Nythe Somset 21 ST4234
Nyton W Susx 14 SU9305

O

Oad Street Kent 28 TQ8762
Oadby Leics 50 SK6200
Oak Cross Devon 8 SX5399
Oak Tree Dur 89 NZ3613
Oakall Green H & W 47 SO8161
Oakamoor Staffs 73 SK0444
Oakbank Loth 117 NT0766
Oakdale Gwent 33 ST1898
Oake Somset 20 ST1525
Oaken Staffs 60 SJ8602
Oakenclough Lancs 80 SD5447
Oakengates Shrops 60 SJ7010
Oakenholt Clwyd 70 SJ2571
Oakenshaw Dur 96 NZ1937
Oakenshaw W York 82 SE1727
Oaker Side Derbys 74 SK2760
Oakerthorpe Derbys 74 SK3854
Oakford Devon 20 SS9121
Oakford Dyfed 42 SN4558
Oakfordbridge Devon 20 SS9122
Oakgrove Ches 79 SJ9169
Oakham Leics 63 SK8608
Oakhanger Ches 72 SJ7754
Oakhanger Hants 14 SU7635
Oakhill Somset 21 ST6347
Oakhurst Kent 27 TQ5550
Oakington Cambs 52 TL4164
Oaklands Powys 45 SO0450
Oakle Street Gloucs 35 SO7517
Oakley Beds 51 TL0153
Oakley Bucks 37 SP6412
Oakley Dorset 11 SZ0198
Oakley Hants 24 SU5650
Oakley Oxon 37 SP7500
Oakley Suffk 54 TM1677
Oakley Green Berks 26 SU9276
Oakley Park Powys 58 SN9886
Oakridge Gloucs 35 SO9103
Oaks Dur 96 NZ1525
Oaks Lancs 81 SD6733
Oaks Shrops 59 SJ4204
Oaks Green Derbys 73 SK1533
Oaksey Wilts 35 ST9993
Oakshaw Cumb 101 NY5176
Oakshott Hants 13 SU7427
Oakthorpe Leics 61 SK3212
Oakwood Nthumb 102 NY9465
Oakwoodhill Surrey 15 TQ1337
Oakworth W York 82 SE0338
Oare Kent 28 TR0063
Oare Somset 19 SS7947
Oare Wilts 23 SU1563
Oasby Lincs 63 TF0039
Oath Somset 21 ST3827
Oathlaw Tays 127 NO4756
Oatlands Park Surrey 26 TQ0865
Oban Strath 122 NM8629
Obley Shrops 46 SO3377
Obney Tays 125 NO0237
Oborne Dorset 11 ST6518
Obthorpe Lincs 64 TF0914
Occlestone Green Ches 72 SJ6962
Occold Suffk 54 TM1570
Ochiltree Strath 107 NS5021
Ockbrook Derbys 62 SK4235
Ocker Hill W Mids 60 SO9793
Ockeridge H & W 47 SO7762
Ockham Surrey 26 TQ0756
Ockle Highld 129 NM5570
Ockley Surrey 15 TQ1440
Ocle Pychard H & W 46 SO5945
Octon Humb 91 TA0369
Odcombe Somset 10 ST5015
Odd Down Avon 22 ST7462
Oddingley H & W 47 SO9159
Oddington Gloucs 48 SP2225
Oddington Oxon 37 SP5515
Odell Beds 51 SP9657
Odham Devon 18 SS4703
Odiham Hants 24 SU7451
Odsal W York 82 SE1529
Odsey Herts 39 TL2938
Odstock Wilts 23 SU1426
Odstone Leics 62 SK3907
Offchurch Warwks 48 SP3565
Offenham H & W 48 SP0546
Offerton T & W 96 NZ3455
Offham E Susx 15 TQ4012
Offham Kent 28 TQ6557
Offham W Susx 14 TQ0208
Offleymarsh Shrops 72 SJ7829
Offord Cluny Cambs 52 TL2267
Offord Darcy Cambs 52 TL2266
Offton Suffk 54 TM0649
Offwell Devon 9 SY1999
Ogbourne Maizey Wilts 36 SU1871
Ogbourne St Andrew Wilts 36 SU1872
Ogbourne St George Wilts 36 SU2074
Ogden W York 82 SE0730
Ogle Nthumb 103 NZ1378
Oglet Mersyd 78 SJ4481
Ogmore M Glam 33 SS8876
Ogmore Vale M Glam 33 SS9390
Ogmore-by-Sea M Glam 33 SS8675
Ogwen Bank Gwynd 69 SH6265
Okeford Fitzpaine Dorset 11 ST8010
Okehampton Devon 8 SX5995
Olchard Devon 9 SX8777
Old Nhants 50 SP7872
Old Aberdeen Gramp 135 NJ9407
Old Alresford Hants 24 SU5834
Old Auchenbrack D & G 107 NX7597
Old Basford Notts 62 SK5543
Old Basing Hants 24 SU6652
Old Bewick Nthumb 111 NU0621
Old Bolingbroke Lincs 77 TF3565
Old Bracknell Berks 25 SU8668
Old Bramhope W York 82 SE2343
Old Brampton Derbys 74 SK3371
Old Bridge of Urr D & G 100 NX7767
Old Buckenham Norfk 66 TM0691
Old Burghclere Hants 24 SU4657
Old Byland N York 90 SE5585
Old Cassop Dur 96 NZ3339
Old Castle M Glam 33 SS9079
Old Church Stoke Powys 58 SO2894
Old Clee Humb 85 TA2808
Old Cleeve Somset 20 ST0441
Old Clipstone Notts 75 SK6064
Old Colwyn Clwyd 69 SH8678
Old Dailly Strath 106 NX2299
Old Dalby Leics 63 SK6723
Old Dam Derbys 74 SK1179
Old Deer Gramp 143 NJ9747
Old Ditch Somset 21 ST5049
Old Edington S York 75 SK5397
Old Eldon Dur 96 NZ2427
Old Ellerby Humb 85 TA1637
Old Felixstowe Suffk 55 TM3135
Old Fletton Cambs 64 TL1997
Old Forge H & W 34 SO5518
Old Furnace H & W 46 SO4923
Old Glossop Derbys 74 SK0494
Old Goole Humb 84 SE7422
Old Grimsby IOS 2 SV8915
Old Hall Green Herts 39 TL3722
Old Hall Street Norfk 67 TG3033
Old Harlow Essex 39 TL4711
Old Heath Essex 41 TM0122
Old Hunstanton Norfk 65 TF6842
Old Hutton Cumb 87 SD5688
Old Kea Cnwll 3 SW8441
Old Kilpatrick Strath 115 NS4672
Old Knebworth Herts 39 TL2320
Old Lakenham Norfk 67 TG2205
Old Langho Lancs 81 SD7035
Old Leake Lincs 77 TF4050
Old Malton N York 90 SE7972
Old Micklefield W York 83 SE4433
Old Milton Hants 12 SZ2394
Old Milverton Warwks 48 SP2967
Old Newton Suffk 54 TM0562
Old Quarrington Dur 96 NZ3237
Old Radford Notts 62 SK5540
Old Radnor Powys 46 SO2558
Old Rayne Gramp 142 NJ6728
Old Romney Kent 17 TR0325
Old Shoreham W Susx 15 TQ2006
Old Shoremore Highld 148 NC2058
Old Soar Kent 27 TQ6254
Old Sodbury Avon 35 ST7581
Old Somerby Lincs 63 SK9633
Old Stratford Nhants 49 SP7741
Old Sunnford W Mids 60 SO9083
Old Tebay Cumb 87 NY6105
Old Thirsk N York 89 SE4382
Old Town Cumb 93 NY4743
Old Town Cumb 87 SD5982
Old Town E Susx 16 TV5999
Old Town IOS 2 SV9110
Old Town Nthumb 102 NY8891
Old Town W York 82 SE0028
Old Trafford Gt Man 79 SJ8196
Old Tupton Derbys 74 SK3865
Old Warden Beds 38 TL1343
Old Weston Cambs 51 TL0977
Old Wick Highld 151 ND3649
Old Windsor Berks 25 SU9874
Old Wives Lees Kent 29 TR0754
Old Woking Surrey 26 TQ0157
Old Wolverton Bucks 38 SP8041
Oldany Highld 148 NC0932
Oldberrow Warwks 48 SP1265
Oldbury Kent 27 TQ5956
Oldbury Shrops 60 SO7192
Oldbury W Mids 60 SO9888
Oldbury Warwks 61 SP3194
Oldbury Naite Avon 35 ST6293
Oldbury on the Hill Gloucs 35 ST8188
Oldbury-on-Severn Avon 34 ST6092
Oldcastle Gwent 46 SO3224
Oldcastle Heath Ches 71 SJ4745
Oldcotes Notts 75 SK5888
Oldfield H & W 47 SO8464
Oldfield W York 82 SE0037
Oldford Somset 22 ST7850
Oldhall Green Suffk 54 TL8956
Oldham Gt Man 79 SD9204
Oldhamstocks Loth 119 NT7470
Oldhurst Cambs 52 TL3077
Oldland Avon 35 ST6771
Oldmeldrum Gramp 143 NJ8127
Oldmill Cnwll 5 SX3673
Oldmixon Avon 21 ST3358
Oldridge Devon 8 SX8296
Oldstead N York 90 SE5379
Oldwall Cumb 101 NY4761
Oldwalls W Glam 32 SS4891
Oldways End Devon 19 SS8724
Oldwhat Gramp 143 NJ8651
Oldwoods Shrops 59 SJ4520
Olive Green Staffs 73 SK1118
Oliver Border 108 NT0924
Oliver's Battery Hants 13 SU4527
Ollaberry Shet 155 HU3680
Ollach Highld 137 NG5137
Ollerton Ches 79 SJ7776
Ollerton Notts 75 SK6567
Ollerton Shrops 72 SJ6425
Olmarch Dyfed 44 SN6255
Olmstead Green Cambs 53 TL6341
Olney Bucks 38 SP8951
Olney Nhants 49 SP6643
Olrig House Highld 151 ND1866
Olton W Mids 61 SP1382
Olveston Avon 34 ST6086
Ombersley H & W 47 SO8463
Ompton Notts 75 SK6865
Onchan IOM 153 SC3978
One House Suffk 54 TM0159
Onecote Staffs 73 SK0455
Onen Gwent 34 SO4314
Ongar Street H & W 46 SO3967
Onibury Shrops 46 SO4579
Onich Highld 130 NN0261
Onllwyn W Glam 33 SN8410
Onneley Staffs 72 SJ7542
Onslow Village Surrey 25 SU9849
Onston Ches 71 SJ5873
Openwoodgate Derbys 62 SK3647
Opinan Highld 137 NG7472
Orbliston Gramp 141 NJ3057
Orbost Highld 136 NG2543
Orby Lincs 77 TF4967
Orchard Portman Somset 20 ST2421
Orcheston Wilts 23 SU0545
Orcop H & W 46 SO4726
Orcop Hill H & W 46 SO4727
Ord Gramp 142 NJ6258
Ord Highld 129 NG6113
Ordhead Gramp 135 NJ6610
Ordie Gramp 134 NJ4501
Ordiequish Gramp 141 NJ3357
Ordley Nthumb 95 NY9459
Ordsall Notts 75 SK7079
Ore E Susx 17 TQ8311
Oreleton Common H & W 46 SO4768
Oreton Shrops 59 SO6580
Orford Ches 78 SJ6190
Orford Suffk 55 TM4250
Organford Dorset 11 SY9392
Orgreave Staffs 73 SK1415
Orlestone Kent 17 TR0034
Orleton H & W 46 SO4967
Orleton H & W 47 SO7067
Orlingbury Nhants 51 SP8572
Ormathwaite Cumb 93 NY2625
Ormesby Cleve 97 NZ5317
Ormesby St Margaret Norfk 67 TG4914
Ormesby St Michael Norfk 67 TG4714
Ormiscaig Highld 144 NG8590
Ormiston Loth 118 NT4169
Ormsaigmore Highld 121 NM4763
Ormsary Strath 113 NR7472
Ormskirk Lancs 78 SD4108
Ornsby Hill Dur 96 NZ1648
Oronsay Strath 112 NR3588
Orphir Ork 155 HY3404
Orpington Gt Lon 27 TQ4666
Orrell Gt Man 78 SD5303
Orrell Mersyd 78 SJ3496
Orrell Post Gt Man 78 SD5305
Orrisdale IOM 153 SC3292
Orroland D & G 92 NX7746
Orsett Essex 40 TQ6482
Orslow Staffs 72 SJ8015
Orston Notts 63 SK7740
Orthwaite Cumb 93 NY2534
Ortner Lancs 80 SD5354
Orton Cumb 87 NY6208
Orton Nhants 51 SP8079
Orton Staffs 60 SO8795
Orton Longueville Cambs 64 TL1796
Orton Rigg Cumb 93 NY3352
Orton Waterville Cambs 64 TL1595
Orton-on-the-Hill Leics 61 SK3003
Orwell Cambs 52 TL3650
Osbaldeston Lancs 81 SD6431
Osbaldeston Green Lancs 81 SD6432
Osbaldwick N York 83 SE6251
Osbaston Leics 62 SK4204
Osbaston Shrops 59 SJ3222
Osborne IOW 13 SZ5194
Osbournby Lincs 64 TF0638
Oscroft Ches 71 SJ5067
Osgathorpe Leics 62 SK4319
Osgodby Lincs 76 TF0792
Osgodby N York 83 SE6433
Osgodby N York 91 TA0584
Oskaig Highld 137 NG5438
Oskamull Strath 121 NM4540
Osmanthorpe W York 83 SE3333
Osmaston Derbys 73 SK1943
Osmington Dorset 11 SY7283
Osmington Mills Dorset 11 SY7381
Osmotherley N York 89 SE4596
Osney Oxon 37 SP4906
Ospringe Kent 28 TR0060
Ossett W York 82 SE2720
Ossington Notts 75 SK7564
Ostend Essex 40 TQ9397
Oswaldkirk N York 90 SE6278
Oswaldtwistle Lancs 81 SD7327
Oswestry Shrops 59 SJ2929
Otford Kent 27 TQ5359
Otham Kent 28 TQ7953
Otham Hole Kent 28 TQ8052
Othery Somset 21 ST3831
Otley Suffk 55 TM2055
Otley W York 82 SE2045
Otley Green Suffk 55 TM2156
Otter Ferry Strath 114 NR9384
Otterbourne Hants 13 SU4522
Otterburn N York 88 SD8857
Otterburn Nthumb 102 NY8893
Otterham Cnwll 4 SX1690
Otterham Quay Kent 28 TQ8366
Otterhampton Somset 20 ST2443
Ottershaw Surrey 26 TQ0263
Otterswick Shet 155 HU5285
Otterton Devon 9 SY0684
Otterwood Hants 13 SU4102
Ottery Devon 6 SX4475
Ottery St Mary Devon 9 SY1095
Ottinge Kent 29 TR1642
Ottringham Humb 85 TA2624
Oughterby Cumb 93 NY2955
Oughtershaw N York 88 SD8780
Oughterside Cumb 92 NY1140
Oughtibridge S York 74 SK3093
Oughtrington Ches 79 SJ6987
Oulston N York 90 SE5474
Oulton Cumb 93 NY2450
Oulton Norfk 66 TG1328
Oulton Staffs 72 SJ7822
Oulton Staffs 72 SJ9035
Oulton Suffk 67 TM5294
Oulton W York 83 SE3628
Oulton Broad Suffk 67 TM5192
Oulton Street Norfk 66 TG1527
Oundle Nhants 51 TL0388
Ounsdale Staffs 60 SO8693
Ousby Cumb 94 NY6134
Ousden Suffk 53 TL7459
Ousefleet Humb 84 SE8323
Ouston Dur 96 NZ2554
Ouston Nthumb 103 NZ0770
Out Newton Humb 85 TA3821
Outchester Nthumb 111 NU1433
Outgate Cumb 87 SD3599
Outhgill Cumb 88 NY7801
Outhill Warwks 48 SP1066
Outlands Staffs 72 SJ7630
Outlane W York 82 SE0817
Outward Gate Gt Man 79 SD7805
Outwell Norfk 65 TF5103
Outwick Hants 12 SU1417
Outwood Surrey 15 TQ3145
Outwood W York 83 SE3323
Outwoods Leics 62 SK4018
Outwoods Staffs 72 SJ7817
Outwoods Warwks 61 SP2484
Ouzlewell Green W York 83 SE3326
Ovenden W York 82 SE0827
Over Avon 34 ST5882
Over Cambs 52 TL3770
Over Ches 71 SJ6365
Over Gloucs 35 SO8119
Over Burrows Derbys 73 SK2639
Over Compton Dorset 10 ST5816
Over End Cambs 51 TL0893
Over Green Warwks 61 SP1694
Over Haddon Derbys 74 SK2066
Over Kellet Lancs 87 SD5169
Over Kiddington Oxon 36 SP4021
Over Monnow Gwent 34 SO5012
Over Norton Oxon 48 SP3128
Over Silton N York 89 SE4493
Over Stenton Fife 117 NT2799
Over Stowey Somset 20 ST1838
Over Stratton Somset 10 ST4315
Over Tabley Ches 79 SJ7279
Over Wallop Hants 23 SU2838
Over Whitacre Warwks 61 SP2590
Over Woodhouse Derbys 75 SK4671
Over Worton Oxon 49 SP4329
Overbury H & W 47 SO9537
Overgreen Derbys 74 SK3273
Overleigh Somset 21 ST4835
Overley Staffs 73 SK1515
Overpool Ches 71 SJ3877
Overscaig Hotel Highld 149 NC4123
Overseal Derbys 73 SK2915
Oversland Kent 28 TR0557
Overstey Green Warwks 48 SP0957
Overstone Nhants 50 SP7966
Overstrand Norfk 67 TG2440
Overstreet Wilts 23 SU0637
Overthorpe Nhants 49 SP4840
Overton Ches 71 SJ5277
Overton Clwyd 71 SJ3741
Overton Gramp 143 NJ8714
Overton Hants 24 SU5149
Overton Lancs 87 SD4358
Overton N York 83 SE5555
Overton Shrops 46 SO5072
Overton W Glam 32 SS4685
Overton W York 82 SE2516
Overton Bridge Clwyd 71 SJ3542
Overton Green Ches 72 SJ8060
Overtown Lancs 87 SD6275
Overtown Strath 116 NS8053
Overtown W York 83 SE3516
Overtown Wilts 36 SU1579
Overy Oxon 37 SU5893
Overy Staithe Norfk 66 TF8444
Oving Bucks 37 SP7821
Oving W Susx 14 SU9004
Ovingdean E Susx 15 TQ3503
Ovingham Nthumb 103 NZ0863
Ovington Dur 89 NZ1314
Ovington Essex 53 TL7642
Ovington Hants 24 SU5631
Ovington Norfk 66 TF9202
Ovington Nthumb 103 NZ0663
Ower Hants 12 SU3215
Ower Hants 13 SU4702
Owermoigne Dorset 11 SY7685
Owl's Green Suffk 55 TM2869
Owlbury Shrops 59 SO3191
Owlerton S York 74 SK3389
Owlpen Gloucs 35 ST7998
Owlsmoor Berks 25 SU8462
Owlswick Bucks 37 SP7806
Owmby Lincs 85 TA0704
Owmby Lincs 76 TF0087
Owslebury Hants 13 SU5123
Owston Leics 63 SK7707
Owston S York 83 SE5511
Owston Ferry Humb 75 SE8000
Owstwick Humb 85 TA2732
Owthorne Humb 85 TA3328
Owthorpe Notts 63 SK6733
Oxborough Norfk 65 TF7401
Oxbridge Dorset 10 SY4797
Oxcombe Lincs 77 TF3177
Oxcroft Derbys 75 SK4873
Oxen End Essex 40 TL6629
Oxen Park Cumb 86 SD3187
Oxenholme Cumb 87 SD5290
Oxenhope W York 82 SE0334
Oxenpill Somset 21 ST4441
Oxenton Gloucs 47 SO9531
Oxenwood Wilts 23 SU3058
Oxford Oxon 37 SP5106
Oxhey Herts 26 TQ1295
Oxhill Dur 96 NZ1852
Oxhill Warwks 48 SP3146
Oxley W Mids 60 SJ9001
Oxley Green Essex 40 TL9014
Oxley's Green E Susx 16 TQ6921
Oxlode Cambs 53 TL4886
Oxnam Border 110 NT6918
Oxnead Norfk 67 TG2224
Oxshott Surrey 26 TQ1460
Oxshott Heath Surrey 26 TQ1361
Oxspring S York 82 SE2601
Oxted Surrey 27 TQ3852
Oxton Border 118 NT4953
Oxton N York 83 SE5043
Oxton Notts 75 SK6351
Oxwich W Glam 32 SS4986
Oxwich Green W Glam 32 SS4985
Oxwick Norfk 66 TF9125
Oykel Bridge Hotel Highld 145 NC3801
Oyne Gramp 142 NJ6725
Oystermouth W Glam 32 SS6187
Ozleworth Gloucs 35 ST7993

P

Packers hill Dorset 11 ST7110
Packington Leics 62 SK3614
Packmoor Staffs 72 SJ8654
Packmores Warwks 48 SP2866
Padanaram Tays 127 NO4251
Padbury Bucks 49 SP7230
Paddington Ches 79 SJ6389
Paddington Gt Lon 27 TQ2681
Paddlesworth Kent 28 TQ6862
Paddlesworth Kent 29 TR1939
Paddock Wood Kent 28 TQ6744
Paddolgreen Shrops 59 SJ5032

Padeswood
Potter Brompton

Padeswood *Clwyd* 70 SJ2762
Padfield *Derbys* 74 SK0296
Padgate *Ches* 79 SJ6389
Padhams Green *Essex* 40 TQ6497
Padiham *Lancs* 81 SD7933
Padside *N York* 89 SE1659
Padstow *Cnwll* 4 SW9175
Padworth *Berks* 24 SU6166
Page Bank *Dur* 96 NZ2335
Pagham *W Susx* 14 SZ8897
Paglesham *Essex* 40 TQ9293
Paignton *Devon* 7 SX8860
Pailton *Warwks* 50 SP4781
Paine's Cross *E Susx* 16 TQ6223
Painleyhill *Staffs* 73 SK0333
Painscastle *Powys* 45 SO1646
Painshawfield *Nthumb* 103 NZ0560
Painsthorpe *Humb* 90 SE8158
Painswick *Gloucs* 35 SO8609
Painter's Forstal *Kent* 28 TQ9958
Paisley *Strath* 115 NS4864
Pakefield *Suffk* 55 TM5390
Pakenham *Suffk* 54 TL9267
Pale *Gwynd* 58 SH9836
Pale Green *Essex* 53 TL6542
Palestine *Hants* 23 SU2640
Paley Street *Berks* 26 SU8776
Palfrey *W Mids* 60 SP0196
Palgrave *Suffk* 54 TM1178
Pallington *Dorset* 11 SY7891
Palmers Green *Gt Lon* 27 TQ3192
Palmersbridge *Cnwll* 5 SX1977
Palmerston *Strath* 107 NS5019
Palmerstown *S Glam* 20 ST1369
Palnackie *D & G* 92 NX8157
Palnure *D & G* 99 NX4563
Palterton *Derbys* 75 SK4768
Pamber End *Hants* 24 SU6158
Pamber Green *Hants* 24 SU6159
Pamber Heath *Hants* 24 SU6162
Pamington *Gloucs* 47 SO9433
Pamphill *Dorset* 11 ST9900
Pampisford *Cambs* 53 TL4948
Panborough *Somset* 21 ST4745
Panbride *Tays* 127 NO5635
Pancrasweek *Devon* 18 SS2905
Pancross *S Glam* 20 ST0469
Pandy *Clwyd* 58 SJ1935
Pandy *Gwent* 34 SO3322
Pandy *Gwynd* 57 SH6202
Pandy *Gwynd* 57 SH8729
Pandy *Powys* 58 SH9004
Pandy Tudur *Clwyd* 69 SH8564
Pandy'r Capel *Clwyd* 70 SJ0850
Panfield *Essex* 40 TL7325
Pangbourne *Berks* 37 SU6376
Pangdean *W Susx* 15 TQ2911
Panks Bridge *H & W* 47 SO6248
Pannal *N York* 82 SE3051
Pannal Ash *N York* 82 SE2953
Pannanich Wells Hotel *Gramp* 134 NO4097
Pant *Shrops* 58 SJ2722
Pant Mawr *Powys* 43 SN8482
Pant-Gwyn *Dyfed* 44 SN5925
Pant-glas *Gwynd* 68 SH4747
Pant-pastynog *Clwyd* 70 SJ0461
Pant-y-dwr *Powys* 45 SN9874
Pant-y-ffridd *Powys* 58 SJ1502
Pant-y-gog *M Glam* 33 SS9090
Pant-y-mwyn *Clwyd* 70 SJ1964
Pantasaph *Clwyd* 70 SJ1675
Pantersbridge *Cnwll* 4 SX1667
Pantglas *Powys* 43 SN7797
Panton *Lincs* 76 TF1778
Pantperthog *Gwynd* 57 SH7404
Pantyffynnon *Dyfed* 32 SN6210
Pantygasseg *Gwent* 34 ST2599
Pantymenyn *Dyfed* 31 SN1426
Panxworth *Norfk* 67 TG3513
Papcastle *Cumb* 92 NY1031
Papigoe *Highld* 151 ND3851
Papple *Loth* 118 NT5972
Papplewick *Notts* 75 SK5451
Papworth Everard *Cambs* 52 TL2862
Papworth St Agnes *Cambs* 52 TL2664
Par *Cnwll* 3 SX0753
Paramour Street *Kent* 29 TR2961
Parbold *Lancs* 80 SD4911
Parbrook *Somset* 21 ST5736
Parbrook *W Susx* 14 TQ0825
Parc *Gwynd* 57 SH8834
Parc Seymour *Gwent* 34 ST4091
Parcllyn *Dyfed* 42 SN2451
Pardshaw *Cumb* 92 NY0924
Parham *Suffk* 55 TM3060
Park *D & G* 100 NX9091
Park *Gramp* 135 NO7898
Park *Nthumb* 102 NY6861
Park Bottom *Cnwll* 2 SW6642
Park Bridge *Gt Man* 79 SD9402
Park Corner *Berks* 26 SU8582
Park Corner *E Susx* 16 TQ5336
Park Corner *Oxon* 37 SU6988
Park End *Beds* 38 SP9952
Park End *Nthumb* 102 NY8675
Park End *Staffs* 72 SJ7851
Park Gate *H & W* 60 SO9371
Park Gate *Hants* 13 SU5108
Park Gate *W York* 82 SE1841
Park Green *Essex* 39 TL4628
Park Green *Suffk* 54 TM1364
Park Head *Cumb* 94 NY5841
Park Head *Derbys* 74 SK3654
Park Head *W York* 82 SE2007
Park Hill *Gloucs* 34 ST5799
Park Royal *Gt Lon* 26 TQ1982
Park Street *W Susx* 14 TQ1131
Parkend *Gloucs* 34 SO6108
Parkers Green *Kent* 16 TQ6148
Parkeston *Essex* 41 TM2332
Parkeston Quay *Essex* 41 TM2332
Parkfield *Bucks* 37 SP8002
Parkfield *Cnwll* 5 SX3167
Parkgate *Ches* 70 SJ2878
Parkgate *Ches* 79 SJ7873
Parkgate *Cumb* 93 NY2146
Parkgate *D & G* 100 NY0288
Parkgate *E Susx* 17 TQ7214
Parkgate *Essex* 40 TL6829
Parkgate *Kent* 27 TQ5064
Parkgate *Kent* 17 TQ8534
Parkgate *Surrey* 15 TQ2043
Parkhall *Strath* 115 NS4871
Parkham *Devon* 18 SS3921
Parkham Ash *Devon* 18 SS3620
Parkhill *Notts* 75 SK6952
Parkhill House *Gramp* 143 NJ8914
Parkhouse *Gwent* 34 SO5003
Parkmill *W Glam* 32 SS5489
Parkside *Clwyd* 71 SJ3855
Parkside *Dur* 96 NZ4248
Parkstone *Dorset* 12 SZ0391
Parley Green *Dorset* 12 SZ1097
Parlington *W York* 83 SE4235
Parmoor *Bucks* 37 SU7989
Parndon *Essex* 39 TL4308
Parr Bridge *Gt Man* 79 SD7001
Parracombe *Devon* 19 SS6745
Parrah Green *Ches* 72 SJ7145
Parrog *Dyfed* 30 SN0539
Parson Drove *Cambs* 64 TF3708
Parson's Cross *S York* 74 SK3492
Parson's Heath *Essex* 41 TM0226
Parson's Hill *Derbys* 73 SK2926
Parsonby *Cumb* 92 NY1438
Partick *Strath* 115 NS5467
Partington *Gt Man* 79 SJ7191
Partney *Lincs* 77 TF4068
Parton *Cumb* 92 NX9820
Parton *D & G* 99 NX6970
Partridge Green *W Susx* 15 TQ1919
Partrishow *Powys* 34 SO2722
Parwich *Derbys* 73 SK1854
Paslow Wood Common *Essex* 27 TL5802
Passenham *Nhants* 38 SP7839
Passfield *Hants* 14 SU8234
Passingford Bridge *Essex* 27 TQ5097
Paston *Cambs* 64 TF1802
Paston *Norfk* 67 TG3234
Pasturefields *Staffs* 73 SJ9924
Patchacott *Devon* 5 SX4798
Patcham *E Susx* 15 TQ3008
Patchetts Green *Herts* 26 TQ1497
Patching *W Susx* 14 TQ0806
Patchole *Devon* 19 SS6142
Patchway *Avon* 34 ST6082
Pateley Bridge *N York* 89 SE1565
Paternoster Heath *Essex* 40 TL9115
Pateshall *H & W* 46 SO5262
Path of Condie *Tays* 125 NO0711
Pathe *Somset* 21 ST3730
Pathhead *Fife* 117 NT2992
Pathhead *Gramp* 135 NO7263
Pathhead *Loth* 118 NT3964
Pathhead *Strath* 107 NS6114
Pathlow *Warwks* 48 SP1758
Patmore Heath *Herts* 39 TL4425
Patna *Strath* 106 NS4110
Patney *Wilts* 23 SU0758
Patrick *IOM* 153 SC2482
Patrick Brompton *N York* 89 SE2190
Patricroft *Gt Man* 79 SJ7597
Patrington *Humb* 85 TA3122
Patrixbourne *Kent* 29 TR1855
Patterdale *Cumb* 93 NY3915
Pattingham *Staffs* 60 SO8299
Pattishall *Nhants* 49 SP6754
Pattiswick Green *Essex* 40 TL8124
Patton *Shrops* 59 SO5895
Paul *Cnwll* 2 SW4627
Paul's Dene *Wilts* 23 SU1432
Paulerspury *Bucks* 49 SP7145
Paull *Humb* 85 TA1626
Paulton *Avon* 21 ST6556
Paunton *H & W* 47 SO6650
Pauperhaugh *Nthumb* 103 NZ1099
Pave Lane *Shrops* 72 SJ7616
Pavenham *Beds* 51 SP9955
Pawlett *Somset* 20 ST2942
Pawston *Nthumb* 110 NT8532
Paxford *Gloucs* 48 SP1837
Paxton *Border* 119 NT9353
Payden Street *Kent* 28 TQ9254
Payhembury *Devon* 9 ST0901
Paythorne *Lancs* 81 SD8251
Paytoe *H & W* 46 SO4171
Peacehaven *E Susx* 15 TQ4101
Peak Dale *Derbys* 74 SK0976
Peak Forest *Derbys* 74 SK1179
Peak Hill *Lincs* 64 TF2615
Peakirk *Cambs* 64 TF1606
Pean *Kent* 29 TR1837
Peanmeanach *Highld* 129 NM7180
Pearsie *Tays* 134 NO3659
Pearson's Green *Kent* 28 TQ6943
Pease Pottage *W Susx* 15 TQ2633
Peasedown St John *Avon* 22 ST7057
Peasehill *Derbys* 74 SK4049
Peaseland Green *Norfk* 66 TG0516
Peasemore *Berks* 37 SU4577
Peasenhall *Suffk* 55 TM3569
Peaslake *Surrey* 14 TQ0844
Peasley Cross *Mersyd* 78 SJ5294
Peasmarsh *E Susx* 17 TQ8822
Peasmarsh *Somset* 10 ST3312
Peasmarsh *Surrey* 25 SU9946
Peat Inn *Fife* 127 NO4509
Peathill *Gramp* 143 NJ9366
Peatling Magna *Leics* 50 SP5992
Peatling Parva *Leics* 50 SP5889
Peaton *Shrops* 59 SO5385
Pebmarsh *Essex* 40 TL8533
Pebworth *H & W* 48 SP1347
Pecket Well *W York* 82 SD9929
Peckforton *Ches* 71 SJ5356
Peckham *Gt Lon* 27 TQ3476
Peckleton *Leics* 62 SK4701
Pedair-ffordd *Powys* 58 SJ1124
Pedlinge *Kent* 17 TR1335
Pedmore *W Mids* 60 SO9182
Pedwell *Somset* 21 ST4236
Peebles *Border* 109 NT2540
Peel *IOM* 153 SC2483
Peel *Lancs* 80 SD3531
Peel Common *Hants* 13 SU5703
Peening Quarter *Kent* 17 TQ8828
Pegsdon *Beds* 38 TL1130
Pegswood *Nthumb* 103 NZ2287
Pegwell *Kent* 29 TR3664
Peinchorran *Highld* 137 NG5233
Peinlich *Highld* 136 NG4158
Pelaw *T & W* 96 NZ3061
Pelcomb *Dyfed* 30 SM9218
Pelcomb Bridge *Dyfed* 30 SM9317
Peldon *Essex* 41 TL9816
Pell Green *E Susx* 16 TQ6432
Pelsall *W Mids* 60 SK0203
Pelsall Wood *W Mids* 60 SK0204
Pelton *Dur* 96 NZ2553
Pelton Fell *Dur* 96 NZ2551
Pelutho *Cumb* 92 NY1249
Pelynt *Cnwll* 5 SX2055
Pemberton *Dyfed* 32 SN5300
Pemberton *Gt Man* 78 SD5503
Pembles Cross *Kent* 28 TQ8947
Pembrey *Dyfed* 31 SN4301
Pembridge *H & W* 46 SO3958
Pembroke *Dyfed* 30 SM9801
Pembroke Dock *Dyfed* 30 SM9603
Pembury *Kent* 16 TQ6240
Pen Rhiwfawr *W Glam* 32 SN7410
Pen-bont Rhydybeddau *Dyfed* 43 SN6783
Pen-ffordd *Dyfed* 31 SN0722
Pen-groes-oped *Gwent* 34 SO3106
Pen-llyn *Gwynd* 68 SH3582
Pen-lon *Gwynd* 68 SH4365
Pen-rhiw *Dyfed* 31 SN2440
Pen-twyn *Gwent* 33 SO2000
Pen-twyn *Gwent* 34 SO2603
Pen-twyn *Gwent* 34 SO5209
Pen-y-Bont-Fawr *Powys* 58 SJ0824
Pen-y-bont *Clwyd* 58 SJ2123
Pen-y-bryn *Dyfed* 31 SN1742
Pen-y-bryn *M Glam* 33 SS8384
Pen-y-cae *Powys* 33 SN8413
Pen-y-cae-mawr *Gwent* 34 ST4195
Pen-y-cefn *Clwyd* 70 SJ1175
Pen-y-clawdd *Gwent* 34 SO4507
Pen-y-coedcae *M Glam* 33 ST0587
Pen-y-cwn *Dyfed* 30 SM8523
Pen-y-darren *M Glam* 33 SO0506
Pen-y-fai *M Glam* 33 SS8981
Pen-y-felin *Clwyd* 70 SJ1569
Pen-y-Gwryd Hotel *Gwynd* 69 SH6655
Pen-y-garn *Dyfed* 43 SN6285
Pen-y-genffordd *Powys* 45 SO1729
Pen-y-graig *Gwynd* 56 SH2033
Pen-y-lan *S Glam* 33 SS9976
Pen-y-pass *Gwynd* 69 SH6455
Pen-y-stryt *Clwyd* 70 SJ1952
Pen-yr-Heol *Gwent* 34 SO4311
Pen-yr-Heolgerrig *M Glam* 33 SO0306
Penair *Cnwll* 3 SW8445
Penallt *Gwent* 34 SO5210
Penally *Dyfed* 31 SS1199
Penalt *H & W* 46 SO5629
Penare *Cnwll* 3 SW9940
Penarth *S Glam* 33 ST1871
Penbryn *Dyfed* 42 SN2951
Pencader *Dyfed* 31 SN4436
Pencaitland *Loth* 118 NT4468
Pencalenick *Cnwll* 3 SW8545
Pencarnisiog *Gwynd* 68 SH3573
Pencarreg *Dyfed* 44 SN5445
Pencarrow *Cnwll* 4 SX1082
Pencelli *Powys* 45 SO0925
Penclawdd *W Glam* 32 SS5495
Pencoed *M Glam* 33 SS9581
Pencombe *H & W* 46 SO5952
Pencoyd *H & W* 46 SO5126
Pencraig *H & W* 34 SO5620
Pencraig *Powys* 58 SJ0426
Pendeen *Cnwll* 2 SW3834
Penderyn *M Glam* 33 SN9408
Pendine *Dyfed* 31 SN2208
Pendlebury *Gt Man* 79 SD7802
Pendleton *Lancs* 81 SD7539
Pendock *H & W* 47 SO7832
Pendoggett *Cnwll* 4 SX0279
Pendomer *Somset* 10 ST5210
Pendoylan *S Glam* 33 ST0576
Pendre *M Glam* 33 SS9181
Penegoes *Powys* 57 SH7600
Penelewey *Cnwll* 3 SW8140
Pengam *Gwent* 33 ST1597
Pengam *S Glam* 33 ST2177
Penge *Gt Lon* 27 TQ3570
Pengelly *Cnwll* 3 SW8551
Pengelly *Cnwll* 4 SX0783
Pengorffwysfa *Gwynd* 68 SH4692
Pengover Green *Cnwll* 5 SX2765
Pengrugla *Cnwll* 3 SW9947
Pengwern *Clwyd* 70 SJ0276
Penhale *Cnwll* 2 SW6918
Penhale *Cnwll* 4 SW9057
Penhale *Cnwll* 4 SX0860
Penhale *Cnwll* 5 SX4153
Penhallow *Cnwll* 3 SW7651
Penhalurick *Cnwll* 2 SW7038
Penhalvean *Cnwll* 2 SW7038
Penhill *Wilts* 36 SU1588
Penhow *Gwent* 34 ST4290
Penhurst *E Susx* 16 TQ6916
Peniarth *Gwynd* 57 SH6105
Penifiler *Highld* 136 NG4841
Peninver *Strath* 105 NR7524
Penisar Waun *Gwynd* 69 SH5563
Penistone *S York* 82 SE2403
Penjerrick *Cnwll* 3 SW7730
Penkelly *Cnwll* 4 SX1854
Penketh *Ches* 78 SJ5587
Penkill *Strath* 106 NX2398
Penkridge *Staffs* 60 SJ9213
Penlean *Cnwll* 5 SX2098
Penley *Clwyd* 71 SJ4040
Penllergaer *W Glam* 32 SS6198
Penllyn *S Glam* 33 SS9775
Penmachno *Gwynd* 69 SH7950
Penmaen *Gwent* 33 ST1897
Penmaen *W Glam* 32 SS5288
Penmaenan *Gwynd* 69 SH7175
Penmaenmawr *Gwynd* 69 SH7276
Penmaenpool *Gwynd* 57 SH6918
Penmark *S Glam* 20 ST0568
Penmon *Gwynd* 69 SH6280
Penmorfa *Gwynd* 57 SH5540
Penmynydd *Gwynd* 68 SH5074
Penn *Bucks* 26 SU9193
Penn *W Mids* 60 SO8895
Penn Street *Bucks* 26 SU9295
Pennal *Gwynd* 57 SH6900
Pennan *Gramp* 143 NJ8465
Pennant *Clwyd* 58 SJ0234
Pennant *Powys* 43 SN8897
Pennant-Melangell *Powys* 58 SJ0226
Pennard *W Glam* 32 SS5688
Pennerley *Shrops* 59 SO3599
Pennicott *Devon* 9 SS8701
Pennington *Cumb* 86 SD2677
Pennington *Hants* 12 SZ3195
Pennington Green *Gt Man* 79 SD6206
Pennorth *Powys* 45 SO1125
Pennsylvania *Avon* 35 ST7473
Penny Bridge *Cumb* 86 SD3083
Penny Green *Notts* 75 SK5475
Penny Hill *Lincs* 64 TF3526
Pennycross *Strath* 121 NM5025
Pennygate *Norfk* 67 TG3423
Pennyghael *Strath* 121 NM5125
Pennyglen *Strath* 106 NS2710
Pennymoor *Devon* 19 SS8611
Penparc *Dyfed* 42 SN2047
Penparcau *Dyfed* 43 SN5980
Penpedairheol *Gwent* 34 SO3303
Penpedairheol *M Glam* 33 ST1497
Penperlleni *Gwent* 34 SO3204
Penpethy *Cnwll* 4 SX0886
Penpillick *Cnwll* 3 SX0856
Penpol *Cnwll* 3 SW8139
Penpoll *Cnwll* 3 SX1454
Penponds *Cnwll* 2 SW6339
Penpont *D & G* 100 NX8494
Penpont *Powys* 45 SN9728
Penquit *Devon* 7 SX6454
Penrest *Cnwll* 5 SX3377
Penrherber *Dyfed* 31 SN2938
Penrhiwceiber *M Glam* 33 ST0597
Penrhiwllan *Dyfed* 31 SN3641
Penrhiwpal *Dyfed* 42 SN3445
Penrhos *Gwent* 34 SO4111
Penrhos *Gwynd* 68 SH2781
Penrhos *Gwynd* 56 SH3433
Penrhos *Powys* 32 SN8011
Penrhos garnedd *Gwynd* 69 SH5670
Penrhyn Bay *Gwynd* 69 SH8281
Penrhyn-side *Gwynd* 69 SH8181
Penrhyncoch *Dyfed* 43 SN6384
Penrhyndeudraeth *Gwynd* 57 SH6139
Penrice *W Glam* 32 SS4987
Penrioch *Strath* 105 NR8744
Penrith *Cumb* 94 NY5130
Penrose *Cnwll* 4 SW8770
Penrose *Cnwll* 5 SX2589
Penruddock *Cumb* 93 NY4227
Penryn *Cnwll* 3 SW7834
Pensarn *Clwyd* 70 SH9578
Pensarn *Dyfed* 31 SN4119
Pensax *H & W* 47 SO7269
Pensby *Mersyd* 78 SJ2782
Penselwood *Somset* 22 ST7531
Pensford *Avon* 21 ST6263
Pensham *H & W* 47 SO9444
Penshaw *T & W* 96 NZ3354
Penshurst *Kent* 16 TQ5243
Penshurst Station *Kent* 16 TQ5246
Pensilva *Cnwll* 5 SX2970
Pensnett *W Mids* 60 SO9189
Pensont *Cnwll* 4 SX0874
Penstone *Devon* 8 SS7700
Penstrowed *Powys* 58 SO0691
Pentewan *Cnwll* 3 SX0147
Pentir *Gwynd* 69 SH5766
Pentire *Cnwll* 4 SW7961
Pentlepoir *Dyfed* 31 SN1105
Pentlow *Essex* 54 TL8146
Pentlow Street *Essex* 54 TL8245
Pentney *Norfk* 65 TF7214
Penton Grafton *Hants* 23 SU3247
Penton Mewsey *Hants* 23 SU3247
Pentraeth *Gwynd* 68 SH5278
Pentre *Clwyd* 70 SJ0862
Pentre *Clwyd* 70 SJ2840
Pentre *Clwyd* 71 SJ3267
Pentre *Gwent* 34 SO3106
Pentre *M Glam* 33 SS9696
Pentre *Powys* 58 SO0685
Pentre *Powys* 58 SO1589
Pentre *Shrops* 59 SJ3617
Pentre Bach *Clwyd* 70 SJ2175
Pentre Berw *Gwynd* 68 SH4772
Pentre bach *Dyfed* 44 SN5547
Pentre Ffwrndan *Clwyd* 70 SJ2572
Pentre Halkyn *Clwyd* 70 SJ2072
Pentre Hodrey *Shrops* 46 SO3277
Pentre Isaf *Clwyd* 70 SH9871
Pentre Llanrhaeadr *Clwyd* 70 SJ0863
Pentre Llifior *Powys* 58 SO1598
Pentre Meyrick *S Glam* 33 SS9675
Pentre ty gwyn *Dyfed* 44 SN8135
Pentre'r Felin *Gwynd* 69 SH8069
Pentre'r-felin *Powys* 45 SN9230
Pentre-bach *Powys* 45 SN9132
Pentre-bont *Gwynd* 69 SH7351
Pentre-cagel *Dyfed* 31 SN3340
Pentre-celyn *Clwyd* 70 SJ1453
Pentre-celyn *Powys* 57 SH8905
Pentre-chwyth *W Glam* 32 SS6794
Pentre-clawdd *Shrops* 59 SJ2931
Pentre-cwrt *Dyfed* 31 SN3838
Pentre-dwr *W Glam* 32 SS6995
Pentre-Gwenlais *Dyfed* 32 SN6016
Pentre-llwyn-llwyd *Powys* 45 SN9654
Pentre-llyn *Dyfed* 43 SN6175
Pentre-llyn-cymmer *Clwyd* 70 SH9752
Pentre-Maw *Powys* 57 SH8803
Pentre-piod *Gwent* 34 SO2601
Pentre-poeth *Gwent* 34 ST2686
Pentre-tafarn-y-fedw *Gwynd* 69 SH8162
Pentrebach *M Glam* 33 SO0604
Pentrebeirdd *Powys* 58 SJ1813
Pentredwr *Clwyd* 70 SJ1946
Pentrefelin *Gwynd* 68 SH4392
Pentrefelin *Gwynd* 57 SH5239
Pentrefoelas *Clwyd* 69 SH8751
Pentregalar *Dyfed* 31 SN1831
Pentregat *Dyfed* 42 SN3551
Pentrich *Derbys* 74 SK3852
Pentridge Hill *Dorset* 12 SU0317
Pentyrch *M Glam* 33 ST1081
Penwithick *Cnwll* 3 SX0256
Penwyllt *Powys* 33 SN8515
Penybanc *Dyfed* 44 SN6123
Penybont *Powys* 45 SO1164
Penycae *Clwyd* 70 SJ2745
Penycaerau *Gwynd* 56 SH1927
Penyffordd *Clwyd* 71 SJ3061
Penygarnedd *Powys* 58 SJ1023
Penygraig *M Glam* 33 ST0090
Penygroes *Dyfed* 32 SN5813
Penygroes *Gwynd* 68 SH4752
Penysarn *Gwynd* 68 SH4590
Penywaun *M Glam* 33 SN9804
Penywern *W Glam* 32 SN7609
Penzance *Cnwll* 2 SW4730
Peopleton *H & W* 47 SO9350
Peover Heath *Ches* 79 SJ7973
Peper Harow *Surrey* 25 SU9344
Peplow *Shrops* 59 SJ6224
Pepper's Green *Essex* 40 TL6110
Peppershill *Oxon* 37 SP6709
Pepperstock *Beds* 38 TL0817
Percie *Gramp* 134 NO5992
Percyhorner *Gramp* 143 NJ9665
Perelle *Guern* 152 GN4608
Periton *Somset* 20 SS9545
Perivale *Gt Lon* 26 TQ1682
Perkins Village *Devon* 9 SY0291
Perkinsville *Dur* 96 NZ2553
Perlethorpe *Notts* 75 SK6470
Perran Wharf *Cnwll* 3 SW7738
Perranarworthal *Cnwll* 3 SW7738
Perranporth *Cnwll* 3 SW7554
Perranuthnoe *Cnwll* 2 SW5329
Perranwell *Cnwll* 3 SW7739
Perranwell *Cnwll* 3 SW7752
Perranzabuloe *Cnwll* 3 SW7752
Perrott's Brook *Gloucs* 35 SP0106
Perry *W Mids* 61 SP0792
Perry Barr *W Mids* 61 SP0791
Perry Green *Essex* 40 TL8022
Perry Green *Herts* 39 TL4317
Perry Green *Wilts* 35 ST9689
Perry Street *Somset* 10 ST3305
Pershall *Staffs* 72 SJ8129
Pershore *H & W* 47 SO9446
Pertenhall *Beds* 51 TL0865
Perth *Tays* 126 NO1123
Perthy *Shrops* 59 SJ3633
Perton *Staffs* 60 SO8699
Pertwood *Wilts* 22 ST8936
Pet Street *Kent* 29 TR0846
Peter Tavy *Devon* 5 SX5177
Peter's Green *Herts* 38 TL1419
Peterborough *Cambs* 64 TL1998
Peterchurch *H & W* 46 SO3438
Peterculter *Gramp* 135 NJ8300
Peterhead *Gramp* 143 NK1246
Peterlee *Dur* 96 NZ4241
Peters Marland *Devon* 18 SS4713
Petersfield *Hants* 13 SU7423
Petersham *Gt Lon* 26 TQ1873
Peterston-Super-Ely *S Glam* 33 ST0876
Peterstone Wentlooge *Gwent* 34 ST2679
Peterstow *H & W* 46 SO5624
Petham *Kent* 29 TR1251
Petherwin Gate *Cnwll* 5 SX2889
Petrockstow *Devon* 19 SS5109
Petsoe End *Bucks* 38 SP8949
Pett *E Susx* 17 TQ8714
Pett Bottom *Kent* 29 TR1552
Pettaugh *Suffk* 54 TM1659
Petterden *Tays* 127 NO4240
Pettinain *Strath* 108 NS9543
Pettistree *Suffk* 55 TM3055
Petton *Devon* 20 ST0124
Petton *Shrops* 59 SJ4326
Petts Wood *Gt Lon* 27 TQ4567
Petty France *Avon* 35 ST7885
Pettycur *Fife* 117 NT2686
Pettymuk *Gramp* 143 NJ9023
Petworth *W Susx* 14 SU9721
Pevensey *E Susx* 16 TQ6405
Pevensey Bay *E Susx* 16 TQ6504
Pewsey *Wilts* 23 SU1660
Pheasant's Hill *Bucks* 37 SU7887
Phepson *H & W* 47 SO9459
Philadelphia *T & W* 96 NZ3352
Philham *Devon* 18 SS2522
Philiphaugh *Border* 109 NT4327
Phillack *Cnwll* 2 SW5638
Philleigh *Cnwll* 3 SW8639
Philpot End *Essex* 40 TL6118
Philpstoun *Loth* 117 NT0577
Phocle Green *H & W* 47 SO6326
Phoenix Green *Hants* 24 SU7555
Phoines *Highld* 132 NN7093
Pibsbury *Somset* 21 ST4426
Pica *Cumb* 92 NY0222
Piccotts End *Herts* 38 TL0409
Pickering *N York* 90 SE7984
Picket Piece *Hants* 23 SU3947
Picket Post *Hants* 12 SU1906
Pickford *W Mids* 61 SP2881
Pickford Green *W Mids* 61 SP2781
Pickhill *N York* 89 SE3483
Picklescott *Shrops* 59 SO4399
Pickmere *Ches* 79 SJ6977
Pickney *Somset* 20 ST1929
Pickstock *Shrops* 72 SJ7223
Pickup Bank *Lancs* 81 SD7122
Pickwell *Devon* 18 SS4540
Pickwell *Leics* 63 SK7811
Pickwick *Wilts* 35 ST8670
Pickworth *Leics* 63 SK9913
Pickworth *Lincs* 64 TF0433
Pict's Cross *H & W* 46 SO5526
Pictillum *Gramp* 142 NJ7317
Picton *Ches* 71 SJ4371
Picton *Clwyd* 70 SJ1182
Picton *N York* 89 NZ4107
Picton Ferry *Dyfed* 31 SN2717
Piddinghoe *E Susx* 16 TQ4303
Piddington *Bucks* 37 SU8094
Piddington *Nhants* 51 SP8054
Piddington *Oxon* 37 SP6317
Piddlehinton *Dorset* 11 SY7197
Piddletrenthide *Dorset* 11 SY7099
Pidley *Cambs* 52 TL3377
Pie Corner *H & W* 47 SO6461
Piercebridge *Dur* 96 NZ2115
Pierowall *Ork* 155 HY4348
Piff's Elm *Gloucs* 47 SO9026
Pig Oak *Dorset* 12 SU0202
Pig Street *H & W* 46 SO3647
Pigdon *Nthumb* 103 NZ1588
Pigeon Green *Warwks* 48 SP2260
Pikehall *Derbys* 74 SK1959
Pilford *Dorset* 12 SU0301
Pilgrims Hatch *Essex* 27 TQ5895
Pilham *Lincs* 76 SK8693
Pill *Avon* 34 ST5275
Pillaton *Cnwll* 5 SX3664
Pillaton *Staffs* 60 SJ9413
Pillatonmill *Cnwll* 5 SX3663
Pillerton Hersey *Warwks* 48 SP2948
Pillerton Priors *Warwks* 48 SP2947
Pilleth *Powys* 46 SO2667
Pilley *Hants* 12 SZ3298
Pilley *S York* 74 SE3300
Pilley Bailey *Hants* 12 SZ3398
Pillgwenlly *Gwent* 34 ST3186
Pillhead *Devon* 18 SS4726
Pilling *Lancs* 80 SD4048
Pilling Lane *Lancs* 80 SD3749
Pilning *Avon* 34 ST5684
Pilot Inn *Kent* 17 TR0818
Pilsbury *Derbys* 74 SK1163
Pilsdon *Dorset* 10 SY4199
Pilsgate *Cambs* 64 TF0605
Pilsley *Derbys* 74 SK2371
Pilsley *Derbys* 74 SK4262
Pilson Green *Norfk* 67 TG3713
Piltdown *E Susx* 16 TQ4422
Pilton *Leics* 63 SK9102
Pilton *Nhants* 51 TL0284
Pilton *Somset* 21 ST5941
Pilton Green *W Glam* 32 SS4487
Pimlico *Lancs* 81 SD7443
Pimlico *Nhants* 49 SP6140
Pimperne *Dorset* 11 ST9009
Pin Green *Herts* 39 TL2525
Pinchbeck *Lincs* 64 TF2425
Pinchbeck Bars *Lincs* 64 TF1925
Pinchbeck West *Lincs* 64 TF2024
Pincheon Green *S York* 83 SE6517
Pinchinthorpe *Cleve* 90 NZ5714
Pincock *Lancs* 80 SD5417
Pindon End *Bucks* 38 SP7847
Pinfold *Lancs* 80 SD3811
Pinford End *Suffk* 54 TL8459
Pinged *Dyfed* 31 SN4203
Pingewood *Berks* 24 SU6969
Pinhoe *Devon* 9 SX9694
Pinkett's Booth *W Mids* 61 SP2781
Pinkney *Wilts* 35 ST8686
Pinley *W Mids* 61 SP3577
Pinley Green *Warwks* 48 SP2066
Pinmill *Suffk* 55 TM2037
Pinminnoch *Strath* 106 NX1993
Pinmore *Strath* 106 NX2091
Pinner *Gt Lon* 26 TQ1289
Pinner Green *Gt Lon* 26 TQ1289
Pinsley Green *Ches* 71 SJ5846
Pinvin *H & W* 47 SO9549
Pinwherry *Strath* 98 NX2086
Pinxton *Derbys* 75 SK4554
Pipe and Lyde *H & W* 46 SO5043
Pipe Gate *Shrops* 72 SJ7340
Pipehill *Staffs* 61 SK0907
Piperhill *Highld* 140 NH8650
Pipers Pool *Cnwll* 5 SX2584
Pipewell *Nhants* 51 SP8485
Pippacott *Devon* 19 SS5237
Pippin Street *Lancs* 81 SD5924
Pipton *Powys* 45 SO1637
Pirbright *Surrey* 25 SU9455
Pirbright Camp *Surrey* 25 SU9356
Pirnie *Border* 110 NT6528
Pirton *H & W* 47 SO8847
Pirton *Herts* 38 TL1431
Pishill *Oxon* 37 SU7389
Pistyll *Gwynd* 56 SH3241
Pitagowan *Tays* 132 NN8165
Pitblae *Gramp* 143 NJ9864
Pitcairngreen *Tays* 125 NO0627
Pitcalnie *Highld* 147 NH8072
Pitcaple *Gramp* 142 NJ7225
Pitcarity *Tays* 134 NO3365
Pitch Green *Bucks* 37 SP7703
Pitch Place *Surrey* 25 SU8839
Pitch Place *Surrey* 25 SU9852
Pitchcombe *Gloucs* 35 SO8508
Pitchcott *Bucks* 37 SP7720
Pitcher Row *Lincs* 64 TF2933
Pitchford *Shrops* 59 SJ5303
Pitchroy *Gramp* 141 NJ1738
Pitcombe *Somset* 22 ST6732
Pitcot *M Glam* 33 SS8974
Pitcox *Loth* 118 NT6475
Pitfichie *Gramp* 142 NJ6716
Pitglassie *Gramp* 142 NJ6943
Pitgrudy *Highld* 147 NH7991
Pitkennedy *Tays* 127 NO5454
Pitlessie *Fife* 126 NO3309
Pitlochry *Tays* 132 NN9458
Pitmachie *Gramp* 142 NJ6728
Pitmain *Highld* 132 NH7400
Pitmedden *Gramp* 143 NJ8827
Pitmuies *Tays* 127 NO5649
Pitmunie *Gramp* 142 NJ6614
Pitney *Somset* 21 ST4528
Pitroddie *Tays* 126 NO2125
Pitscottie *Fife* 126 NO4112
Pitsea *Essex* 40 TQ7488
Pitses *Gt Man* 79 SD9403
Pitsford *Nhants* 50 SP7567
Pitstone *Bucks* 38 SP9415
Pitt *Devon* 9 ST0316
Pitt *Hants* 24 SU4528
Pitt Court *Gloucs* 35 ST7496
Pitt's Wood *Kent* 16 TQ6149
Pittarrow *Gramp* 135 NO7274
Pittenweem *Fife* 127 NO5502
Pitteuchar *Fife* 117 NT2899
Pittington *Dur* 96 NZ3244
Pittodrie House Hotel *Gramp* 142 NJ6924
Pitton *Wilts* 23 SU2131
Pittulie *Gramp* 143 NJ9567
Pity Me *Dur* 96 NZ2645
Pityme *Cnwll* 4 SW9576
Pivington *Kent* 28 TQ9146
Pixey Green *Suffk* 55 TM2475
Pixham *Surrey* 26 TQ1750
Plain Street *Cnwll* 4 SW9778
Plains *Strath* 116 NS7966
Plaish *Shrops* 59 SO5296
Plaistow *Derbys* 74 SK3456
Plaistow *Gt Lon* 27 TQ4082
Plaistow *H & W* 47 SO6939
Plaistow *W Susx* 14 TQ0030
Plaitford *Hants* 12 SU2719
Plas Llanfair *Gwynd* 69 SH5371
Plas Llysyn *Powys* 58 SN9597
Plastow Green *Hants* 24 SU5361
Platt *Kent* 27 TQ6257
Platt Bridge *Gt Man* 78 SD6002
Platt Lane *Shrops* 59 SJ5136
Platts Heath *Kent* 28 TQ8750
Plawsworth *Dur* 96 NZ2647
Plaxtol *Kent* 27 TQ6053
Play Hatch *Oxon* 37 SU7376
Playden *E Susx* 17 TQ9221
Playford *Suffk* 55 TM2147
Playing Place *Cnwll* 3 SW8141
Playley Green *Gloucs* 47 SO7631
Plealey *Shrops* 59 SJ4206
Plean *Cent* 116 NS8386
Pleasance *Fife* 126 NO2312
Pleasington *Lancs* 81 SD6426
Pleasley *Derbys* 75 SK5064
Pleck *Dorset* 11 ST7010
Pledgdon Green *Essex* 40 TL5626
Pledwick *W York* 83 SE3316
Pleinheaume *Guern* 152 GN5111
Plemont *Jersey* 152 JS0616
Plemstall *Ches* 71 SJ4570
Plenmeller *Nthumb* 102 NY7163
Pleshey *Essex* 40 TL6614
Plockton *Highld* 137 NG8033
Ploughfield *H & W* 46 SO3841
Plowden *Shrops* 59 SO3887
Ploxgreen *Shrops* 59 SJ3604
Pluckley *Kent* 28 TQ9245
Pluckley Station *Kent* 28 TQ9243
Pluckley Thorne *Kent* 28 TQ9244
Plucks Gutter *Kent* 29 TR2663
Plumbland *Cumb* 92 NY1539
Plumgarths *Cumb* 87 SD4994
Plumley *Ches* 79 SJ7274
Plumpton *Cumb* 94 NY4937
Plumpton *E Susx* 15 TQ3613
Plumpton End *Nhants* 49 SP7245
Plumpton Green *E Susx* 15 TQ3616
Plumpton Head *Cumb* 94 NY5035
Plumstead *Gt Lon* 27 TQ4478
Plumstead *Norfk* 66 TG1334
Plumstead Green *Norfk* 66 TG1235
Plumtree *Notts* 62 SK6132
Plumtree Green *Kent* 28 TQ8245
Plungar *Leics* 63 SK7634
Plurenden *Kent* 28 TQ9337
Plush *Dorset* 11 ST7102
Plusha *Cnwll* 5 SX2580
Plushabridge *Cnwll* 5 SX3072
Plwmp *Dyfed* 42 SN3652
Plymouth *Devon* 6 SX4754
Plympton *Devon* 6 SX5456
Plymstock *Devon* 6 SX5152
Plymtree *Devon* 9 ST0502
Pockley *N York* 90 SE6385
Pocklington *Humb* 84 SE8048
Pode Hole *Lincs* 64 TF2121
Podimore *Somset* 21 ST5424
Podington *Beds* 51 SP9462
Podmore *Staffs* 72 SJ7835
Point Clear *Essex* 41 TM1015
Pointon *Lincs* 64 TF1131
Pokesdown *Dorset* 12 SZ1292
Polapit Tamar *Cnwll* 5 SX3389
Polbain *Highld* 144 NB9910
Polbathic *Cnwll* 5 SX3456
Polbeth *Loth* 117 NT0264
Polbrock *Cnwll* 4 SX0169
Pole Elm *H & W* 47 SO8450
Pole Moor *W York* 82 SE0615
Polebrook *Nhants* 51 TL0686
Polegate *E Susx* 16 TQ5804
Polelane Ends *Ches* 79 SJ6479
Polesworth *Warwks* 61 SK2602
Polgigga *Cnwll* 2 SW3723
Polglass *Highld* 144 NC0307
Polgooth *Cnwll* 3 SW9950
Polgown *D & G* 107 NS7103
Poling *W Susx* 14 TQ0404
Poling Corner *W Susx* 14 TQ0405
Polkerris *Cnwll* 3 SX0952
Pollard Street *Norfk* 67 TG3332
Pollington *Humb* 83 SE6119
Polloch *Highld* 129 NM7668
Pollokshaws *Strath* 115 NS5661
Pollokshields *Strath* 115 NS5763
Polmassick *Cnwll* 3 SW9745
Polmont *Cent* 116 NS9378
Polnish *Highld* 129 NM7582
Polperro *Cnwll* 5 SX2051
Polruan *Cnwll* 3 SX1250
Polsham *Somset* 21 ST5142
Polstead *Suffk* 54 TL9938
Polstead Heath *Suffk* 54 TL9940
Poltalloch *Strath* 113 NR8196
Poltescoe *Cnwll* 3 SW7215
Poltimore *Devon* 9 SX9696
Polton *Loth* 117 NT2864
Polwarth *Border* 119 NT7450
Polyphant *Cnwll* 5 SX2682
Polzeath *Cnwll* 4 SW9378
Pomathorn *Loth* 117 NT2459
Ponde *Powys* 45 SO1037
Ponders End *Gt Lon* 27 TQ3596
Pondersbridge *Cambs* 64 TL2692
Ponsanooth *Cnwll* 3 SW7537
Ponsonby *Cumb* 86 NY0505
Ponsongath *Cnwll* 3 SW7518
Ponsworthy *Devon* 7 SX7073
Pont Cyfyng *Gwynd* 69 SH7357
Pont Morlais *Dyfed* 32 SN5307
Pont Pen-y-benglog *Gwynd* 69 SH6560
Pont Rhyd-sarn *Gwynd* 57 SH8528
Pont Rhyd-y-cyff *M Glam* 33 SS8788
Pont Robert *Powys* 58 SJ1012
Pont Walby *M Glam* 33 SN8906
Pont-ar-gothi *Dyfed* 32 SN5021
Pont-ar-Hydfer *Powys* 45 SN8627
Pont-ar-llechau *Dyfed* 44 SN7224
Pont-Ebbw *Gwent* 34 ST2985
Pont-faen *Powys* 45 SN9934
Pont-gareg *Dyfed* 31 SN1441
Pont-Nedd-Fechan *Powys* 33 SN9007
Pont-rhyd-y-fen *W Glam* 32 SS7994
Pont-rug *Gwynd* 68 SH5162
Pont-y-blew *Clwyd* 71 SJ3138
Pont-y-pant *Gwynd* 69 SH7554
Pont-yr-hafod *Dyfed* 30 SM9026
Pont-yr-Rhyl *M Glam* 33 SS9089
Pontac *Jersey* 152 JS1807
Pontamman *Dyfed* 32 SN6312
Pontantwn *Dyfed* 32 SN4412
Pontardawe *W Glam* 32 SN7204
Pontarddulais *W Glam* 32 SN5903
Pontarsais *Dyfed* 31 SN4428
Pontblyddyn *Clwyd* 70 SJ2760
Pontdolgoch *Powys* 58 SO0193
Pontefract *W York* 83 SE4521
Ponteland *Nthumb* 103 NZ1672
Ponterwyd *Dyfed* 43 SN7481
Pontesbury Hill *Shrops* 59 SJ3905
Pontesford *Shrops* 59 SJ4106
Pontfadog *Clwyd* 70 SJ2338
Pontfaen *Dyfed* 30 SN0234
Pontgarreg *Dyfed* 42 SN3353
Ponthenry *Dyfed* 32 SN4709
Ponthir *Gwent* 34 ST3292
Ponthirwaun *Dyfed* 42 SN2645
Pontllanfraith *Gwent* 33 ST1895
Pontlliw *W Glam* 57 SN6199
Pontlottyn *M Glam* 33 SO1106
Pontlyfni *Gwynd* 68 SH4352
Pontnewydd *Gwent* 34 ST2896
Pontnewynydd *Gwent* 34 SO2701
Pontop *Dur* 96 NZ1453
Pontrhydfendigaid *Dyfed* 43 SN7366
Pontrhydygroes *Dyfed* 43 SN7472
Pontrhydyrun *Gwent* 34 ST2997
Pontrilas *H & W* 46 SO3927
Ponts Green *E Susx* 16 TQ6715
Pontshaen *Dyfed* 42 SN4446
Pontshill *H & W* 35 SO6421
Pontsticill *M Glam* 33 SO0511
Pontwelly *Dyfed* 31 SN4140
Pontyates *Dyfed* 32 SN4708
Pontyberem *Dyfed* 32 SN5010
Pontybodkin *Clwyd* 70 SJ2759
Pontyclun *M Glam* 33 ST0381
Pontycymer *M Glam* 33 SS9091
Pontyglasier *Dyfed* 31 SN1436
Pontygwaith *M Glam* 33 ST0094
Pontygynon *Dyfed* 31 SN1237
Pontymoel *Gwent* 34 SO2900
Pontypool *Gwent* 34 SO2800
Pontypool Road *Gwent* 34 ST3099
Pontypridd *M Glam* 33 ST0789
Pontywaun *Gwent* 34 ST2292
Pooksgreen *Hants* 12 SU3710
Pool *Cnwll* 2 SW6641
Pool *IOS* 2 SV8714
Pool *W York* 82 SE2445
Pool Head *H & W* 46 SO5550
Pool o'Muckhart *Cent* 117 NO0000
Pool Quay *Powys* 58 SJ2511
Pool Street *Essex* 53 TL7636
Poole *Dorset* 11 SZ0090
Poole Keynes *Wilts* 35 ST9995
Poolewe *Highld* 144 NG8580
Pooley Bridge *Cumb* 93 NY4724
Pooley Street *Norfk* 54 TM0581
Poolfold *Staffs* 72 SJ8959
Poolhill *Gloucs* 47 SO7229
Pooting's *Kent* 16 TQ4549
Popham *Hants* 24 SU5543
Poplar *Gt Lon* 27 TQ3780
Poplar Street *Suffk* 55 TM4465
Porchbrook *H & W* 60 SO7270
Porchfield *IOW* 13 SZ4491
Poringland *Norfk* 67 TG2701
Porkellis *Cnwll* 2 SW6933
Porlock *Somset* 19 SS8846
Porlock Weir *Somset* 19 SS8647
Port Appin *Strath* 122 NM9045
Port Askaig *Strath* 112 NR4369
Port Bannatyne *Strath* 114 NS0767
Port Carlisle *Cumb* 101 NY2461
Port Charlotte *Strath* 112 NR2558
Port Clarence *Cleve* 97 NZ5021
Port Dinorwic *Gwynd* 68 SH5267
Port Dolgarrog *Gwynd* 69 SH7766
Port Driseach *Strath* 114 NR9973
Port Einon *W Glam* 32 SS4685
Port Ellen *Strath* 104 NR3645
Port Elphinstone *Gramp* 142 NJ7720
Port Erin *IOM* 153 SC1969
Port Gaverne *Cnwll* 4 SX0080
Port Glasgow *Strath* 115 NS3274
Port Henderson *Highld* 137 NG7573
Port Isaac *Cnwll* 4 SW9980
Port Logan *D & G* 98 NX0940
Port Mor *Highld* 128 NM4279
Port Mulgrave *N York* 97 NZ7917
Port Na Craig *Tays* 125 NN9357
Port of Menteith *Cent* 115 NN5801
Port of Ness *W Isls* 154 NB5363
Port Quin *Cnwll* 4 SW9780
Port Ramsay *Strath* 122 NM8845
Port Soderick *IOM* 153 SC3472
Port St Mary *IOM* 153 SC2067
Port Sunlight *Mersyd* 78 SJ3384
Port Talbot *W Glam* 32 SS7689
Port Tennant *W Glam* 32 SS6893
Port Wemyss *Strath* 112 NR1651
Port William *D & G* 98 NX3343
Port-an-Eorna *Highld* 137 NG7732
Portachoillan *Strath* 113 NR7557
Portavadie *Strath* 114 NR9369
Portbury *Avon* 34 ST5075
Portchester *Hants* 13 SU6105
Portencalzie *D & G* 98 NX0171
Portencross *Strath* 114 NS1748
Portesham *Dorset* 10 SY6085
Portessie *Gramp* 142 NJ4366
Portfield Gate *Dyfed* 30 SM9215
Portgate *Devon* 5 SX4285
Portgordon *Gramp* 142 NJ3964
Portgower *Highld* 147 ND0013
Porth *Cnwll* 4 SW8362
Porth *M Glam* 33 ST0291
Porth Dinllaen *Gwynd* 56 SH2740
Porth Navas *Cnwll* 3 SW7527
Porth-y-Waen *Shrops* 58 SJ2623
Porthallow *Cnwll* 3 SW7923
Porthallow *Cnwll* 5 SX2251
Porthcawl *M Glam* 33 SS8177
Porthcothan *Cnwll* 4 SW8672
Porthcurno *Cnwll* 2 SW3822
Porthgain *Dyfed* 30 SM8132
Porthgwarra *Cnwll* 2 SW3721
Porthill *Staffs* 72 SJ8448
Porthkea *Cnwll* 3 SW8242
Porthkerry *S Glam* 20 ST0866
Porthleven *Cnwll* 2 SW6225
Porthmadog *Gwynd* 57 SH5638
Porthmeor *Cnwll* 2 SW4337
Portholland *Cnwll* 3 SW9541
Porthoustock *Cnwll* 3 SW8021
Porthpean *Cnwll* 3 SX0250
Porthtowan *Cnwll* 2 SW6947
Porthyrhyd *Dyfed* 32 SN5215
Portincaple *Strath* 114 NS2393
Portinfer *Jersey* 152 JS0615
Portington *Humb* 84 SE7831
Portinnisherrich *Strath* 122 NM9711
Portinscale *Cumb* 93 NY2523
Portishead *Avon* 34 ST4675
Portknockie *Gramp* 142 NJ4868
Portlethen *Gramp* 135 NO9196
Portling *D & G* 92 NX8753
Portloe *Cnwll* 3 SW9339
Portlooe *Cnwll* 5 SX2452
Portmahomack *Highld* 147 NH9184
Portmellon *Cnwll* 3 SX0144
Portmore *Hants* 12 SZ3397
Portnacroish *Strath* 122 NM9247
Portnaguiran *W Isls* 154 NB5537
Portnahaven *Strath* 112 NR1652
Portnalong *Highld* 136 NG3434
Portobello *Loth* 117 NT3073
Portobello *T & W* 96 NZ2856
Portobello *W Mids* 60 SO9598
Porton *Wilts* 23 SU1836
Portontown *Devon* 5 SX4176
Portpatrick *D & G* 98 NW9954
Portreath *Cnwll* 2 SW6545
Portreath *Cnwll* 4 SW9679
Portree *Highld* 136 NG4843
Portrye *Strath* 114 NS1757
Portscatho *Cnwll* 3 SW8735
Portsea *Hants* 13 SU6300
Portskerra *Highld* 150 NC8765
Portskewett *Gwent* 34 ST4988
Portslade *E Susx* 15 TQ2506
Portslade-by-Sea *E Susx* 15 TQ2605
Portslogan *D & G* 98 NW9858
Portsmouth *Hants* 13 SU6400
Portsmouth *W York* 81 SD9026
Portsoy *Gramp* 142 NJ5866
Portswood *Hants* 13 SU4214
Portuairk *Highld* 128 NM4368
Portway *H & W* 46 SO4844
Portway *H & W* 46 SO4935
Portway *W Mids* 60 SO9787
Portwrinkle *Cnwll* 5 SX3553
Portyerrock *D & G* 99 NX4738
Posbury *Devon* 8 SX8197
Posenhall *Shrops* 59 SJ6501
Poslingford *Suffk* 53 TL7648
Posso *Border* 109 NT2033
Post Green *Dorset* 11 SY9593
Postbridge *Devon* 8 SX6579
Postcombe *Oxon* 37 SP7000
Postling *Kent* 29 TR1439
Postwick *Norfk* 67 TG2907
Pothole *Cnwll* 3 SW9750
Potsgrove *Beds* 38 SP9530
Pott Row *Norfk* 65 TF7022
Pott Shrigley *Ches* 79 SJ9479
Pott's Green *Essex* 40 TL9122
Potten End *Herts* 38 TL0109
Potten Street *Kent* 29 TR2567
Potter Brompton *N York* 91 SE9777

Potter Heigham
Rothley

Potter Heigham *Norfk* 67 TG4119
Potter Row *Bucks* 26 SP9002
Potter Somersal *Derbys* 73 SK1335
Potter's Cross *Staffs* 60 SO8484
Potter's Forstal *Kent* 28 TQ8946
Potter's Green *E Susx* 16 TQ5023
Potter's Green *Herts* 39 TL3520
Pottergate Street *Norfk* 66 TM1591
Potterhanworth *Lincs* 76 TF0566
Potterhanworth Booths *Lincs* 76 TF0767
Potterne *Wilts* 22 ST9958
Potterne Wick *Wilts* 22 ST9957
Potters Bar *Herts* 26 TL2401
Potters Brook *Lancs* 80 SD4852
Potters Crouch *Herts* 38 TL1105
Potters Green *W Mids* 61 SP3782
Potters Marston *Leics* 50 SP4996
Pottersheath *Herts* 39 TL2318
Potterspury *Nhants* 49 SP7543
Potterton *W York* 83 SE4038
Potthorpe *Norfk* 66 TF9422
Pottle Street *Wilts* 22 ST8140
Potto *N York* 89 NZ4703
Potton *Beds* 52 TL2249
Poughill *Cnwll* 18 SS2207
Poughill *Devon* 19 SS8508
Poulner *Hants* 12 SU1606
Poulshot *Wilts* 22 ST9659
Poulston *Devon* 7 SX7754
Poulton *Gloucs* 36 SP0901
Poulton *Mersyd* 78 SJ3091
Poulton Priory *Gloucs* 36 SP0900
Poulton-le-Fylde *Lancs* 80 SD3439
Pound Bank *H & W* 60 SO7374
Pound Green *E Susx* 16 TQ5123
Pound Green *H & W* 60 SO7579
Pound Green *Suffk* 53 TL7153
Pound Hill *W Susx* 15 TQ2937
Pound Street *Hants* 24 SU4561
Poundffald *W Glam* 32 SS5694
Poundgates *E Susx* 16 TQ4928
Poundon *Bucks* 49 SP6425
Poundsbridge *Kent* 16 TQ5341
Poundsgate *Devon* 7 SX7072
Poundstock *Cnwll* 18 SX2099
Pounsley *E Susx* 16 TQ5221
Pouton *D & G* 99 NX4645
Povey Cross *Surrey* 15 TQ2642
Pow Green *H & W* 47 SO7144
Powburn *Nthumb* 111 NU0616
Powderham *Devon* 9 SX9684
Powerstock *Dorset* 10 SY5196
Powfoot *D & G* 100 NY1465
Powhill *Cumb* 93 NY2355
Powick *H & W* 47 SO8351
Powmill *Tays* 117 NT0297
Poxwell *Dorset* 11 SY7384
Poyle *Gt Lon* 26 TQ0376
Poynings *W Susx* 15 TQ2611
Poynter's Lane End *Cnwll* 2 SW6743
Poyntington *Dorset* 21 ST6520
Poynton *Ches* 79 SJ9283
Poynton *Shrops* 59 SJ5617
Poynton Green *Shrops* 59 SJ5618
Poys Street *Suffk* 55 TM3570
Poyston Cross *Dyfed* 30 SM9819
Poystreet Green *Suffk* 54 TL9758
Praa Sands *Cnwll* 2 SW5828
Pratt's Bottom *Gt Lon* 27 TQ4762
Praze-an-Beeble *Cnwll* 2 SW6335
Predannack Wollas *Cnwll* 2 SW6616
Prees *Shrops* 59 SJ5533
Prees Green *Shrops* 59 SJ5531
Prees Heath *Shrops* 71 SJ5538
Prees Higher Heath *Shrops* 59 SJ5635
Prees Lower Heath *Shrops* 59 SJ5732
Preesall *Lancs* 80 SD3647
Pren-gwyn *Dyfed* 42 SN4244
Prendwick *Nthumb* 111 NU0012
Prenteg *Gwynd* 57 SH5841
Prenton *Mersyd* 78 SJ3086
Prescot *Mersyd* 78 SJ4692
Prescott *Devon* 9 ST0814
Prescott *Shrops* 59 SJ4220
Prescott *Shrops* 60 SO6681
Presnerb *Tays* 133 NO1866
Pressen *Nthumb* 110 NT8335
Prestatyn *Clwyd* 70 SJ0682
Prestbury *Ches* 79 SJ8976
Prestbury *Gloucs* 47 SO9723
Presteigne *Powys* 46 SO3164
Prestleigh *Somset* 21 ST6340
Prestolee *Gt Man* 79 SD7505
Preston *Border* 119 NT7957
Preston *Devon* 7 SX7451
Preston *Devon* 7 SX8574
Preston *Devon* 7 SX8962
Preston *Dorset* 11 SY7083
Preston *E Susx* 15 TQ3106
Preston *Gloucs* 47 SO6834
Preston *Gloucs* 36 SP0400
Preston *Herts* 39 TL1824
Preston *Humb* 85 TA1830
Preston *Kent* 28 TR0260
Preston *Kent* 29 TR2460
Preston *Lancs* 80 SD5329
Preston *Leics* 63 SK8602
Preston *Loth* 118 NT5977
Preston *Nthumb* 111 NU1825
Preston *Shrops* 59 SJ5211
Preston *Somset* 20 ST0935
Preston *Suffk* 54 TL9450
Preston *Wilts* 36 SU2774
Preston Bagot *Warwks* 48 SP1765
Preston Bissett *Bucks* 49 SP6529
Preston Bowyer *Somset* 20 ST1326
Preston Brockhurst *Shrops* 59 SJ5324
Preston Brook *Ches* 78 SJ5680
Preston Candover *Hants* 24 SU6041
Preston Capes *Nhants* 49 SP5754
Preston Crowmarsh *Oxon* 37 SU6190
Preston Deanery *Nhants* 50 SP7855
Preston Green *Warwks* 48 SP1665
Preston Gubbals *Shrops* 59 SJ4919
Preston Montford *Shrops* 59 SJ4314
Preston on Stour *Warwks* 48 SP2049
Preston on the Hill *Ches* 78 SJ5780
Preston on Wye *H & W* 46 SO3842
Preston Patrick *Cumb* 87 SD5483
Preston Plucknett *Somset* 10 ST5316
Preston Street *Kent* 29 TR2561
Preston upon the Weald Moors *Shrops* 72 SJ6815
Preston Wynne *H & W* 46 SO5546
Preston-under-Scar *N York* 88 SE0691
Prestonpans *Loth* 118 NT3874
Prestwich *Gt Man* 79 SD8104
Prestwick *Nthumb* 103 NZ1872
Prestwick *Strath* 106 NS3525
Prestwood *Bucks* 26 SP8700
Prestwood *Staffs* 60 SO8786
Price Town *M Glam* 33 SS9391
Prickwillow *Cambs* 53 TL5982
Priddy *Somset* 21 ST5250
Priest Hutton *Lancs* 87 SD5273
Priestacott *Devon* 18 SS4206
Priestcliffe *Derbys* 74 SK1471
Priestcliffe Ditch *Derbys* 74 SK1371
Priestend *Bucks* 37 SP6905
Priestley Green *W York* 82 SE1326
Priestweston *Shrops* 59 SO2997
Priestwood Green *Kent* 28 TQ6564
Primethorpe *Leics* 50 SP5293
Primrose Green *Norfk* 66 TG0716
Primrose Hill *Cambs* 52 TL3889
Primrose Hill *Derbys* 75 SK4358
Primrose Hill *Lancs* 78 SD3809
Primrose Hill *W Mids* 60 SO9487
Primrosehill *Border* 119 NT7857
Primsidemill *Border* 110 NT8126
Princes Gate *Dyfed* 31 SN1312
Princes Risborough *Bucks* 38 SP8003
Princethorpe *Warwks* 61 SP4070
Princetown *Devon* 6 SX5873
Prinsted *W Susx* 14 SU7605
Prior Rigg *Cumb* 101 NY4568
Priors Halton *Shrops* 46 SO4975
Priors Hardwick *Warwks* 49 SP4756
Priors Marston *Warwks* 49 SP4957
Priors Norton *Gloucs* 47 SO8624
Priory Wood *H & W* 46 SO2645
Prisk *S Glam* 33 ST0176
Priston *Avon* 22 ST6960
Pristow Green *Norfk* 54 TM1388
Prittlewell *Essex* 40 TQ8687
Privett *Hants* 13 SU6727
Probus *Cnwll* 3 SW8947
Prospect *Cumb* 92 NY1140
Prospidnick *Cnwll* 2 SW6431
Protstonhill *Gramp* 143 NJ8163
Providence *Avon* 34 ST5370
Prudhoe *Nthumb* 103 NZ0962
Prussia Cove *Cnwll* 2 SW5528
Ptarmigan Lodge *Cent* 115 NN3500
Publow *Avon* 21 ST6264
Puckeridge *Herts* 39 TL3823
Puckington *Somset* 10 ST3718
Pucklechurch *Avon* 35 ST6976
Puckrup *Gloucs* 47 SO8836
Puddinglake *Ches* 79 SJ7269
Puddington *Ches* 71 SJ3273
Puddington *Devon* 19 SS8310
Puddledock *Norfk* 66 TM0592
Puddletown *Dorset* 11 SY7594
Pudsey *W York* 82 SE2232
Pulborough *W Susx* 14 TQ0418
Puleston *Shrops* 72 SJ7322
Pulford *Ches* 71 SJ3758
Pulham *Dorset* 11 ST7008
Pulham Market *Norfk* 55 TM1986
Pulham St Mary *Norfk* 55 TM2085
Pullens Green *Avon* 34 ST6192
Pulley *Shrops* 59 SJ4809
Pulloxhill *Beds* 38 TL0634
Pumpherston *Loth* 117 NT0669
Pumsaint *Dyfed* 44 SN6540
Puncheston *Dyfed* 30 SN0129
Puncknowle *Dorset* 10 SY5388
Punnett's Town *E Susx* 16 TQ6220
Purbrook *Hants* 13 SU6707
Purbrook Park *Hants* 13 SU6707
Purfleet *Essex* 27 TQ5578
Puriton *Somset* 21 ST3241
Purleigh *Essex* 40 TL8402
Purley *Berks* 37 SU6675
Purley *Gt Lon* 27 TQ3161
Purlogue *Shrops* 46 SO2877
Purlpit *Wilts* 22 ST8766
Purls Bridge *Cambs* 53 TL4786
Purse Caundle *Dorset* 11 ST6917
Purshall Green *H & W* 60 SO8971
Purslow *Shrops* 59 SO3680
Purston Jaglin *W York* 83 SE4319
Purtington *Somset* 10 ST3908
Purton *Gloucs* 35 SO6904
Purton *Gloucs* 35 SO6705
Purton *Wilts* 36 SU0987
Purton Stoke *Wilts* 36 SU0990
Pury End *Nhants* 49 SP7145
Pusey *Oxon* 36 SU3596
Putley *H & W* 47 SO6337
Putley Green *H & W* 47 SO6437
Putloe *Gloucs* 35 SO7709
Putney *Gt Lon* 26 TQ2374
Putron Village *Guern* 152 GN5306
Putsborough *Devon* 18 SS4440
Puttenham *Herts* 38 SP8814
Puttenham *Surrey* 25 SU9247
Puttock End *Essex* 54 TL8040
Puttock's End *Essex* 40 TL5719
Putton *Dorset* 11 SY6480
Puxley *Nhants* 49 SP7542
Puxton *Avon* 21 ST4063
Pwll *Dyfed* 32 SN4801
Pwll Trap *Dyfed* 31 SN2616
Pwll-du *Gwent* 34 SO2411
Pwll-y-glaw *W Glam* 32 SS7993
Pwllcrochan *Dyfed* 30 SM9202
Pwllglas *Clwyd* 70 SJ1154
Pwllgloyw *Powys* 45 SO0333
Pwllheli *Gwynd* 56 SH3735
Pwllmeyric *Gwent* 34 ST5292
Pydew *Gwynd* 69 SH8079
Pye Bridge *Derbys* 75 SK4452
Pye Corner *Gwent* 34 ST3485
Pye Corner *Herts* 39 TL4412
Pye Green *Staffs* 60 SJ9813
Pyecombe *W Susx* 15 TQ2813
Pyle *M Glam* 33 SS8282
Pyleigh *Somset* 20 ST1330
Pylle *Somset* 21 ST6038
Pymore *Cambs* 53 TL4986
Pymore *Dorset* 10 SY4694
Pyrford *Surrey* 26 TQ0358
Pyrton *Oxon* 37 SU6896
Pytchley *Nhants* 51 SP8574
Pyworthy *Devon* 18 SS3102

Q

Quabbs *Shrops* 58 SO2180
Quadring *Lincs* 64 TF2233
Quadring Eaudike *Lincs* 64 TF2433
Quainton *Bucks* 37 SP7420
Quaker's Yard *M Glam* 33 ST0995
Quaking Houses *Dur* 96 NZ1850
Quarley *Hants* 23 SU2743
Quarndon *Derbys* 62 SK3340
Quarr Hill *IOW* 13 SZ5792
Quarrier's Homes *Strath* 115 NS3666
Quarrington *Lincs* 64 TF0544
Quarrington Hill *Dur* 96 NZ3337
Quarry Bank *W Mids* 60 SO9386
Quarrybank *Ches* 71 SJ5465
Quarrywood *Gramp* 141 NJ1763
Quarter *Strath* 116 NS7251
Quatford *Shrops* 60 SO7391
Quatt *Shrops* 60 SO7588
Quebec *Dur* 96 NZ1743
Quedgeley *Gloucs* 35 SO8014
Queen Adelaide *Cambs* 53 TL5681
Queen Camel *Somset* 21 ST5924
Queen Charlton *Avon* 21 ST6367
Queen Dart *Devon* 19 SS8316
Queen Oak *Dorset* 22 ST7831
Queen Street *Kent* 28 TQ6845
Queen Street *Wilts* 35 SU0287
Queen's Bower *IOW* 13 SZ5684
Queen's Head *Shrops* 59 SJ3327
Queen's Park *Beds* 38 TL0349
Queen's Park *Nhants* 49 SP7562
Queenborough *Kent* 28 TQ9172
Queenhill *H & W* 47 SO8537
Queensbury *W York* 82 SE1030
Queensferry *Clwyd* 71 SJ3168
Queenslie *Strath* 116 NS6565
Queenzieburn *Strath* 116 NS6977
Quendon *Essex* 39 TL5130
Queniborough *Leics* 63 SK6412
Quenington *Gloucs* 36 SP1404
Quernmore *Lancs* 87 SD5160
Quernmore Park Hall *Lancs* 87 SD5162
Queslett *W Mids* 61 SP0695
Quethiock *Cnwll* 5 SX3164
Quick's Green *Berks* 37 SU5876
Quidenham *Norfk* 54 TM0287
Quidhampton *Hants* 24 SU5150
Quidhampton *Wilts* 23 SU1030
Quina Brook *Shrops* 59 SJ5232
Quinberry End *Nhants* 49 SP6250
Quinton *Nhants* 49 SP7754
Quinton *W Mids* 60 SO9984
Quinton Green *Nhants* 50 SP7853
Quintrell Downs *Cnwll* 4 SW8460
Quither *Devon* 5 SX4481
Quixhall *Staffs* 73 SK1041
Quixwood *Border* 119 NT7863
Quoditch *Devon* 5 SX4097
Quorndon *Leics* 62 SK5616
Quothquan *Strath* 108 NS9939
Quoyburray *Ork* 155 HY5005
Quoyloo *Ork* 155 HY2420

R

RAF College (Cranwell) *Lincs* 76 TF0049
Rabbit's Cross *Kent* 28 TQ7847
Rableyheath *Herts* 39 TL2319
Raby *Cumb* 93 NY1951
Raby *Mersyd* 71 SJ3179
Rachan Mill *Border* 108 NT1134
Rachub *Gwynd* 69 SH6267
Rackenford *Devon* 19 SS8518
Rackham *W Susx* 14 TQ0413
Rackheath *Norfk* 67 TG2814
Rackwick *Ork* 155 ND2099
Radbourne *Derbys* 73 SK2836
Radcliffe *Gt Man* 79 SD7806
Radcliffe *Nthumb* 103 NU2602
Radcliffe on Trent *Notts* 63 SK6439
Radclive *Bucks* 49 SP6734
Radcot *Oxon* 36 SU2899
Raddington *Somset* 20 ST0225
Radernie *Fife* 127 NO4609
Radford Semele *Warwks* 48 SP3464
Radlet *Somset* 20 ST2038
Radlett *Herts* 26 TL1600
Radley *Devon* 19 SS7323
Radley *Oxon* 37 SU5398
Radley Green *Essex* 40 TL6205
Radmore Green *Ches* 71 SJ5955
Radnage *Bucks* 37 SU7897
Radstock *Avon* 22 ST6854
Radstone *Nhants* 49 SP5840
Radway *Warwks* 48 SP3648
Radway Green *Ches* 72 SJ7754
Radwell *Beds* 51 TL0057
Radwell *Herts* 39 TL2335
Radwinter *Essex* 53 TL6037
Radwinter End *Essex* 53 TL6139
Radyr *S Glam* 33 ST1280
Raecleugh *D & G* 108 NT0311
Rafford *Gramp* 141 NJ0556
Raftra *Cnwll* 2 SW3723
Ragdale *Leics* 63 SK6619
Ragdon *Shrops* 59 SO4591
Raginnis *Cnwll* 2 SW4625
Raglan *Gwent* 34 SO4107
Ragnall *Notts* 75 SK8073
Raigbeg *Highld* 140 NH8128
Rainbow Hill *H & W* 47 SO8555
Rainford *Mersyd* 78 SD4700
Rainham *Gt Lon* 27 TQ5282
Rainham *Kent* 28 TQ8165
Rainhill *Mersyd* 78 SJ4991
Rainhill Stoops *Mersyd* 78 SJ5090
Rainow *Ches* 79 SJ9475
Rainsough *Gt Man* 79 SD8002
Rainton *N York* 89 SE3675
Rainworth *Notts* 75 SK5858
Raisbeck *Cumb* 87 NY6407
Raise *Cumb* 94 NY7046
Raisthorpe *N York* 90 SE8561
Rait *Tays* 126 NO2226
Raithby *Lincs* 77 TF3084
Raithby *Lincs* 77 TF3766
Raithwaite *N York* 90 NZ8611
Rake *W Susx* 14 SU8027
Rakewood *Gt Man* 82 SD9414
Ralia *Highld* 132 NN7097
Ram *Dyfed* 44 SN5846
Ram Hill *Avon* 35 ST6779
Ram Lane *Kent* 28 TQ9646
Ramasaig *Highld* 136 NG1644
Rame *Cnwll* 3 SW7233
Rame *Cnwll* 6 SX4249
Rampisham *Dorset* 10 ST5602
Rampside *Cumb* 86 SD2366
Rampton *Cambs* 53 TL4267
Rampton *Notts* 75 SK8078
Ramridge End *Beds* 38 TL1023
Ramsbottom *Gt Man* 81 SD7916
Ramsbury *Wilts* 36 SU2771
Ramscraigs *Highld* 151 ND1427
Ramsdean *Hants* 13 SU7022
Ramsdell *Hants* 24 SU5857
Ramsden *H & W* 47 SO9246
Ramsden *Oxon* 36 SP3515
Ramsden Bellhouse *Essex* 40 TQ7194
Ramsden Heath *Essex* 40 TQ7095
Ramsey *Cambs* 52 TL2885
Ramsey *Essex* 41 TM2130
Ramsey *IOM* 153 SC4594
Ramsey Forty Foot *Cambs* 52 TL3087
Ramsey Heights *Cambs* 52 TL2484
Ramsey Island *Essex* 40 TL9405
Ramsey Mereside *Cambs* 52 TL2889
Ramsey St Mary's *Cambs* 52 TL2587
Ramsgate *Kent* 29 TR3865
Ramsgill *N York* 89 SE1170
Ramshaw *Dur* 95 NY9547
Ramsholt *Suffk* 55 TM3141
Ramshope *Nthumb* 102 NT7304
Ramshorn *Staffs* 73 SK0845
Ramsley *Devon* 8 SX6593
Ramsnest Common *Surrey* 14 SU9432
Ranby *Lincs* 76 TF2278
Ranby *Notts* 75 SK6580
Rand *Lincs* 76 TF1078
Randwick *Gloucs* 35 SO8306
Ranfurly *Strath* 115 NS3865
Rangemore *Staffs* 73 SK1822
Rangeworthy *Avon* 35 ST6986
Rank's Green *Essex* 40 TL7418
Rankinston *Strath* 107 NS4513
Ranksborough *Leics* 63 SK8311
Rann *Lancs* 81 SD7124
Rannoch Station *Tays* 124 NN4257
Ranochan *Highld* 129 NM8282
Ranscombe *Somset* 20 SS9443
Ranskill *Notts* 75 SK6587
Ranton *Staffs* 72 SJ8524
Ranton Green *Staffs* 72 SJ8423
Ranworth *Norfk* 67 TG3514
Raploch *Cent* 116 NS7894
Rapness *Ork* 155 HY5141
Rapps *Somset* 10 ST3316
Rascarrel *D & G* 92 NX7948
Rashfield *Strath* 114 NS1483
Rashwood *H & W* 47 SO9165
Raskelf *N York* 90 SE4971
Rassau *Gwent* 33 SO1511
Rastrick *W York* 82 SE1421
Ratagan *Highld* 138 NG9119
Ratby *Leics* 62 SK5105
Ratcliffe Culey *Leics* 61 SP3299
Ratcliffe on Soar *Notts* 62 SK4928
Ratcliffe on the Wreake *Leics* 63 SK6314
Ratfyn *Wilts* 23 SU1642
Rathen *Gramp* 143 NJ9960
Rathillet *Fife* 126 NO3620
Rathmell *N York* 88 SD8059
Ratho *Loth* 117 NT1370
Rathven *Gramp* 142 NJ4465
Ratlake *Hants* 13 SU4123
Ratley *Warwks* 48 SP3847
Ratling *Kent* 29 TR2453
Ratlinghope *Shrops* 59 SO4096
Rattan Row *Norfk* 65 TF5114
Rattar *Highld* 151 ND2673
Ratten Row *Cumb* 93 NY3240
Ratten Row *Cumb* 93 NY3949
Ratten Row *Lancs* 80 SD4241
Rattery *Devon* 7 SX7461
Rattlesden *Suffk* 54 TL9758
Ratton Village *E Susx* 16 TQ5901
Rattray *Tays* 126 NO1845
Raughton *Cumb* 93 NY3947
Raughton Head *Cumb* 93 NY3745
Raunds *Nhants* 51 SP9972
Raven Meols *Mersyd* 78 SD2905
Ravenfield *S York* 75 SK4895
Ravenglass *Cumb* 86 SD0896
Ravenhills Green *H & W* 47 SO7454
Raveningham *Norfk* 67 TM3996
Ravenscar *N York* 91 NZ9801
Ravenscliffe *Staffs* 72 SJ8452
Ravensdale *IOM* 153 SC3592
Ravensden *Beds* 51 TL0754
Ravenshead *Notts* 75 SK5654
Ravensmoor *Ches* 71 SJ6150
Ravensthorpe *Nhants* 50 SP6670
Ravensthorpe *W York* 82 SE2220
Ravenstone *Bucks* 38 SP8451
Ravenstone *Leics* 62 SK4013
Ravenstonedale *Cumb* 88 NY7203
Ravenstruther *Strath* 116 NS9245
Ravensworth *N York* 89 NZ1308
Raw *N York* 91 NZ9305
Rawcliffe *Humb* 83 SE6822
Rawcliffe *N York* 83 SE5854
Rawcliffe Bridge *Humb* 83 SE6921
Rawdon *W York* 82 SE2139
Rawling Street *Kent* 28 TQ9059
Rawmarsh *S York* 75 SK4396
Rawnsley *Staffs* 60 SK0212
Rawreth *Essex* 40 TQ7893
Rawridge *Devon* 9 ST2006
Rawtenstall *Lancs* 81 SD8123
Raydon *Suffk* 54 TM0438
Raylees *Nthumb* 102 NY9291
Rayleigh *Essex* 40 TQ8090
Raymond Hill *Devon* 10 SY3296
Rayne *Essex* 40 TL7222
Raynes Park *Gt Lon* 26 TQ2368
Rea *Gloucs* 35 SO8016
Reach *Cambs* 53 TL5666
Read *Lancs* 81 SD7634
Reading *Berks* 24 SU7173
Reading Street *Kent* 17 TQ9230
Reading Street *Kent* 29 TR3869
Reagill *Cumb* 94 NY6017
Rearquhar *Highld* 146 NH7492
Rearsby *Leics* 63 SK6514
Rease Heath *Shrops* 72 SJ6454
Reay *Highld* 150 NC9664
Reculver *Kent* 29 TR2269
Red Ball *Devon* 9 ST0917
Red Bull *Ches* 72 SJ8254
Red Cross *Cambs* 53 TL4754
Red Cross *Cnwll* 18 SS2605
Red Dial *Cumb* 93 NY2546
Red Hill *Dorset* 12 SZ0995
Red Hill *Warwks* 48 SP1356
Red Lumb *Gt Man* 81 SD8415
Red Rock *Gt Man* 78 SD5809
Red Roses *Dyfed* 31 SN2011
Red Row *T & W* 103 NZ2599
Red Street *Staffs* 72 SJ8251
Red Wharf Bay *Gwynd* 68 SH5281
Redberth *Dyfed* 31 SN0804
Redbourn *Herts* 38 TL1012
Redbourne *Lincs* 76 SK9799
Redbrook *Clwyd* 71 SJ5041
Redbrook *Gloucs* 34 SO5309
Redbrook Street *Kent* 28 TQ9336
Redburn *Highld* 140 NH9447
Redburn *Nthumb* 102 NY7764
Redcar *Cleve* 97 NZ6024
Redcastle *D & G* 100 NX8165
Redcastle *Highld* 139 NH5849
Redding *Cent* 116 NS9278
Reddingmuirhead *Cent* 116 NS9177
Reddish *Gt Man* 79 SJ8993
Redditch *H & W* 48 SP0467
Rede *Suffk* 54 TL8055
Redenhall *Norfk* 55 TM2684
Redenham *Hants* 23 SU3049
Redesmouth *Nthumb* 102 NY8682
Redford *Gramp* 135 NO7570
Redford *Tays* 127 NO5644
Redford *W Susx* 14 SU8626
Redfordgreen *Border* 109 NT3616
Redgate *M Glam* 33 ST0188
Redgorton *Tays* 125 NO0828
Redgrave *Suffk* 54 TM0477
Redhill *Avon* 21 ST4962
Redhill *Gramp* 135 NJ7704
Redhill *Herts* 39 TL3033
Redhill *Surrey* 27 TQ2750
Redisham *Suffk* 55 TM4084
Redland *Avon* 34 ST5775
Redland *Ork* 155 HY3724
Redlingfield *Suffk* 54 TM1870
Redlingfield Green *Suffk* 54 TM1871
Redlodge *Suffk* 53 TL6970
Redlynch *Somset* 22 ST7033
Redlynch *Wilts* 12 SU2021
Redmain *Cumb* 92 NY1333
Redmarley *H & W* 47 SO7666
Redmarley D'Abitot *Gloucs* 47 SO7531
Redmarshall *Cleve* 96 NZ3821
Redmile *Leics* 63 SK7935
Redmire *N York* 88 SE0491
Redmyre *Gramp* 135 NO7575
Rednal *Shrops* 59 SJ3628
Rednal *W Mids* 60 SP0076
Redpath *Border* 110 NT5835
Redruth *Cnwll* 2 SW6942
Redstocks *Wilts* 22 ST9362
Redstone *Tays* 126 NO1834
Redvales *Gt Man* 79 SD8008
Redwick *Avon* 34 ST5486
Redwick *Gwent* 34 ST4184
Redworth *Dur* 96 NZ2423
Reed *Herts* 39 TL3636
Reedham *Norfk* 67 TG4201
Reedness *Humb* 84 SE7923
Reeds Holme *Lancs* 81 SD8024
Reepham *Lincs* 76 TF0473
Reepham *Norfk* 66 TG1022
Reeth *N York* 88 SE0399
Reeves Green *W Mids* 61 SP2677
Reiff *Highld* 144 NB9614
Reigate *Surrey* 27 TQ2550
Reighton *N York* 91 TA1375
Reisque *Gramp* 143 NJ8819
Reiss *Highld* 151 ND3354
Rejerrah *Cnwll* 3 SW7956
Releath *Cnwll* 2 SW6532
Relubbus *Cnwll* 2 SW5631
Relugas *Gramp* 141 NH9948
Remenham *Berks* 37 SU7684
Remenham Hill *Berks* 37 SU7882
Rempstone *Notts* 62 SK5724
Rendcomb *Gloucs* 35 SP0209
Rendham *Suffk* 55 TM3464
Renfrew *Strath* 115 NS5067
Renhold *Beds* 38 TL0852
Renishaw *Derbys* 75 SK4577
Rennington *Nthumb* 111 NU2118
Renton *Strath* 115 NS3877
Renwick *Cumb* 94 NY5943
Repps *Norfk* 67 TG4217
Repton *Derbys* 73 SK3026
Resaurie *Highld* 140 NH7045
Rescassa *Cnwll* 3 SW9842
Rescorla *Cnwll* 3 SW9848
Resipole *Highld* 121 NM7264
Reskadinnick *Cnwll* 2 SW6341
Resolis *Highld* 140 NH6765
Resolven *W Glam* 33 SN8302
Rest and be Thankful *Strath* 123 NN2307
Reston *Border* 119 NT8862
Restronguet *Cnwll* 3 SW8136
Reswallie *Tays* 127 NO5051
Reterth *Cnwll* 4 SW9463
Retew *Cnwll* 4 SW9257
Retford *Notts* 75 SK7081
Retire *Cnwll* 4 SX0064
Rettendon *Essex* 40 TQ7698
Retyn *Cnwll* 4 SW8858
Revesby *Lincs* 77 TF2961
Rew *Devon* 7 SX7570
Rew Street *IOW* 13 SZ4794
Rewe *Devon* 9 SX9499
Rexon *Devon* 5 SX4188
Reydon *Suffk* 55 TM4977
Reymerston *Norfk* 66 TG0206
Reynalton *Dyfed* 31 SN0908
Reynoldston *W Glam* 32 SS4889
Rezare *Cnwll* 5 SX3677
Rhadyr *Gwent* 34 SO3602
Rhandirmwyn *Dyfed* 44 SN7843
Rhayader *Powys* 45 SN9768
Rheindown *Highld* 139 NH5147
Rhes-y-cae *Clwyd* 70 SJ1871
Rhewl *Clwyd* 70 SJ1060
Rhewl *Clwyd* 70 SJ1744
Rhewl Mostyn *Clwyd* 70 SJ1580
Rhewl-fawr *Clwyd* 70 SJ1381
Rhicarn *Highld* 148 NC0825
Rhiconich *Highld* 148 NC2552
Rhicullen *Highld* 146 NH6971
Rhigos *M Glam* 33 SN9205
Rhireavach *Highld* 144 NH0295
Rhives *Highld* 147 NC8200
Rhiwbina *S Glam* 33 ST1682
Rhiwbryfdir *Gwynd* 57 SH6946
Rhiwderyn *Gwent* 34 ST2687
Rhiwen *Gwynd* 69 SH5763
Rhiwinder *M Glam* 33 ST0287
Rhiwlas *Clwyd* 58 SJ1932
Rhiwlas *Gwynd* 69 SH5765
Rhiwlas *Gwynd* 58 SH9237
Rhiwsaeson *M Glam* 33 ST0682
Rhode *Somset* 20 ST2734
Rhoden Green *Kent* 28 TQ6845
Rhodes *Gt Man* 79 SD8505
Rhodes Minnis *Kent* 29 TR1542
Rhodesia *Notts* 75 SK5679
Rhodiad-y-brenin *Dyfed* 30 SM7627
Rhonehouse or Kelton Hill *D & G* 99 NX7459
Rhoose *S Glam* 20 ST0666
Rhos *Clwyd* 70 SJ1261
Rhos *Dyfed* 31 SN3835
Rhos *Powys* 45 SO1731
Rhos *W Glam* 32 SN7302
Rhos Haminiog *Dyfed* 43 SN5464
Rhos Lligwy *Gwynd* 68 SH4886
Rhos y-brithdir *Powys* 58 SJ1323
Rhos-fawr *Gwynd* 56 SH3838
Rhos-hill *Dyfed* 31 SN1940
Rhos-on-Sea *Clwyd* 69 SH8480
Rhos-y-garth *Dyfed* 43 SN6373
Rhos-y-gwaliau *Gwynd* 58 SH9434
Rhos-y-llan *Gwynd* 56 SH2337
Rhos-y-meirch *Powys* 46 SO2769
Rhoscefnhir *Gwynd* 68 SH5276
Rhoscolyn *Gwynd* 68 SH2267
Rhoscrowther *Dyfed* 30 SM9002
Rhosesmor *Clwyd* 70 SJ2168
Rhosgadfan *Gwynd* 68 SH5057
Rhosgoch *Gwynd* 68 SH4089
Rhosgoch *Powys* 45 SO1847
Rhoshirwaun *Gwynd* 56 SH2029
Rhoslan *Gwynd* 56 SH4840
Rhosllanerchrugog *Clwyd* 71 SJ2946
Rhosmaen *Dyfed* 44 SN6423
Rhosmeirch *Gwynd* 68 SH4677
Rhosneigr *Gwynd* 68 SH3173
Rhosnesni *Clwyd* 71 SJ3550
Rhosrobin *Clwyd* 71 SJ3252
Rhossili *W Glam* 31 SS4187
Rhostryfan *Gwynd* 68 SH4957
Rhostyllen *Clwyd* 71 SJ3148
Rhosybol *Gwynd* 68 SH4288
Rhosygadfa *Shrops* 59 SJ3234
Rhosymedre *Clwyd* 70 SJ2842
Rhu *Strath* 115 NS2684
Rhuallt *Clwyd* 70 SJ0775
Rhubodach *Strath* 114 NS0273
Rhuddall Heath *Ches* 71 SJ5562
Rhuddlan *Clwyd* 70 SJ0278
Rhulen *Powys* 45 SO1349
Rhunahaorine *Strath* 105 NR7048
Rhyd *Gwynd* 57 SH6341
Rhyd-Ddu *Gwynd* 69 SH5652
Rhyd-lydan *Clwyd* 69 SH8950
Rhyd-uchaf *Gwynd* 58 SH9037
Rhyd-y pennau *Dyfed* 43 SN6385
Rhyd-y-clafdy *Gwynd* 56 SH3234
Rhyd-y-foel *Clwyd* 70 SH9176
Rhyd-y-groes *Gwynd* 69 SH5867
Rhyd-y-meirch *Gwent* 34 SO3107
Rhyd-y-sarn *Gwynd* 57 SH6842
Rhyd-yr-onnen *Gwynd* 57 SH6102
Rhydargaeau *Dyfed* 31 SN4326
Rhydcymerau *Dyfed* 44 SN5738
Rhydd *H & W* 47 SO8345
Rhydding *W Glam* 32 SS7499
Rhyddlan *Dyfed* 44 SN4943
Rhydgaled *Clwyd* 70 SH9964
Rhydlanfair *Gwynd* 69 SH8252
Rhydlewis *Dyfed* 42 SN3447
Rhydlios *Gwynd* 56 SH1929
Rhydowen *Dyfed* 42 SN4445
Rhydrosser *Dyfed* 43 SN5667
Rhydspence *H & W* 46 SO2447
Rhydtalog *Clwyd* 70 SJ2354
Rhydycroesau *Shrops* 58 SJ2430
Rhydyfelin *Dyfed* 43 SN5979
Rhydyfelin *M Glam* 33 ST0988
Rhydyfro *W Glam* 32 SN7105
Rhydymain *Gwynd* 57 SH7821
Rhydymwyn *Clwyd* 70 SJ2066
Rhyl *Clwyd* 70 SJ0081
Rhymney *M Glam* 33 SO1107
Rhynd *Tays* 126 NO1520
Rhynie *Gramp* 142 NJ4927
Rhynie *Highld* 147 NH8479
Ribbesford *H & W* 60 SO7874
Ribbleton *Lancs* 81 SD5631
Ribby *Lancs* 80 SD4031
Ribchester *Lancs* 81 SD6535
Riber *Derbys* 74 SK3059
Riby *Lincs* 85 TA1807
Riccall *N York* 83 SE6237
Riccarton *Border* 101 NY5494
Riccarton *Strath* 107 NS4236
Richards Castle *H & W* 46 SO4969
Richings Park *Bucks* 26 TQ0278
Richmond *N York* 89 NZ1701
Richmond *S York* 74 SK4085
Richmond Fort *Guern* 152 GN4609
Richmond upon Thames *Gt Lon* 26 TQ1774
Richs Halford *Somset* 20 ST1434
Rickerscote *Staffs* 72 SJ9220
Rickford *Avon* 21 ST4859
Rickham *Devon* 7 SX7537
Rickinghall Inferior *Suffk* 54 TM0475
Rickinghall Superior *Suffk* 54 TM0375
Rickling *Essex* 39 TL4931
Rickling Green *Essex* 39 TL5129
Rickmansworth *Herts* 26 TQ0694
Riddell *Border* 109 NT5124
Riddings *Cumb* 101 NY4075
Riddings *Derbys* 74 SK4252
Riddlecombe *Devon* 19 SS6113
Riddlesden *W York* 82 SE0742
Ridge *Avon* 21 ST5556
Ridge *Dorset* 11 SY9386
Ridge *Herts* 26 TL2100
Ridge *Wilts* 22 ST9531
Ridge Green *Surrey* 15 TQ3048
Ridge Lane *Warwks* 61 SP2994
Ridge Row *Kent* 29 TR2042
Ridgebourne *Powys* 45 SO0560
Ridgehill *Avon* 21 ST5462
Ridgeway *Derbys* 74 SK3551
Ridgeway *Derbys* 74 SK4081
Ridgeway *H & W* 48 SP0461
Ridgeway Cross *H & W* 47 SO7147
Ridgewell *Essex* 53 TL7340
Ridgewood *E Susx* 16 TQ4719
Ridgmont *Beds* 38 SP9736
Riding Mill *Nthumb* 103 NZ0161
Ridley *Kent* 27 TQ6164
Ridley *Nthumb* 102 NY7963
Ridley Green *Ches* 71 SJ5554
Ridlington *Leics* 63 SK8402
Ridlington *Norfk* 67 TG3430
Ridlington Street *Norfk* 67 TG3430
Ridsdale *Nthumb* 102 NY9084
Rievaulx *N York* 90 SE5785
Rigg *D & G* 101 NY2966
Riggend *Strath* 116 NS7670
Righoul *Highld* 140 NH8851
Rigmadon Park *Cumb* 87 SD6184
Rigsby *Lincs* 77 TF4375
Rigside *Strath* 108 NS8735
Riley Green *Lancs* 81 SD6225
Rileyhill *Staffs* 61 SK1114
Rilla Mill *Cnwll* 5 SX2973
Rillaton *Cnwll* 5 SX2973
Rillington *N York* 90 SE8574
Rimington *Lancs* 81 SD8045
Rimpton *Somset* 21 ST6121
Rimswell *Humb* 85 TA3128
Rinaston *Dyfed* 30 SM9825
Rindleford *Shrops* 60 SO7395
Ring o'Bells *Lancs* 78 SD4510
Ring's End *Cambs* 65 TF3902
Ringford *D & G* 99 NX6957
Ringinglow *Derbys* 74 SK2883
Ringland *Norfk* 66 TG1313
Ringles Cross *E Susx* 16 TQ4722
Ringlestone *Kent* 28 TQ8755
Ringley *Gt Man* 79 SD7605
Ringmer *E Susx* 16 TQ4412
Ringmore *Devon* 7 SX6546
Ringmore *Devon* 7 SX9272
Ringorm *Gramp* 141 NJ2644
Ringsfield *Suffk* 55 TM4088
Ringsfield Corner *Suffk* 55 TM4087
Ringshall *Bucks* 38 SP9814
Ringshall *Suffk* 54 TM0452
Ringshall Stocks *Suffk* 54 TM0551
Ringstead *Nhants* 51 SP9875
Ringstead *Norfk* 65 TF7040
Ringwood *Hants* 12 SU1505
Ringwould *Kent* 29 TR3548
Rinsey *Cnwll* 2 SW5927
Rinsey Croft *Cnwll* 2 SW6028
Ripe *E Susx* 16 TQ5110
Ripley *Derbys* 74 SK3950
Ripley *Hants* 12 SZ1698
Ripley *N York* 89 SE2860
Ripley *Surrey* 26 TQ0556
Riplingham *Humb* 84 SE9631
Riplington *Hants* 13 SU6623
Ripon *N York* 89 SE3171
Rippingale *Lincs* 64 TF0927
Ripple *H & W* 47 SO8737
Ripple *Kent* 29 TR3550
Ripponden *W York* 82 SE0319
Risabus *Strath* 104 NR3143
Risbury *H & W* 46 SO5455
Risby *Humb* 84 SE9114
Risby *Suffk* 54 TL8066
Risca *Gwent* 34 ST2391
Rise *Humb* 85 TA1542
Riseden *E Susx* 16 TQ6130
Risedown *Kent* 28 TQ7036
Risegate *Lincs* 64 TF2129
Riseholme *Lincs* 76 SK9775
Risehow *Cumb* 92 NY0234
Riseley *Beds* 51 TL0462
Riseley *Berks* 24 SU7263
Rishangles *Suffk* 54 TM1668
Rishton *Lancs* 81 SD7230
Rishworth *W York* 82 SE0318
Rising Bridge *Lancs* 81 SD7825
Risley *Ches* 79 SJ6592
Risley *Derbys* 62 SK4535
Risplith *N York* 89 SE2468
Rivar *Wilts* 23 SU3161
Rivenhall End *Essex* 40 TL8316
River *Kent* 29 TR2943
River *W Susx* 14 SU9323
River Bank *Cambs* 53 TL5368
Riverford *Highld* 139 NH5454
Riverhead *Kent* 27 TQ5156
Rivers Corner *Dorset* 11 ST7712
Rivington *Lancs* 81 SD6214
Roachill *Devon* 19 SS8522
Road Ashton *Wilts* 22 ST8856
Road Green *Norfk* 67 TM2693
Road Weedon *Nhants* 49 SP6359
Roade *Nhants* 49 SP7651
Roadhead *Cumb* 101 NY5174
Roadmeetings *Strath* 116 NS8649
Roadside *Highld* 151 ND1560
Roadside *Strath* 107 NS5717
Roadside of Catterline *Gramp* 135 NO8579
Roadside of Kinneff *Gramp* 135 NO8477
Roadwater *Somset* 20 ST0338
Roag *Highld* 136 NG2744
Roan of Craigoch *Strath* 106 NS2904
Roast Green *Essex* 39 TL4632
Roath *S Glam* 33 ST1977
Roberton *Border* 109 NT4214
Roberton *Strath* 108 NS9428
Robertsbridge *E Susx* 17 TQ7423
Roberttown *W York* 82 SE1922
Robeston Wathen *Dyfed* 31 SN0815
Robgill Tower *D & G* 101 NY2471
Robin Hill *Staffs* 72 SJ9057
Robin Hood *Lancs* 80 SD5211
Robin Hood *W York* 83 SE3227
Robin Hood's Bay *N York* 91 NZ9505
Robinhood End *Essex* 53 TL7036
Roborough *Devon* 19 SS5717
Roby *Mersyd* 78 SJ4390
Roby Mill *Lancs* 78 SD5107
Rocester *Staffs* 73 SK1039
Roch *Dyfed* 30 SM8821
Roch Gate *Dyfed* 30 SM8720
Rochdale *Gt Man* 81 SD8913
Roche *Cnwll* 4 SW9860
Rochester *Kent* 28 TQ7468
Rochester *Nthumb* 102 NY8298
Rochford *Essex* 40 TQ8790
Rochford *H & W* 47 SO6268
Rochville *Strath* 114 NS2390
Rock *Cnwll* 4 SW9375
Rock *H & W* 60 SO7371
Rock *Nthumb* 111 NU2020
Rock *W Glam* 32 SS7893
Rock *W Susx* 14 TQ1213
Rock Ferry *Mersyd* 78 SJ3386
Rock Hill *H & W* 47 SO9569
Rockbeare *Devon* 9 SY0194
Rockbourne *Hants* 12 SU1118
Rockcliffe *Cumb* 101 NY3561
Rockcliffe *D & G* 92 NX8454
Rockcliffe Cross *Cumb* 101 NY3463
Rockesta *Cnwll* 2 SW3722
Rockfield *Gwent* 34 SO4814
Rockfield *Highld* 147 NH9282
Rockford *Devon* 19 SS7547
Rockford *Hants* 12 SU1607
Rockgreen *Shrops* 46 SO5275
Rockhampton *Gloucs* 35 ST6593
Rockhead *Cnwll* 4 SX0784
Rockhill *Shrops* 46 SO2978
Rockingham *Nhants* 51 SP8691
Rockland All Saints *Norfk* 66 TL9996
Rockland St Mary *Norfk* 67 TG3104
Rockland St Peter *Norfk* 66 TL9897
Rockley *Notts* 75 SK7174
Rockley *Wilts* 36 SU1571
Rockliffe *Lancs* 81 SD8722
Rockwell End *Bucks* 37 SU7988
Rockwell Green *Somset* 20 ST1220
Rodborough *Gloucs* 35 SO8404
Rodborough *Wilts* 36 SU1485
Rodbourne *Wilts* 35 ST9383
Rodd *H & W* 46 SO3262
Rodden *Dorset* 10 SY6184
Roddham *Nthumb* 111 NU0220
Roddymoor *Dur* 96 NZ1536
Rode *Somset* 22 ST8053
Rode Heath *Ches* 72 SJ8056
Rode Heath *Ches* 72 SJ8767
Rodel *W Isls* 154 NG0483
Roden *Shrops* 59 SJ5716
Rodhuish *Somset* 20 ST0139
Rodington *Shrops* 59 SJ5814
Rodington Heath *Shrops* 59 SJ5814
Rodley *Gloucs* 35 SO7411
Rodley *W York* 82 SE2236
Rodmarton *Gloucs* 35 ST9498
Rodmell *E Susx* 15 TQ4106
Rodmersham *Kent* 28 TQ9261
Rodmersham Green *Kent* 28 TQ9161
Rodney Stoke *Somset* 21 ST4849
Rodono Hotel *Border* 109 NT2321
Rodsley *Derbys* 73 SK2040
Rodway *Somset* 20 ST2540
Roe Cross *Gt Man* 79 SJ9896
Roe Green *Gt Man* 79 SD7501
Roe Green *Herts* 39 TL2107
Roe Green *Herts* 39 TL3133
Roecliffe *N York* 89 SE3765
Roehampton *Gt Lon* 26 TQ2273
Roffey *W Susx* 15 TQ1932
Rogart *Highld* 146 NC7202
Rogate *W Susx* 14 SU8023
Roger Ground *Cumb* 87 SD3597
Rogerstone *Gwent* 34 ST2787
Rogiet *Gwent* 34 ST4587
Roke *Oxon* 37 SU6293
Roker *T & W* 96 NZ4058
Rollesby *Norfk* 67 TG4416
Rolleston *Leics* 50 SK7300
Rolleston *Notts* 75 SK7452
Rolleston *Staffs* 73 SK2327
Rolston *Humb* 85 TA2144
Rolstone *Avon* 21 ST3962
Rolvenden *Kent* 17 TQ8431
Rolvenden Layne *Kent* 17 TQ8530
Romaldkirk *Dur* 95 NY9922
Romanby *N York* 89 SE3693
Romanno Bridge *Border* 117 NT1647
Romansleigh *Devon* 19 SS7220
Romden Castle *Kent* 28 TQ8941
Romesdal *Highld* 136 NG4053
Romford *Dorset* 12 SU0709
Romford *Gt Lon* 27 TQ5188
Romiley *Gt Man* 79 SJ9490
Romney Street *Kent* 27 TQ5561
Romsey *Hants* 12 SU3521
Romsley *H & W* 60 SO9680
Romsley *Shrops* 60 SO7883
Ronachan *Strath* 113 NR7454
Rookhope *Dur* 95 NY9342
Rookley *IOW* 13 SZ5084
Rookley Green *IOW* 13 SZ5083
Rooks Bridge *Somset* 21 ST3652
Rooks Nest *Somset* 20 ST0933
Rookwith *N York* 89 SE2086
Roos *Humb* 85 TA2830
Roose *Cumb* 86 SD2269
Roosebeck *Cumb* 86 SD2567
Roothams Green *Beds* 51 TL0957
Ropley *Hants* 24 SU6431
Ropley Dean *Hants* 24 SU6232
Ropley Soke *Hants* 24 SU6533
Ropsley *Lincs* 63 SK9933
Rora *Gramp* 143 NK0650
Rorrington *Shrops* 59 SJ3000
Rosarie *Gramp* 141 NJ3850
Roscroggan *Cnwll* 2 SW6542
Rose *Cnwll* 3 SW7754
Rose Ash *Devon* 19 SS7921
Rose Green *Essex* 40 TL9028
Rose Green *Suffk* 54 TL9337
Rose Green *Suffk* 54 TL9744
Rose Green *W Susx* 14 SZ9099
Rose Hill *E Susx* 16 TQ4516
Rose Hill *Lancs* 81 SD8231
Rose Lands *E Susx* 16 TQ6200
Roseacre *Lancs* 80 SD4336
Rosebank *Strath* 116 NS8049
Rosebush *Dyfed* 31 SN0729
Rosecare *Cnwll* 4 SX1695
Rosecliston *Cnwll* 4 SW8159
Rosedale Abbey *N York* 90 SE7296
Roseden *Nthumb* 111 NU0321
Rosehall *Highld* 146 NC4702
Rosehearty *Gramp* 143 NJ9267
Rosehill *Shrops* 59 SJ4715
Roseisle *Gramp* 141 NJ1466
Rosemarket *Dyfed* 30 SM9508
Rosemarkie *Highld* 140 NH7357
Rosemary Lane *Devon* 9 ST1514
Rosemount *Tays* 126 NO1843
Rosenannon *Cnwll* 4 SW9566
Rosenithon *Cnwll* 3 SW8021
Roser's Cross *E Susx* 16 TQ5420
Rosevean *Cnwll* 4 SX0258
Rosevine *Cnwll* 3 SW8736
Rosewarne *Cnwll* 2 SW6036
Rosewell *Loth* 117 NT2862
Roseworth *Cleve* 96 NZ4221
Roseworthy *Cnwll* 2 SW6139
Rosgill *Cumb* 94 NY5316
Roshven *Highld* 129 NM7078
Roskhill *Highld* 136 NG2744
Roskorwell *Cnwll* 3 SW7923
Roskrow *Cnwll* 3 SW7635
Rosley *Cumb* 93 NY3245
Roslin *Loth* 117 NT2763
Rosliston *Derbys* 73 SK2416
Rosneath *Strath* 114 NS2583
Ross *D & G* 99 NX6444
Ross *Nthumb* 111 NU1337
Ross-on-Wye *H & W* 46 SO5923
Rossett *Clwyd* 71 SJ3657
Rossett Green *N York* 82 SE2952
Rossington *Notts* 75 SK6298
Rosskeen *Highld* 146 NH6869
Rossland *Strath* 115 NS4370
Roster *Highld* 151 ND2639
Rostherne *Ches* 79 SJ7483
Rosthwaite *Cumb* 93 NY2514
Roston *Derbys* 73 SK1340
Rosudgeon *Cnwll* 2 SW5529
Rosyth *Loth* 117 NT1082
Rothbury *Nthumb* 103 NU0501
Rotherby *Leics* 63 SK6716
Rotherfield *E Susx* 16 TQ5529
Rotherfield Greys *Oxon* 37 SU7282
Rotherfield Peppard *Oxon* 37 SU7182
Rotherham *S York* 75 SK4392
Rothersthorpe *Nhants* 49 SP7156
Rotherwick *Hants* 24 SU7156
Rothes *Gramp* 141 NJ2749
Rothesay *Strath* 114 NS0864
Rothiebrisbane *Gramp* 142 NJ7437
Rothiemay *Gramp* 142 NJ5548
Rothienorman *Gramp* 142 NJ7235
Rothley *Leics* 62 SK5812

Rothley *Nthumb* 103 NZ0488
Rothmaise *Gramp* 142 NJ6832
Rothwell *Lincs* 76 TF1499
Rothwell *Nhants* 51 SP8181
Rothwell *W York* 83 SE3428
Rothwell Haigh *W York* 83 SE3328
Rotsea *Humb* 84 TA0651
Rottal Lodge *Tays* 134 NO3769
Rottingdean *E Susx* 15 TQ3602
Rottington *Cumb* 92 NX9613
Roucan *D & G* 100 NY0277
Roud *IOW* 13 SZ5180
Rough Close *Staffs* 72 SJ9239
Rough Common *Kent* 29 TR1259
Rougham *Norfk* 66 TF8320
Rougham Green *Suffk* 54 TL9061
Roughlee *Lancs* 81 SD8440
Roughley *W Mids* 61 SP1399
Roughpark *Gramp* 134 NJ3412
Roughton *Lincs* 77 TF2464
Roughton *Norfk* 67 TG2136
Roughton *Shrops* 60 SO7594
Roughway *Kent* 27 TQ6153
Round Bush *Herts* 26 TQ1498
Round Green *Beds* 38 TL1022
Round Street *Kent* 28 TQ6568
Roundbush *Essex* 40 TL8501
Roundbush Green *Essex* 40 TL5814
Roundham *Somset* 10 ST4209
Roundhay *W York* 83 SE3337
Rounds Green *W Mids* 60 SO9889
Roundstreet Common *W Susx* 14 TQ0528
Roundway *Wilts* 22 SU0163
Roundyhill *Tays* 126 NO3750
Rous Lench *H & W* 47 SP0153
Rousdon *Devon* 10 SY2991
Rousham *Oxon* 49 SP4724
Rout's Green *Bucks* 37 SU7898
Routenbeck *Cumb* 93 NY1930
Routenburn *Strath* 114 NS1961
Routh *Humb* 85 TA0942
Row *Cnwll* 4 SX0976
Row *Cumb* 94 NY6234
Row *Cumb* 87 SD4589
Row Ash *Hants* 13 SU5413
Row Green *Essex* 40 TL7420
Rowanburn *D & G* 101 NY4177
Rowardennan Hotel *Cent* 115 NS3698
Rowarth *Derbys* 79 SK0189
Rowberrow *Somset* 21 ST4558
Rowborough *IOW* 13 SZ4684
Rowde *Wilts* 22 ST9762
Rowden *Devon* 8 SX6499
Rowen *Gwynd* 69 SH7671
Rowfield *Derbys* 73 SK1948
Rowfoot *Nthumb* 102 NY6860
Rowford *Somset* 20 ST2327
Rowhedge *Essex* 41 TM0221
Rowhook *W Susx* 14 TQ1234
Rowington *Warwks* 48 SP2069
Rowland *Derbys* 74 SK2172
Rowland's Castle *Hants* 13 SU7310
Rowland's Gill *T & W* 96 NZ1658
Rowledge *Surrey* 25 SU8243
Rowley *Dur* 95 NZ0848
Rowley *Humb* 84 SE9732
Rowley *Shrops* 59 SJ3006
Rowley Green *W Mids* 61 SP3483
Rowley Hill *W York* 82 SE1914
Rowley Regis *W Mids* 60 SO9787
Rowlstone *H & W* 46 SO3727
Rowly *Surrey* 14 TQ0440
Rowner *Hants* 13 SU5801
Rowney Green *H & W* 61 SP0471
Rownhams *Hants* 12 SU3817
Rows of Trees *Ches* 79 SJ8379
Rowsham *Bucks* 38 SP8417
Rowsley *Derbys* 74 SK2565
Rowstock *Oxon* 37 SU4789
Rowston *Lincs* 76 TF0856
Rowthorne *Derbys* 75 SK4764
Rowton *Ches* 71 SJ4564
Rowton *Shrops* 59 SJ3612
Rowton *Shrops* 59 SJ6119
Rowton *Shrops* 59 SO4180
Rowtown *Surrey* 26 TQ0363
Roxburgh *Border* 110 NT6930
Roxby *Humb* 84 SE9116
Roxby *N York* 97 NZ7616
Roxton *Beds* 52 TL1554
Roxwell *Essex* 40 TL6408
Roy Bridge *Highld* 131 NN2681
Royal Oak *Dur* 96 NZ2023
Royal Oak *Lancs* 78 SD4103
Royal's Green *Ches* 71 SJ6242
Roydhouse *W York* 82 SE2112
Roydon *Essex* 39 TL4010
Roydon *Norfk* 65 TF7023
Roydon *Norfk* 54 TM1080
Roydon Hamlet *Essex* 39 TL4107
Royston *Herts* 39 TL3540
Royston *S York* 83 SE3611
Royton *Gt Man* 79 SD9107
Rozel *Jersey* 152 JS1914
Ruabon *Clwyd* 71 SJ3043
Ruaig *Strath* 120 NM0747
Ruan High Lanes *Cnwll* 3 SW9039
Ruan Lanihorne *Cnwll* 3 SW8942
Ruan Major *Cnwll* 2 SW7016
Ruan Minor *Cnwll* 2 SW7115
Ruardean *Gloucs* 35 SO6217
Ruardean Hill *Gloucs* 35 SO6317
Ruardean Woodside *Gloucs* 35 SO6216
Rubery *H & W* 60 SO9977
Ruckcroft *Cumb* 94 NY5344
Ruckhall Common *H & W* 46 SO4539
Ruckinge *Kent* 17 TR0233
Ruckland *Lincs* 77 TF3378
Ruckley *Shrops* 59 SJ5300
Rudby *N York* 89 NZ4706
Rudchester *Nthumb* 103 NZ1167
Ruddington *Notts* 62 SK5732
Ruddle *Gloucs* 35 SO6811
Ruddlemoor *Cnwll* 3 SX0054
Rudford *Gloucs* 35 SO7721
Rudge *Somset* 22 ST8251
Rudgeway *Avon* 35 ST6386
Rudgwick *W Susx* 14 TQ0834
Rudhall *H & W* 47 SO6225
Rudheath *Ches* 79 SJ6772
Rudheath *Ches* 79 SJ7471
Rudley Green *Essex* 40 TL8303
Rudloe *Wilts* 35 ST8470
Rudry *M Glam* 33 ST2086
Rudston *Humb* 91 TA0967
Rudyard *Staffs* 72 SJ9557
Ruecastle *Border* 110 NT6120
Rufford *Lancs* 80 SD4615
Rufforth *N York* 83 SE5251
Rug *Clwyd* 70 SJ0543
Rugby *Warwks* 50 SP5075
Rugeley *Staffs* 73 SK0418
Ruggaton *Devon* 19 SS5545
Ruishton *Somset* 20 ST2625
Ruislip *Gt Lon* 26 TQ0987
Ruletown Head *Border* 110 NT6113
Rumbach *Gramp* 141 NJ3852
Rumbling Bridge *Tays* 117 NT0199
Rumburgh *Suffk* 55 TM3481
Rumby Hill *Dur* 96 NZ1634
Rumford *Cent* 116 NS9377
Rumford *Cnwll* 4 SW8970
Rumney *S Glam* 33 ST2178
Rumwell *Somset* 20 ST1923
Runcorn *Ches* 78 SJ5182
Runcton *W Susx* 14 SU8802
Runcton Holme *Norfk* 65 TF6109
Runfold *Surrey* 25 SU8647
Runhall *Norfk* 66 TG0507
Runham *Norfk* 67 TG4610
Runham *Norfk* 67 TG5108
Running Waters *Dur* 96 NZ3240
Runnington *Somset* 20 ST1221
Runsell Green *Essex* 40 TL7905
Runshaw Moor *Lancs* 80 SD5319
Runswick *N York* 97 NZ8016
Runtaleave *Tays* 133 NO2867
Runwell *Essex* 40 TQ7594
Ruscombe *Berks* 37 SU7976
Rush Green *Ches* 79 SJ6987
Rush Green *Essex* 41 TM1515
Rush Green *Gt Lon* 27 TQ5187
Rush Green *Herts* 39 TL2123
Rush Green *Herts* 39 TL3325
Rushall *H & W* 47 SO6435
Rushall *Norfk* 55 TM1982
Rushall *W Mids* 60 SK0200
Rushall *Wilts* 23 SU1255
Rushbrooke *Suffk* 54 TL8961
Rushbury *Shrops* 59 SO5191
Rushden *Herts* 39 TL3031
Rushden *Nhants* 51 SP9566
Rushenden *Kent* 28 TQ9071
Rusher's Cross *E Susx* 16 TQ6028
Rushett Common *Surrey* 14 TQ0242
Rushford *Devon* 5 SX4576
Rushford *Norfk* 54 TL9281
Rushlake Green *E Susx* 16 TQ6218
Rushmere *Suffk* 55 TM4986
Rushmere St Andrew *Suffk* 55 TM1946
Rushmoor *Surrey* 25 SU8740
Rushock *H & W* 46 SO3058
Rushock *H & W* 60 SO8871
Rusholme *Gt Man* 79 SJ8594
Rushton *Ches* 71 SJ5863
Rushton *Nhants* 51 SP8482
Rushton *Shrops* 59 SJ6008
Rushton Spencer *Staffs* 72 SJ9362
Rushwick *H & W* 47 SO8254
Rushyford *Dur* 96 NZ2828
Ruskie *Cent* 116 NN6200
Ruskington *Lincs* 76 TF0851
Rusland *Cumb* 87 SD3488
Rusper *W Susx* 15 TQ2037
Ruspidge *Gloucs* 35 SO6611
Russ Hill *Surrey* 15 TQ2240
Russel's Green *Suffk* 55 TM2572
Russell Green *Essex* 40 TL7413
Russell's Green *E Susx* 16 TQ7011
Russell's Water *Oxon* 37 SU7089
Rusthall *Kent* 16 TQ5639
Rustington *W Susx* 14 TQ0402
Ruston *N York* 91 SE9583
Ruston Parva *Humb* 91 TA0661
Ruswarp *N York* 90 NZ8809
Ruthall *Shrops* 59 SO5990
Rutherford *Border* 110 NT6430
Rutherglen *Strath* 116 NS6161
Ruthernbridge *Cnwll* 4 SX0166
Ruthin *Clwyd* 70 SJ1258
Ruthrieston *Gramp* 135 NJ9204
Ruthven *Gramp* 142 NJ5046
Ruthven *Highld* 140 NH8132
Ruthven *Highld* 132 NN7699
Ruthven *Tays* 126 NO2848
Ruthven House *Tays* 126 NO3047
Ruthvoes *Cnwll* 4 SW9260
Ruthwaite *Cumb* 93 NY2336
Ruthwell *D & G* 100 NY0967
Ruxley Corner *Gt Lon* 27 TQ4770
Ruxton Green *H & W* 34 SO5419
Ruyton-XI-Towns *Shrops* 59 SJ3922
Ryal *Nthumb* 103 NZ0174
Ryall *Dorset* 10 SY4095
Ryall *H & W* 47 SO8640
Ryarsh *Kent* 28 TQ6660
Rycote *Oxon* 37 SP6705
Rydal *Cumb* 87 NY3606
Ryde *IOW* 13 SZ5992
Rye *E Susx* 17 TQ9220
Rye Cross *H & W* 47 SO7735
Rye Foreign *E Susx* 17 TQ8922
Rye Harbour *E Susx* 17 TQ9319
Rye Street *H & W* 47 SO7835
Ryebank *Shrops* 59 SJ5131
Ryeford *H & W* 35 SO6322
Ryeish Green *Nhants* 24 SU7267
Ryhall *Leics* 64 TF0310
Ryhill *W York* 83 SE3814
Ryhope *T & W* 96 NZ4152
Rylah *Derbys* 75 SK4667
Ryland *Lincs* 76 TF0179
Rylands *Notts* 62 SK5335
Rylstone *N York* 88 SD9658
Ryme Intrinseca *Dorset* 10 ST5810
Ryther *N York* 83 SE5539
Ryton *N York* 90 SE7975
Ryton *Shrops* 60 SJ7602
Ryton *T & W* 103 NZ1564
Ryton *Warwks* 61 SP4086
Ryton Woodside *T & W* 96 NZ1462
Ryton-on-Dunsmore *Warwks* 61 SP3874

S

Sabden *Lancs* 81 SD7837
Sabine's Green *Essex* 27 TQ5496
Sacombe *Herts* 39 TL3319
Sacombe Green *Herts* 39 TL3419
Sacriston *T & W* 96 NZ2447
Sadberge *Dur* 96 NZ3416
Saddell *Strath* 105 NR7832
Saddington *Leics* 50 SP6691
Saddle Bow *Norfk* 65 TF6015
Saddlescombe *W Susx* 15 TQ2711
Sadgill *Cumb* 87 NY4805
Saffron Walden *Essex* 39 TL5438
Sageston *Dyfed* 30 SN0503
Saham Hills *Norfk* 66 TF9003
Saham Toney *Norfk* 66 TF8901
Saighton *Ches* 71 SJ4462
Saintbury *Gloucs* 48 SP1139
St Abbs *Border* 119 NT9167
St Agnes *Cnwll* 2 SW7150
St Agnes *Loth* 118 NT6763
St Albans *Herts* 38 TL1407
St Allen *Cnwll* 3 SW8250
St Andrew *Guern* 152 GN5007
St Andrew's Major *S Glam* 33 ST1371
St Andrews *Fife* 127 NO5116
St Andrews Well *Dorset* 10 SY4793
St Ann's *D & G* 100 NY0793
St Ann's Chapel *Cnwll* 5 SX4170
St Ann's Chapel *Devon* 7 SX6647
St Anne's *Lancs* 80 SD3228
St Anthony *Cnwll* 3 SW7825
St Anthony's Hill *E Susx* 16 TQ6201
St Arvans *Gwent* 34 ST5296
St Asaph *Clwyd* 70 SJ0374
St Athan *S Glam* 20 ST0167
St Aubin *Jersey* 152 JS1008
St Austell *Cnwll* 3 SX0152
St Bees *Cumb* 86 NX9711
St Blazey *Cnwll* 3 SX0654
St Blazey Gate *Cnwll* 3 SX0653
St Boswells *Border* 110 NT5930
St Brelade *Jersey* 152 JS0809
St Brelades Bay *Jersey* 152 JS0808
St Breock *Cnwll* 4 SW9771
St Breward *Cnwll* 4 SX0977
St Briavels *Gloucs* 34 SO5604
St Bride's Major *M Glam* 33 SS8974
St Brides *Dyfed* 30 SM8010
St Brides Netherwent *Gwent* 34 ST4289
St Brides super-Ely *S Glam* 33 ST0977
St Brides Wentlooge *Gwent* 34 ST2982
St Budeaux *Devon* 6 SX4558
St Buryan *Cnwll* 2 SW4025
St Cadoc *Cnwll* 4 SW8875
St Catherine *Avon* 35 ST7769
St Catherines *Strath* 123 NN1207
St Chloe *Gloucs* 35 SO8401
St Clears *Dyfed* 31 SN2816
St Cleer *Cnwll* 5 SX2468
St Clement *Cnwll* 3 SW8543
St Clement *Jersey* 152 JS1807
St Clether *Cnwll* 5 SX2084
St Colmac *Strath* 114 NS0467
St Columb Major *Cnwll* 4 SW9163
St Columb Minor *Cnwll* 4 SW8362
St Columb Road *Cnwll* 4 SW9159
St Combs *Gramp* 143 NK0563
St Cross South Elmham *Suffk* 55 TM2984
St Cyrus *Gramp* 135 NO7464
St David's *Tays* 125 NN9420
St Davids *Dyfed* 30 SM7525
St Day *Cnwll* 3 SW7242
St Decumans *Somset* 20 ST0642
St Dennis *Cnwll* 4 SW9557
St Devereux *H & W* 46 SO4431
St Dogmaels *Dyfed* 42 SN1645
St Dogwells *Dyfed* 30 SM9727
St Dominick *Cnwll* 5 SX4067
St Donats *S Glam* 20 SS9368
St Edith's Marsh *Wilts* 22 ST9764
St Endellion *Cnwll* 4 SW9978
St Enoder *Cnwll* 3 SW8956
St Erme *Cnwll* 3 SW8449
St Erney *Cnwll* 5 SX3759
St Erth *Cnwll* 2 SW5535
St Erth Praze *Cnwll* 2 SW5735
St Ervan *Cnwll* 4 SW8970
St Ewe *Cnwll* 3 SW9746
St Fagans *S Glam* 33 ST1277
St Fergus *Gramp* 143 NK0952
St Fillans *Tays* 124 NN6924
St Florence *Dyfed* 31 SN0801
St Gennys *Cnwll* 4 SX1497
St George *Clwyd* 70 SH9775
St George's *S Glam* 33 ST1076
St George's Hill *Surrey* 26 TQ0862
St Georges *Avon* 21 ST3762
St Germans *Cnwll* 5 SX3657
St Giles in the Wood *Devon* 19 SS5319
St Giles-on-the-Heath *Cnwll* 5 SX3690
St Harmon *Powys* 45 SN9872
St Helen Auckland *Dur* 96 NZ1826
St Helena *Norfk* 66 TG1816
St Helens *Cumb* 92 NY0232
St Helens *E Susx* 17 TQ8212
St Helens *IOW* 13 SZ6289
St Helens *Mersyd* 78 SJ5195
St Helier *Gt Lon* 27 TQ2567
St Helier *Jersey* 152 JS1508
St Hilary *Cnwll* 2 SW5431
St Hilary *S Glam* 33 ST0173
St Hill *Devon* 9 ST0908
St Hill *W Susx* 15 TQ3835
St Ibbs *Herts* 39 TL1926
St Illtyd *Gwent* 34 SO2202
St Ishmaels *Dyfed* 30 SM8307
St Issey *Cnwll* 4 SW9271
St Ive *Cnwll* 5 SX3167
St Ives *Cambs* 52 TL3171
St Ives *Cnwll* 2 SW5140
St Ives *Dorset* 12 SU1204
St Jame's End *Nhants* 49 SP7460
St James *Norfk* 67 TG2720
St James South Elmham *Suffk* 55 TM3281
St John *Cnwll* 5 SX4053
St John *Jersey* 152 JS1215
St John's *IOM* 153 SC2781
St John's Chapel *Devon* 19 SS5329
St John's Chapel *Dur* 95 NY8837
St John's Fen End *Norfk* 65 TF5312
St John's Highway *Norfk* 65 TF5214
St John's Kirk *Strath* 108 NS9836
St John's Town of Dalry *D & G* 99 NX6281
St John's Wood *Gt Lon* 27 TQ2683
St Johns *Dur* 95 NZ0633
St Johns *H & W* 47 SO8454
St Johns *Kent* 27 TQ5356
St Johns *Surrey* 25 SU9857
St Jude's *IOM* 153 SC3996
St Just *Cnwll* 2 SW3731
St Just *Cnwll* 3 SW8435
St Just Lane *Cnwll* 3 SW8535
St Katherines *Gramp* 142 NJ7834
St Keverne *Cnwll* 3 SW7921
St Kew *Cnwll* 4 SX0276
St Kew Highway *Cnwll* 4 SX0375
St Keyne *Cnwll* 5 SX2461
St Laurence *Kent* 29 TR3665
St Lawrence *Cnwll* 4 SX0466
St Lawrence *Essex* 41 TL9604
St Lawrence *IOW* 13 SZ5376
St Lawrence *Jersey* 152 JS1211
St Leonards *Bucks* 38 SP9007
St Leonards *Dorset* 12 SU1103
St Leonards *E Susx* 17 TQ8009
St Leonards Street *Kent* 28 TQ6756
St Levan *Cnwll* 2 SW3822
St Lythans *S Glam* 33 ST1072
St Mabyn *Cnwll* 4 SX0473
St Madoes *Tays* 126 NO1921
St Margaret South Elmham *Suffk* 55 TM3183
St Margaret's at Cliffe *Kent* 29 TR3544
St Margarets *H & W* 46 SO3533
St Margarets *Herts* 39 TL3811
St Margarets Hope *Ork* 155 ND4493
St Marks *IOM* 153 SC2974
St Martin *Cnwll* 5 SX2555
St Martin *Guern* 152 GN5206
St Martin *Jersey* 152 JS1912
St Martin's *Tays* 126 NO1530
St Martin's Green *Cnwll* 3 SW7323
St Martin's Moor *Shrops* 59 SJ3135
St Martins *Shrops* 59 SJ3236
St Mary *Jersey* 152 JS1014
St Mary Bourne *Hants* 24 SU4250
St Mary Church *S Glam* 33 ST0071
St Mary Cray *Gt Lon* 27 TQ4768
St Mary Hill *S Glam* 33 SS9678
St Mary in the Marsh *Kent* 17 TR0627
St Mary's *Ork* 155 HY4701
St Mary's Bay *Kent* 17 TR0827
St Mary's Grove *Avon* 21 ST4669
St Mary's Hoo *Kent* 28 TQ8076
St Marychurch *Devon* 7 SX9166
St Marylebone *Gt Lon* 27 TQ2782
St Maughans *Gwent* 34 SO4617
St Maughans Green *Gwent* 34 SO4717
St Mawes *Cnwll* 3 SW8433
St Mawgan *Cnwll* 4 SW8765
St Mellion *Cnwll* 5 SX3965
St Mellons *S Glam* 34 ST2281
St Merryn *Cnwll* 4 SW8874
St Mewan *Cnwll* 3 SW9951
St Michael Caerhays *Cnwll* 3 SW9642
St Michael Church *Somset* 20 ST3030
St Michael Penkevil *Cnwll* 3 SW8541
St Michael South Elmham *Suffk* 55 TM3483
St Michael's on Wyre *Lancs* 80 SD4641
St Michaels *H & W* 46 SO5865
St Michaels *Kent* 17 TQ8835
St Minver *Cnwll* 4 SW9677
St Monans *Fife* 127 NO5201
St Neot *Cnwll* 4 SX1868
St Neots *Cambs* 52 TL1860
St Newlyn East *Cnwll* 3 SW8256
St Nicholas *Dyfed* 30 SM9035
St Nicholas *S Glam* 33 ST0974
St Nicholas at Wade *Kent* 29 TR2666
St Ninians *Cent* 116 NS7991
St Olaves *Norfk* 67 TM4599
St Osyth *Essex* 41 TM1215
St Ouen *Jersey* 152 JS0713
St Owens Cross *H & W* 46 SO5324
St Paul's Walden *Herts* 39 TL1922
St Pauls Cray *Gt Lon* 27 TQ4768
St Peter *Jersey* 152 JS0911
St Peter Port *Guern* 152 GN5308
St Peter's *Guern* 152 GN4706
St Peter's *Kent* 29 TR3868
St Peter's Hill *Cambs* 52 TL2372
St Petrox *Dyfed* 30 SR9797
St Pinnock *Cnwll* 5 SX2063
St Quivox *Strath* 106 NS3723
St Ruan *Cnwll* 2 SW7115
St Sampson *Guern* 152 GN5411
St Saviour *Guern* 152 GN4807
St Saviour *Jersey* 152 JS0000
St Stephen *Cnwll* 3 SW9453
St Stephen's Coombe *Cnwll* 3 SW9451
St Stephens *Cnwll* 5 SX3285
St Stephens *Cnwll* 5 SX4158
St Teath *Cnwll* 4 SX0680
St Tudy *Cnwll* 4 SX0676
St Twynnells *Dyfed* 30 SR9597
St Veep *Cnwll* 3 SX1455
St Vigeans *Tays* 127 NO6443
St Wenn *Cnwll* 4 SW9664
St Weonards *H & W* 46 SO4924
Salachail *Strath* 123 NN0551
Salcombe *Devon* 7 SX7439
Salcombe Regis *Devon* 9 SY1588
Salcott *Essex* 40 TL9413
Sale *Gt Man* 79 SJ7991
Sale Green *H & W* 47 SO9358
Saleby *Lincs* 77 TF4578
Salehurst *E Susx* 17 TQ7524
Salem *Dyfed* 44 SN6226
Salem *Dyfed* 43 SN6684
Salem *Gwynd* 69 SH5456
Salen *Highld* 121 NM6864
Salen *Strath* 121 NM5743
Salesbury *Lancs* 81 SD6832
Salford *Beds* 38 SP9339
Salford *Gt Man* 79 SJ8197
Salford *Oxon* 48 SP2828
Salford Priors *Warwks* 48 SP0751
Salfords *Surrey* 15 TQ2846
Salhouse *Norfk* 67 TG3114
Saline *Fife* 117 NT0292
Salisbury *Wilts* 23 SU1429
Salkeld Dykes *Cumb* 94 NY5437
Sallachy *Highld* 146 NC5408
Salle *Norfk* 66 TG1024
Salmonby *Lincs* 77 TF3273
Salperton *Gloucs* 36 SP0720
Salph End *Beds* 38 TL0852
Salsburgh *Strath* 116 NS8262
Salt *Staffs* 72 SJ9527
Salt Cotes *Cumb* 93 NY1853
Salta *Cumb* 92 NY0845
Saltaire *W York* 82 SE1438
Saltash *Cnwll* 6 SX4258
Saltburn *Highld* 146 NH7270
Saltburn-by-the-Sea *Cleve* 97 NZ6621
Saltby *Leics* 63 SK8526
Saltcoats *Cumb* 86 SD0797
Saltcoats *Lancs* 80 SD3728
Saltcoats *Strath* 106 NS2441
Saltdean *E Susx* 15 TQ3802
Salterbeck *Cumb* 92 NX9926
Salterforth *Lancs* 81 SD8845
Salterswall *Ches* 71 SJ6266
Salterton *Wilts* 23 SU1236
Saltfleet *Lincs* 77 TF4593
Saltfleetby All Saints *Lincs* 77 TF4590
Saltfleetby St Clements *Lincs* 77 TF4691
Saltfleetby St Peter *Lincs* 77 TF4489
Saltford *Avon* 22 ST6867
Salthouse *Norfk* 66 TG0743
Saltley *W Mids* 61 SP1088
Saltmarsh *Gwent* 34 ST3482
Saltmarshe *Humb* 84 SE7824
Saltney *Ches* 71 SJ3865
Salton *N York* 90 SE7179
Saltrens *Devon* 18 SS4522
Saltwick *Nthumb* 103 NZ1780
Saltwood *Kent* 29 TR1535
Salvington *W Susx* 14 TQ1205
Salwarpe *H & W* 47 SO8762
Salwayash *Dorset* 10 SY4596
Sambourne *Warwks* 48 SP0662
Sambrook *Shrops* 72 SJ7124
Samlesbury *Lancs* 81 SD5930
Samlesbury Bottoms *Lancs* 81 SD6228
Sampford Arundel *Somset* 20 ST1118
Sampford Brett *Somset* 20 ST0741
Sampford Courtenay *Devon* 8 SS6301
Sampford Moor *Somset* 20 ST1118
Sampford Peverell *Devon* 9 ST0314
Sampford Spiney *Devon* 6 SX5372
Samson's Corner *Essex* 41 TM0818
Samsonlane *Ork* 155 HY6526
Samuelston *Loth* 118 NT4870
Sanaigmore *Strath* 112 NR2370
Sancreed *Cnwll* 2 SW4129
Sancton *Humb* 84 SE8939
Sand *Somset* 21 ST4346
Sand Cross *E Susx* 16 TQ5820
Sand Hills *W York* 83 SE3739
Sand Hole *Humb* 84 SE8137
Sand Hutton *N York* 90 SE6958
Sand Side *Cumb* 86 SD2282
Sandaig *Highld* 129 NG7102
Sandal Magna *W York* 83 SE3417
Sandale *Cumb* 93 NY2440
Sandavore *Highld* 128 NM4785
Sandbach *Ches* 72 SJ7560
Sandbank *Strath* 114 NS1680
Sandbanks *Dorset* 12 SZ0487
Sandend *Gramp* 142 NJ5566
Sanderstead *Gt Lon* 27 TQ3461
Sandford *Avon* 21 ST4259
Sandford *Cumb* 94 NY7316
Sandford *Devon* 8 SS8202
Sandford *Dorset* 11 SY9289
Sandford *Hants* 12 SU1601
Sandford *IOW* 13 SZ5381
Sandford *Shrops* 59 SJ3423
Sandford *Shrops* 59 SJ5833
Sandford *Strath* 107 NS7143
Sandford Orcas *Dorset* 21 ST6220
Sandford St Martin *Oxon* 49 SP4226
Sandford-on-Thames *Oxon* 37 SP5301
Sandgate *Kent* 29 TR2035
Sandhaven *Gramp* 143 NJ9667
Sandhead *D & G* 98 NX0949
Sandhill *S York* 75 SK4496
Sandhills *Dorset* 10 ST5800
Sandhills *Dorset* 11 ST6810
Sandhills *Oxon* 37 SP5507
Sandhills *Staffs* 61 SK0604
Sandhills *Surrey* 14 SU9337
Sandhoe *Nthumb* 102 NY9666
Sandhole *Strath* 114 NS0098
Sandholme *Humb* 84 SE8230
Sandholme *Lincs* 64 TF3337
Sandhurst *Berks* 25 SU8361
Sandhurst *Gloucs* 47 SO8223
Sandhurst *Kent* 17 TQ8028
Sandhurst Cross *Kent* 17 TQ7827
Sandhutton *N York* 89 SE3881
Sandiacre *Derbys* 62 SK4736
Sandilands *Lincs* 77 TF5280
Sandiway *Ches* 71 SJ6070
Sandleheath *Hants* 12 SU1215
Sandley *Dorset* 22 ST7724
Sandling *Kent* 28 TQ7557
Sandlow Green *Ches* 72 SJ7865
Sandness *Shet* 155 HU1957
Sandon *Essex* 40 TL7404
Sandon *Herts* 39 TL3234
Sandon *Staffs* 72 SJ9429
Sandon Bank *Staffs* 72 SJ9428
Sandown *IOW* 13 SZ5984
Sandplace *Cnwll* 5 SX2557
Sandridge *Herts* 39 TL1710
Sandridge *Wilts* 22 ST9465
Sandringham *Norfk* 65 TF6928
Sands *Bucks* 26 SU8493
Sandsend *N York* 90 NZ8612
Sandtoft *Humb* 84 SE7408
Sandwich *Kent* 29 TR3358
Sandwick *Cumb* 93 NY4219
Sandwick *Shet* 155 HU4323
Sandwith *Cumb* 92 NX9614
Sandwith Newtown *Cumb* 92 NX9614
Sandy *Beds* 52 TL1649
Sandy Bank *Lincs* 77 TF2655
Sandy Cross *H & W* 47 SO6757
Sandy Haven *Dyfed* 30 SM8507
Sandy Lane *Clwyd* 71 SJ4040
Sandy Lane *W York* 82 SE1135
Sandy Lane *Wilts* 22 ST9668
Sandy Park *Devon* 8 SX7189
Sandycroft *Clwyd* 71 SJ3366
Sandyford *D & G* 101 NY2093
Sandygate *Devon* 7 SX8674
Sandygate *IOM* 153 SC3797
Sandyhills *D & G* 92 NX8855
Sandylands *Lancs* 87 SD4263
Sandylane *Staffs* 72 SJ7035
Sandylane *W Glam* 32 SS5589
Sandyway *H & W* 46 SO4925
Sangobeg *Highld* 149 NC4266
Sangomore *Highld* 149 NC4067
Sankey Bridges *Ches* 78 SJ5887
Sankyn's Green *H & W* 47 SO7965
Sanna Bay *Highld* 128 NM4469
Sanquhar *D & G* 107 NS7809
Santon *Cumb* 86 NY1001
Santon *IOM* 153 SC3171
Santon Bridge *Cumb* 86 NY1101
Santon Downham *Suffk* 54 TL8187
Sapcote *Leics* 50 SP4893
Sapey Common *H & W* 47 SO7064
Sapiston *Suffk* 54 TL9175
Sapley *Cambs* 52 TL2474
Sapperton *Derbys* 73 SK1834
Sapperton *Gloucs* 35 SO9403
Sapperton *Lincs* 64 TF0133
Saracen's Head *Lincs* 64 TF3427
Sarclet *Highld* 151 ND3443
Sarisbury *Hants* 13 SU5008
Sarn *Gwynd* 56 SH2432
Sarn *M Glam* 33 SS9083
Sarn *Powys* 58 SN9597
Sarn *Powys* 58 SO2090
Sarn-bach *Gwynd* 56 SH3026
Sarn-wen *Powys* 58 SJ2718
Sarnau *Dyfed* 42 SN3150
Sarnau *Dyfed* 31 SN3318
Sarnau *Gwynd* 70 SH9639
Sarnau *Powys* 58 SJ2315
Sarnau *Powys* 45 SO0232
Sarnesfield *H & W* 46 SO3750
Saron *Dyfed* 31 SN3737
Saron *Dyfed* 32 SN6012
Saron *Gwynd* 69 SH5365
Sarratt *Herts* 26 TQ0499
Sarre *Kent* 29 TR2565
Sarsden *Oxon* 36 SP2822
Sarson *Hants* 23 SU3044
Sartfield *IOM* 153 SC3599
Satley *Dur* 95 NZ1143
Satmar *Kent* 29 TR2539
Satron *N York* 88 SD9397
Satterleigh *Devon* 19 SS6622
Satterthwaite *Cumb* 86 SD3392
Satwell *Oxon* 37 SU7083
Sauchen *Gramp* 135 NJ7011
Saucher *Tays* 126 NO1933
Sauchieburn *Gramp* 135 NO6669
Saul *Gloucs* 35 SO7409
Saundby *Notts* 75 SK7888
Saundersfoot *Dyfed* 31 SN1304
Saunderton *Bucks* 37 SP7901
Saunton *Devon* 18 SS4637
Sausthorpe *Lincs* 77 TF3868
Saveock Water *Cnwll* 3 SW7645
Saverley Green *Staffs* 72 SJ9638
Savile Town *W York* 82 SE2420
Sawbridge *Warwks* 50 SP5065
Sawbridgeworth *Herts* 39 TL4814
Sawdon *N York* 91 SE9485
Sawley *Derbys* 62 SK4631
Sawley *Lancs* 81 SD7746
Sawley *N York* 89 SE2467
Sawston *Cambs* 53 TL4849
Sawtry *Cambs* 52 TL1683
Saxby *Leics* 63 SK8219
Saxby *Lincs* 76 TF0086
Saxby *W Susx* 14 SU9604
Saxby All Saints *Humb* 84 SE9816
Saxelbye *Leics* 63 SK6921
Saxham Street *Suffk* 54 TM0861
Saxilby *Lincs* 76 SK8975
Saxlingham *Norfk* 66 TG0239
Saxlingham Green *Norfk* 67 TM2396
Saxlingham Nethergate *Norfk* 67 TM2297
Saxlingham Thorpe *Norfk* 67 TM2197
Saxmundham *Suffk* 55 TM3863
Saxon Street *Cambs* 53 TL6759
Saxondale *Notts* 63 SK6839
Saxtead *Suffk* 55 TM2665
Saxtead Green *Suffk* 55 TM2564
Saxtead Little Green *Suffk* 55 TM2466
Saxthorpe *Norfk* 66 TG1130
Saxton *N York* 83 SE4736
Sayers Common *W Susx* 15 TQ2618
Scackleton *N York* 90 SE6472
Scaftworth *Notts* 75 SK6691
Scagglethorpe *N York* 90 SE8372
Scalasaig *Strath* 112 NR3993
Scalby *Humb* 84 SE8429
Scalby *N York* 91 TA0090
Scald End *Beds* 51 TL0457
Scaldwell *Nhants* 50 SP7672
Scale Houses *Cumb* 94 NY5845
Scaleby *Cumb* 101 NY4463
Scalebyhill *Cumb* 101 NY4463
Scales *Cumb* 93 NY3426
Scales *Cumb* 86 SD2772
Scales *Lancs* 80 SD4531
Scalesceugh *Cumb* 93 NY4449
Scalford *Leics* 63 SK7624
Scaling *N York* 90 NZ7413
Scaling Dam *N York* 90 NZ7412
Scalloway *Shet* 155 HU4039
Scamblesby *Lincs* 77 TF2778
Scammonden *W York* 82 SE0515
Scamodale *Highld* 129 NM8373
Scampston *N York* 90 SE8575
Scampton *Lincs* 76 SK9579
Scaniport *Highld* 140 NH6239
Scapegoat Hill *W York* 82 SE0916
Scarborough *N York* 91 TA0488
Scarcewater *Cnwll* 3 SW9154
Scarcliffe *Derbys* 75 SK4968
Scarcroft *W York* 83 SE3541
Scarcroft Hill *W York* 83 SE3741
Scarfskerry *Highld* 151 ND2674
Scargill *Dur* 88 NZ0510
Scarinish *Strath* 120 NM0444
Scarisbrick *Lancs* 80 SD3713
Scarness *Cumb* 93 NY2230
Scarning *Norfk* 66 TF9512
Scarrington *Notts* 63 SK7341
Scarth Hill *Lancs* 78 SD4206
Scarthingwell *N York* 83 SE4937
Scartho *Humb* 85 TA2606
Scawby *Humb* 84 SE9605
Scawsby *S York* 83 SE5305
Scawthorpe *S York* 83 SE5506
Scawton *N York* 90 SE5483
Scayne's Hill *W Susx* 15 TQ3623
Scethrog *Powys* 45 SO1025
Scholar Green *Staffs* 72 SJ8357
Scholes *Gt Man* 78 SD5905
Scholes *S York* 74 SK3895
Scholes *W York* 82 SE1507
Scholes *W York* 82 SE1625
Scholes *W York* 83 SE3736
Scholey Hill *W York* 83 SE3825
School Aycliffe *Dur* 96 NZ2523
School Green *Ches* 72 SJ6464
School Green *W York* 82 SE1132
School House *Dorset* 10 ST3602
Schoolgreen *Berks* 24 SU7367
Scissett *W York* 82 SE2410
Scleddau *Dyfed* 30 SM9434
Sco Ruston *Norfk* 67 TG2821
Scofton *Notts* 75 SK6280
Scole *Norfk* 54 TM1579
Sconser *Highld* 137 NG5132
Scoonie *Fife* 126 NO3801
Scopwick *Lincs* 76 TF0757
Scoraig *Highld* 144 NH0096
Scorborough *Humb* 84 TA0145
Scorrier *Cnwll* 3 SW7244
Scorriton *Devon* 7 SX7068
Scorton *Lancs* 80 SD5048
Scorton *N York* 89 NZ2500
Scot Hay *Staffs* 72 SJ7947
Scot Lane End *Gt Man* 79 SD6209
Scot's Gap *Nthumb* 103 NZ0386
Scotby *Cumb* 93 NY4455
Scotch Corner *N York* 89 NZ2105
Scotforth *Lancs* 87 SD4859
Scothern *Lincs* 76 TF0377
Scotland *Lincs* 63 TF0030
Scotland *W York* 82 SE2340
Scotland Gate *T & W* 103 NZ2584
Scotlandwell *Tays* 126 NO1801
Scotscalder Station *Highld* 151 ND0956
Scotscraig *Fife* 127 NO4428
Scotsdike *Cumb* 101 NY3872
Scotsmill *Gramp* 142 NJ5618
Scotstoun *Strath* 115 NS5267
Scotswood *T & W* 103 NZ2063
Scotter *Lincs* 76 SE8800
Scotterthorpe *Lincs* 84 SE8701
Scottlethorpe *Lincs* 64 TF0520
Scotton *Lincs* 76 SK8899
Scotton *N York* 89 SE1895
Scotton *N York* 89 SE3259
Scottow *Norfk* 67 TG2823
Scoulton *Norfk* 66 TF9800
Scounslow Green *Staffs* 73 SK0929
Scourie *Highld* 148 NC1544
Scouriemore *Highld* 148 NC1443
Scousburgh *Shet* 155 HU3717
Scouthead *Gt Man* 79 SD9605
Scrabster *Highld* 151 ND1070
Scraesburgh *Border* 110 NT6718
Scrafield *Lincs* 77 TF3068
Scrainwood *Nthumb* 111 NT9808
Scrane End *Lincs* 64 TF3841
Scraptoft *Leics* 63 SK6405
Scratby *Norfk* 67 TG5015
Scrayingham *N York* 90 SE7359
Scrays *E Susx* 17 TQ7619
Scredington *Lincs* 64 TF0940
Screel *D & G* 92 NX8053
Scremby *Lincs* 77 TF4467
Scremerston *Nthumb* 111 NU0148
Screveton *Notts* 63 SK7343
Scrivelby *Lincs* 77 TF2766
Scriven *N York* 89 SE3458
Scrooby *Notts* 75 SK6590
Scropton *Derbys* 73 SK1930
Scrub Hill *Lincs* 76 TF2355
Scruschloch *Tays* 133 NO2357
Scruton *N York* 89 SE2992
Scuggate *Cumb* 101 NY4474
Sculthorpe *Norfk* 66 TF8930
Scunthorpe *Humb* 84 SE8910
Scurlage *W Glam* 32 SS4687
Sea *Somset* 10 ST3412
Sea Palling *Norfk* 67 TG4226
Seaborough *Dorset* 10 ST4206
Seabridge *Staffs* 72 SJ8343
Seabrook *Kent* 29 TR1835
Seaburn *T & W* 96 NZ4059
Seacombe *Mersyd* 78 SJ3290
Seacroft *Lincs* 77 TF5661
Seacroft *W York* 83 SE3635
Seafield *Highld* 136 NG4743
Seafield *Loth* 117 NT0066
Seaford *E Susx* 16 TV4899
Seaforth *Mersyd* 78 SJ3297
Seagrave *Leics* 62 SK6117
Seagry Heath *Wilts* 35 ST9581
Seaham *Dur* 96 NZ4149
Seahouses *Nthumb* 111 NU2231
Seal *Kent* 27 TQ5556
Seale *Surrey* 25 SU8947
Seamer *N York* 90 NZ4910
Seamer *N York* 91 TA0183
Seamill *Strath* 114 NS2047
Searby *Lincs* 85 TA0705
Seasalter *Kent* 29 TR0864
Seascale *Cumb* 86 NY0301
Seathwaite *Cumb* 93 NY2312
Seathwaite *Cumb* 86 SD2295
Seatle *Cumb* 87 SD3783
Seatoller *Cumb* 93 NY2413
Seaton *Cnwll* 5 SX3054
Seaton *Cumb* 92 NY0130
Seaton *Devon* 9 SY2490
Seaton *Dur* 96 NZ3949
Seaton *Humb* 85 TA1646
Seaton *Kent* 29 TR2258
Seaton *Leics* 51 SP9098
Seaton *Nthumb* 103 NZ3276
Seaton Burn *T & W* 103 NZ2373
Seaton Carew *Cleve* 97 NZ5229
Seaton Delaval *Nthumb* 103 NZ3075
Seaton Ross *Humb* 84 SE7840
Seaton Sluice *Nthumb* 103 NZ3376
Seatown *Dorset* 10 SY4291
Seave Green *N York* 90 NZ5500
Seaview *IOW* 13 SZ6291
Seaville *Cumb* 92 NY1553
Seavington St Mary *Somset* 10 ST4014
Seavington St Michael *Somset* 10 ST4015
Sebastopol *Gwent* 34 ST2998
Sebergham *Cumb* 93 NY3641
Seckington *Warwks* 61 SK2507
Sedbergh *Cumb* 87 SD6591
Sedbury *Gloucs* 34 ST5493
Sedbusk *N York* 88 SD8891
Sedgeberrow *H & W* 48 SP0238
Sedgebrook *Lincs* 63 SK8537
Sedgefield *Dur* 96 NZ3528
Sedgeford *Norfk* 65 TF7036
Sedgehill *Wilts* 22 ST8627
Sedgley *W Mids* 60 SO9193
Sedgley Park *Gt Man* 79 SD8202
Sedgwick *Cumb* 87 SD5186
Sedlescombe *E Susx* 17 TQ7818
Sedrup *Bucks* 38 SP8011
Seed *Kent* 28 TQ9456
Seend *Wilts* 22 ST9460
Seend Cleeve *Wilts* 22 ST9360
Seer Green *Bucks* 26 SU9692
Seething *Norfk* 67 TM3197
Sefton *Mersyd* 78 SD3501
Sefton Town *Mersyd* 78 SD3400
Seghill *Nthumb* 103 NZ2874
Seighford *Staffs* 72 SJ8825
Seion *Gwynd* 69 SH5466
Seisdon *Staffs* 60 SO8495
Selattyn *Shrops* 58 SJ2633
Selborne *Hants* 24 SU7433
Selby *N York* 83 SE6132
Selham *W Susx* 14 SU9320
Selhurst *Gt Lon* 27 TQ3267
Selkirk *Border* 109 NT4728
Sellack *H & W* 46 SO5627
Sellafirth *Shet* 155 HU5198
Sellan *Cnwll* 2 SW4230
Sellick's Green *Somset* 20 ST2119
Sellindge *Kent* 29 TR0938
Selling *Kent* 28 TR0456
Sells Green *Wilts* 22 ST9462
Selly Oak *W Mids* 61 SP0482
Selmeston *E Susx* 16 TQ5007
Selsdon *Gt Lon* 27 TQ3562
Selsey *W Susx* 14 SZ8593
Selsfield Common *Gwynd* 15 TQ3434
Selside *Cumb* 87 SD5399
Selside *N York* 88 SD7875
Selstead *Kent* 29 TR2144
Selston *Notts* 75 SK4553
Selworthy *Somset* 20 SS9246
Semer *Suffk* 54 TL9946
Semington *Wilts* 22 ST8960
Semley *Wilts* 22 ST8926
Send *Surrey* 26 TQ0155
Send Marsh *Surrey* 26 TQ0355
Senghenydd *M Glam* 33 ST1190
Sennen *Cnwll* 2 SW3525
Sennen Cove *Cnwll* 2 SW3526
Sennybridge *Powys* 45 SN9228
Serlby *Notts* 75 SK6389
Sessay *N York* 89 SE4575
Setchey *Norfk* 65 TF6313
Setley *Hants* 12 SU3000
Seton Mains *Loth* 118 NT4275
Settle *N York* 88 SD8163
Settlingstones *Nthumb* 102 NY8468
Settrington *N York* 90 SE8370
Seven Ash *Somset* 20 ST1533
Seven Kings *Gt Lon* 27 TQ4587
Seven Sisters *W Glam* 33 SN8208
Seven Springs *Gloucs* 35 SO9617
Seven Star Green *Essex* 40 TL9325
Seven Wells *Gloucs* 48 SP1134
Sevenhampton *Gloucs* 36 SP0321
Sevenhampton *Wilts* 36 SU2090
Sevenoaks *Kent* 27 TQ5255
Sevenoaks Weald *Kent* 27 TQ5250
Severn Beach *Avon* 34 ST5484
Severn Stoke *H & W* 47 SO8644
Sevicks End *Beds* 51 TL0954
Sevington *Kent* 28 TR0340
Sewards End *Essex* 53 TL5738
Sewardstonebury *Gt Lon* 27 TQ3995
Sewell *Beds* 38 SP9922
Sewerby *Humb* 91 TA1968
Seworgan *Cnwll* 2 SW7030
Sewstern *Leics* 63 SK8821
Sexhow *N York* 89 NZ4706
Sezincote *Gloucs* 48 SP1731
Shabbington *Bucks* 37 SP6606
Shackerstone *Leics* 62 SK3706
Shacklecross *Derbys* 62 SK4234
Shackleford *Surrey* 25 SU9345
Shade *W York* 81 SD9323
Shader *W Isls* 154 NB3854
Shadforth *Dur* 96 NZ3440
Shadingfield *Suffk* 55 TM4384
Shadoxhurst *Kent* 28 TQ9737
Shadwell *Norfk* 54 TL9383
Shadwell *W York* 83 SE3439
Shaftenhoe End *Herts* 39 TL4037
Shaftesbury *Dorset* 22 ST8623
Shaftholme *S York* 83 SE5708
Shafton *S York* 83 SE3911
Shafton Two Gates *S York* 83 SE3910
Shalbourne *Wilts* 23 SU3163
Shalcombe *IOW* 13 SZ3985
Shalden *Hants* 24 SU6941
Shalden Green *Hants* 24 SU7043
Shaldon *Devon* 7 SX9372
Shalfleet *IOW* 13 SZ4189
Shalford *Essex* 40 TL7229
Shalford *Surrey* 25 TQ0047
Shalford Green *Essex* 40 TL7127
Shallowford *Staffs* 72 SJ8729
Shalmsford Street *Kent* 29 TR0954
Shalstone *Bucks* 49 SP6436
Shamley Green *Surrey* 14 TQ0343
Shandford *Tays* 134 NO4962
Shandon *Strath* 114 NS2586
Shandwick *Highld* 147 NH8575
Shangton *Leics* 50 SP7196
Shankhouse *Nthumb* 103 NZ2778
Shanklin *IOW* 13 SZ5881
Shap *Cumb* 94 NY5615
Shapwick *Dorset* 11 ST9301
Shapwick *Somset* 21 ST4138
Shard End *W Mids* 61 SP1588
Shardlow *Derbys* 62 SK4330
Shareshill *Staffs* 60 SJ9406
Sharlston *W York* 83 SE3918
Sharlston Common *W York* 83 SE3919
Sharman's Cross *W Mids* 61 SP1279
Sharnal Street *Kent* 28 TQ7974
Sharnbrook *Beds* 51 SP9959
Sharneyford *Lancs* 81 SD8824
Sharnford *Leics* 50 SP4891
Sharnhill Green *Dorset* 11 ST7105
Sharoe Green *Lancs* 80 SD5333
Sharow *N York* 89 SE3371
Sharp Green *Norfk* 67 TG3820
Sharpenhoe *Beds* 38 TL0630
Sharperton *Nthumb* 102 NT9503
Sharpness *Gloucs* 35 SO6702
Sharpthorne *W Susx* 35 TQ3732
Sharptor *Cnwll* 5 SX2573
Sharpway Gate *H & W* 47 SO9565
Sharrington *Norfk* 66 TG0337
Shatterford *H & W* 60 SO7981
Shatterling *Kent* 29 TR2658
Shaugh Prior *Devon* 6 SX5463
Shave Cross *Dorset* 10 SY4198
Shavington *Ches* 72 SJ6951
Shaw *Berks* 24 SU4768
Shaw *Gt Man* 79 SD9308
Shaw *W York* 82 SE0235
Shaw *Wilts* 22 ST8965
Shaw *Wilts* 36 SU1185
Shaw Common *Gloucs* 47 SO6826
Shaw Green *Herts* 39 TL3032
Shaw Green *Lancs* 80 SD5218
Shaw Green *N York* 82 SE2652
Shaw Hill *Lancs* 81 SD5720
Shaw Mills *N York* 89 SE2562
Shawbost *W Isls* 154 NB2646
Shawbury *Shrops* 59 SJ5521
Shawclough *Gt Man* 81 SD8914
Shawdon Hill *Nthumb* 111 NU0813
Shawell *Leics* 50 SP5480
Shawford *Hants* 13 SU4625
Shawforth *Lancs* 81 SD8920
Shawhead *D & G* 100 NX8675
Shear Cross *Wilts* 22 ST8642
Shearington *D & G* 100 NY0266
Shearsby *Leics* 50 SP6290
Shearston *Somset* 20 ST2830
Shebbear *Devon* 18 SS4409
Shebdon *Staffs* 72 SJ7625
Shebster *Highld* 150 ND0164
Shedfield *Hants* 13 SU5613
Sheen *Derbys* 74 SK1161
Sheep Hill *Dur* 96 NZ1757
Sheep-ridge *W York* 82 SE1519
Sheepbridge *Derbys* 74 SK3674
Sheepscar *W York* 82 SE3134
Sheepscombe *Gloucs* 35 SO8910
Sheepstor *Devon* 6 SX5667
Sheepwash *Devon* 18 SS4806
Sheepwash *Nthumb* 103 NZ2585
Sheepway *Avon* 34 ST4976

Stallingborough Humb 85 TA1911
Stallington Staffs 72 SJ9439
Stalmine Lancs 80 SD3745
Stalmine Moss Side Lancs 80 SD3845
Stalybridge Gt Man 79 SJ9698
Stambourne Essex 53 TL7238
Stambourne Green Essex 53 TL6938
Stamford Lincs 64 TF0307
Stamford Nthumb 111 NU2219
Stamford Bridge Ches 71 SJ4667
Stamford Bridge Humb 84 SE7155
Stamford Hill Gt Lon 27 TQ3387
Stamfordham Nthumb 103 NZ0771
Stamton Lees Derbys 74 SK2562
Stanah Lancs 80 SD3542
Stanborough Herts 39 TL2212
Stanbridge Beds 38 SP9624
Stanbridge Dorset 11 SU0004
Stanbury W York 82 SE0137
Stand Gt Man 79 SD7905
Stand Strath 116 NS7668
Standburn Cent 116 NS9274
Standeford Staffs 60 SJ9107
Standen Kent 28 TQ8540
Standen Street Kent 17 TQ8030
Standerwick Somset 22 ST8150
Standford Hants 14 SU8134
Standingstone Cumb 92 NY0533
Standish Gt Man 78 SD5610
Standish Lower Ground Gt Man 78 SD5507
Standlake Oxon 36 SP3903
Standon Hants 13 SU4226
Standon Herts 39 TL3922
Standon Staffs 72 SJ8135
Standon Green End Herts 39 TL3620
Standwell Green Suffk 54 TM1369
Stane Strath 116 NS8859
Stanfield Norfk 66 TF9320
Stanford Beds 39 TL1640
Stanford Kent 29 TR1238
Stanford Shrops 59 SJ3313
Stanford Bishop H & W 47 SO6851
Stanford Bridge H & W 47 SO7265
Stanford Bridge Shrops 72 SJ7024
Stanford Dingley Berks 24 SU5771
Stanford in the Vale Oxon 36 SU3493
Stanford le Hope Essex 40 TQ6882
Stanford on Avon Nhants 50 SP5978
Stanford on Soar Notts 62 SK5421
Stanford on Teme H & W 47 SO7065
Stanford Rivers Essex 27 TL5301
Stanfree Derbys 75 SK4773
Stanghow Cleve 97 NZ6715
Stanground Cambs 64 TL2097
Stanhill Lancs 81 SD7227
Stanhoe Norfk 66 TF8036
Stanhope Border 108 NT1229
Stanhope Dur 95 NY9939
Stanhope Bretby Derbys 73 SK2921
Stanion Nhants 51 SP9186
Stanley Derbys 62 SK4140
Stanley Dur 96 NZ1953
Stanley Notts 75 SK4662
Stanley Shrops 60 SO7483
Stanley Staffs 72 SJ9352
Stanley Tays 126 NO1033
Stanley W York 83 SE3422
Stanley Common Derbys 62 SK4042
Stanley Crook Dur 96 NZ1637
Stanley Gate Lancs 78 SD4405
Stanley Moor Staffs 72 SJ9251
Stanley Pontlarge Gloucs 47 SO9930
Stanmer E Susx 15 TQ3309
Stanmore Berks 37 SU4778
Stanmore Gt Lon 26 TQ1692
Stanmore Hants 24 SU4628
Stannersburn Nthumb 102 NY7286
Stanningley W York 82 SE2234
Stannington Nthumb 103 NZ2179
Stannington S York 74 SK2987
Stansbatch H & W 46 SO3461
Stansfield Suffk 53 TL7852
Stanshope Staffs 73 SK1253
Stanstead Suffk 54 TL8449
Stanstead Abbots Herts 39 TL3811
Stanstead Street Suffk 54 TL8448
Stansted Kent 27 TQ6062
Stansted Mountfitchet Essex 39 TL5125
Stanton Derbys 73 SK2718
Stanton Devon 7 SX7050
Stanton Gloucs 48 SP0634
Stanton Gwent 34 SO3021
Stanton Nthumb 103 NZ1390
Stanton Staffs 73 SK1245
Stanton Suffk 54 TL9673
Stanton Butts Cambs 52 TL2372
Stanton by Bridge Derbys 62 SK3726
Stanton by Dale Derbys 62 SK4637
Stanton Drew Avon 21 ST5963
Stanton Fitzwarren Wilts 36 SU1790
Stanton Harcourt Oxon 36 SP4105
Stanton Hill Notts 75 SK4760
Stanton in Peak Derbys 74 SK2364
Stanton Lacy Shrops 46 SO4978
Stanton Long Shrops 59 SO5791
Stanton on the Wolds Notts 63 SK6330
Stanton Prior Avon 22 ST6762
Stanton St Bernard Wilts 23 SU0961
Stanton St John Oxon 37 SP5709
Stanton St Quintin Wilts 35 ST9079
Stanton Street Suffk 54 TL9566
Stanton under Bardon Leics 62 SK4610
Stanton upon Hine Heath Shrops 59 SJ5624
Stanton Wick Avon 21 ST6162
Stantway Gloucs 35 SO7313
Stanwardine in the Field Shrops 59 SJ4124
Stanwardine in the Wood Shrops 59 SJ4227
Stanway Essex 40 TL9424
Stanway Gloucs 48 SP0632
Stanway Green Essex 40 TL9523
Stanway Green Suffk 55 TM2470
Stanwell Surrey 26 TQ0574
Stanwell Moor Surrey 26 TQ0474
Stanwick Nhants 51 SP9771
Stanwix Cumb 93 NY4057
Stape N York 90 SE7994
Stapehill Dorset 12 SU0500
Stapeley Ches 72 SJ6749
Stapenhill Staffs 73 SK2521
Staple Kent 29 TR2756
Staple Somset 20 ST1141
Staple Cross Devon 20 ST0320
Staple Cross E Susx 17 TQ7822
Staple Fitzpaine Somset 10 ST2618
Staple Hill H & W 60 SO9773
Staplefield W Susx 15 TQ2728
Stapleford Cambs 53 TL4751
Stapleford Herts 39 TL3117
Stapleford Leics 63 SK8018
Stapleford Lincs 76 SK8857
Stapleford Notts 62 SK4837
Stapleford Wilts 23 SU0737
Stapleford Abbotts Essex 27 TQ5194
Stapleford Tawney Essex 27 TQ5099
Staplegrove Somset 20 ST2126
Staplehay Somset 20 ST2121
Staplehurst Kent 28 TQ7843
Staplers IOW 13 SZ5189
Staplestreet Kent 29 TR0660
Stapleton Cumb 101 NY5071
Stapleton H & W 46 SO3265
Stapleton Leics 50 SP4398
Stapleton N York 89 NZ2612
Stapleton Shrops 59 SJ4704
Stapleton Somset 21 ST4621
Stapley Somset 9 ST1913
Staploe Beds 52 TL1560
Staplow H & W 47 SO6941
Star Dyfed 31 SN2434
Star Fife 126 NO3103
Star Somset 21 ST4358
Starbeck N York 83 SE3255
Starbotton N York 88 SD9574
Starcross Devon 9 SX9781
Stareton Warwks 61 SP3371
Starkholmes Derbys 74 SK3058
Starling Gt Man 79 SD7710
Starlings Green Essex 39 TL4631
Starr's Green E Susx 17 TQ7615
Starston Norfk 55 TM2384
Start Devon 7 SX8044
Startforth Dur 95 NZ0415
Startley Wilts 35 ST9482
Statham Ches 79 SJ6787
Station Town Dur 96 NZ4036
Stathe Somset 21 ST3228
Staughton Green Cambs 52 TL1365
Staughton Highway Cambs 52 TL1364
Staunton Gloucs 34 SO5512
Staunton Gloucs 34 SO7829
Staunton Green H & W 46 SO3661

Staunton in the Vale Notts 63 SK8043
Staunton on Arrow H & W 46 SO3660
Staunton on Wye H & W 46 SO3644
Staveley Cumb 87 SD3786
Staveley Cumb 87 SD4698
Staveley Derbys 75 SK4374
Staveley N York 89 SE3962
Staverton Devon 7 SX7964
Staverton Gloucs 47 SO8923
Staverton Nhants 49 SP5361
Staverton Wilts 22 ST8560
Staverton Bridge Gloucs 35 SO8722
Stawell Somset 21 ST3738
Stawley Somset 20 ST0622
Staxigoe Highld 151 ND3852
Staxton N York 91 TA0179
Staylittle Dyfed 43 SN6489
Staylittle Powys 43 SN8891
Staynall Lancs 80 SD3643
Staythorpe Notts 75 SK7554
Stead W York 82 SE1446
Stean N York 89 SE0973
Steane Nhants 49 SP5538
Stearsby N York 90 SE6171
Steart Somset 20 ST2745
Stebbing Essex 40 TL6624
Stebbing Green Essex 40 TL6823
Stebbing Park Essex 40 TL6524
Stechford W Mids 61 SP1287
Stede Quarter Kent 28 TQ8738
Stedham W Susx 14 SU8622
Steel Nthumb 95 NY9458
Steel Cross E Susx 16 TQ5331
Steel Heath Shrops 59 SJ5436
Steele Road Border 101 NY5293
Steen's Bridge H & W 46 SO5357
Steep Hants 13 SU7425
Steep Lane W York 82 SE0223
Steephill IOW 13 SZ5477
Steeple Dorset 11 SY9080
Steeple Essex 40 TL9303
Steeple Ashton Wilts 22 ST9056
Steeple Aston Oxon 49 SP4725
Steeple Barton Oxon 49 SP4424
Steeple Bumpstead Essex 53 TL6841
Steeple Claydon Bucks 49 SP7026
Steeple Gidding Cambs 52 TL1381
Steeple Langford Wilts 23 SU0337
Steeple Morden Cambs 39 TL2842
Steeton W York 82 SE0344
Stein Highld 136 NG2656
Stella T & W 96 NZ1863
Stelling Minnis Kent 29 TR1447
Stembridge Somset 21 ST4220
Stenalees Cnwll 3 SX0156
Stenhouse D & G 100 NX8093
Stenhousemuir Cent 116 NS8783
Stenigot Lincs 77 TF2480
Stenschol Highld 136 NG4767
Stenson Derbys 62 SK3430
Stenton Loth 118 NT6274
Stepaside Dyfed 31 SN1407
Stepney Gt Lon 27 TQ3681
Stepping Hill Gt Man 79 SJ9187
Steppingley Beds 38 TL0035
Stepps Strath 116 NS6568
Sternfield Suffk 55 TM3861
Sterridge Devon 18 SS5545
Stert Wilts 23 SU0259
Stetchworth Cambs 53 TL6459
Steven's Crouch E Susx 17 TQ7115
Stevenage Herts 39 TL2325
Stevenston Strath 106 NS2742
Steventon Hants 24 SU5447
Steventon Oxon 37 SU4691
Steventon End Essex 53 TL5942
Stevington Beds 51 SP9853
Stewartby Beds 38 TL0142
Stewarton Strath 115 NS4245
Stewkley Bucks 38 SP8526
Stewley Somset 10 ST3118
Stewton Lincs 77 TF3587
Steyne Cross IOW 13 SZ6487
Steyning W Susx 15 TQ1711
Steynton Dyfed 30 SM9107
Stibb Cnwll 18 SS2110
Stibb Cross Devon 18 SS4314
Stibb Green Wilts 23 SU2262
Stibbard Norfk 66 TF9828
Stibbington Cambs 51 TL0898
Stichill Border 110 NT7138
Sticker Cnwll 3 SW9750
Stickford Lincs 77 TF3560
Sticklepath Devon 8 SX6494
Sticklepath Somset 20 ST0436
Stickling Green Essex 39 TL4732
Stickney Lincs 77 TF3457
Stiffkey Norfk 66 TF9742
Stifford's Bridge H & W 47 SO7347
Stile Bridge Kent 28 TQ7547
Stillingfleet N York 83 SE5940
Stillington Cleve 96 NZ3723
Stillington N York 90 SE5867
Stilton Cambs 52 TL1689
Stinchcombe Gloucs 35 ST7298
Stinsford Dorset 11 SY7091
Stirchley Shrops 60 SJ6907
Stirchley W Mids 61 SP0581
Stirling Cent 116 NS7993
Stirling Gramp 143 NK1242
Stirtloe Cambs 52 TL1966
Stirton N York 82 SD9752
Stisted Essex 40 TL8024
Stitchcombe Wilts 36 SU2369
Stithians Cnwll 3 SW7336
Stivichall W Mids 61 SP3376
Stixwould Lincs 76 TF1765
Stoak Ches 71 SJ4273
Stobo Border 109 NT1837
Stoborough Dorset 11 SY9286
Stoborough Green Dorset 11 SY9285
Stobs Castle Border 109 NT5008
Stobswood Nthumb 103 NZ2195
Stock Avon 21 ST4561
Stock Essex 40 TQ6998
Stock Green H & W 47 SO9559
Stock Wood H & W 47 SP0058
Stockbridge Hants 23 SU3535
Stockbury Kent 28 TQ8461
Stockcross Berks 24 SU4368
Stockdale Cnwll 3 SW7337
Stockdalewath Cumb 93 NY3845
Stockerston Leics 51 SP8397
Stocking H & W 47 SO6230
Stocking Green Bucks 38 SP8047
Stocking Pelham Herts 39 TL4529
Stockingford Warwks 61 SP3391
Stockland Devon 9 ST2404
Stockland Bristol Somset 20 ST2443
Stockleigh English Devon 8 SS8506
Stockleigh Pomeroy Devon 8 SS8703
Stockley Wilts 22 ST9967
Stockley Hill H & W 46 SO3738
Stocklinch Somset 10 ST3817
Stockmoor H & W 46 SO3954
Stockport Gt Man 79 SJ8990
Stocksbridge S York 74 SK2698
Stocksfield Nthumb 103 NZ0561
Stockstreet Essex 40 TL8222
Stockton H & W 46 SO5261
Stockton Norfk 67 TM3894
Stockton Shrops 59 SJ3301
Stockton Shrops 72 SJ7716
Stockton Warwks 49 SP4363
Stockton Wilts 22 ST9838
Stockton Brook Staffs 72 SJ9151
Stockton Heath Ches 78 SJ6185
Stockton on Teme H & W 47 SO7167
Stockton on the Forest N York 83 SE6556
Stockwell Gloucs 35 SO9414
Stockwell End W Mids 60 SJ8900
Stockwell Heath Staffs 73 SK0521
Stockwood Avon 21 ST6368
Stockwood Dorset 10 ST5906
Stodmarsh Kent 29 TR2160
Stody Norfk 66 TG0535
Stoer Highld 148 NC0328
Stoford Somset 10 ST5613
Stoford Wilts 23 SU0835
Stogumber Somset 20 ST0937
Stogursey Somset 20 ST2042
Stoke Devon 18 SS2324
Stoke Hants 24 SU4051
Stoke Hants 13 SU7202
Stoke Kent 28 TQ8274
Stoke Abbott Dorset 10 ST4500

Stoke Albany Nhants 51 SP8088
Stoke Ash Suffk 54 TM1170
Stoke Bardolph Notts 63 SK6441
Stoke Bliss H & W 47 SO6563
Stoke Bruerne Nhants 49 SP7449
Stoke by Clare Suffk 53 TL7443
Stoke Canon Devon 9 SX9398
Stoke Charity Hants 24 SU4839
Stoke Climsland Cnwll 5 SX3674
Stoke Cross H & W 47 SO6050
Stoke D'Abernon Surrey 26 TQ1258
Stoke Doyle Nhants 51 TL0286
Stoke Dry Leics 51 SP8596
Stoke End Warwks 61 SP1797
Stoke Farthing Wilts 23 SU0525
Stoke Ferry Norfk 65 TF7000
Stoke Fleming Devon 7 SX8648
Stoke Gabriel Devon 7 SX8557
Stoke Gifford Avon 35 ST6279
Stoke Golding Leics 61 SP3997
Stoke Goldington Bucks 38 SP8348
Stoke Green Bucks 26 SU9982
Stoke Hammond Bucks 38 SP8829
Stoke Heath H & W 47 SO9468
Stoke Heath Shrops 72 SJ6529
Stoke Holy Cross Norfk 67 TG2301
Stoke Lacy H & W 47 SO6249
Stoke Lyne Oxon 49 SP5628
Stoke Mandeville Bucks 38 SP8310
Stoke Newington Gt Lon 27 TQ3386
Stoke Orchard Gloucs 47 SO9028
Stoke Poges Bucks 26 SU9783
Stoke Pound H & W 47 SO9667
Stoke Prior H & W 46 SO5256
Stoke Prior H & W 47 SO9467
Stoke Rivers Devon 19 SS6335
Stoke Rochford Lincs 63 SK9127
Stoke Row Oxon 37 SU6884
Stoke St Gregory Somset 21 ST3427
Stoke St Mary Somset 20 ST2622
Stoke St Michael Somset 22 ST6646
Stoke St Milborough Shrops 59 SO5682
Stoke sub Hamdon Somset 10 ST4717
Stoke Talmage Oxon 37 SU6799
Stoke Trister Somset 22 ST7328
Stoke upon Tern Shrops 59 SJ6328
Stoke Wake Dorset 11 ST7606
Stoke Wharf H & W 47 SO9667
Stoke-by-Nayland Suffk 54 TL9836
Stoke-on-Trent Staffs 72 SJ8745
Stoke-upon-Trent Staffs 72 SJ8745
Stokeford Dorset 11 SY8687
Stokeham Notts 75 SK7876
Stokeinteignhead Devon 7 SX9170
Stokenchurch Bucks 37 SU7696
Stokenham Devon 7 SX8042
Stokesay Shrops 59 SO4381
Stokesby Norfk 67 TG4310
Stokesley N York 90 NZ5208
Stolford Somset 20 ST0332
Stolford Somset 20 ST2345
Ston Easton Somset 21 ST6253
Stondon Massey Essex 27 TL5800
Stone Bucks 37 SP7812
Stone Gloucs 35 ST6895
Stone H & W 60 SO8675
Stone Kent 28 TQ5774
Stone Kent 17 TQ9427
Stone S York 75 SK5589
Stone Somset 21 ST5834
Stone Staffs 72 SJ9034
Stone Allerton Somset 21 ST3951
Stone Bridge Corner Cambs 64 TF2700
Stone Chair W York 82 SE1227
Stone Cross E Susx 16 TQ5128
Stone Cross E Susx 16 TQ6104
Stone Cross Kent 16 TQ5339
Stone Cross Kent 28 TR0236
Stone Cross Kent 29 TR3257
Stone Hill S York 84 SE6809
Stone House Cumb 88 SD7685
Stone Rows Leics 61 SK3214
Stone Street Kent 27 TQ5754
Stone Street Suffk 54 TL9639
Stone Street Suffk 54 TM0143
Stone Street Suffk 55 TM3882
Stone-edge-Batch Avon 34 ST4671
Stonebridge Avon 21 ST3859
Stonebridge Norfk 54 TL9290
Stonebridge W Mids 61 SP2182
Stonebroom Derbys 75 SK4059
Stonecross Green Suffk 54 TL8257
Stonecrouch Kent 16 TQ7033
Stoneferry Humb 85 TA1031
Stonefield Castle Hotel Strath 114 NR8671
Stonegarthside Cumb 101 NY4780
Stonegate E Susx 16 TQ6628
Stonegate N York 90 NZ7708
Stonegrave N York 90 SE6577
Stonehall H & W 47 SO8848
Stonehaugh Nthumb 102 NY7976
Stonehaven Gramp 135 NO8786
Stonehouse Ches 71 SJ5070
Stonehouse D & G 100 NX8268
Stonehouse Gloucs 35 SO8005
Stonehouse Nthumb 94 NY6958
Stonehouse Strath 116 NS7546
Stoneleigh Warwks 61 SP3372
Stoner Hill Hants 13 SU7225
Stones Green Essex 41 TM1626
Stonesby Leics 63 SK8224
Stonesfield Oxon 36 SP3917
Stonethwaite Cumb 93 NY2613
Stonewells Gramp 141 NJ2865
Stonewood Kent 27 TQ5972
Stoney Cross Hants 12 SU2611
Stoney Middleton Derbys 74 SK2375
Stoney Stanton Leics 50 SP4994
Stoney Stoke Somset 22 ST7032
Stoney Stratton Somset 22 ST6539
Stoney Stretton Shrops 59 SJ3809
Stoneybridge H & W 60 SO9476
Stoneybridge W Isls 155 HY2508
Stoneyburn Loth 117 NS9862
Stoneygate Leics 50 SK6002
Stoneyhills Essex 40 TQ9597
Stoneykirk D & G 98 NX0853
Stoneywood Cent 116 NS7982
Stoneywood Gramp 135 NJ8811
Stonham Aspal Suffk 54 TM1359
Stonnall Staffs 61 SK0603
Stonor Oxon 37 SU7388
Stonton Wyville Leics 50 SP7395
Stony Cross H & W 46 SO5466
Stony Cross H & W 47 SO7247
Stony Houghton Derbys 75 SK4966
Stony Stratford Bucks 38 SP7840
Stonyford Hants 12 SU3215
Stonywell Staffs 61 SK0712
Stoodleigh Devon 19 SS6532
Stoodleigh Devon 20 SS9218
Stopham W Susx 14 TQ0219
Stopsley Beds 38 TL1023
Stoptide Cnwll 4 SW9475
Storeton Mersyd 78 SJ3084
Storeyard Green H & W 47 SO7144
Storey Corner Lancs 80 SD4707
Stornoway W Isls 154 NB4232
Storridge H & W 47 SO7548
Storrington W Susx 14 TQ0814
Storth Cumb 87 SD4779
Storwood Humb 84 SE7144
Stotfold Beds 39 TL2136
Stottesdon Shrops 60 SO6783
Stoughton Leics 50 SK6402
Stoughton Surrey 25 SU9851
Stoughton W Susx 14 SU8011
Stoul Highld 129 NM7594
Stoulton H & W 47 SO9049
Stour Provost Dorset 22 ST7921
Stour Row Dorset 22 ST8221
Stourbridge W Mids 60 SO8983
Stourpaine Dorset 11 ST8609
Stourport-on-Severn H & W 60 SO8171
Stourton Staffs 60 SO8684
Stourton Warwks 48 SP2936
Stourton Wilts 22 ST7734
Stourton Caundle Dorset 11 ST7115
Stove Shet 155 HU4024
Stoven Suffk 55 TM4481
Stow Border 118 NT4544
Stow Lincs 76 SK8882
Stow Bardolph Norfk 65 TF6206
Stow Bedon Norfk 66 TL9596
Stow cum Quy Cambs 53 TL5260
Stow Longa Cambs 51 TL1070

Stow Maries Essex 40 TQ8399
Stow-on-the-Wold Gloucs 48 SP1925
Stowbridge Norfk 65 TF6007
Stowe Gloucs 34 SO5606
Stowe Shrops 46 SO3173
Stowe Staffs 61 SK1210
Stowe by Chartley Staffs 73 SK0026
Stowehill Nhants 49 SP6458
Stowell Somset 11 ST6822
Stowey Somset 21 ST5959
Stowford Devon 19 SS6541
Stowford Devon 5 SX4387
Stowlangtoft Suffk 54 TL9568
Stowmarket Suffk 54 TM0458
Stowting Kent 29 TR1242
Stowting Common Kent 29 TR1243
Stowupland Suffk 54 TM0760
Straanruie Highld 141 NH8916
Strachan Gramp 135 NO6592
Strachur Strath 114 NN0901
Stradbroke Suffk 55 TM2373
Stradbrook Wilts 22 ST9152
Stradishall Suffk 53 TL7552
Stradsett Norfk 65 TF6606
Stragglethorpe Notts 63 SK6537
Straiton Loth 117 NT2766
Straiton Strath 106 NS3804
Straloch Gramp 134 NJ8620
Straloch Tays 133 NO0463
Stramshall Staffs 73 SK0735
Strang IOM 153 SC3578
Stranford H & W 46 SO5827
Stranraer D & G 98 NX0560
Strata Florida Dyfed 43 SN7465
Stratfield Mortimer Berks 24 SU6664
Stratfield Saye Hants 24 SU6861
Stratfield Turgis Hants 24 SU6858
Stratford Beds 52 TL1748
Stratford St Andrew Suffk 55 TM3560
Stratford St Mary Suffk 54 TM0434
Stratford sub Castle Wilts 23 SU1332
Stratford Tony Wilts 23 SU0926
Stratford-upon-Avon Warwks 48 SP2055
Strath Highld 151 NG2662
Strath Highld 144 NG7978
Strathan Highld 145 NC0521
Strathan Highld 149 NC5764
Strathaven Strath 116 NS7044
Strathblane Cent 115 NS5679
Strathcanaird Highld 145 NC1501
Strathcarron Sta Highld 138 NG9442
Strathcoil Strath 122 NM6830
Strathdon Gramp 134 NJ3512
Strathkinness Fife 126 NO4616
Strathloanhead Loth 116 NS9172
Strathmiglo Fife 126 NO2109
Strathpeffer Highld 139 NH4858
Strathtay Tays 125 NN9153
Strathwhillan Strath 105 NS0235
Strathy Highld 150 NC8464
Strathy Inn Highld 150 NC8365
Strathyre Cent 124 NN5617
Stratton Cnwll 18 SS2306
Stratton Dorset 11 SY6593
Stratton Gloucs 35 SP0103
Stratton Audley Oxon 49 SP6025
Stratton St Margaret Wilts 36 SU1786
Stratton St Michael Norfk 67 TM2093
Stratton Strawless Norfk 67 TG2220
Stratton-on-the-Fosse Somset 22 ST6650
Stravithie Fife 127 NO5313
Stream Somset 20 ST0639
Streat E Susx 15 TQ3515
Streatham Gt Lon 27 TQ3071
Streatley Beds 38 TL0728
Streatley Berks 37 SU5980
Street Devon 9 SY1888
Street N York 90 NZ7304
Street Somset 21 ST4836
Street Ashton Warwks 50 SP4582
Street Dinas Shrops 71 SJ3338
Street End E Susx 16 TQ6023
Street End Kent 29 TR1453
Street End W Susx 14 SZ8599
Street Gate T & W 96 NZ2159
Street Houses N York 83 SE5245
Street on the Fosse Somset 21 ST6139
Streethay Staffs 61 SK1410
Streetlam N York 89 SE3098
Streetly W Mids 61 SP0899
Strefford Shrops 59 SO4485
Strelitz Tays 126 NO1836
Strelley Notts 62 SK5141
Strensall N York 90 SE6360
Strensham H & W 47 SO9040
Stretcholt Somset 20 ST2943
Strete Devon 7 SX8446
Stretford Gt Man 79 SJ7994
Stretford H & W 46 SO4055
Stretford H & W 46 SO5257
Strethall Essex 53 TL4839
Stretham Cambs 53 TL5174
Strettington W Susx 14 SU8907
Stretton Ches 71 SJ4452
Stretton Ches 79 SJ6282
Stretton Derbys 74 SK3961
Stretton Leics 63 SK9415
Stretton Shrops 59 SJ4411
Stretton Staffs 60 SJ8811
Stretton Staffs 73 SK2526
Stretton en le Field Leics 61 SK3011
Stretton Grandison H & W 47 SO6344
Stretton Heath Shrops 59 SJ3610
Stretton on Fosse Warwks 48 SP2238
Stretton Sugwas H & W 46 SO4642
Stretton under Fosse Warwks 50 SP4581
Stretton Westwood Shrops 59 SO5998
Stretton-on-Dunsmore Warwks 61 SP4072
Strichen Gramp 143 NJ9455
Strines Gt Man 79 SJ9786
Stringston Somset 20 ST1742
Strixton Nhants 51 SP9061
Stroat Gloucs 34 ST5797
Stromeferry Highld 138 NG8634
Stromness Ork 155 HY2509
Stronachlachar Cent 123 NN4010
Stronchrubie Highld 145 NC2421
Strone Highld 131 NH3810
Strone Strath 114 NS1980
Stronmilchan Highld 123 NN1528
Stronsay Airport Ork 155 HY6525
Strontian Highld 130 NM8161
Strood Kent 28 TQ7268
Strood Green Surrey 15 TQ2048
Strood Green W Susx 14 TQ0224
Strood Green W Susx 15 TQ1332
Stroud Gloucs 35 SO8505
Stroud Hants 13 SU7223
Stroud Green Essex 40 TQ8690
Stroud Green Gloucs 35 SO8007
Stroude Surrey 25 TQ0068
Stroxton Lincs 63 SK9030
Struan Highld 136 NG3438
Struan Tays 132 NN8065
Strubby Lincs 77 TF4582
Strumpshaw Norfk 67 TG3407
Strutherhill Strath 116 NS7649
Struy Highld 139 NH3940
Stryd-issa Clwyd 70 SJ2845
Stuartfield Gramp 143 NJ9745
Stubbington Hants 13 SU5503
Stubbins Lancs 81 SD7918
Stubb's Green Norfk 67 TM2598
Stubbs Green Norfk 67 TM2598
Stubhampton Dorset 11 ST9113
Stubshaw Cross Gt Man 78 SD5899
Stubton Lincs 76 SK8748
Stuckton Hants 12 SU1613
Stud Green Berks 26 SU8877
Studdal Kent 29 TR3149
Studfold N York 88 SD8169
Studholme Cumb 93 NY2555
Studland Dorset 11 SZ0382
Studley Warwks 48 SP0764
Studley Wilts 22 ST9671
Studley Common H & W 48 SP0763
Studley Roger N York 89 SE2970
Studley Royal N York 89 SE2970
Stump Cross Cambs 53 TL5044
Stuntney Cambs 53 TL5578
Sturbridge Staffs 72 SJ8330
Sturgate Lincs 76 SK8888
Sturmer Essex 53 TL6943
Sturminster Common Dorset 11 ST7812

Sturminster Marshall Dorset 11 ST9500
Sturminster Newton Dorset 11 ST7814
Sturry Kent 29 TR1760
Sturton Humb 84 SE9604
Sturton by Stow Lincs 76 SK8980
Sturton le Steeple Notts 75 SK7883
Stuston Suffk 54 TM1377
Stutton N York 83 SE4841
Stutton Suffk 54 TM1434
Styal Ches 79 SJ8383
Stynie Gramp 141 NJ3360
Styrrup Notts 75 SK6090
Succoth Strath 123 NN2905
Suckley H & W 47 SO7251
Suckley Green H & W 47 SO7253
Sudborough Nhants 51 SP9682
Sudbourne Suffk 55 TM4153
Sudbrook Gwent 34 ST5087
Sudbrook Lincs 63 SK9744
Sudbrooke Lincs 76 TF0376
Sudbury Derbys 73 SK1631
Sudbury Gt Lon 26 TQ1685
Sudbury Suffk 54 TL8741
Suddie Highld 140 NH6554
Suddington H & W 47 SO8463
Sudgrove Gloucs 35 SO9308
Suffield N York 91 SE9890
Suffield Norfk 67 TG2232
Sugdon Staffs 72 SJ7031
Sugnall Staffs 72 SJ7931
Sugwas Pool H & W 46 SO4541
Suisnish Highld 129 NG5816
Sulby IOM 153 SC3894
Sulgrave Nhants 49 SP5544
Sulham Berks 24 SU6474
Sulhamstead Berks 24 SU6368
Sulhamstead Abbots Berks 24 SU6467
Sulhamstead Bannister Berks 24 SU6368
Sullington W Susx 14 TQ0913
Sullom Shet 155 HU3573
Sullom Voe Shet 155 HU4075
Sully S Glam 20 ST1568
Summer Heath Bucks 37 SU7490
Summer Hill Clwyd 71 SJ3153
Summerbridge N York 89 SE2062
Summercourt Cnwll 3 SW8856
Summerfield H & W 60 SO8473
Summerfield Norfk 65 TF7538
Summerhouse Dur 96 NZ2019
Summersdale W Susx 14 SU8606
Summerseat Gt Man 81 SD7914
Summertown Oxon 37 SP5009
Sunbiggin Cumb 94 NY6608
Sunbury Surrey 26 TQ1168
Sunderland Cumb 93 NY1735
Sunderland Lancs 80 SD4255
Sunderland Strath 112 NR2464
Sunderland T & W 96 NZ3957
Sunderland Bridge Dur 96 NZ2637
Sundhope Border 109 NT3325
Sundon Park Beds 38 TL0525
Sundridge Kent 27 TQ4855
Sunk Island Humb 85 TA2619
Sunningdale Surrey 25 SU9567
Sunninghill Surrey 25 SU9367
Sunningwell Oxon 37 SP4900
Sunniside Dur 96 NZ1438
Sunniside T & W 96 NZ2059
Sunny Bank Lancs 81 SD7720
Sunny Brow Dur 96 NZ1934
Sunnyhill Derbys 62 SK3432
Sunnylaw Cent 116 NS7998
Sunnymead Oxon 37 SP5208
Sunton Wilts 23 SU2454
Surbiton Gt Lon 26 TQ1867
Surfleet Lincs 64 TF2528
Surfleet Seas End Lincs 64 TF2628
Surlingham Norfk 67 TG3106
Sustead Norfk 66 TG1837
Susworth Lincs 84 SE8302
Sutcombe Devon 18 SS3411
Sutcombemill Devon 18 SS3411
Suton Norfk 66 TM0999
Sutterby Lincs 77 TF3872
Sutterton Lincs 64 TF2835
Sutton Beds 52 TL2247
Sutton Cambs 53 TL4479
Sutton Cambs 51 TL0998
Sutton Devon 5 SX7042
Sutton Devon 8 SS7202
Sutton Dyfed 30 SM9715
Sutton E Susx 16 TV4999
Sutton Gt Lon 27 TQ2664
Sutton Kent 29 TR3349
Sutton Mersyd 78 SJ5393
Sutton N York 83 SE4925
Sutton Norfk 67 TG3823
Sutton Notts 75 SK6784
Sutton Notts 63 SK7637
Sutton Oxon 36 SP4106
Sutton S York 83 SE5512
Sutton Shrops 60 SO7386
Sutton Shrops 59 SJ5010
Sutton Shrops 72 SJ6631
Sutton Staffs 72 SJ7622
Sutton Suffk 55 TM3046
Sutton W Susx 14 SU9715
Sutton at Hone Kent 27 TQ5569
Sutton Bassett Nhants 50 SP7790
Sutton Benger Wilts 35 ST9478
Sutton Bingham Somset 10 ST5410
Sutton Bonington Notts 62 SK5024
Sutton Bridge Lincs 65 TF4721
Sutton Cheney Leics 50 SK4100
Sutton Coldfield W Mids 61 SP1295
Sutton Courtenay Oxon 37 SU5094
Sutton Crosses Lincs 65 TF4321
Sutton Grange N York 89 SE2873
Sutton Green Clwyd 71 SJ4048
Sutton Green Oxon 36 SP4107
Sutton Green Surrey 25 TQ0054
Sutton Howgrave N York 89 SE3179
Sutton in Ashfield Notts 75 SK4958
Sutton in the Elms Leics 50 SP5193
Sutton le Marsh Lincs 77 TF5280
Sutton Maddock Shrops 60 SJ7201
Sutton Mallet Somset 21 ST3736
Sutton Mandeville Wilts 22 ST9828
Sutton Manor Mersyd 78 SJ5290
Sutton Marsh H & W 46 SO5544
Sutton Montis Somset 21 ST6224
Sutton on Sea Lincs 77 TF5281
Sutton on Trent Notts 75 SK7965
Sutton on the Hill Derbys 73 SK2333
Sutton Scarsdale Derbys 75 SK4468
Sutton Scotney Hants 24 SU4639
Sutton St Edmund Lincs 64 TF3613
Sutton St James Lincs 65 TF3918
Sutton St Nicholas H & W 46 SO5245
Sutton upon Derwent Humb 84 SE7047
Sutton Valence Kent 28 TQ8149
Sutton Veny Wilts 22 SU9041
Sutton Waldron Dorset 11 ST8615
Sutton Weaver Ches 71 SJ5479
Sutton Wick Avon 21 ST5859
Sutton Wick Oxon 37 SU4894
Sutton-in-Craven N York 82 SE0043
Sutton-on-Hull Humb 85 TA1232
Sutton-on-the-Forest N York 90 SE5864
Sutton-under-Brailes Warwks 48 SP3037
Swaby Lincs 77 TF3877
Swadlincote Derbys 73 SK2919
Swaffham Norfk 66 TF8108
Swaffham Bulbeck Cambs 53 TL5562
Swaffham Prior Cambs 53 TL5764
Swafield Norfk 67 TG2832
Swainby N York 90 NZ4701
Swainshill H & W 46 SO4641
Swainsthorpe Norfk 67 TG2201
Swainswick Avon 22 ST7668
Swalcliffe Oxon 48 SP3737
Swalecliffe Kent 29 TR1367
Swallow Lincs 85 TA1703
Swallow Beck Lincs 76 SK9467
Swallow Nest S York 75 SK4585
Swallowcliffe Wilts 22 ST9627
Swallowfield Berks 24 SU7264
Swallows Cross Essex 40 TQ6398
Swampton Hants 24 SU4150
Swan Green Ches 79 SJ7373
Swan Street Essex 40 TL8927
Swan Village W Mids 60 SO9992
Swanage Dorset 12 SZ0278

Swanbourne Bucks 38 SP8026
Swanbridge S Glam 20 ST1667
Swancote Shrops 60 SO7494
Swanland Humb 84 SE9928
Swanley Kent 27 TQ5168
Swanley Village Kent 27 TQ5369
Swanmore Hants 13 SU5716
Swannington Leics 62 SK4116
Swannington Norfk 66 TG1319
Swanscombe Kent 27 TQ6073
Swansea W Glam 32 SS6592
Swanton Abbot Norfk 67 TG2625
Swanton Morley Norfk 66 TG0117
Swanton Novers Norfk 66 TG0231
Swanton Street Kent 28 TQ8759
Swanwick Derbys 74 SK4053
Swanwick Hants 13 SU5109
Swarby Lincs 64 TF0440
Swardeston Norfk 67 TG2002
Swarkestone Derbys 62 SK3728
Swarland Nthumb 103 NU1602
Swarland Estate Nthumb 103 NU1603
Swarraton Hants 24 SU5636
Swartha W York 82 SE0546
Swarthmoor Cumb 86 SD2777
Swaton Lincs 64 TF1337
Swavesey Cambs 52 TL3668
Sway Hants 12 SZ2798
Swayfield Lincs 63 SK9922
Swaything Hants 13 SU4414
Sweet Green H & W 47 SO6462
Sweetham Devon 9 SX8899
Sweethaws E Susx 16 TQ5028
Sweethams Corner Kent 28 TQ7845
Sweets Cnwll 4 SX1595
Sweetshouse Cnwll 4 SX0861
Swefling Suffk 55 TM3463
Swepstone Leics 62 SK3610
Swerford Oxon 48 SP3731
Swettenham Ches 72 SJ8067
Swffryd Gwent 33 ST2198
Swift's Green Kent 28 TQ8744
Swiftsden E Susx 17 TQ7328
Swilland Suffk 54 TM1852
Swillbrook Lancs 80 SD4834
Swillington W York 83 SE3830
Swimbridge Devon 19 SS6230
Swimbridge Newland Devon 19 SS6030
Swinbrook Oxon 36 SP2812
Swincliffe N York 89 SE2458
Swincombe Devon 19 SS6941
Swinden N York 81 SD8554
Swinderby Lincs 76 SK8663
Swindon Gloucs 47 SO9325
Swindon Nthumb 102 NY9799
Swindon Staffs 60 SO8690
Swindon Wilts 36 SU1484
Swine Humb 85 TA1335
Swinefleet Humb 84 SE7621
Swineford Avon 35 ST6969
Swineshead Beds 51 TL0565
Swineshead Lincs 64 TF2340
Swineshead Bridge Lincs 64 TF2242
Swiney Highld 151 ND2335
Swinford Leics 50 SP5679
Swinford Oxon 37 SP4408
Swingfield Minnis Kent 29 TR2142
Swingfield Street Kent 29 TR2343
Swingleton Green Suffk 54 TL9647
Swinhill Strath 116 NS7648
Swinhoe Nthumb 111 NU2128
Swinithwaite N York 88 SE0489
Swinmore Common H & W 47 SO6741
Swinscoe Staffs 73 SK1247
Swinside Cumb 93 NY2421
Swinstead Lincs 64 TF0122
Swinthorpe Lincs 76 TF0680
Swinton Border 110 NT8347
Swinton Gt Man 79 SD7701
Swinton N York 89 SE2179
Swinton N York 90 SE7573
Swinton S York 75 SK4599
Swithland Leics 62 SK5512
Swordale Highld 139 NM7891
Swordland Highld 129 NM7891
Swordly Highld 150 NC7463
Sworton Heath Ches 79 SJ6986
Swyddffynnon Dyfed 43 SN6966
Swynnerton Staffs 72 SJ8535
Swyre Dorset 10 SY5288
Sychant Clwyd 58 SJ2025
Sychnant Powys 45 SN9777
Sychtyn Powys 58 SH9900
Sydallt Clwyd 71 SJ3055
Syde Gloucs 35 SO9511
Sydenham Gt Lon 27 TQ3671
Sydenham Oxon 37 SP7301
Sydenham Damerel Devon 5 SX4176
Sydenhurst Surrey 14 SU9534
Syderstone Norfk 66 TF8332
Sydling St Nicholas Dorset 10 SY6399
Sydmonton Hants 24 SU4857
Sydnal Lane Shrops 60 SJ8005
Syerston Notts 63 SK7447
Sykehouse S York 83 SE6316
Syleham Suffk 55 TM2078
Sylen Dyfed 32 SN5106
Symbister Shet 155 HU5462
Symington Strath 106 NS3831
Symington Strath 108 NS9935
Symonds Yat H & W 34 SO5515
Symondsbury Dorset 10 SY4493
Sympson Green W York 82 SE1838
Synod Inn Dyfed 42 SN3853
Syre Highld 149 NC6943
Syreford Gloucs 35 SO0221
Syresham Nhants 49 SP6241
Syston Leics 62 SK6211
Syston Lincs 63 SK9240
Sytchampton H & W 47 SO8466
Sywell Nhants 51 SP8267

T

Tabley Hill Ches 79 SJ7379
Tackley Oxon 37 SP4719
Tacolneston Norfk 66 TM1495
Taddington Derbys 74 SK1471
Taddiport Devon 18 SS4818
Tadley Hants 24 SU6061
Tadlow Cambs 52 TL2847
Tadmarton Oxon 48 SP3937
Tadwick Avon 22 ST7470
Tadworth Surrey 26 TQ2257
Tafarn-y-bwlch Dyfed 31 SN0834
Tafarn-y-Gelyn Clwyd 70 SJ1961
Taff's Well M Glam 33 ST1283
Tafolwern Powys 57 SH8902
Tai'r Bull Powys 45 SN9925
Taibach W Glam 32 SS7788
Tain Highld 151 NH7781
Tain Highld 140 NH7881
Takeley Essex 40 TL5621
Takeley Street Essex 39 TL5521
Tal-y-Bont Gwynd 69 SH7668
Tal-y-bont Gwynd 57 SH6070
Tal-y-bont Gwynd 69 SH7668
Tal-y-bont Gwynd 69 SH6070
Tal-y-cafn Gwynd 69 SH7871
Tal-y-coed Gwent 34 SO4115
Tal-y-Waun Gwent 34 SO2604
Talachddu Powys 45 SO0833
Talacre Clwyd 70 SJ1183
Talaton Devon 9 SY0699
Talbenny Dyfed 30 SM8411
Talbot Green M Glam 33 ST0382
Talbot Village Dorset 12 SZ0793
Taleford Devon 9 SY0897
Talerddig Powys 58 SH9300
Talgarreg Dyfed 42 SN4251
Talgarth Powys 45 SO1533
Taliesin Dyfed 43 SN6591
Talisker Highld 136 NG3230
Talke Staffs 72 SJ8253
Talke Pits Staffs 72 SJ8253
Talkin Cumb 94 NY5557
Talla Linfoots Border 108 NT1320
Talladale Highld 144 NG9170
Tallaminnock Strath 106 NX4094
Tallarn Green Clwyd 71 SJ4444
Tallentire Cumb 92 NY1035
Talley Dyfed 44 SN6332
Tallington Lincs 64 TF0908
Talmine Highld 149 NC5863
Talog Dyfed 31 SN3325
Talsarn Dyfed 44 SN5456

Talsarnau Trelewis

Talsarnau Gwynd 57 SH6135
Talskiddy Cnwll 4 SW9165
Talwrn Clwyd 71 SJ3847
Talwrn Gwynd 68 SH4877
Talybont Dyfed 43 SN6589
Talybont-on-Usk Powys 33 SO1122
Talysarn Gwynd 68 SH4952
Talywern Powys 57 SH8200
Tamer Lane End Gt Man 79 SD6401
Tamerton Foliot Devon 6 SX4761
Tamworth Staffs 61 SK2003
Tamworth Green Lincs 64 TF3842
Tan Hill N York 88 NY8906
Tan Office Green Suffk 53 TL7858
Tan-y-Bwlch Gwynd 57 SH6540
Tan-y-fron Clwyd 70 SH9564
Tan-y-fron Clwyd 71 SJ2952
Tan-y-groes Dyfed 42 SN2849
Tancred N York 89 SE4558
Tancredston Dyfed 30 SM8826
Tandlemuir Strath 115 NS3361
Tandridge Surrey 27 TQ3750
Tanfield Dur 96 NZ1855
Tanfield Lea Dur 96 NZ1854
Tangiers Dyfed 30 SM9518
Tangley Hants 23 SU3252
Tangmere W Susx 14 SU9006
Tankerness Ork 155 HY5109
Tankersley S York 74 SK3499
Tankerton Kent 29 TR1166
Tannach Highld 151 ND3247
Tannachie Gramp 135 NO7884
Tannadice Tays 134 NO4758
Tanner Green H & W 61 SP0874
Tannington Suffk 55 TM2467
Tannochside Strath 116 NS7061
Tansley Derbys 74 SK3259
Tansor Nhants 51 TL0590
Tantobie Dur 96 NZ1754
Tanton N York 90 NZ5210
Tanworth in Arden Warwks 61 SP1170
Tanygrisiau Gwynd 57 SH6945
Taplow Bucks 26 SU9182
Tarbert Strath 113 NR6551
Tarbert Strath 113 NR8668
Tarbert W Isls 154 NB1500
Tarbet Highld 148 NC1649
Tarbet Highld 129 NM7992
Tarbet Strath 123 NN3104
Tarbock Green Mersyd 78 SJ4687
Tarbolton Strath 107 NS4327
Tarbrax Strath 117 NT0255
Tardebigge H & W 47 SO9969
Tardy Gate Lancs 80 SD5425
Tarfside Tays 134 NO4879
Tarland Gramp 134 NJ4804
Tarleton Lancs 80 SD4520
Tarlscough Lancs 80 SD4314
Tarlton Gloucs 35 ST9599
Tarnock Somset 21 ST3752
Tarns Cumb 92 NY1248
Tarnside Cumb 87 SD4390
Tarporley Ches 71 SJ5562
Tarr Somset 19 SS8632
Tarr Somset 20 ST1030
Tarrant Crawford Dorset 11 ST9203
Tarrant Gunville Dorset 11 ST9213
Tarrant Hinton Dorset 11 ST9311
Tarrant Keynston Dorset 11 ST9204
Tarrant Launceston Dorset 11 ST9409
Tarrant Monkton Dorset 11 ST9408
Tarrant Rawston Dorset 11 ST9306
Tarrant Rushton Dorset 11 ST9305
Tarring Neville E Susx 16 TQ4403
Tarrington H & W 46 SO6140
Tarskavaig Highld 129 NG5810
Tarves Gramp 143 NJ8631
Tarvie Tays 133 NO0164
Tarvin Ches 71 SJ4966
Tarvin Sands Ches 71 SJ4967
Tasburgh Norfk 67 TM1996
Tasley Shrops 60 SO6894
Taston Oxon 36 SP3521
Tatenhill Staffs 73 SK2021
Tathall End Bucks 38 SP8246
Tatham Lancs 87 SD6069
Tathwell Lincs 77 TF3182
Tatsfield Surrey 27 TQ4156
Tattenhall Ches 71 SJ4858
Tatterford Norfk 66 TF8628
Tattersett Norfk 66 TF8429
Tattershall Lincs 76 TF2157
Tattershall Bridge Lincs 76 TF1956
Tattershall Thorpe Lincs 76 TF2159
Tattingstone Suffk 54 TM1337
Tattingstone White Horse Suffk 54 TM1338
Tatworth Somset 10 ST3205
Tauchers Gramp 141 NJ3749
Taunton Somset 20 ST2224
Taverham Norfk 66 TG1613
Taverners Green Essex 40 TL5618
Tavernspite Dyfed 31 SN1812
Tavistock Devon 6 SX4874
Taw green Devon 8 SX6597
Tawstock Devon 19 SS5529
Taxal Derbys 79 SK0079
Taychreggan Hotel Strath 123 NN0421
Tayinloan Strath 105 NR7046
Taynton Gloucs 35 SO7222
Taynton Oxon 36 SP2313
Taynuilt Strath 122 NN0031
Tayport Fife 127 NO4628
Tayvallich Strath 113 NR7487
Tealby Lincs 76 TF1590
Teangue Highld 129 NG6609
Teanord Highld 140 NH5964
Tebay Cumb 87 NY6104
Tebworth Beds 38 SP9926
Tedburn St Mary Devon 8 SX8194
Teddington Gloucs 47 SO9633
Teddington Gt Lon 26 TQ1670
Tedstone Delamere H & W 47 SO6958
Tedstone Wafer H & W 47 SO6759
Teesport Cleve 97 NZ5423
Teeton Nhants 50 SP6970
Teffont Evias Wilts 22 ST9931
Teffont Magna Wilts 22 ST9932
Tegryn Dyfed 31 SN2233
Teigh Leics 63 SK8615
Teigncombe Devon 8 SX6787
Teigngrace Devon 7 SX8574
Teignmouth Devon 7 SX9473
Teindside Border 109 NT4408
Telford Shrops 60 SJ6911
Tellisford Somset 22 ST8055
Telscombe E Susx 15 TQ4003
Telscombe Cliffs E Susx 15 TQ4001
Tempar Tays 124 NN6857
Templand D & G 100 NY0886
Temple Cnwll 4 SX1473
Temple Loth 117 NT3158
Temple Strath 115 NS5469
Temple Balsall W Mids 61 SP2076
Temple Bar Dyfed 44 SN5354
Temple Cloud Avon 21 ST6257
Temple End Suffk 53 TL6650
Temple Ewell Kent 29 TR2844
Temple Grafton Warwks 48 SP1255
Temple Guiting Gloucs 48 SP0928
Temple Hirst N York 83 SE6024
Temple Normanton Derbys 74 SK4167
Temple Pier Highld 139 NH5330
Temple Sowerby Cumb 94 NY6127
Templecombe Somset 22 ST7022
Templeton Devon 19 SS8813
Templeton Dyfed 31 SN1111
Templetown Dur 95 NZ1050
Tempsford Beds 52 TL1653
Ten Mile Bank Norfk 65 TL5996
Tenbury Wells H & W 46 SO5968
Tenby Dyfed 31 SN1300
Tendring Essex 41 TM1424
Tendring Green Essex 41 TM1325
Tendring Heath Essex 41 TM1326
Tenpenny Heath Essex 41 TM0820
Tenterden Kent 17 TQ8833
Terling Essex 40 TL7715
Tern Shrops 59 SJ6216
Ternhill Shrops 59 SJ6332
Terregles D & G 100 NX9377
Terrington N York 90 SE6770
Terrington St Clement Norfk 65 TF5520
Terrington St John Norfk 65 TF5314
Terry's Green Warwks 61 SP1073
Teston Kent 28 TQ7053
Testwood Hants 12 SU3514
Tetbury Gloucs 35 ST8993
Tetbury Upton Gloucs 35 ST8895
Tetchill Shrops 59 SJ3932
Tetcott Devon 5 SX3396
Tetford Lincs 77 TF3374
Tetney Lincs 77 TA3100
Tetney Lock Lincs 85 TA3402
Tetsworth Oxon 37 SP6801
Tettenhall W Mids 60 SJ8800
Tettenhall Wood W Mids 60 SO8899
Tetworth Cambs 52 TL2253
Teversal Notts 75 SK4861
Teversham Cambs 53 TL4958
Teviothead Border 109 NT4005
Tewel Gramp 135 NO8085
Tewin Herts 39 TL2714
Tewkesbury Gloucs 47 SO8932
Teynham Kent 28 TQ9662
Thackley W York 82 SE1738
Thackthwaite Cumb 92 NY1423
Thackthwaite Cumb 93 NY4225
Thakeham W Susx 14 TQ1017
Thame Oxon 37 SP7005
Thames Ditton Surrey 26 TQ1567
Thamesmead Gt Lon 27 TQ4780
Thanington Kent 29 TR1356
Thankerton Strath 108 NS9738
Tharston Norfk 66 TM1894
Thatcham Berks 24 SU5167
Thatto Heath Mersyd 78 SJ5093
Thaxted Essex 40 TL6131
The Bank Ches 72 SJ8457
The Bank Shrops 59 SO6199
The Beeches Gloucs 36 SP0302
The Biggins Cambs 53 TL4788
The Blythe Staffs 73 SK0428
The Bourne H & W 47 SO9856
The Braes Highld 137 NG5234
The Bratch Staffs 60 SO8693
The Broad H & W 46 SO4961
The Brunt Loth 118 NT6873
The Bungalow IOM 153 SC3986
The Bush Kent 28 TQ6649
The Butts Gloucs 35 SO8916
The Chequer Clwyd 71 SJ4840
The City Beds 52 TL1159
The City Bucks 37 SU7896
The Common Oxon 48 SP2927
The Common Wilts 35 SU0285
The Corner Kent 28 TQ7041
The Corner Shrops 59 SO4387
The Den Strath 115 NS3251
The Flatt Cumb 101 NY5678
The Forge H & W 46 SO3459
The Forstal Kent 28 TQ8946
The Forstal Kent 28 TR0438
The Fouralls Shrops 72 SJ6831
The Green Cumb 86 SD1884
The Green Essex 40 TL7719
The Grove H & W 47 SO8741
The Haven W Susx 14 TQ0830
The Haw Gloucs 47 SO8427
The Hill Cumb 86 SD1783
The Hirsel Border 110 NT8240
The Holt Berks 37 SU8078
The Horns Kent 17 TQ7429
The Leacon Kent 17 TQ9833
The Lee Bucks 38 SP9004
The Lhen IOM 153 NX3801
The Marsh Ches 72 SJ8462
The Middles Dur 96 NZ2051
The Moor Kent 17 TQ7529
The Mumbles W Glam 32 SS6187
The Mythe Gloucs 47 SO8934
The Narth Gwent 34 SO5206
The Neuk Gramp 135 NO7397
The Quarry Gloucs 35 ST7499
The Quarter Kent 28 TQ8844
The Reddings Gloucs 35 SO9121
The Rookery Staffs 72 SJ8555
The Ross Tays 124 NN7621
The Rowe Staffs 72 SJ8238
The Sands Surrey 25 SU8846
The Shoe Wilts 35 ST8074
The Smithies Shrops 60 SO6897
The Spike Cambs 53 TL4848
The Spring Warwks 61 SP2873
The Square Gwent 34 ST2796
The Stair Kent 16 TQ6047
The Stocks Kent 17 TQ9127
The Straits Hants 25 SU7839
The Strand Wilts 22 ST9259
The Thrift Herts 39 TL3139
The Towans Cnwll 2 SW5538
The Vauld H & W 46 SO5349
The Wyke Shrops 60 SJ7206
Theakston N York 89 SE3085
Thealby Humb 84 SE8917
Theale Berks 24 SU6471
Theale Somset 21 ST4646
Thearne Humb 85 TA0736
Theberton Suffk 55 TM4365
Thedden Grange Hants 24 SU6839
Theddingworth Leics 50 SP6685
Theddlethorpe All Saints Lincs 77 TF4688
Theddlethorpe St Helen Lincs 77 TF4788
Thelnetham Suffk 54 TM0178
Thelveton Norfk 54 TM1681
Thelwall Ches 79 SJ6587
Themelthorpe Norfk 66 TG0524
Thenford Nhants 49 SP5241
Theobald's Green Wilts 23 SU0268
Therfield Herts 39 TL3337
Thetford Norfk 54 TL8783
Thethwaite Cumb 93 NY3744
Theydon Bois Essex 27 TQ4499
Thicket Prior Humb 83 SE6943
Thickwood Wilts 35 ST8272
Thimbleby Lincs 77 TF2470
Thimbleby N York 89 SE4495
Thingwall Mersyd 78 SJ2784
Thirkleby N York 89 SE4778
Thirlby N York 90 SE4883
Thirlestane Border 118 NT5647
Thirlspot Cumb 93 NY3118
Thirn N York 89 SE2185
Thirsk N York 89 SE4281
Thirtleby Humb 85 TA1634
Thistleton Lancs 80 SD4037
Thistleton Leics 63 SK9118
Thistley Green Suffk 53 TL6676
Thixendale N York 90 SE8460
Thockrington Nthumb 102 NY9578
Tholomas Drove Cambs 65 TF4006
Tholthorpe N York 89 SE4766
Thomas Chapel Dyfed 31 SN1008
Thomas Close Cumb 93 NY4340
Thomastown Gramp 142 NJ5736
Thompson Norfk 66 TL9296
Thomshill Gramp 141 NJ2157
Thong Kent 28 TQ6770
Thoralby N York 88 SE0086
Thoresby Notts 75 SK6371
Thoresthorpe Lincs 77 TF4577
Thoresway Lincs 76 TF1696
Thorganby Lincs 76 TF2097
Thorganby N York 83 SE6841
Thorgill N York 90 SE7096
Thorington Suffk 55 TM4174
Thorington Street Suffk 54 TM0035
Thorlby N York 82 SD9653
Thorley Herts 39 TL4718
Thorley IOW 12 SZ3689
Thorley Houses Herts 39 TL4620
Thorley Street IOW 12 SZ3788
Thormanby N York 90 SE4974
Thorn's Flush Surrey 14 TQ0440
Thornaby-on-Tees Cleve 97 NZ4518
Thornage Norfk 66 TG0536
Thornborough Bucks 49 SP7433
Thornborough N York 89 SE2979
Thornbury Avon 35 ST6390
Thornbury Devon 18 SS4008
Thornbury H & W 47 SO6259
Thornbury W York 82 SE1933
Thornby Cumb 93 NY2851
Thornby Nhants 50 SP6775
Thorncliff Staffs 73 SK0158
Thorncombe Dorset 10 ST3703
Thorncombe Street Surrey 25 SU9941
Thorncott Green Beds 52 TL1547
Thorncross IOW 13 SZ4381
Thorndon Suffk 54 TM1469
Thorndon Cross Devon 8 SX5394
Thorne S York 83 SE6812
Thorne Somset 10 ST5217
Thorne St Margaret Somset 20 ST1020
Thornecroft Devon 7 SX7767
Thornehillhead Devon 18 SS4116
Thorner W York 83 SE3740
Thornes Staffs 61 SK0703
Thornes W York 83 SE3219
Thorney Bucks 26 TQ0379
Thorney Cambs 64 TF2804
Thorney Notts 76 SK8572
Thorney Somset 21 ST4223
Thorney Hill Hants 12 SZ2099
Thorney Toll Cambs 64 TF3404
Thornfalcon Somset 20 ST2823
Thornford Dorset 10 ST6012
Thorngrafton Nthumb 102 NY7865
Thorngrove Somset 21 ST3632
Thorngumbald Humb 85 TA2026
Thornham Norfk 65 TF7343
Thornham Magna Suffk 54 TM1070
Thornham Parva Suffk 54 TM1072
Thornhaugh Cambs 64 TF0600
Thornhill Cent 116 NN6600
Thornhill D & G 100 NX8795
Thornhill Derbys 74 SK1983
Thornhill Hants 13 SU4612
Thornhill M Glam 33 ST1584
Thornhill W York 82 SE2518
Thornhill Lees W York 82 SE2419
Thornhills W York 82 SE1523
Thornholme Humb 91 TA1164
Thornicombe Dorset 11 ST8703
Thornington Nthumb 110 NT8833
Thornley Dur 95 NZ1137
Thornley Dur 96 NZ3639
Thornley Gate Cumb 95 NY8356
Thornliebank Strath 115 NS5559
Thorns Suffk 53 TL7455
Thorns Green Gt Man 79 SJ7884
Thornsett Derbys 79 SK0086
Thornthwaite Cumb 93 NY2225
Thornthwaite N York 89 SE1758
Thornton Bucks 49 SP7435
Thornton Cleve 89 NZ4713
Thornton Dyfed 30 SM9007
Thornton Fife 117 NT2897
Thornton Humb 84 SE7645
Thornton Lancs 80 SD3342
Thornton Leics 62 SK4607
Thornton Lincs 77 TF2467
Thornton Mersyd 78 SD3301
Thornton Nthumb 111 NT9547
Thornton Tays 126 NO3946
Thornton W York 82 SE0932
Thornton Curtis Humb 85 TA0817
Thornton Dale N York 90 SE8383
Thornton Green Ches 71 SJ4473
Thornton Heath Gt Lon 27 TQ3168
Thornton Hough Mersyd 78 SJ3080
Thornton in Lonsdale N York 87 SD6873
Thornton le Moor Lincs 76 TF0496
Thornton Rust N York 88 SD9689
Thornton Steward N York 89 SE1787
Thornton Watlass N York 89 SE2385
Thornton-in-Craven N York 81 SD9048
Thornton-le-Beans N York 89 SE3990
Thornton-le-Clay N York 90 SE6865
Thornton-le-Moor N York 89 SE3988
Thornton-le-Moors Ches 71 SJ4474
Thornton-le-Street N York 89 SE4186
Thorntonhall Strath 115 NS5955
Thorntonloch Loth 119 NT7574
Thornwood Common Essex 39 TL4604
Thornydykes Border 110 NT6148
Thornythwaite Cumb 93 NY3922
Thoroton Notts 63 SK7642
Thorp Arch W York 83 SE4345
Thorpe Derbys 73 SK1550
Thorpe Humb 84 SE9946
Thorpe Lincs 77 TF4981
Thorpe N York 88 SE0161
Thorpe Norfk 67 TM4398
Thorpe Notts 75 SK7649
Thorpe Surrey 26 TQ0168
Thorpe Abbotts Norfk 55 TM1979
Thorpe Acre Leics 62 SK5119
Thorpe Arnold Leics 63 SK7720
Thorpe Audlin W York 83 SE4715
Thorpe Bassett N York 90 SE8673
Thorpe Bay Essex 40 TQ9185
Thorpe by Water Leics 51 SP8996
Thorpe Common S York 74 SK3895
Thorpe Constantine Staffs 61 SK2508
Thorpe End Norfk 67 TG2810
Thorpe Green Essex 41 TM1623
Thorpe Green Lancs 81 SD5923
Thorpe Green Suffk 54 TL9354
Thorpe Hesley S York 74 SK3796
Thorpe in Balne S York 83 SE5910
Thorpe in the Fallows Lincs 76 SK9180
Thorpe Langton Leics 50 SP7492
Thorpe Larches Dur 96 NZ3826
Thorpe Lea Surrey 26 TQ0170
Thorpe le Street Humb 84 SE8343
Thorpe Malsor Nhants 51 SP8378
Thorpe Mandeville Nhants 49 SP5244
Thorpe Market Norfk 67 TG2436
Thorpe Morieux Suffk 54 TL9453
Thorpe on the Hill Lincs 76 SK9065
Thorpe on the Hill W York 82 SE3126
Thorpe Salvin S York 75 SK5281
Thorpe Satchville Leics 63 SK7311
Thorpe St Andrew Norfk 67 TG2508
Thorpe St Peter Lincs 77 TF4860
Thorpe Thewles Cleve 96 NZ3923
Thorpe Tilney Lincs 76 TF1257
Thorpe Underwood N York 89 SE4659
Thorpe Underwood Nhants 50 SP7981
Thorpe Waterville Nhants 51 TL0281
Thorpe Willoughby N York 83 SE5731
Thorpe-le-Soken Essex 41 TM1722
Thorpeness Suffk 55 TM4759
Thorpland Norfk 65 TF6108
Thorrington Essex 41 TM0919
Thorverton Devon 9 SS9202
Thrales End Beds 38 TL1116
Thrandeston Suffk 54 TM1176
Thrapston Nhants 51 SP9978
Threapland Cumb 92 NY1539
Threapland N York 88 SD9860
Threapwood Ches 71 SJ4344
Threapwood Staffs 73 SK0342
Threapwood Head Staffs 73 SK0342
Threave Strath 106 NS3306
Three Ashes H & W 34 SO5122
Three Bridges W Susx 15 TQ2837
Three Burrows Cnwll 3 SW7446
Three Chimneys Kent 28 TQ8238
Three Cocks Powys 45 SO1737
Three Crosses W Glam 32 SS5794
Three Cups Corner E Susx 16 TQ6320
Three Gates H & W 47 SO6862
Three Hammers Cnwll 5 SX2287
Three Holes Norfk 65 TF5000
Three Lane Ends Gt Man 79 SD8309
Three Leg Cross E Susx 16 TQ6831
Three Legged Cross Dorset 12 SU0805
Three Mile Cross Berks 24 SU7167
Three Mile Stone Cnwll 3 SW7745
Three Miletown Loth 117 NT0675
Three Oaks E Susx 17 TQ8314
Threehammer Common Norfk 67 TG3419
Threekingham Lincs 64 TF0836
Threepwood Border 109 NT5143
Threlkeld Cumb 93 NY3125
Threshfield N York 88 SD9863
Thrigby Norfk 67 TG4612
Thringarth Dur 95 NY9322
Thringstone Leics 62 SK4217
Thrintoft N York 89 SE3192
Thriplow Cambs 53 TL4346
Throapham S York 75 SK5387
Throckenhalt Lincs 64 TF3509
Throcking Herts 39 TL3330
Throckley T & W 103 NZ1566
Throckmorton H & W 47 SO9850
Throop Dorset 11 SY8292
Throop Dorset 12 SZ1195
Throphill Nthumb 103 NZ1285
Thropton Nthumb 103 NU0202
Througham Gloucs 35 SO9108
Throughgate D & G 100 NX8784
Throwleigh Devon 8 SX6690
Throwley Kent 28 TQ9955
Throwley Forstal Kent 28 TQ9854
Thrumpton Notts 62 SK5031
Thrumpton Notts 75 SK7080
Thrumster Highld 151 ND3345
Thrunscoe Humb 85 TA3107
Thrup Oxon 36 SU2999
Thrupp Gloucs 35 SO8603
Thrupp Oxon 37 SP4716
Thrushelton Devon 5 SX4487
Thrushesbush Essex 39 TL4909
Thrussington Leics 63 SK6515
Thruxton H & W 46 SO4334
Thruxton Hants 23 SU2945
Thrybergh S York 75 SK4695
Thulston Derbys 62 SK4031
Thundersley Essex 40 TQ7988
Thurcaston Leics 62 SK5610
Thurcroft S York 75 SK4988
Thurdistoft Highld 151 ND2167
Thurdon Cnwll 18 SS2810
Thurgarton Norfk 66 TG1834
Thurgarton Notts 75 SK6949
Thurgoland S York 82 SE2901
Thurlaston Leics 50 SP5099
Thurlaston Warwks 50 SP4670
Thurlbear Somset 20 ST2621
Thurlby Lincs 76 SK9061
Thurlby Lincs 64 TF0916
Thurlby Lincs 77 TF4776
Thurleigh Beds 51 TL0558
Thurlestone Devon 7 SX6742
Thurlow Suffk 53 TL6750
Thurloxton Somset 20 ST2730
Thurlstone S York 82 SE2303
Thurlton Norfk 67 TM4198
Thurlwood Ches 72 SJ8057
Thurmaston Leics 62 SK6109
Thurnby Leics 63 SK6403
Thurne Norfk 67 TG4015
Thurnham Kent 28 TQ8057
Thurning Nhants 51 TL0882
Thurning Norfk 66 TG0729
Thurnscoe S York 83 SE4505
Thursby Cumb 93 NY3250
Thursden Lancs 81 SD9034
Thursford Norfk 66 TF9833
Thursley Surrey 25 SU9039
Thurso Highld 151 ND1168
Thurstaston Mersyd 78 SJ2484
Thurston Suffk 54 TL9265
Thurston Clough Gt Man 82 SD9707
Thurston Planch Suffk 54 TL9364
Thurstonfield Cumb 93 NY3156
Thurstonland W York 82 SE1610
Thurton Norfk 67 TG3200
Thurvaston Derbys 73 SK2437
Thuxton Norfk 66 TG0307
Thwaite N York 88 SD8998
Thwaite Suffk 54 TM1168
Thwaite Head Cumb 87 SD3490
Thwaite St Mary Norfk 67 TM3395
Thwaites W York 82 SE0741
Thwaites Brow W York 82 SE0740
Thwing Humb 91 TA0470
Tibbermore Tays 125 NO0423
Tibbers D & G 100 NX8696
Tibberton Gloucs 35 SO7521
Tibberton H & W 47 SO9057
Tibberton Shrops 72 SJ6820
Tibbie Shiels Inn Border 109 NT2420
Tibenham Norfk 54 TM1389
Tibshelf Derbys 75 SK4461
Tibthorpe Humb 84 SE9555
Ticehurst E Susx 16 TQ6830
Tichborne Hants 24 SU5730
Tickencote Leics 63 SK9809
Tickenham Avon 34 ST4571
Tickford End Bucks 38 SP8843
Tickhill S York 75 SK5993
Ticklerton Shrops 59 SO4890
Ticknall Derbys 62 SK3523
Tickton Humb 84 TA0541
Tidbury Green W Mids 61 SP1075
Tidcombe Wilts 23 SU2858
Tiddington Oxon 37 SP6404
Tiddington Warwks 48 SP2255
Tidebrook E Susx 16 TQ6130
Tideford Cnwll 5 SX3559
Tideford Cross Cnwll 5 SX3461
Tidenham Gloucs 34 ST5595
Tideswell Derbys 74 SK1575
Tidmarsh Berks 24 SU6374
Tidmington Warwks 48 SP2538
Tidpit Hants 12 SU0718
Tiers Cross Dyfed 30 SM9010
Tiffield Nhants 49 SP7051
Tifty Gramp 142 NJ7740
Tigerton Tays 134 NO5364
Tigharry W Isls 154 NF7172
Tighnabruaich Strath 114 NR9873
Tigley Devon 7 SX7660
Tilbrook Cambs 51 TL0869
Tilbury Essex 27 TQ6476
Tilbury Green Essex 53 TL7441
Tile Cross W Mids 61 SP1687
Tile Hill W Mids 61 SP2777
Tilehouse Green W Mids 61 SP1776
Tilehurst Berks 24 SU6673
Tilford Surrey 25 SU8743
Tilgate W Susx 15 TQ2734
Tilgate Forest Row W Susx 15 TQ2632
Tilham Street Somset 21 ST5535
Tillers Green Gloucs 47 SO6932
Tillicoultry Cent 116 NS9197
Tillingham Essex 41 TL9904
Tillington H & W 46 SO4644
Tillington W Susx 14 SU9621
Tillington Common H & W 46 SO4545
Tilly Essex 40 TL5926
Tillybirloch Gramp 135 NJ6807
Tillycairn Gramp 134 NO4697
Tillyfourie Gramp 135 NJ6412
Tillygreig Gramp 143 NJ8822
Tillyrie Tays 126 NO1006
Tilmanstone Kent 29 TR3051
Tiln Notts 75 SK7084
Tilney All Saints Norfk 65 TF5618
Tilney High End Norfk 65 TF5617
Tilney St Lawrence Norfk 65 TF5414
Tilshead Wilts 23 SU0347
Tilstock Shrops 59 SJ5437
Tilston Ches 71 SJ4650
Tilstone Bank Ches 71 SJ5659
Tilstone Fearnall Ches 71 SJ5660
Tilsworth Beds 38 SP9824
Tilton on the Hill Leics 63 SK7405
Tiltups End Gloucs 35 ST8497
Timberland Lincs 76 TF1258
Timbersbrook Ches 72 SJ8962
Timberscombe Somset 20 SS9542
Timble N York 82 SE1853
Timewell Devon 20 SS9625
Timpanheck D & G 101 NY3274
Timperley Gt Man 79 SJ7888
Timsbury Avon 22 ST6758
Timsbury Hants 23 SU3424
Timsgarry W Isls 154 NB0534
Timworth Suffk 54 TL8669
Timworth Green Suffk 54 TL8669
Tincleton Dorset 11 SY7692
Tindale Cumb 94 NY6159
Tindale Crescent Dur 96 NZ1927
Tingewick Bucks 49 SP6532
Tingley W York 82 SE2826
Tingrith Beds 38 TL0032
Tinhay Devon 5 SX3985
Tinker's Hill Hants 24 SU4047
Tinkersley Derbys 74 SK2664
Tinsley S York 74 SK4090
Tinsley Green W Susx 15 TQ2839
Tintagel Cnwll 4 SX0588
Tintern Parva Gwent 34 SO5200
Tintinhull Somset 21 ST4919
Tintwistle Derbys 79 SK0197
Tinwald D & G 100 NY0081
Tinwell Leics 63 TF0006
Tipp's End Norfk 65 TL5095
Tippacott Devon 19 SS7647
Tiptoe Hants 12 SZ2597
Tipton W Mids 60 SO9492
Tipton Green W Mids 60 SO9592
Tipton St John Devon 9 SY0991
Tiptree Essex 40 TL8916
Tiptree Heath Essex 40 TL8815
Tir-y-fron Clwyd 70 SJ2859
Tirabad Powys 45 SN8741
Tiretigan Strath 113 NR7162
Tirley Gloucs 47 SO8328
Tirphil M Glam 33 SO1303
Tirril Cumb 94 NY5026
Tisbury Wilts 22 ST9429
Tisman's Common W Susx 14 TQ0632
Tissington Derbys 73 SK1752
Titchberry Devon 18 SS2427
Titchfield Hants 13 SU5405
Titchfield Common Hants 13 SU5206
Titchmarsh Nhants 51 TL0279
Titchwell Norfk 65 TF7643
Tithby Notts 63 SK6937
Titley H & W 46 SO3360
Titmore Green Herts 39 TL2126
Titsey Surrey 27 TQ4054
Tittensor Staffs 72 SJ8738
Tittleshall Norfk 66 TF8921
Titton H & W 60 SO8370
Tiverton Ches 71 SJ5560
Tiverton Devon 9 SS9512
Tivetshall St Margaret Norfk 54 TM1787
Tivetshall St Mary Norfk 54 TM1686
Tivington Somset 20 SS9345
Tivy Dale S York 82 SE2707
Tixall Staffs 72 SJ9722
Tixover Leics 51 SK9700
Toab Shet 155 HU3811
Toadhole Derbys 74 SK3856
Toadmoor Derbys 74 SK3451
Tobermory Strath 121 NM5055
Toberonochy Strath 122 NM7408
Tocher Gramp 142 NJ6932
Tochieneal Gramp 142 NJ5165
Tockenham Wilts 36 SU0379
Tockenham Wick Wilts 36 SU0381
Tocketts Cleve 97 NZ6217
Tockington Avon 34 ST6086
Tockwith N York 83 SE4652
Todber Dorset 22 ST7919
Todburn Nthumb 103 NZ1295
Toddington Beds 38 TL0128
Toddington Gloucs 48 SP0333
Todds Green Herts 39 TL2226
Todenham Gloucs 48 SP2335
Todhills Cumb 101 NY3762
Todhills Dur 96 NZ2133
Todhills Tays 127 NO4239
Todmorden W York 81 SD9324
Todwick S York 75 SK4984
Toft Cambs 52 TL3656
Toft Ches 79 SJ7576
Toft Lincs 64 TF0717
Toft Shet 155 HU4376
Toft Warwks 50 SP4770
Toft Hill Dur 96 NZ1528
Toft Monks Norfk 67 TM4294
Toft next Newton Lincs 76 TF0388
Toftrees Norfk 66 TF8927
Tofts Highld 151 ND3668
Toftwood Norfk 66 TF9811
Togston Nthumb 103 NU2402
Tokavaig Highld 129 NG6011
Tokers Green Oxon 37 SU7077
Toldavas Cnwll 2 SW4226
Toldish Cnwll 4 SW9259
Toll Bar S York 83 SE5507
Tolland Somset 20 ST1032
Tollard Farnham Dorset 11 ST9515
Tollard Royal Wilts 11 ST9417
Tollbar End W Mids 61 SP3675
Toller Fratrum Dorset 10 SY5797
Toller Porcorum Dorset 10 SY5698
Toller Whelme Dorset 10 ST5101
Tollerton N York 90 SE5164
Tollerton Notts 62 SK6134
Tollesbury Essex 40 TL9510
Tolleshunt D'Arcy Essex 40 TL9211
Tolleshunt Knights Essex 40 TL9114
Tolleshunt Major Essex 40 TL9011
Tolpuddle Dorset 11 SY7994
Tolsta W Isls 154 NB5347
Tolvan Cnwll 2 SW7028
Tolver Cnwll 2 SW4832
Tolworth Gt Lon 26 TQ1966
Tomaknock Tays 125 NN8721
Tomatin Highld 140 NH8028
Tomchrasky Highld 131 NH2512
Tomdoun Highld 131 NH1500
Tomich Highld 146 NC6005
Tomich Highld 139 NH3027
Tomich Highld 139 NH5348
Tomich Highld 146 NH6971
Tomintoul Gramp 141 NJ1619
Tomintoul Gramp 133 NO1490
Tomlow Warwks 49 SP4563
Tomnacross Highld 139 NH5141
Tomnavoulin Gramp 141 NJ2126
Tompkin Staffs 72 SJ9451
Ton Gwent 34 SO3301
Ton Gwent 34 ST3695
Ton-teg M Glam 33 ST0986
Tonbridge Kent 16 TQ5846
Tondu M Glam 33 SS8984
Tonedale Somset 20 ST1321
Tong Kent 28 TQ9556
Tong Shrops 60 SJ7907
Tong W York 82 SE2230
Tong Green Kent 28 TQ9853
Tong Norton Shrops 60 SJ7908
Tong Street W York 82 SE1930
Tonge Leics 62 SK4223
Tongham Surrey 25 SU8848
Tongland D & G 99 NX6954
Tongue Highld 149 NC5956
Tongue End Lincs 64 TF1518
Tongwynlais S Glam 33 ST1382
Tonna W Glam 32 SS7798
Tonwell Herts 39 TL3316
Tonypandy M Glam 33 SS9991
Tonyrefail M Glam 33 ST0188
Toot Baldon Oxon 37 SP5600
Toot Hill Essex 27 TL5102
Toot Hill Hants 12 SU3818
Toothill Wilts 36 SU1183
Tooting Gt Lon 27 TQ2771
Tooting Bec Gt Lon 27 TQ2872
Top of Hebers Gt Man 79 SD8607
Top-y-rhos Clwyd 70 SJ2558
Topcliffe N York 89 SE3976
Topcroft Norfk 67 TM2693
Topcroft Street Norfk 67 TM2691
Topham S York 83 SE6217
Toppesfield Essex 53 TL7437
Toppings Gt Man 81 SD7213
Toprow Norfk 66 TM1698
Topsham Devon 9 SX9688
Torbeg Strath 105 NR8929
Torboll Highld 147 NH7599
Torbreck Highld 140 NH6441
Torbryan Devon 7 SX8266
Torcastle Highld 131 NN1378
Torcross Devon 7 SX8241
Tore Highld 140 NH6052
Torfrey Cnwll 3 SX1154
Torksey Lincs 76 SK8378
Tormarton Avon 35 ST7678
Tormitchell Strath 106 NX2394
Tormore Strath 105 NR8932
Tornagrain Highld 140 NH7650
Tornaveen Gramp 134 NJ6106
Torness Highld 139 NH5826
Tornewton Devon 7 SX8167
Toronto Nthumb 96 NZ1930
Torosay Castle Strath 122 NM7335
Torpenhow Cumb 93 NY2039
Torphichen Loth 117 NS9672
Torphins Gramp 134 NJ6202
Torpoint Cnwll 6 SX4355
Torquay Devon 7 SX9164
Torquhan Border 118 NT4448
Torr Devon 6 SX5851
Torran Highld 137 NG5949
Torrance Strath 116 NS6173
Torranyard Strath 115 NS3544
Torridon Highld 138 NG9055
Torridon House Highld 138 NG8657
Torrin Highld 129 NG5721
Torrisdale Highld 149 NC6761
Torrisdale Square Strath 105 NR7936
Torrish Highld 147 NC9718
Torrisholme Lancs 87 SD4563
Torrobull Highld 146 NC5904
Torry Gramp 135 NJ9405
Torryburn Fife 117 NT0286
Torrylin Strath 105 NR9521
Tortan H & W 60 SO8472
Torteval Guern 152 GN4505
Torthorwald D & G 100 NY0378
Tortington W Susx 14 TQ0004
Tortworth Avon 35 ST7093
Torvaig Highld 136 NG4944
Torver Cumb 86 SD2894
Torwood Cent 116 NS8385
Torwoodlee Border 109 NT4738
Torworth Notts 75 SK6586
Toscaig Highld 137 NG7138
Toseland Cambs 52 TL2462
Tosside Lancs 81 SD7656
Tostock Suffk 54 TL9563
Totaig Highld 136 NG2050
Tote Highld 136 NG4149
Tote Hill W Susx 14 SU8624
Tothill Lincs 77 TF4181
Totland IOW 12 SZ3287
Totley S York 74 SK3079
Totley Brook S York 74 SK3180
Totnes Devon 7 SX8060
Toton Notts 62 SK5034
Totronald Strath 120 NM1656
Totscore Highld 136 NG3866
Tottenham Gt Lon 27 TQ3390
Tottenhill Norfk 65 TF6411
Totteridge Gt Lon 26 TQ2494
Totternhoe Beds 38 SP9821
Tottington Gt Man 81 SD7712
Tottleworth Lancs 81 SD7331
Totton Hants 12 SU3613
Touchen End Berks 26 SU8776
Toulston N York 83 SE4543
Toulton Somset 20 ST1931
Toulvaddie Highld 147 NH8880
Toux Gramp 142 NJ5459
Tovil Kent 28 TQ7554
Tow Law Dur 95 NZ1138
Towan Cnwll 4 SW8774
Towan Cnwll 3 SX0148
Toward Strath 114 NS1368
Toward Quay Strath 114 NS1167
Towcester Nhants 49 SP6948
Towednack Cnwll 2 SW4838
Towersey Oxon 37 SP7305
Towie Gramp 134 NJ4312
Town End Cambs 65 TL4195
Town End Cumb 87 NY3406
Town End Cumb 94 NY6325
Town End Cumb 87 SD3687
Town End Cumb 87 SD4483
Town End Lincs 63 SK9943
Town Green Lancs 78 SD4005
Town Green Norfk 67 TG3612
Town Head Cumb 87 NY4103
Town Head N York 88 SD8258
Town Head N York 82 SE1748
Town Kelloe Dur 96 NZ3536
Town Lane Gt Man 79 SJ6999
Town Littleworth E Susx 15 TQ4117
Town Moor T & W 103 NZ2465
Town of Lowdon Mersyd 78 SJ6196
Town Row E Susx 16 TQ5630
Town Street Suffk 53 TL7785
Town Yetholm Border 110 NT8128
Towngate Cumb 94 NY5246
Towngate Lincs 64 TF1310
Townhead Cumb 92 NY0735
Townhead Cumb 94 NY6334
Townhead D & G 100 NY0088
Townhead S York 82 SE1602
Townhead of Greenlaw D & G 99 NX7464
Townhill Loth 117 NT1089
Townlake Devon 5 SX4074
Towns End Hants 24 SU5659
Townsend Somset 10 ST3614
Townshend Cnwll 2 SW5932
Townwell Avon 35 ST7090
Towthorpe Humb 91 SE8962
Towthorpe N York 90 SE6258
Towton N York 83 SE4839
Towyn Clwyd 70 SH9779
Toxteth Mersyd 78 SJ3588
Toy's Hill Kent 27 TQ4651
Toynton All Saints Lincs 77 TF3963
Toynton Fen Side Lincs 77 TF3961
Toynton St Peter Lincs 77 TF4063
Trabboch Strath 107 NS4421
Trabbochburn Strath 107 NS4621
Traboe Cnwll 3 SW7421
Tracebridge Somset 20 ST0621
Tradespark Highld 140 NH8656
Traethsaith Dyfed 42 SN2851
Trafford Park Gt Man 79 SJ7896
Trallong Powys 45 SN9629
Tranent Loth 118 NT4072
Tranmere Mersyd 78 SJ3187
Trannack Cnwll 2 SW5633
Trantelbeg Highld 150 NC8952
Trantlemore Highld 150 NC8953
Tranwell Nthumb 103 NZ1883
Trap Dyfed 32 SN6518
Trap's Green Warwks 48 SP1069
Trapshill Berks 23 SU3763
Traquair Border 109 NT3334
Trash Green Berks 24 SU6569
Traveller's Rest Devon 19 SS6127
Trawden Lancs 81 SD9138
Trawscoed Dyfed 43 SN6672
Trawsfynydd Gwynd 57 SH7035
Tre Aubrey S Glam 33 ST0372
Tre'r-ddol Dyfed 43 SN6692
Tre-Gibbon M Glam 33 SN9905
Tre-gagle Gwent 34 SO5207
Tre-groes Dyfed 42 SN4044
Tre-Mostyn Clwyd 70 SJ1479
Tre-Vaughan Dyfed 31 SN3921
Tre-wyn Gwent 34 SO3222
Trealaw M Glam 33 ST0092
Treales Lancs 80 SD4332
Treamble Cnwll 3 SW7856
Trearddur Bay Gwynd 68 SH2579
Treaslane Highld 136 NG3953
Treator Cnwll 4 SW9075
Trebanog M Glam 33 ST0190
Trebanos W Glam 32 SN7103
Trebartha Cnwll 5 SX2677
Trebarvah Cnwll 2 SW7130
Trebarwith Cnwll 4 SX0586
Trebeath Cnwll 5 SX2587
Trebehor Cnwll 2 SW3724
Trebelzue Cnwll 4 SW8464
Trebetherick Cnwll 4 SW9378
Trebudannon Cnwll 4 SW8961
Trebullett Cnwll 5 SX3278
Treburgett Cnwll 4 SX0579
Treburick Cnwll 4 SW8971
Treburley Cnwll 5 SX3577
Treburrick Cnwll 4 SW8670
Trebyan Cnwll 4 SX0763
Trecastle Powys 45 SN8829
Trecogo Cnwll 5 SX3080
Trecott Devon 8 SS6300
Trecwn Dyfed 30 SM9632
Trecynon M Glam 33 SN9903
Tredaule Cnwll 5 SX2381
Tredavoe Cnwll 2 SW4528
Tredegar Gwent 33 SO1408
Tredethy Cnwll 4 SX0672
Tredington Gloucs 47 SO9029
Tredington Warwks 48 SP2543
Tredinnick Cnwll 4 SW9270
Tredinnick Cnwll 4 SX0459
Tredinnick Cnwll 4 SX1666
Tredinnick Cnwll 5 SX2357
Tredinnick Cnwll 5 SX2957
Tredomen Powys 45 SO1231
Tredrissi Dyfed 31 SN0742
Tredrizzick Cnwll 4 SW9577
Tredunhock Gwent 34 ST3794
Tredustan Powys 45 SO1332
Treen Cnwll 2 SW3923
Treesmill Cnwll 3 SX0855
Treeton S York 75 SK4387
Trefacca Powys 45 SO1431
Trefasser Dyfed 30 SM8938
Trefdraeth Gwynd 68 SH4170
Trefeglwys Powys 58 SN9690
Trefenter Dyfed 43 SN6068
Treffgarne Dyfed 30 SM9523
Treffgarne Owen Dyfed 30 SM8625
Trefforest M Glam 33 ST0888
Treffynnon Dyfed 30 SM8528
Trefil Gwent 33 SO1212
Trefilan Dyfed 44 SN5456
Treflach Wood Shrops 58 SJ2625
Trefnannau Powys 58 SJ2316
Trefnant Clwyd 70 SJ0570
Trefonen Shrops 58 SJ2526
Trefor Gwynd 68 SH3780
Treforda Cnwll 4 SX0988
Trefrew Cnwll 4 SX1084
Trefriw Gwynd 69 SH7863
Tregadillett Cnwll 5 SX2983
Tregaian Gwynd 68 SH4580
Tregare Gwent 34 SO4110
Tregarne Cnwll 3 SW7823
Tregaron Dyfed 44 SN6759
Tregarth Gwynd 69 SH6067
Tregaswith Cnwll 4 SW8962
Tregatta Cnwll 4 SX0587
Tregawne Cnwll 4 SX0066
Tregear Cnwll 3 SW8650
Tregeare Cnwll 5 SX2486
Tregeiriog Clwyd 58 SJ1733
Tregele Gwynd 68 SH3592
Tregellist Cnwll 4 SX0177
Tregenna Cnwll 3 SW8743
Tregenna Cnwll 4 SX0973
Tregeseal Cnwll 2 SW3731
Tregew Cnwll 3 SW8034
Tregidden Cnwll 3 SW7523
Tregiddle Cnwll 2 SW6723
Tregidgeo Cnwll 3 SW9647
Tregiskey Cnwll 3 SX0146
Treglemais Dyfed 30 SM8229
Tregole Cnwll 5 SX1998
Tregolls Cnwll 3 SW7335
Tregonce Cnwll 4 SW9373
Tregonetha Cnwll 4 SW9563
Tregony Cnwll 3 SW9244
Tregoodwell Cnwll 4 SX1183
Tregoose Cnwll 2 SW6823
Tregoss Cnwll 4 SW9660
Tregowris Cnwll 3 SW7722
Tregoyd Powys 45 SO1937
Tregrehan Mills Cnwll 3 SX0453
Tregullon Cnwll 4 SX0664
Tregunna Cnwll 4 SW9673
Tregunnon Cnwll 5 SX2283
Tregurrian Cnwll 4 SW8565
Tregustick Cnwll 4 SW9866
Tregynon Powys 58 SO0998
Trehafod M Glam 33 ST0490
Trehan Cnwll 5 SX4058
Treharris M Glam 33 ST0996
Treharrock Cnwll 4 SX0178
Trehemborne Cnwll 4 SW8773
Treherbert Dyfed 44 SN5847
Treherbert M Glam 33 SS9498
Treheveras Cnwll 3 SW8046
Trehunist Cnwll 5 SX3263
Trekelland Cnwll 5 SX3480
Trekenner Cnwll 5 SX3478
Treknow Cnwll 4 SX0586
Trelan Cnwll 3 SW7418
Trelash Cnwll 4 SX1890
Trelassick Cnwll 3 SW8752
Trelawne Cnwll 5 SX2154
Trelawnyd Clwyd 70 SJ0979
Treleague Cnwll 3 SW7821
Treleaver Cnwll 3 SW7716
Trelech Dyfed 31 SN2830
Trelech a'r Betws Dyfed 31 SN3026
Treleddyd-fawr Dyfed 30 SM7528
Trelew Cnwll 3 SW8135
Trelewis M Glam 33 ST1096

Treligga

Wargate

Treligga Cnwll 4 SX0484
Trelights Cnwll 4 SW9979
Trelill Cnwll 4 SX0478
Trelinnoe Cnwll 5 SX3181
Trelion Cnwll 3 SW9252
Trelissick Cnwll 3 SW8339
Trelleck Gwent 34 SO5005
Trelleck Grange Gwent 34 SO4901
Trelogan Clwyd 70 SJ1180
Trelonk Cnwll 3 SW8941
Trelow Cnwll 4 SW9269
Trelowarren Cnwll 2 SW7124
Trelowia Cnwll 5 SX2956
Treluggan Cnwll 3 SW8838
Trelystan Powys 58 SJ2503
Tremadog Gwynd 57 SH5640
Tremail Cnwll 4 SX1686
Tremaine Cnwll 5 SX2389
Tremar Cnwll 5 SX2568
Trematon Cnwll 5 SX3959
Trembraze Cnwll 5 SX2565
Tremeirchion Clwyd 70 SJ0873
Tremethick Cross Cnwll 2 SW4430
Tremollett Cnwll 5 SX2975
Tremore Cnwll 4 SX0164
Trenance Cnwll 3 SW8022
Trenance Cnwll 4 SW8568
Trenance Cnwll 4 SW9270
Trenarren Cnwll 3 SX0348
Trenault Cnwll 5 SX2683
Trench Shrops 60 SJ6912
Trench Green Oxon 37 SU6877
Trencreek Cnwll 4 SW8260
Trencreek Cnwll 4 SX1896
Trendeal Cnwll 3 SW8952
Trendrine Cnwll 2 SW4739
Treneague Cnwll 4 SW9871
Trenear Cnwll 2 SW6731
Treneglos Cnwll 5 SX2088
Trenerth Cnwll 2 SW6035
Trenewan Cnwll 4 SX1753
Trenewth Cnwll 4 SX0778
Trengothal Cnwll 2 SW3724
Trengune Cnwll 4 SX1893
Treninnick Cnwll 4 SW8160
Trenowah Cnwll 4 SW7959
Trenoweth Cnwll 3 SW7533
Trent Dorset 10 ST5918
Trent Port Lincs 76 SK8381
Trent Vale Staffs 72 SJ8643
Trentham Staffs 72 SJ8740
Trentishoe Devon 19 SS6448
Trentlock Derbys 62 SK4831
Treoes S Glam 33 SS9478
Treorchy M Glam 33 SS9597
Trequite Cnwll 4 SX0377
Trerhyngyll S Glam 33 ST0077
Trerulefoot Cnwll 5 SX3358
Tresahor Cnwll 3 SW7431
Tresawle Cnwll 3 SW8846
Trescott Staffs 60 SO8597
Trescowe Cnwll 2 SW5731
Tresean Cnwll 4 SW7858
Tresham Avon 35 ST7991
Tresillian Cnwll 3 SW8646
Tresinney Cnwll 4 SX1081
Treskinnick Cross Cnwll 5 SX2098
Treslea Cnwll 4 SX1368
Tresmeer Cnwll 5 SX2387
Tresparrett Cnwll 4 SX1491
Tressait Tays 132 NN8160
Tresta Shet 155 HU3650
Tresta Shet 155 HU6090
Treswell Notts 75 SK7879
Treswithian Cnwll 2 SW6241
Trethawle Cnwll 5 SX2662
Trethevey Cnwll 4 SX0789
Trethewey Cnwll 2 SW3823
Trethomas M Glam 33 ST1888
Trethosa Cnwll 3 SW9454
Trethurgy Cnwll 3 SX0355
Tretio Dyfed 30 SM7829
Tretire H & W 46 SO5123
Tretower Powys 33 SO1821
Treuddyn Clwyd 70 SJ2557
Trevadlock Cnwll 5 SX2679
Trevague Cnwll 5 SX2379
Trevalga Cnwll 4 SX0890
Trevalyn Clwyd 71 SJ3856
Trevanger Cnwll 4 SW9677
Trevanson Cnwll 4 SW9773
Trevarrack Cnwll 2 SW4731
Trevarren Cnwll 4 SW9160
Trevarrian Cnwll 4 SW8566
Trevarrick Cnwll 3 SW9843
Trevarth Cnwll 3 SW7240
Trevaughan Dyfed 31 SN2015
Treveal Cnwll 2 SW4740
Treveal Cnwll 4 SW7858
Treveale Cnwll 3 SW8751
Treveighan Cnwll 4 SX0779
Trevellas Downs Cnwll 3 SW7452
Trevelmond Cnwll 5 SX2063
Trevempor Cnwll 4 SW8159
Treveneague Cnwll 2 SW5432
Treveor Cnwll 3 SW9841
Treverbyn Cnwll 3 SW8849
Treverbyn Cnwll 4 SX0157
Treverva Cnwll 3 SW7531
Trevescan Cnwll 2 SW3524
Trevethin Gwent 34 SO2801
Trevia Cnwll 4 SX0983
Trevigro Cnwll 5 SX3369
Trevilla Cnwll 3 SW8239
Trevilledor Cnwll 4 SW8867
Trevilson Cnwll 3 SW8455
Trevine Dyfed 30 SM8432
Treviscoe Cnwll 3 SW9455
Treviskey Cnwll 3 SW9340
Trevissick Cnwll 3 SX0248
Trevithal Cnwll 2 SW4626
Trevithick Cnwll 4 SW8862
Trevithick Cnwll 3 SW9645
Trevivian Cnwll 4 SX1785
Trevoll Cnwll 4 SW8358
Trevone Cnwll 4 SW8975
Trevor Clwyd 70 SJ2742
Trevor Gwynd 56 SH3746
Trevorgans Cnwll 2 SW4025
Trevorrick Cnwll 4 SW8672
Trevorrick Cnwll 4 SW9273
Trevose Cnwll 4 SW8675
Trew Cnwll 2 SW6129
Trewalder Cnwll 4 SX0782
Trewalkin Powys 45 SO1531
Trewarlett Cnwll 5 SX3380
Trewarmett Cnwll 4 SX0686
Trewarthenick Cnwll 3 SW9044
Trewassa Cnwll 4 SX1486
Trewaves Cnwll 2 SW5926
Treween Cnwll 5 SX2182
Trewellard Cnwll 2 SW3733
Trewen Cnwll 4 SX0577
Trewennack Cnwll 2 SW6728
Trewent Dyfed 30 SS0197
Trewern Powys 58 SJ2811
Trewetha Cnwll 4 SX0080
Trewethern Cnwll 4 SX0076
Trewidland Cnwll 5 SX2559
Trewillis Cnwll 3 SW7717
Trewince Cnwll 3 SW8633
Trewint Cnwll 4 SX1072
Trewint Cnwll 5 SX2180
Trewint Cnwll 5 SX2963
Trewirgie Cnwll 3 SW8845
Trewithian Cnwll 3 SW8737
Trewoodloe Cnwll 5 SX3271
Trewoofe Cnwll 2 SW4425
Trewoon Cnwll 2 SW6819
Trewoon Cnwll 3 SW9952
Treworgan Cnwll 3 SW8349
Treworlas Cnwll 3 SW8938
Treworld Cnwll 4 SX1190
Treworthal Cnwll 3 SW8839
Treyarnon Cnwll 4 SW8673
Treyford W Susx 14 SU8218
Triangle W York 82 SE0422
Trickett's Cross Dorset 12 SU0800
Triermain Cumb 102 NY5966
Triffleton Dyfed 30 SM9724
Trillacott Cnwll 5 SX2689
Trimdon Dur 96 NZ3634
Trimdon Colliery Dur 96 NZ3735
Trimdon Grange Dur 96 NZ3635
Trimingham Norfk 67 TG2838
Trimley Suffk 55 TM2737
Trimley Heath Suffk 55 TM2738
Trimley Lower Street Suffk 55 TM2636
Trimpley H & W 60 SO7978
Trimsaran Dyfed 32 SN4504
Trimstone Devon 19 SS5043
Trinafour Tays 132 NN7264
Trinant Gwent 33 ST2099
Tring Herts 38 SP9211
Tring Wharf Herts 38 SP9212
Tringford Herts 38 SP9113
Trinity Jersey 152 JS1614
Trinity Tays 134 NO6061
Trinity Gask Tays 125 NN9718
Triscombe Somset 20 SS9237
Triscombe Somset 20 ST1535
Trislaig Highld 130 NN0874
Trispen Cnwll 3 SW8450
Tritlington Nthumb 103 NZ2092
Troan Cnwll 4 SW8957
Trochry Tays 125 NN9740
Troedrhiwfuwch M Glam 33 SO1204
Troedyraur Dyfed 42 SN3245
Troedyrhiw M Glam 33 SO0702
Trofarth Clwyd 69 SH8571
Trois Bois Jersey 152 JS1212
Troon Cnwll 2 SW6638
Troon Strath 106 NS3230
Trossachs Hotel Cent 124 NN5107
Troston Suffk 54 TL8972
Troswell Cnwll 5 SX2592
Trots Hill H & W 47 SO8855
Trottiscliffe Kent 27 TQ6460
Trotton W Susx 14 SU8322
Trough Gate Lancs 81 SD8821
Troughend Nthumb 102 NY8692
Troutbeck Cumb 93 NY3825
Troutbeck Cumb 87 NY4002
Troutbeck Bridge Cumb 87 NY4000
Troway Derbys 74 SK3879
Trowbridge Wilts 22 ST8558
Trowell Notts 62 SK4839
Trowle Common Wilts 22 ST8458
Trowse Newton Norfk 67 TG2406
Troy W York 82 SE2439
Trudoxhill Somset 22 ST7443
Trull Somset 20 ST2122
Trumfleet S York 83 SE6011
Trumpan Highld 136 NG2261
Trumpet H & W 47 SO6539
Trumpington Cambs 53 TL4454
Trumpsgreen Surrey 25 SU9967
Trunch Norfk 67 TG2834
Trunnah Lancs 80 SD3442
Truro Cnwll 3 SW8244
Truscott Cnwll 5 SX2985
Trusham Devon 8 SX8582
Trusley Derbys 73 SK2535
Trysull Staffs 60 SO8594
Tubney Oxon 36 SU4399
Tuckenhay Devon 7 SX8156
Tuckhill Shrops 60 SO7888
Tuckingmill Cnwll 2 SW6540
Tuckingmill Wilts 22 ST9329
Tuckton Dorset 12 SZ1492
Tucoyse Cnwll 3 SW9645
Tuddenham Suffk 53 TL7371
Tuddenham Suffk 55 TM1948
Tudeley Kent 16 TQ6245
Tudhoe Dur 96 NZ2535
Tudweiloig Gwynd 56 SH2436
Tuesley Surrey 25 SU9642
Tuffley Gloucs 35 SO8314
Tufton Dyfed 30 SN0428
Tufton Hants 24 SU4546
Tugby Leics 63 SK7601
Tugford Shrops 59 SO5587
Tughall Nthumb 111 NU2126
Tullibody Cent 116 NS8595
Tullich Highld 140 NH6328
Tullich Highld 147 NH8576
Tullich Strath 123 NN0815
Tulliemet Tays 125 NO0052
Tulloch Cent 124 NN5120
Tulloch Gramp 143 NJ8031
Tulloch Station Highld 131 NN3580
Tullochgorm Strath 114 NR9695
Tullybeagles Lodge Tays 125 NO0136
Tullynessle Gramp 142 NJ5519
Tumble Dyfed 32 SN5411
Tumbler's Green Essex 40 TL8025
Tumby Lincs 76 TF2359
Tumby Woodside Lincs 77 TF2757
Tummel Bridge Tays 132 NN7659
Tunbridge Wells Kent 16 TQ5839
Tundergarth D & G 101 NY1780
Tungate Norfk 67 TG2629
Tunstall Humb 85 TA3031
Tunstall Kent 28 TQ8961
Tunstall Lancs 87 SD6073
Tunstall N York 89 SE2196
Tunstall Norfk 67 TG4107
Tunstall Staffs 72 SJ7727
Tunstall Staffs 72 SJ8651
Tunstall Suffk 55 TM3655
Tunstall T & W 96 NZ3953
Tunstead Derbys 74 SK1074
Tunstead Norfk 67 TG3022
Tunstead Milton Derbys 79 SK0180
Tunworth Hants 24 SU6748
Tupsley H & W 46 SO5340
Tur Langton Leics 50 SP7194
Turgis Green Hants 24 SU6959
Turkdean Gloucs 36 SP1017
Turleigh Wilts 22 ST8060
Turleygreen Shrops 60 SO7685
Turn Lancs 81 SD8118
Turnastone H & W 46 SO3536
Turnberry Strath 106 NS2005
Turnchapel Devon 6 SX4953
Turnditch Derbys 73 SK2946
Turner Green Lancs 81 SD6030
Turner's Green E Susx 16 TQ6319
Turner's Green Warwks 48 SP1969
Turner's Hill W Susx 15 TQ3435
Turners Puddle Dorset 11 SY8393
Turnworth Dorset 11 ST8207
Turriff Gramp 142 NJ7250
Turton Bottoms Gt Man 81 SD7315
Turvey Beds 38 SP9452
Turville Bucks 37 SU7691
Turville Heath Bucks 37 SU7490
Turweston Bucks 49 SP6037
Tushielaw Inn Border 109 NT3017
Tushingham cum Grindley Ches 71 SJ5246
Tutbury Staffs 73 SK2128
Tutnall H & W 60 SO9970
Tutshill Gloucs 34 ST5494
Tuttington Norfk 67 TG2227
Tutwell Cnwll 5 SX3875
Tuxford Notts 75 SK7471
Twatt Ork 155 HY2724
Twatt Shet 155 HU3253
Twechar Strath 116 NS6975
Tweedmouth Nthumb 119 NT9952
Tweedsmuir Border 108 NT1024
Twelve Oaks E Susx 16 TQ6820
Twelveheads Cnwll 3 SW7542
Twemlow Green Ches 79 SJ7868
Twenty Lincs 64 TF1520
Twerton Avon 22 ST7264
Twickenham Gt Lon 26 TQ1673
Twigworth Gloucs 35 SO8422
Twineham W Susx 15 TQ2519
Twineham Green W Susx 15 TQ2520
Twinhoe Avon 22 ST7559
Twinstead Essex 54 TL8636
Twiss Green Ches 79 SJ6595
Twitchen Devon 19 SS7930
Twitchen Shrops 46 SO3779
Twitham Kent 29 TR2656
Two Bridges Devon 6 SX6174
Two Dales Derbys 74 SK2763
Two Gates Staffs 61 SK2101
Two Mile Oak Cross Devon 7 SX8468
Two Pots Devon 19 SS5344
Two Waters Herts 38 TL0505
Twycross Leics 62 SK3304
Twyford Berks 37 SU7976
Twyford Bucks 49 SP6626
Twyford Derbys 62 SK3228
Twyford Hants 13 SU4824
Twyford Leics 63 SK7210
Twyford Lincs 63 SK9323
Twyford Norfk 66 TG0123
Twyford Common H & W 46 SO5135
Twyn-carno M Glam 33 SO1108
Twyn-y-Sheriff Gwent 34 SO4005
Twyn-yr-Odyn S Glam 33 ST1173
Twynholm D & G 99 NX6654
Twyning Gloucs 47 SO8936
Twyning Green Gloucs 47 SO9036
Twynllanan Dyfed 44 SN7524
Twywell Nhants 51 SP9578
Ty'n-dwr Clwyd 70 SJ2341
Ty'n-y-coedcae M Glam 33 ST1988
Ty'n-y-groes Gwynd 69 SH7771
Ty-croes Dyfed 32 SN6010
Ty-nant Clwyd 70 SH9944
Ty-nant Gwynd 58 SH9026
Tyberton H & W 46 SO3839
Tyburn W Mids 61 SP1391
Tycrwyn Powys 58 SJ1018
Tydd Gote Lincs 65 TF4518
Tydd St Giles Cambs 65 TF4216
Tydd St Mary Lincs 65 TF4418
Tye Hants 13 SU7302
Tye Green Essex 39 TL5424
Tye Green Essex 53 TL5935
Tye Green Essex 40 TL7821
Tyersal W York 82 SE1932
Tyldesley Gt Man 79 SD6802
Tyler Hill Kent 29 TR1461
Tyler's Green Essex 39 TL5005
Tylers Green Bucks 26 SU9093
Tylers Green Surrey 27 TQ3552
Tylorstown M Glam 33 ST0095
Tylwch Powys 58 SN9780
Tyn-y-nant M Glam 33 ST0685
Tyndrum Cent 123 NN3230
Tyneham Dorset 11 SY8880
Tynemouth T & W 103 NZ3669
Tynewydd M Glam 33 SS9398
Tyninghame Loth 118 NT6179
Tynron D & G 100 NX8093
Tynygongl Gwynd 68 SH5082
Tynygraig Dyfed 43 SN6969
Tyringham Bucks 38 SP8547
Tyseley W Mids 61 SP1184
Tythegston M Glam 33 SS8578
Tytherington Avon 35 ST6688
Tytherington Ches 79 SJ9175
Tytherington Somset 22 ST7644
Tytherington Wilts 22 ST9141
Tytherleigh Devon 10 ST3103
Tywardreath Cnwll 3 SX0854
Tywardreath Highway Cnwll 3 SX0755
Tywyn Gwynd 57 SH5800
Tywyn Gwynd 69 SH7878

U

Ubbeston Green Suffk 55 TM3271
Ubley Avon 21 ST5258
Uckerby N York 89 NZ2402
Uckfield E Susx 16 TQ4721
Uckinghall H & W 47 SO8637
Uckington Gloucs 47 SO9124
Uckington Shrops 59 SJ5709
Uddingston Strath 116 NS6960
Uddington Strath 108 NS8633
Udimore E Susx 17 TQ8719
Udny Green Gramp 143 NJ8726
Udny Station Gramp 143 NJ9024
Uffcott Wilts 36 SU1277
Uffculme Devon 9 ST0612
Uffington Oxon 36 SU3089
Uffington Shrops 59 SJ5313
Ufford Cambs 64 TF0903
Ufford Suffk 55 TM2952
Ufton Warwks 48 SP3762
Ufton Nervet Berks 24 SU6367
Ugadale Strath 105 NR7828
Ugborough Devon 7 SX6755
Uggeshall Suffk 55 TM4480
Ugglebarnby N York 90 NZ8707
Ughill Derbys 74 SK2590
Ugley Essex 39 TL5228
Ugley Green Essex 39 TL5227
Ugthorpe N York 90 NZ7911
Uig Highld 136 NG1952
Uig Highld 136 NG3963
Uig Strath 120 NM1654
Uig W Isls 154 NB0533
Uigshader Highld 136 NG4346
Uisken Strath 121 NM3919
Ulbster Highld 151 ND3241
Ulcat Row Cumb 93 NY4022
Ulceby Humb 85 TA1014
Ulceby Lincs 77 TF4272
Ulceby Skitter Humb 85 TA1215
Ulcombe Kent 28 TQ8448
Uldale Cumb 93 NY2437
Uley Gloucs 35 ST7898
Ulgham Nthumb 103 NZ2392
Ullapool Highld 145 NH1294
Ullceby Cross Lincs 77 TF4173
Ullenhall Warwks 48 SP1267
Ullenwood Gloucs 35 SO9416
Ulleskelf N York 83 SE5239
Ullesthorpe Leics 50 SP5087
Ulley S York 75 SK4687
Ullingswick H & W 46 SO5949
Ullinish Lodge Hotel Highld 136 NG3237
Ullock Cumb 92 NY0724
Ulpha Cumb 86 SD1993
Ulpha Cumb 87 SD4581
Ulrome Humb 85 TA1656
Ulsta Shet 155 HU4680
Ulting Wick Essex 40 TL8009
Ulverley Green W Mids 61 SP1382
Ulverston Cumb 86 SD2878
Ulwell Dorset 12 SZ0280
Umachan Highld 137 NG6050
Umberleigh Devon 19 SS6023
Unapool Highld 148 NC2333
Under Burnmouth D & G 101 NY4783
Under River Kent 27 TQ5552
Underbarrow Cumb 87 SD4692
Undercliffe W York 82 SE1834
Underdale Shrops 59 SJ5013
Underley Hall Cumb 87 SD6179
Underling Green Kent 28 TQ7546
Underwood Notts 75 SK4750
Undley Suffk 53 TL6981
Undy Gwent 34 ST4386
Union Mills IOM 153 SC3577
Union Street E Susx 16 TQ7031
Unstone Derbys 74 SK3777
Unstone Green Derbys 74 SK3776
Unsworth Gt Man 79 SD8207
Unthank Cumb 93 NY3948
Unthank Cumb 93 NY4536
Unthank Cumb 94 NY6040
Unthank Derbys 74 SK3075
Unthank Nthumb 111 NT9848
Unthank End Cumb 93 NY4535
Up Cerne Dorset 11 ST6502
Up Exe Devon 9 SS9402
Up Holland Lancs 78 SD5205
Up Marden W Susx 14 SU7913
Up Mudford Somset 10 ST5718
Up Nately Hants 24 SU6951
Up Somborne Hants 23 SU3932
Up Sydling Dorset 10 ST6201
Upavon Wilts 23 SU1354
Upchurch Kent 28 TQ8467
Upcott Devon 19 SS5838
Upcott Devon 19 SS7529
Upcott H & W 46 SO3250
Upcott Somset 20 SS9025
Updown Hill Surrey 25 SU9363
Upend Cambs 53 TL7058
Upgate Norfk 66 TG1318
Upgate Street Norfk 66 TM0992
Upgate Street Norfk 67 TM2891
Uphall Dorset 10 ST5502
Uphall Loth 117 NT0671
Upham Devon 19 SS8808
Upham Hants 13 SU5320
Uphampton H & W 46 SO3963
Uphampton H & W 47 SO8364
Uphill Avon 21 ST3158
Uplawmoor Strath 115 NS4355
Upleadon Gloucs 47 SO7527
Upleatham Cleve 97 NZ6319
Uplees Kent 28 TR0064
Uploders Dorset 10 SY5093
Uplowman Devon 9 ST0115
Uplyme Devon 10 SY3293
Upminster Gt Lon 27 TQ5686
Upottery Devon 9 ST2007
Uppaton Devon 5 SX4380
Upper Affcot Shrops 59 SO4486
Upper Ardchronie Highld 146 NH6188
Upper Arley H & W 60 SO7680
Upper Arncott Oxon 37 SP6117
Upper Astrop Nhants 49 SP5137
Upper Basildon Berks 37 SU5976
Upper Batley W York 82 SE2325
Upper Beeding W Susx 15 TQ1910
Upper Benefield Nhants 51 SP9789
Upper Bentley H & W 47 SO9966
Upper Bighouse Highld 150 NC8856
Upper Birchwood Derbys 75 SK4355
Upper Boat M Glam 33 ST1086
Upper Boddington Nhants 49 SP4852
Upper Borth Dyfed 43 SN6088
Upper Brailes Warwks 48 SP3039
Upper Breakish Highld 129 NG6823
Upper Breinton H & W 46 SO4640
Upper Broadheath H & W 47 SO8056
Upper Broughton Notts 63 SK6826
Upper Bucklebury Berks 24 SU5468
Upper Burgate Hants 12 SU1516
Upper Bush Kent 28 TQ6966
Upper Cairn D & G 107 NS6912
Upper Caldecote Beds 52 TL1645
Upper Canada Avon 21 ST3658
Upper Canterton Hants 12 SU2612
Upper Catesby Nhants 49 SP5259
Upper Catshill H & W 60 SO9674
Upper Chapel Powys 45 SO0040
Upper Cheddon Somset 20 ST2328
Upper Chicksgrove Wilts 22 ST9529
Upper Chute Wilts 23 SU2953
Upper Clapton Gt Lon 27 TQ3487
Upper Clatford Hants 23 SU3543
Upper Clynnog Gwynd 56 SH4646
Upper Coberley Gloucs 35 SO9816
Upper Cokeham W Susx 15 TQ1605
Upper Cotton Staffs 73 SK0547
Upper Cound Shrops 59 SJ5505
Upper Cudworth S York 83 SE3909
Upper Cumberworth W York 82 SE2008
Upper Cwmtwrch Powys 32 SN7511
Upper Dallachy Gramp 141 NJ3662
Upper Deal Kent 29 TR3651
Upper Dean Beds 51 TL0467
Upper Denby W York 82 SE2207
Upper Denton Cumb 102 NY6165
Upper Dicker E Susx 16 TQ5509
Upper Dinchope Shrops 59 SO4583
Upper Dovercourt Essex 41 TM2330
Upper Drumbane Cent 124 NN6606
Upper Dunsforth N York 89 SE4463
Upper Eashing Surrey 25 SU9543
Upper Egleton H & W 47 SO6344
Upper Elkstone Staffs 74 SK0558
Upper Ellastone Staffs 73 SK1043
Upper End Derbys 74 SK0875
Upper Enham Hants 23 SU3650
Upper Ethrie Highld 140 NH7662
Upper Farmcote Shrops 60 SO7791
Upper Farringdon Hants 24 SU7135
Upper Framilode Gloucs 35 SO7510
Upper Froyle Hants 24 SU7543
Upper Godney Somset 21 ST4842
Upper Gravenhurst Beds 38 TL1136
Upper Green Berks 23 SU3763
Upper Green Essex 53 TL5935
Upper Green Gwent 34 SO3818
Upper Green Suffk 53 TL7464
Upper Grove Common H & W 46 SO5526
Upper Hackney Derbys 74 SK2861
Upper Hale Surrey 25 SU8349
Upper Halliford Surrey 26 TQ0968
Upper Halling Kent 28 TQ6964
Upper Hambleton Leics 63 SK9007
Upper Harbledown Kent 29 TR1158
Upper Hardres Court Kent 29 TR1550
Upper Hardwick H & W 46 SO4057
Upper Hartfield E Susx 16 TQ4634
Upper Hartshay Derbys 74 SK3850
Upper Hatherley Gloucs 35 SO9220
Upper Hatton Staffs 72 SJ8237
Upper Haugh S York 74 SK4297
Upper Hayton Shrops 59 SO5181
Upper Heaton W York 82 SE1719
Upper Helmsley N York 83 SE6956
Upper Hergest H & W 46 SO2654
Upper Heyford Nhants 49 SP6659
Upper Heyford Oxon 49 SP4925
Upper Hill H & W 46 SO4753
Upper Hockenden Kent 27 TQ5069
Upper Hopton W York 82 SE1918
Upper Howsell H & W 47 SO7848
Upper Hulme Staffs 73 SK0160
Upper Ifold Surrey 14 TQ0033
Upper Inglesham Wilts 36 SU2096
Upper Keith Loth 118 NT4562
Upper Kilcott Avon 35 ST7988
Upper Killay W Glam 32 SS5892
Upper Kinchrackine Strath 123 NN1627
Upper Lambourn Berks 36 SU3080
Upper Landywood Staffs 60 SJ9805
Upper Langford Avon 21 ST4659
Upper Langwith Derbys 75 SK5169
Upper Largo Fife 127 NO4203
Upper Leigh Staffs 73 SK0136
Upper Ley Gloucs 35 SO7217
Upper Littleton Avon 21 ST5564
Upper Lochton Gramp 135 NO6997
Upper Longdon Staffs 61 SK0614
Upper Ludstone Shrops 60 SO8095
Upper Lybster Highld 151 ND2537
Upper Lydbrook Gloucs 34 SO6015
Upper Lyde H & W 46 SO4944
Upper Lye H & W 46 SO3965
Upper Maes-coed H & W 46 SO3334
Upper Midhope Derbys 74 SK2199
Upper Milton H & W 60 SO8172
Upper Minety Wilts 35 SU0091
Upper Moor H & W 47 SO9747
Upper Moor Side W York 82 SE2430
Upper Mulben Gramp 141 NJ3551
Upper Nesbet Border 110 NT6727
Upper Netchwood Shrops 59 SO6092
Upper Nobut Staffs 73 SK0335
Upper Norwood W Susx 14 SU9317
Upper Padley Derbys 74 SK2478
Upper Pennington Hants 12 SZ3095
Upper Pickwick Wilts 35 ST8571
Upper Pollicott Bucks 37 SP7013
Upper Pond Street Essex 39 TL4636
Upper Poppleton N York 83 SE5553
Upper Pulley Shrops 59 SJ4808
Upper Quinton Warwks 48 SP1846
Upper Ratley Hants 23 SU3223
Upper Rochford H & W 47 SO6367
Upper Ruscoe D & G 99 NX5661
Upper Sapey H & W 47 SO6863
Upper Seagry Wilts 35 ST9480
Upper Shelton Beds 38 SP9843
Upper Sheringham Norfk 66 TG1441
Upper Shuckburgh Warwks 49 SP5061
Upper Slaughter Gloucs 48 SP1523
Upper Soudley Gloucs 35 SO6510
Upper Spond H & W 46 SO3152
Upper Standen Kent 29 TR2139
Upper Staploe Beds 52 TL1459
Upper Stepford D & G 100 NX8681
Upper Stoke Norfk 67 TG2502
Upper Stondon Beds 38 TL1435
Upper Stowe Nhants 49 SP6456
Upper Street Hants 12 SU1518
Upper Street Norfk 67 TG3217
Upper Street Norfk 67 TG3616
Upper Street Norfk 54 TM1779
Upper Street Suffk 53 TL7851
Upper Street Suffk 54 TM1050
Upper Street Suffk 54 TM1434
Upper Sundon Beds 38 TL0428
Upper Swell Gloucs 48 SP1726
Upper Tankersley S York 74 SK3499
Upper Tasburgh Norfk 67 TM2095
Upper Tean Staffs 73 SK0139
Upper Threapwood Ches 71 SJ4345
Upper Town Avon 21 ST5265
Upper Town Derbys 73 SK2351
Upper Town Derbys 74 SK2361
Upper Town Dur 95 NZ0737
Upper Town H & W 46 SO5848
Upper Town Suffk 54 TL9267
Upper Tysoe Warwks 48 SP3343
Upper Ufford Suffk 55 TM2952
Upper Upham Wilts 36 SU2277
Upper Upnor Kent 28 TQ7570
Upper Victoria Tays 127 NO5336
Upper Vobster Somset 22 ST7049
Upper Wardington Oxon 49 SP4945
Upper Weald Bucks 38 SP8037
Upper Weedon Nhants 49 SP6258
Upper Wellingham E Susx 16 TQ4313
Upper Weston Avon 22 ST7267
Upper Weybread Suffk 55 TM2379
Upper Wick H & W 47 SO8252
Upper Wield Hants 24 SU6238
Upper Winchendon Bucks 37 SP7414
Upper Witton W Mids 61 SP0891
Upper Woodford Wilts 23 SU1237
Upper Wootton Hants 24 SU5754
Upper Wraxall Wilts 35 ST8074
Upper Wyche H & W 47 SO7643
Upperby Cumb 93 NY4153
Upperglen Highld 136 NG3151
Uppermill Gt Man 82 SD9905
Upperthong W York 82 SE1208
Upperthorpe Derbys 75 SK4580
Upperton W Susx 14 SU9522
Uppertown Derbys 74 SK3264
Uppertown Highld 151 ND3576
Upperup Gloucs 36 SU0496
Upperwood Derbys 73 SK2956
Uppincott Devon 9 SS9006
Uppingham Leics 51 SP8699
Uppington Dorset 12 SU0206
Uppington Shrops 59 SJ5909
Upsall N York 89 SE4586
Upsettlington Border 110 NT8846
Upshire Essex 27 TL4101
Upstreet Kent 29 TR2263
Upthorpe Suffk 54 TL9772
Upton Berks 26 SU9779
Upton Bucks 37 SP7711
Upton Cambs 64 TF1000
Upton Cambs 52 TL1778
Upton Ches 71 SJ4069
Upton Ches 78 SJ5087
Upton Cnwll 18 SS2004
Upton Cnwll 5 SX2772
Upton Cumb 93 NY3139
Upton Devon 9 ST0902
Upton Devon 7 SX7043
Upton Dorset 11 SY7483
Upton Dorset 11 SY9893
Upton Dyfed 30 SN0204
Upton Hants 23 SU3555
Upton Hants 12 SU3716
Upton Humb 85 TA1454
Upton Leics 61 SP3699
Upton Lincs 76 SK8686
Upton Mersyd 78 SJ2788
Upton Nhants 49 SP7159
Upton Norfk 67 TG3912
Upton Notts 75 SK7354
Upton Notts 75 SK7476
Upton Oxon 36 SP2312
Upton Oxon 37 SU5187
Upton Somset 20 SS9928
Upton Somset 21 ST4526
Upton W York 83 SE4713
Upton Warwks 48 SP1257
Upton Cheyney Avon 35 ST6970
Upton Cressett Shrops 59 SO6592
Upton Crews H & W 47 SO6527
Upton Cross Cnwll 5 SX2872
Upton End Beds 38 TL1234
Upton Grey Hants 24 SU6948
Upton Heath Ches 71 SJ4169
Upton Hellions Devon 8 SS8403
Upton Lovell Wilts 22 ST9440
Upton Magna Shrops 59 SJ5512
Upton Noble Somset 22 ST7139
Upton Pyne Devon 9 SX9198
Upton Scudamore Wilts 22 ST8647
Upton Snodsbury H & W 47 SO9454
Upton St Leonards Gloucs 35 SO8615
Upton Towans Cnwll 2 SW5740
Upton upon Severn H & W 47 SO8540
Upton Warren H & W 47 SO9267
Upwaltham W Susx 14 SU9413
Upware Cambs 53 TL5470
Upwell Norfk 65 TF4902
Upwey Dorset 11 SY6685
Upwick Green Herts 39 TL4524
Upwood Cambs 52 TL2582
Urchfont Wilts 23 SU0357
Urdimarsh H & W 46 SO5248
Ure Bank N York 89 SE3172
Urlay Nook Cleve 89 NZ4014
Urmston Gt Man 79 SJ7694
Urquhart Gramp 141 NJ2862
Urra N York 90 NZ5601
Urray Highld 139 NH5052
Usan Tays 127 NO7254
Ushaw Moor Dur 96 NZ2242
Usk Gwent 34 SO3700
Usselby Lincs 76 TF0993
Usworth T & W 96 NZ3057
Utley W York 82 SE0542
Uton Devon 8 SX8298
Utterby Lincs 77 TF3093
Uttoxeter Staffs 73 SK0933
Uwchmynydd Gwynd 56 SH1525
Uxbridge Gt Lon 26 TQ0584
Uyeasound Shet 155 HP5901
Uzmaston Dyfed 30 SM9714

V

Vale Guern 152 GN5312
Valley Gwynd 68 SH2979
Valley End Surrey 25 SU9564
Valley Truckle Cnwll 4 SX0982
Valtos Highld 137 NG5163
Valtos W Isls 154 NB0936
Van M Glam 33 ST1686
Vange Essex 40 TQ7186
Varteg Gwent 34 SO2606
Vatsetter Shet 155 HU5389
Vatten Highld 136 NG2843
Vaynor M Glam 33 SO0410
Velindre Powys 45 SO1836
Vellow Somset 20 ST0938
Velly Devon 18 SS2924
Venn Devon 7 SX8549
Venn Ottery Devon 9 SY0891
Venngreen Devon 18 SS3711
Vennington Shrops 59 SJ3309
Venny Tedburn Devon 8 SX8297
Venterdon Cnwll 5 SX3675
Ventnor IOW 13 SZ5677
Venton Devon 6 SX5956
Vernham Dean Hants 23 SU3356
Vernham Street Hants 23 SU3457
Vernolds Common Shrops 59 SO4780
Verwood Dorset 12 SU0809
Veryan Cnwll 3 SW9139
Veryan Green Cnwll 3 SW9140
Vickerstown Cumb 86 SD1868
Victoria Cnwll 4 SW9861
Victoria Gwent 33 SO1707
Victoria S York 82 SE1705
Vidlin Shet 155 HU4765
Viewfield Gramp 141 NJ2864
Viewpark Strath 116 NS7061
Vigo Kent 27 TQ6361
Ville la Bas Jersey 152 JS0515
Villiaze Guern 152 GN4906
Vine's Cross E Susx 16 TQ5917
Vinehall Street E Susx 17 TQ7520
Virginia Water Surrey 25 TQ0067
Virginstow Devon 5 SX3792
Virley Essex 40 TL9414
Vobster Somset 22 ST7048
Voe Shet 155 HU4062
Vowchurch H & W 46 SO3636
Vulcan Village Ches 78 SJ5894

W

Wackerfield Dur 96 NZ1522
Wacton Norfk 66 TM1791
Wadborough H & W 47 SO9047
Waddesdon Bucks 37 SP7416
Waddeton Devon 7 SX8756
Waddicar Mersyd 78 SJ3999
Waddingham Lincs 76 SK9896
Waddington Lancs 81 SD7343
Waddington Lincs 76 SK9764
Waddon Dorset 10 SY6285
Wadebridge Cnwll 4 SW9972
Wadeford Somset 10 ST3110
Wadenhoe Nhants 51 TL0183
Wadesmill Herts 39 TL3617
Wadhurst E Susx 16 TQ6431
Wadshelf Derbys 74 SK3170
Wadswick Wilts 22 ST8467
Wadworth S York 75 SK5696
Waen Clwyd 70 SH9962
Waen Clwyd 70 SJ1065
Waen Powys 58 SJ2319
Waen Fach Powys 58 SJ2017
Waen-pentir Gwynd 69 SH5766
Waen-wen Gwynd 69 SH5768
Wagbeach Shrops 59 SJ3602
Wainfelin Gwent 34 SO2701
Wainfleet All Saints Lincs 77 TF4959
Wainfleet Bank Lincs 77 TF4759
Wainford Norfk 55 TM3490
Wainhouse Corner Cnwll 4 SX1895
Wains Hill Avon 34 ST3970
Wainscott Kent 28 TQ7470
Wainstalls W York 82 SE0428
Waitby Cumb 88 NY7508
Waithe Lincs 77 TA2800
Wake Green W Mids 61 SP0982
Wakefield W York 83 SE3320
Wakerley Nhants 51 SP9599
Wakes Colne Essex 40 TL8928
Wal-wen Clwyd 70 SJ2076
Walberswick Suffk 55 TM4974
Walberton W Susx 14 SU9705
Walbottle T & W 103 NZ1666
Walbutt D & G 99 NX7468
Walby Cumb 101 NY4460
Walcombe Somset 21 ST5546
Walcot Humb 84 SE8720
Walcot Lincs 64 TF0635
Walcot Lincs 76 TF1356
Walcot Shrops 59 SJ5912
Walcot Shrops 59 SO3485
Walcot Warwks 48 SP1358
Walcot Wilts 36 SU1684
Walcot Green Norfk 54 TM1280
Walcote Leics 50 SP5683
Walcott Norfk 67 TG3532
Walden N York 88 SE0082
Walden Head N York 88 SD9880
Walden Stubbs N York 83 SE5516
Walderslade Kent 28 TQ7663
Walderton W Susx 14 SU7910
Walditch Dorset 10 SY4892
Waldley Derbys 73 SK1236
Waldridge Dur 96 NZ2549
Waldringfield Suffk 55 TM2845
Waldron E Susx 16 TQ5419
Wales S York 75 SK4882
Wales Somset 21 ST5824
Walesby Lincs 76 TF1392
Walesby Notts 75 SK6870
Walford H & W 46 SO3872
Walford H & W 34 SO5820
Walford Shrops 59 SJ4320
Walford Staffs 72 SJ8133
Walford Heath Shrops 59 SJ4419
Walgherton Ches 72 SJ6948
Walgrave Nhants 51 SP8071
Walhampton Hants 12 SZ3396
Walk Mill Lancs 81 SD8729
Walkden Gt Man 79 SD7302
Walker T & W 103 NZ2864
Walker Fold Lancs 81 SD6741
Walker's Green H & W 46 SO5247
Walker's Heath W Mids 61 SP0578
Walkerburn Border 109 NT3637
Walkeringham Notts 75 SK7792
Walkerith Notts 75 SK7892
Walkern Herts 39 TL2826
Walkerton Fife 126 NO2301
Walkhampton Devon 6 SX5369
Walkington Humb 84 SE9936
Walkley S York 74 SK3388
Walkwood H & W 48 SP0364
Wall Border 109 NT4622
Wall Cnwll 2 SW6036
Wall Nthumb 102 NY9168
Wall Staffs 61 SK1006
Wall End Cumb 86 SD2383
Wall End H & W 46 SO4457
Wall Heath W Mids 60 SO8889
Wall under Haywood Shrops 59 SO5092
Wallacetown Strath 106 NS2703
Wallacetown Strath 106 NS3422
Wallands Park E Susx 15 TQ4010
Wallasey Mersyd 78 SJ2992
Wallend Kent 28 TQ8775
Waller's Green H & W 47 SO6739
Wallfield Fife 126 NO1909
Wallhead Cumb 101 NY4660
Wallingford Oxon 37 SU6089
Wallington Gt Lon 27 TQ2864
Wallington Hants 13 SU5806
Wallington Herts 39 TL2933
Wallington Heath W Mids 60 SJ9903
Wallis Dyfed 30 SN0125
Wallisdown Dorset 12 SZ0694
Walliswood W Susx 14 TQ1138
Walls Shet 155 HU2449
Wallsend T & W 103 NZ2966
Wallthwaite Cumb 93 NY3526
Wallyford Loth 118 NT3671
Walmer Kent 29 TR3750
Walmer Bridge Lancs 80 SD4724
Walmersley Gt Man 81 SD8013
Walmestone Kent 29 TR2559
Walmley W Mids 61 SP1393
Walmley Ash W Mids 61 SP1492
Walmsgate Lincs 77 TF3677
Walpole Somset 20 ST3042
Walpole Suffk 55 TM3674
Walpole Cross Keys Norfk 65 TF5119
Walpole Highway Norfk 65 TF5114
Walpole St Andrew Norfk 65 TF5017
Walpole St Peter Norfk 65 TF5016
Walrow Somset 21 ST3447
Walsall W Mids 60 SP0198
Walsall Wood W Mids 61 SK0403
Walsden W York 81 SD9321
Walsgrave on Sowe W Mids 61 SP3881
Walshall Green Herts 39 TL4430
Walsham le Willows Suffk 54 TM0071
Walshaw Gt Man 81 SD7711
Walshaw W York 82 SD9731
Walshford N York 83 SE4153
Walsoken Norfk 65 TF4710
Walston Strath 117 NT0545
Walsworth Herts 39 TL1930
Walter Ash Bucks 37 SU8398
Walters Green Kent 16 TQ5140
Walterston S Glam 33 ST0671
Walterstone H & W 46 SO3425
Waltham Humb 85 TA2603
Waltham Kent 29 TR1048
Waltham Abbey Essex 27 TL3800
Waltham Chase Hants 13 SU5614
Waltham Cross Herts 27 TL3600
Waltham on the Wolds Leics 63 SK8024
Waltham St Lawrence Berks 37 SU8276
Waltham's Cross Essex 40 TL6930
Walthamstow Gt Lon 27 TQ3689
Walton Bucks 38 SP8936
Walton Cambs 64 TF1702
Walton Cumb 101 NY5264
Walton Derbys 74 SK3568
Walton Leics 50 SP5987
Walton Powys 46 SO2559
Walton Shrops 59 SJ5818
Walton Shrops 46 SO4679
Walton Somset 21 ST4636
Walton Staffs 72 SJ8528
Walton Staffs 72 SJ8932
Walton Suffk 55 TM2935
Walton W Susx 14 SU8104
Walton W York 83 SE3516
Walton W York 83 SE4447
Walton Warwks 48 SP2853
Walton Cardiff Gloucs 47 SO9032
Walton East Dyfed 30 SN0223
Walton Elm Dorset 11 ST7717
Walton Grounds Nhants 49 SP5135
Walton Lower Street Suffk 55 TM2834
Walton on the Hill Surrey 26 TQ2255
Walton on the Naze Essex 41 TM2522
Walton on the Wolds Leics 62 SK5919
Walton Park Avon 34 ST4172
Walton West Dyfed 30 SM8612
Walton-in-Gordano Avon 34 ST4273
Walton-le-Dale Lancs 81 SD5628
Walton-on-Thames Surrey 26 TQ1066
Walton-on-Trent Derbys 73 SK2118
Walton-on-the-Hill Staffs 72 SJ9520
Walwen Clwyd 70 SJ1179
Walwen Clwyd 70 SJ1771
Walwick Nthumb 102 NY9070
Walworth Dur 96 NZ2318
Walworth Gate Dur 96 NZ2320
Walwyn's Castle Dyfed 30 SM8711
Wambrook Somset 10 ST2907
Wamphray D & G 100 NY1295
Wampool Cumb 93 NY2454
Wanborough Surrey 25 SU9348
Wanborough Wilts 36 SU2082
Wandel Strath 108 NS9427
Wandon End Herts 38 TL1322
Wandsworth Gt Lon 27 TQ2574
Wangford Suffk 55 TM4679
Wanlip Leics 62 SK5910
Wanlockhead D & G 108 NS8712
Wannock E Susx 16 TQ5703
Wansford Cambs 64 TL0799
Wansford Humb 84 TA0656
Wanshurst Green Kent 28 TQ7645
Wanstead Gt Lon 27 TQ4088
Wanstrow Somset 22 ST7141
Wanswell Gloucs 35 SO6801
Wantage Oxon 36 SU3988
Wants Green H & W 47 SO7557
Wapley Avon 35 ST7179
Wappenbury Warwks 48 SP3769
Wappenham Nhants 49 SP6245
Warbister Ork 155 HY3932
Warbleton E Susx 16 TQ6018
Warborough Oxon 37 SU5993
Warboys Cambs 52 TL3080
Warbreck Lancs 80 SD3238
Warbstow Cnwll 5 SX2090
Warburton Gt Man 79 SJ7089
Warcop Cumb 94 NY7415
Ward End W Mids 61 SP1188
Ward Green Suffk 54 TM0464
Warden Kent 28 TR0271
Warden Nthumb 102 NY9166
Warden Law T & W 96 NZ3649
Warden Street Beds 38 TL1244
Wardhedges Beds 38 TL0635
Wardington Oxon 49 SP4846
Wardle Ches 71 SJ6156
Wardle Gt Man 81 SD9116
Wardley Gt Man 79 SD7602
Wardley Leics 51 SK8300
Wardlow Derbys 74 SK1874
Wardsend Ches 79 SJ9382
Wardy Hill Cambs 53 TL4782
Ware Herts 39 TL3514
Ware Street Kent 28 TQ7956
Wareham Dorset 11 SY9287
Warehorne Kent 17 TQ9832
Waren Mill Nthumb 111 NU1434
Warenford Nthumb 111 NU1328
Warenton Nthumb 111 NU1030
Wareside Herts 39 TL3915
Waresley Cambs 52 TL2554
Waresley H & W 60 SO8470
Warfield Berks 25 SU8872
Warfleet Devon 7 SX8750
Wargate Lincs 64 TF2330

Wargrave Whittington

Wargrave Berks 37 SU7978
Warham H & W 46 SO4838
Warham All Saints Norfk 66 TF9541
Warham St Mary Norfk 66 TF9441
Wark Nthumb 110 NT8238
Wark Nthumb 102 NY8577
Warkleigh Devon 19 SS6422
Warkton Nhants 51 SP8979
Warkworth Nhants 49 SP4840
Warkworth Nthumb 111 NU2406
Warlaby N York 89 SE3491
Warland W York 82 SD9420
Warleggan Cnwll 4 SX1569
Warleigh Avon 22 ST7964
Warley Town W York 82 SE0524
Warlingham Surrey 27 TQ3658
Warmanbie D & G 101 NY1969
Warmbrook Derbys 73 SK2853
Warmfield W York 83 SE3720
Warmingham Ches 72 SJ7061
Warmington Nhants 51 TL0790
Warmington Warwks 49 SP4147
Warminster Wilts 22 ST8745
Warmley Avon 35 ST6673
Warmsworth S York 75 SE5400
Warmwell Dorset 11 SY7585
Warndon H & W 47 SO8856
Warnford Hants 13 SU6223
Warnham W Susx 15 TQ1533
Warnham Court W Susx 15 TQ1533
Warningcamp W Susx 14 TQ0307
Warninglid W Susx 15 TQ2426
Warren Ches 79 SJ8870
Warren Dyfed 30 SR9397
Warren Row Berks 37 SU8180
Warren Street Kent 28 TQ9252
Warren's Green Herts 39 TL2628
Warrenhill Strath 108 NS9438
Warrington Bucks 51 SP8953
Warrington Ches 78 SJ6088
Warriston Loth 117 NT2575
Warsash Hants 13 SU4906
Warslow Staffs 74 SK0858
Warsop Notts 75 SK5667
Warter Humb 84 SE8750
Warter Priory Humb 84 SE8449
Warthermaske N York 89 SE2078
Warthill N York 83 SE6755
Wartling E Susx 16 TQ6509
Wartnaby Leics 63 SK7123
Warton Lancs 80 SD4128
Warton Lancs 87 SD4972
Warton Nthumb 103 NU0002
Warton Warwks 61 SK2803
Warwick Cumb 93 NY4656
Warwick Warwks 48 SP2865
Warwick Bridge Cumb 93 NY4756
Warwicksland Cumb 101 NY4577
Wasdale Head Cumb 86 NY1808
Wash Derbys 74 SK0682
Wash Devon 7 SX7665
Washaway Cnwll 4 SX0369
Washbourne Devon 7 SX7954
Washbrook Somset 21 ST4250
Washbrook Suffk 54 TM1142
Washfield Devon 9 SS9315
Washfold N York 88 NZ0502
Washford Somset 20 ST0541
Washford Pyne Devon 19 SS8111
Washingborough Lincs 76 TF0170
Washington T & W 96 NZ3155
Washington W Susx 14 TQ1112
Washwood Heath W Mids 61 SP1088
Wasing Berks 24 SU5764
Waskerley Dur 95 NZ0445
Wasperton Warwks 48 SP2658
Wasps Nest Lincs 76 TF0764
Wass N York 90 SE5579
Watchet Somset 20 ST0743
Watchfield Oxon 36 SU2490
Watchfield Somset 21 ST3446
Watchgate Cumb 87 SD5398
Watchill Cumb 93 NY1842
Watcombe Devon 7 SX9267
Watendlath Cumb 93 NY2716
Water Devon 8 SX7580
Water Lancs 81 SD8425
Water Eaton Oxon 37 SP5112
Water Eaton Staffs 60 SJ9011
Water End Beds 38 TL0637
Water End Beds 38 TL1047
Water End Beds 38 TL1051
Water End Essex 53 TL5840
Water End Herts 38 TL0310
Water End Herts 39 TL2304
Water End Humb 84 SE7938
Water Fryston W York 83 SE4726
Water Newton Cambs 51 TL1097
Water Orton Warwks 61 SP1790
Water Stratford Bucks 49 SP6534
Water Street M Glam 32 SS8083
Water Yeat Cumb 86 SD2889
Water's Nook Gt Man 79 SD6605
Waterbeach Cambs 53 TL4965
Waterbeach W Susx 14 SU8908
Waterbeck D & G 101 NY2477
Watercombe Dorset 11 SY7585
Waterden Norfk 66 TF8836
Waterend Cumb 92 NY1122
Waterfall Staffs 73 SK0851
Waterfoot Lancs 81 SD8321
Waterfoot Strath 115 NS5655
Waterford Herts 39 TL3114
Watergate Cnwll 4 SX1181
Waterhead Cumb 87 NY3703
Waterhead Strath 107 NS5411
Waterheads Border 117 NT2451
Waterhouses Dur 96 NZ1841
Waterhouses Staffs 73 SK0850
Wateringbury Kent 28 TQ6853
Waterlane Gloucs 35 SO9204
Waterloo Cnwll 4 SX1072
Waterloo Derbys 74 SK4163
Waterloo Dorset 11 SZ0193
Waterloo Dyfed 30 SM9803
Waterloo H & W 46 SO3447
Waterloo Highld 129 NG6623
Waterloo Mersyd 78 SJ3298
Waterloo Norfk 67 TG2219
Waterloo Strath 116 NS8154
Waterloo Tays 125 NO0537
Waterloo Cross Devon 9 ST0514
Waterloo Port Gwynd 68 SH4964
Waterlooville Hants 13 SU6809
Watermillock Cumb 93 NY4422
Waterperry Oxon 37 SP6206
Waterrow Somset 20 ST0525
Waters Upton Shrops 59 SJ6319
Watersfield W Susx 14 TQ0115
Waterside Bucks 26 SP9600
Waterside Cumb 93 NY2245
Waterside Lancs 81 SD7123
Waterside S York 83 SE6714
Waterside Strath 107 NS4308
Waterside Strath 107 NS4843
Waterside Strath 116 NS6773
Waterstock Oxon 37 SP6305
Waterston Dyfed 30 SM9305
Watford Herts 26 TQ1196
Watford Nhants 50 SP6069
Wath N York 89 SE1467
Wath N York 89 SE3277
Wath upon Dearne S York 75 SE4300
Watlington Norfk 65 TF6111
Watlington Oxon 37 SU6894
Watnall Notts 62 SK5046
Watten Highld 151 ND2454
Wattisfield Suffk 54 TM0074
Wattisham Suffk 54 TM0151
Watton Dorset 10 SY4591
Watton Humb 84 TA0150
Watton Norfk 66 TF9100
Watton Green Norfk 66 TF9201
Watton-at-Stone Herts 39 TL3019
Wattons Green Essex 27 TQ5295
Wattstown M Glam 33 ST0193
Wattsville Gwent 33 ST2091
Wauldby Humb 84 SE9629
Waulkmill Gramp 135 NO6492
Waunarlwydd W Glam 32 SS6095
Waunfawr Dyfed 43 SN6081
Waunfawr Gwynd 68 SH5259
Waungron W Glam 32 SN5901
Waunlwyd Gwent 33 SO1806
Wavendon Bucks 38 SP9137
Waverbridge Cumb 93 NY2249
Waverton Ches 71 SJ4663
Waverton Cumb 93 NY2247
Wawne Humb 85 TA0936
Waxham Norfk 67 TG4426
Waxholme Humb 85 TA3229
Way Kent 29 TR3265
Way Village Devon 19 SS8810
Way Wick Avon 21 ST3862
Waye Devon 7 SX7771
Wayford Somset 10 ST4006
Waytown Dorset 10 SY4797
Weacombe Somset 20 ST1140
Weald Cambs 52 TL2259
Weald Oxon 36 SP3002
Wealdstone Gt Lon 26 TQ1589
Wear Head Dur 95 NY8539
Weardley W York 82 SE2944
Weare Somset 21 ST4152
Weare Giffard Devon 18 SS4721
Wearne Somset 21 ST4228
Weasdale Cumb 87 NY6903
Weasenham All Saints Norfk 66 TF8421
Weasenham St Peter Norfk 66 TF8522
Weasle Gt Man 79 SJ8098
Weatheroak Hill H & W 61 SP0674
Weaverham Ches 71 SJ6174
Weaverslake Staffs 73 SK1319
Weaverthorpe N York 91 SE9670
Webb's Heath Avon 35 ST6873
Webbington Somset 21 ST3855
Webheath H & W 48 SP0266
Webton H & W 46 SO4136
Wedderlairs Gramp 143 NJ8532
Wedding Hall Fold N York 82 SD9445
Weddington Kent 29 TR2959
Weddington Warwks 61 SP3693
Wedhampton Wilts 23 SU0557
Wedmore Somset 21 ST4347
Wednesbury W Mids 60 SO9895
Wednesfield W Mids 60 SJ9400
Weecar Notts 75 SK8266
Weedon Bucks 38 SP8118
Weedon Lois Nhants 49 SP6046
Weeford Staffs 61 SK1403
Week Devon 19 SS5727
Week Devon 19 SS7316
Week Devon 7 SX7862
Week Somset 20 SS9133
Week St Mary Cnwll 5 SX2397
Weeke Devon 8 SS7606
Weeke Hants 24 SU4630
Weekley Nhants 51 SP8881
Weel Humb 84 TA0639
Weeley Essex 41 TM1422
Weeley Heath Essex 41 TM1520
Weem Tays 125 NN8449
Weeping Cross Staffs 72 SJ9421
Weethley Hamlet Warwks 48 SP0555
Weeting Norfk 53 TL7788
Weeton Humb 85 TA3520
Weeton Lancs 80 SD3834
Weeton W York 82 SE2847
Weetwood W York 82 SE2737
Weir Lancs 81 SD8625
Weir Quay Devon 6 SX4365
Weirbrook Shrops 59 SJ3424
Welbeck Abbey Notts 75 SK5574
Welborne Norfk 66 TG0610
Welbourn Lincs 76 SK9654
Welburn N York 90 SE7267
Welbury N York 89 NZ3902
Welby Lincs 63 SK9738
Welches Dam Cambs 53 TL4686
Welcombe Devon 18 SS2318
Welford Berks 24 SU4073
Welford Nhants 50 SP6480
Welford-on-Avon Warwks 48 SP1452
Welham Leics 50 SP7692
Welham Notts 75 SK7281
Welham Green Herts 39 TL2305
Well Hants 24 SU7646
Well Lincs 77 TF4473
Well N York 89 SE2681
Well End Bucks 26 SU8888
Well End Herts 26 TQ2098
Well Fold W York 82 SE2024
Well Head Herts 39 TL1727
Well Hill Kent 27 TQ4963
Welland H & W 47 SO7940
Welland Stone H & W 47 SO8138
Wellbank Tays 127 NO4737
Wellbury Herts 38 TL1329
Wellesbourne Warwks 48 SP2855
Wellesbourne Mountford Warwks 48 SP2755
Wellhouse Berks 24 SU5272
Welling Gt Lon 27 TQ4675
Wellingborough Nhants 51 SP8967
Wellingham Norfk 66 TF8722
Wellingore Lincs 76 SK9856
Wellington Cumb 86 NY0704
Wellington H & W 46 SO4948
Wellington Shrops 59 SJ6511
Wellington Somset 20 ST1320
Wellington Heath H & W 47 SO7140
Wellington Marsh H & W 46 SO4946
Wellow Avon 22 ST7458
Wellow IOW 12 SZ3888
Wellow Notts 75 SK6766
Wellpond Green Herts 39 TL4122
Wells Somset 21 ST5445
Wells Green Ches 72 SJ6853
Wells Head W York 82 SE0833
Wells-Next-The-Sea Norfk 66 TF9143
Wellsborough Leics 62 SK3602
Wellstye Green Essex 40 TL6318
Welltree Tays 125 NN9622
Wellwood Fife 117 NT0988
Welney Norfk 65 TL5293
Welsh End Shrops 59 SJ5135
Welsh Frankton Shrops 59 SJ3533
Welsh Hook Dyfed 30 SM9327
Welsh Newton H & W 34 SO5017
Welsh St Donats S Glam 33 ST0276
Welshampton Shrops 59 SJ4335
Welshpool Powys 58 SJ2207
Welton Cumb 93 NY3544
Welton Humb 84 SE9627
Welton Lincs 76 TF0179
Welton Nhants 50 SP5865
Welton le Marsh Lincs 77 TF4768
Welton le Wold Lincs 77 TF2787
Welwick Humb 85 TA3421
Welwyn Herts 39 TL2316
Welwyn Garden City Herts 39 TL2312
Wem Shrops 59 SJ5128
Wembdon Somset 20 ST2837
Wembley Gt Lon 26 TQ1885
Wembury Devon 6 SX5248
Wembworthy Devon 19 SS6609
Wemyss Bay Strath 114 NS1969
Wenallt Dyfed 43 SN6771
Wendens Ambo Essex 39 TL5136
Wendlebury Oxon 37 SP5619
Wendling Norfk 66 TF9312
Wendover Bucks 38 SP8607
Wendron Cnwll 2 SW6731
Wendy Cambs 52 TL3247
Wenfordbridge Cnwll 4 SX0875
Wenhaston Suffk 55 TM4275
Wennington Cambs 52 TL2379
Wennington Gt Lon 27 TQ5381
Wennington Lancs 87 SD6170
Wensley Derbys 74 SK2661
Wensley N York 89 SE0989
Wentbridge W York 83 SE4817
Wentnor Shrops 59 SO3892
Wentworth Cambs 53 TL4878
Wentworth S York 74 SK3898
Wentworth Castle S York 83 SE3202
Wenvoe S Glam 33 ST1272
Weobley H & W 46 SO4051
Weobley Marsh H & W 46 SO4151
Wepham W Susx 14 TQ0408
Wereham Norfk 65 TF6801
Wergs Staffs 60 SJ8700
Wern Powys 58 SH9612
Wern Powys 58 SJ2513
Wern Powys 33 SO1217
Wern Shrops 58 SJ2734
Wern-y-gaer Clwyd 70 SJ2068
Werneth Low Gt Man 79 SJ9592
Wernffrwd W Glam 32 SS5194
Werrington Cambs 64 TF1603
Werrington Cnwll 5 SX3287
Werrington Staffs 72 SJ9447
Wervin Ches 71 SJ4271
Wesham Lancs 80 SD4133
Wessington Derbys 74 SK3757
West Aberthaw S Glam 20 ST0266
West Acre Norfk 65 TF7815
West Allerdean Nthumb 111 NT9646
West Alvington Devon 7 SX7243
West Amesbury Wilts 23 SU1341
West Anstey Devon 19 SS8527
West Appleton N York 89 SE2294
West Ashby Lincs 77 TF2672
West Ashling W Susx 14 SU8107
West Ashton Wilts 22 ST8755
West Auckland Dur 96 NZ1826
West Ayton N York 91 SE9884
West Bagborough Somset 20 ST1733
West Balsdon Cnwll 5 SX2798
West Bank Ches 78 SJ5183
West Bank Gwent 33 SO2105
West Barkwith Lincs 76 TF1580
West Barnby N York 90 NZ8212
West Barnham W Susx 14 SU9505
West Barns Loth 118 NT6578
West Barsham Norfk 66 TF9033
West Bay Dorset 10 SY4690
West Beckham Norfk 66 TG1439
West Bedfont Surrey 26 TQ0674
West Bergholt Essex 40 TL9527
West Bexington Dorset 10 SY5386
West Bilney Norfk 65 TF7115
West Blatchington E Susx 15 TQ2707
West Boldon T & W 96 NZ3561
West Bourton Dorset 22 ST7629
West Bowling W York 82 SE1630
West Brabourne Kent 29 TR0842
West Bradenham Norfk 66 TF9108
West Bradford Lancs 81 SD7444
West Bradley Somset 21 ST5536
West Bretton W York 82 SE2813
West Bridgford Notts 62 SK5836
West Briscoe Dur 95 NY9619
West Bromwich W Mids 60 SP0091
West Buccleigh Hotel Border 109 NT3214
West Buckland Devon 19 SS6531
West Buckland Somset 20 ST1720
West Burton N York 88 SE0186
West Burton W Susx 14 SU9914
West Butsfield Dur 95 NZ1044
West Butterwick Humb 84 SE8305
West Byfleet Surrey 26 TQ0461
West Cairngaan D & G 98 NX1231
West Caister Norfk 67 TG5011
West Calder Loth 117 NT0163
West Camel Somset 21 ST5724
West Chaldon Dorset 11 SY7782
West Challow Oxon 36 SU3688
West Charleton Devon 7 SX7542
West Chelborough Dorset 10 ST5405
West Chevington Nthumb 103 NZ2297
West Chiltington W Susx 14 TQ0818
West Chinnock Somset 10 ST4613
West Chisenbury Wilts 23 SU1352
West Clandon Surrey 26 TQ0552
West Cliffe Kent 29 TR3444
West Coker Somset 10 ST5113
West Combe Devon 7 SX7662
West Compton Dorset 10 SY5694
West Compton Somset 21 ST5942
West Cottingwith N York 83 SE6942
West Cowick Humb 83 SE6421
West Cross W Glam 32 SS6189
West Curry Cnwll 5 SX2893
West Curthwaite Cumb 93 NY3249
West Dean W Susx 14 SU8612
West Dean Wilts 23 SU2526
West Deeping Lincs 64 TF1008
West Derby Mersyd 78 SJ3993
West Dereham Norfk 65 TF6500
West Down Devon 19 SS5142
West Drayton Gt Lon 26 TQ0579
West Drayton Notts 75 SK7074
West Dunnet Highld 151 ND2171
West Ella Humb 84 TA0029
West End Avon 21 ST4569
West End Avon 35 ST7188
West End Beds 51 SP9853
West End Berks 37 SU8275
West End Cambs 52 TL3168
West End Cumb 93 NY3258
West End Gwent 33 ST2195
West End Hants 13 SU4614
West End Hants 24 SU6335
West End Herts 39 TL2608
West End Herts 39 TL3306
West End Humb 84 SE9130
West End Humb 85 TA1830
West End Humb 85 TA2627
West End Lancs 81 SD7328
West End Lincs 77 TF3598
West End N York 89 SE1457
West End N York 83 SE5140
West End Norfk 66 TF9009
West End Norfk 67 TG5011
West End Oxon 37 SU5886
West End Somset 22 ST6734
West End Surrey 25 SU9461
West End Surrey 26 TQ1263
West End W Susx 15 TQ2016
West End W York 82 SE2238
West End Wilts 22 ST9124
West End Wilts 35 ST9777
West End Wilts 22 ST9824
West End Green Hants 24 SU6661
West Ewell Surrey 26 TQ2063
West Farleigh Kent 28 TQ7152
West Farndon Nhants 49 SP5251
West Felton Shrops 59 SJ3425
West Firle E Susx 16 TQ4707
West Firsby Lincs 76 SK9784
West Flotmanby N York 91 TA0779
West Garforth W York 83 SE3932
West Ginge Oxon 37 SU4486
West Grafton Wilts 23 SU2460
West Green Hants 24 SU7456
West Grimstead Wilts 23 SU2026
West Grinstead W Susx 15 TQ1720
West Haddlesey N York 83 SE5626
West Haddon Nhants 50 SP6371
West Hagbourne Oxon 37 SU5187
West Hagley H & W 60 SO9080
West Hallam Derbys 62 SK4341
West Hallam Common Derbys 62 SK4241
West Halton Humb 84 SE9020
West Ham Gt Lon 27 TQ3983
West Handley Derbys 74 SK3977
West Hanney Oxon 36 SU4092
West Hanningfield Essex 40 TQ7399
West Harnham Wilts 23 SU1329
West Harptree Avon 21 ST5556
West Harting W Susx 14 SU7820
West Hatch Somset 20 ST2821
West Hatch Wilts 22 ST9227
West Haven Tays 127 NO5735
West Head Norfk 65 TF5705
West Heath Hants 24 SU5858
West Heath W Mids 60 SP0277
West Helmsdale Highld 147 ND0115
West Hendred Oxon 37 SU4488
West Heslerton N York 91 SE9176
West Hewish Avon 21 ST3963
West Hill Devon 9 SY0794
West Hoathly W Susx 15 TQ3632
West Holme Dorset 11 SY8885
West Holywell T & W 103 NZ3072
West Horndon Essex 40 TQ6288
West Horrington Somset 21 ST5747
West Horsley Surrey 26 TQ0752
West Horton Nthumb 111 NU0230
West Hougham Kent 29 TR2640
West Howe Dorset 12 SZ0595
West Howetown Somset 20 SS9134
West Huntingtower Tays 125 NO0724
West Huntspill Somset 20 ST3044
West Hyde Beds 38 TL1117
West Hyde Herts 26 TQ0391
West Hythe Kent 17 TR1234
West Ilkerton Devon 19 SS7046
West Ilsley Berks 37 SU4782
West Itchenor W Susx 14 SU7901
West Keal Lincs 77 TF3663
West Kennet Wilts 23 SU1168
West Kilbride Strath 114 NS2048
West Kingsdown Kent 27 TQ5763
West Kington Wilts 35 ST8077
West Kirby Mersyd 78 SJ2186
West Knapton N York 90 SE8775
West Knighton Dorset 11 SY7387
West Knoyle Wilts 22 ST8632
West Lambrook Somset 10 ST4118
West Langdon Kent 29 TR3247
West Laroch Highld 130 NN0758
West Lavington W Susx 14 SU8920
West Lavington Wilts 22 SU0052
West Layton N York 89 NZ1410
West Leake Notts 62 SK5226
West Learmouth Nthumb 110 NT8437
West Lees N York 89 NZ4702
West Leigh Devon 8 SS6805
West Leigh Devon 7 SX7557
West Leigh Somset 20 ST1230
West Lexham Norfk 66 TF8417
West Lilling N York 90 SE6465
West Linton Border 117 NT1551
West Littleton Avon 35 ST7675
West Lockinge Oxon 36 SU4187
West Lulworth Dorset 11 SY8280
West Lutton N York 91 SE9369
West Lydford Somset 21 ST5631
West Lyn Devon 19 SS7248
West Lyng Somset 21 ST3128
West Lynn Norfk 65 TF6120
West Malling Kent 28 TQ6757
West Malvern H & W 47 SO7646
West Marden W Susx 14 SU7713
West Markham Notts 75 SK7272
West Marsh Humb 85 TA2509
West Marton N York 81 SD8950
West Melbury Dorset 22 ST8720
West Melton S York 83 SE4201
West Meon Hants 13 SU6423
West Meon Hut Hants 13 SU6526
West Meon Woodlands Hants 13 SU6426
West Mersea Essex 41 TM0112
West Milton Dorset 10 SY5096
West Minster Kent 28 TQ9073
West Monkton Somset 20 ST2628
West Moor T & W 103 NZ2770
West Moors Dorset 12 SU0802
West Morden Dorset 11 SY9095
West Morton W York 82 SE0942
West Mudford Somset 21 ST5620
West Ness N York 90 SE6879
West Newbiggin Dur 96 NZ3518
West Newton Humb 85 TA2037
West Newton Norfk 65 TF6928
West Newton Somset 20 ST2829
West Norwood Gt Lon 27 TQ3171
West Ogwell Devon 7 SX8270
West Orchard Dorset 11 ST8216
West Overton Wilts 23 SU1267
West Panson Devon 5 SX3491
West Parley Dorset 12 SZ0896
West Peckham Kent 27 TQ6452
West Pelton Dur 96 NZ2353
West Pennard Somset 21 ST5438
West Pentire Cnwll 4 SW7760
West Perry Cambs 52 TL1466
West Prawle Devon 7 SX7637
West Preston W Susx 14 TQ0602
West Pulham Dorset 11 ST7008
West Putford Devon 18 SS3616
West Quantoxhead Somset 20 ST1141
West Raddon Devon 9 SS8902
West Rainton T & W 96 NZ3246
West Rasen Lincs 76 TF0689
West Ravendale Humb 76 TF2299
West Raynham Norfk 66 TF8725
West Retford Notts 75 SK6981
West Rounton N York 89 NZ4103
West Row Suffk 53 TL6775
West Rudham Norfk 66 TF8127
West Runton Norfk 66 TG1842
West Saltoun Loth 118 NT4667
West Sandford Devon 8 SS8102
West Sandwick Shet 155 HU4588
West Scrafton N York 88 SE0783
West Sleekburn Nthumb 103 NZ2884
West Somerton Norfk 67 TG4620
West Stafford Dorset 11 SY7289
West Stockwith Notts 75 SK7895
West Stoke W Susx 14 SU8208
West Stonesdale N York 88 NY8801
West Stoughton Somset 21 ST4148
West Stour Dorset 22 ST7822
West Stourmouth Kent 29 TR2562
West Stow Suffk 54 TL8171
West Stowell Wilts 23 SU1361
West Stratton Hants 24 SU5240
West Street Kent 28 TQ7376
West Street Kent 28 TQ9054
West Street Kent 29 TR3254
West Street Suffk 54 TL9871
West Tanfield N York 89 SE2678
West Taphouse Cnwll 4 SX1463
West Tarbert Strath 113 NR8467
West Tarring W Susx 14 TQ1103
West Thorney W Susx 14 SU7602
West Thorpe Notts 62 SK6225
West Thurrock Essex 27 TQ5877
West Tilbury Essex 40 TQ6678
West Tisted Hants 24 SU6529
West Torrington Lincs 76 TF1381
West Town Avon 21 ST4868
West Town Avon 21 ST5160
West Town H & W 46 SO4361
West Town Hants 13 SZ7199
West Town Somset 21 ST5335
West Town Somset 22 ST7042
West Tytherley Hants 23 SU2729
West Tytherton Wilts 35 ST9474
West Walton Norfk 65 TF4613
West Walton Highway Norfk 65 TF4913
West Weetwood Nthumb 111 NU0028
West Wellow Hants 12 SU2819
West Wembury Devon 6 SX5249
West Wemyss Fife 118 NT3294
West Wick Avon 21 ST3761
West Wickham Cambs 53 TL6149
West Wickham Gt Lon 27 TQ3766
West Williamston Dyfed 30 SN0305
West Winch Norfk 65 TF6316
West Winterslow Wilts 23 SU2331
West Wittering W Susx 14 SZ7898
West Witton N York 88 SE0588
West Woodburn Nthumb 102 NY8987
West Woodhay Berks 23 SU3963
West Woodlands Somset 22 ST7743
West Woodside Cumb 93 NY3049
West Worldham Hants 24 SU7436
West Worthing W Susx 15 TQ1302
West Wratting Essex 53 TL6052
West Wycombe Bucks 37 SU8294
West Wylam Nthumb 103 NZ1063
West Yatton Wilts 35 ST8575
West Yoke Kent 27 TQ6065
West Youlstone Cnwll 18 SS2615
Westbere Kent 29 TR1961
Westborough Lincs 63 SK8544
Westbourne W Susx 13 SU7507
Westbrook Berks 24 SU4272
Westbrook Kent 29 TR3470
Westbrook Wilts 22 ST9565
Westbury Bucks 49 SP6235
Westbury Shrops 59 SJ3509
Westbury Wilts 22 ST8751
Westbury Leigh Wilts 22 ST8649
Westbury on Severn Gloucs 35 SO7114
Westbury-on-Trym Avon 34 ST5777
Westbury-sub-Mendip Somset 21 ST5049
Westby Lancs 80 SD3831
Westcliff-on-Sea Essex 40 TQ8685
Westcombe Somset 22 ST6739
Westcote Gloucs 36 SP2120
Westcott Bucks 37 SP7116
Westcott Devon 9 ST0204
Westcott Somset 19 SS8720
Westcott Surrey 15 TQ1448
Westcott Barton Oxon 49 SP4325
Westcourt Wilts 23 SU2261
Westdean E Susx 16 TV5299
Westdown Camp Wilts 23 SU0447
Westdowns Cnwll 4 SX0582
Wested Kent 27 TQ5166
Westend Gloucs 35 SO7807
Westend Town Nthumb 102 NY7865
Westenhanger Kent 29 TR1237
Wester Drumashie Highld 140 NH6032
Wester Essenside Border 109 NT4320
Wester Ochiltree Loth 117 NT0374
Wester Pitkierie Fife 127 NO5505
Westerdale Highld 151 ND1251
Westerdale N York 90 NZ6605
Westerfield Suffk 54 TM1747
Westergate W Susx 14 SU9305
Westerham Kent 27 TQ4454
Westerhope T & W 103 NZ1966
Westerland Devon 7 SX8662
Westerleigh Avon 35 ST6979
Westerton Tays 127 NO6754
Westfield Avon 22 ST6753
Westfield D & G 92 NX9926
Westfield E Susx 17 TQ8115
Westfield Loth 116 NS9472
Westfield Norfk 66 TF9909
Westfield Sole Kent 28 TQ7761
Westfields Dorset 11 ST7206
Westfields H & W 46 SO4941
Westfields of Rattray Tays 126 NO1746
Westford Somset 20 ST1220
Westgate Dur 95 NY9038
Westgate Humb 84 SE7707
Westgate Norfk 66 TF9740
Westgate Hill W York 82 SE2029
Westgate on Sea Kent 29 TR3270
Westgate Street Norfk 67 TG1921
Westhall Suffk 55 TM4280
Westham Dorset 11 SY6679
Westham E Susx 16 TQ6404
Westham Somset 21 ST4046
Westhampnett W Susx 14 SU8806
Westhay Somset 21 ST4342
Westhead Lancs 78 SD4407
Westhide H & W 46 SO5843
Westhill Gramp 135 NJ8307
Westholme Somset 21 ST5741
Westhope H & W 46 SO4651
Westhope Shrops 59 SO4786
Westhorp Nhants 49 SP5152
Westhorpe Lincs 64 TF2231
Westhorpe Suffk 54 TM0468
Westhoughton Gt Man 79 SD6506
Westhouse N York 87 SD6773
Westhouses Derbys 74 SK4157
Westhumble Surrey 26 TQ1651
Westlake Devon 6 SX6253
Westland Green Herts 39 TL4222
Westleigh Devon 18 SS4728
Westleigh Devon 9 ST0617
Westleton Suffk 55 TM4369
Westley Shrops 59 SJ3607
Westley Suffk 54 TL8264
Westley Waterless Cambs 53 TL6156
Westlington Bucks 37 SP7610
Westlinton Cumb 101 NY3964
Westmarsh Kent 29 TR2761
Westmeston E Susx 15 TQ3313
Westmill Herts 39 TL3627
Westmuir Tays 126 NO3652
Westnewton Cumb 92 NY1344
Westoe T & W 103 NZ3765
Weston Avon 22 ST7366
Weston Berks 36 SU3973
Weston Ches 78 SJ5080
Weston Ches 72 SJ7352
Weston Devon 9 ST1400
Weston Devon 9 SY1688
Weston Dorset 11 SY6871
Weston H & W 46 SO3656
Weston Hants 13 SU7221
Weston Herts 39 TL2530
Weston Lincs 64 TF2924
Weston Nhants 49 SP5846
Weston Notts 75 SK7767
Weston Shrops 59 SJ2927
Weston Shrops 59 SJ5629
Weston Shrops 46 SO3273
Weston Staffs 72 SJ9726
Weston W York 82 SE1747
Weston Beggard H & W 46 SO5841
Weston by Welland Nhants 50 SP7791
Weston Colley Hants 24 SU5039
Weston Colville Cambs 53 TL6153
Weston Corbett Hants 24 SU6846
Weston Coyney Staffs 72 SJ9343
Weston Favell Nhants 50 SP7962
Weston Green Cambs 53 TL6252
Weston Heath Shrops 60 SJ7713
Weston Hills Lincs 64 TF2720
Weston in Arden Warwks 61 SP3886
Weston Jones Staffs 72 SJ7624
Weston Longville Norfk 66 TG1115
Weston Lullingfields Shrops 59 SJ4224
Weston Patrick Hants 24 SU6946
Weston Rhyn Shrops 58 SJ2835
Weston Subedge Gloucs 48 SP1241
Weston Turville Bucks 38 SP8510
Weston Underwood Bucks 38 SP8650
Weston Underwood Derbys 73 SK2942
Weston under Penyard H & W 35 SO6322
Weston under Wetherley Warwks 48 SP3669
Weston-in-Gordano Avon 34 ST4474
Weston-on-Trent Derbys 62 SK4027
Weston-on-the-Green Oxon 37 SP5318
Weston-Super-Mare Avon 21 ST3260
Weston-under-Lizard Staffs 60 SJ8010
Westonbirt Gloucs 35 ST8589
Westoning Beds 38 TL0332
Westoning Woodend Beds 38 TL0232
Westonzoyland Somset 21 ST3534
Westover Hants 23 SU3640
Westow N York 90 SE7565
Westpeek Devon 5 SX3493
Westport Somset 21 ST3820
Westport Strath 104 NR6526
Westquarter Cent 116 NS9178
Westra S Glam 33 ST1470
Westridge Green Berks 37 SU5679
Westrigg Loth 116 NS9067
Westrop Wilts 36 SU2093
Westruther Border 110 NT6349
Westry Cambs 65 TL4098
Westthorpe Derbys 75 SK4579
Westward Cumb 93 NY2744
Westward Ho Devon 18 SS4329
Westwell Kent 28 TQ9947
Westwell Oxon 36 SP2209
Westwell Leacon Kent 28 TQ9647
Westwick Cambs 53 TL4265
Westwick Dur 95 NZ0715
Westwick Norfk 67 TG2726
Westwood Devon 9 SY0199
Westwood Kent 27 TQ6070
Westwood Kent 29 TR3667
Westwood Notts 75 SK4551
Westwood Wilts 22 ST8059
Westwood Heath W Mids 61 SP2776
Westwoodside Humb 75 SE7400
Wetham Green Kent 28 TQ8468
Wetheral Cumb 93 NY4654
Wetherby W York 83 SE4048
Wetherden Suffk 54 TM0062
Wetheringsett Suffk 54 TM1266
Wethersfield Essex 40 TL7131
Wetherup Street Suffk 54 TM1464
Wetley Rocks Staffs 72 SJ9649
Wettenhall Ches 71 SJ6261
Wetton Staffs 73 SK1055
Wetwang Humb 91 SE9359
Wetwood Staffs 72 SJ7733
Wexcombe Wilts 23 SU2758
Wexham Bucks 26 SU9882
Wexham Street Bucks 26 SU9883
Weybourne Norfk 66 TG1142
Weybread Suffk 55 TM2480
Weybread Street Suffk 55 TM2479
Weybridge Surrey 26 TQ0764
Weydale Highld 151 ND1564
Weyhill Hants 23 SU3146
Weymouth Dorset 11 SY6779
Whaddon Bucks 38 SP8034
Whaddon Cambs 52 TL3546
Whaddon Gloucs 35 SO8313
Whaddon Wilts 22 ST8861
Whaddon Wilts 23 SU1926
Whale Cumb 94 NY5221
Whaley Derbys 75 SK5171
Whaley Bridge Derbys 79 SK0180
Whaligoe Highld 151 ND3140
Whalley Lancs 81 SD7336
Whalley Banks Lancs 81 SD7335
Whalton Nthumb 96 NZ1318
Whamley Nthumb 102 NY8766
Whaplode Lincs 64 TF3224
Whaplode Drove Lincs 64 TF3213
Wharf Warwks 49 SP4352
Wharfe N York 88 SD7869
Wharles Lancs 80 SD4435
Wharley End Beds 38 SP9442
Wharncliffe Side S York 74 SK2994
Wharram-le-Street N York 90 SE8665
Wharton Ches 72 SJ6666
Wharton H & W 46 SO5055
Whashton Green N York 89 NZ1405
Whasset Cumb 87 SD5080
Whaston N York 89 NZ1506
Whatcote Warwks 48 SP2944
Whateley Warwks 61 SP2299
Whatfield Suffk 54 TM0246
Whatley Somset 10 ST3607
Whatley Somset 22 ST7347
Whatley's End Avon 35 ST6581
Whatlington E Susx 17 TQ7618
Whatsole Street Kent 29 TR1144
Whatstandwell Derbys 74 SK3354
Whatton Notts 63 SK7439
Whauphill D & G 99 NX4049
Whaw N York 88 NY9804
Wheal Rose Cnwll 2 SW7144
Wheatacre Norfk 67 TM4694
Wheatfield Oxon 37 SU6899
Wheathampstead Herts 39 TL1714
Wheathill Shrops 59 SO6282
Wheathill Somset 21 ST5830
Wheatley Hants 25 SU7840
Wheatley Oxon 37 SP5905
Wheatley W York 82 SE0726
Wheatley Hill Dur 96 NZ3738
Wheatley Hills S York 83 SE5904
Wheatley Lane Lancs 81 SD8337
Wheaton Aston Staffs 60 SJ8512
Wheatsheaf Clwyd 71 SJ3253
Wheddon Cross Somset 20 SS9238
Wheel Inn Cnwll 2 SW6921
Wheelbarrow Town Kent 29 TR1445
Wheeler's Green Oxon 24 SU7672
Wheeler's Street Kent 28 TQ8444
Wheelerend Common Bucks 37 SU8093
Wheelerstreet Surrey 25 SU9440
Wheelock Ches 72 SJ7559
Wheelock Heath Ches 72 SJ7557
Wheelton Lancs 81 SD6021
Wheldale W York 83 SE4526
Wheldrake N York 83 SE6844
Whelpley Hill Bucks 38 SP9904
Whelpo Cumb 93 NY3139
Whelston Clwyd 70 SJ2076
Whempstead Herts 39 TL3221
Whenby N York 90 SE6369
Whepstead Suffk 54 TL8358
Wherstead Suffk 54 TM1540
Wherwell Hants 23 SU3841
Wheston Derbys 74 SK1376
Whetsted Kent 28 TQ6646
Whetstone Gt Lon 27 TQ2693
Whetstone Leics 50 SP5597
Wheyrigg Cumb 93 NY1948
Whicham Cumb 86 SD1382
Whichford Warwks 48 SP3134
Whickham T & W 96 NZ2061
Whiddon Devon 18 SX4799
Whiddon Down Devon 8 SX6992
Whight's Corner Suffk 54 TM1242
Whigstreet Tays 127 NO4844
Whiligh E Susx 16 TQ6431
Whilton Nhants 49 SP6364
Whimble Devon 18 SS3503
Whimple Devon 9 SY0497
Whimpwell Green Norfk 67 TG3829
Whin Lane End Lancs 80 SD3941
Whinburgh Norfk 66 TG0009
Whinnie Liggate D & G 99 NX7252
Whinnow Cumb 93 NY3051
Whinny Hill Cleve 96 NZ3818
Whinnyfold Gramp 143 NK0733
Whippingham IOW 13 SZ5193
Whipsnade Beds 38 TL0117
Whipton Devon 9 SX9493
Whisby Lincs 76 SK9067
Whissendine Leics 63 SK8214
Whissonsett Norfk 66 TF9123
Whistlefield Inn Strath 114 NS1492
Whistley Green Berks 25 SU7974
Whiston Mersyd 78 SJ4791
Whiston Nhants 51 SP8460
Whiston S York 75 SK4489
Whiston Staffs 60 SJ8914
Whiston Staffs 73 SK0347
Whiston Cross Shrops 60 SJ7903
Whiston Eaves Staffs 73 SK0446
Whiston Lane End Mersyd 78 SJ4690
Whitacre Fields Warwks 61 SP2592
Whitbeck Cumb 86 SD1184
Whitbourne H & W 47 SO7257
Whitburn Loth 116 NS9464
Whitburn T & W 96 NZ4062
Whitby Ches 71 SJ3975
Whitby N York 91 NZ8910
Whitbyheath Ches 71 SJ3974
Whitchurch Avon 21 ST6167
Whitchurch Bucks 38 SP8020
Whitchurch Devon 6 SX4972
Whitchurch Dyfed 30 SM8025
Whitchurch H & W 34 SO5517
Whitchurch Hants 24 SU4648
Whitchurch Oxon 37 SU6377
Whitchurch S Glam 33 ST1579
Whitchurch Shrops 71 SJ5341
Whitchurch Canonicorum Dorset 10 SY3995
Whitchurch Hill Oxon 37 SU6378
Whitcombe Dorset 11 SY7188
Whitcot Shrops 59 SO3791
Whitcott Keysett Shrops 58 SO2782
White Ball Somset 20 ST1019
White Chapel H & W 48 SP0740
White Chapel Lancs 81 SD5541
White Colne Essex 40 TL8729
White Coppice Lancs 81 SD6118
White Cross Cnwll 2 SW6821
White End H & W 47 SO7834
White Lackington Dorset 11 SY7198
White Ladies Aston H & W 47 SO9252
White Notley Essex 40 TL7818
White Ox Mead Avon 22 ST7258
White Pit Lincs 77 TF3777
White Roding Essex 40 TL5613
White Stake Lancs 80 SD5125
White Stone H & W 46 SO5642
White Waltham Berks 26 SU8577
White-le-Head Dur 96 NZ1654
Whiteacre Kent 29 TR1148
Whiteacre Heath Warwks 61 SP2292
Whiteash Green Essex 40 TL7930
Whitebirk Lancs 81 SD7028
Whitebridge Highld 139 NH4815
Whitebrook Gwent 34 SO5306
Whitecairns Gramp 143 NJ9218
Whitechapel Gt Lon 27 TQ3381
Whitechurch Dyfed 31 SN1536
Whitecliffe Gloucs 34 SO5609
Whitecraig Loth 118 NT3470
Whitecroft Gloucs 35 SO6206
Whitecrook D & G 98 NX1656
Whitecross Cnwll 2 SW5234
Whitecross Cnwll 4 SW9672
Whiteface Highld 146 NH7088
Whitefarland Strath 105 NR8642
Whitefield Devon 19 SS7035
Whitefield Gt Man 79 SD8006
Whitefield Lane End Mersyd 78 SJ4589
Whiteford Gramp 142 NJ7126
Whitegate Ches 71 SJ6269
Whitehall Hants 24 SU7452
Whitehall Ork 155 HY6528
Whitehall W Susx 15 TQ1321
Whitehaven Cumb 92 NX9718
Whitehill Hants 14 SU7934
Whitehill Kent 28 TR0059
Whitehills Gramp 142 NJ6565
Whitehouse Gramp 142 NJ6114
Whitehouse Strath 113 NR8161
Whitehouse Common W Mids 61 SP1397
Whitekirk Loth 118 NT5981
Whitelackington Somset 10 ST3815
Whiteley Hants 13 SU5209
Whiteley Bank IOW 13 SZ5581
Whiteley Green Ches 79 SJ9278
Whiteley Village Surrey 26 TQ0962
Whitemans Green W Susx 15 TQ3025
Whitemire Gramp 140 NH9854
Whitemoor Cnwll 4 SW9757
Whitemoor Derbys 62 SK3647
Whitemoor Notts 62 SK5441
Whitemoor Staffs 72 SJ8861
Whitenap Hants 12 SU3620
Whiteness Shet 155 HU3844
Whiteoak Green Oxon 36 SP3414
Whiteparish Wilts 23 SU2423
Whiterashes Gramp 143 NJ8523
Whiterow Gramp 141 NJ0257
Whiterow Highld 151 ND3648
Whiteshill Gloucs 35 SO8406
Whitesmith E Susx 16 TQ5213
Whitestaunton Somset 10 ST2810
Whitestone Devon 9 SX8694
Whitestone Cross Devon 9 SX8993
Whitestreet Green Suffk 54 TL9739
Whitewall Corner N York 90 SE7969
Whiteway Avon 22 ST7264
Whitewell Lancs 81 SD6646
Whiteworks Devon 6 SX6171
Whitfield Avon 35 ST6791
Whitfield Kent 29 TR3045
Whitfield Nhants 49 SP6039
Whitfield Nthumb 94 NY7758
Whitfield Hall Nthumb 94 NY7756
Whitford Clwyd 70 SJ1478
Whitford Devon 10 SY2595
Whitgift Humb 84 SE8122
Whitgreave Staffs 72 SJ9028
Whithorn D & G 99 NX4440
Whiting Bay Strath 105 NS0425
Whitington Norfk 65 TL7199
Whitkirk W York 83 SE3633
Whitland Dyfed 31 SN1916
Whitlaw Border 109 NT5012
Whitletts Strath 106 NS3623
Whitley Berks 24 SU7270
Whitley N York 83 SE5620
Whitley S York 74 SK3494
Whitley Wilts 22 ST8866
Whitley Bay T & W 103 NZ3571
Whitley Chapel Nthumb 95 NY9257
Whitley Heath Staffs 72 SJ8126
Whitley Lower W York 82 SE2217
Whitley Row Kent 27 TQ4952
Whitlock's End W Mids 61 SP1076
Whitlow S York 74 SK3182
Whitminster Gloucs 35 SO7708
Whitmore Dorset 12 SU0609
Whitmore Staffs 72 SJ8140
Whitnage Devon 9 ST0215
Whitnash Warwks 48 SP3263
Whitney H & W 46 SO2747
Whitrigg Cumb 93 NY2038
Whitrigg Cumb 93 NY2257
Whitrigglees Cumb 93 NY2457
Whitsbury Hants 12 SU1219
Whitsford Devon 19 SS6633
Whitsome Border 119 NT8650
Whitson Gwent 34 ST3883
Whitstable Kent 29 TR1066
Whitstone Cnwll 5 SX2698
Whittingehame Loth 118 NT6073
Whittingham Nthumb 111 NU0611
Whittingslow Shrops 59 SO4388
Whittington Derbys 74 SK3875
Whittington Gloucs 35 SP0120
Whittington H & W 47 SO8753
Whittington Lancs 87 SD6075

Whittington
Zouch

Whittington Shrops 59 SJ3231
Whittington Staffs 61 SK1508
Whittington Staffs 60 SO8682
Whittington Warwks 61 SP2999
Whittle-le-Woods Lancs 81 SD5821
Whittlebury Nhants 49 SP6943
Whittlesey Cambs 64 TL2697
Whittlesford Cambs 53 TL4748
Whittlestone Head Lancs 81 SD7119
Whitton Cleve 96 NZ3822
Whitton Humb 84 SE9024
Whitton Powys 46 SO2767
Whitton Shrops 46 SO5772
Whitton Suffk 54 TM1447
Whittonditch Wilts 36 SU2872
Whittonstall Nthumb 95 NZ0757
Whitway Hants 24 SU4559
Whitwell Derbys 75 SK5276
Whitwell Herts 39 TL1820
Whitwell IOW 13 SZ5277
Whitwell Leics 63 SK9208
Whitwell N York 89 SE2899
Whitwell Street Norfk 66 TG1022
Whitwell-on-the-Hill N York 90 SE7265
Whitwick Leics 62 SK4315
Whitwood W York 83 SE4024
Whitworth Lancs 81 SD8818
Whixall Shrops 59 SJ5134
Whixley N York 89 SE4458
Whorlton Dur 95 NZ1014
Whorlton N York 90 NZ4802
Whyle H & W 46 SO5561
Whyteleafe Surrey 27 TQ3358
Wibdon Gloucs 34 ST5797
Wibsey W York 82 SE1430
Wibtoft Warwks 50 SP4887
Wichenford H & W 47 SO7860
Wichling Kent 28 TQ9256
Wick Avon 35 ST7072
Wick Devon 9 ST1704
Wick Dorset 12 SZ1591
Wick H & W 47 SO9645
Wick Highld 151 ND3650
Wick M Glam 33 SS9271
Wick Somset 20 ST2144
Wick Somset 21 ST4026
Wick W Susx 14 TQ0203
Wick Wilts 12 SU1621
Wick End Beds 38 SP9850
Wick Rissington Gloucs 36 SP1821
Wick St Lawrence Avon 21 ST3665
Wicken Cambs 53 TL5770
Wicken Nhants 49 SP7439
Wicken Bonhunt Essex 39 TL4933
Wickenby Lincs 76 TF0982
Wicker Street Green Suffk 54 TL9742
Wickersley S York 75 SK4791
Wickford Essex 40 TQ7493
Wickham Berks 36 SU3971
Wickham Hants 13 SU5711
Wickham Bishops Essex 40 TL8412
Wickham Green Berks 24 SU4072
Wickham Green Suffk 54 TM0969
Wickham Heath Berks 24 SU4169
Wickham Market Suffk 55 TM3055
Wickham Skeith Suffk 54 TM0969
Wickham St Paul Essex 54 TL8336
Wickham Street Suffk 53 TL7654
Wickham Street Suffk 54 TM0869
Wickhambreaux Kent 29 TR2158
Wickhambrook Suffk 53 TL7554
Wickhamford H & W 48 SP0641
Wickhampton Norfk 67 TG4205
Wicklewood Norfk 66 TG0702
Wickmere Norfk 66 TG1733
Wickstreet E Susx 16 TQ5308
Wickwar Avon 35 ST7288
Widdington Essex 39 TL5331
Widdop Lancs 81 SD9233
Widdrington T & W 103 NZ2595
Widdrington Station T & W 103 NZ2494
Wide Open T & W 103 NZ2472
Widecombe in the Moor Devon 8 SX7176
Widegates Cnwll 5 SX2858
Widemouth Bay Cnwll 18 SS2002
Widford Essex 40 TL6904
Widford Herts 39 TL4216
Widford Oxon 36 SP2712
Widham Wilts 36 SU0988
Widmer End Bucks 26 SU8896
Widmerpool Notts 63 SK6327
Widmore Gt Lon 27 TQ4268
Widnes Ches 78 SJ5184
Wigan Gt Man 78 SD5805
Wigborough Somset 10 ST4415
Wiggaton Devon 9 SY1093
Wiggenhall St Germans Norfk 65 TF5914
Wiggenhall St Mary Magdalen Norfk 65 TF5911
Wiggenhall St Mary the Virgin Norfk 65 TF5813
Wiggens Green Essex 53 TL6642
Wiggenstall Staffs 74 SK0960
Wiggington Shrops 59 SJ3335
Wigginton Herts 38 SP9310
Wigginton N York 90 SE6058
Wigginton Oxon 48 SP3833
Wigginton Staffs 61 SK2006
Wigglesworth N York 81 SD8156
Wiggold Gloucs 36 SP0404
Wiggonby Cumb 93 NY2952
Wiggonholt W Susx 14 TQ0616
Wighill N York 83 SE4746
Wighton Norfk 66 TF9439
Wigley Hants 12 SU3217
Wigmore H & W 46 SO4169
Wigmore Kent 28 TQ7964
Wigsley Notts 76 SK8570
Wigsthorpe Nhants 51 TL0482
Wigston Leics 50 SP6198
Wigston Fields Leics 50 SK6000
Wigston Parva Leics 50 SP4689
Wigthorpe Notts 75 SK5983
Wigtoft Lincs 64 TF2636
Wigton Cumb 93 NY2548
Wigtown D & G 99 NX4355
Wigtwizzle S York 74 SK2495
Wike W York 83 SE3342
Wilbarston Nhants 51 SP8188
Wilberfoss Humb 84 SE7350
Wilburton Cambs 53 TL4775
Wilby Nhants 51 SP8666
Wilby Norfk 54 TM0389
Wilby Suffk 55 TM2472
Wilcot Wilts 23 SU1360
Wilcrick Gwent 34 ST4088
Wilday Green Derbys 74 SK3274
Wildboarclough Ches 79 SJ9868
Wilden Beds 51 TL0955
Wilden H & W 60 SO8272
Wildhern Hants 23 SU3550
Wildhill Herts 39 TL2606
Wildmanbridge Strath 116 NS8253
Wildmoor H & W 60 SO9575
Wildsworth Lincs 75 SK8097
Wilford Notts 62 SK5637
Wilkesley Ches 71 SJ6241
Wilkhaven Highld 147 NH9486
Wilkieston Fife 117 NT1268
Wilkin's Green Herts 39 TL1907
Wilksby Lincs 77 TF2862
Willand Devon 9 ST0310
Willards Hill E Susx 17 TQ7124
Willaston Ches 71 SJ3377
Willaston Ches 72 SJ6852
Willcott Shrops 59 SJ3718
Willen Bucks 38 SP8741
Willenhall W Mids 60 SO9798
Willenhall W Mids 61 SP3676
Willerby Humb 84 TA0230
Willerby N York 91 TA0079
Willersey Gloucs 48 SP1039
Willersley H & W 46 SO3147
Willesborough Kent 28 TR0441
Willesborough Lees Kent 28 TR0342
Willesden Gt Lon 26 TQ2284
Willesleigh Devon 19 SS6033
Willesley Wilts 35 ST8588
Willett Somset 20 ST1033
Willey Shrops 60 SO6799
Willey Warwks 50 SP4984
Willey Green Surrey 25 SU9351
Williamscot Oxon 49 SP4845
Williamstown M Glam 33 ST0090
Willian Herts 39 TL2230
Willingale Essex 40 TL5907
Willingdon E Susx 16 TQ5902
Willingham Cambs 52 TL4070
Willingham Lincs 76 SK8784
Willingham Green Cambs 53 TL6254
Willington Beds 52 TL1150
Willington Derbys 73 SK2928
Willington Dur 96 NZ1935
Willington Kent 28 TQ7853
Willington Warwks 48 SP2639
Willington Corner Ches 71 SJ5266
Willington Quay T & W 103 NZ3267
Willitoft Humb 84 SE7434
Williton Somset 20 ST0840
Willoughbridge Staffs 72 SJ7440
Willoughby Lincs 64 TF0537
Willoughby Lincs 77 TF4771
Willoughby Warwks 50 SP5167
Willoughby Hills Lincs 64 TF3545
Willoughby Waterleys Leics 50 SP5792
Willoughby-on-the-Wolds Notts 63 SK6325
Willoughton Lincs 76 SK9293
Willow Green Ches 71 SJ6076
Willows Green Essex 40 TL7219
Willsbridge Avon 35 ST6670
Willsworthy Devon 8 SX5381
Willtown Somset 21 ST3924
Wilmcote Warwks 48 SP1658
Wilmington Avon 22 ST6962
Wilmington Devon 9 SY2199
Wilmington E Susx 16 TQ5404
Wilmington Kent 27 TQ5372
Wilmslow Ches 79 SJ8481
Wilnecote Staffs 61 SK2200
Wilpshire Lancs 81 SD6832
Wilsden W York 82 SE0936
Wilsford Lincs 63 TF0042
Wilsford Wilts 23 SU1057
Wilsford Wilts 23 SU1339
Wilsham Devon 19 SS7548
Wilshaw W York 82 SE1109
Wilsill N York 89 SE1864
Wilsley Green Kent 28 TQ7736
Wilsley Pound Kent 28 TQ7837
Wilson H & W 46 SO5523
Wilson Leics 62 SK4024
Wilsontown Strath 116 NS9455
Wilstead Beds 38 TL0643
Wilsthorpe Lincs 64 TF0913
Wilstone Herts 38 SP9014
Wilstone Green Herts 38 SP9013
Wilton Cleve 97 NZ5819
Wilton Cumb 86 NY0311
Wilton H & W 46 SO5824
Wilton N York 90 SE8582
Wilton Wilts 23 SU0931
Wilton Wilts 23 SU2661
Wilton Dean Border 109 NT4914
Wimbish Essex 53 TL5936
Wimbish Green Essex 53 TL6035
Wimblebury Staffs 60 SK0111
Wimbledon Gt Lon 26 TQ2370
Wimblington Cambs 65 TL4192
Wimborne Minster Dorset 11 SZ0199
Wimborne St Giles Dorset 12 SU0311
Wimbotsham Norfk 65 TF6205
Wimpstone Warwks 48 SP2148
Wincanton Somset 22 ST7128
Winceby Lincs 77 TF3268
Wincham Ches 79 SJ6775
Winchburgh Loth 117 NT0975
Winchcombe Gloucs 48 SP0228
Winchelsea E Susx 17 TQ9017
Winchelsea Beach E Susx 17 TQ9116
Winchester Hants 24 SU4829
Winchet Hill Kent 28 TQ7340
Winchfield Hants 24 SU7654
Winchmore Hill Bucks 26 SU9395
Winchmore Hill Gt Lon 27 TQ3194
Wincle Ches 72 SJ9566
Wincobank S York 74 SK3891
Winder Cumb 92 NY0417
Windermere Cumb 87 SD4098
Winderton Warwks 48 SP3240
Windhill Highld 139 NH5348
Windlehurst Gt Man 79 SJ9586
Windlesham Surrey 25 SU9364
Windmill Cnwll 4 SW8974
Windmill Derbys 74 SK1677
Windmill Hill E Susx 16 TQ6412
Windmill Hill Somset 10 ST3116
Windrush Gloucs 36 SP1913
Windsole Gramp 142 NJ5560
Windsor Berks 26 SU9576
Windsor Green Suffk 54 TL8954
Windsoredge Gloucs 35 SO8400
Windy Arbour Warwks 61 SP2971
Windy Hill Clwyd 71 SJ3054
Windygates Fife 118 NO3500
Windyharbour Ches 79 SJ8270
Wineham W Susx 15 TQ2320
Winestead Humb 85 TA2924
Winewall Lancs 81 SD9140
Winfarthing Norfk 54 TM1085
Winford Avon 21 ST5464
Winford IOW 13 SZ5584
Winforton H & W 46 SO2946
Winfrith Newburgh Dorset 11 SY8084
Wing Bucks 38 SP8822
Wing Leics 63 SK8903
Wingate Dur 96 NZ4036
Wingates Gt Man 79 SD6507
Wingates Nthumb 103 NZ0995
Wingerworth Derbys 74 SK3867
Wingfield Beds 38 TL0026
Wingfield Suffk 55 TM2277
Wingfield Wilts 22 ST8256
Wingfield Green Suffk 55 TM2177
Wingham Kent 29 TR2457
Wingham Well Kent 29 TR2356
Wingmore Kent 29 TR1946
Wingrave Bucks 38 SP8719
Winkburn Notts 75 SK7058
Winkfield Berks 25 SU9072
Winkfield Row Berks 25 SU8971
Winkfield Street Berks 25 SU8972
Winkhill Staffs 73 SK0651
Winkhurst Green Kent 16 TQ4949
Winkleigh Devon 19 SS6308
Winksley N York 89 SE2571
Winkton Dorset 12 SZ1696
Winlaton T & W 96 NZ1762
Winlaton Mill T & W 96 NZ1860
Winless Highld 151 ND3054
Winllan Powys 58 SJ2221
Winmarleigh Lancs 80 SD4647
Winnall H & W 47 SO8167
Winnall Hants 24 SU4829
Winnersh Berks 25 SU7870
Winnington Ches 79 SJ6474
Winscales Cumb 92 NY0226
Winscombe Avon 21 ST4257
Winsford Ches 72 SJ6566
Winsford Somset 20 SS9034
Winsham Devon 19 SS5038
Winsham Somset 10 ST3706
Winshill Staffs 73 SK2623
Winshwen W Glam 32 SS6896
Winskill Cumb 94 NY5834
Winslade Hants 24 SU6548
Winsley Wilts 22 ST7960
Winslow Bucks 49 SP7727
Winslow Oxon 36 SU2685
Winson Gloucs 36 SP0808
Winsor Hants 12 SU3114
Winster Cumb 87 SD4193
Winster Derbys 74 SK2460
Winston Dur 96 NZ1416
Winston Suffk 54 TM1861
Winston Green Suffk 54 TM1761
Winstone Gloucs 35 SO9509
Winswell Devon 18 SS4913
Winterborne Came Dorset 11 SY7088
Winterborne Clenston Dorset 11 ST8303
Winterborne Herringston Dorset 11 SY6888
Winterborne Houghton Dorset 11 ST8204
Winterborne Kingston Dorset 11 SY8697
Winterborne Monkton Dorset 11 SY6787
Winterborne Stickland Dorset 11 ST8304
Winterborne Tomson Dorset 11 SY8897
Winterborne Whitechurch Dorset 11 ST8300
Winterborne Zelston Dorset 11 SY8997
Winterbourne Avon 35 ST6480
Winterbourne Berks 24 SU4572
Winterbourne Abbas Dorset 10 SY6190
Winterbourne Bassett Wilts 36 SU0974
Winterbourne Dauntsey Wilts 23 SU1734
Winterbourne Earls Wilts 23 SU1734
Winterbourne Gunner Wilts 23 SU1735
Winterbourne Monkton Wilts 36 SU0971
Winterbourne Steepleton Dorset 10 SY6289
Winterbourne Stoke Wilts 23 SU0741
Winterbrook Oxon 37 SU6088
Winterburn N York 88 SD9358
Winteringham Humb 84 SE9221
Winterley Ches 72 SJ7457
Wintersett W York 83 SE3815
Winterslow Wilts 23 SU2332
Winterton Humb 84 SE9218
Winterton-on-Sea Norfk 67 TG4919
Winthorpe Lincs 77 TF5665
Winthorpe Notts 75 SK8156
Winton Cumb 88 NY7810
Winton Dorset 12 SZ0893
Winton E Susx 16 TQ5103
Winton N York 89 SE4196
Wintringham N York 90 SE8873
Winwick Cambs 51 TL1080
Winwick Ches 78 SJ6092
Winwick Nhants 50 SP6273
Wirksworth Derbys 73 SK2854
Wirswall Ches 71 SJ5444
Wisbech Cambs 65 TF4609
Wisbech St Mary Cambs 65 TF4208
Wisborough Green W Susx 14 TQ0525
Wiseman's Bridge Dyfed 31 SN1406
Wiseton Notts 75 SK7189
Wishanger Gloucs 35 SO9109
Wishaw Strath 116 NS7955
Wishaw Warwks 61 SP1794
Wisley Surrey 26 TQ0659
Wispington Lincs 76 TF2071
Wissenden Kent 28 TQ9041
Wissett Suffk 55 TM3679
Wissington Suffk 40 TL9533
Wistanstow Shrops 59 SO4385
Wistanswick Shrops 72 SJ6629
Wistaston Ches 72 SJ6853
Wistaston Green Ches 72 SJ6854
Wisterfield Ches 79 SJ8371
Wiston Dyfed 30 SN0218
Wiston Strath 108 NS9532
Wiston W Susx 15 TQ1512
Wistow Cambs 52 TL2780
Wistow N York 83 SE5935
Wiswell Lancs 81 SD7437
Witby Mills Avon 22 ST6657
Witcham Cambs 53 TL4680
Witchampton Dorset 11 ST9806
Witchford Cambs 53 TL5078
Witcombe Somset 21 ST4721
Witham Essex 40 TL8214
Witham Friary Somset 22 ST7441
Witham on the Hill Lincs 64 TF0516
Withcall Lincs 77 TF2883
Withdean E Susx 15 TQ3007
Witherenden Hill E Susx 16 TQ6426
Witheridge Devon 19 SS8014
Witherley Leics 61 SP3297
Withern Lincs 77 TF4282
Withernsea Humb 85 TA3427
Withernwick Humb 85 TA1940
Withersdale Street Suffk 55 TM2680
Withersfield Essex 53 TL6548
Witherslack Cumb 87 SD4384
Witherslack Hall Cumb 87 SD4385
Withiel Cnwll 4 SW9965
Withiel Florey Somset 20 SS9833
Withielgoose Cnwll 4 SX0065
Withington Ches 79 SJ8169
Withington Gloucs 35 SP0215
Withington Gt Man 79 SJ8492
Withington H & W 46 SO5643
Withington Shrops 59 SJ5713
Withington Staffs 73 SK0335
Withington Green Ches 79 SJ8071
Withleigh Devon 9 SS9012
Withnell Lancs 81 SD6322
Withybed Green H & W 60 SP0172
Withybrook Warwks 50 SP4383
Withycombe Somset 20 ST0141
Withyditch Avon 22 ST6959
Withyham E Susx 16 TQ4935
Withypool Devon 19 SS8435
Witley Surrey 25 SU9439
Witnesham Suffk 54 TM1751
Witney Oxon 36 SP3510
Wittering Cambs 64 TF0502
Wittersham Kent 17 TQ9027
Witton H & W 47 SO8962
Witton Norfk 67 TG3109
Witton Norfk 67 TG3331
Witton Gilbert Dur 96 NZ2345
Witton Green Norfk 67 TG4102
Witton le Wear Dur 96 NZ1431
Witton Park Dur 96 NZ1730
Wiveliscombe Somset 20 ST0827
Wivelrod Hants 24 SU6738
Wivelsfield E Susx 15 TQ3420
Wivelsfield Green E Susx 15 TQ3519
Wivelsfield Station W Susx 15 TQ3219
Wivenhoe Essex 41 TM0321
Wivenhoe Cross Essex 41 TM0423
Wiveton Norfk 66 TG0442
Wix Essex 41 TM1628
Wix Green Essex 41 TM1728
Wixford Warwks 48 SP0854
Wixhill Shrops 59 SJ5528
Wixoe Essex 53 TL7143
Woburn Beds 38 SP9433
Woburn Sands Bucks 38 SP9235
Wokefield Park Berks 24 SU6765
Woking Surrey 25 TQ0058
Wokingham Berks 25 SU8168
Wolborough Devon 7 SX8570
Wold Newton Humb 91 TA0473
Wold Newton Humb 77 TF2496
Woldingham Surrey 27 TQ3755
Wolf Hills Nthumb 94 NY7258
Wolf's Castle Dyfed 30 SM9526
Wolfclyde Strath 108 NT0236
Wolferlow H & W 47 SO6661
Wolferton Norfk 65 TF6528
Wolfhampcote Warwks 50 SP5265
Wolfhill Tays 126 NO1533
Wolfsdale Dyfed 30 SM9321
Wollaston Nhants 51 SP9062
Wollaston Shrops 59 SJ3212
Wollaton Notts 62 SK5239
Wollerton Shrops 59 SJ6130
Wollescote W Mids 60 SO9283
Wolseley Staffs 73 SK0220
Wolsingham Dur 95 NZ0737
Wolstanton Staffs 72 SJ8548
Wolstenholme Gt Man 81 SD8414
Wolston Warwks 50 SP4175
Wolsty Cumb 92 NY1050
Wolvercote Oxon 37 SP4910
Wolverhampton W Mids 60 SO9198
Wolverley H & W 60 SO8379
Wolverley Shrops 59 SJ4731
Wolverton Bucks 38 SP8141
Wolverton Hants 24 SU5558
Wolverton Kent 29 TR2642
Wolverton Warwks 48 SP2062
Wolverton Wilts 22 ST7831
Wolverton Common Hants 24 SU5659
Wolvesnewton Gwent 34 ST4599
Wolvey Warwks 50 SP4387
Wolvey Heath Warwks 50 SP4388
Wolviston Cleve 97 NZ4525
Wombleton N York 90 SE6683
Wombourne Staffs 60 SO8793
Wombwell S York 83 SE4002
Womenswold Kent 29 TR2250
Womersley N York 83 SE5319
Wonastow Gwent 34 SO4810
Wonersh Surrey 14 TQ0145
Wonford Devon 9 SX9491
Wonson Devon 8 SX6789
Wonston Hants 24 SU4739
Wooburn Bucks 26 SU9087
Wooburn Green Bucks 26 SU9188
Wooburn Moor Bucks 26 SU9189
Wood Bevington Warwks 48 SP0554
Wood Burcot Nhants 49 SP6946
Wood Dalling Norfk 66 TG0827
Wood Eaton Staffs 72 SJ8417
Wood End Beds 38 TL0046
Wood End Beds 51 TL0866
Wood End Cambs 52 TL3675
Wood End Gt Lon 26 TQ1385
Wood End Herts 39 TL3225
Wood End W Mids 60 SJ9400
Wood End Warwks 61 SP1171
Wood End Warwks 61 SP2498
Wood End Warwks 61 SP2987
Wood Enderby Lincs 77 TF2764
Wood Green Gt Lon 27 TQ3090
Wood Hayes W Mids 60 SJ9402
Wood Lane Shrops 59 SJ4132
Wood Lane Staffs 72 SJ8149
Wood Norton Norfk 66 TG0127
Wood Row W York 83 SE3827
Wood Street Norfk 67 TG3722
Wood Street Surrey 25 SU9550
Wood Top Lancs 81 SD5643
Wood Walton Cambs 52 TL2180
Wood's Corner E Susx 16 TQ6619
Wood's Green E Susx 16 TQ6333
Woodale N York 88 SE0279
Woodall S York 75 SK4880
Woodbastwick Norfk 67 TG3315
Woodbeck Notts 75 SK7777
Woodborough Notts 63 SK6347
Woodborough Wilts 23 SU1159
Woodbridge Dorset 22 ST8518
Woodbridge Suffk 55 TM2649
Woodbury Devon 9 SY0087
Woodbury Salterton Devon 9 SY0189
Woodchester Gloucs 35 SO8302
Woodchurch Kent 17 TQ9434
Woodchurch Mersyd 78 SJ2786
Woodcombe Somset 20 SS9546
Woodcote Oxon 37 SU6482
Woodcote Shrops 72 SJ7615
Woodcote Green H & W 60 SO9172
Woodcott Hants 24 SU4354
Woodcroft Gloucs 34 ST5495
Woodcutts Dorset 11 ST9717
Woodditton Cambs 53 TL6559
Woodeaton Oxon 37 SP5312
Woodend Highld 130 NM7861
Woodend Loth 116 NS9269
Woodend Nhants 49 SP6149
Woodend Staffs 73 SK1726
Woodend W Susx 14 SU8108
Woodend Green Essex 39 TL5528
Woodfalls Wilts 12 SU1920
Woodford Devon 7 SX7950
Woodford Gloucs 35 ST6995
Woodford Gt Man 79 SJ8882
Woodford Nhants 51 SP9676
Woodford Bridge Gt Lon 27 TQ4291
Woodford Halse Nhants 49 SP5452
Woodford Wells Gt Lon 27 TQ4092
Woodgate Devon 9 ST1015
Woodgate H & W 47 SO9666
Woodgate Norfk 66 TF8915
Woodgate Norfk 66 TG0215
Woodgate W Mids 60 SO9982
Woodgate W Susx 14 SU9304
Woodgreen Hants 12 SU1717
Woodgreen Oxon 36 SP3610
Woodhall N York 88 SD9790
Woodhall Hill W York 82 SE2035
Woodhall Spa Lincs 76 TF1963
Woodham Bucks 37 SP7018
Woodham Dur 96 NZ2826
Woodham Lincs 76 TF2267
Woodham Ferrers Essex 40 TQ7999
Woodham Mortimer Essex 40 TL8104
Woodham Walter Essex 40 TL8007
Woodhaven Fife 126 NO4126
Woodhead Gramp 142 NJ7838
Woodhill Somset 21 ST3527
Woodhorn Nthumb 103 NZ2988
Woodhorn Demesne Nthumb 103 NZ3088
Woodhouse Leics 62 SK5314
Woodhouse S York 74 SK4284
Woodhouse W York 82 SE2935
Woodhouse W York 83 SE3821
Woodhouse Eaves Leics 62 SK5214
Woodhouse Green Staffs 72 SJ9162
Woodhouse Mill S York 75 SK4385
Woodhouselee Loth 117 NT2364
Woodhouselees D & G 101 NY3975
Woodhouses Cumb 93 NY3252
Woodhouses Gt Man 79 SD9100
Woodhouses Staffs 61 SK0709
Woodhouses Staffs 73 SK1518
Woodhuish Devon 7 SX9152
Woodhurst Cambs 52 TL3176
Woodingdean E Susx 15 TQ3505
Woodkirk W York 82 SE2725
Woodland Devon 7 SX7968
Woodland Dur 95 NZ0726
Woodland Gramp 143 NJ8723
Woodland Kent 29 TR1441
Woodland Strath 106 NX1795
Woodland Head Devon 8 SX7796
Woodland Street Somset 21 ST5337
Woodland View S York 74 SK3188
Woodlands Dorset 12 SU0509
Woodlands Gramp 135 NO7895
Woodlands Hants 12 SU3211
Woodlands Kent 27 TQ5660
Woodlands N York 83 SE3254
Woodlands S York 83 SE5308
Woodlands Park Berks 26 SU8678
Woodlands St Mary Berks 36 SU3375
Woodleigh Devon 7 SX7349
Woodlesford W York 83 SE3629
Woodley Berks 25 SU7773
Woodley Gt Man 79 SJ9392
Woodley Green Berks 26 SU8480
Woodmancote Gloucs 47 SO9727
Woodmancote Gloucs 35 SP0008
Woodmancote Gloucs 35 ST7597
Woodmancote H & W 47 SO9142
Woodmancote W Susx 14 SU7707
Woodmancote W Susx 15 TQ2314
Woodmancott Hants 24 SU5642
Woodmansey Humb 84 TA0538
Woodmansgreen W Susx 14 SU8627
Woodmansterne Surrey 27 TQ2759
Woodmarsh Wilts 22 ST8555
Woodmill Staffs 73 SK1320
Woodminton Wilts 22 SU0022
Woodnesborough Kent 29 TR3157
Woodnewton Nhants 51 TL0394
Woodnook Notts 75 SK4752
Woodplumpton Lancs 80 SD4934
Woodrising Norfk 66 TF9803
Woodrow H & W 60 SO8974
Woodseaves Shrops 72 SJ6831
Woodseaves Staffs 72 SJ7925
Woodsend Wilts 36 SU2176
Woodsetts S York 75 SK5483
Woodsford Dorset 11 SY7590
Woodside Berks 25 SU9371
Woodside Cumb 92 NY0434
Woodside Essex 39 TL4704
Woodside Fife 127 NO4207
Woodside Gt Lon 27 TQ3467
Woodside Hants 12 SZ3294
Woodside Herts 39 TL2406
Woodside Tays 126 NO2037
Woodside Green Kent 28 TQ9053
Woodstock Dyfed 30 SN0325
Woodstock Oxon 37 SP4416
Woodston Cambs 64 TL1897
Woodthorpe Derbys 75 SK4574
Woodthorpe Leics 62 SK5417
Woodthorpe Lincs 77 TF4380
Woodton Norfk 67 TM2994
Woodtown Devon 18 SS4123
Woodvale Mersyd 78 SD3010
Woodville Derbys 62 SK3118
Woodwall Green Staffs 72 SJ7831
Woody Bay Devon 19 SS6748
Woodyates Dorset 12 SU0219
Woofferton Shrops 46 SO5268
Wookey Somset 21 ST5145
Wookey Hole Somset 21 ST5347
Wool Dorset 11 SY8486
Woolacombe Devon 18 SS4643
Woolage Green Kent 29 TR2349
Woolaston Gloucs 34 ST5899
Woolaston Common Gloucs 34 SO5801
Woolavington Somset 21 ST3441
Woolbeding W Susx 14 SU8722
Woolcotts Somset 20 SS9631
Wooldale W York 82 SE1508
Wooler Nthumb 111 NT9927
Wooley Bridge Derbys 79 SK0194
Woolfardisworthy Devon 18 SS3321
Woolfardisworthy Devon 19 SS8208
Woolfold Gt Man 81 SD7811
Woolfords Strath 117 NT0056
Woolhampton Berks 24 SU5766
Woolhanger Devon 19 SS6945
Woolhope H & W 46 SO6135
Woolland Dorset 11 ST7707
Woollard Avon 21 ST6364
Woollensbrook Herts 39 TL3609
Woolley Avon 22 ST7468
Woolley Cambs 52 TL1574
Woolley Cnwll 18 SS2516
Woolley Derbys 74 SK3760
Woolley W York 83 SE3212
Woolmer Green Herts 39 TL2518
Woolmere Green H & W 47 SO9663
Woolmerston Somset 20 ST2833
Woolminstone Somset 10 ST4108
Woolpack Kent 28 TQ8537
Woolpit Suffk 54 TL9762
Woolpit Green Suffk 54 TL9761
Woolscott Warwks 50 SP5068
Woolsgrove Devon 8 SS7902
Woolsington T & W 103 NZ1870
Woolstaston Shrops 59 SO4598
Woolsthorpe Lincs 63 SK8333
Woolsthorpe Lincs 63 SK9224
Woolston Ches 79 SJ6489
Woolston Devon 7 SX7141
Woolston Devon 7 SX7150
Woolston Hants 13 SU4310
Woolston Shrops 59 SJ3224
Woolston Shrops 59 SO4287
Woolston Somset 20 ST0939
Woolston Somset 21 ST6527
Woolston Green Devon 7 SX7766
Woolstone Bucks 38 SP8738
Woolstone Gloucs 47 SO9630
Woolstone Oxon 36 SU2987
Woolton Mersyd 78 SJ4286
Woolton Hill Hants 24 SU4361
Woolverstone Suffk 54 TM1738
Woolverton Somset 22 ST7953
Woolwich Gt Lon 27 TQ4478
Woonton H & W 46 SO3552
Wooperton Nthumb 111 NU0420
Woore Shrops 72 SJ7342
Wootten Breadmead Beds 38 TL0243
Wootten Green Suffk 55 TM2372
Wootton Beds 38 TL0044
Wootton H & W 46 SO3252
Wootton Hants 12 SZ2498
Wootton Humb 85 TA0815
Wootton IOW 13 SZ5392
Wootton Kent 29 TR2246
Wootton Nhants 49 SP7656
Wootton Oxon 37 SP4419
Wootton Oxon 37 SP4701
Wootton Shrops 59 SJ3327
Wootton Staffs 72 SJ8227
Wootton Staffs 73 SK1044
Wootton Bassett Wilts 36 SU0682
Wootton Bridge IOW 13 SZ5492
Wootton Common IOW 13 SZ5391
Wootton Courtenay Somset 20 SS9343
Wootton Fitzpaine Dorset 10 SY3695
Wootton Rivers Wilts 23 SU1962
Wootton St Lawrence Hants 24 SU5953
Wootton Wawen Warwks 48 SP1563
Worbarrow Dorset 11 SY8779
Worcester H & W 47 SO8554
Worcester Park Gt Lon 26 TQ2165
Wordsley W Mids 60 SO8987
Worfield Shrops 60 SO7595
Worgret Dorset 11 SY9087
Workington Cumb 92 NY0028
Worksop Notts 75 SK5879
Worlaby Humb 84 TA0113
Worlaby Lincs 77 TF3476
World's End Berks 37 SU4877
Worlds End Bucks 38 SP8509
Worlds End Hants 13 SU6311
Worlds End W Susx 15 TQ3220
Worle Avon 21 ST3562
Worleston Ches 72 SJ6556
Worlingham Suffk 55 TM4489
Worlington Devon 19 SS7713
Worlington Suffk 53 TL6973
Worlingworth Suffk 55 TM2368
Wormald Green N York 89 SE3065
Wormbridge H & W 46 SO4230
Wormegay Norfk 65 TF6611
Wormelow Tump H & W 46 SO4930
Wormhill Derbys 74 SK1274
Wormhill H & W 46 SO4239
Wormingford Essex 40 TL9332
Worminghall Bucks 37 SP6308
Wormington Gloucs 48 SP0336
Worminster Somset 21 ST5743
Wormiston Border 117 NT2345
Wormit Tays 126 NO4026
Wormleighton Warwks 49 SP4553
Wormley Herts 39 TL3605
Wormley Surrey 25 SU9438
Wormley Hill S York 83 SE6616
Wormleybury Herts 39 TL3506
Wormshill Kent 28 TQ8857
Wormsley H & W 46 SO4247
Worplesdon Surrey 25 SU9753
Worrall S York 74 SK3092
Worrall Hill Gloucs 34 SO6014
Worsbrough S York 83 SE3602
Worsbrough Bridge S York 83 SE3503
Worsbrough Dale S York 83 SE3604
Worsley Gt Man 79 SD7500
Worsley Mesnes Gt Man 78 SD5703
Worstead Norfk 67 TG3025
Worsthorne Lancs 81 SD8732
Worston Devon 6 SX5953
Worston Lancs 81 SD7742
Worth Kent 29 TR3355
Worth Somset 21 ST5144
Worth W Susx 15 TQ3036
Worth Abbey Surrey 15 TQ3134
Worth Matravers Dorset 11 SY9777
Wortham Suffk 54 TM0877
Worthen Shrops 59 SJ3204
Worthenbury Clwyd 71 SJ4146
Worthing Norfk 66 TF9919
Worthing W Susx 15 TQ1403
Worthington Leics 62 SK4020
Worthybrook Gwent 34 SO4711
Worting Hants 24 SU5952
Wortley S York 74 SK3099
Wortley W York 82 SE2732
Worton N York 88 SD9589
Worton Wilts 22 ST9757
Wortwell Norfk 55 TM2784
Wotherton Shrops 58 SJ2800
Wothorpe Cambs 64 TF0205
Wotter Devon 6 SX5661
Wotton Surrey 14 TQ1247
Wotton Underwood Bucks 37 SP6815
Wotton-under-Edge Gloucs 35 ST7593
Woughton on the Green Bucks 38 SP8737
Wouldham Kent 28 TQ7164
Woundale Shrops 60 SO7793
Wrabness Essex 41 TM1731
Wrafton Devon 18 SS4935
Wragby Lincs 76 TF1378
Wragby W York 83 SE4116
Wramplingham Norfk 66 TG1106
Wrangaton Devon 7 SX6758
Wrangbrook W York 83 SE4913
Wrangle Lincs 77 TF4250
Wrangle Common Lincs 77 TF4253
Wrangle Lowgate Lincs 77 TF4451
Wrangway Somset 20 ST1218
Wrantage Somset 20 ST3022
Wrawby Humb 84 TA0108
Wraxall Avon 34 ST4971
Wraxall Somset 21 ST6036
Wray Lancs 87 SD6067
Wray Castle Cumb 87 NY3700
Wraysbury Berks 25 TQ0074
Wrayton Lancs 87 SD6172
Wrea Green Lancs 80 SD3931
Wreaks End Cumb 86 SD2286
Wreay Cumb 93 NY4348
Wreay Cumb 93 NY4423
Wrecclesham Surrey 25 SU8244
Wrekenton T & W 96 NZ2759
Wrelton N York 90 SE7686
Wrenbury Ches 71 SJ5947
Wrench Green N York 91 SE9689
Wreningham Norfk 66 TM1698
Wrentham Suffk 55 TM4982
Wrenthorpe W York 82 SE3122
Wrentnall Shrops 59 SJ4203
Wressle Humb 84 SE7131
Wressle Humb 84 SE9709
Wrestlingworth Beds 52 TL2547
Wretton Norfk 65 TF6900
Wrexham Clwyd 71 SJ3350
Wribbenhall H & W 60 SO7975
Wrickton Shrops 59 SO6486
Wright's Green Essex 39 TL5017
Wrightington Bar Lancs 80 SD5313
Wrinehill Staffs 72 SJ7547
Wrington Avon 21 ST4762
Wringworthy Cnwll 5 SX2658
Writhlington Somset 22 ST6954
Writtle Essex 40 TL6706
Wrockwardine Shrops 59 SJ6212
Wroot Humb 84 SE7103
Wrose W York 82 SE1636
Wrotham Kent 27 TQ6158
Wrotham Heath Kent 27 TQ6357
Wrottesley Staffs 60 SJ8200
Wroughton Wilts 36 SU1480
Wroxall IOW 13 SZ5579
Wroxall Warwks 61 SP2271
Wroxeter Shrops 59 SJ5608
Wroxham Norfk 67 TG3017
Wroxton Oxon 49 SP4141
Wyaston Derbys 73 SK1842
Wyatt's Green Essex 40 TQ5999
Wyberton Lincs 64 TF3240
Wyboston Beds 52 TL1656
Wybunbury Ches 72 SJ6949
Wych Dorset 10 SY4791
Wych Cross E Susx 15 TQ4131
Wychbold H & W 47 SO9266
Wychnor Staffs 73 SK1715
Wyck Hants 24 SU7539
Wycliffe Dur 95 NZ1114
Wycoller Lancs 81 SD9339
Wycomb Leics 63 SK7724
Wycombe Marsh Bucks 26 SU8892
Wyddial Herts 39 TL3731
Wye Kent 28 TR0546
Wyesham Gwent 34 SO5211
Wyfordby Leics 63 SK7918
Wyke Devon 9 SX8799
Wyke Devon 10 SY2996
Wyke Dorset 22 ST7926
Wyke Shrops 59 SJ6402
Wyke Surrey 25 SU9251
Wyke W York 82 SE1526
Wyke Champflower Somset 22 ST6634
Wyke Regis Dorset 11 SY6677
Wykeham N York 90 SE8175
Wykeham N York 91 SE9683
Wyken Shrops 60 SO7695
Wyken W Mids 61 SP3780
Wykey Shrops 59 SJ3824
Wykin Leics 61 SP4095
Wylam Nthumb 103 NZ1164
Wylde Green W Mids 61 SP1294
Wylye Wilts 22 SU0037
Wymeswold Leics 62 SK6023
Wymington Beds 51 SP9564
Wymondham Leics 63 SK8418
Wymondham Norfk 66 TG1001
Wyndham M Glam 33 SS9392
Wynds Point H & W 47 SO7640
Wynford Eagle Dorset 10 SY5896
Wyre Piddle H & W 47 SO9647
Wysall Notts 62 SK6027
Wyson H & W 46 SO5267
Wythall H & W 61 SP0774
Wytham Oxon 37 SP4708
Wythburn Cumb 93 NY3214
Wythenshawe Gt Man 79 SJ8386
Wythop Mill Cumb 93 NY1729
Wyton Cambs 52 TL2772
Wyton Humb 85 TA1733
Wyverstone Suffk 54 TM0468
Wyverstone Street Suffk 54 TM0367
Wyville Lincs 63 SK8729

Y

Y Ferwig Dyfed 42 SN1849
Y Gyffylliog Clwyd 70 SJ0557
Y Maerdy Clwyd 70 SJ0144
Y Nant Clwyd 70 SJ2850
Y Rhiw Gwynd 56 SH2227
Yaddlethorpe Humb 84 SE8806
Yafford IOW 13 SZ4481
Yafforth N York 89 SE3494
Yalberton Devon 7 SX8658
Yalding Kent 28 TQ6950
Yalverton Devon 6 SX5267
Yanwath Cumb 94 NY5127
Yanworth Gloucs 36 SP0713
Yapham Humb 84 SE7851
Yapton W Susx 14 SU9703
Yarborough Avon 21 ST3857
Yarbridge IOW 13 SZ6086
Yarburgh Lincs 77 TF3592
Yarcombe Devon 9 ST2408
Yard Devon 19 SS7721
Yardley W Mids 61 SP1386
Yardley Gobion Nhants 49 SP7644
Yardley Hastings Nhants 51 SP8657
Yardley Wood W Mids 61 SP1079
Yardro Powys 45 SO2258
Yarford Somset 20 ST2029
Yarkhill H & W 46 SO6042
Yarlet Staffs 72 SJ9129
Yarley Somset 21 ST5044
Yarlington Somset 21 ST6529
Yarlsber N York 87 SD7072
Yarm Cleve 89 NZ4112
Yarmouth IOW 12 SZ3589
Yarnacott Devon 19 SS6230
Yarnbrook Wilts 22 ST8654
Yarnfield Staffs 72 SJ8632
Yarnscombe Devon 19 SS5623
Yarnton Oxon 37 SP4711
Yarpole H & W 46 SO4764
Yarrow Border 109 NT3528
Yarrow Somset 21 ST3746
Yarrow Feus Border 109 NT3325
Yarrowford Border 109 NT4030
Yarsop H & W 46 SO4047
Yarwell Nhants 51 TL0697
Yate Avon 35 ST7081
Yateley Hants 25 SU8161
Yatesbury Wilts 36 SU0671
Yattendon Berks 24 SU5574
Yatton Avon 21 ST4365
Yatton H & W 46 SO4366
Yatton H & W 47 SO6330
Yatton Keynell Wilts 35 ST8676
Yaverland IOW 13 SZ6185
Yawl Devon 10 SY3194
Yawthorpe Lincs 76 SK8992
Yaxham Norfk 66 TG0010
Yaxley Cambs 64 TL1891
Yaxley Suffk 54 TM1273
Yazor H & W 46 SO4046
Yeading Gt Lon 26 TQ1182
Yeadon W York 82 SE2041
Yealand Conyers Lancs 87 SD5074
Yealand Redmayne Lancs 87 SD4975
Yealand Storrs Lancs 87 SD5075
Yealmpton Devon 6 SX5851
Yearby Cleve 97 NZ5921
Yearngill Cumb 92 NY1443
Yearsley N York 90 SE5874
Yeaton Shrops 59 SJ4319
Yeaveley Derbys 73 SK1840
Yeavering Nthumb 110 NT9330
Yedingham N York 91 SE8979
Yelford Oxon 36 SP3604
Yelland Devon 18 SS4931
Yelling Cambs 52 TL2662
Yelvertoft Nhants 50 SP5975
Yelverton Norfk 67 TG2902
Yenston Somset 22 ST7121
Yeo Mill Somset 19 SS8426
Yeo Vale Devon 18 SS4223
Yeoford Devon 8 SX7899
Yeolmbridge Cnwll 5 SX3187
Yeovil Somset 10 ST5515
Yeovil Marsh Somset 10 ST5418
Yeovilton Somset 21 ST5423
Yerbeston Dyfed 30 SN0609
Yesnaby Ork 155 HY2215
Yetlington Nthumb 111 NU0209
Yetminster Dorset 10 ST5910
Yetson Devon 7 SX8056
Yettington Devon 9 SY0585
Yetts o'Muckhart Cent 117 NO0001
Yew Green Warwks 48 SP2367
Yews Green W York 82 SE0931
Yielden Beds 51 TL0167
Yieldingtree H & W 60 SO8977
Yieldshields Strath 116 NS8750
Yiewsley Gt Lon 26 TQ0680
Ynysboeth M Glam 33 ST0695
Ynysddu Gwent 33 ST1792
Ynysforgan W Glam 32 SS6799
Ynyshir M Glam 33 ST0292
Ynyslas Dyfed 43 SN6193
Ynysmaerdy M Glam 33 ST0383
Ynysmeudwy W Glam 32 SN7305
Ynyswen M Glam 33 SS9597
Ynyswen Powys 33 SN8313
Ynysybwl M Glam 33 ST0594
Ynysymaengwyn Gwynd 57 SH5902
Yockenthwaite N York 88 SD9078
Yockleton Shrops 59 SJ3910
Yokefleet Humb 84 SE8124
Yoker Strath 115 NS5069
Yonder Bognie Gramp 142 NJ6046
York Lancs 81 SD7133
York N York 83 SE6051
York Town Hants 25 SU8660
Yorkletts Kent 29 TR0963
Yorkley Gloucs 35 SO6307
Yorton Heath Shrops 59 SJ5022
Youlgreave Derbys 74 SK2064
Youlthorpe Humb 84 SE7655
Youlton N York 90 SE4963
Young's End Essex 40 TL7319
Youngsbury Herts 39 TL3618
Yoxall Staffs 73 SK1418
Yoxford Suffk 55 TM3969
Yoxford Little Street Suffk 55 TM3869
Ysbyty Cynfyn Dyfed 43 SN7578
Ysbyty Ifan Gwynd 69 SH8448
Ysbyty Ystwyth Dyfed 43 SN7371
Ysceifiog Clwyd 70 SJ1571
Ysgubor-y-Coed Dyfed 43 SN6895
Ystalyfera W Glam 32 SN7608
Ystrad M Glam 33 SS9895
Ystrad Aeron Dyfed 44 SN5256
Ystrad Meurig Dyfed 43 SN7067
Ystrad Mynach M Glam 33 ST1494
Ystrad-ffyn Dyfed 44 SN7846
Ystradfellte Powys 33 SN9313
Ystradgynlais Powys 32 SN7910
Ystradowen S Glam 33 ST0077
Ystumtuen Dyfed 43 SN7378
Ythanwells Gramp 142 NJ6338
Ythsie Gramp 143 NJ8830

Z

Zeal Monachorum Devon 8 SS7204
Zeals Wilts 22 ST7831
Zelah Cnwll 3 SW8151
Zennor Cnwll 2 SW4538
Zoar Cnwll 3 SW7619
Zouch Notts 62 SK5023

Restricted motorway junctions

M1 LONDON - LEEDS

Northbound	Junction	Southbound
No exit. Access only from northbound lane of A1	2	No access. Only exit is to southbound lane of A1
No exit . Access only from northbound lane of A41	4	No access. Only exit is to southbound lane of A41
No exit . Access only from M25	6A	No access. Exit only to M25
No exit . Access only from M1	7	No access. Exit only to M10
No access. Exit only to M45	17	No exit. Access only from M45
No access. Exit only to M6	19	No exit. Access only from M6
No access. Exit only to A616	35A	No exit. Access only from A616
No exit. Access only	44	No access. Exit only
No exit. Access only	45	No access. Exit only
No restriction	46	No restriction
Full interchange between M1, M621 & A653 using gyratory system	47	Access only by slip road from A653 Dewsbury Road gyratory

M2 ROCHESTER - FAVERSHAM

Westbound	Junction	Eastbound
Only exit is to A2 westbound	1	Access only from A2 eastbound

M3 SUNBURY - SOUTHAMPTON

South-westbound	Junction	North-eastbound
No access. Exit only to A303	8	No exit. Access only from A303
Only exit is to A33 southbound	10	Access is from A33 northbound
No access from A335 to eastbound lane of M27	13	No restriction
The only exit is to M27 & A33	14	The only access is from M27 & A33

M4 LONDON - SOUTH WALES

Westbound	Junction	Eastbound
Access only from A4 westbound	1	Only exit is to A4 eastbound
Access/exit available to/from westbound lane of A4 only	2	Access/exit available to/from eastbound lane of A4 only
No access. Exit only to A48(M)	29	No access. Access only from A48(M)
No access from A48	38	No restriction
No exit. Access only from A48	39	No exit or access
No exit. Access only from A48	41	No access. Exit only to A48
No access. Exit only from A48	46	No exit. Access only from A48

M5 BIRMINGHAM - EXETER

Southbound	Junction	Northbound
No access. Exit only to A4019	10	No exit. Access only from A4019
No exit. Access only from A38	12	No access. Exit only to A38
No exit. The only access is from the westbound lane of A30	29	No access. The only exit is to eastbound lane of A30

M6 RUGBY - CARLISLE

Northbound	Junction	Southbound
Access is from M1 northbound	M1	Only exit is to M1 southbound
No exit to northbound lane of M42. No access from M42 southbound	4	No exit to M42. No access from southbound lane of M42
No exit. Access only from southbound spur of M42	4A	No access. Exit only to M42
No access. Exit only to A452	5	No exit. Access only from A452
No exit. Access only to M54	10A	No access. Exit only from M54
No direct access to eastbound lane of M56 (use A50 junction)	20	No direct access from westbound lane of M56 (use A50 junction)
No access. Exit only from A58	24	No exit. Access only to A58
No access. Exit only to A49	25	No access. Exit only from A49
No exit. Access only from M61	30	No access. Exit only to M61

M8 EDINBURGH-GLASGOW-BISHOPTON

Westbound	Junction	Eastbound
No access from southbound lane of M73 or from A8 & A89 eastbound	8	No exit to northbound lane of M73 or to A8 & A89 westbound
No exit. Access only	9	No access. Exit only
The only access is from M80	13	The only exit is to M80
No exit. Access only	14	No access. Exit only
No access. Exit only to A804	16	No exit. Access only from A804
The only exit is to A82	17	The only access is from A82
No access. Exit only to Charing Cross	18	No access. Exit only to Charing Cross
No access from Argyle Street A814	19	No exit to Argyle Street A814
No exit. Access only	20	No access. Exit only
No exit. Access only	21	No access. Exit only
No exit. Access only to M77	22	No access. Exit only from M77
No access. Exit only to B768	23	No exit. Access only from B768
The only exit/access is to/from Clyde Tunnel A739	25	The only exit/access is to/from Clyde Tunnel A739

M9 EDINBURGH - DUNBLANE

North-westbound	Junction	South-eastbound
No access. Exit only to A8000 spur	1	No exit. Access only from A8000
No exit. Access only from B8046	2	No access. Exit only to B8046
No access. Exit only to A803	3	No exit. Access only from A803
No exit. Access from A904 & A905	6	No access. Exit only to A905
No access. Exit only to M876	8	No exit. Access only from M876

M10 ST ALBANS BYPASS

Northbound	Junction	Southbound
The only exit is to M1 northbound	M1	Only access is from M1 s'thbound

M11 LONDON - CAMBRIDGE

Northbound	Junction	Southbound
The only access is from A406	4	The only exit is to A406
No exit. Access only to A1168	5	No access. Exit only from A1168
No exit. Access only to A11 spur	9	No access. Exit only from M11 spur
No exit. Access only to A1303	13	No access. Exit only from A1303
No exit to A1307 or A45 westbound.	14	No entry from A1307 or A45
No access from A45 eastbound		

M20 SWANLEY - FOLKESTONE

South-eastbound	Junction	North-westbound
No exit. Access only to A20	2	No exit. Access from A20 & A227
No exit. Access only from M26	3	No access. Exit only to M26

M23 HOOLEY - CRAWLEY

Northbound	Junction	Southbound
The only exit is to A23 northbound	7	Only access is from A23 s'bound

M25 LONDON ORBITAL MOTORWAY

Clockwise	Junction	Anti-clockwise
Exit only to A225 & A296. No access (use slip road via Jct 2)	1B	Access only from A225 & A296. No exit (use slip road via Junction 2)
No exit to M26	5	No access from M26
No restriction	9 (south)	No exit or access
No access	9 (north)	No restriction
No access. Exit only to A41 spur	19	No exit. Access only from A41 spur

	21	
The only exit is to northbound lane of M1. The only access is from southbound lane of M1	21	The only exit is to northbound lane of M1. The only access is from southbound lane of M1
No link from M1 to A405	21A	No link from A405 to M1
Access only from A13 & A1306. No exit (use slip road via Junction 30)	31	Exit only to A13 & A1306. No access (use slip road via Jct 30)

M26 SEVENOAKS - WROTHAM

Eastbound	Junction	Westbound
The only access is from the anti-clockwise (eastbound) lane of M25	M25 Jct 5	The only exit is to the clockwise (westbound) lane of M25.
The only exit is to the south-eastbound lane of M20	M20 Jct 3	The only access is from the north-westbound lane of M20

M27 CADNAM - PORTSMOUTH

Eastbound	Junction	Westbound
The only exit is to northbound lane of M3. No access from northbound lane of A33	4	The only exit is to northbound lane of M3. No access from A335 or northbound lane of A33
No exit. Access only from A32	10	No access. Exit only to A32
No access from A27 spur	12 (west)	No exit to A27 spur
The only exit is to A27 eastbound	12 (east)	Access is from A27 Westbound

M40 LONDON - BIRMINGHAM

North-westbound	Junction	South-eastbound
No access. Exit only to A40	3	No exit. Access only from A40
No access. Exit only to A329	7	No exit. Access only from A329
No access. Exit only to A452	13	No exit. Access only from A452
No exit. Access only from A452	14	No access. Exit only to A452
No exit. Access only from A3400	16	No access. Exit only to A3400

M42 BROMSGROVE - MEASHAM

North-eastbound	Junction	South-westbound
No exit. Access only from A38	1	No access. Exit only to A38
No access. The only exit is to M6	7/7A	No exit. The only access is from northbound lane of M6
No exit. Access only from southbound lane of M6	8	Exit only to northbound lane of M6. Access is from M6 southbound

M45 DUNCHURCH SPUR

Eastbound	Junction	Westbound
The only exit is to M1 southbound	M1	Access is from M1 northbound
No access from A45 east of Dunchurch. Exit only	With A45	No exit to A45 east of Dunchurch. Access only

M53 WALLASEY - CHESTER

Southbound	Junction	Northbound
The only exit is to eastbound lane of M56. The only access is from westbound lane of M56	11	The only exit is to eastbound lane off M56. The only access is from westbound lane of M56

M54 TELFORD MOTORWAY

Westbound	Junction	Eastbound
Access is from M6 northbound	M6	The only exit is to M6 southbound

M56 NORTH CHESHIRE MOTORWAY

Westbound	Junction	Eastbound
The only access is from the westbound lane of M63 or southbound lane of A34	1	The only exit is to the eastbound lane of M63 or northbound lane of A34
No access. Exit only to A560	2	No exit. Access only from A560
No exit. Access only from A5103	3	No access. Exit only to A5103
No access. Exit only	4	No exit. Access only
Access via slip road from A556	7	No restriction
No exit to southbound lane of M6 (possible via A50 interchange)	9	No access from northbound lane of M6 (possible via A50 interchange)
No access. Exit only to M53	15	No exit. Access only from M53

M57 LIVERPOOL OUTER RING ROAD

Northbound	Junction	Southbound
No exit. Access only from A526	3	No access. Exit only to A526
No exit (use Jct 4). Access only from westbound lane of A580	5	No access (use Jct 4). Exit only to eastbound lane of A580

M58 LIVERPOOL - WIGAN

Eastbound	Junction	Westbound
No exit. Access only	1	No access. Exit only

M61 GREATER MANCHESTER - PRESTON

North-westbound	Junction	South-eastbound
The only access is from M62	1	The only exit is to M62
No exit. The only access is via spur from westbound lane of A580	2	The only exit is via spur to eastbound lane of A580
No access. Exit only to A666 spur	3	No restriction
No access. Exit only to A6 spur	9	No exit. Access only from A6 spur
The only exit is to M6 northbound	M6	Access only from M6 southbound

M62 LIVERPOOL - HULL

Eastbound	Junction	Westbound
The only access is from M61 & spur from eastbound lane of A580. The only exit is to M61	14	The only access is from M61. The only exit is to M61 and spur to westbound lane of A580
No exit. Access only from A666	15	No access. Exit only to A666
No access. Exit only to A640	20	No exit. Access only from A640

M63 MANCHESTER OUTER RING ROAD

Southeast/Eastbound	Junction	West/North-westbound
No exit (use slip road via Jct 6). Access only from A56	7	No access (use slip road via Jct 6). Exit only to A56
No access from or exit to northbound lane of A5103	9	No access from or exit to southbound lane of A5103
No exit to M56 or northbound lane of A34. No access from southbound lane of A34	10	No exit to northbound lane of A34. No access from M56 or southbound lane of A34
No access. Exit only to A560 spur	11	No exit. Access only from A560
No access. Exit only to A560	13	No exit. Access only from A560
No exit or access	14	No restriction
No restriction	15	No access from A560 & A6017

M65 CALDER VALLEY MOTORWAY

North-eastbound	Junction	South-westbound
No exit. Access only to A679	9	No access. Exit only from A679
No access. Exit only	11	No exit. Access only

M66 GREATER MANCHESTER

Southbound	Junction	Northbound
Access is from A56 southbound	With A56	Only exit is to A56 northbound
No exit. Access only from A56	1	No access. Exit only to A56

M67 HYDE BYPASS

Eastbound	Junction	Westbound
No exit. Access only from A6017	1	No access. Exit only from A6017
No exit. Access only from A57	2	No access. Exit only to A57

M69 COVENTRY - LEICESTER

Northbound	Junction	Southbound
No exit. Access only from A5070	2	No access. Exit only to A5070

M73 HAMILTON BYPASS - MOLLINSBURN

Northbound	Junction	Southbound
No access to or from A89. No access from eastbound lane of M8	2	No access to or from A89. No exit to westbound lane of M8
The only exit is to north-eastbound lane of A80	3	The only access is from the south-westbound lane of A80

M74 GLASGOW - GRETNA

Southbound	Junction	Northbound
The only access is from A74	A74/A721	Only exit is to A74 westbound
No access. Exit only to A72	7	No exit. Access only from A72
No exit. Access only to B7078	9	No exit or access
No exit. Access only from B7078	10	No restriction
No access. Exit only to B7078	11	No exit. Access only from B7078
No exit. Access only from A70	12	No access. Exit only to A70

M77 DUMBRECK SPUR, GLASGOW

Southbound	Junction	Northbound
Access is from M8 westbound	M8:	Only exit is to M8 eastbound

M80 BONNYBRIDGE - STIRLING

Northbound	Junction	Southbound
No access. Exit only to M876	5	No exit. Access only from M876

M80 STEPPS BYPASS

North-eastbound	Junction	South-westbound
No access. Exit only	Hornshill	No exit. Access only

M85 PERTH EASTERN BYPASS

Southbound	Junction	Northbound
No exit to A912	M90	No access from A912

M90 FORTH ROAD BRIDGE - PERTH

Northbound	Junction	Southbound
No exit. Access only from A91	7	No access. Exit only to A91
No access. Exit only to A91	8	No exit. Access only from A91
No access from A912. No exit to southbound lane of A912	10	No exit to A912. No access from northbound lane of A912

M180 THORNE - BRIGG

Eastbound	Junction	Westbound
No access. Exit only to A18 & A614	1	No exit. Access from A18 & A164

M606 BRADFORD SPUR

Northbound	Junction	Southbound
No access. Exit only	Merrydale Road	No restriction

M621 LEEDS - GLIDERSOME

South-westbound	Junction	North-eastbound
No restriction	M1	Access to M1 via gyratory system
No access. Exit only	A621	No exit. Access only

M876 BONNYBRIDGE - KINCARDINE BRIDGE

North-eastbound	Junction	South-westbound
Access is from M80 northbound	M80	The only exit is to M80 southbound
No access. Exit only to A9 & A88	2	No exit. Access from A9 & A88
No exit to north-westbound lane of M9	M9: Jct 8	No access from south-eastbound lane of M9

A1(M) SOUTH MIMMS - BALDOCK

Northbound	Junction	Southbound
No restriction	2	No exit. Access only from A1001
No restriction	3	No access. Exit to A414 & A1001
No access only from B197	5	No exit or access

A1(M) SCOTCH CORNER - TYNESIDE

Northbound	Junction	Southbound
No access. Exit only to A66(M)	A66(M)	No exit. Access only from A66(M)
Only exits are to A194(M) & A1	A194(M)	Only access is from A194(M) & A1

A3(M) HORNDEAN - HAVANT

Southbound	Junction	Northbound
The only access at Horndean is from southbound lane of A3	A3	The only exit at Horndean is to northbound lane of A3
No exit. Access only	Purbrook Way	No access. Exit only

A38(M) ASTON EXPRESSWAY, BIRMINGHAM

Northbound	Junction	Southbound
No exit. Access only	Victoria Rd	No access. Exit only

A40(M) WESTWAY, LONDON

Eastbound	Junction	Westbound
No access. Exit only to Westbourne Terrace	Paddington	No exit. Access only from Gloucester Terrace
The only access is onto the Marylebone Flyover	Marylebone Flyover	The only access is via Marylebone Flyover

A48(M) CARDIFF SPUR

Westbound	Junction	Eastbound
Only access is from M4 westbound	M4	The only exit is to M4 eastbound
Only exit is to A48 eastbound	29A(A48)	Only access is from A48 eastbound

A57(M) MANCUNIAN WAY, MANCHESTER

Eastbound	Junction	Westbound
No access (use Cambridge Street)	A5103	No exit (use Cambridge Street)
No exit (use A5103 junction)	Cambridge St	No access (use A5103 jct)
No access. The only exit is to southbound lane of Brook St.	A34	No exit. Access only from Brook Street, A34

A58(M) A64(M) LEEDS INNER RING ROAD

Eastbound	Junction	Westbound
No restriction	Westgate	No access. Exit only
No direct access from northbound lane of A660	A660	No direct access from northbound lane of A660
No access form Clay Pit Lane, A58	A58	No exit to Clay Pit Lane, A58
No exit to North Street	North St	Access available via New Briggate
No exit to A61	Eastgate	No access from A61

A66(M) DARLINGTON SPUR

North-eastbound	Junction	South-westbound
Access is from A1(M) northbound	A1(M)	Only exit is to A1(M) southbound

A102(M) BLACKWALL TUNNEL APPROACH ROADS

Northbound	Junction	Southbound
No exit to Blackwall Lane A2203	A2203	No restriction
No restriction	Hackney	Access only. No exit to Wick Rd
The only exit is to the eastbound lane of Eastway, A106	Eastway	The only access is from the westbound lane of Eastway, A106

A167(M) NEWCASTLE CENTRAL MOTORWAY

Northbound	Junction	Southbound
No exit. Access only	Camden St	No exit or access

A194(M) TYNESIDE

Southbound	Junction	Northbound
Only exit is to A1(M) southbound	A1(M)	Access only from A1(M) n'bound